Language Skills in Elementary Education

Language Skills in Elementary Education

THIRD EDITION

Paul S. Anderson **Diane Lapp**

Boston University

Macmillan Publishing Co., Inc.
New York
Collier Macmillan Publishers
London

Macmillan Publishing Co., Inc.
866 Third Avenue, New York, New York 10022

Collier Macmillan Canada, Ltd.

Library of Congress Cataloging in Publication Data

Anderson, Paul S
  Language skills in elementary education.

  Includes bibliographies and index.
  1. Language arts (Elementary)   I. Lapp, Diane,
joint author.   II. Title.
LB1576.A616   1979   372.6'044   78-6498
ISBN 0-02-303140-9

Printing: 1 2 3 4 5 6 7 8   Year: 9 0 1 2 3 4 5

ACKNOWLEDGMENTS

ALAMEDA COUNTY PUBLIC SCHOOLS *Listening Habits and Speech Sound Discrimination* by M. Smith, Haywood, California, 1963. Used by permission.

ALBUQUERQUE PUBLIC SCHOOLS *Albuquerque Public Schools Journal,* March 1970. Used by permission.

ALLYN AND BACON, INC. "Cooperative Poetry—A Creative project," by S. G. Gilburt in *Language Art News,* Fall 1957.

AMERICAN BOOK COMPANY *Composition Through Literature* by H. T. Fillmer et al., 1967.

APPLETON-CENTURY-CROFTS, INC. *Teaching English Grammar* by Robert C. Pooley. Copyright 1957 by Appleton-Century-Crofts, Inc. Reprinted by permission of the publisher, Appleton-Century-Crofts.

ASSOCIATION FOR CHILDHOOD EDUCATION INTERNATIONAL "Helping Children to Create," by Lois Lenski. From *Childhood Education,* November 1949, Vol. 26, No. 3. Reprinted by permission of Lois Lenski and the Association for Childhood Education International, 3615 Wisconsin Avenue, N.W., Washington, D.C. 20016. Copyright © 1949 by the Association. "Building with Children a Better Tomorrow" by Leland Jacobs. Reprinted by permission of the author and the Association for Childhood Education International. From *Childhood Education,* November 1961, Vol. 38, No.

3. "Curiosities of Children that Literature Can Satisfy" by Roy Eugene Toothaker. From *Childhood Education,* March 1976, pp. 262–267. Reprinted by permission of Roy Eugene Toothaker and the Association for Childhood Education International. Copyright © 1976 by the Association.

BATTLE CREEK, MICHIGAN, PUBLIC SCHOOLS Chart, "Reading Readiness Handicaps and Their Correction," Battle Creek, Michigan. Used by permission.

BENNETT, JOAN "Locomotive" by Rodney Bennett, copyright 1941 by Rodney Bennett, Reprinted by permission of Joan Bennett and the author's estate.

BOARD OF EDUCATION OF THE CITY OF NEW YORK *Teaching Spelling,* Brooklyn, New York. Used by permission. Cursive writing lesson plan for the fifth and sixth grades. Used by permission.

BROWN, SALOME "The First Grade Child Not Quite Ready for Beginning Reading Instruction," *Proceedings of Summer Conference,* Vol. XX, Western Washington State College, Bellingham, Washington, January 1968.

BURGESS PUBLISHING COMPANY *Resource Materials for Teachers of Spelling* by Paul S. Anderson. Copyright 1964 by Paul S. Anderson. Reprinted by permission of the publisher.

CALIFORNIA STATE DEPARTMENT OF EDUCATION "Syllabus for

Speech'' by A. Frye. *California Journal of Elementary Education,* Sacramento, California, 1961.

CCM PROFESSIONAL MAGAZINES, INC. "Slang 20 Years Ago" by Anna McCormic and Norma Dove. Reprinted from the February, 1969, issue of *Grade Teacher* magazine with permission of the publisher. This article is copyrighted. © 1969 by CCM Professional Magazines, Inc. All rights reserved.

THE UNIVERSITY OF CHICAGO PRESS List of one hundred words, from "Johnson's Basic Vocabulary: Words for Grades 1 and 2," by D. D. Johnson and E. Majer, *Elementary School Journal,* September 1976, pp. 74–82. Used by permission of the University of Chicago Press.

THE CHRISTIAN SCIENCE PUBLISHING SOCIETY "Clouds," by Helen Wing, from *The Christian Science Monitor,* reprinted by permission of the publisher.

COLUMBIA UNIVERSITY *Listening Aids Through the Grades* by D. Russell and E. F. Russell, Bureau of Publications, Teachers College, Columbia University, 1959. Used by permission.

DENVER PUBLIC SCHOOLS English Language Program, "Language and Learning in a Modern World." Denver, Colorado, 1968. Used by permission.

DOUBLEDAY & COMPANY, INC. "Very Lovely" by Rose Fyleman. Used by permission of Doubleday & Company, Inc.

DOUBLEDAY & COMPANY, INC., and WORLD'S WORK LTD. "The Wonderful Words" from *Words, Words, Words* by Mary Gibbons O'Neill. Copyright © 1966 by Mary Gibbons O'Neill. Reprinted by permission of Doubleday & Company, Inc., and World's Work Ltd.

E. P. DUTTON & CO., INC., and THE BODLEY HEAD From the book *My Side of the Mountain* by Jean George. Illus. by the author. Copyright, © 1959 by Jean George. Published by E. P. Dutton & Co., Inc., and used with their permission and that of The Bodley Head.

ENCYCLOPAEDIA BRITTANICA Encyclopaedia Brittanica Language Experiences. Used by permission.

ESCONDIDO UNION SCHOOL DISTRICT "Fifty Writing Demons." From a spelling handbook compiled by Paul S. Anderson, Escondido, California, 1957. Used by permission.

FISHER, AILEEN "Coffeepot Face," copyright by Aileen Fisher and reprinted by permission of the author.

FOLLETT EDUCATIONAL CORPORATION *The World of Language,* Book 4, Muriel Crosby, Ed. D., General Editor. Copyright © 1970 by Follett Educational Corporation. Used by permission of Follett Educational Corporation.

GALE RESEARCH COMPANY Handwriting examples from *Date Book Calendar.*

GARY PUBLIC SCHOOLS *Reading and Language in the Elementary School,* Board of Education, Gary, Indiana, 1962. Used by permission.

GINN AND COMPANY From the *Manual for Teaching the Reading Readiness Program, Revised Edition,* by David Russell et al., of The Ginn Basic Readers. © Copyright 1961 by Ginn and Company. Used with permission. *Initial Placement Test:* Class Work Sheet; Teacher's Editions, Levels 2–13: "Components of READING 720 Management System"; Level 2, *Reading Achievement Card,* Side 1; Level 5, *May I Come In?:* pp. 60 and 78 (text and art); Level 12, *Measure Me, Sky:* pp. 404 and 405 (art only).

GOTT, MARGARET E. "Teaching Reading to Spanish Speaking Children," unpublished thesis, San Diego State College, San Diego, California, 1955. Used by permission of the author.

GROSSE POINT PUBLIC SCHOOLS *Thinking About Spelling,* "Generalizations." Grosse Point, Michigan. Used by permission.

HARCOURT BRACE JOVANOVICH, INC. "Little Sounds," from *Something Special,* © 1958 by Beatrice Schenk de Regniers. Reprinted by permission of Harcourt Brace Jovanovich, Inc. and Wm. Collins Sons & Co. Ltd. "Counting," from *Windy Morning,* copyright 1953 by Harry Behn. Reprinted by permission of Harcourt Brace Jovanovich, Inc. "Good Night," from *Smoke and Steel* by Carl Sandburg, copyright 1920 by Harcourt Brace Jovanovich, Inc.; copyright 1948 by Carl Sandburg. Reprinted by permission of the publisher. "The Secret Cavern," from *Little Girl and Boy Land* by Margaret Widdemer, copyright 1924 by Harcourt Brace Jovanovich, Inc.; copyright 1952 by Margaret Widdemer Schauffler. Reprinted by permission of the publisher. Figure of nasal and oral cavities and phonetic chart, from *Working with Aspects of Language,* Second Edition, by Mansoor Alyeshmerni and Paul Tauber, Copyright © 1975 by Harcourt Brace Jovanovich, Inc. Reprinted (reproduced for the figure) by permission of the publishers. Books 8 and 19 from *The Palo Alto Reading Program,* Second Edition, by Theodore E. Glim, copyright © 1973 by Harcourt Brace Jovanovich, Inc. Reproduced and reprinted by permission of the publishers.

HARPER & ROW, PUBLISHERS *New Directions in English,* 1968. Used by permission. *How to Make Sense* by Rudolf Flesch. Used by permission of Harper & Row, Publishers.

HARPER & ROW, PUBLISHERS and LUTTERWORTH PRESS *Farmer Boy* by Laura Ingalls Wilder. Copyright © 1933 by Harper & Brothers. Renewed 1961 by Roger L. MacBride. Reprinted with permission of Harper & Row, Publishers, and Lutterworth Press.

D. C. HEATH AND COMPANY Reprinted by permission of the publisher from H. L. J. Carter and J. J. McGinnis, *Teaching Individuals to Read* (Lexington, Mass.: D. C. Heath and Company, 1962).

HISPANIA Excerpts from a presentation given at the San Diego Conference on the Teaching of English to Speakers of Other Languages, March 12, 1965. Reprinted from *Hispania,* May 1966, Vol. 49, No. 2, pp. 293–296.

THE HORN BOOK, INC. "One Day When We Went Walking," by Valine Hobbs, copyright 1945 by The Horn Book, Inc., reprinted by permission of the publisher.

HOUGHTON MIFFLIN COMPANY *Improving Your Language* by Paul McKee, copyright 1957 by Houghton Mifflin Company. *Come Along* Teacher's Manual by Paul McKee, copyright 1957 by Houghton Mifflin Company. *Bright Peaks,* teacher's edition, by

Paul McKee, copyright 1958 by Houghton Mifflin Company. *Student Centered Language Arts Curriculum* by James Moffett, copyright 1968 by Houghton Mifflin Company. Reprinted by permission of the publisher.

IMPERIAL BEACH PUBLIC SCHOOLS *Emory Epitaph*, Imperial Beach, California. Used by permission.

INDIANA UNIVERSITY PRESS *Bibliography of Child Language* by D. I. Slobin, 1972.

THE INSTRUCTOR PUBLICATIONS, INC. "Three Cheers for Peter" by Alice Hartich, © 1961, by the Instructor Publications, Inc. Used by permission. "You Can Teach Handwriting with Only Six Rules," by Max Rosenhaus, © 1957, by the Instructor Publications, Inc. Used by permission. "Phonics Clinic" by Selma E. Herr, copyright 1957 by Selma Herr. Used by permission.

INTERNATIONAL READING ASSOCIATION "Usefulness of Phonic Generalizations," by Lou E. Burmeister, *The Reading Teacher,* January, 1968, pp. 352–356. Reprinted with permission of Lou E. Burmeister and the International Reading Association.

BERTHA KLAUSNER INTERNATIONAL LITERARY AGENCY, INC. "Funny the Way Different Cars Start" by Dorothy Baruch.

LAIDLAW BROTHERS, PUBLISHERS "Song of the Pop-Corn" by Louise Abney, from *On the Way to Storyland,* 1961. "The American Flag" By Louise Abney, from *From Every Land,* book 6, copyright 1961 by Laidlaw Brothers, reprinted by permission of the publisher.

LE CRON, HELEN COWLES "Little Charlie Chipmunk," reprinted by permission of the author.

J. B. LIPPINCOTT COMPANY *Poetry Therapy* by J. J. Leedy, 1969. "A Letter Is a Gypsy Elf " from the book *For Days and Days,* by Annette Wynne. Copyright, 1919, by J. B. Lippincott Company. Renewal, 1947, by Annette Wynne. Reprinted by permission of J. B. Lippincott Company.

LONGMAN GROUP LTD. "Hints on Pronunciation for Foreigners," cited by Macky and Thompson in *Programme in Linguistics and English Teaching,* Paper No. 3, p. 45.

LOS ANGELES CITY SCHOOLS *Speech in the Elementary School,* Publication No. 479, 1949. Used by permission.

LOVELL, MARIE *Independent Activities*. Used by permission.

MACMILLAN PUBLISHING CO., INC. "The Cat," from Menagerie, by Mary Britton Miller, copyright 1929 by Macmillan Publishing Co., Inc., reprinted by permission of the author and publisher. *A Basic Vocabulary of Elementary School Children,* by Henry D. Rinsland, copyright 1945. Used by permission of Macmillan Publishing Co., Inc., and the author. *My City, A Bank Street Reader,* Bank Street College of Education, Irma Simonton Black, Senior Editor. Reprinted with permission of Macmillan Publishing Co., Inc. © Copyright Macmillan Publishing Co., Inc., 1966. *Teaching Reading to Every Child* by Diane Lapp and James E. Flood. Copyright © 1978, Macmillan Publishing Co., Inc. Reprinted by permission.

MACMILLAN PROFESSIONAL MAGAZINES, INC. "Soft Is the Hush of Falling Snow" by Emily Carey Alleman. Reprinted from the March 1953 issue of *Grade Teacher* magazine with permission of the publisher. This article is copyrighted. © 1953 by Macmillan Professional Magazines, Inc. All rights reserved.

MC CULLOUGH, CONSTANCE M., and PARAGON PUBLICATIONS *Handbook for Teaching the Language Arts,* copyright 1958 by Constance McCullough, reprinted by permission of the author and Paragon Publications.

MC GRAW-HILL BOOK COMPANY *Are You Listening?* by Ralph G. Nichols and Leonard A. Stevens, copyright © 1957 by the McGraw-Hill Book Company, Inc., and Willis Kinsley Wing. *Remedial Techniques in Basic School Subjects* by Grace M. Fernald. Copyright 1943, McGraw-Hill Book Company. Used by permission.

MC INTOSH AND OTIS, INC. *The Two Worlds of Damyan* by Marie Halun Bloch. Copyright © 1966 by Marie Halun Bloch. Reprinted by permission of McIntosh and Otis, Inc.

CHARLES E. MERRILL PUBLISHING COMPANY *I Can* by Wayne Otto et al., Merrill Linguistic Reading Program, Columbus, Ohio, 1975. *Reader 2* by Charles E. Fries et al., Merrill Linguistic Readers, Columbus, Ohio, 1966.

MINNEAPOLIS PUBLIC SCHOOLS "The First Thanksgiving," video script. From *Communication* (1953), p. 24. Used by permission.

UNIVERSITY OF MINNESOTA "Finger Plays for Young Children," Leaflet No. 11, reprinted by permission of the Institute of Child Development and Welfare.

MOUTON PUBLISHERS Chart of speech sounds in *Fundamentals of Language* by R. Jakobson and M. Halle, 1956. Used by permission of Mouton & Co., Publishers, Noordeinde 41, 2514 GC The Hague, The Netherlands.

NATIONAL ASSOCIATION OF ELEMENTARY SCHOOL PRINCIPALS "Helping the Disadvantaged Build Language," by Theda Wilson. *National Elementary School Principal,* November 1965. Copyright 1965, National Association of Elementary School Principals, National Education Association. All rights reserved.

NATIONAL CONFERENCE OF CHRISTIANS AND JEWS, INC. "Role Playing the Problem Story," by George and Fannie Shaftel, 1952.

NATIONAL COUNCIL OF TEACHERS OF ENGLISH "Instant Enrichment" by Marie E. Taylor, *Elementary English,* February 1968. Copyright © 1968 by the National Council of Teachers of English. Reprinted by permission of the publisher and Marie E. Taylor. Eldonna L. Everts in Alexander Frazier, *New Directors in Elementary English,* 1967. Copyright © 1967 by the National Council of Teachers of English. Reprinted by permission of the publisher and Alexander Frazier. Map of dialects by Raven I. McDavid, Jr., *American Speaking,* 1967. Copyright © 1967 by the National Council of Teachers of English. Reprinted by permission of the publisher and the author.

NATIONAL SOCIETY FOR THE STUDY OF EDUCATION Word count study table by Dr. Ernest Horn, Twenty-third Yearbook of the National Society for the Study of Education. Used by permission of the National Society for the Study of Education and the author.

UNIVERSITY OF NEBRASKA PRESS Reprinted from A Curriculum for English Poetry for the Elementary Grades, 1966, by permission of the University of Nebraska Press. Copyright © 1966 by the University of Nebraska Press.

NEW IOWA SPELLING SCALE   Statistical data on the words *elephant* and *school* by Dr. Harry A. Greene. Used by permission.

PHI DELTA KAPPAN   Table of spelling errors by George C. Kyte. *Phi Delta Kappan,* May 1958. Used by permission of the *Phi Delta Kappan* and the author.

PLAYS, INC.   *A Kettle of Brains* by Gweniera Williams. Reprinted from *Thirty Plays for Classroom Reading,* Donald D. Durrell and B. Alice Crossley, eds. Copyright © 1957 by Plays, Inc., Publishers, 8 Arlington Street, Boston, Massachusetts 02116. *The Wonderful Circus of Words* by Claire Boiko. Reprinted by permission from *Children's Plays for Creative Actors,* by Claire Boiko. Copyright © 1961 by Plays, Inc. This play is for reading purposes only. For permission to produce this play, write to Plays, Inc., 8 Arlington Street, Boston, Massachusetts 02116.

PRATT, MARIA   ''A Mortifying Mistake.'' Used by permission.

PRENTICE-HALL, INC.   Nila Banton Smith, *Reading Instruction for Today's Children,* © 1963. Reprinted by permission of Prentice-Hall, Inc., Englewood Cliffs, New Jersey.

RECREATION MAGAZINE   ''My Mother Read to Me'' by E. H. Frierwood, *Recreation* magazine, February 1950. Used by permission.

RICHARDS, ROSALIND   ''Antonio'' by Laura E. Richards. Used by permission.

THE RONALD PRESS COMPANY   *Speech Methods in the Elementary School* by Carrie Rasmussen. Copyright 1949 by The Ronald Press Company.

SAN BERNARDINO COUNTY SCHOOLS   *Arts and Skills of Communication for Democracy's Children,* San Bernardino, California, 1954. Used by permission.

SAN DIEGO CITY SCHOOLS   A Blitz Handwriting Program by Nathan Naiman, San Diego, California, 1960. Used by permission. *Oral and Written Language,* San Diego, California, with special acknowledgment to Elizabeth Stocker.

SAN DIEGO STATE COLLEGE   Lists of frequently used words, Campus Laboratory School. Used by permission.

SCOTT, FORESMAN AND COMPANY   *Language and How to Use It,* books 3 and 4, by Andrew Schiller et al. Copyright © 1969 by Scott, Foresman and Company.

CHARLES SCRIBNER'S SONS and WILLIAM HEINEMAN LTD.   Reprinted by permission of Charles Scribner's Sons and William Heineman Ltd., from *The Yearling,* page 279, by Marjorie Kinnan Rawlings. Copyright 1938 Marjorie Kinnan Rawlings; renewal copyright © 1966 Norton Baskin.

W. A. SHEAFFER PEN CO.   Handwriting evaluation form, *My Handwriting Quotient,* Madison, Wisconsin, 1960. Used by permission.

SIDGWICK & JACKSON LTD.   ''Choosing Shoes,'' from *The Very Thing,* by ffrida Wolfe, reprinted by permission of the author's representatives and the publishers, Sidgwick & Jackson Ltd.

SMYTHE, ISABEL   ''Soliloquy on Phonics and Spelling,'' By Isabel Smythe. Used by permission.

SOUTH BAY PUBLIC SCHOOLS   *Our Writing,* Emory School, South Bay School District, San Diego, California. Used by permission.

TASH, MERRY LEE   ''To the Boy That Sits in Front of Me''; ''Hobbies''; ''Dear Mom''; reprinted by permission of the author and Clover C. Tash and Lloyd C. Tash.

TULARE COUNTY SCHOOLS   Language Arts Course of Study, pp. 26–72. Tulare County, California, 1949. Used by permission.

H. W. WILSON COMPANY   ''Helping Childldren Enjoy Poetry'' by May Hill Arbuthnot. Reprinted by permission from the January 1962 issue of the *Wilson Library Bulletin.* Copyright © 1962 by the H. W. Wilson Company.

WISCONSIN DEPARTMENT OF PUBLIC INSTRUCTION   *English Language Arts in Wisconsin,* 1968. Used by permission.

YALE UNIVERSITY PRESS   ''Bundles'' from *Songs for Parents* by John Farrar, © 1921 by Yale University Press, reprinted by permission of the publisher.

Special thanks are extended to Susan Melanson for her patience and typing efforts, to Elizabeth Fox for her editing skills, and to Linda Lungren for her expertise in photography and layout.

Dedicated to Eric and Shannon,
who are having lots of fun with language

Preface

This book is designed for you, the language arts teacher, as you plan learning experiences that will "make a difference" in the lives of your students. If you are questioning the fact that you are a "language arts teacher," remember that regardless of your content specialization, you will be required to teach the language arts—which consist of *language, listening, writing,* and *reading*—because learning in any content area is dependent on prior acquisition of one or more of these skills. *All* teachers at *all* grade levels in *all* content areas are language arts teachers.

Teaching in the elementary schools involves hundreds of tasks. No one has ever made an effort to list all of them. Teachers have acquired skill in much the same way that good parents learn to care for a family or physicians learn to treat their patients. Part of teaching proficiency comes from the memory of the way we were taught, part comes by learning from the experience of others, and part is based on our own

willingness to work at tasks that we feel must be accomplished. A methods course in the language arts is designed to prepare you to teach by having you relate your own childhood efforts to speak, read, and write to those of young learners, to inform you about what others have learned who have worked in this area, and to present ways of working with problems you will face. Some of these problems will have rather specific solutions; others are predicaments that are never completely resolved. But with better teacher training and greater awareness of child psychology, more and more children are learning to read well, write with ease, speak expressively, and think efficiently.

Understanding and teaching the language arts skills are the basic concepts around which this book is organized; herein are described the participants in the language arts program, the place of the language arts in the school curriculum, the interrelationships of language and culture, and the development of a managed language arts curriculum. Several chapters emphasize the *many* ways teachers accomplish their goals. Do not hesitate to evaluate the ideas and procedures presented in these chapters. Select those that are most appropriate for your students. Because this is the third edition of the text, there are numerous similarities between this and earlier versions. The original topics have all been extended by exploration of current theories regarding language acquisition, development, and heritage and by further analysis of the processes involved in comprehending written discourse.

Throughout the text, specific techniques, exercises, and activities are suggested. What happens in these classroom experiences must be something read, something written, something learned. Theory is practical in that it helps a teacher determine which of many activities and techniques to use. The great unknown to anyone outside your classroom is a knowledge of the individual child with whom you work. It is your ability to know this child and combine this knowledge with the information of a methods course that will determine your success as a teacher. The complexity of this task is a sign of how important your role as a teacher will be.

Contents

Part I
Participants
in the
Learning
Process

Chapter 1
The Teacher Is You!

The teacher asked of the child,
"What would you have of me?"
And the child replied,
"Because you are you, only you know some of the things
I would have of you.
But because I am I,
I do know some of what I would have of you."

The teacher asked again,
"What would you have of me?"
And the child replied,
"I would have of you what
You are and what you know.
I would have you speaking and silent,
Sure and unsure, seeking for surety,
Vibrant and pensive.
I would have you talking and letting me tell,
Going my way with my wonderings and enthusiasms,
And going your way that I may know new curiosities,
I would have you leading step by step
You letting me step things off in my own fashion."

"Teach me," said the child,
"With simplicity and imagination—
Simply that the paraphernalia and the gadgets
Do not get between us;
Imaginatively that I may sense and catch your enthusiasm,
And the quickening thrill of never having been this way be-
  fore.
Too, I would have you watching over me, yet not too watch-
  ful,
Caring for me, yet not too carefully,
Holding me to you, yet not with bindings,
So when the day comes, as it must,
    that we, each, go our separate ways,
I can go free.
Let me take you with me not because
    I must, but because I would have it so.
Let me take you with me because you have become, in me,
Not just today—
Tomorrow!"

Leland B. Jacobs

Building with Children a Better Tomorrow

Your desire to teach can open the doors to an exciting adventure, the adventure of learning. Each day offers many new dimensions for you and for those you teach. You and your students can be stimulated by each other's ideas and experiences, feelings of success and satisfaction, and constant desire to grow in many cognitive and affective areas. The rewards of teaching, and of learning, are many.

Coupled with the unique rewards of your profession are the frustrations of reaching each individual, of knowing the "right way," and of predicting the consequences of each action you take. Your desire to grow as a teacher and as an individual, along with an intense commitment to meet each challenge with an open mind and a positive attitude, will play a vital role in the success of the learning adventures ahead.

As a teacher you will be involved in the task of aiding students in developing the skills and knowledge necessary for continually extending their learning bases. In order to accomplish this task, ability in the following areas is a necessity.

1. *Classroom preparation.* Well-planned instructional material and interesting methods of presentation are essential for effective teaching. Plan books are useful tools for budgeting class time and recording well-thought-through procedures for the development of new learnings. Lack of preparation of teaching sequence and student activity is usually quite obvious and hinders the fruitfulness of a school day.
2. *Planning for individual differences.* Recognition of individual differences among your students is a beginning step; then you must plan a range of purposeful activities to meet those differences.
3. *Motivation.* The desire to learn is a strong factor in the child's academic success in school. As a teacher, you can become a source of inspiration to your students. The best motivation will result when pupils and teacher have similar purposes.
4. *Knowledge of subject matter.* A teacher must have a clear understanding of a subject in order to teach it effectively. Therefore, you must continually acquaint yourself with methods and materials that are part of current curricula. If you feel you lack the necessary skill to teach specific skills and content, it is time to *ready yourself* for the task.
5. *Teaching methods.* Teaching methods are too numerous to mention; they are ever-changing and multiplying. Effective methods utilize positive rather than negative reinforcement, consist of various techniques, and make wide use of materials that can be touched as well as seen.
6. *Classroom atmosphere.* The atmosphere of the classroom is the result of many factors. Heat and light, color combinations, use of display areas and bulletin boards, organization of instructional materials and equipment, arrangement of interest centers and quiet areas, and the nature of human relations that are encouraged and reinforced are integrated with the personalities of the students and teacher. Classroom management is facilitated by the positive interaction of these factors. Expertise in managing the classroom is gradually acquired through the development of a comfortable, well-organized, and stimulating environment.
7. *Classroom organization.* From the beginning of your career, it is important to realize that children expect the teacher to be a leader and the arbiter of classroom behavior. Although students enjoy warm, friendly interaction with an adult, they are also looking for a person who will direct their academic experiences and provide a secure learning environment.

Strategies for managing behavior in the classroom are varied. Some teachers spend their school lives in a desperate effort to "hold the line," whereas others lead their classes with the magic wands of interest, cooperation, fair play, and mutual respect. There are few discipline problems in a classroom when children are motivated by an important goal. Children who are involved in learning find satisfaction in their achievement and provide positive role models for each other.

Emergencies, both major and minor, may occur in

the course of the school day. The teacher must react professionally to problems of illness, fire drills, and civil defense procedures. She must anticipate such minor catastrophes as spilled paint, missing lunches, emergency phone calls, a visit by an angry parent, broken equipment, and the many embarrassing moments of childhood that later become anecdotes.

Since classroom management is built on the application of common sense and experience, the following points may be helpful in developing a successful rapport with your students:

1. *See that initial interactions are positive.* Friendly interactions with children aid in developing a warm atmosphere. Be friendly, but also be efficient.
2. *Avoid disruptive consequences.* Plan well and have materials ready. Be composed, calm, and dignified. Provide a program with variety and enough mental stimulation for even the cleverest children.
3. *Don't let minor incidents go uncorrected.* Be alert to minor negative incidents, for if you allow children to practice disorder they soon become experts at it. Children tend to imitate the behavior of their peers.
4. *Be tactful, mannerly, and just.* A good-tempered, tactful teacher can achieve positive goals more effectively than the authoritarian, sarcastic teacher. Children have a strong sense of justice and seldom forget when the teacher shows favoritism. Remember, children are real people who model the examples of behavior that you provide.
5. *Be persistent and exhibit consistent behavior.* Emphasize important matters, without allowing for exceptions, until the desired form of conduct is habitual. Don't be severe one day and lenient the next. Showing self-control at all times demonstrates professional poise.
6. *Be a decision maker.* Consider all problems with a clear mind and make careful decisions. Once you make a judgment, show confidence in upholding it.
7. *Avoid conflicts.* Don't try to "fight it out" with a child. One of the simplest ways to solve a difficult situation is to provide the child with an either-or choice and then follow through on the decision by

reinforcement of the positive behavior or the loss of a privilege for the negative choice.

Teaching Is a Complex Process

Teaching in the elementary school is an art. Techniques and materials can be shared, but the human relationships of the teaching-learning process cannot be learned through words alone. In recent years paint-by-number kits have been designed for "do-it-yourself" painters, using key numbering to indicate which areas are to be painted a certain color. If one follows the directions, one can produce something that resembles the original painting, but at best it is only a copy of another's creative expression and planning. One's first efforts at original painting will perhaps betray uncertainties of line and form, but the result, however labored, is a creation rather than an imitation. With talent, training, and determination, the amateur painter may in time produce a genuine work of art. In teaching, some start with great talent and seem to know not only how to work with children but also how to use suggestions for the best results. Others start with nothing more than interest and must master the skills by hard work. But the rewards are worth the effort. Few professions offer the satisfactions that a teacher knows as children develop the communication skills that will help them face with confidence their responsibilities as adults.

The longer you teach, the more you will realize that it is difficult to separate the art of teaching from the science of education. Some teachers are able to gain amazing results with the simple resources of their environment; others, surrounded by texts, films, typewriters, and the latest audiovisual devices, manage only to reduce those who would learn to boredom.

We look at life through our attitudes. If yours is that each child has a worthy contribution to make and your task is to help him achieve the maximum that his stage of growth and capacity will permit, you will have made a major step in the direction of teaching success. Such an attitude will also cause you continually to seek improved ways of meeting the needs of children.

Any art that cannot be specified in detail cannot be

transmitted by specific prescriptions alone. It can best be passed on by example from master to apprentice. Colleges educate some who are fine teachers, others who are fine scholars, and still others who have enough credits to graduate. The difference seems to be the quality of craftsmanship displayed by those with whom the future teacher associates. One aspect of this association is supervision. Beginning teachers should seek employment in a district where there is adequate service to guide them through the beginning years of their professional apprenticeship. Many great teachers are unknown except to parents and children, who have no basis for comparison. These teachers may be unaware of their own excellence or conversely of their incompetence.

Your task as a teacher is to identify your most effective style of relating to students so that comfortable teacher-student interactions and maximum learning will be encouraged.
(PHOTO BY LINDA LUNGREN.)

There are many who could be much better teachers if they had guidance from their fellow professionals. If you choose to "spend" your life teaching, give it the best of your talent, remembering that it is on the wings of words that children claim their cultural identity. There is no more rewarding role for an elementary teacher than sharing such growth.

How Important Is the Teacher in the Learning Process?

In many research studies the teacher has been shown to be the most important factor involved in the child's reading success. Malmquist (1973) reviewed the massive federally funded study entitled "The Cooperative Research Program in First-Grade Reading Instruction" and concluded: "the teacher is a more important variable in reading instruction than are the teaching methods and instructional materials."

After analyzing the results of first-grade studies that attempted to compare several methods of reading instruction, George Spache reaffirmed the importance of the teacher:

our reading research into the effectiveness of various instructional methods in classroom or remedial situations is often pointless. Such comparative research tends to ignore the fact that the dynamic practices of the teacher and the kinds of teacher-pupil interaction she promotes are the most important determinants of pupils' achievements. The collected results of the large scale First Grade Reading Studies . . . strongly reaffirm this fact. Hardly any real differences in pupil achievement were found in comparisons among a half-dozen different approaches in carefully equated populations. Rather, in almost every study, achievement varied more from one teacher's classroom to the next than it varied according to the methods or materials employed. [Spache, 1973]

Tinker and McCullough (1975) concluded that the teacher is a greater factor in the achievement of better reading scores than are specific methods or materials. King (1973), agreeing with Tinker and McCullough, stated that the differences in teaching styles and professional competencies among teachers have a definite ef-

fect on children's language arts achievement. Goldbecker (1975) further emphasized the importance of the teacher: "The salient point remains that no reading program operates by itself. The teacher is still the single catalyst who can determine success or failure of a reading program, no matter where its emphasis lies."

Thus the teacher emerges as a prime factor in the learning encounter. It is therefore very important for you, the teacher, to think through your values and your approach, to assess your philosophy of teaching, and to learn as much as you can about each child you teach. Consider all facets of learning, including the theories that have been proposed to explain the learning process and the patterns of physical, mental, psychological, and sociological development. All of this information should be integrated into your approach to teaching.

One of your roles as a classroom teacher will be to facilitate the learning process. In your relationship with students, never impose yourself. Your role is that of facilitator, providing a variety of educationally rich environments, confirming and encouraging each student by your positive regard. Whether limited to your own classroom or given responsibility in the entire school, you must strive to create learning environments that are congruent with the learning patterns of children. This may be accomplished by continually asking yourself the following questions.

Questions Concerning My Role as a Teacher

1. What is my role as a teacher? Who am I to my students?
2. What are my values? Do I encourage children to accept my value structure, or do I foster individual development and selection of values?
3. What type of communication do I promote between my students and myself? Am I most comfortable with one-way or two-way, open-ended or planned communication?
4. What types of motivation do I promote? Are the students self-motivated, or is there a materialistic reward system?
5. What types of discipline do I employ? What are the

emotional and educational results of my disciplinary techniques?

Questions Concerning My Students

1. What expectations do I have for my students? What is their relationship to me?
2. How do my students learn?
3. How are my students evaluated? What purpose does this evaluative process serve?

Curriculum

1. What will be the learning climate, and how will it be determined? Will it be friendly or impersonal, quiet or active, individually oriented or teacher dominated, task oriented or unstructured?
2. What will be the major goals of the classroom? What specific social, psychological, emotional, and cognitive learning will occur within the classroom?

The process of answering these and similar questions may seem burdensome. However, you are encouraged to think about each of these questions, since they contribute to your beliefs about the education of children.

As well as thinking about these questions it is important for you to attempt to formulate the basic principles of your philosophy and hypothesize the effects of these principles on your students. Then consider the practical implementation of these principles in a classroom setting. Once you have analyzed your beliefs, you can begin to plan a curriculum that will provide your students with positive learning experiences.

This text will provide you with a comprehensive view of language arts literature and methods for implementing such theory. Thus you as a teacher will be guided by a clear understanding of the theory that underlies meaningful language teaching and successful language learning.

Bibliography

Barzun, J. *Teacher in America.* Boston: Little, Brown, 1945.

Bigge, M. L. *Learning Theories for Teachers.* New York: Harper & Row, 1971.

Davis, A. *Social-Class Influences upon Learning.* Cambridge, Mass.: Harvard University Press, 1961.

Goldbecker, S. S. "Reading: Instructional Approaches." Washington, D.C.: National Education Association, 1975.

Gorman, A. H. *Teachers and Learners.* Boston: Allyn and Bacon, 1974.

Greene, M. *Teacher as Stranger.* Belmont, Calif.: Wadsworth, 1973.

Gross, R. (ed.). *The Teacher and the Taught.* New York: Dell, 1963.

Harmin, M., and T. Gregory. *Teaching Is* . . . . Chicago: Science Research Associates, 1974.

Highet, G. *The Art of Teaching.* New York: Random House, 1950.

Hunt, R. L. "Why Teachers Fail." *The Clearing House,* **12**(8) (April 1938), 176.

James, W. *Talks to Teachers.* New York: Norton, 1958.

Jersild, A. T. *When Teachers Face Themselves.* New York: Teachers College Press, Columbia University, 1955.

King, E. M. "The Influence of Teaching on Reading Achievement." *Reading for All,* ed. by Robert Karlin. Proceedings of the Fourth IRA World Congress on Reading. Newark, Del.: International Reading Association, 1973, pp. 110–115.

Malmquist, E. "Perspectives on Reading Research." *Reading for All,* ed. by Robert Karlin. Proceedings of the Fourth IRA World Congress on Reading. Newark, Del.: International Reading Association, 1973, pp. 142–155.

Spache, G. D. "Psychological and Cultural Factors in Learning to Read." *Reading for All,* ed. by Robert Karlin. Proceedings of the Fourth IRA World Congress on Reading. Newark, Del.: International Reading Association, 1973, pp. 43–50.

Tinker, M., and C. M. McCullough. *Teaching Elementary Reading,* 4th ed. Englewood Cliffs, N.J.: Prentice-Hall, 1975.

White, N. J. "I've Taught Them All." *The Clearing House,* **12**(3) (November 1937), 151, 192.

Chapter 2
Who Are Your Students?

As a teacher of language arts it is essential that you appreciate *many* factors about students, because for decades educational theorists (Rousseau, 1964; Drucker, 1957; Dewey, 1938) have encouraged the teacher to be concerned with the "gestalt" or *total* development of each child.

To understand the dimensions involved in saying "the total development of each child," it is advisable that the prospective teacher become acquainted with the large body of background information on learning potential and motivation.

What Principles of Learning Guide the Teacher of Language Arts?

Learning has been described in many ways. For our purposes it might be described as a change of behavior that persists and that is not due to maturation alone.

This rules out those behavioral changes associated with physical growing up. When a child begins to substitute a carefully drawn letter in the first grade for the scribbling he did before coming to school and uses this acquired skill to further develop his writing, he is learning.

Learning involves more than the acquisition of skills. It is a combination of *knowledge* and *skill* with a goal, supported by an attitude of *confidence*. As we influence the behavior of children in a learning situation, we are aware of these three factors. Often our task is not to teach a skill but to establish a goal for the learner so that he will employ knowledge he already has; or it may be encouragement to instill the confidence needed by the child in directing his skills toward a goal.

To a college student it may well seem that learning means the gathering of information. A history course might be considered an example of this kind of learning. Why did you take the history course? Your goal

A study of man's effort to communicate through signs helps children become objective about their own language skills. (COURTESY OF SAN DIEGO STATE COLLEGE.)

may have been to learn more about the United States. Did it change your behavior in any way? Will it influence your actions as a citizen? Will it influence your interests as you select recreational reading? Is your attitude the same with respect to political decisions you are asked to make? Your answers may be negative to all of these questions, yet the fact remains that you chose to take the course because of some personal motivation. Usually a college instructor attempts to make his classes interesting and to motivate your participation. In the back of his mind there is the comforting thought that you are there to learn about a subject he thoroughly enjoys and can help you learn. In addition, he may not face any special problems of communication. If you do not understand his language, you can review the subject matter in books or other reference materials with his aid. If you then fail to understand you are notified of that in the form of a low grade or through a conference.

The teacher of grade school children faces a different situation. Many a well-informed adult has failed completely as an elementary teacher because he or she could not guide the learning of individuals. The child is in your classroom because of cultural pressure rather than any specific decision of his own. As a matter of fact, he had no alternative but to go to school, because attendance is required by law. Fortunately, he has two culturally important goals that make school an attractive place. First, the young child wants to learn to read and write and, second, he desires to be accepted and loved. Because of this he strives to please the adults who are his associates. A child does many things through no other motivation than to please his parents or other family members and his teachers. One of the tragedies of childhood is to be in a situation where the tasks assigned cannot be accomplished in a way that wins approval.

Modern psychology has much to offer the teacher of language arts. The following principles emphasize some results of the work in psychology that may make learning more effective.

Teacher-Student Planning

The first principle is that teaching effort is most effective when the learner has a basic understanding of established goals and sees the relationship between what is taught and those goals. A visit to an elementary classroom will reveal that the teacher knows a great deal about each child. One of her concerns is interest. As she plans she asks, "What will interest Eric?" Or she will remember, "Lynne is very interested in insects." She also knows that children follow patterns of interests as they develop. Home, parents, babies, and fun are universal interests of the beginners. As their environment expands, interests will include neighbors, children far away, foods of different countries. Schools often plan their curriculum units around these known common interests. Such interests establish purposes for reading, writing, and research; they therefore provide goals for the child in undertaking certain tasks.

When children have rather limited interests, the effective elementary teacher plans situations that will arouse curiosity and questions. Sometimes a film will awaken interest in volcanoes or animals. An exhibit of pioneer objects that can be handled may lead to further study of history. When this is accomplished, the teacher has motivated an interest. Sometimes a teacher is criticized for forcing interests on children rather than developing interests that already exist. The problem faced by most teachers is one of working with a large group of children rather than with just one or two. With one or two, a teacher could well teach language in association with the emerging interests of each child. With a total

The teacher plans situations that will arouse curiosity and questions. (PHOTO BY LINDA LUNGREN.)

class a teacher faces such practical problems as meeting certain expected achievement standards and having enough material on hand to gain certain objectives, as well as the social responsibility of controlling youthful energy so that learning can receive some direction. Motivation that results only in acceptance by children of teacher-determined goals will never be as effective as goals mutually desired by teacher and pupil. At times during the day motivation can come from each individual child; at other times it must be group determined.

The word *attainable* is significant with respect to goals. The child who is constantly asked to do more than he can accomplish is in a difficult position. The adult can simply walk away from the situation by resigning from a job, changing courses, or moving to another town. The child cannot meet frustrating conditions in the same way. He may misbehave or move into a dream world and ignore what is happening to him. Some will put forth extra effort to master a task for a time if they feel the pressure from home or the teacher. Eventually, for the sake of relieving tension, these children create for themselves an acceptable self-image that does not value the specific skill. It is safe to say that few children are motivated for any length of time by continuous failure. Of equal importance in considering the word *attainable* is the child who achieves without effort. For some children the tasks of education present little challenge. Proficiency with the yo-yo is not an especially satisfying skill for a college student. In almost any classroom there is one child who is completely bored by the situation. Frequently we exploit these children by making little teachers out of them. This action at least recognizes their superior knowledge, although it seldom helps them toward greater educational growth. The most effective effort is put forth by children when they attempt tasks that fall into the "range of challenge"—not too easy and not too hard—where success seems quite possible but not certain.

Personalizing Learning

A second basic understanding about directing the learning of children is that you as a teacher must consider individual differences. A college classroom of future teachers studying the language arts is a fairly homogeneous group. Not only have the students passed through a number of educational filters so that they all must be good learners, but also they have made a common vocational choice. No elementary classroom can be made this homogeneous. Yet there are differences within the college classroom; some students are married and have children; others have traveled widely; others belong to campus organizations. Although they may have a common interest in teaching, their other interests may vary widely.

A classroom of children will reveal differences in rate of learning, interests, social and economic backgrounds, and dozens of other factors that must be recognized. The teacher knows that the *whole* child comes to school, not just a mind to be taught. Some of the differences that the teacher considers would be the child without a breakfast, the child who is worried because he heard his parents quarreling the night before, and the child who had a nightmare after seeing a TV movie. The differences have a direct influence on the goals established for each child.

It should not be assumed that all instruction must be individualized because of these differences. There are common needs that might be considered with respect to the group. There are many similar interests based on ages and years in school that form the basis for group instruction. The important thing to remember is that a competitive rating is not appropriate in many elementary classrooms. To let a child who reads very well set the expected standard for the class would be as foolish as to let the one who sings the best establish the only acceptable vocal standard for all. Yet we sometimes act as if we were saying that unless you read as well as Daryl you cannot get an A in reading. A more common way of ignoring the significance of individual differences is to use an average score as the means of measurement. This is simply a numerical manipulation that has an apparent authority far beyond any defensible reason. If we give a spelling test and add the scores made and divide by the total number of students, we can find the average score. If all those taking the test were of equal ability and aptitude, the results might indicate those who put forth the greatest effort and least effort to study the words. But if those taking the test represented the normal range in ability, the average would not tell us what we need to know. It is only as we consider the work exhibited by each child in terms of his personal idiosyncrasies that we can make any judgment worthy of a professional teacher.

It is especially important that as a teacher you accept individual differences as well as recognize them. Some teachers spend a career trying to make people alike in the area of reading and writing. One hears them say, "If Harold would only try as hard as Dennis!" the inference being that with more effort Harold could be like Dennis. As children advance through the school years, the differences in the skills taught at school will become greater. The span of reading ability in a first grade will be small, usually ranging from six months to three years. The span of reading ability in a sixth grade will range from the second-grade level to the adult reading level. The device most frequently used to make dissimilar groups alike is to hold the top ones back by limiting material to sixth-grade books while providing special training for those "below grade level," with the assumption that through some teaching magic those who read second-grade material can be brought to the sixth-grade level.

As a teacher it is also important to be careful as to the predictions made about children based on present performance or potential level of achievement. Some "late bloomers" may eventually surpass pupils who seem far ahead of them in grade school. It is well to remember that it is only in school that success is limited to success in reading.

Simulated Learning Situations

A third basic principle of teaching children is to present the skills or information in situations similar to those in which they will be used. Language is functional when it is used in conversation, reports, letter writing, listening to the radio, viewing television, telling a story, or any other of the communicative acts of daily life. Effective expression, legibility in writing, correctness in usage, or thoughtfulness in listening and reading will develop only to the extent that children discover these skills to be of value in the daily, functional use of language. To isolate instruction on any aspect of language without this understanding on the part of the learner produces very limited results.

This does not mean that drill is entirely out of place in the language arts program. But to be effective the drill must be self-assigned by the learner in terms of a specific goal he desires to achieve. Drill on a specific word in spelling may involve writing the word many times, just as drill in basketball may involve shooting toward the basket over and over again.

The same is true of worksheets that involve selection of such correct usage items as *set* and *sit* or *lie* and *lay*. They are true learning devices only when the student does them with an understanding of the possible error and the desire to correct an error he has made. Some children in filling in blanks on worksheets make the same errors year after year, and the teachers carefully record scores made on these assignments. Some teachers have the students correct errors and think that they are doing a good job of teaching. Teachers may defend this procedure by saying that all judgments concerning the language arts are based on standardized test results. The teachers feel that they are preparing the children for this measurement by such drills, and in that they are correct. But it should be recognized that they are teaching for testing rather than for any functional use of the language.

An example of an effective application of this learning principle can be found in association with letter writing. During the year the need to write a business letter will develop in connection with the work of the students. At that time instruction should be given concerning the form of such letters, and careful attention should be given to their content. If the letter is actually mailed, children will welcome the experience and remember the information taught.

Related to this is the care that must be taken to assure that something once taught will be used when needed. As a new language skill is introduced, it becomes a standard to be applied in all work. Throughout the year students will add to the list of standards that they expect to maintain as they write and speak, and as new knowledge is employed and habits are established.

Developing Concepts

A fourth basic principle of teaching is that concepts are best established by using many firsthand perceptual experiences. How easy our task would be if it were only a matter of "telling" the child. If concepts were built by lectures, an oral reading of the law would make good citizens of all of us. However, a concept is a *word* or *phrase* that identifies or classifies a group of objects, events, or ideas. Given any group of objects, we are concerned with finding distinguishing features that can be classified or given a concept label. A concept may be concrete: *cat* or *truck;* or it may be abstract: *friendship* or *maturity.* The concept may be more or less inclusive as well. *Animal* is more inclusive than *dog;* and *dog* is more inclusive than *German shepherd.*

Concept Formation

Concept formation is the process of building an understanding of objects and experiences, particularly in relation to others. The product of concept formation, or conception, is a *concept.* We often designate a concept as a *term.*

Perception, or mere awareness, becomes conception. This development is quite complex, and there remains a great deal to be learned about it. In his observations of the transition from perception to conception, Piaget (1963) concluded that (1) the amount of redundant material decreases, (2) the amount of irrelevant information that can be tolerated without affecting the responses increases, and (3) the spatial and temporal separation increases over which the total information contained in the stimulus field can be integrated. As the concept forms, the learner requires less repetition, is less distracted by irrelevant information, and can deal with greater time and space separation.

The complex process of concept formation has been studied in some detail by L. S. Vygotsky (1962). He has concluded that the child, during his early years, associates a number of objects with a single word. This association can be based only on an impression, such as "leggedness." For example, to the child *doggie* may equal *horse, cat, donkey, cow, teddy bear,* and *chair.* From this large grouping of objects, the child exercises

trial-and-error methods to improve his organization of this "heap" (as Vygotsky calls it). He organizes his visual field and reorganizes heaps by associating elements from different heaps with a new word. As the child matures, he continues to reorganize and reassociate various elements, he begins to make these decisions on the basis of more concrete features. The child does not yet distinguish between relevant and irrelevant attributes of objects, since he may associate objects on the basis of similarities, contrasts, proximity in space or time, or his own practical experiences. In this phase of concept formation, however, the child still groups objects *in toto* with all of their attributes.

In the final stage of concept formation the child is able to consider single elements apart from the concrete *experience* in which they were first encountered. The process of concept formation, seen in all of its complexity, appears as a *movement* of thought within the pyramid of concepts. This movement constantly alternates between two directions—from the particular to the general and from the general to the particular (Vygotsky, 1962, pp. 80–81).

Concept formation, in its simplest form, consists of three basic steps:

1. Delineating global wholes into specific elements.
2. Grouping these elements on the basis of common characteristics.
3. Naming, labeling, or categorizing the elements.

Because young children are growing both mentally and physically, they need many opportunities to examine and reorganize the concepts they have developed. They need many experiences that will expose them to new objects, events, and ideas. The child's ability to comprehend what he reads and his ability to think evaluatively will be facilitated by his having carefully defined concepts.

Concept Attainment

Concept attainment is affected by several factors, including the nature of the concept (whether it is abstract or concrete), the child's developmental stage, and the kinds of experiences he has had in his lifetime. This suggests that there is a time and a kind of experience appropriate for a child—a ''teachable moment'' or the *''right kind* of experience at the right time for the developing organism'' (Hooper, 1968, p. 423).

Much of Piaget's work deals with how the individual attains concepts. He discusses *accommodation* and *assimiliation* in the developing child. *Accommodation* refers to the individual's modification or reorganization of his existing mental structure. When he encounters something new that is not part of his existing mental structure, he must accommodate the new information to the old. *Assimilation* refers to the individual's internalization of the change. Once he can handle the new experience with ease, he has assimilated the new information.

The accommodation–assimilation process is a form of *adaptation*. The individual is learning to deal with new experiences and information, and is therefore adapting to new elements in the environment. Ginsberg and Opper give a prime example of infant accommodation:

Suppose an infant of 4 months is presented with a rattle. He has never before had the opportunity to play with rattles or similar toys. The rattle, then, is a feature of the environment to which he needs to adapt. His subsequent behavior reveals the tendencies of assimilation and accommodation. The infant tries to grasp the rattle. In order to do this successfully he must accommodate in more ways than are immediately apparent. First, he must accommodate his visual activities to perceive the rattle correctly; then he must reach out and accommodate his movements to the distance between himself and the rattle; in grasping the rattle he must adjust his fingers to its shape; and in lifting the rattle he must accommodate his muscular exertion to its weight. In sum, the grasping of the rattle involves a series of acts of accommodation, or modifications of the infant's behavioral structures to suit the demands of the environment. [Ginsberg and Opper, 1969, p. 19]

Developmental Stages

In dealing with children, one must allow time for the accommodation process Piaget has discussed in the stages of thought development in the growing child. He suggests that the evolution of thought coincides *roughly* with age-developmental stages:

1. *Sensorimotor* stage or preverbal intelligence, roughly from birth to eighteen months or two years.
2. *Preoperational,* roughly from two to seven years. This is the stage in which children group and categorize according to function. For example, the child might group pencil with paper, or hat with coat. A child grouped a knife with a carrot and potato because ''you can peel them with it.''
3. *Concrete operations,* roughly from seven to eleven years. This is the stage of thinking while mentally or physically manipulating specific objects or concrete events.
4. *Formal operations,* from about eleven years on. This is the stage of conceptual or formal thought, during which the child likes to think in abstract terms and enjoys hypothesizing.

As a true developmental stage theorist, Piaget suggests that cognitive growth stages stem from the preceding stages, and emerge in a logical pattern. The stages are irreversible and unavoidable. ''According to Piaget, every child must pass through the stages of cognitive development in the same order'' (Wadsworth, 1971, p. 28). Therefore, the child cannot go through the concrete operations stage and then the preoperational stage, nor can he go directly from the sensorimotor stage to the concrete operations stage. The child must accomplish certain learning tasks before going on to more complex tasks. Thus one cannot skip and/or reverse stages.

Although the developmental stages are identified with certain age ranges, these ranges are only approximations. ''Cognitive development flows along, but the stages are useful to the observer conceptualizing the developmental process'' (Wadsworth, 1971, p. 26). The rate at which children pass through the developmental processes is not fixed, but is an approximation that may be affected by intelligence, physical and mental health, social conditions, and other variables.

Children can learn only what they have experienced. All meanings are limited by the experiences of the learner. The understanding of democracy may start from such basic behaviors as taking turns, participating in a group decision, acting as chairman of a group, or being on the school safety patrol. Eventually we hope that these illustrations will aid the child in developing an understanding of our way of life.

Fortunately the imagination of a child is so vivid that some concepts will develop as he identifies himself with characters in a story or with great personages in history. Some children can do this as they read, others as they participate in role-playing dramatizations, and still others through discussion of problems and situations.

Some of the concepts are developed in association with other learning. The teacher may think she is doing a fine job teaching speech by means of a verse choir, yet the child may actually be learning to like or dislike poetry rather than to enunciate correctly. All learning situations have an emotional content. Often the feeling about a learning situation remains long after the facts taught are forgotten. One teacher reports remembering a composition he had written on Italy in the fifth grade. The contents are forgotten except that for his cover he drew a flag of Italy. He does remember vividly a mental picture of the teacher mounting his composition on the bulletin board. He also reports that since that time Italy and things Italian have held a special attraction for him.

Retaining What Has Been Learned

A fifth basic principle has been implied in the other four but for the purpose of emphasis should be noted by itself. It is simply that, to be retained, learning must be used. Learning for a specific situation—such as memorizing a part in a play or studying Japanese while visiting Japan—disappears in a very few years if not used. Nearly every college student reading this page once knew how to solve a problem involving square root. Now if you try to obtain the square root of any four-figure number without referring to the tables, you will probably find you have completely forgotten how to do it, simply because the knowledge has not been used recently. Usually we plan instruction with respect to specific learning in what might be called a spiral organization. We start with the known, go to the new, then return to the known. We call this reteaching, reinforc-

ing knowledge, integration of knowledge, or simply review. Seldom do we attempt to move toward the new by climbing stairs where each step represents new knowledge.

This reteaching principle places a responsibility on the teacher. The teacher, as the mature individual in the teaching-learning situation, is expected to plan and select experiences that are useful to the child at his present stage of development. In the language arts curriculum of today this can be illustrated by the way phonics is taught. A few years ago the school day provided a separate period for phonics. Children were drilled in the sounds of the English language. Some were able to transfer this knowledge so that it could be used in reading and spelling. Others failed to make the transfer. In order to render this knowledge more useful, teachers were told to teach the specific phonics needed to meet a specific reading or spelling need. As soon as the child knew two words that started with the same sound, he was taught to note the beginning letter and to apply its sound in a new word. Thus the immediate usefulness of phonics was apparent to the learner.

Later, when we discuss the parts of speech, we will see that this problem has reference to teaching sentence analysis. No matter how sincerely we drill children in identification of nouns, verbs, adjectives, and other parts of speech, few children remember this information. For some reason we have not taught this subject in a way useful to the learner in the elementary grades. Application of this principle means that teachers must first find a way in which the language skills we teach children can be of immediate service to them and then see that it is used with frequency to prevent forgetting.

External Learning Stimulants

A sixth basic principle that greatly influences learning involves external learning stimulants: family, home environment, and parent involvement.

Family

VERBAL DISCOURSE WITHIN FAMILIES. The child's oral language experiences are a vital factor in his reading success. Oral language provides a foundation on which the child is able to build many other language skills. To encourage optimum language development, parents need to talk a great deal, even to their youngest child. This will provide the child with the language model needed for learning. The family, therefore, begins influencing the child's attitude toward the language arts as early as the child is able to respond to language.

One of the most valuable experiences that the parent can provide is reading stories aloud to the maturing child. The parent can hold the book so the child can see both the illustrations and the printed page, and therefore establish and reinforce an understanding of the relationship between the spoken word and the printed page. This also serves to promote discussions of the story and pictures by the parent and child and may introduce new words into the child's vocabulary. Enjoyment of good literature also offers the child new language models and may initiate a growing interest in becoming an independent reader.

ROLE MODELING. That children who view their parents reading, who are read to by adults on a regular basis, and who have books and educational toys are successful at prereading tasks is supported by many research studies. In all cases, modeling results in higher child performance than parental noninvolvement, as shown by Hess and Shipman (1965), Klaus and Gray (1968), and many other researchers. Most of the modeling research studies, however, have not related to readiness for reading. The exceptions are Durkin's (1966) studies, which showed that modeling was an important predictor of reading success in cases of early readers.

PARENT-CHILD VERBAL INTERACTION FACTORS.
Verbal interaction between mother and child also appears to be of extreme importance in understanding the child's current level of development. Family factors that contribute to the relationship of modeling to reading success include the amount and quality of verbal interaction between the parent and the child. McCarthy (1954) postulated that a degree of verbal reading efficiency depended on the frequency and quality of contact between parent and child. The child's performance on cognitive tasks was associated with the "teaching style" of the mother in studies by Hess and Shipman (1965). In reading episodes between parent and child, this maternal teaching style becomes evident.

As early as the child is able to respond to language, members of the family can begin responding to the child, holding the book so that the illustrations as well as the printed page can be seen. (PHOTO BY LINDA LUNGREN.)

Studies have shown that modeling results in higher performance by children. (PHOTO BY LINDA LUNGREN.)

READING EPISODES BETWEEN PARENT AND TEACHER. The notion that reading to young children enhances language development and relates to reading success is supported by an extensive body of literature (Templin, 1957; MacKinnon, 1973; Durkin, 1974, 1976; Bullock, 1975; Almy, 1958). Several reading methods texts strongly urge parents to read to young children because books and stories offer children important "models of book language" (Durkin, 1974) and models of "life-lifting language" (Martin, 1960).

Children should also be read to as part of each school day. Chapparo (1975) maintains: "Storytime reading to children should be an integral part of every reading program—children need models." Durkin (1974) argues in favor of reading to young children on the premise that an oral reading episode "can be a vehicle for learning about children's readiness for reading."

The need for reading to young children has been acclaimed by most educators, but few researchers have investigated the most effective ways in which this reading should be done. Sir Allan Bullock's report, "A Language for Life" (1975), advised: "The best way to prepare the very young child for reading is to hold him on your lap and read aloud to him stories he likes—over and over again."

One of the few studies on the effects of reading style on the child's cognitive growth was conducted by Swift (1970). His very successful parent training program, called *Get Set,* first presented the value of reading to young children. The parents were taught to retell certain parts of stories in order to extend the verbalization and communication skills of their children, and were taught to ask experiential questions during the readings in order to encourage children to explore their thoughts verbally. The purpose of the program was to enable mothers to lengthen their children's thought, elaborate on their ideas, and improve their observational skills.

Adult-child interaction has been directly related to reading and language success by many researchers. Durkin (1966, 1974) and many others have reported that language growth in children is fostered in an environment in which there is much interaction of adults with children. Reading episodes therefore can provide both parents and teachers with valuable opportunities for enhancing the language abilities of children.

PARENTAL EVALUATION OF THE CHILD. There has been very little research on parents' knowledge of their child's cognitive abilities. Many parents make assertions based on few criteria. Jones (1972) found that mothers of ten- to twelve-year-old boys of high verbal attainment did not differ from mothers of boys of low verbal attainment "with respect to their knowledge of the child's academic progress at the .0 level of significance." There seems to be no comparable research for young children. In the field of parent and child relations this represents an uncharted area of potential interest for researchers.

Home Environment and Parental Influence

EDUCATIONAL RESOURCES. Family influences and verbal interaction have been discussed as factors related to the child's reading success. Children also need books and materials (toys, chalkboards, and so on) in order to prepare for reading (Bernstein, 1967; Beck, 1973; Durkin, 1974). The availability and use of reading materials and organizational opportunities by the child in the home environment have been cited as important to the development of reading skills (Jones, 1972).

Television viewing may very well be the single greatest home environmental influence on the child's later cognitive abilities, including reading ability. Let us examine the effect of television on early language development.

TELEVISION. Today's question is not whether educational television *is* effective, but rather to what degree it affects the growing child. Templin recognized the influence of television on changing norms of language ability when she argued for periodic language studies many years ago. In the introduction to *Certain Language Skills in Children,* she states:

The present study was begun after the introduction of television into many homes. Thus it is likely that more adult language was present in the environment than would have been true earlier. . . . It may be that the effect of such language stimulation in the child's environment would be even greater today than when the first data for this study were gathered just a few years ago. [Templin, 1957]

In response to the need for updated norms to account for the influence of television, there has been a great deal of research on the social and cognitive effects of television on children. However, there has been very little research on the interrelationship of television and language learning, reading, and the role of parents in the cognitive development of children.

Several researchers have demonstrated that parents play an important role in shaping attitudes toward television. Lyle and Hoffman (1972) report: "Mothers who watch television at least three hours per day are likely to have children who watch a great deal of television." Leifer (1974) suggests that parents must be especially active in limiting and guiding their children's exposure to television. Unfortunately, studies show that only one third of parents have established television-viewing rules for their children (Lyle and Hoffman, 1972).

Although general television viewing may or may not affect children's language growth, there is a significant body of literature suggesting that educational television in general and the Children's Television Workshop in particular are beneficial for children.

The *Sesame Street* program is a production of the Children's Television Workshop, resulting from a joint venture of the Carnegie and Ford Foundations and the U.S. Office of Education. As a result of their evaluation of *Sesame Street* for the Educational Testing Service, Ball and Bogatz stated:

The facts are that the show was seen to have a marked effect, not only in the areas of role learning of basic skills such as counting and in simple contiguity association learning as in learning the names of letters and numbers, but also in higher areas of cognitive activity such as sorting and classifying pictorial representations. [Ball and Bogatz, 1972]

Ball and Bogatz also maintain that "we should think of beginning with younger than 4-year-old children and perhaps raise our expectations of what these young children can learn."

What are the specific goals of a prereading program? What are the objectives of educational television? Bill Blanton has studied these questions and has developed objectives for prereading programs to serve as the basis for the educational television curriculum:

BLANTON'S EDUCATIONAL TELEVISION PREREADING OBJECTIVES

Letters

1. *Matching.* Given a printed letter, the child can select the identical letter from a set of printed letters.
2. *Recognition.* Given the verbal label for a letter, the child can select the appropriate letter from a set of printed letters.
3. *Labeling.* Given a printed letter, the child can provide the verbal sound.
4. *Letter Sounds.*
   a. For sustaining consonants (*f, l, m, n, r, s, v*), given the printed letter the child can produce the letter's corresponding sound.
   b. Given a set of words presented orally, all beginning with the same letter sound, the child can select from a set of words another word with the same initial letter sound.
5. *Recitation of the Alphabet.* The child can recite the alphabet.

Words

1. *Matching.* Given a printed word, the child can select an identical word from a set of printed words.
2. *Boundaries of a Word.* Given a printed sentence, the child can correctly point to each word in the sentence.
3. *Temporal-Sequence/Spatial-Sequence Correspondence.* (Words and sentences are read from left to right.)
   a. Given a printed word, the child can point to the first and last letter.
   b. Given a printed sentence, the child can point to the first and last word.
4. *Decoding.* Given the first five words on the reading vocabulary list (*ran, set, big, mop, fun*), the child can decode other related words generated by substitutions of a new initial consonant. (Example, given the word *ran* the child can decode *man* and *can.*)
5. *Word Recognition.* For any of the words on the *Sesame Street* word list, the child can recognize the given word when it is presented in a variety of contexts.
6. *Reading.* The child can read each of the 20 words on the *Sesame Street* word list.
[Blanton, 1972, p. 807]

The Electric Company, also developed by Children's Television Workshop, was designed to further develop reading skills. Its purpose is to supplement the reading of seven- to ten-year-olds.

As outlined by Roser, *The Electric Company* program emphasizes these curricular areas:

1. The left-to-right sequence of print corresponds to the temporal sequence of speech.
2. Written symbols stand for speech sounds. They "track" the stream of speech.
3. The relationship between written symbols and speech sounds is sufficiently reliable to produce successful decoding most of the time.
4. Reading is facilitated by learning a set of strategies for figuring out sound-symbol relationships.
[Roser, 1974]

Ball and Bogatz (1972) have also studied the effectiveness of *The Electric Company.* Their study was based on one hundred classes of children, half of whom viewed *The Electric Company* program as part of their school day. The other half was encouraged by the teachers to view the program at home. The classes who viewed the program at school achieved significantly larger gain scores than the other group. The results, however, did not show change in the students' attitudes toward school and toward reading.

Television therefore can be a vehicle of tremendous potential in children's learning. Our concern should not be only with reading via the printed page, for it can also be facilitated by television. The world of television is here to stay, and we should explore the many possibilities it offers for the development of language skills.

Modern psychology has taught us much more with respect to the way children learn, but the preceding principles should help the teacher begin to understand many of the factors involved in planning instruction for children.

How Do Schools Meet the Special Needs of Individual Students?

As a classroom teacher attempting to meet the extreme ranges of talent and abilities encountered in your classroom, you will need to individualize the curriculum by modifying the requirements of the regular curriculum. Usually we modify the requirements for children who, for many reasons, have an experiential or cognitive readiness below the norm, and also for those whose readiness for learning exceeds the classroom norm. Motivation for the child who far exceeds the norm may in some schools involve promoting him to a class where he works with students much older than himself but where he finds the content a stimulating challenge. However, if the classroom teacher understands the concept of "individualized instruction" and "meeting the needs of all children," every child may be kept with children of his own age and yet work in books suitable to his ability level.

Some individualized settings have been designed so that several teachers are with a large group of children who are divided according to interests or purpose. There may be a great deal of student tutoring when we group students. The room is carpeted, and children may be working on the floor, in large boxes under and on tables, or sometimes outside the classroom in a comfortable, secluded spot. There are many materials easily available to the learner. These may include individual sound tapes, film cassettes, games, animals, reference books, records with listening headphones, or objects such as a gasoline motor. The atmosphere is one of freedom to explore as well as achieve. In some there are continuous rewards in the form of stamps or other recognition. In none is there a predetermined achievement level that would create a sense of failure. Time is usually organized by the learners in conference with the teacher. Some are far more skill oriented than traditional classrooms in that progress is based on a sense of

Rooms are designed to facilitate individualized or small-group instruction. The atmosphere is one of freedom, and many materials are easily available to the learner. (PHOTO BY LINDA LUNGREN.)

mastering rather than covering a book or preset curriculum.

Some teachers have always followed such a program because of their orientation to children and their educational goals. Nearly all kindergartens have been such classrooms in the past.

Many activities are available that encourage the development of individual abilities. Guided reading in the world of literature, research reports from encyclopedias, creative expression in original stories, plays, and poems, and surveys relating to a personal interest are but a few of these. Procedures will differ according to the abilities or needs of the child.

There may be a difference between highly creative individuals and those with high intelligence potential. One study reports that creative talents do not seek conformity with teacher-approved models, nor do they seek to possess now the qualities that will lead to adult success. The investigators report, "It is as if the high-IQ children seek and like safety and security of the known while the highly creative seem to enjoy the risk and uncertainty of the unknown." These creatively gifted individuals consider high marks, IQ, pep and energy, character, and goal-directedness less important than does the high-IQ group. They do rate a wide range of interests and a sense of humor higher than the high-IQ group. Indeed, humor is marked among the creatively talented. Apparently these children do not find a comfortable place in many classrooms, yet they possess a gift more rare than academic intelligence (Guilford, 1959).

There is one special group that a beginning teacher needs to understand well to avoid serious error in judgment and practice. These are the children who come from homes where English is not spoken. Common sense tells us that their primary need is a knowledge of the English language. They are not necessarily slow learners and should not be treated as such. Of course, they appear slow in a world where the printed books and all instruction are in a foreign language.

In the language program there will be a greater emphasis on oral speech experiences based on actually shared experiences of the group. These children need a lot of directed "doing" of the type associated with kindergarten activities. They need to handle things. Early reading will be limited to basic signs such as "Stop" and "Go." Much of the learning is situational—what we do and say when we visit the principal's office, when we go to the cafeteria, when we watch a program.

All children want praise and honor as much as anyone else does. It should be given to them when they achieve growth or improvement. Just as the gifted need to be challenged, so do all other children. It is sometimes difficult to think of a challenge for the gifted. It is equally difficult to appreciate what may be a challenge for the less ready child. With an understanding teacher all children become steady, stable, dependable workers.

How Do You Work with Very Young Children in School?

At the nursery school and kindergarten level each day is one of wonder and discovery. There are new things to see, new words to use, and new ideas to try. No day is long enough to see it all, and tomorrow seems so far away. As a teacher, you will be amazed at children's energy and constant need for activity.

In order to work well with very young children, you must learn to use a very different technique from that suitable for a group of young adults. In the Orient a form of wrestling called judo has been developed. It is a method of using an opponent's strength and energy so that it reacts against him. When the opponent makes a rushing attack, the master of judo estimates his force and momentum and instead of meeting them with an opposite force attempts to direct them so that the opponent is thrown to the floor. Although the analogy is a bit strained, it suggests how you can manage the energy of young children. You should not try to stop it or even keep up with it; but you should attempt to understand it, and provide ways for directing this energy so that the child's needs are met.

A visit to a kindergarten will reveal the physical characteristics of the age. Children are active and must move their large muscles. There are room centers where movement is possible because of the play equipment. Because this is the age of chickenpox, measles, and mumps, there are frequent physical checkups and absences. Because vision is not yet mature, the child is protected from activities that call for frequent refocusing of the eyes. Rest periods and quiet times alternate with periods of activity because fatigue is a natural result of expending so much energy.

Intellectually, children of this age are beginning to understand time patterns, follow simple directions, and see differences more readily than similarities. They are not quite certain about the distinction between reality and fantasy, and are able to tell or retell simple stories. The teacher provides opportunities to talk about and distinguish between imaginary and real things. The group shares experiences in order to build a common background. There is freedom to ask questions. Perhaps most important of all, children have an opportunity to listen and to be aware of the things they have learned through listening.

Emotionally, the young child demands affection and attention. The desire to please is powerful, and many ways are used to gain status. Some show evidence of fear of the unknown, and the wise teacher is careful about phobic response to punishment. At this age the threat of being sent to the principal's office can become, in the imagination of a child, almost equal to that of capital punishment for an adult. On the playground children become combative but are beginning to substitute language for force, using namecalling or verbal quarreling instead of hitting and kicking.

In the classroom there are outlets for emotions through dramatic play, listening to verse, and creative use of paints, clay, and paper. There is freedom to express opinions without fear of criticism, and there is freedom from pressure to work beyond abilities. Encouragement is given to the child to enable him to recognize himself as an individual and to respect the individuality of others. Limits to behavior are clearly defined so that the child is aware of how things are done while sitting on the rug, while tinkering with toys or equipment, or while playing outdoors or moving in single file through the halls.

Socially, children of this age are self-centered in their contacts with others. They learn how to work in a group, find sharing of prized objects a bit difficult, and look to adults for approval.

In the classroom the children are given an opportunity to participate in group activities and to be creative in social situations by dictating stories, poems, and experiences to the teacher, who records them. Opportunities to look at the work or behavior of the group, or of other small groups, provide occasions to define limits and expectations.

The children are taught such specifics as what to reply when a visitor comes to our room and says,

"Good morning, girls and boys." How may we show a visitor what we are doing? How can this block house be made better? What might we do to improve the way we played at the swing today?

Much of what is done in school at this age is important to the immediate needs of the child, but teachers must anticipate the future needs that must be satisfied as the child masters reading, writing, and other skills needed by educated persons in our society. The term used to describe this is *promotion of readiness*. Among the many factors involved in language readiness are the following:

Broad, rich experience

Vocabulary development

Ability to attend (stories, completion of work, participation)

Seeing likeness and difference

Hearing likeness and difference

Organizing thought in sequence

Being able to classify and generalize

Ability to follow instructions

Ability to speak clearly

Interest in books and experience of others

Ability to draw conclusions

Ability to recall details

A wise teacher looks at the language needs of children at the kindergarten level and asks two questions: "What skill do they need now as they live and work together in this room?" and "What later needs will be influenced by what we do now?" These children may not have a formal reading, spelling, or writing program; however, nearly every activity will be related to later development of these skills. As children learn to identify their own clothes hangers, as they watch the teacher put labels on objects in the room or write the day of the week on the chalkboard, each child begins to understand the meaning of reading. When a particular sound appeals to a child and he repeats it in a song or verse, he is mastering the sounds of our language that will later help him in spelling. The pictures done with great concentration at the easel are expressive experiences almost identical with writing in that they express an idea or experience visually.

From the moment the child enters the room and is greeted in a friendly manner until he leaves with a satisfactory feeling about the day, he has many language experiences. As he makes an airplane, he enjoys using the words that he has heard: *jet, pilot, hostess, fuel,* and maybe *supersonic.* As he paints the plane, color words take on meaning. A feeling of orderliness, neatness, and appropriateness accompanies his activities throughout the day. In cleanup, he used words like *over, under, behind, beside,* which have indefinite associations. Dramatic play in the home, store, and other interest centers calls for conversations that explain sentence structure, choice of words, and organization of ideas. On his walks he learns to see, listen to, and appreciate the sights and sounds of nature. When his sensory experiences are vivid, he bubbles over with ideas and loves to talk about what he saw, what he did, how things look, and how he feels.

Throughout the day you may find the right moment to bring literature either to one child alone or to a group of children. As a child works with others to build a play road, church, or bridge, you may find an occasion to read to the group such poems as James Tippet's "Trains," "Trucks," "Tugs," and "The River Bridge." A teacher who can go to her file and find "My Dog" and read, "His nose is short and stubby, his ears hang rather low," ending with the thought "Oh, puppy, I love you so," has given the children an expression for their inner feeling. If she teaches them the action play or finger play that starts, "My dog, Duchess, knows many tricks," and substitutes the name of Shannon's dog, new experience is shared.

At times, the teacher is wisest who remains silent and waits for children to react. She realizes that truly educative experiences mean not only active presentation of ideas, questions, and materials but also a quiet alertness to and observation of the child's responses to the environment and to her.

There is much "planned" listening for these children. While they close their eyes, they listen to the fire crackling, the sound of a truck passing, or an object being tapped. They listen to you reading and to each other telling about the events at home. It has been said that "the child who listens is one who has been listened to." In order to serve the child's listening needs, we establish standards not only for what children will tell us but also for how they will listen. The group decides that today we will only tell about happy things, beautiful things, pets, or things that make sounds. The very shy may tell only the teacher; the very vocal must limit himself to only one incident of his trip.

The child leaves the kindergarten with the beginnings of many skills. Among those closely related to language, one should note these:

Beginning Language Skills

Ability to listen:
When a story is read aloud.
When a speaker is telling of an experience.
To different sounds and tones.
To directions.
To hear likenesses and differences.
To rhythms.
To gain ideas.

Ability to speak:
In complete thoughts.
Repeating sounds.
Imitating good speech patterns.
In a pleasant voice.
Telling of his own experience.
Showing feeling in manner of expression.

Abilities related to future reading:
Recognizing simple sequence.
Recognizing likenesses and differences in letter forms.
Connecting symbols with ideas.
Care in handling picture books.
Interpreting the events in a picture.

Abilities related to future writing:
Learning to use paintbrush, chalk, pencil.
Putting teacher-made signs and labels on objects.

Expressing oral ideas that the teacher records.

Experimenting with paint, chalk, crayon, and pencil in imitating writing.

What Will Children in the Elementary Grades Be Like?

As children progress through the first and second grades, their standards often exceed their abilities. There is much dissatisfied crumpling of paper or erasing. One writer describes this as the "eraser" age. Teachers sometimes make it a rule that all erasing will be done by the teacher in order to keep children from rubbing holes through the paper. This behavior is only one aspect of the child's awareness of criticism from peers or age mates. The world is no longer made for him alone, but for the group or gang with whom he identifies himself. What others think, the praise or punishment that others receive, and other children's opinions about things now have much greater influence on his conduct than they did previously.

There is a loss of personal freedom of expression in art and story. Where the child once wanted to paint simply what he felt or saw, he is now concerned about the effect his work will produce on others. Group judgment or practice will influence his clothes, eating habits, books read, language used, and personal conduct.

By the age of eight, definite speech patterns have developed. The eye is more adapted to the tasks of reading and writing. There is a sense of hurry and untidiness that is related to tendency toward accidents. These accidents are also associated with curiosity and interests that outdistance caution. Exploring the unknown is a favorite activity.

Emotionally, primary children desire and seek prestige. The Cub Scout or Brownie uniform is worn with pride. Those who do not belong show jealousy, and, because feelings are still near the surface, violent outbursts or sullen withdrawal can be expected at times. Boy-girl relationships are either at the companion level or ignored. These children look for recognition from adults through use of social courtesies and individual association, but at the same time they seek independence through peer group approval. Most want adults to keep "hands off," literally and figuratively.

The older children of this age range are sometimes referred to as being in the latency period rather than preadolescence. Because they have already mastered the basic skills, they can follow their interests in all directions. Teachers of these groups are true generalists from the educational point of view. One day they may be learning how humans can breathe in outer space, the next how the United Nations is organized, and the next how the Aztec Indians told time.

In the sixth grade many of the girls have entered adolescence. They find emotions difficult to control. Trivial sights or events can cause a major crisis. Some overt emotional display may belie underlying causes. Sometimes these children cry when happy and show antagonism toward persons they admire. Ordinarily, the girls are taller and weigh more than the boys throughout the intermediate grades.

Intermediates like to plan and organize. Clubs are organized almost solely for the fun of organizing them, although such activity may express a yearning for great achievement. There is little regret when nothing of much significance happens in a club meeting. The important thing seems to be that the meeting took place. Close friends also constitute an aspect of this period, and new friendships explain some of the changed classroom behavior. Elections are often little more than popularity contests. New students go through a period of popularity as individuals seek them as friends. Note passing and in a few cases actual flaunting of a boy or girl friend are other common forms of social behavior at this time.

Working with these children requires a fine balance of permissiveness and control. At times free rein must be given to permit maximum use of abilities and extension of interest. At other times the control of the adult leader must be exercised to prevent immature judgments and emotional actions. This control requires a knowledge of each individual and of the nature of group interaction.

Beginning teachers are usually unprepared for the

wide range of abilities encountered in groups of children. A study conducted by Ketcham and Lafitte (1960) in Ferndale, Michigan, showed a reading range among children aged seven of thirty-two months, whereas among those aged twelve it was 107 months. The range in mental age increased from sixty-five months at age seven to 107 months at age twelve. Excluded from this study were children who had been placed in special rooms, so in some classrooms teachers would expect a greater range than this. Ferndale is a suburban city near Detroit. The range is probably similar in most American communities. This means that we must expect great variability in the results of teaching effort. There are many common interests and needs toward which teaching energies are directed, but by no effort or magic can we produce common achievement or "fifth-grade work" or "sixth-grade norms" with a total class. We have not failed as teachers, nor have some children failed as students. Although teaching and learning took place, the responses were influenced by the individual abilities of those with whom we work.

Previous studies of the growth patterns of individual children reveal that each child's pattern is uniquely his own. Some start early and continue to grow rapidly; others start late and are always behind their age mates. Yet we cannot be certain that one who starts early will be always ahead of his group. The following case study reveals why teachers hesitate to make absolute predictions.

At 78 months of chronological age all of Mary's growth measurements but one were below her chronological age. Her mental age was 64 months, reading age 74 months, weight age 76 months, and height age 84 months. By 138 months of chronological age, all of her growth measurements were above her chronological age. The child's IQ was 100 when she was 78 months old and 131 when she was 137 months old. By age twelve she had a reading age of fifteen although her reading did not equal her chronological age until age 8. [Ketcham and Lafitte, 1960]

Such children are not unusual. Parents will sometimes say, "My boy did not like reading until he had Miss Lungren in the fifth grade." With all due credit to Miss Lungren, the child was probably like the girl just described. However, it may have been the efforts of a Miss Lungren that prevented this child from accepting a self-image of being slow to learn or poor in scholarship.

Children move through this sequence of language growth in the elementary school—no two at the same rate or in the same way. The following is an approximate age sequence of the developmental stages of growth of preschool and elementary school-age children as prepared by the Tulare County Schools, California. With minor changes, this listing still seems appropriate today.

KINDERGARTEN (4½–6 YEARS)

Listening: Listen to peers in play groups. Develop an increasingly long attention span to stories. Can remember simple directions and messages.

Speaking: A few will still be developing speech sounds, using them correctly in some words and not in others. Use simple direct sentences. The vocabulary ranges from 2,000 to over 10,000 words.

Reading: Interpret books, explore books. Can identify some signs such as STOP or displayed words on television. About 1 in 600 can read children's books.

Writing: Like to watch adults write. Experiment with crayola and paints.

GRADE ONE (5½–7 YEARS)

Listening: Listen to clarify thinking or for answers to questions. Can repeat accurately what is heard. Listen for specific sounds in words and the environment.

Speaking: Can share experiences before the group in an established way. Use compound and complex sentences. Use the grammar patterns of the home. Some speech repetition takes place as they try to remember words for ideas they wish to express.

Reading: Read charts, preprimers and primers, and master a vocabulary of 300 to 600 words. Understand the use of many consonant sounds.

Writing: Write names, labels for pictures, and stories to illustrate art work. The spelling applies the phonics of reading.

GRADE TWO (6½–8 YEARS)

Listening: Listen with increasing discrimination. Making suggestions and asking questions to check their understanding. Are aware of situations when it is best not to listen.

Speaking: Have mastered all sounds of speech and use them correctly. Use some of the "shock" words of our language without complete understanding.

Reading: Read with increasing attention to meaning, enjoy selecting their own stories, read their own writing. Usually start the year in a first reader of a commercial reading series.

Writing: Write well with print script. Use dictionary books or notebooks as references for spelling. Seek to correct misspellings.

THIRD TO FOURTH GRADE (7½–10 YEARS)

Listening: Are increasingly aware of the value of listening as a source of information and enjoyment. Listen to the reports of others, tapes of their own reports, and radio broadcasts with purpose and pertinent questions. Display arrogance with words or expressions they do not understand.

Speaking: Re-enact and interpret creatively radio, movie, and story situations as they play. Speak fairly well to adults and can make themselves understood. Are praised in most school-associated social situations. Vocabulary of some children may be as high as 60,000 words.

Reading: Read with interpretive expression. Grow in reading speed as they read silently. Most children succeed in using reading as a study skill.

Writing: Reports are written in all subject areas. Creative stories and poems are written. Write rough copies with a willingness to recopy to improve legibility, ideas, and punctuation.

FIFTH TO SIXTH GRADE (9½–12 YEARS)

Listening: Listen critically for errors, propaganda, false claims. Listen to a wide variety of stories, poetry, rhyme and find pleasure in exploring new types.

Speaking: Show an increasing awareness of the social value of conversation and try to get what they want through persuasion. Become increasingly competent in the use of inflections, modulation, and other methods of voice control. Employ singing, yelling, whispering, and talking. Can conduct club meeting and present organized talks or dramatic recitations.

Reading: Show increased interest in factual material and how-to-do-it books. Many read independent of instruction. Use reading with greater purpose, such as getting information for a trip, checking references, or following a personal interest. Adapt method and speed of reading to the content and purpose.

Writing: Make between 1½ to 2 errors in each sentence at first. Find new uses for writing as they answer advertisements and do creative work. Are interested in the writing techniques of others and will note good and poor composition in the newspapers. Like to see their writing in print. Use the dictionary as a spelling aid.

[Tulare County Schools, 1949]

Although a general age range of language arts development has been suggested, a wide range of skill development will be obvious in any elementary classroom. This occurs because you are working with *individuals,* all with varying degrees of experience and readiness. You may group them for instruction, but do not for one moment lose sight of the dimensions and needs of *each individual*. Each child, for ten months, will be dependent on you to provide learning experiences that nurture his cognitive and emotional growth. Indeed, teaching is an entailed task.

Bibliography

Almy, M. "The Importance of Children's Experience to Success in Beginning Reading." *Research in the Three R's,* ed. by Hunnicutt and Iverson. New York: Harper & Row, 1958.

Ball, S., and G. A. Bogatz. "Research on *Sesame Street:* Some Implications for Compensatory Education." Paper presented at the Second Annual Blumbery Symposium in Early Childhood Education. Baltimore: Johns Hopkins University Press, 1972.

Beck, I. L. *A Longitudinal Study of the Reading Achievement Effects of Formal Reading Instruction in the Kindergarten: A Summative and Formative Evaluation.* Unpublished doctoral dissertation, University of Pittsburgh, 1973.

Bernstein, B. "Elaborated and Restricted Codes: Their Social Origin and Some Consequences." *The Ethnography of Communication,* ed. by B. Gumperz and D. Mymes. American Anthropologist Publication, 1967.

Blanton, W. "How Effective Is Sesame Street?" ERIC/CRIER column, *The Reading Teacher* (May 1972), 807.

Brown, R. *Words and Things.* New York: Free Press, 1958, p. 69.

Bullock, Sir A. "A Language for Life." Report for the British Government, 1975.

Chapparo, J. "A New Look at Language Experience." *A Successful Foundation for Reading in a Second Language.* Conference, San Diego, Calif., 1975.

Chase, W. G. (ed.). *Visual Information Processing.* New York: Academic Press, 1973.

Chomsky, C. S. *The Acquisition of Syntax in Children from 5 to 10.* Cambridge, Mass.: MIT Press, 1969.

Chomsky, N. *Aspects of the Theory of Syntax.* Cambridge, Mass.: MIT Press, 1965.

Chomsky, N. *Language and Mind.* New York: Harcourt Brace Jovanovich, 1972.

Chomsky, N. "Phonology of Reading." *Basic Studies in Reading,* ed. by M. Levin and J. Williams. New York: Harper & Row, 1970.

Chomsky, N. *Syntactic Structures.* The Hague: Mouton, 1957.

Dewey, J. *Experience and Education.* New York: Macmillan Publishing Co., Inc., 1938.

Drucker, P. "The New Philosophy Comes to Life." *Harpers Magazine* (August 1957), 37–40.

Durkin, D. *Children Who Read Early: Two Longitudinal Studies.* New York: Teachers College Press, Columbia University, 1966.

Durkin, D. *Teaching Them to Read.* Boston: Allyn and Bacon, 1974.

Durkin, D. *Teaching Young Children to Read.* Boston: Allyn and Bacon, 1976.

Gallagher, J. J. "Productive Thinking." *Review of Child Development Research,* Vol. I, ed. by M. L. Hoffman and L. W. Hoffman. New York: Russell Sage Foundation, 1964.

Ginsberg, H., and Opper, S. *Piaget's Theory of Intellectual Development.* Englewood Cliffs, N.J.: Prentice-Hall, 1969.

Gordon, W. J. J. *Synetics—The Development of Creative Capacity.* New York: Harper & Row, 1961.

Guilford, J. P. "Convergent and Divergent Aspects of Behavior." Lecture, San Diego County, October 1960. See also his *Personality.* New York: McGraw-Hill, 1959, Chapters 15 and 17.

Hess, R. D., and V. C. Shipman. "Early Experience and the Socialization of Cognitive Modes in Children." *Child Development,* **36** (1965), 869–886.

Hooper, I. H. "Piagetian Research and Children." *Logical Thinking in Children,* ed. by I. E. Sigel and F. H. Hooper. New York: Holt, Rinehart and Winston, 1968.

Jones, J. P. *Intersensory Transfer, Perceptual Shifting, Modal Preference and Reading.* Newark, Del.: International Reading Association, 1972.

Kagen, J. *Change and Continuity in Infancy.* New York: Wiley, 1971.

Ketcham, W. A., and R. G. Lafitte. "A Description and Analysis of Longitudinal Records of Development of Elementary School Children in Ferndale, Michigan." Ferndale Public Schools, 1960.

Klaus, R. A., and W. S. Gray. *The Early Training Project for Disadvantaged Children: A Report After Five Years.* Society for Research in Child Development Monographs, Serial No. 120, 1968, pp. 33 and 34.

Leifer, G. "Children's Theater Workshop." Harvard Educational Workshop, 1974.

Lenneberg, E. H. *Biological Foundations of Language.* New York: Wiley, 1967.

Lyle, L., and M. Hoffman. "Children's Use of Television

and Other Media." *Television and Social Behavior,* Vol. 4, ed. by E. A. Rubinstein, G. A. Comstock, and J. P. Murray. Washington, D.C.: U.S. Government Printing Office, 1972.

MacKinnon, E. M. "Language, Speech, and Speech-Arts." *Philosophy and Phenomenological Research,* **34**(2) (1973), 224–238.

Mankiewicz, F. "Two Tributes." *Look Magazine Tribute to Robert Kennedy,* Special Issue (1968).

Martin, J. G. *Mediated Transfer in Two Verbal Learning Paradigms.* Unpublished doctoral dissertation, University of Minnesota, 1960.

McCarthy, D. "Language Development in Children." *Manual of Child Psychology,* 2nd ed., ed. by L. Carmichael. New York: Wiley, 1954, pp. 492–630.

Neisser, U. *Cognitive Psychology.* New York: Appleton-Century-Crofts, 1967.

O'Shea, M. V. *Linguistic Development and Education.* New York: Macmillan Publishing Co., Inc., 1970, pp. 234–35.

Piaget, J. *The Origins of Intelligence in Children.* New York: Norton, 1963.

Poincaré, H. *Science and Hypothesis.* New York: Dover, 1952.

Posner, M. I. *Cognition: An Introduction.* New York: Scott, Foresman, 1974.

Pribram, K. A. "Neurological Notes in the Art of Educating." *Theories of Learning and Instruction.* National Society for the Study of Education. Chicago: University of Chicago Press, 1964.

Robeck, M. C., and J. A. Wilson. *Psychology of Reading: Foundations of Instruction.* New York: Wiley, 1974.

Roser, N. L. "Electric Company Critique: Can Great Be Good Enough?" *The Reading Teacher,* **27**(7) (April 1974), 680–684.

Rousseau, J.-J. *Emile, Julie, and Other Writings.* New York: Barrow's Educational Services, 1964.

Schroder, H., M. Driver, and S. Streufert. *Human Information Processing.* New York: Holt, Rinehart and Winston, 1967.

Silbiger, F., and D. Woolf. "Perceptual Difficulties Associated with Reading Disability." *College Reading Association Proceedings,* **6** (Fall 1965), 98–102.

Smith, H. K. "The Responses of Good and Poor Readers When Asked to Read for Different Purposes." *Reading Research Quarterly,* **3** (1967), 53–83.

Spache, G. D., and E. B. Spache. *Reading in the Elementary School.* Boston: Allyn and Bacon, 1973.

Swift, M. "Training Poverty Mothers in Communication Skills." *The Reading Teacher,* **24** (January 1970), 360–367.

Templin, M. *Certain Language Skills in Children.* Minneapolis: University of Minnesota Press, 1957.

Tulare County Schools. *Tulare County Cooperative Language Arts Guide.* Visalia, Calif., 1949.

Vernon, M. D. "The Perceptual Process in Reading." *The Reading Teacher,* **13** (October 1959), 2–8.

Vygotsky, L. S. *Thought and Language.* Cambridge, Mass.: MIT Press, 1962.

Wadsworth, B. J. *Piaget's Theory of Cognitive Development.* New York: David McKay Co., 1971.

Wattenberg, W. W. *Adolescent Years.* New York: Harcourt Brace Jovanovich, 1973.

Part II
The Components of a Managed Language Arts Curriculum

Chapter 3
Language Arts Defined

THE WONDERFUL CIRCUS OF WORDS*

Characters

JAMIE
GRAMMARIAN
FOUR PENNANT BEARERS
PERIOD

WORDS:

ARTICLE

nouns		adjectives	
JIM		BEAUTIFUL	
JANE		SPARKLING	
JAPAN	nouns	RED	adjectives
BALL		WHITE	
BOOK		BLUE	

verbs		adverbs	
THROWS		SLOWLY	
BRINGS		QUICKLY	
RUNS	verbs	CLUMSILY	adverbs
LEAPS		SKILLFULLY	
MAKES		HAPPILY	

*Reprinted from Claire Boiko, *Children's Plays for Creative Actors* (Boston: Plays, Inc. 1967), pp. 35–44.

SETTING: *Jamie's living room.*

AT RISE: JAMIE *is sitting at the table, bent over a book of English grammar.*

JAMIE: Let's see. The teacher said to compose ten sentences. I'd better look up the definition of "sentence" in the grammar book. (*He flips pages of book.*) What a bore! (*Reads*) "A sentence is an association of words so ordered as to convey a completed idea." I wish I were outside playing baseball. (*Reads again*) "For example, 'The pencil is on the desk' is an example of a simple sentence." Boy! What a dull subject. Who cares about whether the pencil is on the desk, or the floor, or in the wastebasket. (JAMIE *waves his pencil, then grins as he imagines it is a bat. He holds it bat fashion.*) Batter up! (*He crumples a piece of paper into a ball.*) And the pitcher winds up for a super-special sizzle ball. (*Throws paper upstage*) And the ball streaks across the plate like a meteor . . . And it's a strrrike, ball fans! A strike! (*As* JAMIE *does this,* GRAMMARIAN, *dressed as a ringmaster, enters and sits on table. As* JAMIE *recovers the*

33

paper ball upstage, GRAMMARIAN *blows his whistle sharply.* JAMIE *turns, startled.*) Who are you?

GRAMMARIAN (*Bowing*): Flammarian Grammarian, Impresario of the English Language.

JAMIE: Where did you come from? I didn't see you a minute ago.

GRAMMARIAN: Oh, I've always been here. Every time you speak to someone or write a letter or read a book, I'm here. Now, Jamie, do I really look dull to you?

JAMIE: No, you don't, Mr. Grammarian. It's the grammar book. It's a lot of old mumbo-jumbo. But you look like a ringmaster.

GRAMMARIAN: That's just what I am. Grammar is the ringmaster, so to speak, of that wonderful three-ring circus, the English language. Once you glimpse the excitement of words, you will never again say that English is a dull subject.

JAMIE: I don't understand.

GRAMMARIAN: Let me demonstrate. (*He strides to center and blows his whistle, as the music of "Ta Ra Ra Boom De Ay" is heard.* FOUR PENNANT BEARERS *march on, followed by the* WORDS. *Each* PENNANT BEARER *carries a pennant marked "Nouns," "Verbs," "Adjectives," or "Adverbs," and is followed by the* WORDS *in that category. Each* WORD *may wear a name card.* ARTICLE *follows the other* WORDS, *beating time with a small drum. The* WORDS *arrange themselves in four columns, face the audience, and mark time until the* GRAMMARIAN *finishes.*) Ladies and gentlemen, teachers and students! We are about to present the most stupendous, most colossal, most difficult-to-spell language in the entire world! You are about to behold complex sentences full of intricate infinitives, scintillating syntax and red-hot rhetoric. Feast your optics on the first ring as your ringmaster presents the death-defying trapeze act, the Dangling Participles. Hold your breath as the Volatile Verbs, strong men of the sentence, tumble tenses and juggle conjugations. In ring number two, see the Adjectives in bangles and spangles, each one a princess of the polysyllables, and the clowns, those merry mix-ups of modification. And finally, in ring number three, the trained adverbs, each one especially educated to modify his own verb, adverb or adjective. And last but not least the Nouns! Twenty thousand—you count them— twenty thousand exotic, extraordinary Nouns, from "aardvark" to "Zanzibar," brought to you at enormous expense all the way from Noah Webster's Dictionary. Hurry! Hurry! Hurry! The show is about to begin! (*He*

blows his whistle; the WORDS *break ranks and mill about aimlessly.* JAMIE *pulls at* GRAMMARIAN'S *sleeve.*)

JAMIE: Mr. Grammarian—your words! They are just wandering around. Shouldn't somebody take them in hand— organize them?

GRAMMARIAN: Certainly! That is my task. You see, Jamie, grammar makes sense out of nonsense; (*He blows whistle;* WORDS *begin to arrange themselves back into columns.*) order out of chaos; sentences out of higgledy-piggledy words. (WORDS *are in order again, marking time quietly.*) Attention, words! Prepare yourselves to make a sentence! (WORDS *stop marking time and stand still.*) All right. Jamie. Help yourself to a subject. You may have any of my nouns.

JAMIE: I hate to be so thickheaded, Mr. Grammarian, but I don't know what a noun is. (*At this, the* NOUNS *march forward and arrange themselves horizontally along the stage as they speak in unison.*)

NOUNS:
A noun is a name
That means the same
As a person, a thing, or a place.

JIM: A noun can be—

JANE: The sky or the sea—

JAPAN: Yokohama—(*She bows.*)

BALL: Mickey Mantle.

BOOK (*Pointing to nose*): Or the nose on your face.

JAMIE: If I choose one of these nouns, will it be the subject of the sentence? What the sentence will be about?

GRAMMARIAN: That is correct.

JAMIE (*Inspecting the* NOUNS): I choose . . . Jim. He looks a little bit like me. I think I could make up a good story about him. (JIM *stands at attention, as the other* NOUNS *go back behind their* PENNANT BEARER, *in column form again.*)

JIM (*Stiffly, in robot fashion*): My name is Jim. I am a Proper Noun.

JAMIE: He's just standing there, Mr. Grammarian. He isn't doing anything.

GRAMMARIAN: You need a bit of action for your friend Jim. Why don't you try adding a verb? (*He whistles. The* VERBS *line up across the stage. As* JAMIE *inspects them, they pantomime their appropriate actions.*)

JAMIE: (*Pointing, as* THROWS, *dressed as discus thrower, throws*): He's throwing. (*As* RUNS, *in shorts and shirt, runs*) He's running. (*As* BRINGS, *dressed as weight lifter, brings dumbbells to him*) He's bringing. (*As* LEAPS, *dressed in Superman costume with cape, leaps*) He's leaping. (*As* MAKES, *dressed as carpenter, pretends to hammer a nail*) He's making something. Say, those verbs are hard workers, aren't they!

GRAMMARIAN: Indeed they are, Jamie. They make statements, give commands, ask questions, and behave like the muscles of the sentence. Watch Jim come alive when you choose a verb for him.

JAMIE: Let's see. . . . Baseball is my favorite sport, so I'll choose "throws." (THROWS *stands beside* JIM. *He pumps* JIM's *arm up and down in throwing motion.* JIM *smiles and winds up.*)

JIM (*Proudly*): Jim throws!

GRAMMARIAN: There! That is a genuine, twenty-four carat sentence.

JAMIE: That's a sentence? But there are only two words.

GRAMMARIAN: Very true, but those two words are all you need to express a complete thought.

JAMIE: But I don't know what Jim is throwing. It could be a rock, a bean bag, a pillow, or a ball.

GRAMMARIAN: What sort of word do you need?

JAMIE: A thing word . . . a . . . a . . .

NOUNS: You need a noun.

GRAMMARIAN: And a small article. (ARTICLE *and* BALL *come forward.* BALL *gives a tennis ball to* JIM, *and takes his place beside* ARTICLE *and* THROWS.)

JIM (*Winding up and throwing the ball offstage*): Jim throws the ball.

GRAMMARIAN: Are you satisfied with your sentence as it stands now?

JAMIE: Not quite. I don't know much about the ball. Maybe it's a big ball, like a basketball. Or a small one, like a ping-pong ball. Or a red and blue one, like a beach ball.

ADJECTIVES (*Stepping forward in line across stage*): You need an adjective. An adjective is a word that describes a noun. Listen to what we can do to Jim. Happy Jim. Sad Jim. Good Jim. Bad Jim. Fat Jim. Slim Jim. Bright Jim. Dim Jim.

JAMIE: Oh, is that what you are? I thought an adjective was something horrible.

ADJECTIVES: We can be horrible. Dreadful, deadly, doleful, desperate, demonic Jim!

JAMIE: Wow! Adjectives pack a lot of power. I'll use the adjective "white." (WHITE *takes her place in the sentence. She gives a white ball to* BALL, *who gives it to* JIM.)

JIM (*Throwing offstage*): Jim throws the white ball.

GRAMMARIAN: A fine, upstanding sentence. You may be proud of it.

JAMIE: Wait, Mr. Grammarian. I'm still not finished. It's that word "throws." The sentence doesn't tell *how* Jim is throwing the ball.

GRAMMARIAN: Is that important, Jamie?

JAMIE: Well, it certainly is. Say you are a pitcher—if you throw the ball slowly, the batter may hit a home run. If you throw clumsily, the umpire may call a ball. If you throw skillfully, you may strike the batter out. See?

GRAMMARIAN: I see. And I have just the words you need. The adverbs. (*He whistles. The* ADVERBS *take their places. Each one performs in pantomime as* JAMIE *inspects him.*)

JAMIE (*As* SLOWLY, *dressed as a turtle, crawls by*): That must be "slowly." (*As* QUICKLY, *dressed as a rabbit, hops by*) That's "quickly." (*As* CLUMSILY, *dressed as a bear, lumbers along*) "Clumsily"—that's how he's walking. (SKILLFULLY, *dressed as a monkey, juggles balls deftly*) The monkey is juggling "skillfully." (*As* HAPPILY, *dressed as a canary, smiles and whistles sweetly*) The canary sounds as if it's whistling "happily." Well, I like Jim. I want him to play a good game of ball, so I'll choose "skillfully." (SKILLFULLY *takes his place after* BALL. WHITE *gives another ball to* BALL *who gives it to* JIM. JIM *gives an extra special wind-up and throws the ball offstage.*)

SKILLFULLY (*Holding up three fingers like an umpire*): Strike three!

WORDS (*In unison*): Hooray for Jim! Jim throws the white ball skillfully! Jim throws the white ball skillfully!

JAMIE (*Proudly*): There now! That's a sentence. My very first real sentence.

GRAMMARIAN (*Smiling*): Are you quite sure you have finished?

JIM: Jim—

THROWS: Throws—

ARTICLE: The—

WHITE: White—

BALL: Ball—

SKILLFULLY: Skillfully—(*They keep repeating the sentence, one word at a time. After they have repeated it several times,* JAMIE *tries to quiet them down and motions them to stop, but they keep on going.*)

JAMIE: Hey! The sentence is going on and on. I can't stop it!

GRAMMARIAN: Yes, you can. Think a moment. What stops a sentence?

JAMIE: Oh! A period!

PERIOD (*Bouncing out and doffing beanie*): Did someone call me?

JAMIE: Can you stop my sentence?

PERIOD: Young man, I may look small, but I've stopped more sentences than a Philadelphia lawyer. (*He sits down firmly at the end of the sentence. The sentence stops at "skillfully."*)

JAMIE: There!

GRAMMARIAN: There! Now, do you feel happier about learning English grammar, Jamie?

JAMIE: Sure I do. But I've only started my sentences about Jim. I could go on and write a paragraph—or a composition.

GRAMMARIAN: Just a minute, Jamie. Do you know what time it is?

JAMIE (*Looking at the clock*): Nine o'clock! Why, I've never spent more than ten minutes on grammar before.

GRAMMARIAN: I must pack up my circus of words. I have an urgent appointment at the White House this evening.

JAMIE: Boy! The White House! Do you know the President?

GRAMMARIAN: I've known them all, my boy. When Mr. Jefferson first sat down with quill pen and ink, I was at his right hand, guiding him as he wrote, "When in the course of human events—" We did rather well on that document, Mr. Jefferson and I, if I do say so myself. But, I'll be back. This was only a smattering. Wait until you meet the Conjunctions, Prepositions, Pronouns, and Punctuation Marks.

JAMIE: Conjunctions! Pronouns! Punctuation Marks!

GRAMMARIAN (*Whistles*): Attention! Now hear this, all you words. Prepare to embark for Washington. (WORDS *form columns, march in place.*)

NOUNS:
Apples, animals, aspirin, ants!
Peanuts, pineapples, pots and plants!
Saturday, Sunday, Susan, Sam!
Timbuktu and Amsterdam!
We are nouns,
Whose voices sing
Of person, quality, place and thing.
(*They march off stage.*)

VERBS:
Dancing, prancing, jumping, bumping!
Doing, wooing, howling, scowling!
Reading, writing, weeding, fighting!
Being, seeing, fleeing, freeing!
Verbs command, and act, and ask—
Verbs can tackle any task!
(*They march offstage.*)

ADJECTIVES:
Scarlet, silver, sapphire, gold!
Toasty-warm, icy-cold!
Sugar-sweet, fleecy-white!
Dangerous, glamorous, dismal, bright!
Adjectives, gaudy as tropical birds,
Paint a picture with colorful words!
(*They march offstage.*)

ADVERBS:
Happily, sadly, snappily, madly!
Afterwards, almost, rarely, badly!
Also, always, sometimes, never!
Forward, backward, seldom, ever!
Adverbs answer: here? or there?
How much, how many, when and where?
(*They march offstage, followed by* ARTICLE, *who has been beating drum.*)

JAMIE (*At desk, writing*): "After Jim threw the white ball skillfully, Red Jones came up to bat. Red Jones was a good batter." No, I need something more interesting than that. I have it! "Red Jones was known far and near as the terror of the pitchers." That's better. "Jim wound up for the next pitch—"

GRAMMARIAN: Come on, Period. We'll have to leave Jim winding up for the next pitch. But we'll return one of these days and see if he's struck out Red Jones. (*He holds up a hoop which is decorated with tissue paper and a circus design in the center.* PERIOD *makes a running jump through the center of the hoop, doffs his beanie to the audience, and turns his back. On his back is written in bold letters, "The End." Curtain.*)

The Wonderful World of Language

The world of language is a truly dynamic world. This chapter is designed to aid the teacher in discovering the dimensions of this world and to provide a plethora of ideas for sharing these discoveries with students. As the Grammarian in *The Wonderful Circus of Words* says, "Once you glimpse the excitement of words, you will never again say that English is a dull subject."

Let us begin our discussion of the language arts by considering the remarkable power of language.

The Power of Language

Language is the one attribute that sets humans apart from all other creatures and binds humans together across all geographic barriers. A word can cause us to sink into the deepest despair or lift us to inspired action. Language can be the tool for great achievement in art, engineering, and social progress or for confusion, war, and destruction. The choice is ours, and the tool is powerful.

The mere sound of poetry gives intense pleasure, to which form and the various levels of meaning can only add. The story of the tower of Babel tells symbolically how a civilization without communication must fall. Without language, there is no way to accumulate or pass on cultural knowledge.

Whose life may not be changed by the utterance of a single sentence of promise or perjury? How many civilizations are now only memories because they failed to understand the importance of signing or failing to sign a treaty or because they could not express their intentions clearly to an opponent? After the atomic explosion at Hiroshima, the Japanese were warned to surrender. It is said that their carefully worded return statement asked for a delay but was mistakenly interpreted by the Allies as a refusal. So the city of Nagasaki paid dearly for a misunderstood phrase.

Yet whole civilizations, their palaces and city walls long since crumbled, are still alive through songs, poems, and histories. Through the poetry of Homer, we can still feel the crushing despair of the people of Troy when their hero Hector died.

When a way to write words was discovered, man was no longer dependent on the memory of listening. Meanings became clearer and understanding more certain. Written words are a link with all generations to

Teachers can foster learning by integrating the language arts, individualizing instruction, and encouraging active involvement.
(PHOTO BY LINDA LUNGREN.)

come and with all past generations. If there are no written clues, relics and ruins can only hint at lost civilizations. Other cultures, although buried under desert
sands, seem almost contemporary because of written
records that tell us about their religion, education, busi-
nesses, and even the intimate gossip of their times.

The Symbolic Nature of Language

Sounds and symbols *mean* nothing unless we agree
to use them as representations of objects and concepts.
Lip movements and handspelling meant nothing to
Helen Keller until she could conceive of them as naming something specific. Language requires agreement
about the specific connections between the symbols and
the things or ideas to which they refer.

The use of language as a symbolic system is more
than the manipulation of abstractions. A language can
be seen as behavior, a set of activities with much
broader nature than that of other systems. Language is a
habitual, even unconscious response instead of something new and unfamiliar in each situation. To a greater
degree than the visual or the plastic arts, language arts
are anchored in a set of shared conventions. Unlike
mathematical expression, language carries emotional
connotations and expresses subjective feelings. Mastery
of language requires complex and sophisticated effects.
Just as a parent is proud of the first words a child
speaks, so is a teacher justly proud of the child's first
written vocabulary, first written story, and comprehension of written discourse. Teachers must realize that the
child who does not develop the language skills demanded by the modern world is at a disadvantage, because this weakness will limit his options for work and
narrow his horizons for learning.

Language—The Art of Communication

Communication is an interesting word. When two or
more individuals have a successful communication,
they share an understanding or feeling; normally, this
communion is an exchange of ideas on a common basis
of understanding.

Language is the foremost means of communicating
most ideas and feelings. Language can speak to us from
the far distant past, but it can also travel around the
planet and into space. Communication today can be almost instantaneously transmitted everywhere on earth
electronically. Through television, telephone, and
radio, as well as the printed and spoken word, language
is humanity's common bond.

The capacity for language is a specific human trait;
any language may theoretically be learned by any child
or adult. Communication is therefore always a possibility, if not a reality. A child's earliest babbling is nonna-
tional; there is no initial predisposition to one language
or another. Instead, exposure, practice, and maturity
seem to be the determinants of speech. Increased language arts skills increase the individual's power to learn
and to share, whatever language is employed.

The Content of Communication

If we separate the ideas communicated from the
means of communication (the reading, speaking, writing, or listening), we have the content of communication. It is sometimes claimed that language arts
instruction must use social studies, science, or other information in order for there to be ideas to share. This
notion has at times resulted in the tendency of some
teachers to teach facts and neglect instruction in language skills, their logic being that skills will develop
without planned instruction if the student has enough to
talk and write and think about.

Another belief is that children need skill mastery in
order to deal competently with the world's ever-increasing body of knowledge. For an individual who reads
with ease and expresses himself clearly and comfortably, learning and sharing continue throughout life. But
if the attempt is made to master many volumes of facts
during the elementary school years, the pressure on
teachers and students may result in inadequate competence in language skills.

One guiding principle of a language arts curriculum
is that language skills, like motor skills, are best developed in an integrated fashion. Learning experiences
should involve several or all language skills instead of

Plays, games, and class presentations are multidimensional activities that can involve the whole language system. (PHOTO BY TOM WOLFE.)

one at a time. Plays, games, and class presentations are multidimensional activities that can involve the whole language system.

Language Learning in the Curriculum

In view of the state of the world, communication is vital but not easy to achieve. As a thinking individual, one is always concerned with communication. For you as a teacher the concern is paramount. Just as you may remember a college teacher who seemed at times incomprehensible, children can find you hard to follow if you take too much for granted. (Do you say "certainly" when something is not at all certain for a first grader?) Sometimes we compromise meaning and communication by using words in ways others do not. Past a certain degree of imaginative novelty, this creates trouble instead of interest. However, two individuals would have to have exactly the same experiences, moods, and memories of words between them to have the same response to a situation, and in that case what would be the need for communication? Because we are not mechanical in the way we think and speak, our

words are not limited to rigid, universal meanings that never change. Without the great connotative richness of language, we would lose metaphor, allegory, and the other "figures" of speech. Fortunately, language has the flexibility to operate at almost any level of meaning.

Defining "Language Arts"

Art is something expressive, creative, original, and usually personal. The term *skill* is reserved for an acquired ability that is mechanical, exact, and impersonal. Learning the proper spelling of a word is certainly learning a skill, whereas the writing of a poem or personal letter is considered the expression of language art. Both are part of language instruction; any modern language curriculum must show concern for both skills and arts. In reality and in practice, they are not as separate as they might seem.

Language can be seen as a code system. The term *encoding* applies to the functions of putting meaning into code, as speech and writing do. *Decoding* refers to the language functions of extracting meaning, which are listening and reading. Gough (1972), among others, maintains that reading involves a process called *recoding*, through which print is received as sound and is then decoded. There is some doubt as to whether this is performed by all competent readers, but the controversy is important in the psychology of reading. Other skills and modes do interact closely, whether or not a limited form of speech occurs in reading. Taking notes on a lecture coordinates listening with writing skills, and good conversation involves intense listening and speech efforts.

The word *teach* derives from the Anglo-Saxon *taecean* and from the German *zeigen,* meaning "to show." The teacher's role is to show, to make available, to open, to point the way. This introduces a second important principle of the language arts curriculum—the necessity for active involvement of the learner in the process of education. Gone, we hope, is the image of the stern pedagogue enumerating facts that the student must commit to memory or fail. George Orwell says he was taught in school that "Disraeli brought peace with honor" but was never allowed to wonder to whom or how this was done. Memories and instances of this kind of teaching remain, although research in educational psychology since the time of John Dewey has stressed the need for the learner to participate actively in the learning process. A language arts curriculum should compel the teacher to match the level of the child's learning instead of insisting that the child get in stride with the teacher's teaching. This way the child must be active and responsive, and so must the teacher.

"Language arts" describes a major portion of the elementary curriculum, which includes the *communication process* of *listening, speaking, reading,* and *writing.* The development of these interrelated communication processes serves the learner when *gaining* (intake) information as well as *giving* (output) information.

Integrating the Language Arts

We must view the art of communication as an interrelated process, for more often than not we utilize more than one of the processes (listening, speaking, reading, writing) at a time. Loban (1976) has found that students evidencing low abilities in oral language also evidence difficulty in reading and writing, and further that students with adequate language abilities evidence little if any difficulty in acquiring other communication skills.

As a classroom teacher, your task will be not only that of integrating the language arts among themselves but also that of integrating them throughout the entire curriculum. When a student engages in a science, math, or social studies activity, is he not required to employ language arts processes? Doesn't he often *listen* to instructions or shared ideas? Isn't he often required to *speak* about his ideas? He may be involved in the *reading* of these content materials as well as the *writing* of detailed reports to express his ideas. Throughout the curriculum, students are employing the language arts. Therefore, it seems quite unrealistic to believe that for forty minutes each day one can have a separate period devoted to the communication processes.

Individualizing Instruction

As with any approach, individualization is based on and formed by an appreciation of the ways skills complement each other. Existing facilities can be used for horizontal or vertical development. No skill is unconnected to others in the curriculum, yet skill mastery for various situations may develop in different children at different rates. Therefore, a teacher must understand the child's developmental level and be able to stress each of the language arts components as they relate to each other. A good understanding of the capabilities and needs of the individual child and a sound knowledge and belief in the goals of the language arts program are vital factors in successful individualization of instruction.

It is important for a teacher not to lose sight of the larger purposes of language while teaching exactness in spelling or speech. Language is the means through which thought is organized, refined, and expressed. The famous Sapir-Whorf hypothesis about the influence of different languages on expression of thought and the theories of Piaget and Vygotsky debate the exact functions of language, yet its role as a tool in conceptual thinking is undeniable. Individual or cultural intellectual gains could not accumulate to much complexity or be preserved for posterity without language.

Institutional philosophies can be slow to change, as can teaching traditions; the three R's are still considered fundamental for success in life. There are, however, many different ways to organize the materials to be learned. A body of knowledge organized in terms of its own structure is logically organized, and philosophers would call this "objective" or "empirical," strictly according to what is to be found in the world. If the knowledge is organized in terms of how it is acquired by the learner, this is more a developmental or psychological approach, and often very useful. The good teacher uses both types of organization along with some of the great variety of learning and teaching styles that exist.

The Objective of a Language Arts Program

In any endeavor, objectives are a function of values. If a teacher values silence in the classroom, mistake-free papers, proper modes of address, and rote responses, the objectives of the program will reflect these values, much to the discomfort of the learners. Similarly, if a teacher values the enriching exploration of language, investigation of its playful and creative aspects, self-expression, and appreciation of literature, the objectives of the program will encompass broader goals and deeper experiences. This type of teacher will present a class with poems, songs, pictures, and films; she will generally be a model of one who is responsive to the intellectual, moral, and aesthetic powers of language. If children are free to exercise their taste and pleasure in selecting materials and in expressing themselves, they will develop their aesthetic sensibilities and their evaluative skills. If language learning is not separated from the learning of other arts and skills, then reading, writing, speaking, and listening will be learned as the closely related functions of cognitive abilities that they are. Exercises in spelling, punctuation, and grammar should not be ignored, but they need not head the cur-

riculum or be used as a bludgeon. Sybil Marshall explains how she would present such exercises:

> I would give them enough patterns, but not in the form of exercises. I would give them patterns in speech, in books, in poetry, and in plays. I would not subject my pupils to ten minutes a day under the ultraviolet lamp of intense grammatical exercises, but would instead seek out every patch of literary sunshine and see to it that the pupils worked and played in its warmth and light until grammatical usage and good style, the balance and cadence of sentences, and the happy choice of the most significant words soaked into them through every one of their senses. . . . It is much more important, surely, to be bursting with things to write about and not know precisely how to write them, than to know all the rules and not have anything to write. [Marshall, 1963, p. 9]

Let us look at an example of the goals set forth for one language arts program. The following is a description of the goals and beliefs of the English Language Program in the Denver, Colorado, Public Schools.

Language and Learning in a Modern World

In an age in which knowledge multiplies during every decade and in which technological advances are changing the typical worker's tasks every few years, education takes on an even greater importance than it has in the past; in a school system seeking to educate young people who can be expected to retrain themselves at least three times during their working years, learning *how to learn* takes on additional significance. The importance of the role of language in the learning process cannot be overestimated. Language plays a key role in unifying a vast and complex nation and in providing individuals with outlets for developing diverse skills and abilities.

Principles

The following principles reflect an attempt to translate the goals and beliefs expressed above into a form which is more practical and workable in the daily classroom environment. The principles are intended to apply to the teaching of the English language and its literature at each age level from the time the young child enters school until the young adult graduates.

1. There exists a common body of English which is taught and used in all courses at all levels of instruction.

2. Language, as social behavior, is both a structured system of symbols and a means of communication.
3. At an early age children are in possession of the essential elements of language in its spoken form. The conventions of the English language are taught on the basis of need, experience, and background of pupils as well as on previous attainment.

Structure

4. At a preschool age, native speakers have usually acquired unconsciously the basic sentence structure of the English language.
5. English has its roots in many languages.
6. A study of the history of language will reveal its dynamic character and will foster an appreciation of its literary and colloquial variation.
7. Word order is the predominant factor in the structure of the English language.
8. English takes different forms in varying situations.
9. All language skills are interrelated.
10. Use of language can develop critical thinking and self-evaluation.

Thinking

11. A high correlation exists between thought and proficiency in communication.
12. Language is an instrument of personal development and social communication.
13. Language enables one to release creative potential.
14. Literature, as an art form, reveals the culture from which it springs.
15. Specific literary types have definite structure.
16. Literature has sensory as well as intellectual appeal.

Literature

17. Literature makes use of imaginative and figurative language.
18. Literature broadens experience, deepens understanding, improves judgment, and provides for esthetic response.
19. Listening to good literature read aloud enhances appreciation through sensory appeal and the union of sound and sense.
20. Facts are important only as they contribute to the understanding, as a whole, of the literary selection of any other type of communication.
21. Exposure to good speakers and writers will improve competence in communication.

Composition

22. As pupils have opportunities to recognize and experiment with structures, competence in clear, forceful, appropriate expression will be increased.
23. Composition, both oral and written, should be a challenge which enables pupils to see relationships and to draw valid conclusions.

Speaking

24. Students should be encouraged to develop an inquiring mind which understands the reasoning processes and is able to interpret the evidence necessary to solve problems and make decisions.
25. Spoken language, which is basic to all communication and most widely used, occupies a prior position of importance in relation to other communication skills.

Listening

26. Pupils must be taught how to listen for directions, facts, ideas, concepts, and appreciation; for listening is more than hearing.
27. Listening must go beyond hearing to become a response with understanding, feeling, and critical analysis.

Method

28. The inductive process is basic to learning.
29. Classroom emphasis should stress learning rather than teaching.
30. Classroom climate should be such to encourage constructive expression on the part of the pupil.
31. The responsibility for teaching English is shared by all teachers.

[Denver Public Schools, 1968]

It is obvious that this outline reflects the language values of the educators involved. Let us now consider your present values and goals as a teacher of the language arts.

Self-appraisal as a Growth Tool

Humility and honesty in self-appraisal are good traits for any teacher or student; none of us maintains facility without practice. The following is a self-evaluation form for language teachers. It is only a partial inventory of teaching knowledge but can be a useful tool in recognizing areas in which you may feel a need for improvement. Use the form and refer back to it as you progress in your professional and personal development.

Your Role as a Language Arts Teacher

Your role as a teacher is that of a *catalyst* to the child's learning. You can foster learning by integrating the language arts, by personalizing instruction, and by actively

Self-evaluation form for language teachers

Rate your present skill or knowledge for each of the following aspects of teaching language arts as follows:	Satisfactory	Improving	Needs attention

1. I understand the historical background of the language I teach.
2. I know how children master language before starting to school.
3. I know how language instruction fits into the school day.
4. I can explain how reading, writing, listening, and speaking are related.
5. I know what the National Council of Teachers of English is and have read the publications of that group.
6. I know the educational leaders in the field of language arts instruction.
7. I can give a parent a reference that will help guide the recreational reading of her children.
8. I can purchase books intelligently for a classroom library.
9. I know of books that should be read to children.
10. I can hold children's attention as I tell a story.
11. I know how to share a picture book with little children.
12. I can teach a finger play to a child and explain its importance to his parents.
13. I know many things to do that will encourage children to read good literature.
14. I can involve children in dramatic play and creative dramatics.
15. I can suggest a variety of book-sharing techniques to children.
16. I know where to get information concerning a book fair.
17. I know the sources of poetry that are appropriate to the children in my class.
18. I can read poetry well.
19. I know how to direct children in simple verse choir experiences.
20. I can recognize different types of speech defects.
21. I know how to distinguish the speech defects that I can help and those that need a speech specialist.
22. I understand why it is important to listen to children.
23. I can discuss with a supervisor the importance of teaching listening in my classroom and give examples of classroom emphasis on listening.
24. I can write print script.
25. I can write neatly and legibly on the chalkboard.
26. I can write a note to a parent and not be embarrassed by my handwriting.
27. I know the reasons why I teach handwriting the way I do.
28. I know how to help a left-handed child write well.
29. I know how to teach skills of spelling.
30. I know how to individualize spelling instruction.
31. I know how to make the spelling period interesting to children.
32. I am able to help children to write creatively.
33. I know the relationship between oral and written composition and use it in my teaching.
34. I understand how standards of performance are established and how to use them to foster improvement in composition.
35. I can plan and produce an assembly program.
36. I know what type of work in composition to expect of children in the separate grades.
37. I understand the fundamentals of grammar.
38. I understand the conflict between teaching grammar and functional usage in the grades.

Self-evaluation form for language teachers (continued)

Rate your present skill or knowledge for each of the following aspects of teaching language arts as follows:	Satisfactory	Improving	Needs attention
39. I understand the significance of readiness in all learning experience.			
40. I know how the textbooks in spelling, penmanship, language, and reading are usually organized and used.			
41. I can teach a beginner to read.			
42. I understand the strengths and weaknesses of phonics as applied to spelling and reading.			
43. I know of material designed to be used with children who are below grade level in reading.			
44. I know these magazines and read them to keep informed concerning the language arts: *Elementary English, N.E.A. Journal, The Reading Teacher, Elementary School Journal, The Instructor,* and *The Grade Teacher.*			
45. I can identify these authors of children's books: Doris Gates, Florence Means, Laura I. Wilder, Marjorie Flack, Virginia Lee Burton, Dr. Seuss, Beatrix Potter, Lois Lenski, Astrid Lindgren, Holling C. Holling, and others who have received special awards.			
46. I can plan a lesson for one period of instruction, and for three groups in a single skill for a week.			
47. I can make purposeful worksheets in handwriting and reading or know sources of such material.			
48. I can give a talk at the P.T.A. explaining the significance of the skills of language arts for children in the space age.			
49. I recognize the issues that exist in the language program and seek solutions that will work in my classroom.			
50. I am aware of the importance of research in education and seek to keep informed.			

involving the child in all kinds of language experiences.

As a beginning teacher, you will not find immediate answers to the many issues related to the teaching of language. Educators do not have exact or absolute answers. Authorities often differ in their conclusions, and these conclusions change as new knowledge is gained. As a growing teacher, therefore, you should set as one of your goals a constant awareness of the current methods, materials, and literature in the language arts field.

As an effective language arts teacher, it is important to consider that the way a child uses language is important to him both as a student learning to communicate his needs and feelings to others and as a future adult who will require mature language skills in order to meet the problems of a complex society. Your own mastery of such skills as handwriting, spelling, reading, and speaking should be coupled with a sensitivity to the beauty expressed through words in poetry and prose, an understanding that words are the tools of personal and worldwide communication, and an awareness that thoughts and expression are the ends or goals for which such skills are perfected. Your desire to grow in language power as you teach and work with children will be of utmost importance as you establish yourself as an individual growing in teaching competence. Your excitement with the wonderful world of language may well be contagious to those around you.

Bibliography

Boiko, C. "The Wonderful Circus of Words," in *Children's Plays for Creative Actors.* Boston: Plays, Inc., 1967, pp. 35–44.

Denver Public Schools. *Denver Public Schools Preliminary English Course of Study.* 1968.

Dewey, J. *Experience and Education.* New York: Collier-Macmillan, 1938.

Gough, P. "One Second of Reading." *Language by Ear and Eye,* ed. by J. F. Kavanagh and I. G. Mattingly. Cambridge, Mass.: MIT Press, 1972, pp. 331–358.

Homer. *The Iliad,* translated with an introduction by Richard Lattimore. New York: McGraw-Hill, 1968.

Jakobson, R., and M. Halle. *Fundamentals of Language.* The Hague: Mouton, 1956.

Loban, W. *Language Development: Kindergarten Through Grade Twelve.* Champaign, Ill.: National Council of Teachers of English, 1976.

Marshall, S. *Experiment in Education.* New York: Cambridge University Press, 1963.

Orwell, G. *Nineteen Eighty-four.* New York: Harcourt Brace Jovanovich, 1949.

Piaget, J. *The Origins of Intelligence in Children.* New York: Norton, 1963.

Sapir, E. *Selected Writings of Edward Sapir,* ed. by D. G. Mandelbaum. Berkeley and Los Angeles: University of California Press, 1949.

Vygotsky, L. S. *Thought and Language.* Cambridge, Mass.: MIT Press, 1962.

Whorf, B. L. *Language, Thought and Reality: Selected Writings of B. L. Whorf,* ed. by J. B. Carroll. New York: Wiley, 1958.

Chapter 4
Our Language Heritage

Language . . . the ever repeating working-out of the Spirit.

Wilhelm von Humboldt, *Über die Verschiedenheit des menschlicher Sprachbaues und ihren Einfluss auf die geistige Entwickelung des Menschengeschlechts* (Berlin: Konigliche Akademie der Wissenschaften, 1836), p. LVII

Language Is Fun

THE WONDERFUL WORDS

Never let a thought shrivel and die
For want of a way to say it,
For English is a wonderful game
And all of you can play it.
All that you do is match the words
To the brightest thoughts in your head
So that they come out clear and true
And handsomely groomed and fed—
For many of the loveliest things
Have never yet been said.

Words are the food and dress of thought,
They give it its body and swing,
And everyone's longing today to hear
Some fresh and beautiful thing.
But only words can free a thought
From its prison behind your eyes.
Maybe your mind is holding now
A marvelous new surprise!

Mary O'Neill

HINTS ON PRONUNCIATION FOR FOREIGNERS

I take it you already know
Of tough and bough and cough and dough?
Others may stumble but not you,
On hiccough, thorough, laugh and through.
Well done! And now you wish, perhaps,
To learn of less familiar traps?

Beware of heard, a dreadful word
That looks like beard and sounds like bird,

And dead: it's said like bed, not bead—
For goodness' sake don't call it "deed"!
Watch out for meat and great and threat
(They rhyme with suite and straight and debt.)

A moth is not a moth in mother
Nor both in bother, broth in brother,
And here is not a match for there
Nor dear and fear for bear and pear,
And then there's dose and rose and lose—
Just look them up—and goose and choose,
And cork and work and card and ward,
And font and front and word and sword,
And do and go and thwart and cart—
Come, come, I've hardly made a start!
A dreadful language? Man alive,
I'd mastered it when I was five.

T.S.W.
(*only initials of writer known*)

Cultural Influences on Language

Do you realize that the simplest words in our language are items in a vast chronicle that tell the story of a dynamic people and their language? Have you ever wondered why surnames seem to fall into groups, some ending in *-ton* and others in *-son?* Why there are Latin words where English ones might do as well, such as *post meridian* and *ante meridian?* Why we don't have the profusion of verb and noun endings that French, German, Italian, and other languages have? Why we hear the Greek *hoi polloi* and the French *savoir faire?* Why there are so many "little" words in English (look at the opening quotation in German). How "good" a language English is, and what it means for a language to be "good"?

The purpose of this chapter is to illustrate the historical development and cultural significance of the English language. It is important for you as a language arts teacher to have a broad understanding of the forces that have shaped our language in order to share with your students a sense of the dynamic qualities of their language.

Language abilities in speaking, listening, thinking, reading, and writing are not developed independently of each other; neither is any individual's language ability developed independently of a group life in which he can find his securities, his values, and his language patterns. This group life is what we call a culture: the sum total of all the material achievements, customs, beliefs, and values of any group of people. Culture includes the people themselves and their ways of communicating and interacting with each other within their institutions. A culture cannot be viewed merely as an aggregate of parts but must be seen as a functionally integrated whole. Art, literature, and philosophy emerge from the group's social experiences and provide more experience and a cultural heritage. Thus a culture is a dynamic and changing pattern, always being created by its members and in turn influencing the behavior of its creators and participants.

The American culture furnishes the context in which all American schools function. Together with democratic values and methods, a common basic language makes it possible for the United States to be a national, cultural unit.

Culturally determined goals in language teaching make language a social tool for such purposes as understanding oneself and other people, relating oneself to the world through literature, finding personal satisfaction through expressive and creative use of language to solve personal and group problems, developing discriminative power to detect the purposes behind the written or spoken symbols, and evaluating the reliability of the spoken and printed messages. These goals have grown out of the modern setting of cultural activities. The conditions of living in today's world make it important to listen to and evaluate a radio or TV broadcast, to read and interpret a newspaper intelligently, and to speak, write, read, and listen with concern for integrity, logic, and honesty of expression.

The establishment of newer goals in a position of primary importance demands a new cultural integration of values and events. This integration is a slow process. It is not easy for people to see that the familiar, fundamental three R's may become still more fundamental with a recognition of the purpose for which reading, writing, speaking, and other language tools are used.

The culture holds the values that determine the opportunities for learning in the schools. Such questions as who will go to school, for how long, and in what kind of building and who should teach are answered in different ways by different cultures. Laura Ingalls Wilder in *These Happy Golden Years* describes a culture that felt that a few weeks of school in midwinter were adequate.

The culture determines what the interests and experiences of schoolchildren will be. What a child reads, speaks, and writes about is influenced by the family and community in which he lives. Children are most interested in the learning activities they can experience in their learning environments.

The culture determines the meanings that children attach to words and statements. A child raised on the prairies of eastern Colorado has no experience to relate to the word *woods*. Eventually, through pictures and descriptions he finds a meaning, but it will never be as complete as that of a child who has watched a forest change through the seasons, known the fun of seeking wild fruit and nuts, or participated in the gathering of maple sap. The Navajo child whose dwelling has always been a hogan does not use, hear, or read the word *house* with the same meaning as the child who has lived in a brick bungalow.

The culture determines when learning experiences shall be introduced and the sequence in which skills shall be developed. As knowledge from the fields of child development and social anthropology has accumulated, leaders in education are finding that the cultural patterns of age and grade expectations in a middle-class society do not always agree with what is known about children's intimate growth patterns; the culture often expects learning to occur before the child is ready for it. However, the expectations provide a strong stimulus for learning, and when the timing of the expectation is not out of adjustment with the individual's growth pattern, this cultural influence is in favor of educational achievement.

It is unfortunate that our culture has defined types of speech that are expected of boys and of girls. The little boy has often been respected for speaking like a "male" but scolded, teased, or otherwise punished for speaking like a "female." The father serves as a model

of the sex culture that the boy is encouraged to learn. The works of Key (1975) and Lakoff (1975) provide us with many insights regarding sex stereotyping in our language.

A child speaks the way his family and neighborhood speak because this is the group with which he has made first identifications. To identify with a person or group means to form a strong emotional attachment. A child's first identifications are the result of his human need for love and membership in the group. When a child identifies with someone, he unconsciously imitates that person's speech patterns. He is prone to retain these early speech habits, for they give him an identification badge; they are the symbols by which he proves his belongingness to a group. The extent to which a child speaks correctly or according to the school standards indicates the patterns that are in the security-giving group life surrounding him.

It is significant to note that the social group, even more than the family, provides the pattern for speech imitations after early childhood—more specifically, the peer group to which an individual belongs during later childhood and adolescence. The school must then *accept* as well as *extend* the language of the child.

When teachers begin to understand the middle-class expectations for rapid training, they will more clearly see why early reading and writing have become symbols of status. A child who learns to read early proves his and his parents' worthiness by this important cultural achievement. Fear of losing face with their group causes some parents to pressure children into reading before they show readiness for it. Teachers, too, are sometimes sensitive to their status position and exert similar pressures on children for early reading performance.

The cultural expectation for learning to read during the first year of school experience was established at a time when children were beginning the first reader at the age of seven, eight, or even nine years. It has persisted in the culture pattern, although the age for beginning first grade has been lowered. It was once culturally acceptable to leave school without having mastered reading.

Language instruction is dependent not only on a

child's inner maturational pattern but also on his experience background and his opportunities for learning. A teacher must respect every child's commonplace experiences. She should dignify some of the everyday incidents of life and thereby help the child feel comfortable about his own home life and group experiences. An example of how this may happen is related by a teacher at a small school. Ten-year-old Denny, who seemed active and interested outside of the schoolroom but who had never volunteered to share any of his interests in writing, said that he "didn't want to write anything." Denny had never been to a circus. His only experience with airplanes consisted of watching them fly overhead. He did not have a horse or a pet. The teacher's concern for Denny's lack of interest in sharing experiences led her to a discovery. Hitherto she had asked children to write about the unusual, or the exciting, or the very, very new experiences that only certain children had. She now changed her approach and encouraged them to write about such everyday occurrences as skinning a knee, getting wet in the rain, or running a race; Denny then made some attempts to write about these "commonplace" experiences. Later he wrote rather well about "Hurting My Thumb."

Similarly, a child who comes from a home where a foreign language is spoken may not be ready to read English. The school program must both supplement and complement the cultural nurturing of language growth.

We must understand language and language history to foster language growth. Human language is certainly unique among communicative systems. Aside from the sound in a handful of onomatopoetic words such as *buzz* and *clang,* there is little within the sounds or shapes of words and phrases to indicate the idea being communicated; yet through language we can examine cultures thousands of years old or thousands of miles away, we can send astronauts into space, we can provide education and legal protection for billions of individuals. What makes language so flexible for different needs, so precise in a specific case, and so common that we take such a sophisticated system for granted?

The Language System

Linguists make the distinction between a sign system and a symbol system of communication. An arm raised with the palm outward is a passable symbol for "stop!" and the sounds combined in /stɔp/ constitute a sign for the same notion. The language community of which you are a part has agreed to let both sign and symbol convey the meaning of "stop," although this may not have been true a thousand years ago, nor may it continue to be the case for hundreds of years to come. If we see that language is conventional, we must also note that it is arbitrary. A four-wheeled freight-carrying vehicle is known as a "truck" in the United States and a "lorry" in much of Great Britain. This example of different naming conventions illustrates their arbitrary nature, yet people have chosen for any of a large number of reasons to use either "truck" or "lorry" or both, if they travel. As we noted before, there is nothing inherent in the orthography or spelling of words to convey meaning. Symbol and sign systems are conventional and arbitrary.

Both of these aspects point to other features of language: it is *changeable* and *adaptable* over time. If convention and habit determine vocabulary, inflections, and spelling, new conventions and new habits can determine new forms of language. This is, in fact, the process that has made our English language into the system we now use.

It is helpful to distinguish between the structure and the function of language. This book is written in a language structure that all English speakers will be able to understand. It would succeed just as well in its function as a text about language arts instruction if it were translated to the structure of another language. Any language user may request, congratulate, daydream, hypothesize, describe, or interrogate. Linguists agree that all human languages perform much the same functions and are equally "good" at them. The structure is what varies from one language to another and within one language over time.

No one language or dialect is "best" either structurally or functionally, in the way German was once judged "best" for scientific communications, because language is dynamic and can change as its users and their world change. Classical Latin is one of the few examples to the contrary. It is called "dead" because it is not used in conversation and therefore is not susceptible to influences outside its written form. The language of Latin literature has a consistency that anyone who has studied the classical form can understand.

Because convention determines change, a language can develop irregularities and lapses in logic while it fulfills the needs of a speaking community. Irregular forms and the fact that some nouns can be verbs, whereas others cannot, illustrate that language and logic are not always partners in the English language. This does not mean that the language is not efficient, for it has changed to serve our purposes admirably.

What Cultural Influences Are Reflected in the History of the English Language?

Language is of major importance in our culture. Familiarity with the great literature of our language can help us with philosophical issues, but we must also concern ourselves with the historical development of language in order to comprehend orthography, sentence structure, and the changes in vocabulary and usage.

Similarities in vocabulary and structure among many languages of Europe and the Middle East were of great interest to linguists during the nineteenth century. It became apparent that these languages formed a group or family of languages, and it was hypothesized that there must have been a common parent language. Some characteristics of this prehistoric parent language, called Indo-European, can be reconstructed from the common characteristics of its offspring. Eleven major subgroups to the base language, believed to have originated in East Central Europe, have been postulated. Three language subgroups have particular relevance to English: Hellenic, Italic, and Teutonic.

The Hellenic and Italic groups gave rise to Greek and Latin, respectively, from which many English words were borrowed directly, whereas others came indirectly via French. It is the Teutonic group, though, from which English has largely developed, as we shall soon see.

The original speakers of the tongue from which English arose were Germanic dwellers on the eastern or European coast of the North Sea from Denmark to Holland. These Anglo-Saxons and Jutes had undoubtedly raided the British shores even before the Roman departure in A.D. 410.

When the last legions were summoned back to defend their Italian homeland, the Britons started fighting among themselves. The Jutes were called in by the British King Vostigen to assist him, after which they settled in Kent. The Saxons did not arrive until 477 or the Angles until 547. Many of these came as mercenaries lured by the promise of land, which was divided as war booty.

A number of the early outside influences on the language of Britain came from Rome. As early as 54 B.C., Julius Caesar reconnoitered on British soil and established friendly contacts with various chieftains. The Roman conquest was not completed until a century later and was marked by periods of savage resistance. The completeness of the cultural impact on the Britons is not known; the many Roman ruins throughout Britain would indicate a thoroughgoing Romanization of the country. For a period of almost four hundred years the Romans were in complete control of Britain.

Later the influence of Latin was extended by the activities of the Church. By the sixth century Christianity had spread throughout all of England. Christian converts were among the Anglo-Saxons, who conquered England after the Romans left; the Welsh and British inhabitants were for the most part Christians before this time.

There are over 450 words of Latin origin found in Old English; these include *cheese* (cāseus), *mint* (monēta), *seal* (sigillum), *street* (strata), *kitchen* (coquīna), *cup, plum, inch, wine, abbot, candle, chapter, minister, noon, nun, offer, priest, inscribe* (scribere), *cap, silk* (sericus), *sack, pear, cook, box, school, master, circle, spend, paper, term, title.*

The influence of Latin has continued through the years. Sometimes the borrowed words have come

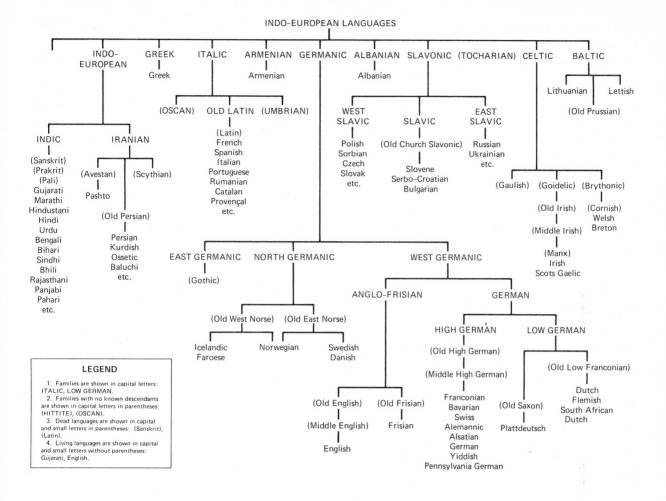

INDO-EUROPEAN LANGUAGES

through French, Spanish, or Italian, but many retain their original form or drop an ending. One recognizes the Latin derivation of words like *censor, census, genius, inferior, quiet, reject, legal, history, individual, necessary, picture, nervous, lunatic, interrupt.* The Latin prefixes *pre-, pro-, sub-, super-* and endings *-al, -ty, -ble, -ate, -tion, -ize* are often used with words from other sources. Of the 20,000 words in full use today about 12,000 are of Latin, Greek, or French origin.

During the Roman Empire, the Teutonic tribes inhabited the forested area of present-day Germany. Their language can be divided into three dialects: *Eastern,* or Gothic, for which there is no remaining language; *Northern,* which gave rise to Danish, Swedish, and Norwegian; and *Western,* which was spoken by coastal tribes including the Angles, Saxons, and Jutes.

Old English 600–1100 A.D.

By the beginning of the seventh century the Germanic language that we call Anglo-Saxon emerged from the confusion and turmoil of the British conquest to take its place among the modern tongues of Europe. Among the factors thought to have influenced this development were the wide acceptance of a single religion and the unity of the seven kingdoms to resist the Danish invasions.

The sounds of the language resembled those of modern German rather than those of modern English. The little *c* always had the hard *k* sound. The letters *j*, *g*, *v* were not used; *f* suggested our *v* sound; *h* was more like the *ach* of German. One additional letter, þ, called *thorn*, was used for one of the *th* sounds; we still use it in such signs as *Ye Olde Shoppe*. We have lost the *u* sound and *i* has replaced *y* in many words. Nouns had four cases: nominative, genitive, dative, and accusative. Adjectives were declined to agree with the word modified. Our little word *the* could assume any one of twelve different forms to show gender, number, and case. There were only present and past tenses.

Only a small percentage of our vocabulary today is Anglo-Saxon. If one were to take two thousand Anglo-Saxon words at random, one would find only a little more than five hundred still in use; however, these would include many of our most common words, such as *man, wife, child, horn, harp, coat, hat, glove, hall, yard, room, bread, fish, milk, house, home, hand, thumb, head, nose, ear, eye, arm, leg, eat, work,* and *play.*

The Anglo-Saxon ability to form compounds led to expressions in which the original elements are almost lost. *Good-by* or *good-bye* is a corruption of "God be with you."

Some words from the Anglo-Saxon have picturesque word origins. *Spider* means "spinner" and *beetle* "biter." *Strawberries* once were strung on a straw. The "poll" in *poll tax* is the old word for *head*.

In spite of the Latin influence in the Church, such Anglo-Saxon words as *god, gospel, lord, Holy Ghost, sin,* and *doomsday* survived. In isolated dialects some Anglo-Saxon forms have resisted change; *larned* is used for *taught, hundreder* for *centurion, foresayer* for *prophet,* and *gainraising* for *resurrection.*

In the year 787 piratical rovers from Scandinavia first visited England, and for more than a hundred years continued to make landings primarily for the sake of pillage. In 840, thirty-five shiploads of Danes landed in Dorset; in 851, 350 ships came up the Thames and ap-

parently for the first time wintered in England. Eventually they became so numerous that, for the sake of order, Alfred the Great made a settlement in 986 whereby half of England had its own Danish king; at one time all of England was ruled by these Danish kings. (When you say "They are ill," you are speaking old Norse, from which has descended modern Danish.) At least 1,400 localities in England have Scandinavian names.

Such words as *steak, knife, dirt, birth, fellow, guess, loan, sister, slaughter, trust, wart, window, odd, tight, skin, happy, ugly, wrong, scare,* and *though* are among our language heritage from the Danes. The *-son* of our family names replaced the *-ing* of the Saxon. (*Washington* actually means "Wasa's children's farm.")

Such doublets as *no–nay, rear–raise, fro–from, shatter–scatter, shirt–skirt, ditch–dike,* and *whole–hole* are a part of the divided language loyalties of the Islanders. The first is Saxon, the second Norse. Because of language mixing and the Teutonic stress on the first syllable or root word, English moved away from inflections to its largely noninflected present state. There has since been a steady decline in the number of English inflections.

The future tense (which had hitherto been expressed by the present, "I go tomorrow"); the pronouns *they, their, them;* and the omission of the relative pronoun *that* in such expressions as "the house I saw" were Scandinavian introductions in our language.

The Scandinavian invasion was not limited to the British Isles. Just as the Danes were settling in England, other Norsemen were invading the coast of France. As the British secured peace by granting an area to the invaders, so those in France were granted the reign centering about Rouen. These Normans accepted both the religion and the customs of the Franks. Indeed, this acceptance was so rapid that the grandson of their Viking leader Rolf (or Rollo) could not learn his ancestral language at home but was sent away to learn Norse. Thus it was that when these Normans invaded England they brought with them not only the French language but vestiges of Scandinavian as well; indeed, other languages than these were spoken by the forces under William, Duke of Normandy. There were mercenaries from Spain, Italy, and Germany.

Middle English 1100–1500 A.D.

The struggle between the hardy race that had been developed in England under the wise policies of Alfred the Great and this Norman force was a long and bitter one. The Anglo-Saxon nobility finally was reduced to the level of its own peasantry. Their language was scorned as being fit only for inferiors. With their defeat, the land was divided among the conquerors. William of Normandy displaced the Anglo-Saxon ruling class in 1066 and replaced it with French-speaking Normans.

At the dawn of the thirteenth century there were three languages in England: French was the literary and courtly tongue, Latin the language of the Church and legal documents, and Anglo-Saxon that of the marketplace.

Conquerors clung to their own ways since they planned eventually to return to their homeland. While the Normans were occupying England their forces were defeated in France, in 1204, and most of them gave up all thought of returning to that land. This changed their attitude toward the Anglo-Saxons and the language they spoke. At the same time the French spoken in England became mocked as provincial by Parisians. In 1349 English was reinstated in the schools, and in 1362 Parliament was reopened in English. During this time, hundreds of words came into the language. Some were words that one class might acquire from another, such as *baron*, *noble*, *dame*, *servant*, *messenger*, *story*, *rime*, *lay*. French law terms remain in use: *fee simple*, *attorney general*, *body politic*, *malice aforethought*. In our kitchens we use *sauce*, *boil*, *fry*, *roast*, *toast*, *pastry*, *soup*, *jelly*, *gravy*, *biscuit*, *venison*, *supper*, *salad*, *saucer*, *cream*. The French words *beef*, *veal*, and *pork* remain along with the Saxon *ox*, *calf*, and *swine*. Our present word *island* represents a blend of Saxon *iegland* and the French word *isle*. Among our synonyms, we have French and Saxon words in *acknowledge*, *confess*; *assemble*, *meet*; *pray*, *beseech*; *perceive*, *know*; and *power*, *might*. The words associated with the arts are French, or Late Latin through French: *amusement*, *dancing*, *leisure*, *painting*, *sculpture*, *beauty*, *color*, *poetry*, *prose*, *study*, *grammar*, *title*, *volume*, *paper*, *pen*, *copy*, *medicine*, *grief*, *joy*, *marriage*, *flower*.

Many of the terms of the modern square dance are French. When one "sashays to the corner" the word is an adaptation of *chasser*, which means *to chase;* and *do si do* is *dos-à-dos*, or *back-to-back*. Many military terms are French: *army*, *navy*, *enemy*, *arms*, *battle*, *siege*, *sortie*, *soldier*, *guard*, *spy*, *lieutenant*, *rank*, *vanquished*, *conquer*.

But the most important thing that happened during these years was a tremendous simplification of the language. No longer were nouns and adjectives declined. One form of each word emerged as that most frequently used. One authority says with a note of regret that if the language had remained neglected by scholars for another hundred years it might have emerged with a great purity of expression and meaning determined on basic usefulness to a people blessed with considerable common sense.

In review, then, the English language contains words, patterns of speech, and spellings that were influenced by historical developments. Starting with the ancient Celtic, we next found the Latin influence of the Roman invaders. The basic language structure is Teutonic as introduced to the British Isles by the Angles, Saxons, and Jutes. This in time was influenced by the Danes. With the Norman invasion, we have noted both the French and continuing Scandinavian influences. Because of the Church, the Latin influence continued through the years. Although trade with other lands has influenced our vocabulary, these are the major historical sources of the English language we use today.

Modern English 1500 A.D. to Present

With the development of printing, a number of important changes came into the language. The English printer William Caxton (1422–1491) made the works of Chaucer (1343–1400) available to the general public beginning in 1477; he is famous for printing the first book in English in 1475 (*The Reccuyell of the Historyes of Troye*).

Something happens when words are reproduced in

print; they achieve an importance and dignity they did not possess in manuscript form. The very act of duplication or making copies seems to grant authority to the printed word. The spelling of a word or the sentence structure that appears in such an important literary effort places the stamp of social and cultural approval on the form; at any rate, we can trace many of our instructional problems in language to these first printed books.

One of the problems was that of spelling. The word *guest* appears as *gest, geste, ghest, gheste; peasant* as *pesant* or *pezant; publicly* as *publickly, publikely, publiquely; yield* as *yeild, yielde,* and *yilde.*

Often it was a printer's effort to make words seem more consistent or even more scholarly that determined the form used. The silent *b* in *debt* and *doubt* originated on the premise that the original Latin forms had *b.* An early form was *det* or *dette.* The *gh* in *delight* and *tight* is a result of analogy with *light* and *night.* A number of words such as *won* in which the *o* represents the sound of *u* were an effort toward spelling reform. When such words are spelled with *u,* the handwriting tends to become a confusing series of upstrokes.

Geoffrey Chaucer helped to take English from its fourteenth-century position as a major London dialect to the beginning of modern Standard English. Writers during the next two hundred years made conscious efforts to invest English with the range and flexibility to compete with French as the language of culture and Latin as the language of scholarly instruction. Chaucer wrote in a composite of dialects that is fairly easily read by a modern reader. Here is a selection from the General Prologue to the *Canterbury Tales* (c. 1390 A.D., lines 43–46):

A knyght ther was, and that a worthy man
That fro the tyme that he first bigan
To riden out, he loved chivalrie,
Trouthe and honour, fredom and curteisie.

Chaucer's English contains many French words and spellings, but it is recognizable English.

Shakespeare's English is even more familiar, and it is truly modern English, although it differs from what we use today, almost four centuries later. The fact that literature four hundred years old does not seem foreign to us points out the decelerated pace of change. There are several reasons for the slower rate of language change and for a different style of change. Here is one example to keep in mind: in Old English a new term was frequently the result of joining two older ones, such as *woruld+had* for *worldhood.* Our modern term *secular life* shows the French and Latin influence of a word borrowed directly from other languages, part of the Renaissance spirit.

Along with increased availability of books, the prominence of London as a cultural city and the increase of the reading public due to the rise of the middle class placed conservative constraints on the language. Two other events gave English its present shape. One is the "great vowel shift" in the years 1500 to 1650, when the sounds of English vowels underwent an extensive sound change.

The sounds of Middle English vowels shifted in length, with those that were already long becoming a combination of two vowel sounds. This difference gives the same word quite a different sound in Modern English from the one it had in Middle English. The other major influence in Modern English was the English Renaissance, which followed the Italian Renaissance by roughly one century. The sixteenth and seventeenth centuries were the age of humanism, and literary figures were much enamored of the Greek and Latin languages. These structures, it was thought, were more suitable for abstract thought. Dryden later claimed that it was necessarry to translate his more significant thoughts from Latin, in which he could think more deeply. One result of the revival of classicism was a massive borrowing of Latin words. Of the thousands brought by scholars into English, many took hold; others—like *canicular, ossoany, diuturnity,* and *clenches*—did not.

It was during this time that English spawned a peculiar but predictable observer—the purist, or one who wishes to see the language cleansed and preserved from the ruin of foreign frills and corruptions. A purist, of course, is faced with a conundrum—English incorporates many influences, and without them it might not have developed into a distinct language. The people whom the purists were largely at odds with were the classicists, grammarians trying to fit English grammar into a Latin mold and including the apparently unnecessary declensions of English verbs in the lessons of English schoolchildren. The purist tradition is alive today in those who decry the use of latinate constructions or technical jargon where simple English might do. The classicist tradition, which helps us make sense of language, is alive and well in the dicta regarding *lie* and *lay* and *irregardless*. We call the codifying of the way people "ought" to use language "prescriptive grammar" as opposed to "descriptive grammar," or the way people *do* use language.

It has been estimated that 10,000 words were added to the language during the Renaissance, and they became widespread through the press. Shakespeare added such words or expressions as *accommodating, apostrophe, dislocate, frugal, heartsick, needle-like, long-haired, green-eyed, hot-blooded*. Words such as *capacity, celebrate, fertile, native, confidence*, and *relinquish* were called barbarisms and were understood by few readers.

No description of this time would be complete without reference to the King James Bible of 1611. It is estimated that fewer than 6,000 different words are used in this translation and that fully 94 per cent of these were part of the common speech of the day. The translators were apparently concerned with reaching the masses in a language that would be understood by all. Hence it was up to them to use the best-known words.

Some words are repeated with great frequency (*and* is used 46,277 times). Although there is monotony in some parts, the text is usually very clear in spite of the profound ideas expressed. Shakespeare shows us the range of thought that can be expressed with many (15,000 to 17,000) words, and the Bible demonstrates almost the same range with only 6,000.

Today a highly literate adult is not likely to have a recognition vocabulary of much more than 150,000 words. Of this number a few will be used over and over again. One fourth of all our spoken words consist of repetition of the words *and, be, have, it, of, the, to, will, you, I, a, on, that*, and *is*.

Since the invention of printing, new words have been added to English in many ways. Some are borrowed from other languages; others have been created for new products; and still others seem to be accidents or the results of misunderstanding foreign speech. If a person who spoke Anglo-Saxon were to listen to us today, he would have a very difficult task understanding all that is said.

From the Italian we find these words: *design, piazza, portico, stanza, violin, volcano, alto, piano, torso, cello, vogue, serenade, trombone, broccoli, boloney, confetti* (hard candy), *cash, carnival, cartoon, studio, solo, opera*.

Spanish words include *alligator, banana, canoe, cocoa, hammock, hurricane, mosquito, potato, tobacco, rodeo, cockroach, cork, tornado, sombrero*. In the western United States many towns, hills, and rivers are Spanish-named as a result of the early exploration and settlement in those states during the seventeenth and eighteenth centuries. The terms of ranch life and of the cowboy and his equipment are usually Spanish in origin: *hacienda, mustang, corral, lasso, lariat*.

The Dutch are responsible for such words as *chapter, yacht, schooner, boor, drawl, deck, boom, cruiser, furlough, landscape, tub, scum, freight, jeer, snap, cookie, toy, switch, cole slaw, yankee*.

The Arabic language gave us *candy, lemon, orange, spinach, sugar, algebra, alkali, alcohol, assassin, syrup, sofa, divan, mattress, magazine, safari*.

From Hebrew we have *camel, ebony, sapphire, seraph, cherub, cabal, rabbi*.

From India come *loot, pundit, rajah, punch, coolie, bungalow, calico, cot, polo, thug, khaki*.

Kimono, samurai, kamikaze are Japanese.

Malay gave us *caddy*.

The tribes of Africa are responsible for *gorilla, voodoo, zebra*, and probably *jazz*.

The American Indians are the creators of many of our words; among these are *moccasin, raccoon, skunk, totem, woodchuck, hominy, caucus, tomahawk*. Every state contains Indian place names: *Chicago* means "a place that smells like skunks," *Peoria* "a place of fat beasts," and *Manhattan* "the place where all got drunk."

You may be wondering what changes have occurred in the English language. New words come into our language almost daily. Some are changes in the word root: *edit* from *editor, peddle* from *peddler, jell* from *jelly*. Others are abbreviations, such as *pub* from *public house, cad* from *cadet, pup* from *puppy*. Some imitate other words: *motorcade* and *aquacade* from *cavalcade, litterbug* from *jitterbug, telethon* from *marathon*. We combine words to make new ones, with *smoke* and *fog* becoming *smog, motor* and *hotel* becoming *motel*, and *liquid oxygen* becoming *lox* (used for fuel in rockets).

Old words are used in new ways or as different parts of speech. A master of ceremonies is abbreviated *emcee;* this in turn becomes a verb in such usages as "Allen may emcee the show." An example of one word used to serve different parts of a sentence is the newspaper headline that reads, "Police Police Police Show."

Words change in meaning. *Harlot* once meant "servant," *wanton* and *lewd* meant "untaught" or "ignorant." *Notorious* was simply "well known." A *governor* was a "pilot," *rheumatism* meant a "head cold," and a *nice person* was "foolish person."

In the years since World War II many words have been added to our language: *Cinerama, countdown, zoorama, fallout, readout, sonic boom,* and *astronaut* are examples.

Trends Throughout the Development of English

The primacy of root words, the dropping of inflections, the use of initial syllable stress, the decline of the practice of word coinage by the joining of two root words, and the tendency to borrow words from other languages all caused English to move in the direction of one-syllable words. This tendency has been arrested somewhat with the borrowing of Latin and Greek and the fashion of dressing one's speech with these words for the appearance of scholarliness.

English shamelessly lifts words from other languages; and it is likely that this efficient and cosmopolitan process will continue. This is an attribute that makes some linguists back English as the world language of the future, if not of the present.

There will probably always be those who wish to prescribe how English is to be used. Since Jonathan Swift's ironic proposal to set up an Academy to oversee and control the proper evolution of English, there have been arguments over what is right and wrong in English. In the prescriptive attitude is revealed a failure to understand that English is arbitrary and unfixed. The schoolchild who says *run slow* or *run bad* as opposed to *slowly* and *badly* is violating American school grammar as taught in many places. However, these words come from a class of adjectives in Old English that were not inflected when used as adverbs. So the child's usage is historically correct, but only a minority of "educated" Americans is likely to realize this. "Correctness" is therefore a slightly ambiguous notion, although language arts teachers are often expected to teach the "correct" ways to speak.

Linguistic Terms

Linguists have their own jargon with which to communicate regarding language *phonology,* or sounds, *semantics,* or meaning, and *syntax,* or lexical ordering. Familiarity with the following terms should provide you with a clearer understanding of the technical vocabulary of linguistics.

In this section we will look at the constituents of language and how they have changed throughout the development of English. The chapter on language acquisition will discuss language constituents in greater depth.

Phonology

Phonology is the sound pattern of a language. As we have seen, there have been wholesale shifts in the sounds of English vowels as well as the development of a great number of mutually intelligible dialects. The language is essentially Germanic in sound patterns, although some sounds have been lost, such as the German *h* and *u,* and we have gained the French *qu* and the

Danish *sk*. Sounds in English are not completely predictable from written form, e.g., *thoughts, could.*

Morphology

The morpheme is the basic unit of meaning. The word *sings* is made up of two morphemes—a lexical morpheme *sing* and a grammatic morpheme *-s,* which indicates the tense. Tense and case morphemes have largely been dropped in English. Plural is still marked with an *-s* or *-es* (something pronounced *-ez*) and possession is marked with an *'s.* Verb tense is now usually conveyed by auxiliary verbs, and this is intimately tied to the decelerated tendency to use one-syllable morphemes. English shows great liberality and variety toward options for changing a word's form or meaning slightly with suffixes such as *-ness, -ity, -tion, -y,* and *-ly,* as in *jump→jumpiness, jumpy; scarce→scarcity, scarcely.* It is sometimes difficult to refrain from "creating" a word this way when the accepted term for our meaning eludes us.

Syntax

Syntax is the structure of the language. The most important point about English syntax is that English has become a word-order language, depending on position in the sentence to indicate meaningful relationships among words. In a language in which three relationships are indicated by word endings, there is great latitude of word position. English depends on the subject-verb-object order or accepted deviations that are well marked by auxiliaries or other markers. Case is marked by position also, instead of by the ten forms of Latin.

Semantics

Semantics has to do with meaning. The vocabulary of a language is one source of meaning, but definitions of words alone are insufficient to explicate the "deep structure" of a word pattern presented. Words must be arranged according to the rules of syntax, producing a "surface structure" to convey the relationship among words. Vocabulary growth in English has been enormous, as we have seen, and idioms and word fashions have come and gone. English adapts to the need for new concepts quickly, whether by coining or by borrowing. Science and government are two areas in which words and phrases are often coined; art and cultural vocabularies draw heavily on other languages.

Pragmatics

Pragmatics is a relatively new area of language research that has to do with how language is used, i.e., with the intended meaning of an utterance. All languages serve much the same functions, but there have been changes over time in the style of using language for various purposes. Have there been changes in the strategies for being polite, for being deferential, for ordering or requesting, for lying, for informing? Switching language styles to talk to people of different age, sex, or status creates complex and confusing language variations for children to absorb. English shows great variety over time and within individuals for effecting various language functions.

Orthography

We mentioned before that English is a museum containing the fossils of former fashions in spelling. Printing has brought a general agreement of spelling conventions, and it has also retarded further change in this area. If word sounds and spellings are not phonetically regular, the relationships among words connected by a root form are largely preserved. In addition, the written language is highly distinctive visually, which aids reading and writing. Those who argue for a phonetic script have yet to establish the connection between predictability and ease of reading. Therefore, the present orthography will probably continue, despite periodically energetic reform movements.

Modern Influences in English

Turns of phrases and newly coined words are constantly infiltrating the language of print and other media, often called "Standard English." Although expressions like *y'all* for the second person plural are frowned on by many, they do find their way into common use. However, their meanings vary among the many regions of the country. The larger and more culturally diverse a land area, the more likely it is that subcultures, including sublanguages or dialects, will develop. The greater the differences among various environments, the greater will be the differences in language styles.

Do You Speak a Dialect?

The term *dialect* refers to the form of a spoken language that is peculiar to a particular group of people. *American Speaking,* a National Council of Teachers of English (1967) recording, provides samples of dialect variations. Each speaker who participated in making the record was from one of the major dialect regions of the United States. The map on page 59 illustrates these regions.

Slang and technical jargon have also been mighty contributors to the language of late. Slang and other newly coined terms will survive or subside on their own merits; generally the mortality rate is very high. *Keen* and *super* have a hollow sound now, although they are not a generation old. *Blurb* and *go-getter* seem to be useful and have taken hold. Purists who object that slang is an empty-headed shortcut to nonthinking should remember that language itself is the decisive and deliberative judge of what will become part of its lexicon.

Another important influence on the language today is what might be called "hyperliteracy." As the efforts of Noah Webster suggest, a strange process seems to be occurring, through which letters present in the written word come to be pronounced even if they generally had been omitted in speaking. *Often* is one example of this, in which the *t* is pronounced by some highly educated people. Even the second *c* in Connecticut is sometimes heard. This is a process that may be unique to our era.

Our language has systematically changed as a means to facilitate communication. As lexicons have been added or deleted, meanings have also changed. The following eight basic principles should enable you to better understand your language heritage.

1. *Language is a system.* It is a system of complex patterns and a basic structure. There are individual units that work together with other units. Thus linguistically we look at grammar not to identify parts of speech but to learn the forms and patterns within the system. Children learn a language by learning to *use* these structured patterns rather than by analyzing them.

2. *Language is vocal.* Only speech provides all the essential signals of a language. The unit parts are those sounds that make a difference in meaning when used; they are called *phonemes.* Letters are an attempt to represent the sounds of a language. Reading is first of all a recoding of print to sound, then a decoding of the language to meaning. This is why a reading program should be based on the child's existing language knowledge.

3. *Language is composed of arbitrary symbols.* This means that the relationship between symbol and meaning is also arbitrary. It is wrong to argue that one should say *pail* rather than *bucket* or *shades* instead of *curtains* or *blinds* and that there should be only one correct pronunciation of a word. The recognition that language symbols are arbitrary may keep us from *being* arbitrary.

4. *Language is unique.* No two languages have the same set of patterns, sounds, words, or syntax. English is neither German nor Latin. For many years our school grammar has misled students by providing Latin grammatical statements as if they were true about English. It would have been equally erroneous to have insisted that students follow the grammatical rules for German.

5. *Language is composed of habits.* Our use of the system itself is on the habit level. Our ways of pronouncing a sound or ordering words in a sentence are done as automatically as walking. Teachers are not going to get anyone to speak English by telling him about the language or having the learner memorize language forms. Learning a language is governed by situations that require the use of language. The situations control the vocabulary and the syntax.

6. *Language is for communication.* Language must first make sense to the user—but it must also make sense to others. If the pronunciation is misunder-

American English dialects. (1) N.E. New England; (2) S.E. New England; (3) S.W. New England; (4) Upstate New York and W. Vermont; (5) Hudson Valley; (6) Metropolitan New York; (7) Delaware Valley; (8) Susquehanna Valley; (9) Upper Potomac and Shenandoah valleys; (10) Upper Ohio Valley; (11) N.W. Virginia; (12) S.W. Virginia; (13) W. North Carolina and W. South Carolina; (14) Delmarva (E. shore of Maryland and Virginia and S. Delaware); (15) Virginia Piedmont; (16) N.E. North Carolina (Albemarle Sound and Neuse Valley); (17) Cape Fear and Peedee valleys; (18) South Carolina; (19) Eastern Southern; (20) Central Southern; (21) Western Southern; (22) South Midlands; (23) North Midlands; (24) Northern.

stood, or forms indicate a meaning other than the one intended, the language fails to communicate. This demands an audience analysis. If this is done, it is apparent why standard usage is essential and at the scholarly level an exactness is necessary. Getting a job, participation in group discussions, writing to be understood require a high quality of language. Although there is less concern about the best way to speak and write, there will always be a concern for grammatical adequacy to assure the exchange of meaning.

7. *Language is related to the culture in which it exists.* Language exists in speakers who are in certain places doing certain things. Almost every trade has words and expressions understood only by the in-group. Sometimes this is called jargon, a kind of occupational slang. At other times it is highly technical language requiring similar experiences to assure communication.

8. *Language changes.* One teacher illustrated this to a group by having the following dialogue of slang used twenty years ago recorded on a tape. The children were asked to interpret what was meant.

Bilingual children are not disadvantaged. It is important to create meaningful contexts that stimulate communication in the new language. (PHOTO BY LINDA LUNGREN.)

Slang 20 Years Ago [1]

School has been dismissed for the day.
Jim and Kathy meet outside Jim's homeroom.

JIM: Hi, Kathy! Howzit?

KATHY: Hi, Jim. Say, what gives in your class these days? Jeepers, I never saw so much junk!

JIM: Not junk, sister. Pyramids. We're building Egyptian doodads in social studies.

KATHY: How come?

JIM: It's for the glass gadget in the hall. We're going to stash the stuff in there so the other kids can glim it.

KATHY: Terrif! That's a lot more fun than eyeballing the old books all day. This brain factory's looking up.

JIM: Well, I gotta beat it now. Time to put on the feed bag. Dig ya later?

KATHY: Natch.

Slang words such as *neat, square, cool, dough, bread, pad, sharp* were discussed, noting both established meaning and the slang interpretation.

[1] From Anita McCormic and Norma Dove, "Teaching Slang, It's a Gas!" *Grade Teacher* (February 1969), 116.

Bilingual Education in the United States

Many teachers who are not specifically trained to teach bilingual and non-English-speaking children are confronted with this task. Familiarity with the following terminology may help you to understand the role of bilingual education in your school:

1. Bilingual program. Teaching in a bilingual setting; students are taught in two languages.
2. TESOL or TESL. Teaching English to Speakers of Other Languages, Teaching English as a Second Language.
3. TEFL. Teaching English as a Foreign Language.

ESL (English as a Second Language) is often a component of a bilingual program. EFL (English as a Foreign Language) would not be used as a component of a bilingual program in the United States. Bilingual children are *not* disadvantaged, an obvious but important fact to remember. The child whose native language is not English and who is learning the English language will, with proper teaching, soon be able to communicate in *two* languages. So bilingual children are more fortunate than many because they have this privilege of knowing two languages. When we teach language arts to these children, we must deal with language abundance, a situation that sometimes calls for instruction in English, in the native language, or in both languages. The teacher's linguistic capabilities may therefore limit the desired instruction.

Linguistic Influences on Second Language Teaching

The history of second language teaching reflects changes in theory about the nature of language. Fifty years ago grammarians believed that language had a set of rules that prescribed a best way to form sentences. Dialect differences were viewed as aberrations from Standard English. In the past, second language teachers emphasized both the learning of formal rules about the new language and the memorization of individual lexical items. These were usually studied without the benefit of context. Teachers often taught the formal written language, and they used the students' native language as the language of instruction.

Structural linguists such as Leonard Bloomfield rejected the ideas of the traditional grammarians, who believed that language was a set of speech habits acquired through a series of conditional responses. The structural linguists eliminated standards of good and bad and proper and improper. They did not consider classroom English superior to nonstandard dialects, and the only criterion for judgment regarding the correctness or incorrectness of an utterance was a native speaker's judgment. Psycholinguistics emphasized that children learned language by imitating what they heard. Incorrect utterances and incorrect pronunciation were self-corrected when they failed to communicate effectively.

Second language teachers who were influenced by these theories began teaching oral language through patterns of mimicry and memorization. They rejected the notion of teaching the grammatical rules about language; they emphasized phonology and the acquisition of nativelike pronunciation by language learners. The assumption of this approach was that in memorizing enough samples of natural speech the learner would be able to make proper use of them when the appropriate context arose. This approach demonstrated that learners could perfect their accent in a second language even if they learned it after childhood.

The influence of a third group, transformational/generative grammarians, has been most significant. By stressing the unique ability of all children to generate in their native language sentences that they have neither imitated nor memorized, these linguists have changed many of the objectives of second language teachers. Instead of emphasizing either reading or speaking exclusively, the second language teacher may explore many dimensions of language with new students. The key is to create meaningful contexts that stimulate communication in the new language. Although reading is not to be ignored, in this approach it has been assumed that one cannot, in the early stages, read what one cannot produce orally. As one moves to a more advanced level in the new language, reading reinforces language and develops it through exposure to new vocabulary, syntactic structures, and cultural contexts.

Children come to school with a variety of language skills in reading, writing, listening, and speaking. The teacher's task is to help children to develop and extend these skills. It is in the nature of human development that all children learn to listen and speak before they learn to read and write. If a speaker and a listener share the same set of oral symbols for objects and relationships in their experience, oral language conveys meaning. Written language also conveys meaning if its symbols, based on these oral symbols, are shared by the reader and the writer. Therefore, the language arts teacher must build on the child's oral language base in order to enhance both the reading and writing processes. Without a strong oral language base, reading and writing are senseless to the child.

Most reading programs being developed today for bilingual students support the need for a strong oral language base. These programs are designed to teach children to read their native language while doing oral work in the second language. Reading is not introduced in the second language until the child evidences an oral base sufficient to support the development of other skills. A survey done by the United Nations in 1953 concluded that an oral language base must precede learning to read and write, and also cited studies showing that students who first learned to read in the vernacular made better progress, even in the second language reading programs, than did students who had spent the same length of time working only on reading in a second language. This evidence seems to indicate the importance of helping children view reading and writing as important additions to the communicative abilities they already possess. When reading skill has meaning for children, they learn it more easily and are also able to transfer much of what they know toward literacy in the second language.

The question "How do I proceed in the task of teaching English structures to nonnative speakers?" is certainly complex. Again, researchers and teachers are not in total agreement on an appropriate sequence of instruction. The sequence you choose will probably reflect the individual differences of your students. The following scope and sequence chart designed by Lapp and Flood will serve as *one* model for you. You will probably alter this within your own classroom.

A Scope and Sequence Chart for Use in Teaching English to Speakers of Other Languages[2]

Vocabulary development

Beginning level

A basic flexible-content vocabulary should include items relevant to the students' everyday experiences, i.e.:

eating and cooking utensils	colors
common foods	names of occupations
parts of the body	days of the week
articles of clothing	months of the year, seasons
furniture	common animals
telling time	various materials: wood, plastic, etc.
numbers; cardinal, ordinal	holidays
family relationships	most important geographic names
	words used to ask directions

[2] From Diane Lapp and James Flood, *Teaching Reading to Every Child* (New York: Macmillan Publishing Co., Inc., 1978), pp. 524–525, 519–523, 526.

Pictures and/or objects should be used to explain all of the above.

In addition:

Several basic two-word verbs (verbs + particle): pick up, wait for, hang up, get up, etc.

Concepts of directionality: in front of, behind, before, after, etc.

Countable and noncountable nouns; *cup* as opposed to *cereal*, etc.

Following simple directions

Simple synonyms, antonyms, especially adjectives and prepositions such as good–bad, on–off, etc.

Intermediate Level

Extension of vocabulary introduced above, plus:

Shopping expressions
Further occupations and responsibilities
Health and health practices
Further synonyms and antonyms
Family—names of more distant relatives
Government agencies
Clothing materials

Intermediate-advanced level

Daily living skills
　Purchasing suggestions
　Driving
　Traffic regulations
　Postal procedures
　Insurance procedures
Music, literature, the arts
Educational opportunities
Leisuretime activities
Travel
Government
Directions involving choice
Derivations
Structural analysis: prefixes, suffixes, hyphenation of words
Synonyms, antonyms, homonyms (more advanced)

Advanced level

Study skills information—locating and organizing information, synthesizing information, and making cross-comparisons

Propaganda techniques—discerning fact and fiction

The human body and its actions
  Evening and morning activities

Special problems: Idiomatic expressions
  Multiple meanings of words

Advanced descriptive terminology
  Attributes of objects (size, shape, etc.)
  Attributes of people (including personality, etc.)

Buying and selling

Transportation and communication

Personal and professional contacts (job applications, etc.)

Further government interaction (law, courts, taxes, etc.)

Oral and written reports: books, movies, trips, etc.

Discussions on American history, geography, climate

Syntactic Structure

Beginning level

A. Declarative and question sentence structures
  1. Word order of declaratives contrasted with different word order of questions with *be* verbs (They are leaving, Are they leaving?)
  2. Use of contracted forms of *be* verbs (he's, they're, I'm)
    (a) Use of pronouns with corresponding forms of *be* verb (*she is, they are*)
  3. Use of *be* verbs to show action:
    (a) in progress
    (b) of repetitive nature
  4. Use of determiners (*the, a, an*)
  5. Affirmative and negative short answers to questions with *be* verbs (*I'm going, He's not going*)
B. Verbs other than *be*
  1. Word order for declaratives compared to order for questions with *do* and *does*
  2. Affirmative and negative short answers to questions with *do* and *does*
  3. *-s* forms of third person singular used with pronouns (*he, she, it*) and other singular nouns in declaratives, contrasted to plural nouns (*he runs, we run*)
C. Expression of time (tense)
  1. Use of *be* in expressions of past tense in statements and questions. (*I was walking, Were they singing?*)
  2. Irregular verbs which form past tense without *-ed* (Use of vowel and consonant contrast)

3. Formation of verbs other than *be* to express past tense using regular rule (*-ed*)
  a. Past tense forms and placement of verbs other than *be* in declaratives and questions
  4. Forms of short responses to questions asked in past tense (use of *be* or *do* appropriately)
  5. Use of *be* verbs + *going to* to express future tense. (*She is going to ride home, They are going to sing*)
D. Formation of questions with interrogative words or word order
E. Negatives
  1. Use and placement of *not* in declaratives (past, present, future) with verb *be*
  2. Use of *not* in questions with *be*
  3. Use of *not* in sentences (declarative and question) with *do* and verbs other than *be*
  4. Use of *any, rarely, seldom, few,* etc.
F. Frequency words
  1. Different positions of frequency words with *be* contrasted with positions with verbs other than *be* (*He sometimes walks, He is always late*)
  2. Use of *ever* in question patterns; *never* in declarative sentences

Articulation

A. Contrasted intonation contours of declarative sentences, questions, and short answers
B. Stress and accent patterns of requests
C. Articulation of contracted forms of *be* with pronouns, *he, she, we, you, it, there*
D. Articulation of the /s/, /z/, and /-əz/ of third person singular verbs and plurals as in words such as *eats, wins, smashes* and contractions such as *it's, there's.*
E. Unstressed forms of *a, an, the*
F. Articulation of /k/, /g/, /ŋ/: *kick, go, sing*
G. Stress and accent patterns of compound words
H. Articulation of /t/, /d/, and *-ed* endings as in *foot, wood, hunted*
I. Articulation of /p/ and /b/ as in *pay, boy*
J. Articulation of /f/ and /v/ as in *calf, move*
K. Articulation of /θ/ and /ə/: *thin, those*
    a. Contrasting /t-/ with /θ/: *boat, both*
    b. Contrasting /d/ with /ə/: *day, they*
L. Articulation of /š/, /ž/, /č/, and / ǰ/: *mash, pleasure, choose, fudge*
M. Articulation of /m/ and /n/: *moon, no*
N. Articulation of /l/ and /r/: *lose, read*
O. Articulation of /w/ and /y/: *wood, yellow*
P. Articulation of front vowels:
    a. /i/ and /I/: *seat, sit*
    b. /e/ and /ε/: *say, pet*
    c. Contrast of /ε/ with /I/: *set, sit*

d. Contrast of /I/, /ɛ/, and /i/: *sit, set, seat*
e. /æ/: *hat*
Q. Articulation of middle vowels:
  a. /ə/ and /a/: *nut, hot*
  b. Contrast of /a/ with /æ/: *hot, hat*
  c. /ai/: *tie*
  d. /ər/: *hurt*
R. Articulation of glides and back vowels:
  a. /u/ and /U/: *food, foot*
  b. /aU/: *cow*
  c. /o/ and /ɔ/: *boat, bought*
  d. /oI/: *toy*
A. Review of patterns introduced at beginning level
B. Modification constructions: use of substitute words
  1. How *other* and *another* can be substituted for nouns, contrasted with their use as modifiers of nouns
  2. Use of objective forms of personal pronouns in object position
C. Structures in which *me, to me,* and *for me* are used with certain verbs
D. Patterns of word order when expressing manner (*John runs quickly*)
E. Modals: use of *must, can, will, should, may,* and *might* in appropriate place in sentence
F. Techniques for connecting statements:
  1. *and . . . either* contrasted with *and . . . too*
  2. Use of *but*
G. Structures with two-word verbs (verb + particle): *call up, put on*
  1. Structures in which they are unseparated
  2. Structures in which they are separated
H. Patterns for answers to *Why* and *How* questions
I. Special patterns using *to* and *for:*
  1. *for* and *to* + other words as modifiers following some terms of quality
  2. Placement of *very, too, enough*
  3. Patterns in which nouns or pronouns are used after certain action words
J. *it* or *there* as subject of the sentence
K. *-'s* as a contraction and as a possessive marker
L. Comparisons:
  1. Structures for comparisons with *different from, same as, like, the same as, as . . . as*
  2. Patterns of comparison using *-er than* and *more than, of the, -est,* and *the most*

Articulation

A. Articulation of consonant cluster: /sp/ as in *special*
B. Articulation of consonant cluster: /st/, /sk/, /sn/, /sm/, /sl/, and /sw/ as in *step, skip, snap, smell*
C. Articulation of final consonant clusters: consonant + /s/, consonant + /t/, consonant + /d/, as in *cats, dropped, flags, used*

D. Articulation of final consonant clusters: two consonants + /s/, as in *helps*
E. Articulation of final consonant clusters: two consonants + /t/, as in *jumped*
F. Intonation patterns used in comparisons

Intermediate-advanced level

A. Review of structures introduced at earlier levels
B. Word order pattern and use of relative clauses or embedded sentences to modify nouns:
  1. Words used as subject of the embedded sentence (*that, which, who,* etc.)
  2. *that* and related words in other positions
C. *what, when, who,* etc. in object position
D. Embedded sentences of different statement pattern type used in object positions
E. Patterns with *have* and *be* in the auxiliary
  1. Present perfect complete *have (has)* + *-ed/-en* form of verb
  2. *be* + *-ing* verb form (used with *yet, anymore, still,* etc.)
  3. *have* + *been* + *-ing* verb forms in continuous present perfect structures
  4. Using *be* + *-ed/-en* verb forms
  5. Using *be* with *-ed/-en* and *-ing* in descriptions
  6. Special cases:
    (a) *be* + two-word verbs and *-ing* form
    (b) Use of *had* in the above structures
Special structural patterns:
A. Verb modification
  1. *hope* }*wish* (*that*) + declarative sentence
  2. *to* omitted after certain verbs
B. Conditionals
  1. Patterns with *should, might, could, must*
  2. Cause and effect sentence structures
C. Object structures and modification
  1. Use of *-ing* endings of verbs
  2. Patterns for verbs followed by an object and one or more describing words, and/or an *-ing* form
  3. Verbs followed by two nouns with the same reference
  4. *-ing* endings used in subject position contrasted to their use at the beginning of sentences (referring to the subject)
D. Logical order of sentences in sequence
  1. Ordering for sentences related by *however, therefore, also, but*
  2. Ordering for sentences related by terms of time or place (*before, after that, then*)

Advanced level

A. Review of all levels above
B. Review of function words

1. auxiliaries: *will, may, can, could, should, might, would, must, have, be, shall, do*
2. Preposition adverbs:
   (a) Frequently used: *at, by, in, into, for, from, with, to, on, of, off*
   (b) Location
   (c) Direction
   (d) Time
   (e) Comparison
C. Conjunction patterns with *but* and *or*
D. Other complement structures
   1. *believe*
      want
      think } + declarative sentence
      expect
   2. Use of appropriate complementizer words in the above

Articulation

A. Articulation of final consonant cluster: two consonants + /z/ as in *holds*
B. Articulation of final consonant cluster: two consonants + /d/ as in *solved*

Articulation–advanced level

Intonation and stress patterns used with comparisons, manner and time words, and prepositions
Intonation patterns for modals: *could, would, must, should,* etc.
Conjunction and intonation pattern with *or* and *but*
Words for degree and for generalizing
Articulation of *to* and *too*

Reading and writing

Beginning level

In beginning English, writing is quite limited. It should be directly related to the student's understanding and use of vocabulary and structures in the class. At this level, the comma, period, question mark, and apostrophe should be taught in order to develop proper intonation. The use of capital letters at the beginning of sentences should be introduced.

The following is a suggested guide for allotting time for the teaching of language skills at this level: listening—40%; speaking—40%; reading—15%; and writing—5%.

Intermediate level

As in the beginning, writing should be a direct outgrowth of the student's mastery of the spoken word in class. Simple dictation and writing answers to questions generated by reading and conversation materials can be used as effective exercises.

Reading activities should include silent reading, group oral reading, and individual oral reading, with emphasis on the intonation patterns of language, such as rhythm and stress.

Proportions of time that might be spent in developing skills: listening and speaking—45%; reading—35%; writing—20%.

Intermediate-advanced level

At this stage, more time should be devoted to reading and writing. Advanced reading comprehension should be evaluated both orally and in written form, and should include knowledge of literal, interpretive, and critical levels of cognition.

Writing skills should be directly related to the needs of daily living as well as the more formal requirements of education. Reference and study skills should also be emphasized.

Suggested proportions of time: listening and speaking—40%; reading—40%; writing—20%.

Advanced level

At this stage, emphasis should be on the expansion of the material introduced at previous levels. The student should be encouraged to use his reading and writing skills to enable him to gain insight into all realms of our society.

Bibliography

Alexander, H. *The Story of Our Language.* Garden City, N.Y.: Doubleday, 1940.

Baugh, A. C. *The History of the English Language.* Englewood Cliffs, N.J.: Prentice-Hall, 1957.

Bloomfield, L., and C. L. Barnhart. *Let's Read.* Detroit: Wayne State University Press, 1961.

Brook, G. L. *A History of the English Language.* New York: Norton, 1958.

Jespersen, O. *Growth and Structure of the English Language.* New York: Free Press, 1968.

Key, M. R. *Male/Female Language.* Metuchen, N.Y.: Scarecrow Press, 1975.

Lakoff, R. *Language and Woman's Place.* New York: Harper & Row, 1975.

Lapp, D., and J. Flood. *Teaching Reading to Every Child.* New York: Macmillan Publishing Co., Inc., 1978.

Pei, M. *The Story of Language.* New York: New American Library, 1965.

Trapp, J. B. *The Oxford Anthology of English Literature: Medieval English Literature.* London: Oxford University Press, 1973.

Chapter 5
Language Acquisition and Development

Linguistically speaking, man is not born free. He inherits a language full of quaint sayings, archaisms, and a ponderous grammar; even more important, he inherits certain fixed ways of expression that may shackle his thoughts. Language becomes man's shaper of ideas rather than simply his tool for reporting ideas.
—Peter Farb, "Man at the Mercy of His Language," 1974, p. 86.

Language is something more than a system of communicating; it is also a social convention which one must observe under penalty of being misjudged. Ignorance or improper use of language can easily interfere with your success or advancement.
—Mario Pei, *Language for Everybody,* 1956, pp. 4–5

Silence is golden: The ability to speak several languages is an asset, but to be able to hold your tongue in one language is priceless.

—Sidney Smith

The second flame in the universe is
    the flame of language.
People look for each other with
    words of fire
and a tongue of fire
    that stammers
is better than a head
    full of brains
that is silent.
    —from a Chassidic Tale adapted
     by Marc Lee Raphael

How Children Acquire Language

From the field of physiology we have learned that the human infant is neurologically immature at birth, with the central nervous system (the brain and spinal cord) more developed than the peripheral nervous system. As the infant learns to control his muscles, this maturation enables him to discriminate among sets of sounds, shapes, and colors. By the end of a baby's first month of life, his mother can often detect pain, rage, or mere exuberance in his vocalizations. Just as the baby's random movements with his arms and legs are exercise and help him to gain control over his body, so are such vocalizations the baby's way of exercising his speech mechanism.

A child when born is physically equipped to perceive and produce speech. However, many of the sounds made by the infant are not directly related to the sounds of his later language. According to Lenneberg (1966, 1967) and other investigators, there is an age range for the stages of language development, and these stages occur in a sequential order. Noam Chomsky (1965) and others have postulated that humans possess an innate specific language acquisition device (LAD). They tell us that all infants acquire this language tool without overt teaching. Every physiologically "normal" child learns to talk, given a minimal amount of language input. Even mentally retarded children with IQs of 60 learn to talk, although often not as rapidly as the normal child, and often with more limited vocabulary.

A child entering first grade can send as well as receive spoken messages. Because of his early ability to communicate, we may deduce that formal instruction is not required for the development of two basic skills: listening and speaking. These skills have been developed through the child's involvement in a language-rich environment. In sending and receiving messages within this environment, the child evidences internalization of a working grammar of his native language. Children of this age have not acquired all of the structures of adult grammar, but they have developed the basic grammatical structures of their native language.

Imitation plays an important role in linguistic development. This is shown by the fact that the congenitally deaf child cannot learn normal speech because his inability to hear makes it impossible for him to imitate sounds. Of equal importance to the imitation of others is the child's self-imitation of his own sounds. Nearly everyone is familiar with the "babbling" of an infant; it is thought that a desire to hear himself talk contributes to this activity. When the infant is in the presence of his parents and accidentally or purposely makes a speech-like sound, they are likely to pronounce the word that approximates the sound he has just made. This is good training because it provides auditory strengthening and stimulates the child to remake the sound he has produced.

According to a report by Brown and Bellugi (1964) on the early language of two children, young talkers concern themselves with syntax (sentence arrangement) in remarkably efficient ways. Two children, a boy aged twenty-seven months and a girl aged eighteen months, imitated their mothers' sentences, and although they left out words, they never changed the original order of words they repeated. "Frazer will be unhappy" became "Frazer unhappy." "He's going out" became "He go out." Words and parts of words that carry meaning were retained in these and other samples. "No, you can't write on Mr. Cromer's shoe" was condensed to "Write Cromer's shoe." It was never "Shoe write Cromer." The investigators remind us that in speaking such sentences as "Frazer will be unhappy" the adult spontaneously stresses the most important words, here "Frazer" and "unhappy." This is an essential facet of our language; we do, indeed, stress the meaning-bearing words. Children learn the stress system as easily as they learn to talk. Innumerable repetitions make it automatic.

Loban (1976) has completed a fascinating study of the language of a group of children from their entrance into kindergarten through their graduation from high school. In this study the pupils were asked in an interview to tell what they saw in a carefully selected group of pictures and what they thought about them. The responses were recorded and the language was analyzed according to a scheme devised by a board of linguists.

One of the major problems in any such analysis is the presence in the speech of children and young people of certain "tangles" of language. They are hesitations, false starts, and meaningless repetitions that interrupt the sentence patterns. These "tangles" were extracted and studied separately from the remaining sentences. During kindergarten and the first three grades, the total group and the high subgroup showed a steady decrease in the number of tangles (35 per cent) and the number of words per tangle (50 per cent). The low group, on the other hand, increased both the number of tangles and the average number of words per tangle during the same four-year period. Throughout the study, the low group said less, had more difficulty saying it, and had a smaller vocabulary with which to say it. The high group was distinguished from the kindergarten by the ability to express tentative thinking, as revealed by such phraseology as "Perhaps," "Maybe," and "I'm not exactly sure." The gifted sensed alternatives; the weak made flat, dogmatic statements. Although the pictures invited generalizations and figurative language, little of either was used by any of the children.

Logan's study used the same analytical scheme that Strickland (1962) used for her study of the oral language of children from sixteen public schools in Bloomington, Indiana. Her purpose was to contrast the intricacy of children's patterns of speech with the simplicity of sentence structures in reading textbooks commonly used in first through sixth grades. The latter structures proved to be extremely simple compared to forms used by the children in their own speech. Whether they should be so or not is an issue still in dispute.

How Children Learn to Use Language

Speech is often a social overture (for example, the asking of a question that requires no answer). Talking often accompanies action in other motor areas. The child appears to fill every waking moment with oral expression; indeed, it seems that talking is almost compulsive in nature.

For a child as young as three years, language serves the purpose of simple narration, with the incidents related usually being telescoped into a single simple sentence. For example, "We went downtown" may be used to cover all the exciting things that happened. Occasionally children of three can enlarge upon this, and some children of four can tell enough of an incident to hold the attention of other children. Imaginative elements often crop up, possibly reflecting the

stories that are read to children of this age. For example, a child may relate, "Once there was a big engine. It came right up to the door and asked for breakfast."

Shirley (1933) found that in a single day her three-year-old-child asked 376 questions and that her four-year-old child asked 397. This is probably somewhat high for average children but gives an idea of why this age is referred to as the "question age."

The most complicated and advanced use of language is to express reasoning: "If I don't wear my mittens, I don't get them dirty," or "Where does my dinner go when I eat it?" As the child's experiences enlarge and as his mastery of vocabulary increases, his reasoning becomes increasingly complex.

The Content of the Language of Young Children

In the early years egocentricity predominates in language content. The six-year-old's insistent "Look at me" is familiar to every parent and teacher.

Almost all studies of children's language have noted the lateness with which pronouns are added to the child's vocabulary. It is not unusual to hear a three-year-old refer to himself as "Jimmy" instead of saying "I," "me," or "myself."

Developmental trends explain the peculiar flavor of the very young child's speech. Carmichael (1954) has described McCarthy's study of recorded responses from twenty children at each of seven age levels from eighteen to fifty-four months. McCarthy found that nouns constitute about 50 per cent of the total speech of very young children. Verbs increase from about 14 per cent of the total speech at eighteen months to about 25 per cent at fifty-four months. Adjectives increase over the same interval from about 10 to about 20 per cent. Connectives do not appear until about two years of age; after that age they steadily increase in proportion. Therefore, the young child typically uses many nouns and verbs, very few pronouns, and practically no connectives. His speech is thus direct, unadorned, and essentially disconnected.

Measuring the vocabulary of an individual presents

many problems. The words used will be limited by the occasion or situation. Decisions must be made as to what constitutes a word. Should *chairs* be counted as a separate word from *chair?* Should *moo-moo* be accepted as a word for *cow?* Should each meaning of a word be counted as a separate vocabulary understanding?

Vocabulary studies have been made in a number of situations. Conversations have been recorded; the written material of an individual has been analyzed; children have been stimulated to write all the words they know by showing them pictures or giving them key words; lists have been used to check recognition.

One research study by Larrick (1959) used a pocket dictionary of 18,000 words to check vocabulary; it was concluded that a twelve-year-old knew 7,200 words. When another study used a dictionary of 371,000 words, it was concluded that a child that age knew 55,000 words. With respect to the vocabulary of first-grade children, some studies indicate that a vocabulary of 2,500 words is normal whereas others indicate that 24,000 words is normal.

Repeated tests with college undergraduates indicate a vocabulary of over 100,000 words, probably over 200,000. It seems likely that such vocabulary development must occur gradually throughout the individual's growth, so the evidence indicates that the vocabulary of children has probably been underestimated.

An additional consideration is the fact that an individual's speaking vocabulary differs from his listening and reading vocabularies. Children understand many words spoken to them that they never use in their own speech, and adults read and sometimes write words that they do not use in their spoken vocabulary.

The Phenomenon of Language Acquisition

The notion of a "critical period" in language development refers to a stage in which the human organism is especially sensitive to a specific component of language. It is possible that there are certain periods that are extremely sensitive for the development of each of the language components of phonology, syntax, morphology, semantics, and pragmatics. These periods of heightened sensitivity may parallel Piaget's (1963) stages of cognitive development; for example, the first growth spurt between two and four years of age *might* be the most sensitive period for phonological development. It is important to note that "critical period" here refers to a period of particular sensitivity to language development, not a terminal point after which no language development will occur.

Let us look at some of the factors that affect a child's sensitivity to language development. Three of the major determinants are neurophysiology, psychology, and environment.

Neurophysiology

The "critical period" hypothesis is derived from behavior observed in animals such as geese (Lorenze, 1970). In applying this biological concept of critical period to the acquisition and development of language, Lenneberg (1966, 1967) and others have claimed that language cannot be learned as easily after the completion of the lateralization of the brain, a phenomenon that Lenneberg believes to occur at puberty.

Krashen (1972) claims that lateralization is complete by age five, but others such as Eimas and Corbit (1973) suggest that lateralization occurs even earlier. Kinsbourne and Smith (1974) suggest that lateralization has much in common with Piaget's concept of the sensorimotor stage, which may lead researchers to an investigation of the relationship between the sensorimotor period and the critical period of language development.

Psychology and Environment

A second determinant of language development is the psychological composition of the individual. Psychology includes such factors as cognition, intellectual functioning, experience, attitude, motivation, and culture, all of which must be considered when proposing a theory to explain a sensitive stage of development.

One must also consider environmental influences such as auditory input/stimulation, semantic input, and syntactic input. The case of "Genie" (Curtiss et al., 1974; Fromkin and Robman, 1974)—a fictitious name—demonstrates the profound effect of environment on language. Genie was a thirteen-year-old girl who was brought to the Children's Hospital in Los Angeles in November 1970 after having been virtually locked in a closet for most of her life. The actual details of the case are unknown for the most part. But at the time of her entry into Children's Hospital she had no speech, had few signs of any nonverbal language, and was barely able to control the vocal muscles that allow speech production, chewing, and swallowing. After several years of life in a normal foster home and work with educators, psychologists, and speech pathologists, Genie has exhibited an incredible amount of growth. She is able to comprehend speech, use expressive speech, and understand cognitive relationships far beyond the expectations of many researchers who would hold to a strict critical period theory of development. Although her phonology is far from perfect, her syntax, in general, far exceeds what is expected of a typical five- or six-year-old who has been learning English for that number of years. The case of Genie certainly is relevant to Lenneberg's theory of a critical period for language acquisition, which he suggests occurs between birth and puberty. Lenneberg's theory may not be totally valid, because Genie's language acquisition *began* at the onset of puberty.

It should be emphasized that neurophysiological, psychological, and environmental factors are not separable in their effects on an individual's sensitivity to language development. It is simply not clear which factor may operate first or which is most significant for the acquisition of language.

The Nature of Language

Language has a fairly definite structure that can be described by a set of rules we call "grammar." These rules or statements about the nature of language meet with fairly wide agreement. In this section we will discuss these generalizations as they apply to the English language system.

Language is usually discussed in terms of four components:

1. Phonology (the sound system).
2. Morphology (the word-formation systems).
3. Syntax (the system of word relations).
4. Semantics (the meaning system for words and sentences).

Phonology

Young children, during their first year of life, develop consonantlike sounds from back to front in the mouth. For vowellike sounds, the direction of development is from front to back for the first part of the year but switches during the last part (Irwin, 1947a, 1947b, 1947c; McCarthy, 1954).

According to Jakobson (1941, translated to English in 1968), children establish a series of oppositions within a sound continuum in order to impose order on the speech sounds they hear. The first oppositions they produce are usually between a consonant and a vowel: usually between the vowel /a/ and the consonant /p/. The consonant-vowel opposition appears in the production of the syllable *pa,* which explains the frequency of /papa/ as a first syllable sequence in young children. When there is less than optimal control over the larynx and the velum (the soft palate), the first syllable sequences are usually /baba/ or /mama/. This is why "papa," "baba," and "mama" are often the child's first quoted sequences and why these terms are used as parental names in many cultures.

The infant experiments with the vocal mechanism in producing various sounds. By about four months of age he has almost totally mastered the basic principles of its effective use. He can gurgle, chuckle, laugh, blow bubbles, and experiment with the use of breath control, the tongue, and the larynx. During this period, usually called the babbling stage, the infant learns to modify the tension of his vocal cords and to vary the positions of tongue and lips in order to imitate sounds he hears. At this time he has command of most vowel sounds and a few of the consonants. Some children are able to produce all consonants and some diphthong sounds by six or seven months of age. At approximately nine months the child's babbling usually softens into the rhythm of the speech he hears in his environment. The child's first real word is uttered between nine and fourteen months of age. The child's active vocabulary at eleven or twelve months usually consists of "mama," "daddy," and one or two other words.

The exact point at which actual words are substituted for babbling is unclear. We usually depend on parents for these records, and the data may not be reliable, for first words are so anxiously awaited by parents that word formation can be more imagined than real.

The child's first words, usually monosyllables or repetitions of monosyllables such as "ma" and "mama," serve as interjections or nouns. The child, with gestures, can convey a variety of meanings with only one word. The single word "water" or "wa-wa" may mean "I want a drink," "See the pool," "It's raining," "I want that glass," and so on. The infant's first words usually have an emotional quality, as he expresses a wish, feeling, or need. Some authorities believe that the production of the word is secondary to the general emotional status of the child at that time. Words may often be used to supplement emotional expression, body movement, and other devices used to express wants.

Principles of Phonology

Phonology is a rulebound system in which the smallest meaningful speech sound unit is called the phoneme. The English language is composed of approximately forty of these distinct speech sounds, which are related by the presence or absence of distinctive features. For example, the words *but* and *putt* are the same except for the voicing, or vocal cord involvement, of the initial phoneme. Both /b/ and /p/ are articulated in the same place, with the lips together, and in the same manner, with a slight puff of air when the lips are opened. In contrast, /k/ and /p/ are alike in being unvoiced and also are alike in manner of articulation because both involve an air stop; but they differ in place of articulation, with /k/ far back at the velum instead of at the lips.

Positions of Articulation

Most of the contrasts in the sounds of speech are made by modifying the relation of the lower jaw and tongue to the upper jaw. The generally stationary organs of the upper jaw are called points of articulation. They are the upper lip and the teeth, the alveolar ridge, the (hard) palate, the velum (soft palate), and the uvula. The uvula and upper lip are the only organs in the upper jaw that move. The organs along the lower jaw are called articulators. They are the lower lip and teeth, and the apex (tip), front, and dorsum (back) of the tongue. The six major positions of articulation made by the relation of the articulator to the point of articulation in the different phonemes are defined as follows:

The glottal position is described as follows: When no organs other than the vocal folds are used in producing a sound, the sounds are called glottal. The /h/ in *he*

Articulator	Point of Articulation	Position of Articulation	Examples
1. Lower lip	Upper lip	Bilabial	/p/, /b/, /m/
2. Lower lip	Upper teeth	Labiodental	/f/, /v/
3. Apex of the tongue and lower teeth	Upper teeth	Interdental	/th/ in *thin*, as in *then*
4. Apex of the tongue	Alveolar ridge	Apicoalveolar	/t/, /d/, /s/, /z/, /n/, /l/, /r/
5. Front of the tongue	Palate	Frontopalatal	/c/ (*chip*), /j/ (*jet*) /s/ (*ship*), /z/ (*azure*) /y/ (*boy*)
6. Dorsum of the tongue	Velum	Dorsovelar	/k/, /g/ (*ring*), /w/

From M. Alyeshmerni and P. Tauber, *Working with Aspects of Language* (New York: Harcourt Brace Jovanovich, 1975).

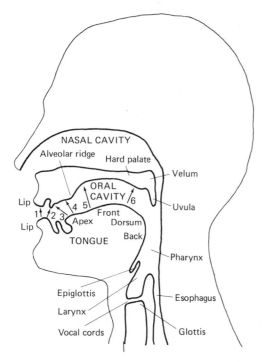

From M. Alyeshmerni and P. Tauber, Working with Aspects of Language *(New York: Harcourt Brace Jovanovich, 1975).*

and the sound heard between the two parts of the colloquial negative *hunh-uh* are examples of this position of articulation.

Distinctive Features

Following is a chart that illustrates development distinctions between speech sounds and how and where they are formed in the mouth. They are illustrations of Jakobson and Halle's theory of distinctive features.

Consonants	Dental vs. labial (/t/ vs. /p/)
Vowels	Narrow vs. wide (/i/ vs. /a/)
Narrow vowels	Palatal vs. velar* (/i/ vs. /u/)
Wide vowels	Palatal vs. velar*
Narrow palatal vowels	Rounded vs. unrounded*
Wide palatal vowels	Rounded vs. unrounded*
Velar vowels	Rounded vs. unrounded (/a/ vs. /u/)
Consonants	Velopalatal vs. labial and dental (/k/ vs. /t/)
Consonants	Palatal vs. velar (/s/ vs. /k/)
Consonants	Rounded vs. unrounded or pharyngealized vs. nonpharyngealized
Consonants	Palatalized vs. nonpalatalized*

*No English examples.
From R. Jakobson and M. Halle, *Fundamentals of Language* (The Hague: Mouton, 1956).

Phonetic Chart

The following phonetic chart illustrates the relationship between manner and position of articulation in the production of the consonant sounds of English. It does not indicate voicing, which can be imagined as a third dimension to the two axes presented. Although the terminology of the English phonetic system is complex, it is important for language arts teachers to become familiar with these terms.

Morphology

Morphology is the study of the smallest units of meaning in language, morphemes. Inflectional endings and tense markers as well as the root words to which they are attached all represent types of morphemes. Here we are interested in looking briefly at how the child demonstrates a growth of understanding about the effects that changes in inflectional endings and tense markers have on meaning in language.

The word *boy* is one morpheme, whereas *boys* is two: *boy* plus plurality conferred by the suffix *-s* (or *-es* in some words). In this example there are two classes of morpheme, the lexical *boy* and the grammatical *-s*. Lexical morphemes have inherent meaning, whereas grammatical morphemes structure the sentence or add meaning to lexical morphemes. The following examples further illustrate this difference:

The Phonetic Chart

Manner of Articulation		Bilabial	Labiodental	Interdental	Apicoalveolar	Frontopalatal	Dorsovelar	Glottal
Stop	VL	p (pit)			t (tip)		k (kit)	
	V	†b (bit)			d° (dip)		g (get)	
Affricate	VL					c (chip)		
	V					j (jet)		
Fricative	VL		f (fit)	Θ (thin)	s (sit)	s (ship)		h (hit)
	V		v (vex)	(then)	z (zip)	z (azure)		
Nasal	(V)	m (moon)			n (noon)		n (ring)	
Lateral	(V)				l (loom)			
Semi-vowel	(V)				‡r (bar)	y (boy)	w (bow)	
Vowel	(V)							

(Left-margin groupings: Stop — Continuant — Resonant — Oral — Central — Nasal — Lateral)

Vowel chart:

	Front	Central	Back
High			u (boot)
Lower high	i (beat)		
	I (bit)	i§	u (put)
Mid	e (bait)	e§ o§	o (boat)
Lower mid	ε (bet)	ə§	e (bought)
		ʌ (but)	
Low	æ (bat)		ɑ (pot)

Tongue height → / Degree of Frontness →

Note: The vowel qualities in the examples will not match those of every speaker. You will have to find examples in your own speech that fit the definition of the vowels.

°The flap sound [ə] appears in words such as butter and ladder in American speech and in British speech.

†This is similar in articulation to an aspirated voiceless vowel.

‡The r is not pronounced in New England and much of the South. In this chart semivowel = semiconsonant.

The three reduced vowels i (many) ə, often called shwa (sofa), and I (willow) represent vowels usually found in unstressed positions in words.

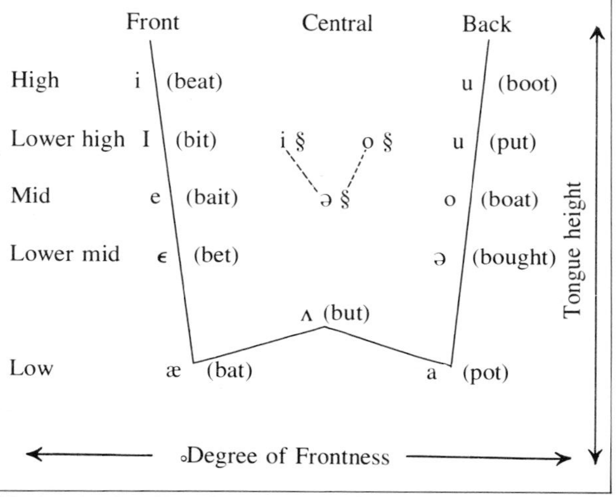

From Working with Aspects of Language, Second Edition, by Mansoor Alyeshmerni and Paul Tauber © 1975 by Harcourt Brace Jovanovich, Inc. and reprinted with their permission.

Lexical Morphemes	Grammatical Morphemes
boy	-s, -es
green	-d, -ed
	to (in infinitive)
swim	that (as in "the fact that")
chase	's
soon	-ing
from	

In one important study on the acquisition of morphology, Jean Berko-Gleason (1958) showed children a picture of a cartoon figure, telling them, "This is a *wug*." She then told the children that there were two animals, showed them a picture, and said: "There are two _____," expecting the children to supply the plural "wugs" (/wəgz/). She used nonsense words that took all three types of English plural morphemes into consideration (/-s/ as in *hats*, /-z/ as in *rugs*, and /-iz/ as in *doses*). Berko-Gleason found that children in the age range of four to five years made 6 per cent errors with the /-iz/ forms but only 25 per cent errors with /-z/ forms. She also found that the children did have /-iz/ forms in their lexicons, for 91 per cent had the correct plural for *glass*. Thus at a relatively early age, children are able to account for morphological changes in language.

The work of Brown (1963) as well as others suggests that English-speaking children acquire use of grammatical morphemes in a predictable sequence. The following chart illustrates such a sequence:

1. Present progressive
   - -ing Eric's sleep*ing*
2. Prepositions
   - in *in* house
3. on *on* chairs
4. Plural
   - -s shoe*s*
5. Past irregular
   - went he *went*
   - broke it *broke*
6. Possessive
   - 's Shannon'*s* ball
7. Uncontractible linking verb
   - is *Is* the dog brown?
8. Articles
   - the *the* wagon
   - a *a* toy
   - an *an* apple
9. Past regular
   - -ed snow*ed*
10. Third person regular
    - -s play*s*
11. Third person irregular
    - -s ha*s*
12. Uncontractible auxiliary verb
    - is *Is* Denise playing?
13. Contractible linking verb
    - s Beverly'*s* sleepy
14. Contractible auxiliary verb
    - s Daryl'*s* smiling

A curious thing happens while the child is acquiring morphemic knowledge: the phenomenon of overgeneralization or inappropriate rule formation. An example will help to explain what happens. In learning the tense forms of the verb *to run*, a child may use both *run* and *ran* appropriately for a while. After learning the regular past tense marker -d/-ed, however, he may begin to say *runned* or *runnded* before using both *ran* and *run* correctly again. The explanation for this phenomenon is that *ran* and *run* are originally learned as separate lexical items. When the regular past tense rule is learned later, it is overgeneralized in application to irregular verbs and *ran* is forgotten or ignored. The proper past tense forms are finally acquired as irregular instances. The significance of the process is that it demonstrates the tendency of the language learner to formulate, apply, and then modify rules. We will return to this important principle when we discuss grammar.

Syntax

Syntax refers to the structuring of language or the rules that order and relate words within a sentence. Adults have extensive sets of rules for their communications, but these are largely inappropriate for children's language. What is the structure of children's language? Let us review briefly.

Children produce their first words in the wide normal age range of nine to fourteen months. Before this age they have been able to produce many phonemes of all languages with their vocal apparatus, but not to convey meaning. The first words often have emotional and egocentric content, and early one-word utterances can also serve as what is called holophrastic speech. This kind of speech has a largely social function of labeling and pointing out objects in the environment, condensing into one word both the name of an object and the fact that it is noticed. Examples include "dada," "doggy," "car," "go," "gone," "book." At approximately twenty months, or when the vocabulary is about fifty words, two-word utterances begin as the individual words are combined. Most of these early combinations are "telegraphic." According to Brown and Fraser (1963), articles, prepositions, and auxiliaries are not used. Here are some samples of telegraphic speech: "mommy glass," "baby book."

Shortly after this, children begin to use some of their words as "pivots"; that is, some of these words are fixed and other words are attached to them. This division shows the operation of some kind of rule system, or grammar. Here are some examples of utterances with pivot words:

"byebye daddy"
"byebye mommy"
"byebye truck"

"allgone milk"
"allgone car"
"allgone candy"

Brown and Fraser (1963) also indicate that the child at this point has divided his lexicon into "function" words and "object" words. These divisions may be the basis of functional divisions that later become formal word classes (e.g., nouns, verbs, adjectives).

Slobin (1972) presents examples of some of these pivot structures:

Function	English		
Modify, qualify	pretty ____		here ____
	my ____		see ____
	allgone ____		it ____
	all ____		that ____
	big ____		____ on-there
	other ____		____ up-there
	there ____		
Describe act	____ away		____ it
	____ on		____ do
	____ off		____ come
Demand	I ____		give ____
	more ____		want ____
Negate	no ____		don't ____

Questions

English has two ways to form a question: (1) beginning the sentence with a verb or auxiliary (*do, did*), e.g., "Does Big Boy have the salad?" and (2) beginning the sentence with a "*wh-* word" (*who, what, where, when, why, how*). Studies by Menyuk (1969) suggest that from the earliest stages of language development children, through intonation, patterns, and simple transformations, learn to produce questions. The first type of question is called a "yes/no" question. *Wh-* questions are called "information" questions.

When children learn to ask questions, they do so first by incorporating the rising intonation typical of English questions into the same sentences they use for statements and demands, e.g., "Lynne happy?" The second step in the acquisition process is the use of *wh-* questions. When yes/no questions occur for the first time, the auxiliary *do* takes on a unique function in inverted questions and in negatives. The system is similar to an adult system, but auxiliaries are still not inverted in *wh-* questions, e.g., "Does he say why?" There are no combinations of auxiliaries in the children's speech, e.g., "Has he had the operation?" although these combinations can occur in adult English. The auxiliary form of *be* does not usually appear in early children's speech, e.g., "He has been having a good time in New Orleans."

Relative Clauses

Carol Chomsky (1969) showed that many children do not fully comprehend relative clauses until quite late; many eight-year-olds do not thoroughly understand sentences like "Tell Linda when to water the plants" and "Ask Nancy which chair to sit at." If pushed, some young children will say, "Nancy, which chair to sit at?"

Chomsky, like Clark (1972), suggests that most children who are five to ten years of age regard the first noun phrase in a sentence as the subject and the second noun phrase as the object, so that "The pie was eaten by Bob Hill" is thought of as subject–pie, object–Bob Hill.

Some psychologists have suggested that acquisition of grammar and modification of rules go on not just throughout childhood but rather throughout life. Carol Chomsky (1969) found that many children ten years old still adhere rigidly to the "minimal distance principle" that assumes that the subject of a verb is the noun phrase immediately before it. In the sentence "Harold promised Mary to make dinner" it is Harold who will be the chef, yet many school-age children will believe the chef to be Mary. These children have not learned to modify the often-correct minimal distance principle to accommodate verbs like *promise* that take indirect objects. Following is a chart (Lenneberg, 1964) showing when certain linguistic performances are likely to occur in normally developing children:

Age	Vocalization
At birth	Crying
1–2 months	Cooing, crying
3–6 months	Babbling, cooing, and crying
9–14 months	First words
18–24 months	First sentences
3–4 years	Almost all basic syntactic structure
4–8 years	Almost all speech sounds correctly articulated
9–11 years	Semantic distinctions established

Semantics

Semantics is the study of word meanings, including phonology, syntax, and pragmatics. Single words can have multiple meanings, and "fixed" multiple meanings can be altered by syntactic and contextual constraints. A four-year-old child understands that a figurative meaning is being attached to the word *devil* when his mother says, "Jimmy, you're acting like a little *devil*." He also knows if *devil* is used in a positive or negative way by his mother's tone and by contextual considerations (his actions).

Using Jakobson's (1941, 1968) notion of binary oppositions, H. H. Clark (1970) has proposed a theory of distinctive features in phonology. Jakobson maintained that young children interpret *less* as though it means *more*. Clark argued that when young children learn polar adjectives and comparatives, they first learn that *more/less, big/little, near/far* refer to the same concept: *having*. Next, the child learns that dimension is involved and proceeds to use both words positively—therefore, *big-little*. Finally, the child realizes that the dimension is polar and he begins to use the words correctly.

Clark's semantic feature theory may look like this:

	CAT	COW
	+ animal	+ animal
	+ four legs	+ four legs
Later development:	+ little	+ big

Chomsky (1972), attempting to minimize semantics, claimed, "it has been found that semantic reference . . . does not apparently affect the manner in which acquisition of syntax proceeds; that is, it plays no role in determining which hypotheses are selected by the learner" (p. 33).

Disagreeing with Chomsky, E. V. Clark (1971) stated, "semantic information does affect the manner in which the subject (or child) approaches the learning of syntactic rules, contrary to Chomsky's (1965) assumption. Without any semantic information, subjects simply tried to learn the relative positions of words'' (p. 56).

Ferguson (1971), Berko-Gleason (1973), Shatz and Gelman (1973), and others have provided information that has contributed to the reformulation of the language-acquisition-device (LAD) theory to include mechanisms that will handle the acquisition of semantics as well as the acquisition of syntax.

The Nature of a Grammar

How do native speakers develop a language? It can be said somewhat simplistically that they gather information about language, form hypotheses about the underlying principles of the language's organization, and test those hypotheses in the world. Children, then, are striving to acquire the concepts that control language rather than merely the words that compose language. One's knowledge of the rules of a language and the concepts that underlie it is regarded as one's language competence. As suggested by Noam Chomsky (1965), a description of this linguistic competence possessed by the native speakers of a language is called a grammar. A grammar describes what is known, however unconsciously, by the speakers of a language. Chomsky (1965) as well as Lenneberg (1967) claims that the capacity to acquire language competence is an innate attribute of the human organism. There is considerable support for this position, but we will only say now that all humans in reasonable environments acquire language, and the possibility of forgetting how to use language seems unlikely. Before we treat the nature of the knowledge possessed by a natural language user, it might be worthwhile to explore the criteria used in evaluating a grammar. A grammar must first of all be descriptively adequate, which means that it must account for all the data that can be observed. When you call a friend in the evening and no one answers the phone, there are several theories to explain why, all of which are descriptively adequate. We will suggest three:

Theory 1: He has not come home.
Theory 2: He has gone out for the evening.
Theory 3: A marauding band of Martians swooped in and kidnapped him.

All theories account for the observed facts and are, in that sense, descriptively adequate. The second criterion, explanatory adequacy, requires that the theory makes as few assumptions as possible and at the same time express as many relevant generalizations as possible. Certainly theory 3 does not meet this criterion, because it makes unaccountable assumptions and fails to express the generalization that, in fact, people often are away from home of their own free will.

One grammar that attempts to satisfy the two criteria of descriptive and explanatory accuracy is generally attributed to Noam Chomsky (1957, 1965) and has been applied to children's acquisition of language by Menyuk (1963). This is the theory of generative transformational grammar.

Transformational Grammar

Most people agree that sentences such as

1. John loves Mary.
2. Mary is loved by John.

are pretty closely related. But how are they related, and what underlies their relationship? They seem to have the same meaning but a different structure. Now consider the sentences:

1. The shooting of the hunters frightened us.
2. Sailing ships can be exciting.

Each of these sentences can be interpreted in two different ways. For example, in the first sentence it can be the hunters' use of guns or the hunters' having been shot that we find frightening.

One proposed explanation of the differing interpretations follows: Language has a meaning level (which is called its deep structure) and a level consisting of actual sentences used in communication (which is called its surface structure). Noam Chomsky (1957) originally suggested simple, active declarative sentences as the deep structures that are then subjected to certain transformations, such as the passive transformation through substitution of a reflexive pronoun and through conjoining. Transformation produces the surface structure we hear, which differs in construction but not in meaning from the original deep structure. The hearer can transform this sentence back into its deep structure and assimilate the intended meaning.

In the sentences "John loves Mary" and "Mary is loved by John" the deep structure and therefore the meaning are identical. The sentence "Sailing ships can be exciting" is ambiguous because it could arise from either of two different deep structures: "The sailing of ships can be exciting," or "Ships with sails can be exciting."

We have, then, meaning or semantics on one level and phonological form on the "surface" level above meaning. The link between these two is syntax—the vehicle for bringing meaning to the surface. Transformational grammar allows four basic kinds of operations on base sentences (deep structure). These operations can occur in any order, any number of times, and operate on specific elements in the sentence.

Transformation can

1. Move elements:
   from   "The chairman began the financial review after introducing the board members."
   to   "After introducing the board members, the chairman began the financial review."
   The adverbial phrase has been shifted.

2. Delete elements:
   from   "He was stung on the arm by a bee."
   to   "He was stung on the arm."
   The phrase "by a bee" has been deleted (called agent deletion).

3. Insert elements:
   from   "He is baking bread."
   to   "He is not baking bread."

Linguists do not entirely agree about negative insertion transformations.

4. Transpose elements:
   from   "John loves Mary."
   to   "Mary is loved by John."
   This passive transformation transposes the subject and object of the sentence.

The capacity for this linguistic behavior is innate, and therefore the child's language normally develops according to a conventional set of patterns. In transformational terms a grammar is the set of rules for bringing meanings to the surface. We will borrow from transformational or T-grammar to explain much that is observed in children's language.

Rule Formation Theory

As has been said before, a child learns language by acquiring the concepts behind language performance. The child wants to know not only how to form the plural of *candy* but also how to form the plurals of all words. This apparent fact contradicts the notion that children learn items one at a time and progress in a linear fashion. Children strive instead to learn the rules that will bring the ideas to the surface. In this attempt is language structure learned.

The first item of support for this notion of the child's role as a systematic language processor is the presence of identifiable grammars in children. A pivot/open grammar is one example of a ruled grammar. Support also comes from the previously mentioned overgeneralization of learned structures in children. When a child acquires a new morphemic ending, it usually sweeps over all possible areas, whether correct or not. Most children cannot know or guess that *ox* comes from a Southern England dialect and is made plural with the addition of *-en*. They apply the rule they know, which is to add *-es* to a word that ends in a voiceless stop.

Support also comes from the behavior of children

called on to repeat phrases that contain constructions too sophisticated for their current grammatical knowledge or in violation of whatever grammatical rules they have at the time. If asked to repeat "I haven't any candy," the child of two or three is likely to say "I got no candy." Neither shaping, correcting, nor rehearsing seems effective in eliciting an exact repetition. Obviously the child is incorporating what he hears into his rule system and expressing it via that same rule system. Although incorporation shares the same deep structure, expression takes a different surface structure.

The Development of Language

Language continues to develop beyond childhood, of course, and it is important to know how this happens. Here we shall talk about two important kinds of language development that proceed long after the acquisition of a language's structuring in grammar. Both can be greatly influenced by education.

Pragmatic Development

Throughout life we use language, but clearly language can be used well, poorly, or indifferently. To expand, it can be used effectively, ineffectively, humorously, persuasively, deceptively, artistically, or in many other ways. The knowledge of how to use language is called pragmatics, and it is what a writer might call style. To say that we all differ in terms of command of style is to understate the case greatly. We may all possess basically the same knowledge of language structure, but we differ greatly in how we use it. The language arts curriculum can and should be effective in giving students many styles of language use, including those for formal social expression, informal correspondence, spontaneous expression, logical argument, criticism, and diplomacy. Language arts teachers should explore the whole intriguing area of how language can be used most effectively in particular situations. How would a letter written to a mail-order business be different from one written to the editor of a newspaper? If you were writing a repair manual, why would the style you used be different from that of a fairy tale?

Metalinguistic Development

Certainly we all possess some common knowledge of language—its basics of pronunciation, vocabulary, grammar. However, another area where we differ greatly is in our knowledge of what we know. Think a minute; this merely means knowing what we are doing when we use language. The fact that some of us, more than others, can dwell on, analyze, criticize, subvert, or play with language is significant. This self-knowledge of one's linguistic processes is called metalinguistic awareness. The user of puns, riddles, and paradoxes is showing an acute knowledge of language that allows him to manipulate it. In *The Taming of the Shrew* a character orders his servant to "knock me soundly upon this door," and the servant is befuddled, not wishing to believe that he should swat his master against the door. In this example, Shakespeare is mocking an affected style of speech and at the same time playing with language. This is also true for "Jam every other day," which Alice is promised in wages from the Queen. She later learns that "every other day" is every day except today.

It is said that reading requires bringing to conscious awareness what we know *about* language; and what we know about language we must have learned, whether in the classroom or elsewhere. It can even be hypothesized that the differences in individuals' performance in school are ultimately differences in metalinguistic ability. Here there is much need for research and workable knowledge of how and what to teach people about language that will help them use it to increase their own knowledge of the world. Here, too, is where metalinguistics and pragmatics intersect. Knowledge about styles, modes, and structure of language is clearly connected to both metalinguistic and pragmatic knowledge. These areas of expertise can develop throughout life and must be given careful attention when one plans for language instruction. The teacher will never really provide anyone with language, but he or she can certainly help to provide an increased awareness of how to use that language.

Other Aspects of Language Acquisition

Second Language Acquisition

There is much controversy among those linguists who study the learning of second languages, and the implications of this controversy are significant for educators. There are those who claim with Lenneberg that the ability to acquire language is actually dependent on certain maturational stages, such as the range of two to three years old when a great deal of phonological information is acquired. As one matures, the theory runs, one loses the ability to learn a language in a "natural" way. Noam Chomsky and other linguists, however, hold that the language acquisition device has full potency throughout life. The implication of the former theory is that a second language must be learned via metalinguistic awareness. The development of awareness of the rules of a second language can refer to rules from the first one, but second language acquisition can never be unconscious and "natural." It must be very conscious, with intense drill and evaluation of rules, conjugation of verbs, and so on. The latter theory holds that unconscious acquisition of a second language is always possible and so an immersion or language experience approach is the more legitimate one. The contrast between these two approaches underscores how our assumptions about language determine our teaching styles and points to the need for research on teaching effectiveness and on learning stages.

Language Disability

What can language disabilities tell us about language acquisition? Do people with aphasia or autism, for example, have delayed linguistic development, or are they in fact experiencing a different linguistic development? This is another difficult yet researchable question whose answer will largely determine how these individuals will be taught. Suffice it to say that much more needs to be known about the language of individuals with central nervous system disorders, although it most likely will prove difficult to draw inferences from the language competence of individuals with impaired neurology that are relevant to the language of others who are not impaired.

Implications for Language Learning

In summary, language acquisition and development can be seen as rulebound activities. The child strives to learn the grammar of his linguistic community by a process of forming linguistic hypotheses and testing them out on others. The claim has been made that this capacity is innate and coded in the gene structure of humans. This capacity for language is a uniform one possessed by all undamaged human beings and is unmatched by any other species. By and large, language is everywhere acquired via the same invariant stages and is processed by the same kinds of operations; which is to suggest that language production is dominated by some mechanism dependent on deep structures that undergo any number of transformations before an utterance is delivered in its surface form. Language comprehension works in the opposite direction, deriving deep structure from its surface forms.

Language arts teachers need to be aware of what effect they can have on the development of a child's language. They must make children aware of the power of language as a tool for personal, professional, and global communication. This knowledge is what linguists slightly mystify with the name "pragmatics," which simply means the effective and appropriate use of language.

Another area where teachers can make an impact is in metalinguistic awareness. Increased familiarity with the workings of language makes its use that much more adept, in the same way that knowledge of how a sewing machine or car works can improve a user's performance. There are, of course, many ways to approach metalinguistics in the classroom. Beware the pedantic teacher who thinks children need to know tedious structural rules merely for their own sake. Language instruction can be a joy. For example, etymology is by nature fascinating, as is exercise of the human facility for punning and otherwise joking with words. Believing that language arts is a dull subject is like believing that the telephone's best use is as a paperweight.

Bibliography

Alyeshmerni, M., and P. Tauber. *Working with Aspects of Language.* New York: Harcourt Brace Jovanovich, 1975.

Bellugi, U., and R. Brown. *The Acquisition of Language.* Chicago: University of Chicago Press, 1971.

Berko-Gleason, J. "The Child's Learning of English Morphology." *Word,* **14:** 150–177, 1958.

Berko-Gleason, J. "Language and Social Context: Selected Readings." *Contemporary Psychology,* **18** (4): 178–179, 1973.

Berry, M. F., and J. Eisenson. *Speech Disorders: Principles and Practices of Therapy.* New York: Appleton-Century-Crofts, 1956.

Brown, R., and U. Bellugi. "Three Processes in the Child's Acquisition of Syntax." In E. H. Lenneberg, ed., *New Directions in the Study of Language.* Cambridge, Mass.: MIT Press, 1964.

Brown, R., and C. Fraser. "The Acquisition of Syntax." In C. N. Cofer and Barbara S. Musgrave, eds., *Verbal Behavior and Learning: Problems and Processes.* New York: McGraw-Hill, 1963, pp. 158–197.

Chomsky, C. S. *The Acquisition of Syntax in Children from 5 to 10.* Cambridge, Mass.: MIT Press, 1969.

Chomsky, N. *Aspects of the Theory of Syntax.* Cambridge, Mass.: MIT Press, 1965.

Chomsky, N. *Language and Mind.* New York: Harcourt Brace Jovanovich, 1972.

Chomsky, N. *Syntactic Structures.* The Hague: Mouton, 1957.

Clark, E. V. "On Acquisition of the Meaning of 'Before' and 'After,' " *Journal of Verbal Learning and Verbal Behavior,* **10:** 266–275, 1971.

Clark, H. "Information of Language on Solving Three-Term Series Problems." *Journal of Experimental Psychology,* **82** (2): 205–215, 1969.

Clark, H. "Memory for Semantic Features in the Verb." *Journal of Experimental Psychology,* **80:** 326–334, 1969.

Clark, H. "Role of Semantics in Remembering Comparative Sentences." *Journal of Experimental Psychology,* **82** (3): 545–553, 1969.

Clark, H. "The Primitive Nature of Children's Relational Concepts." In *Cognition and the Development of Language,* ed. by J. R. Hayes. New York: John Wiley and Sons, Inc., 1970.

Clark, H. "Difficulties People Have in Answering the Question, 'Where Is It?' " *Journal of Verbal Learning and Verbal Behavior,* **11** (3): 265–277, 1972.

Curtiss, S., and others. "The Linguistic Development of Genie." *Language,* 1974.

Eimas, P. D., and J. D. Corbit. "Selective Adaptations of Linguistic Feature Detectors." *Cognitive Psychology,* 1973.

Epstein, C. *Affective Subjects in the Classroom: Exploring Race, Sex and Drugs.* Scranton, Pa.: Intext Educational Publishers, 1972.

Farb, P. "Man at the Mercy of His Language." In R. L. Cherry et al., eds., *A Return to Vision.* 2nd ed. Boston: Houghton Mifflin, 1974.

Ferguson, C. A. *Language and Language Use.* Stanford, Calif.: Stanford University Press, 1971.

Fromkin, V., and R. Robman. *An Introduction to Language.* New York: Holt, Rinehart and Winston, 1974.

Geschwind, N. *Selected Papers on Language and the Brain.* Dordrecht, Holland: D. Reidel, 1974.

Irwin, O. C. "Infant Speech: Consonantal Sounds According to Manner of Articulation." *Journal of Speech and Hearing Disorders,* **12:** 402–404, 1947a.

Irwin, O. C. "Infant Speech: Consonantal Sounds According to Place of Articulation.' *Journal of Speech and Hearing Disorders,* **12:** 397–401, 1947.

Irwin, O. C. "Infant Speech: Variability and the Problem of Diagnosis." *Journal of Speech and Hearing Disorders,* **12:** 287–289, 1947.

Jakobson, R. *Child Language, Aphasia and General Sounds.* The Hague: Mouton, 1968.

Jakobson, R., and M. Halle. *Fundamentals of Language.* The Hague: Mouton, 1956.

Kinsbourne, M., and W. L. Smith. *Hemispheric Disconnection and Cerebral Function.* Springfield, Ill.: C. C. Thomas, 1974.

Larrick, N. *Your Child and His Reading: How Parents Can Help.* New York: Public Affairs Committee, 1959.

Lenneberg, E. H. *Biological Foundations of Language.* New York: Wiley, 1967.

Lenneberg, E. H. "A Biological Perspective of Language." In E. H. Lenneberg, ed., *New Directions in the Study of Language.* Cambridge, Mass.: MIT Press, 1964.

Lenneberg, E. H. "The Natural History of Language." In F.

Smith and G. Miller, eds., *The Genesis of Language*. Cambridge, Mass.: MIT Press, 1966.

Loban, W. *Language Development: Kindergarten Through Grade Twelve*. Champagne, Ill.: National Council of Teachers of English, 1976.

Lorenze, K. Z. "On Killing Members of One's Own Species," *Bulletin of the Atomic Scientists,* **26:** 2–5, October 1970.

Krashen, S. D. "Language and the Left Hemisphere." *University of California Working Papers in Phonetics, 1972.*

McCarthy, D. "Language Development in Children." In *Manual of Child Psychology,* 2nd ed., edited by L. Carmichael. New York: Wiley, 1934, pp. 492–630.

McNeill, D. *The Acquisition of Language.* New York: Harper & Row, 1970.

McNeill, D. "Developmental Psycholinguistics." In F. Smith and G. Miller, eds., *The Genesis of Language.* Cambridge, Mass.: MIT Press, 1966.

Menyuk, P. *Sentences Children Use.* Cambridge, Mass.: MIT Press, 1969.

Menyuk, P. "Syntactic Structures in the Language of Children," *Journal of Child Development,* **34:** 407–422, 1963.

Pei, M. *Language for Everybody.* New York: Devin-Adair, 1956.

Piaget, J. *The Origins of Intelligence in Children.* New York: Norton, 1963.

Raphael, M. L. *Chassidic Tales Adapted.* Columbus, Ohio: Department of Jewish Studies, Ohio State University.

Shatz, M., and R. Gelman. *The Development of Communication Skills: Modifications in the Speech of Young Children as a Function of Listener.* Chicago: University of Chicago Press, 1973.

Shirley, M. M. *The First Two Years: A Study of Twenty-five Babies.* Minneapolis: University of Minnesota Press, 1933.

Slobin, D. I. Universals of grammatical development in children, *Advances in Psycholinguistics,* edited by G. B. Flores d'Arcais and W. J. M. Levelt. Amsterdam: North-Holland, 1970.

Strickland, R. G. "The Language of Elementary School Children: Its Relationship to the Language of Reading Textbooks and the Quality of Reading in Selected Children." *Bulletin of the School of Education, Indiana University,* **38:** 4, 1962.

Strickland, R. G. *Some Approaches to Reading.* Washington, D.C.: Association for Childhood Education International, 1969.

Chapter 6
Speech and Listening

How Are Skills in Oral Communication Fostered?

The development of language skills is a topic of constant research in education. Theorists such as Lenneberg (1970) stress the innate aspects of language acquisition, whereas others such as Skinner (1972) emphasize behavioral reinforcement as a prime factor in language development. Still others such as Piaget (1962) focus on the child's interactions within his environment as an essential factor in establishing concepts that will later be communicated through language. After reviewing, grouping, and labeling existing theories as "nativistic, behavioristic, and cognitive," Wanat states:

group differences have generally been ignored in research on language development. Thus, dialect differences, possible ethnic differences in capacities and strategies for processing information, differences in thinking style, and emotionally related factors are not adequately taken under consideration. None of the theories reviewed (Nativistic, Behavioristic, Cognitive) gives an adequate explanation of the way a child acquires his language. Each of the theories is wrong in that each unjustifiably claims to provide a complete explanation. Yet, each of these theories is valuable in that each provides part of the information we need to understand language. [Wanat, 1971, p. 147]

Although there is a need for continued research involving larger sample populations with greater sociological and motivational controls, existing theories *do* offer much of what is needed in order to understand the language base of the communication process. A child may enter school with a "private" language as well as a "public" language (Patin, 1964). Because the private language is often better developed than the public lan-

A child may enter school with a "private" language as well as a "public" language. The child learns to use the appropriate language in the appropriate setting. (PHOTO BY LINDA LUNGREN.)

tween them. With this growing knowledge, the child learns, respects, and applies the appropriate language in the appropriate setting.

With the belief that language refinement and growth are highly dependent on teacher acceptance, you are encouraged to accept and extend the language presented by the child. Through your examples, you can provide further learning; for example, if your first-grader says, "I busted it!" you can reply, "I see that you *broke* it. Delicate things *break* easily. *Broken* things are hard to repair, but let's try." You are beginning to help the child acquire "public" language skills while you are accepting his "private" language. If you can offer children such nonthreatening verbal interactions, they will continually *learn* language by *using* it.

This human need to continually refine one's language through using it is also expressed in interactions within the home. A child of four is probably silent nineteen minutes of his waking day. Given some direction, such oral practice has great potential for learning. A study of the relationship between the early reading experiences and patterns of parent-child relationships showed that children who engage in two-way conversations at mealtime with parents who encourage them to talk can be distinguished from other children denied this experience. The child in a home where both parents are often absent because of work or social activities may get such experience by relating with another adult, such as a grandmother or babysitter.

It is certain that exposure to television does not do the same thing for a child. First, the child watching television does not get practice in speaking. There is limited interaction. Second, much that demands a child's attention on television is limited with respect to language. Many children's cartoons are based on sophisticated visual humor, and many of the words that are used mean little to a child. Third, television vocabulary is limited to the relatively few situations portrayed on this medium, such as the imagined life of the Western cowboy. However, it is quite possible that some television programs especially designed for children with an educational goal may influence their speech in a positive way.

guage, some children may find reading a difficult task in that most reading materials are written in public language, which linguists often call Standard English. All children must be encouraged to accept both their private and public languages through instruction about the phonological and grammatical variations that exist be-

Extending the Public and Private Language Patterns of All Children

Experience with young children who speak a combination of English and another language such as Hawaiian or who speak a Spanish-English dialect suggests that teachers must provide a model that demonstrates a desired "public" speaking form.

By the time the native child reaches the age of seven, his cultural and language patterns have been set, and his parents are required by law to send him to school. Until this time he is likely to speak only his own local dialect of Indian, Aleut, or Eskimo or, if his parents have had some formal schooling, he may speak a kind of halting English.

He now enters a completely foreign setting—a Western classroom. His teacher is likely to be a Caucasian who knows little or nothing about his cultural background. He is taught to read the Dick and Jane series. Many things confuse him: Dick and Jane are two gussuk (Eskimo term for "white person," derived from the Russian *Cossack*) children who play together. Yet, he knows that boys and girls do not play together and do not share toys. They have a dog named Spot who comes indoors and does not work. They have a father who leaves for some mysterious place called "office" each day and never brings any food home with him. He drives a machine called an automobile on a hard-covered road called a street which has a policeman on each corner. These policemen always smile, wear funny clothing, and spend their time helping children to cross the street. Why do these children need this help? Dick and Jane's mother spends a lot of time in the kitchen cooking a strange food called "cookies" on a stove which has no flame in it, but the most bewildering part is yet to come. One day they drive out to the country, which is a place where Dick and Jane's grandparents are kept. They do not live with the family and they are so glad to see Dick and Jane that one is certain that they have been ostracized from the rest of the family for some terrible reason. The old people live on something called a "farm" which is a place where many strange animals are kept: a peculiar beast called a "cow," some odd-looking birds called "chickens," and a "horse" which looks like a deformed moose. . . .

So it is not surprising that 60 percent of the native youngsters never reach the eighth grade. [*Bilingual Schooling in the United States,* 1972]

The bilingual child encounters some difficulty in reading materials written in English, often because he is exposed to a life-style and language unlike his own. He therefore has special needs in the following areas: (1) ethnic heritage, (2) self-image, (3) language.

Culture

Zintz aptly explains some cultural interference problems that teachers and students may experience:

Too many teachers are inadequately prepared to understand or accept these dissimilar cultural values. Teachers come from homes where the drive for success and achievement has been internalized early, where "work for work's sake" is rewarded, and where time and energy are spent building for the future. Many children come to the classroom with a set of values and background of experiences radically different from that of the average American child. To teach these children successfully, the teacher must be cognizant of these differences and must above all else seek to understand without disparagement those ideas, values and practices different from his own [Zintz, 1975]

Self-image

Perhaps the most important characteristic of any good teacher is her ability to accept each child without prejudice or preconception. Children quickly and thoroughly sense rejection by their teacher. In the case of the bilingual child, the teacher must be quick to accept the child's language because it is the language of his home. Language and self-concept are so closely intertwined that a child can be made to feel foolish and worthless when his "accent" or dialect is ridiculed by his teacher or peers. Trust and confidence between the teacher and the child must precede linguistic corrections.

Language

Any statement to the effect that bilingual children need to learn to speak English before they can read English obviously needs qualification. Adults who can read their native language often read English before speaking it. But the young child who does not read his native language probably needs to learn to speak English and to hear English spoken before he can read it or write it.

There are four linguistic categories in which bilingual children may need instruction: [1]

1. Experiential - conceptual - informational background. Children often need experiences in English to tap their conceptual knowledge. A child from a farm may find it difficult to read about a bazaar because he has never experienced such an event.

2. Auditory discrimination. Children from language backgrounds other than English will possess a phonemic system that differs considerably from the English phonemic system; e.g., Spanish-speaking children often have difficulty discriminating between pairs in English:

hit	ship	beet
heat	sheep	bit

3. Vocabulary. There are several factors that teachers of bilingual children must take into consideration when teaching vocabulary. First, the child may have an English word for a phenomenon that is culturally determined. This meaning may not be shared by native English speakers. Second, there are many words in other languages that sound like English words but have different meanings. These words are called false cognates; some examples in Spanish are

salvar	to save a life, not to save money
libreria	bookstore, not library
chanza	joke, not chance

4. Syntax. Many languages of the world do not have the same syntactic structure as English. The bilingual child needs time and practice to acquire a second syntactic structure. Possible difficulties may include:

   a. Reversed/inverted word order:
      The house white
      (*La casa blanca*)
      I don't know where is the boat.

[1] From Diane Lapp and James Flood, *Teaching Reading to Every Child* (New York: Macmillan Publishing Co., Inc., 1978), p. 499.

b. Grammatical elements:

Copula confusion:	Today he working downtown.
Pluralization:	My foots are sore.
Comparison:	She is more big.
Possession:	The pen of Maria is black.

These sources of possible confusion can be the basis of instruction. With time, practice, and competent teachers, bilingual children can learn to communicate and read in their native language and English.

When a child asks, *"Hay tees?"* (What's this?), answer, "That is an elephant" rather than "An elephant." Say, "This is a soldier's hat," not "A soldier's hat" or "A hat." Thus the speech pattern for labeling is established. Through these and similar interactions children are helped in their understanding of generalized concepts needed for classification. Say, "That *color* is pink," "This *color* is red." Say, "That *animal* is a horse" rather than "A horse," when a picture is shown. Children will only be confused by "This is rough; this is smooth," even when objects are handled. Use "The sandpaper is rough," "The floor is smooth."

Activities involving matching should involve more than identification. Children should say *how* things match: "Yes, the toys are the same *color*," "The wheel and the apple have the same *shape*." Be careful about the so-called big and little hands on the clock. *Longer* and *shorter* may be more accurate.

When a child gropes in his effort to communicate, such as sticking out a foot with a new shoe on it, respond, "Yes, I see your new shoe." This form of echo procedure provides the words the child needs—in this case, "See my new shoe." When a child says, "Hus got one dem flowers, dem Sann Slause—our house," the teacher says, "You have a Christmas tree at your house, too." Or when he shouts, "Eu-ahhee-ee me uh," the teacher can sympathize by saying, "Yes, I saw Carl hit you."

This procedure may be extended using the child's original expression. "You have a Christmas tree at your house, too. Some of the children are making decorations for the tree. You can make some for our tree and some to take home to put on your tree." Expanded and recast sentences have been shown to facilitate syntactic development.

Vocabulary is developed by having children be actively, physically involved in the demonstrations of the use of words. Real objects rather than pictures are starting points. The children see, feel, put together, take apart, smell, listen to, and eat as aids to learning language. Activities are planned to involve such motor-response—the child puts his hand in *front* of him, *behind* him, *between* his knees, *over* his head, *on* his head.

A narrow focus on the right word should be avoided: as long as the meaning is clear, all should be accepted.

The ball that is beside the box may also be next to the box, at the side of the box, by the box, in front of the teacher, on the floor, on the rug, between George and the box. Remember how you felt when a teacher had a "right" answer that was so narrow that others equally correct were not accepted.

Such language activities are not a part of special drill periods but a part of every activity the child experiences. Teachers do not need to be concerned about talking too much if they know the purpose to be served by such activity.

Oral language use shows positive results even at the college level. Dillard University planned a prefreshman program to help students who wished to offset a background of limited language, little access to books, and inadequate opportunity to think about and discuss current affairs. For six weeks the students read two hours a day, talked over what they read with a teacher, and listened to a selected television broadcast and discussed it. In addition, the students studied one subject of their own choosing. Such a program uses the techniques that research and common sense suggest are important for the development of language power and thinking.

Specific Methods

The following special methods are suggested as you attempt to extend the communication skills of both the native-speaking and bilingual children within your classroom.

A group of Spanish-speaking first-graders in San Antonio, Texas, was studied in terms of their problems of learning to read English. In addition to the language problem, observation revealed a lack of experience related to the material in the reading texts; a short attention span; general unfamiliarity with such tasks as using a pencil and scissors; minimal auditory and visual discrimination (many seemed unaware of or indifferent to differences); lack of information about such topics as their names, how many were in their family, and so on; fear or apathy toward the school environment and the world around them; and inability to classify objects and follow a sequence of directions even when given in Spanish.

To meet the communication needs of your children, you may wish to use audiolingual techniques applicable to specific environmental topics in science such as weather, animals, and materials. This approach is inductive and uses objects. The task is to accustom the pupils to the basic language structure. "Is this a _____?" "Yes, it is. It is a _____." From this pattern, in which the children have individual objects to use, you eventually move to words with more abstract meanings (for example, *shape*). But more is needed than just language patterns in English. Children need a sense of pride in what they do know.

Plan lessons that will give children a feeling of accomplishment. The place to start may be with the child's name. One's name needs to be more than a label if one is to be more than an object; therefore, a child's name should be treated as a part of him. This is implied in the pattern, "Who are you?" "I am _____." In such a lesson the child answers the teacher's question "Who are you?" only after looking into a full-length mirror. Variations may be to have others respond to questions about the child before the mirror; they would be asked, for example, "Who is he?" The word *teacher* and the teacher's name may be introduced similarly. The use of "talking dolls" may permit some objectivity. A reading booklet based on oral language can be developed with the title "All About Me." It may contain such items as "What color is your hair?" "My hair is _____."

Language Experience Approach

The language experience approach also builds on existing skills to integrate development of listening, speaking, reading, and writing. The philosophy behind this approach is based on Allen's frequently quoted statement:

What I can think about, I can talk about.
What I can say, I can write.
What I can write, I can read.
I can read what I write and what other people can write for me to read. [Allen, 1961, p. 880]

One view of the language experience approach is that the teacher guides students to realize that written material is "talk written down." Because some of the important aspects of oral presentation (such as gestures, facial expression, voice inflection and control, and rate of speech) are seldom recorded as "talk written down," this view is inaccurate. It is, however, desirable to help children realize the connections among listening, oral expression, writing, and reading.

Although this method integrates activities in all four areas of language arts skills, it does not include a heavy reliance on published materials. Instead, activities are meant to grow out of children's group or individual experience. Recess games, art activities, celebrations of holidays, and field trips are examples of the kinds of activity that stimulate interest and language growth. To coordinate the visual, oral, auditory, and kinesthetic impact of the experience, children need freedom to discuss feelings in their own words. These impressions can be recorded and then written where the class can see what they have produced. Large chart paper makes a more permanent record than a chalkboard. Individual reports can also be written or typed so that each child has a tangible representation of his or

Recess games, art activities, holiday celebrations, and field trips are examples of the kinds of activity that stimulate interest and language growth. (PHOTO BY LINDA LUNGREN.)

her own reactions. Both of these writing activities lead to improvement of reading and enlargement of sight vocabulary. With the reports as texts, phonics and word attack skills can be learned without the difficulties involved in isolating units of work. The great strength of the language experience approach is its tying together of all language activities. Here is an example of a language experience lesson:

Mrs. Fredericks, a beginning-level reading teacher, is working with a group of five children who came to school very excited about a television program they had watched the previous evening. The program had followed a particular bird family from the nest-building stage through the leaving-the-nest stage. Mrs. Fredericks decided to take advantage of their interest and excitement and develop a reading story. She called the group together in one corner of the room near the chalkboard. She invited the children to think of one thing they would like to say or ask about the birds. They knew from previous experience that she would write the things they said. The following are the things she recorded.

The two birds worked very hard to build their nest.
The birds used grass and real little sticks.
The nest was high up in a tree.
Little birds hatched.
The big birds fed the little birds.
The big birds pushed the babies out of the nest.

As Mrs. Fredericks recorded each sentence, she repeated what the speaker had said. Then she asked all children to look at the written form of the sentence while one child repeated the sentence. She moved her hand from left to right to help the children follow. When composing had been completed, the group reread the story. Then individual children volunteered to read different sentences. They discussed a name for the story and chose "The Bird Family."

Children in the group already knew some of the words: the, was, of, to, birds, and big. Mrs. Fredericks asked them to identify some words they would like to add to their word banks. (These were individual word files that the children kept. Each file had two compartments: one for words already learned; one for words the child wanted to learn.) Children took turns telling Mrs. Fredericks three words they wanted to put in their files. She wrote the words on individual cards for them. After each child's words were written, he looked at the words and pronounced them. It was understood by each child that he would say the words for her again later in the day.

Each child in the group also made his own copy of the story to put in his personal storybook. When he had finished copying the story, he took his copy for Mrs. Fredericks' examination and read the story to her from it. If any significant errors had been made in copying, the child corrected his work before putting the story in his book folder.

Mrs. Fredericks made two chart copies of the story. She put one copy of the story on a chart board for children who wished to read or refer to it. She asked each child to draw an illustration for the sentence he had contributed to the story. These were placed around the chart as they were completed.

During her next session with this group, Mrs. Fredericks used sentence strips from the second copy of the story. These were distributed to different children who read their sentences to the class. Then they stood in line according to the sentence order in the story. In addition, each child read the words from the "to learn" compartment of his word file to Mrs. Fredericks. When a word had been identified without help during three different reading sessions, it could be filed in the "learned" compartment. Soon Mrs. Fredericks hoped to advance to the individual composition of stories. The words in the word files could be used independently in these stories.

Mrs. Fredericks uses a procedure, or pattern, common to many language-experience programs. She encourages oral expression and tries to help children to be more aware of new words they hear and may pick up. She moves into group composition, and then, as children are able, she moves them into individual composition.

As she works with children she learns their interests and selects trade books to bring from the library into the classroom. She reads books to children and encourages them to look at and if possible read these books. She also encourages and provides opportunities for children to read their own stories to others.

Mrs. Fredericks recognizes two potential problems in a language experience program. One relates to the teaching of word recognition skills. Mrs. Fredericks tries to use words that occur in children's stories as a basis for teaching as many phonic principles as possible, although she does recognize the danger inherent in such a program of limited development of phonics skills.

She realizes that some children have a wealth of background experiences from which stories can be generated, whereas others have limited story resources. She tries to provide many new and appropriate experiences for her children. She also realizes the necessity of pulling in new vocabulary through these experiences. She encourages children to use new words in communication through conversation and writing.

Mrs. Fredericks is well aware of the factors that need to be developed in an effective reading program. She is adept at learning children's interests and concerns and at getting them to express themselves verbally. She also views the language experience reading program as a stepping stone to another type of program and works to integrate other reading materials into the program. She does not recommend that the language experience approach be used as the major plan for helping children learn to read after the primary levels. She does feel that it can be used well in conjunction with some other approach in the intermediate levels. Perhaps at those levels the emphasis in its use should shift to creative and informative writing rather than reading instruction.

D. Lapp and J. Flood, *Teaching Reading to Every Child.* New York: Macmillan, 1978, pp. 469–470.

News Time

Have individual students become experts on a person of their choice, such as the President, an astronaut, a sports figure, a music group, the governor, the mayor. When appropriate, the class is given a briefing about the activities of the person.

Have individuals or small groups follow a single problem or activity and keep a bulletin board or notebook for periodic reporting of the collected data. Suitable topics might include air pollution, effects of DDT on animal life, political changes in other countries, Africa (or a single country), nutrition health news, the new school building, the new bridge, the strike.

When a student reports a news item, he might first locate the place on a map, put two words (or more) on the board that may be new to the class, ask a question at the end or give a question to the teacher to be put in a listening test at the end of the week. Such procedures help the child prepare his report with the listeners in mind.

All news reporting may be centered on a large topic until the students become expert; such topics may include an election, a war, our national policy, use of

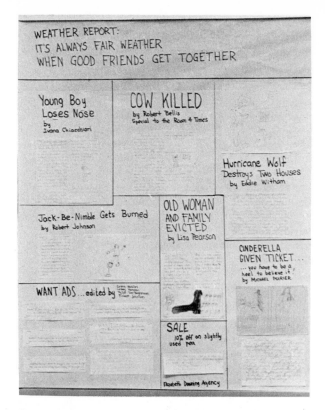

To generate interest in news reporting, the teachers and students may design a large "newspaper page" to be displayed in the school corridor. (PHOTO BY LINDA LUNGREN.)

leisure time, animals in the news, humor in the news, human interest stories, and characters in comic strips. Alternate groups should use news of the class and home. This can be dictated and written as *Our Day* or *Our Week* for future reference. This should be done at the end of the period.

Editorials also have a place in News Time. In turn, each one who wishes might talk on such topics as

"How I think TV could be improved," "Why I think ten-year-old students should be in bed by 10 o'clock," "Our school lunch program needs to be changed," "Safety hazards in our school," "Our school needs _____," "My parents understand me," "Ugly spots in our neighborhood that can be

Sharing an experience orally gains form when purposes are well defined. (COURTESY OF THE BURBANK PUBLIC SCHOOLS.)

changed," "There should be a special period for _____," "Let's write to the mayor (governor) about _____."

Interviewing and Surveying

Planned interviews also provide exceptional opportunities for oral communication practice. The interview subjects may range from family and friends to important figures in the community. The child will need help setting up the questions, which should be written ahead of time.

Children are often asked, "What did you do at school today?" The teacher might introduce interviewing with such a question (which would also prepare the children to promote good public relations at home). Preference surveys are a common commercial practice. A committee might make a preference survey of the class with respect to favorite toothpaste, soap, cold drink, music, or television program.

This activity may be extended to planning interviews with the principal (ask him what he does), the superintendent of schools (have him come to the classroom), the school secretary, the janitor, the oldest person in a child's family or neighborhood, or a neighbor with a hobby (tropical fish, cooking, collecting). Interviewing others in the class in order to write a short biography increases the interest in reading biographies and in the author's techniques.

Surveys provide an equally interesting extension of the interview. Each child might interview one adult on a problem and pool the results. Such questions as the following might be used: "What do you think is the greatest problem our city must solve?" "If you were my age, what business would you prepare for?" "What gives you the most enjoyment?" Some surveys can be made without interviews, such as "How many cars stop between 8 and 8:30 A.M. for the traffic patrol?" "What is the most popular make of car in the school parking lot?"

To give meaning to the occasion the interview and survey may be used during such special weeks as Education Week, Book Week, Safety Week, or such days as Poetry Day, Veterans' Day, Arbor Day. On Arbor Day a nursery might be visited to learn which trees grow well in the area, or a survey of different varieties of trees in one block might be made.

Demonstrations and Directions

Children who have traveled can demonstrate a skill they learned (instead of "What I did on my vacation"). This might involve the use of chopsticks to eat, Japanese paper folding, hobby or craft projects, magic tricks, slides, post cards, photographic talks, care of plants or pets, or experiences earning money (newsboys and babysitters have adventures and problems).

Teach the class a game to play on a rainy day or at a picnic, or imagine you were telling an Eskimo about baseball, football, tennis, horseshoes, and so on.

Play "How do I get there?" One child asks how to get to a place in the community, school, or state. Volunteers who answer may be given one to five points for their accuracy, simplicity, and brevity.

Talks on "How does it work?" stimulate a great deal of research either in books or through field trips. A vocational slant can be given by interviewing neighbors and parents on "What do they do at the _____ (bakery, movie theater, clinic, service station, supermarket, and so on).

Selling, Describing, Persuading

Your Scout troop is selling cookies (or peanuts, tickets, and so on). What should you say as you go to potential customers?

Take any object in the room, including clothing worn, and make a commercial for it such as one you might hear on the radio.

Describe "The car (bicycle) I want," "The dress I need," "The best meal I remember," "My grandparents," "My old school."

You need a quarter (a larger allowance, a new pair of shoes, and so on). What would you say to your parents?

Creative-Imaginative Situations

Many suggestions for creative writing are impressively effective in increasing the oral vocabularies of some children.

Show any three objects and ask how they might be related. Examples of such objects might be a pen, paper, and a book; a book, a lamp, and a toy; pictures of a house, a dog, and an airplane. Let the children think of the most unrelated objects possible and show how they might be associated through imagination. A salt shaker, an old tire, and a worn hat might be a challenge. A student teacher brought a sack to school with three strange items in it. She explained, "I found these in the old house I bought. What do you suppose the people were like who lived there?"

To make children aware of the ordinary, it might be good for some classes to start the day at least once each week with a creativity exercise. Such an exercise might proceed from the following questions:

1. What would happen if you woke up and the ground was covered with red snow?
2. What would happen if we could talk with insects?
3. What would happen if you had an experience like Rip

Van Winkle and today was a day twenty years from now?

Role-playing experiences are exceptional opportunities for language growth. The child must project his personality into that of another. This may require changes in dialect, age, sex, class, or color.

A friend borrowed a book from you. When he returns it you see that someone has spilled ink on it. What do you say? Why?

Newspaper accounts can be made into role situations by asking, "If you had been _____ what would you have done?"

Telephoning

In many communities the telephone company will arrange a conference interview for a class. It may be with a local author, an official, or another classroom— sometimes in a distant state. The entire class can listen while individuals participate. All aspects of telephone courtesy and use can become a part of the preparations of such a call.

Some schools select a student to help in the principal's office at noon hour. A specific task is to answer the telephone and take messages.

As a science activity, two fourth-grade boys in Poway, California, installed a telephone between their classrooms. As an independent reading activity students read aloud to each other on the telephone during a scheduled period.

Listening Centers and Environment

The use of listening posts and the tape recorder has provided substantial aid in teaching listening and speaking. Records, tape cassettes, and reels are valuable accessories; they provide stories, instructions for exercises, and commercials and reports to evaluate. Other materials children will enjoy include signs, decorations, displays, and of course books. Along with stimulating materials teachers must provide the freedom for boys and girls to use them and share their experiences.

These efforts should include attention to environmental factors that promote communication develop-

The use of listening posts and the tape recorder has provided substantial aid in teaching listening and reading. (PHOTO BY LINDA LUNGREN.)

ment. Proper ventilation and lighting, comfortable chairs, attractive materials, and low levels of noise "pollution" from outside sources are all important to a pleasant physical environment. Methods of improving the social and emotional environment are components of any beneficial language activity and will be discussed later in the chapter. The concrete physical environment can be altered to complement any activity if the class is fortunate enough to have lightweight chairs and desks. Modern furniture and a tolerant custodial staff enable a class to make frequent changes of seating arrangements. Horseshoe and semicircular seatings stimulate learning when visual and auditory perception are possible, as in any presentation to a group. Children enjoy creating new seating patterns and can be solicited for ideas and energy. These arrangements also accommodate variations in hearing acuity.

Tutoring

Speaking-listening activities are prominent in many tutoring situations. One child may check another with respect to beginning sounds in a series of words presented on separate cards or in sentence blocks. Sets of cards with similar pictures on them may be given a pair of people and a screen put between them. One describes the picture on his card in such a way that the other identifies the picture from the description. Each identified card is surrendered. Reading along with another to assist with words or simply reading a story aloud may be a reinforcement for a student who has recently mastered a skill or a step in reading development.

Attention to the following aspects of speaking, accompanied by training and practice, can assure teachers of the continuous growth of students in their command of spoken English:[2]

> *Vocabulary.* Words are the basic units of spoken language. Experiences of home, school, and community provide the opportunity for an ever-expanding vocabulary. But command of words, except in limited numbers, does not arise by itself. Children need to be led

continually to recognize new words, to relate them to context, and to practice their use in purposeful communication. Ideally each child should have an opportunity to speak briefly using new words every day. Conscious encouragement by teachers can do much to expand vocabulary.

Voice. Many children need sympathetic guidance in developing a good speaking voice. Pitch should be brought within a reasonable range and volume adjusted to the class group. Frequent practice in choral reading and speaking can allow the teacher to note and correct voice deficiencies of individual pupils without the embarrassment of a solo performance. Since boys' voices change with adolescence, they need readjustment of pitch and volume in junior high school and early senior high school years. Great tact is required in helping such students.

Stamina. Standing easily and gracefully before others is difficult for children and is a particular problem for young adolescents. Much of their reluctance to speak before a group arises from this factor. From the primary grades on, every possible opportunity should be seized to make appearance before others a natural classroom situation. Children should take it for granted that they will perform before their fellows as pantomimists, oral readers, actors in impromptu plays, makers of oral reports, and expressers of ideas. Where such experience is habitual, much uneasiness will disappear. By private conference the teacher can help an awkward child assume a better posture, use his hands more freely, and acquire relaxation before a group.

Planning. Children's speaking progresses from the utterance of a few scattered ideas to the presentation of a well-planned, organized discourse. This progression seldom happens by accident. Therefore, training in organization is an important factor in the growth of speaking. It begins with the child's arranging a few items he wishes to express in an order which he deems best for his purpose. The second stage is the formation of a brief outline on paper to allow the speaker to present his ideas in an order which he has planned in advance. The culmination is the highly organized outline of a prepared speech in which a central idea is supported by properly subordinated contributing ideas. The latter stage is for mature students only; in general, a simple card outline will suffice.

Sentence patterns. Oral sentences are much more loosely constructed than written sentences. Neverthe-

[2] From *English Language Arts in Wisconsin*, Robert Pooley, Project Director (Madison, Wis.: Madison Department of Public Instruction, 1968), p. 160.

One child may check another with respect to beginning sounds in a series of words presented on word charts. (PHOTO BY TOM WOLFE.)

less, there is a definite growth in spoken sentence patterns which marks the experienced speaker over the beginner. Young children often get into "mazes," which are confused patterns they cannot complete. An illustration: "This boy, he didn't understand this man, well, so he, I mean the man, took and. . . ." This kind of pattern confusion can be reduced by helping students make shorter statement units and avoid vague references such as "this boy," "this man," etc. Thinking sentences before speaking them also tends to improve spoken sentence structure, and learning to begin sentences with clear, unmistakable subjects is another aid. There is no need to make speech sound like written English. It can be free and informal, but expressed in those simple patterns of the English sentence which avoid confusion of structure and reference.

Audience response. Very often, schoolroom speaking practice becomes a dialogue between pupil and teacher. The wise teacher will direct the pupil's speech

to his fellow students and will expect critical but friendly listening. When possible the teacher should retire to the audience, training pupils to conduct the speaking exercises as well as to participate in them. The teacher will help each pupil become aware of his audience, learn to speak to it, and become sensitive to its reactions. As the speaker learns to direct his remarks to a live audience, he will increasingly recognize how he is "getting across." His own desire for success is the best motivation.

One of the important aspects of speech is the observation of certain courtesies between speaker and listener. Many of these can be taught indirectly by the teacher in his own speaking to students as individuals or as a class. Preserving the dignity of the individual, no matter how young, refraining from unnecessary interruption of a speaker, using courteous terms when addressing students (even when one is provoked!) and encouraging the expression of independent views are important courtesies of speaking. It is of little use to teach as lessons what one violates in practice.

One principal reported the following experiences with emphasis upon oral language: [3]

Vocabulary building goes on constantly as teachers chart key words for children, promote dictionary skills, utilize the resources of the special teachers, tell stories and have children re-tell them, use jokes, riddles, conversation, discussion, telephoning, reading and poetry.

Two effective media for promoting vocabulary growth and fluency of expression have been 1) the intercom for students to give the daily news and special announcements and 2) the Storytellers Club where children learn how to tell stories.

When using the intercom, children learned to listen to one another as they took turns giving the daily news reports. They also learned how to write to get attention and the importance of saying things in a variety of ways in order to keep attention. They grew in confidence and prestige when they identified themselves as the announcers.

The children selected the announcers and showed astuteness in their selections. They did not only select the good readers; they selected the children who needed recognition. When selections were made this way, the need to excel was important. Some children memorized their scripts by studying them with the family at night. Others asked parents to come to school to listen to them as they made the announcements.

The Storytellers Club met weekly with its membership drawn from grades three through six. It started quite simply. For the children its major goal was to tell stories to children in kindergarten and first grade. For the teachers, the goals were to

1. Encourage reluctant readers by having them read simple material with no stigma attached.
2. Get more inflection in children's voices.
3. Promote vocabulary.
4. Develop thinking.

In an environment where relationships are good, . . . children seem to say by their actions, "I don't understand everything my teacher says, but I like her and I am trying to talk like her. . . ."

[3] From Theda M. Wilson, "Helping the Disadvantaged Build Language," *National Elementary School Principal* (November 1965), 456–459.

[Children] like their teachers very much and want to please them. Teachers have strong influences on attitudes and behavior as well as on the acquisition of skills and the development of concepts.

Knowledge of the structural parts of the English language (parts of speech, kinds of sentences, etc.) is not essential in the elementary school, and there certainly is little evidence to indicate that such knowledge improves the grammar or usage of children. . . .

Successful [extensions of language patterns are] being made by teachers who

Set good examples in their own oral expressions, since children tend to imitate adults.

Realize that the cultural setting of the home has a definite influence on the language skills of children. [Extensions will be made] more slowly when children have regular contact with teachers, parents, and playmates who express themselves understandably in more than one idiom. . . .

Provide many opportunities for oral expression in order to develop aural consciousness of forms and construction. Children need much practice in using preferred forms in regular class activities as well as in controlled practice.

Emphasize what the child says rather than how he says it. We are dealing with thinking when we deal with language. . . . Expressions can be emphasized at another time when a child is not developing a thought.

Help vocabulary and fluency to develop by providing many firsthand as well as vicarious experiences. Words and expressions that children repeat do not always have correct meaning for them.

Encourage children to convey feelings and ideas through their own original efforts, especially through the media of letter writing, diaries, and short stories. This will bring increasing satisfaction as the gap is narrowed between their speaking and writing vocabularies and between their oral structure and skill in manipulating words and structures in writing.

In the exciting, interesting, accepting climate of the classrooms of sensitive and creative teachers, children . . . search for meanings and find opportunities to imagine, to exchange ideas, to think, to discover, and to create. As they listen, speak, read, and write, they develop their own individualities and form the basic foundations for their futures.

They have inherited the right to express themselves.

They are becoming free to do that with clarity and with confidence.

For Discussion

1. A city child may have a cultural background quite different from those presented in reading textbooks. The same would be true of a rural child with a Mexican or Indian heritage. What should be the content of their early reading material?

2. Current textbooks for language instruction contain a great deal about the linguistic history and structure of English. Is this content more appropriate to social science than a language text? How much help does the teacher find in current textbooks with respect to oral composition?

What Should Be Taught About Listening?

A teacher once complained, "The children all have that tuned-out look." A marriage counselor reports that the most frequent complaint by either spouse is, "You're not listening to a thing I say!" Nonlistening may be a natural defense against the bombardment of partially useless information and sound that assaults the ear in our mechanized society. Or nonlistening may be the result of limited auditory perception and/or understanding on the part of an audience. For some people, listening to music may be only a pleasant physical experience comparable at best to basking idly in the sunshine; for others the music may have a deep intellectual and spiritual significance, involving perception of inner harmonies and complex rhythmical patterns.

No one questions the importance of listening as a means of learning for all of us. Paul Rankin's pioneering study showed that high school students in Detroit spent 30 per cent of the time they devote to language each day in speaking, 16 per cent in reading, 9 per cent in writing, and 45 per cent in listening. Miriam Wilt more recently found that elementary school children spent about two and one half hours of the five-hour school day in listening. This was nearly twice as much time as their teachers estimate the children spent in listening. Some feel that in the usual classroom the chances are about 60 to 1 against any given pupil speaking, compared to the possibility of others speaking and a pupil listening.

Undoubtedly, there is as wide an individual difference in the area of listening as in other skills. We speak of some people as being auditory-minded and of others as visual-minded. Speech and music teachers have long been aware of the differences among children in hearing specific sounds.

It has been suggested that some of these differences are culturally determined. Some sociologists explained the fact that boys in the elementary school are apt to have more reading problems than girls by the observation that in many families the mother talks more frequently with the little girl than with the little boy. The result of such "preferential" talking, according to the theory, is that girls are more advanced in language than boys of the same age, especially in the primary grades. In Japan, just the opposite has been noticed. Little girls were long considered academically "inferior" until it was realized that boy children were getting much more attention at home and at school. In some classrooms over 80 per cent of the questions were being directed to the boys until the inequity was brought to the attention of the teachers.

Another cultural influence on listening is provided by radio and television. Kindergarten teachers are reporting that children come to school with a much wider knowledge than the curriculum assumes. In India, where there is a high degree of illiteracy, one might assume that the population would be relatively uninformed about world events. This, however, is not the case. The availability of free radios in many community teahouses has resulted in a surprisingly well-informed adult population.

Don Brown (1954) suggests that the terms *learning* and *listening* are both limited in meaning, and that the gerund *auding,* based on the neologic verb *to aud,* more accurately describes the skill that concerns teachers. "Auding is to the ears what reading is to the eyes." If reading is the gross process of looking at, recognizing, and interpreting written symbols, auding may be defined as the gross process of listening to, recognizing, and interpreting spoken symbols.

Russell and Russell (1959) use the following formula to contrast reading and auding further:

Seeing is to Hearing
as
Observing is to Listening
as
Reading is to Auding

To aud, then, means to listen with comprehension and appreciation.

Children *hear* the whistle of a train, the chirp of a bird, or the noise of traffic. They *listen* either passively or actively to a popular song or news broadcast. But when they listen attentively to a teacher to follow directions, or to get facts from a classmate's report, or to understand two sides of a debate, they may be said to be *auding*, for they are listening to verbal symbols with comprehension and interpretation. Throughout this discussion, the term *listening* will be used in referring both to the response that Brown describes as auding and to the other styles of listening.

Different levels of listening are really different degrees of involvement. Some activities call for much less involvement to be satisfying than do others that demand a higher degree of concentration.

1. Hearing sounds of words but not reacting to the ideas expressed: a mother knows that Daryl is speaking.
2. Intermittent listening—turning the speaker on and off: hearing one idea in a sermon but none of the rest of it.
3. Half listening—following the discussion only well enough to find an opportunity to express your own idea: listening to a conversation to find a place to tell how you handled a child.
4. Listening passively with little observable response: the child knows the teacher is telling him once again how to walk in the hall.
5. Narrow listening in which the main significance or emphasis is lost as the listener selects details that are familiar or agreeable to him: a good Democrat listening to a candidate from another party.
6. Listening and forming associations with related items from one's own experiences: a first-grade child hears the beginning sound of *Sally, says,* and *said,* and relates it to the letter *s.*
7. Listening to a report to get main ideas and supporting details or follow directions: listening to the rules and descriptions of a new spelling game.
8. Listening critically: a listener notices the emotional appeal of words in a radio advertisement.
9. Appreciative and creative listening with genuine mental and emotional response: a child listens to the teacher read *Miracle on Maple Hill* and shares the excitement of sugar making.

These levels overlap, but they do describe listening with respect to situations that teachers know. In the classroom it is possible to guide a child's listening so that his auding may be selective, purposeful, accurate, critical, and creative, just as we guide growth in the skills of reading. A format for such instruction still seems applicable today:[4]

A. Social Listening
   1. Listening courteously and attentively to conversation in social situations with a purpose. K–6
   2. Understanding the roles of the speaker and listener in the communication process. K–6
B. Secondary Listening
   1. Listening to music that accompanies rhythms or folk dances. K–6
   2. Enjoying music while participating in certain types of school activities such as painting, working with clay, sketching, and handwriting practice. K–6
C. Aesthetic Listening
   1. Listening to music, poetry, choral reading, or drama heard on radio or on recordings. K–6
   2. Enjoying stories, poems, riddles, jingles, and plays as read or told by the teacher or pupils. K–6
D. Critical Listening
   1. Noting correct speech habits, word usage, and sentence elements of others. K–6
   2. Listening to determine the reason "why." 1–6

[4] From *Reading and Language in the Elementary School* (Gary, Ind.: Board of Education, Gary Public Schools, 1962).

3. Listening to understand meanings from context clues. 1–6
4. Listening to distinguish between fact and fancy, relevance and irrelevance. 1–6
5. Listening to draw inferences. 1–6
6. Listening to make judgments. 1–6
7. Listening to find new or additional information on a topic. 2–6
8. Listening to find the answers to specific questions which require selectivity and concentration. 4–6
9. Listening to interpret idioms and unusual language. 5–6
10. Listening objectively and appraisingly to determine authenticity or the presence of bias and inaccuracies. 5–6

E. Concentrative Listening (a study-type listening)
1. Listening to follow directions. K–6
2. Perceiving relationships such as class, place, quantity, time, sequence, and cause and effect. 4–6
3. Listening for a definite purpose to elicit specific items of information. 4–6
4. Attaining understanding through intent listening. 4–6
5. Listening for sequence of ideas. 4–6
6. Perceiving a speaker's or a group's main objective and organization of ideas. 4–6
7. Taking notes of important facts. 4–6

F. Creative Listening
1. Associating meanings with all kinds of listening experiences. K–6
2. Constructing visual images while listening. K–6
3. Adapting imagery from imaginative thinking to create new results in writing, painting, and dramatizing. 1–6
4. Listening to arrive at solutions for problems as well as checking and verifying the results of the problems solved. 4–6

Listening in some respects is more difficult than reading. In the process of reading, a strange word may be the signal to stop, look at other words in the sentence or pictures on the page, or refer to the glossary. In listening this is not possible. One must make a hasty guess as the speaker continues, rethink what the speaker has said while keeping up with the current ideas being spoken. Most college students know the experience expressed by a freshman when he commented, "I was with him until he mentioned the macrocephalic measurement, then he lost me." Children too have their "frustration level" in listening. The "tuned-out look" familiar to teachers can be a signal about either the interest or the difficulty of what is being said.

The fact that we listen from six to ten times faster than a person can talk means that dedicated concentration must be practiced in some listening situations to avoid distractions. The printed page demands attention and can be read at a rate equal to that of our mental reactions. In listening, this happens only if the listener disciplines himself to attend to what the speaker is saying. Interruptions to an oral explanation by a classroom visitor, outside noises, or any disruptive incident mean the explanation must be repeated. Once listening is accepted as important, the learner must accept the responsibility of putting forth an active listening effort to learn. This activity should approach the effort to gain information from reading.

One element that makes listening more difficult than reading is that a person usually listens for the main idea rather than specific parts. In reading, one has a record of the specifics and usually remembers where they may be found. In listening, the speaker has designed the material to highlight a major idea that he wants the audience to remember. To do this he uses facts, stories, and emotional appeals. These are recalled only if the listener relates them to the total effect of the talk. Political speeches and college lectures are good examples; a person may tell a friend that he heard a good speech or lecture, but when asked what was said may be able to recall only that it was "about brotherhood."

Related to this is the problem of listening to a discussion or conversation. Such speech is frequently disorganized as the speakers explore various ideas or aspects of a topic. Strange to say, people seem to remember as much or more from such situations as from a well-organized lecture. Apparently the careful organization and fixed pattern lull some listeners into a comfortable enjoyment that is less involving than the disorganized rambling that permits or requires involvement with random changes of topic or subject matter.

Many bad habits develop in the listening area. Both

children and adults have a way of avoiding difficult or unpleasant listening. Every parent knows the "Surely, he is not talking about me!" attitude of a child who is being corrected. Emotions interfere with listening to ideas. "Who is he to be saying that?" "They will never convince me that those ugly things are art" and "How would she know, she's never been a mother!" are emotional statements that reveal limited reception.

It is interesting to note the wide variation of response to a distraction in a classroom. A lawn mower operating outside the window or music being played in the next room will command the complete attention of some and be ignored by others. Some individuals have a habit of seeking distraction even though they may be interested in the speaker or topic.

The expression of ego is as obvious in listening as it is in the constant use of *I* in speech. This is especially obvious in little children. A teacher or speaker may be telling about a trip to Europe or showing a cowboy lariat. A hand will pop up and a child will volunteer, "Tomorrow is my birthday" or "We have some baby chickens at our house." For some this is an innocent way to "say something, too." Usually it is an indication of lack of interest in others. Adults will be listening or participating in a conversation about a topic, then suddenly will say, "I think I'll have my hair done tomorrow" or "When do we eat?" Or there may be a not too subtle attempt to impress, as in "When I was in Mexico" or "The President said to my cousin."

Teachers are frequently poor listeners. For some, teaching limits their interests to such an extent that they dismiss many subjects prematurely as "uninteresting." At one university club the matron said she felt sorry for many of the people who lived there: "They are such specialists they cannot listen to each other." Some teachers develop the habit of not listening for ideas but are always judging the manner of expression or organization of speech. They are actually evaluating or grading the manners of those they hear.

Good listening habits involve not only thinking with the speaker but also anticipating the direction of his thoughts, objectively evaluating the verbal evidence offered in terms of the speaker's purpose (rather than arguing with it item by item as it is presented), and reviewing mentally some of the facts presented. Taking notes of ideas or phrases helps many people. There are others who find notetaking a distraction. Some report that they find the ideas in their notes rather than in their heads. Brief summaries are probably better than detailed stenographic reports. This kind of critical listening must be done often and well. It has been shown by Giannangelo and Frazer (1975) that the necessary skills can be taught. Teachers bear the responsibility to provide opportunities for this kind of learning.

There is no more attentive listener than the child who asks a question that truly concerns him. These are probably the most "teachable moments" in any classroom. Choosing the question to ask a visitor or the principal or when planning material before a unit sets the stage for careful listening. Before oral reading, attention is assured if children are listening in order to answer a question. A good story writer builds this interest or suspense into his plots. The reason the reader gets involved in a story is usually because he wants to know how a problem will be solved.

In the classroom the language arts teacher wants to be sure that the listening experience will be worth the children's time and effort. The sharing period can be improved by having each child think first of his audience and how he wants them to respond. At one time this period was considered valuable simply as a spontaneous period of free expression. At the beginning that may be its purpose. But such items as "I have a new petticoat" or "Our cat had kittens" belong in the free conversational exchange of children rather than the crowded school curriculum. The following suggestions provide the same practice in language but add a concern for the listeners:

1. Share the signs of the change of a season noted while going to and from school.
2. Share things that happened at home or play that were pleasant or humorous.
3. Share the most important thing that happened on a trip.
4. Share one toy by telling about it or demonstrating its use.

5. Share something good or kind that a person has done.
6. Share the local or national news. Some classrooms have a television committee, a radio committee, and a picture committee. These children report events they have learned from these sources. In the intermediate grades some teachers provide the clippings from which children select their reports. Others give a little quiz at the end of the week on the news reported. Sometimes better preparation will result if the listeners may ask one question about a report. Two standards should apply—the news must be told rather than being read orally, and it must not concern crime.
7. Share something an individual has made.
8. Share a riddle or joke (after first checking with the teacher).
9. Share a fact or interesting bit of knowledge about a bird, rock, stamp, coin, insect, star, airplane, sea shell, object from a foreign land, book, or "believe-it-or-not" item.
10. Share a new word and its meaning or history. This might be a word in a foreign language if there are children from homes where a foreign language is spoken.

Material shared is better if children have to plan ahead a bit. Children may sign on the chalkboard today for sharing tomorrow, or each row or cluster may have a day that is their sharing day. The teacher is responsible for the quality of material shared in literature. If children are to listen to material read, it should be material that offers true enrichment. Poetry appropriate to the child's interests that is read well will reveal the beauty of words. Stories that add stature to the child's value concepts should be told and read.

The responsibility of the listener should be discussed. There is the point of courtesy to a speaker that all children understand: "You listen to me and I will listen to you." Listening for meaning is just as important as reading for meaning. A listener may *disagree* but should not *misinterpret*. Causes of misinterpretation might be discussed with benefit to both speaker and listener.

The attitude of the teacher toward listening will influence children. Teaching is as much listening as telling. We listen to discover interest and needs. Those trained in nondirective guidance know how important it is for the therapist to listen. The psychologist listens a great deal as the patient talks. A good salesman listens to discover what customers want. The wise teacher listens to encourage the expression of children. At times a teacher listens because a child, or parent, needs an audience for a personal concern. The following suggestions will help in such situations: [5]

1. Take time to listen. When someone is troubled or needs to talk, give him the time if at all possible. It will help clarify communication between you.
2. Be attentive. Let tirades flow uninterrupted. Try to indicate that you want to understand.
3. Employ three kinds of verbal reactions only—"H-m-mm," "Oh," or "I see." Remain silent, nodding to show understanding. If the talker is unreasonable, restate what he said, putting it in the form of a question.
4. Never probe for additional facts. There is a difference between willingness to listen and curiosity. Your purpose in therapeutic listening is seldom to obtain information.
5. Avoid evaluating what has been said. Avoid moral judgments and the temptation to advise. The talker is clarifying his problem through talking and then must define alternative solutions.
6. Never lose faith in the ability of the speaker to solve his own problems. The speaker is really talking things over with himself as he talks with you.

Start instruction in listening by establishing standards. The discussion might be centered about situations where listening is important: You are a waiter taking an order; you are to go to the principal's office with a message and return with his; you are to interview a famous person; you are to report on a news broadcast. These imaginative exercises could lead to an inventory of listening habits. A checklist like the following may be used:

1. Do I get ready to listen?
2. Do I give the speaker my attention?

[5] Adapted from R. G. Nichols and Leonard A. Stevens, *Are You Listening?* (New York: McGraw-Hill, 1957).

Classroom activities may be designed to include informal listening centers. Here three students are following instructions and performing tasks given them on the teacher-made tapes. (PHOTO BY LINDA LUNGREN.)

3. Do I think with the speaker?
4. Can I select the main idea?
5. Can I recall things in order?
6. Can I follow directions?
7. Can I retell what I hear?

Children learn from discussions of this nature that a good listener is polite, gets the facts, listens thoughtfully, listens for a reason, and makes intelligent use of what he hears.

The following lesson is from a fourth-grade textbook. Determine what skills are taught by such a lesson. These classroom activities emphasize the skills of listening:[6]

1. Develop a routine of giving directions only once in a lesson. Select one subject and introduce the challenge of a "One-Time Club" or "First-Time Club" with re-

[6] From Andrew Schiller and others, *Language and How to Use It,* Book 4 (Glenview, Ill.: Scott, Foresman, 1969), p. 90.

spect to assignments or directions. If a child misses the first time, he is not a club member but may get the information from a member. For some groups the teacher might say, "I will give the assignment only once, then I will ask some of those in the 'First-Time Club' to repeat what I have said."

2. Use oral tests frequently that require more than one-word answers. Dramatize the test if the group responds to that type of motivation by imitating the pattern of a television quiz program.

3. Ask children to review the work of the previous day in a subject for a child who was absent.

4. Practice oral summarization of the information presented in a film.

5. Read a descriptive paragraph, have children paint or draw the picture presented, then read the story again as a check.

6. Play a listening game by giving increasingly difficult instructions to one child and then another. To the first child you might say, "Jim, take the apple from the desk and place it on the chair." To the next child, "Linda, take the apple from the chair, show it to Mary and re-

turn it to the desk." The game increases in difficulty until someone fails to follow directions correctly.

7. Ask the pupils, in pairs, to interview each other on hobbies or special interests. After the interviews talk about the possibilities of learning by this method. Discuss the advantages and disadvantages of interviewing as compared to reading.

8. A game called "Efficient Secretary" is designed to challenge children to write entire sentences from dicta-

tion. The sentences are read only once. At first the sentences are short, but they are increased in length as the child's ability increases. This exercise has a natural correlation with spelling.

9. Second-chance listening is valuable in the social studies. The teacher reads an informative article, which is followed by questions. After this the article is read again and children check their answers or answer the questions a second time.

EMPHASIS

This lesson gives children further practice in visualizing while they listen. It is a step up over previous exercises in that both the objects described and the identifying terms will be new to children.

EXPLANATION

List these words on the chalkboard: *jump scooter, whirligig, muff, foot stove, tailor's goose, quern, piggy churn, hex signs.* Tell children that the words are names of the objects pictured on page 90. Invite pupils to read the two paragraphs on the page to learn a little more about these objects.

Since the appearance of many objects described in this lesson will be strange to pupils and the names will be equally strange, you may want to (1) let children listen with their books open, and/or (2) let pupils jot down brief clues while listening (such as "piggy churn —looks like a pig").

Give boys and girls explicit instructions that they are to make only two notes concerning each object: (1) the name of the object, and (2) one characteristic that will help them to remember how it looks or how it works. Children should not be allowed to take unlimited notes, or the purpose of note-taking is defeated.

For your convenience, the articles are identified below.

1. jump scooter   5. tailor's goose
2. hex signs   6. muff
3. whirligig   7. quern
4. foot stove   8. piggy churn

After children have made their responses and checked them with each other's opinions, replay the record as a final check. Exercises 1 and 2 on pages 97-98 of this *Guidebook* are extensions of this lesson.

Let's Listen

All the objects on this page played some part in the life of early America. Most of them have passed from daily use. You may guess the purpose of some from looking at the pictures, but how many can you name?

Listen now to a description of how these things were used and what they were called.

10. The game "Lost Child" is good for both oral description and listening. One player is the policeman. Another player describes someone in the room who is his "lost child." If a class member can guess who it is before the policeman does, the two exchange places.

Russell and Russell have collected a group of listening activities called *Listening Aids Through the Grades* which will be helpful in extending the listening skills of the children in your classroom.[7]

For Discussion

1. A visual-minded individual is one who remembers best things that he sees. An auditory-minded person would be one who remembers more of what he hears. Which of your memories are most vivid—things you hear or see?

2. Do you know of any way of measuring individual differences in this respect? How might it be done by a classroom teacher?

What Is the Relationship Between Listening and Reading?

Both reading and listening require the learner to have a readiness for accomplishment. This includes his mental maturity, vocabulary, ability to follow sequence of ideas, and his interest in language.

In general, the purposes of reading and auding are both functional and appreciative. In functional reading and auding, children are concerned with finding facts, getting a general idea, following directions, or putting the material to work in some way. In appreciative reading and auding, children are ready to enjoy a selection for its own sake—a story for its humor, or a poem for its expression. Or they may combine function and appreciation in reading or listening with a view to creating a dramatization.

In both reading and auding, the word is not usually the unit of comprehension, but it affects comprehension of the phrase, the sentence, and the paragraph. Children must hear certain key words clearly (e.g., *world* vs. *whirled*) if they are to understand an oral passage, and they must see them clearly (*bond* vs. *board*) if they are to read them exactly. But along with exact perception in both activities must go understanding of word meaning. The grasp and interpretation of both oral and written paragraphs depend on understanding the meaning of individual words in their context and in varied relationships.

In both reading and auding, the unit of comprehension is either the phrase, the sentence, or the paragraph—rather than the single word. Comprehension is aided if the speaker or writer avoids common errors of pronunciation, spelling, and usage. Both reading and auding make use of "signals" in the form of written or oral punctuation.

In addition to an exact understanding of a sentence or passage, both reading and auding may involve critical or creative interpretation of the material. In both situations the receiver may critically question the reliability of the source, the relevance of the argument, or the emotive power of the language employed. In both cases the receiver may utilize his previous experiences to combine the materials into some fresh, original, and personal interpretation.

Reading and auding may take place in either individual or social situations. Critical, analytical activities often flourish best in the individual situation; creative and appreciative reactions, under the stimulus of the group situation. Analysis of the propaganda devices in a political speech is easier when the printed version of the speech is read in a quiet room than when a speaker delivers it in a crowded hall. Conversely, appreciation of the choral reading of a poem may be heightened by an enthusiastic group response.

In order to improve reading, each listening skill should be followed by its reading counterpart. As students advance, the material used for these activities should necessarily become more difficult in order to meet their growing needs. The listening-reading skills need to be approached through direct and indirect instruction, with more emphasis on the direct than has been the practice in recent years. As early as 1957,

[7] From D. H. Russell and E. F. Russell, *Listening Aids Through the Grades* (New York: Bureau of Publications, Teachers College, Columbia University, 1959).

readers by McKee provided listening exercises in the teacher's manual: [8]

> Sue's big brother, Jerry, has made a model airplane. He is going to fly it in the contest Saturday. The contest is going to be at White Park. Prizes will be given there for the best made airplane, the airplane that flies the longest, and the airplane that makes the best take-off and landing. One of the prizes is a motor for a model airplane. Jerry hopes he can win that.
>
> Here are the questions: What I read said, "Sue's brother, Jerry, has made a model airplane. He is going to fly it in the contest Saturday." Who is meant by the word *he* in those lines, John? . . . Yes, the word *he* means Jerry. What is meant by the word *it* in those lines, Carl? . . . Yes, the model airplane.
>
> Then what I read said, "The contest is going to be at White Park. Prizes will be given there for the best made airplane, the airplane that flies the longest, and the airplane that makes the best take-off and landing." What did I mean by the word *there* in those lines, Jim? . . . Yes, I meant White Park.
>
> The last two sentences said, "One of the prizes is a motor for a model airplane. Jerry hopes he can win that." What does the word *that* mean in those lines, Ann? . . . Yes, it means the motor for a model airplane.

Deciding Which of Several Meanings a Word Has in Statements

> When Harry said, "It's a long way to our house from here," the word *way* meant distance. When Paul asked, "Which way do we go from here?" the word *way* meant direction. When I say, "I like the way in which you are fixing your hair," the word *way* means manner.
>
> Listen while I read three sentences to you. Decide what the word *way* means in each sentence.
>
> Here is the first sentence. "John swims in the same way that Bob swims." What did I mean by the word *way* in that sentence, Ben? . . . Yes, I meant manner.
>
> Here is the second sentence. "Which way is the zoo from here?" What did the word *way* mean in that sentence, Ruth? . . . That's right. It meant direction.
>
> Here is the third sentence. "It's not a very long way from our house to Betty's house." What did the word *way* mean in that sentence, Carl? . . . Yes, it meant distance.

[8] From Paul McKee, *Reading for Meaning: Come Along*, Teacher's Manual (Boston: Houghton Mifflin, 1957).

You can see that one word can have many different meanings. To decide what a word means each time it is used, you have to think of the meaning of the words that are used with it.

The chart on p. 106 further illustrates the relationship between listening and reading.

For Discussion

1. Why is it often ineffective to correct the behavior of children by giving the class a lecture?

2. What listening experience had the greatest learning effect on you?

How May Correct Public Usage Habits Be Established?

Correct public usage is concerned with proper form. The agreement of verb and subject in number and tense, the form of the pronoun in various positions in the sentence, and the word order in sentences are some of the situations that present learning problems of proper form. The child who says, "I done my work" is using the wrong verb form. Another who says, "Him and me are friends" is using the wrong form of the pronoun. Children use these forms because they hear them at home, on television, and in the playground.

First of all, the teacher will encourage the child to enjoy his private language. He will be accepted, no matter what he says or how he says it. His language is a verbal expression of his thoughts and feelings. If we reject it, we reject him. Furthermore, we reject by implication the family who has taught him to speak and with whom he has strong emotional ties that he needs as he develops as a human being.

A child's speech patterns are discovered and extended by encouraging him to talk. During the early school years the content of his "talk" will often be centered about himself, his home, and his family. At first the teacher will accept the child's own word groupings, if they are in communication units, whether or not he considers them to be complete. But he may also listen for and take note of patterns of substandard usage that can be brought to the children's attention later.

Listening goal	Reading activity
1. To discriminate and locate phonetic and structural elements of the spoken word.	Use selections with rhyming words.
2. To discover and to identify sounds, words, or ideas new to the listener.	Close eyes and identify sounds—man-made as well as natural. The tape recorder can be used.
3. To listen for details in order to interpret the main idea and to respond accurately.	After listening show the main idea, with details radiating from it.
4. To listen to a selection for the purpose of answering a previously stated question.	
5. To listen for the main idea when stated in the topic or key sentence.	Have the key sentence occur in various positions.
6. To discriminate between spoken fact and opinion.	Listen to selections. Students write *Fact* or *Opinion*. Discussion and reading to verify should follow.
7. To distinguish between relevant and irrelevant details.	List relevant details in one column and irrelevant ones in another.
8. To listen to select the type of writing: narrative, descriptive, or expositive.	Use various sentences and paragraphs. Students select type.
9. To listen to music to determine mood.	After listening, select and discuss words that could be used to reflect the same mood.
10. To listen to poetry or prose to determine mood.	After listening, select and discuss words and phrases that were used to set mood.
11. To listen in order to visualize a scene.	After listening, draw the scene. Follow this by reading to verify the visual concept. Discuss.
12. To determine oral story sequence.	a. Ask for the sequence of events for a paragraph heard. b. Listen to a story and act out the story sequentially (possibly with puppets).
13. To list the stated facts used to obtain an inference.	Stated facts }Inference
14. To listen in order to understand space and time relationships.	
15. To associate descriptive ideas heard with more concrete objects and life situations.	Listen to descriptions of familiar people and determine the identities.
16. To draw conclusions or form opinions based on facts heard.	Use discussions on a topic followed by conclusions drawn. Group decides the validity of conclusions.
17. To recognize bias.	Use the tape recorder and reproductions of speeches and commercials. What indicates the bias? Are *all* facts given?

Important as it is to accept the child along with any immature patterns of usage, we cannot leave him here. As he develops to take his place in his ever-widening world, a corresponding development in his language patterns will be necessary. We can provide for this continuous sequential growth through carefully organized instruction.

At this point individual deviations will be handled with respect for the child. He is aided in expressing himself by modeling his speech after a classroom dialect. The teacher may say something like "I understand what you mean, but in our classroom we say it this way," and then give him the substitute form. The time and manner in which these substitute forms are given depend on the feeling of belonging that the child has in his classroom, a state to which the teacher will always be sensitive. In order to acquire this delicate balance it is important to acquaint children with the need for both public and private language.

The teacher's attitude, too, plays a major role in achieving a standard classroom dialect. If the teacher is consistent in what is expected from the class and communicates this expectation firmly yet kindly, the pupils will respond with their best. The teacher will want to carry over this consistent attitude into the other subjects as she continues incidental correcting throughout the day.

Forms that might help to establish the public language of the classroom include the following:

1. A transition from all "baby-talk" and "cute" expressions.
2. The acceptable uses in speech and writing of *I, me, him, her, she, they,* and *them.* (Accepted: "It's me.")
3. The appropriate uses of *is, are, was, were* with respect to number and tense.
4. Standard past tenses of common irregular verbs, such as *saw, gave, took, brought, stuck.*
5. Elimination of the double negative: "We don't have no apples."
6. Elimination of analogical forms: *ain't, hisn, hern, ourn, hisself, theirselves,* and so on.
7. Appropriate use of possessive pronouns: *my, mine, his, hers, theirs, ours.*
8. Mastery of the distinction between *its* (possessive pronoun) and *it's* (it is, the contraction). (This applies only to written English.)
9. Elimination of *this here* and *that there.*
10. Approved use of personal pronouns in compound constructions: as subject (*Mary and I*), as object (*Mary and me*), as object of preposition (*to Mary and me*).
11. Attention to number agreement with the phrases *there is, there are, there was, there were.*
12. Elimination of *he don't, she don't, it don't.*
13. Elimination of *learn* for *teach, leave* for *let.*
14. Avoidance of pleonastic subjects: *my brother he; my mother she; that fellow he.*
15. Sensing the distinction between *good* as adjective

and *well* as adverb (for example, "He spoke well").

The English language is constantly changing. The meaning difference between *shall* and *will* that is still taught in language books has for all practical purposes disappeared in usage. The pronoun *whom* has reached the stage where it is frequently used incorrectly, and seldom used in conversation.

There are very few research studies available on which grades are best for usage practice. Those that do exist are usually surveys of city courses of study and textbooks. This means that teacher judgment, as much as any other factor, has influenced when usage practice is desirable. Textbook writers must consider the practical problem of the total amount of material to be put in a book. As a result, the teacher may find an item such as *take–took* listed in an index with three page references. Further examination will often reveal that these refer to one sentence in a test of ten items in which the child has to make a choice between two forms. Frequently children guess the correct form in such an exercise, even though they misuse the verb in their own speech and writing. *If a child is making an error, the teacher must plan more corrective instruction than that found in many textbooks.*

A peculiar problem of usage errors is the fact that a child who has acceptable public speech in the primary grades may start making errors in later grades. Perhaps this is because he hears incorrect usage on television and in the playground or reads comic books. Exercises in the textbook may help to counteract these factors by reinforcing existing correct habits.

One other factor concerning textbook drill material should be noted. The sentence may require the child to select between *was* and *were.* If the problem is only one of selecting between the singular and plural, it will not serve the child who says, "You was." The drill or test should concern the error the learner makes.

To change a usage habit three things are necessary: the error should be identified, oral practice should be stressed until the established form sounds correct to the learner, and written practice should be given to maintain the desired habit and to test the learner. Oral exercises provide opportunities in listening to the correct form. The drill is for the listener as well as the speaker. "Game" situations provide such practice.

A child cannot learn to *improve* his language unless he first feels free to *use* language. Errors in the use of language, therefore, should be called to his attention only after he feels accepted by the group and sufficiently self-confident so that correction will not silence him. The spirit in which corrections are made is perhaps the most important single factor in the child's language development.

These steps have proved effective in practice:

1. Discuss the need for both public and private language.
2. Listen to the children talk and note the type of patterns common to the group and to individuals.
3. Select the most common patterns of error for correction.
4. Choose a few errors at a time for concentrated effort.
5. Call attention to the correct use of words as well as to errors in usage.
6. Correct the child at the time the error is made, but after he has finished what he has to say.
7. Follow a period of oral expression with a short drill period in which the child hears the correct form repeated several times.
8. Play games in which the correct form is used over and over again.

Note how Shannon is complimented on correct word usage in first grade.

The children were saying "I got" repeatedly. Shannon said, "I have."

TEACHER: I am so glad to hear Shannon say "I have."

This approval made the others eager to use "I have."

The children correct a common error in second grade:

TEACHER: This morning I heard someone say, "The bird he was building a nest." Let's all think of something you have seen a bird do and see if we can leave out the *he*.

CHILD 1: The bird was feeding his babies.
CHILD 2: The bird was hopping on the ground.
TEACHER: This morning I heard someone say, "This here book is mine." It would be acceptable public language to say, "This book is mine." Let's all take something out of our desks that belongs to us and tell about it.
CHILD 1: This pencil is mine.
CHILD 2: This chalk is yours.

The children begin to drop *ain't* when assisted to make proper substitutions.

TEACHER: Lately I've been hearing some of you say, "I ain't got a pencil. I ain't going with you." Does anyone know a better way of saying it?
CHILD 1: I haven't a pencil.
CHILD 2: I'm not going with you.
TEACHER: That's better.

Pooley suggests that using toy telephones for conversation between two children is a helpful device to alert teachers to inappropriate usage such as "Me and my brother," or "I seen." [9] Here, too, we detect baby talk that has been permitted in the home. Many five- and six-year-olds begin school unable to sound several of the consonants. A few examples are *fadder* for *father*, *Zimmy* for *Jimmy*, *yittle* for *little*, *won* for *run*.

By listening and speaking to each other in the form of these "pretended" phone calls, children grow in the knowledge of a standard classroom dialect. The tape recorder is also a valuable instructional aid at this point as the child is able to hear his own voice and listen to it critically.

The best drills to teach English as a foreign language are known as pattern practice drills. The drills are something like the following: Suppose the teacher wants to make automatic the use of *there are* and *there is*. The problem, of course, is that the student wants to say, "There is two spoons on the table." We can set up a series of key frames thus:

There's one spoon on the table.

There're two spoons on the table.

[9] Throughout this chapter, examples have been drawn from *English Language Arts in Wisconsin*, op. cit.

There's a spoon on the table.

There're some spoons on the table.

There're several spoons on the table.

The teacher will say each one of these sentences and then ask the class to repeat each orally. Next she can ask for individual repetition. Then she can extend the exercise by giving a series of cues—words that will substitute in the patterns: *toast, dishes, bread, glasses, forks, two vases, several napkins, some food,* and so on. This can be varied further as follows:

CUE: How many spoons are there on the table?
RESPONSE: There're two spoons on the table.
CUE: Is there a spoon on the table?
RESPONSE: Yes, there's a spoon on the table.
CUE: There's . . . .
RESPONSE: There's a spoon on the table. There's a dish on the table.
CUE: There're . . . .
RESPONSE: There're forks on the table.

Or take another example: Our problem here is that the student says ''them things.'' We can set up a series of frames as follows:

I don't like that thing.
I don't like those things.
That book's on the table.
Those books are on the table.

The students will repeat these and similar frames after the teacher, and then the teacher can proceed thus:

CUE: That man is my friend. (*Men.*)
RESPONSE: Those men are my friends.
CUE: That thing is on the table. (*Things.*)
RESPONSE: Those things are on the table.

Later a student may provide cues.

''Chain Practice'' can be played to substitute *he doesn't* for *he don't.* In this game each child asks a question, and the child in the next desk responds and then forms the question for the next, who then responds and forms a question for the next child, and so on. The teacher may ask the first question:

TEACHER (*to Eric*): What doesn't Eric like to do?
ERIC (*to teacher*): Eric doesn't like to mow the lawn.
ERIC (*to Denise*): What doesn't Denise like to do?
DENISE (*to Eric*): Denise doesn't like to wash the dishes.
DENISE (*to Mahar*): What doesn't Mahar like to do?

Chain practice is more fun if it moves along quickly.

An imaginative pupil or the teacher may make a puppet for this activity by coloring a face on a lunch size bag with the mouth at the bottom of the sack so that the puppet can appear to be talking. Children may take turns talking for the puppet. The teacher will ask the puppet (the pupil) questions that he will answer using standard classroom dialect. Here the pupils will practice negative answers.

TEACHER (*to puppet*): Ronnie, do you have any candy?
RONNIE (*to teacher*): No, I don't have any candy.
TEACHER (*to Ronnie*): Ronnie, do you have any marbles in your pocket?
RONNIE (*to teacher*): No, I haven't any marbles in my pocket.

The responses to the teacher's questions are intended to replace ''I haven't got no . . .'' or ''I ain't got no . . .'' with the more desirable ''No, I haven't any . . .'' Ronnie might develop as a special character who makes the errors the class is committing.

The next language game is designed to substitute deviant words with acceptable ones (such as *isn't* for *ain't*). The teacher will list some words on the chalkboard. For example,

troposphere	ionosphere
scientific	satellite
barometer	prediction
humidity	forecast
atmosphere	thermometer

These are scientific words that might be selected for a sixth-grade class that had become familiar with them in science. One student is chosen to begin. He thinks of one of the words on the list. Then he begins by saying, ''What word am I thinking of?''

CLASSMATE: Is it *humidity*?
STUDENT: No, it isn't *humidity*.

ANOTHER CLASSMATE: Is it *prediction?*
STUDENT: No, it isn't *prediction.*

This game may be scaled down to almost any level by the use of more simple words.

A sixth-grade class prepared the following material:

Script for an Exercise Using Did *and* Done *Correctly*

Good morning. This is station WDSC bringing you another in the series called "Aids to English Usage." Have you ever heard a person say, "I done wrong"? Now, does this sound like a good use of English to you? How about saying it this way? "I have done wrong." The use of *did* and *done* causes a lot of children trouble, so this morning we are going to try and help you use these two words correctly. Listen to the following sentences. Can you explain why we use *done* instead of *did*? Does the word *done* seem to stand alone?

1. I have done the job well.
2. We have done the work quickly.
3. They have done the lesson well.

In these sentences did you notice that *done* has a helper word, *have?* When used, as it was in these sentences, *done* requires a helper word. The word *did* may stand alone. Listen and you will see that *did* stands alone.

1. I did the work for the teacher.
2. We did our homework in the kitchen.
3. Our class did well in arithmetic this week.

Did you notice that the word *did* was able to stand alone? It did not need a helper word. Now, listen to this story and try to fill in the missing word. The speaker will pause when he comes to a place where you could use either *did* or *done.* Write the correct word on your paper. Number your answers from 1 through 5 so we may correct them afterwards. Let's begin the story.

Paul said to Bob, "Look, I (*pause*) my work paper already." Bob laughed and said, "You are slow, Paul. I have (*pause*) my paper already. Mike has (*pause*) his paper, too." Mike looked up from his desk and smiled. "I (*pause*) mine when the teacher was going over the problem." It looks like all three boys have (*pause*) their lesson well.

Now I shall repeat the story so that you can proof-read your answers before we grade the exercise. (*Repeat story.*)

The correct words are (1) *did,* (2) *done,* (3) *done,* (4) *did,* (5) *done.* Did you get them all correct? Tune in tomorrow for a special lesson on two more demons, *saw* and *seen.* See you then.

Children at the intermediate level can learn a manner of speaking for the classroom and still retain a homely dialect that they learn from their parents. They can also begin to appreciate other dialects. For example, stories in dialects once spoken in the South have been preserved. In some classes the familiar Uncle Remus stories might be used. At the outset children may be reminded that few black people now speak, or perhaps ever spoke, this way. If the teacher feels comfortable with the dialect, she may read the stories to the children; if she is uneasy about the pronunciation, she may use records.

The lesson may be structured this way: Tell the children that these stories are different from other stories they have heard and that they will have to listen carefully to the way that the storyteller uses words. Explain who the speaker is. The first listening is just for the fun of the story. *The Wonderful Tar Baby* or the language patterns in the regional books by Lois Lenski would be a good beginning.

After the reading or the record is finished, children will want to talk about it and tell about different ways of talking that they have heard or regional dialects to which they have been exposed. The record might be played a second time for the children to listen for interesting ways of expression which they hear. A second lesson could be set up by asking the children to look in the library for stories using dialects. Give them some help by suggesting that they might find conversations between Southern people or between Western people. Suggest that people from different areas have a dialect the children will find different from their own. Set a time for the children to read the dialects that they have discovered for themselves.

A whole week could be devoted to dialects if the children become enthusiastic about them. The music teacher could help out by giving some time during music to songs with lyrics in dialect. For instance, some of the Western cowboy ballads offer excellent experiences in dialect. Stories using dialect could be written by some children.

For Discussion

1. How can correct public usage be stressed without establishing the discourteous habit of correcting each other? Should children ever politely correct adults or other children?

2. Are there programs on television such as "60 Minutes" that could be adapted for classroom use?

What Voice Qualities Should a Classroom Teacher Possess?

Speech instruction in the elementary classroom starts with the voice of the teacher. The tone used, the manner of speaking, and the vocabulary employed all influence the quality of instruction. A voice that is too low to be heard or that has a high, irritating quality produces classroom tension and behavior problems. A monotonous voice robs literature of its emotional content. Voice is a major aspect of personality. When we think of someone as gracious or poised, our judgment is partly based on that person's style of vocal expression.

The teacher's words carry meaning not only because she conceives and expresses her thoughts accurately but also because her voice is properly attuned and controlled to convey this meaning. The tonal quality of her voice may make the difference between interested and inattentive children. A thin voice gives an impression of weakness, causing the listener to shift his attention. Clarity of enunciation and resonance quality or timbre determine whether or not a teacher's directions and suggestions will be followed. The teacher's voice is of greatest value when it is calm yet firm, well modulated yet sufficiently loud to be heard in a busy classroom, and suitably inflected to convey the varied feelings encountered in oral reading.

There are two ways to discover how you sound to others. One is to make a tape recording and then to listen critically to yourself. The other is to cup your hands behind your ears and read aloud either a paragraph of a story or a verse of poetry. If the results are not pleasing, there are a number of things you can do.

Start by learning to control your breathing and posture. Standing "tall," head up, shoulders back, and breathing deeply will do much to improve the sound of your voice. Listening attentively to people whose voices you find attractive while consciously imitating some of the patterns of speech will also help. Speaking with relaxed throat and lips well apart helps to produce full, rounded tones, as do proper sitting and standing. Barring a physical deformity in the throat or mouth, anyone can learn to speak distinctly and agreeably.

Voice modulation means a "toning down," or tempering, of the voice to avoid nasal twang, harshness, stridency, shrillness, or shouting. A man with a high-pitched voice or a woman with a hoarse or low-pitched voice may wish to alter these qualities. Speech exercises can provide a pattern of speech to imitate that will modify disturbing qualities. At first one may feel a bit self-conscious saying, "How now, brown cow?" over and over again, but this exercise is just as therapeutic as those used in a gym class to correct posture.

Relaxation is fundamental in all speech training. Not only the muscles used for speech but all other parts of the body as well should be free from tension in order to produce relaxed, clear voice tones and harmonious coordination of the many elements composing the speech mechanism. Relaxation may be gained by reading a quiet story or a short poem or by looking at a restful scene or painting.

Flexibility and control of the lips are important in the projection of correct "labial" sounds. Proper placement of the tongue is essential to the production of well-rounded vowels and to the formation of distinct, clear consonants and other "velar" and "glottal" sounds. This type of exercise is best done at home. The object is to "throw" the sounds toward the back of the room and to imagine that they are bouncing off the wall. The sounds should be thrown with an explosive breath effort.

ba,
ba, be;
ba, be, bi;
ba, be, bi, bo;
ba, be, bi, bo, boo.

The same exercise may be used with *p, m, v,* and *f* as well. The following poem provides practice in lip movement.

Antonio

Antonio, Antonio
Was tired of living alonio.
He thought he would woo
Miss Lissamy Lu,
Miss Lissamy Lucy Malonio.

Antonio, Antonio
Rode off on his polo-ponio.
He found the fair maid
In a bowery shade,
Sitting and knitting alonio.

"Oh, nonio, Antonio!
You're far too bleak and bonio!
And all that I wish,
You singular fish,
Is that you would quickly begonio."

Antonio, Antonio,
He uttered a dismal moanio;
Then ran off and hid
(Or I'm told that he did)
In the Antarctical Zonio.
Laura E. Richards

Flexible tongue practice can be obtained by the same type of exercise used for the lips:

ta,
ta, te;
ta, te, ti;
ta, te, ti, to;
ta, te, ti, to, too.

These letters may also be used: *l, n, d, k, g.*

Insufficient breath and lack of volume are often the speech characteristics of timid, insecure individuals.

With a group or alone, the timid child can be reassured through the device of projecting himself into a character. Have these children pretend to be newsboys crying, "Extra! Extra! Read all about it." Or peddlers selling fruit, "Big, ripe bananas. Buy your bananas here!" Or cheerleaders, "Team! Team! Team! Fight! Fight! Fight!" Of equal value and far easier is the singing of familiar songs that help the individual project his voice and interpret feelings.

The roof of the mouth or hard palate forms the top of a cavity that amplifies sound vibrations in addition to giving them a strong and more pleasing quality. Voice resonance can be cultivated by the way the oral cavity is used. Dull voices are frequently associated with dull faces. A smile and a happy state of mind will help increase resonance. Humming is also good for this purpose.

Intonation and emphasis give variety to the voice. The voice may come down emphatically at the end of an important idea, or go up in suspense and wonderment. Parts of words, entire words, or complete phrases may be lowered or raised.

Practice in Raising or Lowering the Voice [10]

Read the following sentences up and down as they are written:

```
                    hear me?
          do          you           Stop
1. Don't     that! Do                    I say.
_____

   Put           not
      it    here,        there.
2.       up         down
_____

                     I'll
      you          here        there.
3. If    don't come        come
_____

              do?      help you? Thank
   How   you    May
4.    do          I                you.
```

[10] From Agnes Frye, "Syllabus for Speech," mimeographed (Sacramento, Calif.: California State Department of Instruction, 1956).

	That's		What is
			rodent?

5.   an unusual animal.   it? A

Make the voice go up or down as the lines indicate:

1. Police horses are trained by encouragement, not by punishment.
2. He was a bully, not a hero—a cheat, not a conqueror.
3. You would vote for that stupid, that hateful, that impossible beast?
4. Here were strangers to face, tasks to conquer, opportunities to grasp.
5. The game was almost a landslide for our boys.

Emphasize the underlined word and note the change in meaning of the sentence:

1. I am going to the show.
2. I am going to the show.
3. I am going to the show.
4. I am going to the show.

Read the different interpretations of this sentence:

1. Naturally he'd like some cake. (of course he would)
2. Naturally he'd like some cake. (whether anyone else does or not)
3. Naturally he'd like some cake. (but he can't have any)
4. Naturally he'd like some cake. (he wouldn't need much)
5. Naturally he'd like some cake. (he wouldn't like bread)

Carrie Rasmussen suggests that teachers use the following questions to decide how qualified they are in the speech area of the language arts: [11]

Do my visible actions add meaning to my words?
Does my facial expression reinforce my words?
Is my whole body alive?
Do I appear free physically?

Do I talk loud enough to be heard easily?
Do I pronounce my words carefully?
Is my voice pleasant?
Is my tone quality (pitch) good?
Does my voice have variety?
Do I speak clearly?

Do I know what I am talking about; is my information accurate?
Is my vocabulary good?

[11] Carrie Rasmussen, *Speech Methods in the Elementary School*. Copyright 1949. The Ronald Press Company.

Do I understand my audience—one, four or forty in number?
Do I make clear what I am saying? Is my choice of words good?

Do I try to understand others?
Do I talk too much?
Do I know how to listen?
Do I know how to make things interesting?
Do I have a sense of humor?
Do I get the other person's point of view?

Do I have ideas?
Do I know how to create things?
Do I know how important creating is in the life of man?
What do I know about Creative Dramatics?
Am I teaching poetry in my class and are they enjoying it?
What do I know about discussion, storytelling, giving a talk?
Can I direct a play?
Can I integrate one subject with several others and make it fun?

You can tell from this that Rasmussen considers speech far more inclusive than voice. Her definition is an interesting one:

Speech is the blending of those elements: thought—mental processes; language—the molding of thought and feelings into words; voice—carrying thought and words through vocal sound to someone else; action—bodily bearing and response and listening. Speech is designed to transmit belief, emotion, or attitude on the part of the speaker, and our chief reason for speaking is to arouse corresponding ideas, meanings, and actions in others. It is sometimes called a code, but whatever we call it, we use it almost constantly; it is one of our most necessary tools. [Rasmussen, 1949, p. 8]

For Discussion

1. Should a teacher who moves from Georgia to California attempt to change her speech pattern to conform to her new classroom?

2. Should college students with speech faults, such as lisping or high-pitched voices, be admitted to a teacher-training program?

3. Observe a classroom. Note the different tones of voice the teacher uses as she explains material to the total class, talks with an individual child, or gains attention of a group.

4. Do you have a speech habit that you would not wish children to imitate?

5. Can you tell from a person's voice if he is tired or emotionally upset?

What Speech Activities Are Presented in the Primary Grades?

Some children come to school who have not yet mastered all the sounds of our language. Studies indicate that we can expect this development of speech sounds:

Age	Consonants
3½	p, b, m, h, w (lip sounds)
4½	d, n (tip-of-the-tongue sounds)
5–5½	f, j, w, h, s, z
6–6½	v, th, sh, zh, l
7–7½	ch, r, th (voiceless)
8	such blends as pl, br, st, sk, str

[Poole, 1934, p. 60]

The sounds most frequently defective are: *s, z, sh, zh* (as in pleasure), *ch, j, th, l, r, wh,* and the *-ing* ending, which is shortened to *-en.*

With young children the following letters have more than names—they are given a personality to focus attention on the sound they represent:

In order to do this, key words or sounds are used as the children practice the sounds. Naming objects in pictures and talking for dolls or animals aid sound identification.

Some sounds are twins. They look the same when we make them but some whisper in words and some talk out loud: *p–b; t–d; k–g; f–v; th–th; s–z; sh–zh; ch–j.* The second is the "talker" because it adds the vibration of vocal chords.

Ear training is important if the children are to improve speech habits. Until they hear the difference between the way they are pronouncing a word or produc-
ing a voice sound and the way it should be pronounced or produced, they will not change their pattern of speech. Ear training to develop auditory discrimination for the sounds of speech is the first step in speech correction and improvement.

Do not try to correct an *s* or *r* before easier sounds have been mastered. Instead, give much ear training on these sounds. Of course, there is no sense working on blends if the *l* and *r* have not been perfected.

A picture test can be made by the teacher to check the child's ability to say the initial consonants. Frequently, an alphabet book or picture dictionary will provide the pictures needed. These are suggestions that might be used: *h*, hat; *m*, man; *wh*, whistle; *w*, wagon; *p*, pig; *b*, ball; *n*, nail; *y*, yellow; *t*, table; *d*, day; *k*, kite; *g*, gun; *ng*, ring; *f*, fish; *v*, valentine; *l*, lamp; *th*, thumb; *th*, feather; *sh*, shoe; *zh*, tape measure; *s*, sun; *z*, zebra; *r*, rabbit; *ch*, chair; *j*, jar.

A still more comprehensive test uses separate pictures for each sound in all three positions—initial, medial, and final. As the teacher points to the picture, the child names it, with the teacher recording all errors. Teachers may make this test themselves with pictures cut from magazines, or they may purchase any of the commercial tests that are available. Many authorities feel that at the kindergarten level testing for errors in the initial position only is sufficient.

An individual test that is interesting for the child is a story using the rebus method of picture insertion. The tester reads the words and the child "fills in" by giving the words for the pictures. One in the Los Angeles City Speech Course of Study goes like this: "Jimmy sat up in (picture of bed). He looked through the (window) at the bright (sun). It was time to get up. He put on his (coat) and (pants), his (stockings) and (shoes). He put his magic (ring) on his (finger) and went downstairs." The story continues until all sounds have been tested.

Auditory discrimination is an essential skill in both reading and spelling. The following lessons indicate how the sounds may be isolated in words: [12]

[12] From Mary Smith, *Listening Habits and Speech Sound Discrimination* (Haywood, Calif.: Alameda County Schools Department, 1963).

Lip sounds	p	the *pop* sound (not *puh*)
	b	the *bubble* sound (not *buh*)
	m	the *humming* sound
	w	the *soft wind* sound
	y	the *smile* sound
Lip–breath sounds	h	the *little puff* sound
	wh	the *big puff* sound
Tip-of-the-tongue sounds	t	the *ticking watch* sound
	d	the *tapping* sound
	n	the *spinning* sound
Back-of-the-tongue sounds	k	the *little cough* sound
	g	the *gurgle* sound
	ng	the *ring* sound (*ding-a-ling, ting-a-ling*)
Lip–teeth sounds	f	the *cross kitty* sound
	v	the *airplane* sound
Tongue–teeth sounds	th	(as in *this*) the *flat tire* sound
	th	(as in *the*) the *motor* sound
Teeth sounds	s	the *steam* sound
	z	the *buzz* sound
	sh	the *baby's asleep* sound
	zh	the *vacuum cleaner* sound
	ch	the *train* sound
	j	the *jump* sound
Tongue and voice sounds	l	the *bell* sound
	r	the *rooster* sound

Words Beginning with S—Paper Bag Game

Teacher, "Today we are going to play a guessing game. In each of these paper bags is a toy or an article. The name of each thing starts with *s* as in sun. One person will be it. He will peek into one of these bags and give you one clue about what he sees. He might say, 'I see something we wear.' Then we will take turns guessing what he saw." (These items can be in the paper bags.)

sock   sailboat   soap
salt (small package as served on airplanes)

"The game must be played using complete sentences. When you guess, you say, 'Is it _____?' putting in the name of what you want to guess. The person who is it must answer you using the name of what you have guessed. If after everyone has had one turn and no one has guessed correctly, a second clue will be given."

(Stress the need for all questions and answers to be complete sentences using the forms: Is it a _____? No, it is not a _____! Depending upon the ability of your group, you may wish to add the following step in the lesson.)

"Let's write the names of all the things we have guessed and any other words we have used that begin with *s* sounds. Tell me what to write on the chalkboard."
Note: The lesson that follows should be used soon after this one.

Initial, Medial, and Final S Words—Paper Bag Game

Teacher, "The game today uses words that have *s* sounds in the beginning, the middle, and the end. Your main clue is that there is an *s* sound somewhere in the word you are to guess. The things in the paper bags all have an *s* sound somewhere in their name."

(See preceding lesson for detailed instructions for playing this game.) The items in the paper bags can be

basket   bus   sunglasses   nest
stone   purse   mouse

(Stress the need for all questions and answers to be complete sentences using the forms: Is it a _____? No, it is not a _____. Write the words they have guessed and have the class tell whether the *s* is in the beginning, middle, or end of the word.)

Auditory Discrimination Between S and Z

Teacher, "When the letter *s* is in front of a word, sometimes it says *s* and sometimes it says *z*. "Scissors" is a word that has lots of *s*'s. See if you can tell which ones say *s* and which ones say *z*. Hold your throat as you say *sizorz*. Yes, it begins with *s* and has a *z* sound in the middle and on the end."

(Put these words on the chalkboard in *mixed* order and have the children tell you whether they belong in the *s* column or *z* column.)

S *column*	Z *column*
sister	rose
salt	houses (note that both *s*'s have the
seven	*z* sound in the plural of house)
house	his
this	flowers
guess	please
school	does
sleep	ears
just	nose
said	these
across	present

The following games are speech centered and may be used with positive results in the primary grades:

I See Something You May See

A child makes three statements to describe something he sees. Children guess what it is by saying, "Do you see _____?"

Lip-Reading Game

TEACHER: "I am going to say names of children in the class but I am not going to use my voice. Watch for your name. Stand when your name is said on my lips."

CH Guessing Game

Guess the answer. Example: two sides of the face (*cheeks*). I write on the board with (*chalk*).

I Have Something in My Sack

In a large box put many small paper bags, in each of which is a small toy.

The names of the toys may contain specific sounds for improvement. A child chooses a sack from the box, peeks in, and discovers his toy. He then describes the toy without naming it. The child who guesses correctly then chooses a sack from the box and the game continues.

Telephone Games

One child orders from a list of toys and telephones order to Toy Store. He then goes to the storekeeper and asks if his package is ready. Storekeeper answers, "What is your name?" "My name is _____." "Yes, your package is ready," etc.

Fishing Game

Select pictures representing words that contain sounds you have been working on. Put paper clips on each picture, then put pictures in a pail or box. Attach a magnet to a string hanging from a pole. After lifting the picture out of the pail, the child tries to say the name of the picture. If he does, he keeps the picture; if he does

From Mary Finocchiaro, English as a Second Language: From Theory to Practice *(New York: Regents, 1965), p. 54. By permission.*

A very effective device is to sketch a large profile on a cardboard, indicating the lips, teeth, palate, and bottom of the mouth. Omit the tongue. Cut out the cardboard to show the mouth cavity. Make a red mitten for your right hand. As you teach a sound, use your gloved hand in the open mouth cavity to simulate the tongue. Move it against or between the teeth, bunch it up in the back, curl it up to the palate for /r/, or indicate movement from one sound to another.

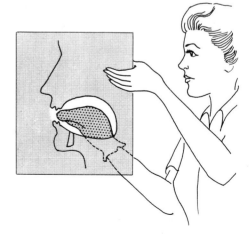

not, he must put the picture back (after having practiced it a little) and try again.

Sound Ladder or Word Ladder

Draw an outline ladder on paper on the blackboard. Place syllables or words you are practicing on each rung of the ladder. The child begins at bottom and climbs ladder by pronouncing each of the words or syllables correctly. The game is to see if he can climb to the top and back down again without "falling off." If he misses he must start at the bottom again.

Animal Talk

The sounds *quack-quack, moo-moo, baa-baa, oink-oink,* and *peep-peep* are good for lip movement. Pictures of animals may be shown and the children imitate that animal. A story may be told about a farmer and when an animal is mentioned the children make the proper sounds.

Noisy Cards

Make picture cards that suggest sound effects. The pictures are face down in a stack. A child takes the top card. Questions and answers should be in sentences.

CHILD: "My picture says _____. What do I have?"
ANSWER: "Do you have _____?"
CHILD: "Yes (or no), I have a _____."

Sound Boxes

Collect and place in boxes small objects starting with easily confused sounds; example *s–z, th–s, th–f, w–r.* Review the contents of the boxes periodically, letting children use names of objects in sentences.

I See Something

Use sound boxes mentioned above. Teacher says, "I see something in this box that starts with _____." Child chooses object and says, "Is it a _____?"

Balloons

Make colored paper balloons about six inches in diameter with a string fastened to each one.

FIRST CHILD: I am the balloon man. Balloons! Balloons for sale!
 Who will buy my balloons?
SECOND CHILD: I will buy a balloon.
FIRST CHILD: What color would you like?
SECOND CHILD: I would like a _____ balloon.

(Continue game until all balloons have been choosen.) After all balloons have been chosen, ask for them to be returned by colors, using only the lips to form the words without a voice. Do not exaggerate lip movements when forming the words.

For Discussion

1. Should a child be expected to read a word containing a sound that is not present in his speech?

2. Should a child be expected to read a word containing a sound that he cannot or does not hear?

3. What games to play at home would you suggest for a child who has not mastered the major speech sounds?

4. How might singing games help in the development of a child's speech?

How May the Classroom Teacher Help Children with Speech Needs?

Speech is defective when it deviates so far from the speech of other people in the group that it calls attention to itself, interferes with communication, or causes the possessor to be maladjusted to his environment. [Van Riper and Butler, 1953]

About one of every ten children in the public schools has a speech defect as defined in the preceding quote. About half of these defects are relatively simple problems, such as substituting *wun* for *run* or saying *pay* for *play*. The remaining are more serious. These include hearing impairment, physical defects such as cleft palate, stuttering, and delayed speech resulting from psychological causes. The first group can be cared for by a classroom teacher; the second needs the help of a specialist. However, many of those receiving special training will be in regular classrooms, and in all other respects their education is the responsibility of the regular teacher.

In all cases early recognition and treatment of the defect will help the child. Even if some of these defects cannot be corrected, the child, like other handicapped individuals, can be shown how to adjust to his limitations. The teacher can aid in this recognition, but in so doing she must also recognize and be able to distinguish between those defects that can be corrected and those that cannot. It is as unprofessional to attempt to remove some of these speech defects without special training as it would be to treat serious illnesses without medical training.

Parents and regular teachers can assist the child in correcting simple articulation errors. Articulation errors of sound substitution, addition, and omission may be identified in a number of ways. Conversation, questions, counting, and naming the days of the week or objects in a room will reveal the existence of the error. Further identification of the habit can be made by test sentences or picture of objects that contain the sound in different parts of words. Sometimes the child can say the sound in some words that he fails to articulate in others.

The first step toward correction is to have the child recognize his error and decide to change it. The teacher might say

John, sometimes you use a sound in a word that other people do not use. Listen while I read a story and pronounce some words the way you do. I'll put my hand behind my ear when I say those words. Then I'll read the story again and say the words as others do. If you hear the difference put your hand behind your ear. You say "shine crackers," others say "fine crackers." Here are two pictures of a fine cracker. One has a X across the picture. Listen to me. If I say "fine cracker" hold up the picture without the X. If I say "shine cracker" hold up the one with the X. [Van Riper, 1972, pp. 243–244]

Once errors have been identified by the one making them, the emphasis is on listening. "It is not sufficient to isolate and identify the correct sound during the pre-liminary period of ear training. The student must be stimulated with the sound so thoroughly that it may almost be said to ring in his ears." (Van Riper, 1972, p. 251). Names, faces, symbols, stories are used to identify the incorrect sounds. Discrimination consists of comparing and contrasting the correct and incorrect sounds both in isolation and in incorporation within regular speech. Without the ability to differentiate correct sound from incorrect sound, the student becomes discouraged and treatment becomes blind drill.

Therapy should involve ear training to the extent that the learner hears himself. Hearing his own error is the foundation for corrective habit formation.

Some speech problems are beyond the treatment of the classroom teacher. The teacher will have children with such problems in class and needs to understand some of the problems these children have.

Cleft palate designates the pathological condition in which the roof of the mouth has failed to grow together before the child was born. Surgery can correct this, but sometimes the condition is neglected until after the child has developed speech, when correction requires relearning breath control. Ordinarily a classroom teacher is not trained to meet this problem, but she may have such a child in her class. The sounds made by these children are distorted, because they have no sounding board except the throat and nose chambers. A film is available, titled "The Wisconsin Cleft Palate Story," which might be used to help a child's parents understand this problem or to enlist the aid of others. During the long period of reeducation that follows a cleft palate operation these children need patient understanding by teachers, parents, and peers.

Malocclusion denotes a failure of the teeth to mesh—usually at the front of the mouth. During the intermediate grades this is a frequent condition of new teeth in the as yet undeveloped jaw. A large number of these situations adjust themselves with growth. It is a frequent (and expensive) practice to correct malocclusion during the junior high school years.

Probably the most misunderstood of all speech defects is *stuttering*. In this situation the speech problem may be a symptom of a deeper psychological difficulty.

Correction may not always be possible, since stuttering may be caused by pressure and tension at some critical moment in a child's life. The tragedy is that stuttering is sometimes caused by the school itself.

In the American culture stuttering is more frequent among boys than among girls, but in some cultures stuttering does not exist at all. At times when the child is facing considerable speech development, as at the age of three or in the first grade, ideas sometimes come faster than the sounds or words can be recalled and produced. Nearly every child "clutters" or says "ah-ah-ah" while seeking the word. Concern by parents or teachers during this period seems to cause some to stutter.

We may forget the inner sensitivity of the child. A remark of concern, such as "I am afraid Susan is going to stutter," overheard at this time may actually cause stuttering. Even an attempt by the parent to correct the speech by saying "Stop and start again" may cause damage.

Because stuttering is misunderstood, parents of older children frequently think they are clinging to a childish habit and can stop stuttering if they want to. Stutterers can usually sing, speak, or read in a group; take part in a memorized play that involves them physically (such as sweeping with a broom); and talk while dancing without stuttering. Increased language facility that is the result of much writing and a growth in confidence and security usually helps a person who stutters.

The most important thing a classroom teacher can do for a stutterer is to help him accept this defect without embarrassment. The child who can accept this speech pattern as one accepts being left-handed is a long way toward satisfactory educational and social adjustment. These suggestions may be shared with the child's parents:

1. Do not provide words, finish a sentence, or act impatient when listening to a stuttering child.
2. Do see that the child is not subject to physical or emotional strain. Stuttering may be the weak and weary nervous system protecting itself from complete exhaustion.
3. Do praise the child's efforts and make him feel both worthy and loved.
4. Do not put the stuttering child in an exciting and highly competitive position. Overly ambitious parents or those who expect high behavior standards sometimes create ulcers for themselves at the same time that they make a stutterer of their child. Far too many stutterers are the sons of highly ambitious professional men.
5. Do not correct or reprimand the child for stuttering or call attention to it. He is already building up fears in meeting speech situations and is extremely conscious of his trouble. Anticipate some speech situations—such as telephoning, meeting strangers, answering questions—and provide confidence-building practice.
6. Help him accept himself as a stutterer. "Sure I stutter sometimes but I'm trying to get over it" is a healthy attitude. All of us on occasion do what the stutterer does more frequently.

For Discussion

1. There are other speech defects than those described here. Can you describe some of them?

2. Would you advise a parent to send a child with a speech defect to some of the special speech camps held during the summer months? What would you want to know before doing anything?

3. Would there be any advantage in clustering all children with speech defects in a few rooms?

4. A child with a speech defect in your classroom has been accepted by the other children as a humorous clown. The speech-defective child likes this role and plays it well. What actions would you take?

5. One teacher reports "My A/V Club is a very small group, usually six boys. I have had students with speech deviations, and find that these boys feel free to participate in oral discussions and demonstrations, and have overcome a great deal of their timidity about speaking as they become interested in operating the equipment." How would you justify such a grouping based upon speech needs?

How Does a Teacher Work with Children Who Do Not Speak English?

Some schools place children who do not speak English in special orientation classes regardless of grade until language is mastered. For little children a year of "prefirst" following kindergarten is considered essential. When the problem concerns only a single child, a buddy system in which the buddy is changed at times usually works well. This is an excellent learning experience for the English-speaking child in that he is forced to note the structure of his language.

Although the great stress will be on listening and on reproduction of oral language, there will be some reading. Anyone who has traveled in a foreign country knows that it is easier to read some of the basic signs than it is to speak the language.

The very first day of school the foreign-speaking child has one word in common in both languages—his name. His experience with language should begin with this one word. First the teacher must make sure that the child recognizes his name orally. Some parents use a different name or an abbreviation but give the school the full formal name. This results in difficulty for the child. Frequently the teacher pronounces the name differently from the way the parents do.

The teacher presents the name cards by attaching one set to the child's table or chair or coat hook, and teaches the child to find his own place. Then she gathers them in small groups and presents the cards, holding one up, saying the name, and handing it to the child. The following games provide needed practice. Although designed for Spanish-speaking children, these activities are appropriate for any child learning the English language.[13]

[13] From Margaret E. Gott, "Teaching Reading to Spanish Speaking Children" (unpublished thesis, San Diego State College, 1955).

1. *Mailman* (tests the "mailman"). A child who is chosen to be mailman tries to pass out the name cards of his group, giving each one his own card. If a recipient gets the wrong card and does not realize it, the teacher may call for an inspector to check on the mail delivery. The game is good because it involves no competition.
2. *Going to the Store* (tests each participant). The teacher places all the name cards of the group in the pocket chart. She then calls a child to "go to the store" and get his name. This is especially valuable when there are names that begin alike, as it calls for careful discrimination. It can be varied by telling the child to get another child's name.
3. *Storekeeper* (tests the storekeeper). The teacher places all the names in the pocket chart. One child is the storekeeper. The others go up one by one, say their names, and the storekeeper tries to give out the correct card. If he misses, the one to whom he gave the wrong card is the new storekeeper. This game provides opportunity to teach new English phrases orally, such as "Good morning," "What do you want?" "I want," and "Thank you."
4. *Find the Stranger* (tests discrimination of each participant). The teacher uses a double set of name cards. She arranges each line in the pocket chart so that it contains two identical names and one different name. The children in turn study one line and point out the stranger.
5. *Find the Twins* (tests discrimination of each participant). Using a double set of name cards, the teacher arranges the pocket chart so that each line contains three different names, one of which is repeated. The children in turn study one line and point out the twins.

It is usual for most first grades to have many labels around the room, such as *window, door,* and *books.* If the class will contain many non-English-speaking children it is better not to put up these labels at the beginning of the term, for the children may associate the label with the language they know. The words should be used in every possible classroom situation before being presented in written form. The first word chosen might be *chair.* When the teacher can say the word *chair* and get a satisfactory response from the child, such as touching the chair or pointing at it, she is ready to present the word. She presents a card to the child with the word *chair* on it and attaches a duplicate card to the chair. The child then takes the card to the chair to prove that it is identical, saying the words as he does this. This is called *matching* and will be used in many other lessons.

In presenting the nouns, it is best to present the singular form first and avoid the plural as much as possible. In Spanish, the final *s* is usually preceded by a vowel, and it is difficult for the child to pronounce the plurals that have a consonant preceding the *s*. There is also another difficulty because the final *s* sometimes has a *z* sound. When the plural form is used in the course of schoolroom activities, the teacher should try to establish the correct pronunciation as soon as possible.

The following list of words is divided according to the number of pronunciation difficulties. They should be presented slowly and practiced in enjoyable situations. They provide the Spanish-speaking child with the satisfaction of reading achievement while he is learning speech.

Few pronunciation difficulties:

ball	game	chair	toy	crayola
clay	house	nail	clock	playhouse

One pronunciation difficulty:

table—*bl*	paper—final *r*
door—final *r*	saw—*aw*
window—short *i*	box—short *o*
book—short *oo*	car—final *r*
paint—final *nt*	airplane—no vowel between *rp*
pencil—short *i*	top—short *o*
rug—short *u*	crayon—*on*

Two pronunciation difficulties:

hammer—short *a*, final *r*
sharpener—*sh*, final *r*

Three or more pronunciation difficulties:

blackboard—short *a*, final *d*, no vowel between syllables
puzzles—short *u*, *z*, final *s*
playthings—*th*, short *i*, *ng*, final *s*
scissors—short *i*, *zr*, final *s*
picture—short *i*, *tu*, final *r*, no vowel between *ct*
drawing—*aw*, short *i*, *ng*, no consonant sound between syllables

Games

1. *Matching* (tests discrimination of each participant). This should be played with no competition and as much bodily movement as needed. Each child is handed a card and tries to match it with the label on the object before the teacher rings her bell. When he finds the correch object, he stands quietly until it is his turn to read his word to the group.

2. *Where Are You Going?* (tests recognition of words by each participant). In this game the teacher holds up a card and asks a child, "Where are you going?" He tries to remember the word on the card and points to the place where he is going to try to match it up. Then he is given the card and goes to prove the correctness of his recognition, matching the word with the proper label and reading it aloud. If he is in error, he is allowed to go about the room and hunt for the correct label. This game teaches silent reading with comprehension.

3. *Picture Match*. The teacher prepares a set of small pictures mounted on cards about 3×4 inches and places the pictures in the pocket chart. The children try to place the word cards under the correct pictures. A card incorrectly placed is checked against the labeled object in the room. The children may place one card in each turn, or one child may try to place them all. If this game is used at the stage where the child has been taught only two words, and then each new word is added to the set, there will be no confusion.

After the words *door* and *window* have been taught, the teacher may play an oral language game of "Open the Door; Open the Window." This may be done first in the group with a cardboard house and later in the room. The words *open* and *shut* need not be presented in printed form, for they seldom occur below primer or first-reader level. The child hears the word *the* in the complete sentence first. Later the teacher uses it just with the noun. She shows the cardboard house and says, "The door." The child points to the door. After the child has shown that he is familiar with the article in oral language, the time has come to present it in written form.

For the first presentation the teacher says the words *the door* while showing the phrase on a card, and a child responds by indicating the door. The label on the classroom door has only the noun. Some bright child sees this at once and calls the teacher's attention to it. Her card is different! The teacher then holds up the card with the noun only, saying, "Door," then holds up the other saying, "The door." Ask children to add *the* to other words.

Pictures drawn by the children supply a good medium for the first sentences. The child brings his picture to his small group to show. If he knows no English he can quickly learn to hold it up and say, "See." The children will quickly learn to express appreciation for the picture by saying, "Oh! Oh!" These words are easy for the child to say. The teacher can employ them many times daily. She should use only a simple paraphrase of the meaning of *pleasure* and *approval* at first; later on she can add *excitement, dismay,* and *disapproval.*

A number of pictures are now placed in the chalkrail or hung along the chalkboard. Then the children learn to indicate their own by saying, "My boat" or "My airplane." The teacher can very easily facilitate this by having all the children or all the group draw the same thing. The word *my* is also easily taught, as soon as the children know the word *chair,* by having each child indicate his chair with his name on it and say, "My chair."

On the wall or on a bulletin board the teacher arranges an ever-changing display of children's pictures. As the child shows his drawing, he says, "See my boat." The teacher selects, with the children voting, a picture of the day, and puts it up, writing on the tagboard label what the child said, "See my boat." The child goes to the bulletin board, points to the picture, and says, "See my boat." The teacher then indicates the label, and moving her whole arm under the line of words in a horizontal position from left to right, repeats the phrase. Some pictures are left up for several days and the children play matching games with the duplicate labels. Two or three pictures may be mounted on large sheets of tagboard or paper and hung on the chart rack with the labels printed below. These are the first experience charts used by the children.

The New York City Schools have summarized their experience as a result of working with many emigrants from Puerto Rico in the following: [14]

The elementary school child will learn English better if he is placed in a class where the majority of the children are English-speaking. This arrangement builds into the language learner's day a natural and forceful motivation for speaking English as well as many native models of English speech to which he may listen and respond.

The language learner's classmates should be English-speaking children of average and above average academic ability in order to give him a verbally stimulating environment and classmates whose attitudes toward learning are positive.

The language learner will adjust better if he is placed as closely as possible and desirable with his age peers, regardless of his previous schooling.

English will be learned best if taught by a native speaker of the language.

The classroom teacher needs special assistance in acquiring the skills of teaching English as a second language as well as additional instructional aids.

Teachers who have an understanding and appreciation of the cultural heritage of their language learners are more apt to relate better to their pupils and thus establish a better climate for the teaching-learning process. Children who are learning English as a second language should not be referred to as "culturally deprived" regardless of the economic status of their parents. The term "culturally diverse" appears to be more accurate.

The terms *oral* and *aural* are difficult to contrast as we speak English. For that reason *audiolingual* is used to describe the oral approach to teaching language. In a sense this is no more than a planned drill-centered repetition of the way a child would learn English as a native. There is one important difference. The learner knows another language pattern and thought organization. Young children accept such differences and seldom make comparisons except in vocabulary. An older student does continue to think in his first language and translate thought and words into the second. Space per-

[14] Reprinted from *Hispania,* **49:** No. 2 (May 1966), 293–296. Excerpts from a presentation given at the San Diego Conference on the Teaching of English to Speakers of Other Languages, March 12, 1965.

mits only a summary of suggestions for those who use the audiolingual approach. It should be noted that highly motivated adults sent to the English Language Institute at the University of Michigan were able to speak a workable oral English in about three months. During World War II many in the armed forces learned oral Japanese as a result of intensive work for about six months. No effort is made to teach the reading of a language until the oral patterns and vocabulary are mastered. The following are tips for teaching English through the audiolingual approach:

1. Limit the English to experiences the learners know.
2. Repeat the sample language patterns rather than isolating individual words. (Piaget says all people learn language from the whole to the part.)
3. Repeat the pattern several times before asking a learner to say it. Move around the group so that all can see your lips and face while speaking.
4. Always use the normal speed and natural conversational intonation. Exaggerations will be imitated.
5. Add variety to the responses by having the groups speak—one table or row, then the boys, then the girls, and so on.
6. If you speak the learner's language, use it sparingly and only when gesture, pantomime, pictures, objects, or other materials have failed.
7. Do not rush the learner. Speed should not be a factor in gaining early responses.
8. If you isolate a word or sound in order to correct an individual, repeat the entire language pattern naturally and have the pupils do this as well.
9. Move from individual, to group, to individual, and so on. All should be involved, instead of waiting for a turn.
10. After three or four efforts to correct an individual, go on to others. Later return to the first pupil after he has heard the others.
11. Individual differences, short attention spans, and monotony of drill call for variety. Sing a phrase, act a phrase, let students move about. Do not advance rapidly. You are establishing habits that take years of practice.
12. Postpone reading and writing in all forms until lan-

guage patterns are established. In time some reading and writing may maintain skills. Don't be tempted to seek a quite busy classroom that may mean the learners will never gain the oral practice needed.
13. Use routine (some order of practice) and avoid oral directives. Gestures can be used for *you speak, you listen, you stand, you sit* if such words would distract from the practice.

A practical problem of working with children whose language is limited is reported by a principal.[15] The approach is also applicable when social skills are limited.

Fighting and name-calling are problems in areas where children and adults are not articulate enough to be able to discuss differences of opinion and to reconcile them. A principal helped some children to make words work for them by keeping a small tape recorder on her desk. When children were sent to her office because of fighting, they followed a simple formula:

1. Tell exactly what you did even if you feel it was wrong.
2. Tell what you might have done differently.
3. Decide what you are going to do about it.

As the children talked, she recorded each version, and if they came to no agreement on what could be done about the dispute, she played the tape for them to hear each account. The playback always had a profound effect. When children had to listen and were not grouping words, they found it easier to solve their problems.

She noticed that these phrases were generally used as children told what happened:

"talking about my mother"
"got all big and bad"
"got up in my face"
"get off my back"
"flipped me"
"rooted me"

The principal helped the children to see that these phrases did not specify what had happened, and the children were encouraged to be more specific. They learned to tell events in sequence. The principal learned that what are

[15] Theda M. Wilson, "Helping the Disadvantaged Build Language," *National Elementary School Principal* (November 1965), 44.

common meanings to certain groups are uncommon in general use. In communicating with people, one must understand the implications of what is said as well as what is meant.

For Discussion

1. Why have many adults studied a foreign language for the purpose of reading it rather than speaking it?

2. Would it be wise to have foreign-speaking children learn to read their language prior to reading English? What is their learning goal?

3. The term *bicultural* is used with respect to some programs. In what respect does such a concept include more than language? Do you see any reasons for seeking a one-culture population?

How May Oral Reading Skills Be Improved?

A good oral reader is eager to share with his listeners something that seems important. It may be new information, an experience, a vivid description, an interesting character, a bit of humor, or a poetic phrase. Without a motive of this kind, oral reading is impersonal and lifeless. The reader should know his audience's interests and needs and interpret the material accordingly. To read aloud well, the reader must have mastered the skills of perception so that he recognizes words quickly and accurately. Equally important is the ability to group words together in thought units and to read smoothly. To help his listeners grasp the author's meaning, the reader uses various devices. He highlights new ideas through the use of emphasis; makes clear the transition from one idea to another; indicates by proper phrasing the units of thought within a sentence; relates the ideas of a series by keeping his voice up until the end is reached; and indicates climax by force and vigor of expression.

Most teachers will ask, "Does such reading really take place in the elementary school?" They are thinking of the slow, halting oral reading of the reading circle.

Day by day teachers have urged children to read as if they were talking, to read to find the answer to a question, or to read the part of a story they liked best. But seldom has such reading produced anything like that just described. It was usually thought good if the child knew all the words. Nor was anyone in the listening group charmed by what was read. After all, they had read the same material.

Unfortunately, most oral reading in a classroom has been for the single purpose of evaluation. In addition, there has been an emphasis on speed as an indication of growth. Children have sat before machines to increase eye movement, have taken timed tests, have been taught how to skim, and have been given vast amounts of materials to read for information. Little wonder, then, that few read well orally.

The skills of oral reading are most naturally developed in the reading of plays. The reading of plays adds many values to reading: it enlists the delight in dramatization that appears in the everyday make-believe of all children; it enriches imagery in the reading of fiction; it provides disciplines not found in other types of reading; it enhances comprehension, vocabulary development, phrase reading, expression, and general speech skills.

Children with varying reading abilities may be cast in a play. Undiscovered personality qualities are often brought out in play reading. When a child is "someone else" while reading a play, new and delightful aspects of his personality are revealed. Plays are good for reducing shyness in timid children and for revealing sympathetic qualities in aggressive ones. Plays allow discussion of personal qualities, manners, habits, and ethical choices without self-consciousness on the part of pupils or moralizing by the teacher. The children can talk objectively about the actions of the characters, knowing that the roles they have played are only "make-believe."

Play reading requires discipline not encountered in other reading. Alertness to timing of speeches, coming in on cue, keeping one's place on the page, reading words and phrases correctly, expressing oneself well—these and other factors are recognized by the child as important in the success of the play.

The motivating power of the true audience situation

Carefully prepared oral reading is an excellent small-group activity. (COURTESY OF THE SAN DIEGO CITY SCHOOLS.)

is always found in play reading. Comprehension is assured; the child cannot interpret his lines unless he understands them. Phrase reading is improved by play reading. The child who is inclined to read a word at a time or to ignore commas and periods in oral reading will strive for complete phrases and attend to punctuation when he interprets his role. Improvement of expression through emphasis, pauses, and interpretation of mood and feeling is the main outcome of play reading.

Modern elementary readers contain plays designed to achieve these goals. But children need more experience with this form of literature than that provided in a reading series. Those in the format of radio plays provide excellent practice in oral skills. The radio format is modern and appeals to the children. It also has great appeal for the teacher, because costumes and scenery are not needed.

Durrell and Crossley state that college students enjoy reading the following play, although it is planned for the intermediate grades: [16]

As soon as you have read the play decide who will take the different parts.

Now practice reading aloud together. Your big job is to see that each person comes in on time.

Betsy, Clem, and the Wise Woman all get impatient with Noodle at some time or other. *Be sure you show this impatience in your voice.*

Noodle is not very bright. His speech is slow and hesitant. *Try to sound stupid as you read his lines.*

After you have read the play over two or three times, decide together how well you are doing these things:

1. Does Noodle sound stupid?
2. Does Betsy sound quick, alert and confident?
3. Are your voices clear and loud enough to be heard?

[16] From Donald D. Durrell and B. Alice Crossley, *Thirty Plays for Classroom Reading* (Boston: Plays, Inc., 1957).

4. Are you pronouncing every word carefully?

5. Is each person ready to come in "on cue" with his lines?

6. Are you paying attention to the punctuation?

If you cannot truly say yes to these things, get busy and practice again.

Don't read the whole play. Work on the parts that are not coming right.

When you are sure you are ready to read the play for others, let your teacher know. You can then decide with her when it is best to read to the class.

A KETTLE OF BRAINS

adapted from an old folk tale by Gweneira M. Williams

Characters
(2 boys, 1 girl, 1 woman and the narrator)
NARRATOR
NOODLE, *a stupid boy who wants a kettleful of brains.*
CLEM, *Noodle's friend who is trying to help him to get some brains.*
THE WISE WOMAN, *who is old and a little impatient with Noodle. She is really poking fun at him.*
BETSY, *a smart girl who decides Noodle needs her care.*

NARRATOR: Noodle, a stupid boy, is being brought to the hut of the Wise Woman. His friend, Clem, is showing him the way. Noodle is hanging back.

NOODLE (*fearfully*): But I'm afraid.

CLEM: You want brains, don't you?

NOODLE: I need a whole kettleful, I do.

CLEM: Well, then, go to the Wise Woman's hut there and knock at the door. Maybe she knows a way to get you some brains.

NOODLE: Aw, Clem, I'm scared.

CLEM: Noodle, don't be more of a fool than you can help, will you? Go on!

NOODLE: Hello, in there!

WISE WOMAN: What do you want, fool?

NOODLE (*hesitantly*): Well . . . well . . . well . . .

CLEM: Noodle, you're a fool.

NOODLE (*hopefully*): It's a fine day, isn't it?

WISE WOMAN: Maybe.

NOODLE: Maybe it'll rain, though.

WISE WOMAN: Maybe.

NOODLE (*gulping*): Or on the other hand, maybe it won't.

WISE WOMAN: Maybe.

NOODLE: Well, I can't think of anything else to say about the weather. But, but . . .

WISE WOMAN: Maybe.

NOODLE (*in a rush*): The crops are getting on fine, aren't they?

WISE WOMAN: Maybe.

NOODLE: The cows are getting fat.

WISE WOMAN: Maybe.

NOODLE: Wise Woman, I thought maybe you could help me.

WISE WOMAN: Maybe.

NOODLE (*desperately*): I need brains. Do you have any to sell?

WISE WOMAN: Maybe.

NOODLE: What d'you mean, maybe?

WISE WOMAN: Maybe I have and maybe I haven't. It depends on what kind of brains you want. Do you want a king's brains?

NOODLE (*astonished*): Ooh, no!

WISE WOMAN: Or a teacher's brains?

NOODLE (*startled*): Lawkamercy, no!

WISE WOMAN: Or a wizard's brains?

NOODLE: Heavens to Betsy, no!

WISE WOMAN: Well, what kind do you want?

NOODLE: Just ordinary brains. You see, I don't have any at all!

WISE WOMAN: Maybe I can help you.

NOODLE: Maybe? How?

WISE WOMAN: You'll have to help yourself first.

NOODLE (*eagerly*): Oh, if I can, I will.

WISE WOMAN: You'll have to bring me the thing you love best.

NOODLE: How can I do that?

WISE WOMAN: That's not for me to say. But when you bring it here, you must answer a riddle for me, so I'll be sure you can use the brains.

NOODLE: Oh, gosh to goodness!

NARRATOR: Noodle hurried home and now we see him dragging a big bag toward the Wise Woman's hut.

NOODLE (*eagerly*): Here it is, Wise Woman.

WISE WOMAN: Here's what?

NOODLE: The thing I love best.

WISE WOMAN: What is it?

NOODLE: My pig!

WISE WOMAN: Well, now that you're here, can you answer this riddle?

NOODLE: I'll try.

WISE WOMAN: Tell me, what runs without feet?

NOODLE (*stupidly*): Maybe . . . caterpillars?

WISE WOMAN (*angrily*): Idiot! You're not ready for brains! Come back again when you've decided what you love next best!

NOODLE (*thoughtfully*): What runs without feet? . . . Gosh I loved my pig best. What do I love best after him? . . . I know! My hen, my little hen! Wait a minute, hey, wait! Just wait a minute! I'll be back in a jiffy! Wait!

WISE WOMAN: Burn, fire, burn,
                        Burn to a turn,
                        One thing's sure as sky and fire,
                        Fools never learn!

NOODLE: Here it is! Wait, here it is! Gosh, my goodness, heavens to Betsy, wait! Don't sell that kettle of brains! Here it is!

WISE WOMAN: Here's what?

NOODLE: Here's the thing I love best next to my pig!

WISE WOMAN: What is it?

NOODLE: My hen!

WISE WOMAN: Are you ready to answer another riddle?

NOODLE (*bravely*): I'll try!

WISE WOMAN: Well, tell me this. What is yellow, and shining, and isn't gold?

NOODLE (*hopefully*): Cheese, maybe?

WISE WOMAN: Fool! . . . What do you love best next to your hen?

NOODLE (*crying*): What'll I do? What'll I do? I've lost the two things I love best! And I still haven't any brains! Whatever will I do now? They were the only two things I loved in the whole world! . . . Who are you?

NARRATOR: As Noodle looks around helplessly a girl comes in. When she sees him, this is what she says.

BETSY: Well, for heaven's sake!

NOODLE (*still crying*): Who are you?

BETSY: My name's Betsy. What's the matter with you?

NOODLE: Oh, I wanted some brains.

BETSY: Why?

NOODLE: I don't have any.

BETSY: Well, where did you think you could get some?

NOODLE (*sobbing*): The Wise Woman in there said she'd give me some if I brought her the things I loved best in the world.

BETSY: Well, did she?

NOODLE: No-o-o!

BETSY: You poor fool, why not?

NOODLE: I c-c-c-couldn't answer the r-r-rid-dles sh-sh-she asked m-me!

BETSY (*kindly*): There, there, don't cry. Don't you have anyone to take care of you, silly?

NOODLE: No.

BETSY: No one?

NOODLE: No one.

BETSY: Well, I wouldn't mind taking care of you myself!

NOODLE: Lawkamercy!

BETSY: Well?

NOODLE: You mean . . . (Hesitating) *marry* me?

BETSY: Well, yes.

NOODLE: Can you cook?

BETSY: Yes.

NOODLE: Can you sew?

BETSY: Yes.

NOODLE: Can you scrub?

BETSY: Yes, I can. Will you have me? I'd be a good wife.

NOODLE: Well, I guess you'd do as well as anyone else.

BETSY: That's fine.

NOODLE: But, but . . .

BETSY: But what?

NOODLE: What shall I do about the Wise Woman?

BETSY: Let *me* talk to her!

NOODLE: Oh, no, no!

BETSY: Why not?

NOODLE: I'm afraid!

BETSY: I'm not! Don't you need brains?

NOODLE: Well, yes.

BETSY: Come on, then, come on!

WISE WOMAN: What do you want, young woman?

BETSY: Brains for my husband here!

WISE WOMAN: Your husband, eh?

BETSY: We're going to be married.

WISE WOMAN: Does he love you the best of anything in the world?

BETSY: Go on, tell her!

NOODLE: I reckon I do.

WISE WOMAN: Not so fast, not so fast. He'll have to answer the riddles first.

NOODLE (*sadly*): Oh, the riddles.

BETSY (*unafraid*): What are they?

WISE WOMAN: What runs without feet?

NARRATOR: Betsy nudges him and whispers something. Noodle speaks.

NOODLE: Well, my goodness, water!

WISE WOMAN: H'm.

BETSY: Give him the next riddle.

WISE WOMAN: What's yellow and shining and isn't gold?

NARRATOR: Betsy whispers something to Noodle. He answers again.

NOODLE: Well, heavens to Betsy, the sun!

WISE WOMAN: H'm. Here's the third riddle. What has first no legs, then two legs, then four legs?

NARRATOR: Noodle looks at Betsy. Betsy makes swimming motions with her hands. Then she whispers something.

NOODLE (*happily*): A tadpole!

WISE WOMAN (*crossly*): That's right. Now go away!

NOODLE: But where is the kettleful of brains?

WISE WOMAN: You already have them.

NOODLE: Where? I can't see them.

WISE WOMAN: In your wife's head, silly. The only cure for a fool is a good wife. And you have one . . . or will have one. I can't help you any more. Be off with you! Good day!

NOODLE: Maybe she's right. . . . You'll marry me, lass? I won't have any brains if you don't.

BETSY: Of course I will! I have brains enough for two, anyway! Come on!

THE END

There are other ways of practicing oral reading. One very good practice in many schools is that of having children in the intermediate grades prepare a library book to read to a small group in the kindergarten or first grade. One fourth grade motivates this by keeping a record of "Books I Have Read to Others."

Some selections in great literature especially lend themselves to oral reading. The whitewashing of the fence in *The Adventures of Tom Sawyer* is written as if it were a play. Some of the scenes in *Freddie the Pig* by Walter R. Brooks consist almost exclusively of conversation that makes delightful oral reading.

For the lower grades parts of *Pooh* by A. A. Milne may be presented as a Readers' Theater. *Charlotte's Web* can be an excellent assembly or P.T.A. program, with a narrator and four readers sometimes reading dialogue and at other times reading exposition.

Have three members of the class read the following from *Tom Sawyer* to demonstrate the fun of oral reading.

NARRATOR: When school broke up at noon, Tom flew to Becky Thatcher and whispered in her ear:

TOM: Put on your bonnet and let on you're going home; and when you get to the corner give the rest of 'em the slip and turn down through the lane and come back. I'll go the other way and come it over 'em the same way.

NARRATOR: So the one went off with one group of scholars, and the other with another. In a little while the two met at the bottom of the lane, and when they reached the school they had it all to themselves. Then they sat together, with a slate before them, and Tom gave Becky the pencil and held her hand in his, guiding it, and so created another surprising house. When the interest in art began to wane, the two fell to talking. Tom was swimming in bliss. He said:

TOM: Do you love rats?

BECKY: No! I hate them!

TOM: Well, I do, too—*live* ones. But I mean dead ones, to swing round your head with a string.

BECKY: No, I don't care for rats much, anyway. What *I* like is chewing gum.

TOM: Oh, I should say so. I wish I had some now.

BECKY: Do you? I've got some. I'll let you chew it awhile, but you must give it back to me.

NARRATOR: That was agreeable, so they chewed it turn about, and dangled their legs against the bench in excess of contentment.

TOM: Was you ever at a circus?

BECKY: Yes, and my pa's going to take me again sometime, if I'm good.

TOM: I been to the circus three or four times—lots of times. Church ain't shucks to a circus. There's things going on at a circus all the time. I'm going to be a clown in a circus when I grow up.

BECKY: Oh, are you! That will be nice. They're so lovely, all spotted up.

TOM: Yes, that's so. And they get slathers of money—most a dollar a day, Ben Rogers says. Say, Becky, was you ever engaged?

BECKY: What's that?

TOM: Why, engaged to be married.

BECKY: No.

TOM: Would you like to?

BECKY: I reckon so. I don't know. What is it like?

TOM: Like? Why, it ain't like anything. You only just tell a boy you won't ever have anybody but him, ever ever *ever,* and then you kiss and that's all. Anybody can do it.

BECKY: Kiss? What do you kiss for?

TOM: Why, that, you know, is to—well, they always do that.

BECKY: Everybody?

TOM: Why, yes, everybody that's in love with each other. Do you remember what I wrote on the slate?

BECKY: Ye—yes.

TOM: What was it?

BECKY: I shan't tell you.

TOM: Shall I tell *you?*

BECKY: Ye—yes—but some other time.

TOM: No, now.

BECKY: No, not now—tomorrow.

TOM: Oh, no, *now.* Please, Becky—I'll whisper it, I'll whisper it ever so easy.

NARRATOR: Becky hesitating, Tom took silence for consent, and passed his arm about her waist and whispered the tale ever so softly, with his mouth close to her ear. And then he added:

TOM: Now you whisper it to me—just the same.

NARRATOR: She resisted for a while, and then said:

BECKY: You turn your face away so you can't see, and then I will. But you mustn't ever tell anybody—*will* you, Tom? Now you won't, *will* you?

TOM: No, indeed, indeed I won't. Now, Becky.

NARRATOR: He turned his face away. She bent timidly around till her breath stirred his curls and whispered,

BECKY: I—love—you!

NARRATOR: Then she sprang away and ran around and around the desks and benches, with Tom after her, and took refuge in a corner at last, with her little white apron to her face. Tom clasped her about her neck and pleaded:

TOM: Now, Becky, it's all done—all over but the kiss. Don't you be afraid of that—it ain't anything at all. Please, Becky.

NARRATOR: By and by she gave up, and let her hands drop; her face, all glowing with the struggle, came up and submitted. Tom kissed the red lips and said:

TOM: Now it's all done, Becky. And always after this, you know, you ain't ever to love anybody but me, and you ain't ever to marry anybody but me, never never and forever. Will you?

BECKY: No, I'll never love anybody but you, Tom, and I'll never marry anybody but you—and you ain't to ever marry anybody but me, either.

TOM: Certainly. Of course. That's *part* of it. And always coming to school or when we're going home, you're to walk with me, when there ain't anybody looking—and you choose me and I choose you at parties, because that's the way you do when you're engaged.

BECKY: It's so nice. I never heard of it before.

TOM: Oh, it's ever so gay! Why, me and Amy Lawrence—

NARRATOR: The big eyes told Tom his blunder and he stopped, confused.

BECKY: Oh, Tom! Then I ain't the first you've ever been engaged to!

NARRATOR: The child began to cry.

TOM: Oh, don't cry, Becky, I don't care for her any more.

BECKY: Yes, you do, Tom—you know you do.

For Discussion

1. It is reported that high school and college students dislike reading aloud in class. Can you explain why?

2. Because reading ahead of the voice with the eyes is necessary in oral reading, do you think oral reading can be done by children having reading difficulty?

3. Give reasons for agreeing or disagreeing with this statement: "Oral reading at sight of new material is the most difficult of all reading tasks."

Books of Plays Designed for Oral Reading

Durrell, Donald D., and B. Alice Crossley. *Thirty Plays for Classroom Reading.* Boston: Plays, Inc., 1957.

Kissen, Fran. *Bag of Fire, The Straw Ox, The Four Winds.* Boston: Houghton, 1941–1952.

Schneideman, Rose. *Radio Plays for Young People to Act.* New York: Dutton, 1960.

Stevenson, Augusta. *Dramatic Readers.* Boston: Houghton, 1930–1954.

Ward, Winifred. *Stories to Dramatize.* Anchorage, Ky.: Children's Theater Press, 1952.

What Is the Place of Dramatics in the Classroom?

Creative dramatics starts with the simple, natural play of the preschool or kindergarten. Here the children play house in the roles of father, mother, child, and the lady next door. In these roles the children try out the vocabulary they hear spoken in the situations of the adult world around them. There is no better way to teach children the social amenities of greeting and farewell. Teacher suggestion as to what should be said is usually welcomed and frequently sought. Some of the more imaginative children will provide patterns that others will imitate.

Children will observe the storekeeper, bus driver, and waiter with new interest after playing any of these roles in the classroom. Although the teacher is seldom imitated in the classroom, playing school is a favorite home activity. Parents frequently know many of the teacher's mannerisms and practices as a result of this. However, most children seem to invest the role of teacher with a crossness and severity that is more a part of childhood's folklore than actuality. The influence of television will reveal itself in the children's acting. Where once children saw a movie once a week, they now see one daily. It is only natural that free play will reflect some of the behavior they observe. To avoid some of the noise and violence it is well to establish through discussion and practice the "acting" techniques that are appropriate to the classroom.

As the children get older, the influence of television can be converted to an asset. No generation of children has had wider experience with dramatic form. Many children by the age of twelve have seen more of the great dramatic personalities and literature than past generations have known in a lifetime. The attention-getting exposition, the involvement of the main character with a problem, the gradual working out of that problem, and the final resolution become almost second nature after so much familiarity with this form. Many of the favorite children's programs follow a theme as simple and obvious as that of old folk stories so that the concept of unity, which once seemed such a difficult idea, can be easily understood. Unfortunately, some of these comedy shows have a degree of sophistication of theme and action that is inappropriate for the classroom.

A few items to use as props help children give realism to a role. An apron establishes a grandmother, just as a cane identifies a grandfather. A hat makes a boy a man, and nothing gives a girl more maturity than a long skirt.

Creative dramatics in the school is not concerned with making children into "actors" or with producing story plays for a guest audience. In some situations the presence of an audience may make the children self-conscious of their roles as actors rather than assist the process of creating the play. The stage may be the front of the classroom, but the whole room may be involved in order to indicate a change of scene. Aisles are used as roads, scenery is drawn on the chalkboard, and tables become bridges, mountaintops, or castle towers.

In the primary grades the attitude is one of creative play. "Let's play that story," the teacher will suggest. "Who wants to be the mother bear?" Some children are quite content to be a tree in the forest, others will need suggestions as to what to say, but the values of released imagination, language practice, and dramatic interest are always there.

In the intermediate grades children imagine that they are the Pilgrims or pioneers. Such dramatics frequently becomes organized to the extent that the main ideas are outlined, children experiment with different scenes, select the ones that seem most effective, and actually write a script that is later presented as a formal production.

It may help some students to start with simple pantomime, such as pretending to walk through deep snow or falling leaves; pretending to eat ice cream, a pickle, or cotton candy; pretending to toss a baseball, a chunk of ice, a hot potato, or a pillow. Stand facing another student and act as his reflection in a mirror, moving slowly at first and then faster.

From such pantomimes move to sketches involving one-way dialogue. For example, you get a telephone call inviting you to a party, telling you that your parents were in an accident, informing you that you won a contest, announcing that your team lost.

Situations involving two or more may be suggested by the teacher. For example:

1. Your friend has asked you to go to the movie; your mother has said you must stay home. She is nearby.
2. A shy schoolmate has just returned from being ill and absent from school and you want him to feel at home at school again.

A few items to use as theater props help children add realism to their roles. (PHOTO BY TOM WOLFE.)

3. You are taking a test and a schoolmate asks for your help.
4. A classmate has just had a religious holiday. You want to know about it.
5. Your mother wants you to go to camp, but you want to stay home.
6. You have borrowed a camera and broken it. Return it to the owner.
7. Your class is going to elect a president. You want a friend to run, but he is reluctant.

Ordinarily the group decides who will take the various roles in a play. After discussing what a character should be like, it is wise to have different individuals "try out" for the part. The king should walk with lordly mien, speak deliberately and loudly because of his vast authority, and perhaps flourish a wooden sword. After such a character is established in the minds of the children, let them take turns feeling like a king or whatever character is being developed. At the beginning most teachers cast parts by type. This means using the child whose personality most nearly fits the part. But after children have had some experience with dramatics there will be opportunity to use the story to help a child with a social or personality problem. All the parts, however, should not be assigned on a "problem" basis or children will lose interest. One case of "play therapy" at a time is enough for most teachers to handle.

Sociodrama is closely related to group dramatics as an aid to personality adjustment. Its main purpose is to assist children in being aware of the feelings and problems of others. "How does it feel to be the only child in a room not asked to a party? Let's act it out in a story." The situation may be centered in any problem: the child who acts as a bully and mistreats little children, the child who does not speak English, the lonely lady who complains about the noise children make.

Shaftel and Shaftel suggest that children sometimes write stories that lend themselves to role playing. This example was guided and supervised by Barbara Celse of the Orange County, California, schools:[17]

Work at Home

My name is Jim and I want to tell you a story of my life. My house has six living in it. They are my mother, father, brother, sister and brother-in-law. The reason my brother-in-law is living with us is because they are fixing their house.

I want to write this story because I don't think it's fair. Every night after six people have dinner at the house, they go to the other part of the house. My mother says, "Do the dishes, son." I am the only living thing in the kitchen. I have to do the dishes and they go watch TV.

The class role-played this story. Jim, who wrote this problem, did not participate in the first enactment. However, he helped arrange the seating at the dinner table.

A. Family Around the Table

(*The adults did most of the talking. They tried to find someone else to do the dishes.*)

MOTHER: Well, I think Jean (*older brother, aged 19*) should stop gadding around every night with his girlfriend. He should help, too. Now Jean, you just stay home tonight and do the dishes. It won't hurt you.

JEAN: I got a date. Why doesn't Pat (*married sister*) help?

(*They suggested everyone in the family at one time or another. They also proposed:*

That everyone take turns.

That a dishwasher be bought—but this was immediately vetoed because of cost.)

At this point, the class questioned Jim to get more information about the family. It was discovered that:

Sister just had a baby.
Jean (the older brother) works all day and sometimes helps build a house at night. He's engaged.
Father and brother-in-law work on the house they are building at night.
Jim gets paid for doing the dishes.

[17] From George and Fannie R. Shaftel, *Role Playing, The Problem Story* (New York: National Conference of Christians and Jews, 1952), pp. 69–70.

B. Family Around the Table

(*In this second enactment Jim plays his own role.*)

FATHER: Well, I think the women should wash the dishes.

JIM (*to brother*): Why don't you help out?

JEAN: I'm too busy.

JIM: But I want to see my TV program. I think he should help.

JEAN: You need the money more than I do.

BROTHER-IN-LAW: I don't think Jim should have to do it all. Let's do them before we go to the house.

FATHER: Well, you know, you aren't going to be living with us much longer. Your house is almost finished. It will be different then.

Then the class again began to question the family members.
To Jean:

Question: Why don't you bring your girlfriend over and both of you help?

Answer: We'll be all dressed up!

Question: Well, she can wear an apron. I do.

Answer: Gosh, I work all day. I have to have some time for fun. Besides, I help on the house some nights, too.

To Mother:

Question: Why don't you help?

Answer: I work all day, too. Jim gets paid for this job.

To Jim:

Question: How long does it take you to do the dishes?

Answer: Last night it took me about two hours!

Question: You don't know how to do them!

The discussion then became a sharing of experiences in dish-washing, and rules for efficiency in doing the job.

The final consensus of the class's thinking was:

Jim should have help sometimes.
He needs to be more efficient.
He could arrange his time better.
Everybody has some job to do.
And, furthermore, Jim gets *paid* to wash those dishes!

Puppets are used as a vehicle for dramatic work in all grades. Some shy children find it easier to project their language through a puppet actor. Certain dramatic effects can be achieved with puppets that make the productions much more satisfying. Animal actors, folklore characters, magic changes, and exotic areas (such as the bottom of the sea) are much easier to manage with puppets than with human actors. Somehow the simple plays written by children seem more spirited when given with puppets.

Puppets should be kept simple. Finger puppets, figures on a stick, sacks on the fist, and even the toy hand puppets that can be purchased are better than elaborate string marionettes. Marionette making is an art rather than a language project. The time taken to make and manipulate these figures does not stimulate enough language activity to warrant the effort.

Formal dramatics, involving the memorization of a well-written play, has many values for children able to participate in it. The discipline of memorization, the work on characterization, the team spirit developed in presenting the material, and the gratifying applause of a truly appreciative audience are valuable experiences. The beginning teacher is often tempted to start with a play that is too difficult. The professional children's theaters with well-equipped stages and trained staffs can produce elaborate plays with such apparent ease that a teacher is tempted to try the same in the classroom. Don't do it unless you are willing to spend hours rehearsing after school, devote weekends to painting scenery and making costumes, and act as a military policeman during rehearsal and the performance. Perhaps in a summer school or with an especially talented group you can realize your ambitions. In the meantime, be content with less professional material. By all means avoid plays that require large casts or run more than an hour.

Plays such as *Why the Chimes Ring, Strawberry Red, King of Nomania, Knights of the Silver Shield, Elmer,* and *Cabbages* are favorites for the junior high school age group. The little plays published in the magazines *Teacher, Instructor,* and *Plays* are widely used in the lower grades and are relatively simple to prepare. Most children will learn their parts in six or eight readings. By the time of the production most of the children will know all the lines. Get parents involved in making costumes, and on the day of the show have at least one adult supervise children backstage who are not performing. If makeup is used, keep it simple. A little rouge on the cheeks, a dab of lipstick, and a stroke or two with the grease pencil will transform most child actors sufficiently. No matter how well it is put on, a beard never looks right on a child. Crepe hair applied with spirit gum, available at all theatrical supply stores, is about as satisfactory a method of "aging" as any.

Most scenery problems can be solved by using sets of folding screens on which the outline of a forest, window, or fireplace has been drawn in colored chalk or water colors. Children's imaginations are so vivid that anything more than this is lost effort. Various sound effects are available on records or they can be put on a tape and amplified at the proper time.

Children are usually excited after a performance. If possible, plan to have a post-performance period with refreshments and general relaxation while costumes are put away and other details attended to. Children are seldom ready for a scheduled class after a play, and the wise teacher will recognize this fact in making plans. Avoid showing concern over forgotten lines or things that did not go just right, but instead find much to praise.

Radio and television scripts offer excellent possibilities at the elementary level for group composition and speech. The definite pattern in which action and dialogue must be cast gives pupils a needed support as they plan what scenes the cameras should focus on, or what sounds the microphone can pick up. In a television script the scenes for the cameras ("video") are placed on the left-hand side of the page; the words spoken, music, and sound effects ("audio") are placed on the right, opposite the scenes they will accompany.

The First Thanksgiving was first produced in the school auditorium by a fifth grade and then on local television. The "script" is actually a continuity sheet.

Children should be told to speak in a clear and natural voice without "rushing" their lines, yet moving along as though they were talking normally to other students. They should not try to imitate or exaggerate. This does not mean, however, they should not strive to get some feeling into their voices.

On most educational television shows, all colors are seen as shades from black to white. Blacks, grays, and light grays give good contrasts. Pure white is not good because it produces "halo" effects and shapes are blurred. This does not exclude murals and drawings

THE FIRST THANKSGIVING[18]

Video

1. Announcer.
2. Pupils stage left.
3. Play given stage right and center; scenes as follows:
4. The Lullaby:
   Mistress Hopkins at home, taking care of her baby when Squanto arrives.
5. Squanto exits.
   Mother and baby at home.
6. Other Pilgrim mothers and children come to visit Mistress Hopkins.
7. Priscilla enters. Priscilla and children begin preparations for the feast.
8. Priscilla sends two boys on an errand.

Audio

1. Opening announcement.
2. Short reports on Pilgrims settling in Massachusetts.
3. (Dialogue from play.)
4. Squanto tells Mistress Hopkins that Governor Bradford and Chief Massasoit have agreed upon a feast of Thanksgiving.
5. Mother sings Old Lullaby.
6. Women discuss the coming feast.
7. Priscilla directs the children in preparation for the feast.
8. Priscilla sends boys out to get corn.

(The script continues through ten more scenes and ends as follows.)

21. Governor Bradford advances and holds out hand to Massasoit.

22. Massasoit shakes Governor's hand, nodding head solemnly. Then waves his hand toward distance, as if game had been laid down there.
23. Governor Bradford exits followed by Standish, Massasoit, braves, Squanto and Pilgrims.

24. Pilgrims and Indians worship, Elder Brewster leading meeting. Tithing man has a stick with rabbit's foot on one end and hard ball on the other. Pilgrims seated on benches. Taller Pilgrim men stand in rear. During service the tithing man quietly touches a small girl who has fallen asleep with her head on her neighbor's shoulder.
25. All stand and sing.

21. *Gov. Bradford:* Welcome, Massasoit! Welcome to the great Sachem! Welcome to all your braves. The palefaces (gestures toward Pilgrims) welcome the Red Men. We are happy to be here.
22. *Massasoit:* Massasoit brings heap buck, turkey, rabbit for white man's feast.
23. *Gov. Bradford:* We thank you. And now follow me (*beckons*). I will show you to your tents till the feasting begins.
24. Elder Brewster offers prayer.
   "Lord, we come before Thee, now,
   At thy feet we humbly bow,
   Oh do not our suit disdain,
   Shall we seek Thee, Lord, in vain?
   May the Lord abide with us till our next meeting."
25. Song ("O God, Beneath Thy Guiding Hand")
26. SIGN OFF

done in color, but if you are preparing "props" for the show, use blacks, grays, and light grays in order to obtain desirable contrasts. Values are easier to control with these colors than with yellows, reds, blues, and greens.

Lettering on posters should be large and simple,

not less than two inches in height. Remember that lower case is more legible than capitals. Do not use "fancy" lettering. Try to use black letters when possible.

Prints or photographs can be used to show specific objects, scenery, or people. They should be mounted on 11- × 14-inch board, preferably horizontally.

Normally there are at least two TV cameras on each show; one takes all "placement" or long shots and

[18] From Minneapolis Public School Board of Education, *Communications* (1953).

the other the closeups. This is important to know, for if you want to show something you have made you must hold it a little above waist height—tilted slightly forward to prevent glare—very steady for about ten to fifteen seconds in the direction of the closeup camera.

For Discussion

1. Do you feel that every child in a classroom should have a part in a program presented for an audience?

2. You work in a school where assembly programs and PTA programs are assigned to teachers a year in advance. As a result the teachers put on elaborate productions and compete with each other. This year you have drawn the Thanksgiving assembly. What would you do?

3. You have a class with many emotionally disturbed children. These children come from broken homes, attend clinics, and so on. Should you attempt creative dramatics?

4. In order to encourage participation and expression, teachers sometimes permit or encourage children to participate in activities of questionable taste. Should a second-grade girl dance a hula and sing *Lovely Hula Hands?* The love songs that constitute the popular music of the day have their place, but should one be sung by primary children simply because their childish innocence adds cuteness? Sometimes boys appear on TV singing in the manner of popular singers whose facial and bodily expressions accentuate the sexual suggestions of the lyrics. Are there aspects of taste and propriety that students might discuss with respect to such programs?

How Is Courtesy Taught in the Language Arts Program?

A part of the awkwardness of children in a social situation arises from not knowing the proper thing to say. Greetings, introductions, apologies, interruptions, and expressions of appreciation involve established patterns of language. At first these may be taught as examples to

be imitated. "Say bye-bye," a mother urges the infant. Or the parent will, by asking the child, "What do we say when someone gives us something?" eventually elicit a "Thank you."

A student teacher working with a group of small children knows that it is a disturbance when an adult enters the classroom. Naturally, children are curious about the stranger. The teacher can maintain control, keep the class moving ahead, and teach some courtesy by stopping a minute and saying, "Girls and boys. This is Mr. Vanek from the college. He is here to watch me teach. What do we say when we have a visitor in the room?" The children chorus, "Good morning, Mr. Vanek," then return to their work. In upper grades a monitor will go to the visitor, show him where to sit, and hand him a copy of the book in use. Then at a convenient time the teacher greets the visitor. Many states require that a record of all visitors be maintained. Even if this is not required, it provides an interesting way to greet a visitor. Prepare a "Visitor's Register." Have a child make an attractive cover for it. After the visitor has registered, it is sometimes a good idea to have the courtesy monitor introduce him to the class.

Courtesy instruction will seem a bit silly to children unless it is presented in terms of situations. These situations should reveal the need for some type of social convention. At the time when the school is having an open house or a parents' evening, present the problem of just how we should introduce a parent to the teacher, a parent to a classmate, or one child's parents to other parents.

In a social studies class there will be times when opposing opinions must be expressed. How do we express disagreement without offending people or starting an argument? And if we should offend a person, how can we express our apologies? It will interest children to learn how these problems have been solved in other lands. Many of our concepts of courtesy reflect our democratic belief that everyone has certain rights and freedoms. We do not avoid direct contests in athletics even though we know someone will lose, whereas in other cultures direct contests are avoided, and ideas are generally expressed indirectly.

There is no better place to discuss table manners

than in a health class. Start with problems like this: "Do you like to sit at a table where someone is messy with food? Talks with his mouth full? Shouts and plays at the table?" Lessons about the use of knife and fork, setting the table, refusing food you don't like, discussing certain topics at the table, and even ordering food at the restaurant all involve language skills in this area.

In the third grade, children are growing in social awareness and are anxious to know ways of behaving.

Etiquette that requires girls to precede boys through doorways, to walk "on the inside," and to make the initial greeting does not seem quite so trivial at this age as it may later. A party at Halloween or Valentine's Day can be rich in lessons in courtesy. Some classes make little guidebooks on good manners.

Basic to all courtesy are two concepts, respect and kindness. Respect is shown to our parents and to older people, to our country and its flag, to those who serve

Good manners: Concepts to discuss	*Learning activities*
People use good manners and courtesy because they make living and working together more enjoyable.	The children can be asked to speculate on what the room would be like if no one used manners and courtesy.
What things can we do to make our classroom more enjoyable? 1. Hang up clothes on hangers. 2. Clean up spilled paint and water. 3. Leave the easel clean and ready for the next person. 4. Keep desks clean and neat. 5. Respect the rights of others. Try to help other people. 6. Equipment in the room belongs to all of us. We each have the privilege of using it, and the responsibility of taking care of it.	*Why Have Good Manners,* filmstrip (Eyegate House), gives many ideas on why people use good manners. Children will mention most of these specifics and probably add many more. The song "It's Good to Share" (*New Music Horizons, Book III*, p. 70) fits in nicely. Young America Films' *We Plan Together* is an excellent filmstrip to use prior to committee work. The group will profit from planning and executing a "model" work and clean-up period. Afterward, the values of all working to achieve a common purpose can be pointed out.

Flag courtesy: Concepts to discuss	*Learning activities*
Why do we show respect for our country's flag? 1. To show that we are thankful for our country. How do we show respect for the flag? 1. When giving the pledge, stand and face the flag, place right hand over heart. 2. When the flag is brought into a room, stand and remain standing until the flag is in place in its holder. 3. When the flag is raised or lowered on the flagpole, stand still, face the flag, and place hand over heart. 4. When the national anthem is played, face the flag and salute. If the flag is not displayed, face the music but do not salute. (This holds true only for "live" music and is generally not done if the music is recorded.) 5. Cubs and Brownies, when inside a room, salute instead of placing hand over heart, only if they are in full uniform.	The film *The Flag Speaks* will make an especially valuable contribution. It discusses our national pride for the flag and demonstrates correct flag courtesy. Members of the class who are Cub Scouts or Brownies can be called on to share what they know about flag courtesy. The filmstrip *Flag Etiquette* (Young America Films) will provide an excellent summary of what has been learned. A committee can be formed to learn and demonstrate these rules for the class. This might also be shared at an assembly. This is a good time to learn or relearn "The Star-Spangled Banner" and "America, the Beautiful."

us, and to our friends and neighbors. Kindness covers a broad area of human virtue and includes good will, compassion, generosity, and love for one's fellow man. Rudeness is the opposite of kindness in that it makes another person suffer. Even following the rules of etiquette can be unkind if it causes others to be embarrassed. The story of Queen Victoria blowing on her soup to cover up a guest's bad manners can be told as a true act of courtesy.

Both respect and kindness are implied when we speak of consideration of others. This must go much deeper than the language aspect, but knowing the language is a way of establishing the behavior desired as well as the inner sensitivity that is true courtesy.

Again the importance of example must not be forgotten. The teacher's everyday manners will provide many object lessons in this area. It might be well for the children to know more about the teacher's prerogatives and responsibilities.

After consideration is given to the social amenities that come into use in the classroom and on the playground, the children can be guided into a study of manners and courtesy on a broader scope that includes the whole school and the school's personnel.

Playground: Concepts to discuss	*Learning activities*
What are some things a good citizen tries to do on the playground? 1. Learn the rules of the game, and play according to the rules. 2. Observe safety rules for the swings, slide, and other equipment. 3. Avoid picking fights. 4. Try to include new children in games. Do not tease. 5. Take care of school equipment. 6. The equipment belongs to everyone at our school; therefore, all must share it.	The filmstrip *Good Manners at Play* (Eyegate House) is a helpful aid to introduce playground manners. Have a problem-solving discussion centered around difficulties that can be prevented by learning and knowing rules. A small committee can undertake the writing down of game rules. Copies of these could be run off. Another group might prepare a bulletin-board display on playground manners. Dramatic play could be used to demonstrate several ways of handling a "touchy" situation. Role playing might be used in regard to the "new child" on the playground. Use the filmstrip *New Classmate* (Popular Science Films).

Home, school, and elsewhere: Concepts to discuss	*Learning activities*
Why do we need to use courtesy and manners at home, at school, with friends, and in other places? 1. Use of good manners will make our school a more enjoyable place.	Some of the ideas that were developed in answer to discussion about the need for courtesy in the room and on the playground can be reviewed and enlarged upon.
Besides the teacher, who are some of the people at school who need our help in order to do their jobs? 1. The principal.	This will be a good opportunity to invite resource people to the classroom. The principal may be asked to explain the "whys and wherefores" of the various school rules. She might also help develop a cooperative attitude toward these.
2. The school secretary.	She can tell of her job and its complexities. The need for manners in the school office should be emphasized, as her job is often complicated by children who forget to use good manners.

3. The custodian.

The school custodian will appreciate the opportunity of talking to the group. He can help them in many ways by stressing the need for conservation of paper and soap in lavatories, explaining the need for respecting property, etc. He may also wish to express his appreciation to those who help him keep the school clean.

4. Patrols and school safeties.

Because the patrols and safeties make such a valuable contribution to the school, they should be given a chance to speak to the group.

What can we do to help these people help us?

1. Be courteous and remember that what they say is to help us.
2. Follow the rules because rules are like manners in that they help everyone get along better.

Children are naturally grateful for things done for them. They may want to discuss ways of expressing their gratitude to the people who have come to the room and helped them learn. This can lead to a consideration of *ways* of saying "thank you."

When someone has done something nice for you, what can you do to show you appreciate it? (Children need to be introduced to other ways besides verbal thanks.)

1. Write "thank-you" notes.
2. Make things to show our appreciation.
3. Do something.

The language period can be used to study the mechanics of letter writing. Emphasis should be placed on individuality. Children should see this as a pleasurable activity rather than a disagreeable task.

Are there other times and places at school when we need to use good manners and courtesy?

1. The cafeteria:
   Wait in line patiently.
   Use good table manners.
2. Auditorium.
   Find seat and sit down quietly.
   Give attention to the program.
   Applaud politely.
3. Corridors.
   Walk on the right side.
   Say "excuse me" when necessary.
   Keep voices low.
Look where you are going, or go where you are looking.
4. The school bus.

Committees can be organized so that each child is given the chance to say "thank you" in his own way. Some groups may write "thank-you" notes, whereas others express their gratitude by making things such as clay paperweights, calendars, or pictures.

The filmstrip *Good Manners at School* (Eyegate House) discusses many situations at school calling for the use of good manners. This will provide an opportunity for small-group work. Each group may choose a specific situation such as the auditorium. The group can find out what manners and courtesies are in order at these places. A report can be prepared and a presentation given to the class such as a puppet play or illustrated talk.

(The school bus deserves special consideration, since difficulties often arise in such situations where children are without close supervision. Children need to know that certain behavior is very dangerous on the bus. Riding the bus is a privilege that, if not respected, may be lost.)

Why do we *especially need* to use courtesy and manners on the school bus?

1. Safety factors.
2. Buses are usually crowded. Consideration for others helps make it a pleasant trip.

A good lead-in discussion about the school bus might be centered around what the bus driver does for us. An excursion will provide the best learning opportunity for this concept.

How can we show respect for public and private property? 1. By treating it as if it were ours. 2. Public property is just like school equipment. We all have a share in maintaining it. 3. You may be trespassing if you are on someone's private property without the owner's permission. (Teacher may explain that the property owner is entitled to certain legal protection from trespassers.)	When respect for property is being discussed, the teacher can share the "Golden Rule" or similar object story. Role playing can be meaningful in a situation such as this: Several children are picking flowers as they wait for the bus. What would you do if you were the person who planted these flowers and how would you feel about this?
If you find something that you think someone has lost, what is the right thing to do? 1. Do everything you can to find the owner. 2. The more valuable a thing is, the more reason a person has to try to find the owner.	A spontaneous puppet play can be used in connection with lost-and-found concepts. This can demonstrate how the loser feels and how the finder reacts.

For Discussion

1. Do you think that a "courtesy week" would be effective in a school? What would you suggest as activities?

2. What understandings should children have concerning telephone courtesy?

3. Who had the greatest influence on your own habits of courtesy? Your mother? Father? Scout leader? Teacher?

4. In the primary grades it is sometimes effective to have a "boy of the day" and "girl of the day." Sometimes these children wear a special badge or crown. This is an honor given as a reward for desirable behavior. Would such a device work with intermediate-grade children?

Suggestions for Projects

1. Evaluate parliamentary procedure as a speech activity and illustrate its use.

2. Show how certain radio and television program ideas or techniques might be adapted to classroom use.

3. Evaluate educational television and illustrate how a class might prepare a program for broadcast.

4. Plan a way to use puppets to gain better speech habits.

5. Discuss and illustrate how the sharing time may be made an effective language learning experience.

6. Evaluate some of the listening tests. Examine the Brown-Carlsen Listening Test, World Book Company (9–12) California Auding Test, Council on Auding Research, 146 Columbia Avenue, Redwood City, California (9–12), Listening Test, Educational Testing Service, Princeton, New Jersey, four levels.

7. Make a courtesy handbook to use in an intermediate classroom.

8. Make a collection of speech drills and verse to use with children who have articulation problems.

9. Some school systems have "listening posts" in some rooms. These consist of sets of earphones that the child uses while a recording is played. Investigate the literature relating to these or evaluate one in use.

Bibliography

Allen, R. Van. *Report of the Reading Study Project*, monograph. San Diego, Calif.: Department of Education, San Diego County, 1961.

Bilingual Schooling in the United States. Washington, D.C.: Office of Education, 1972.

Board of Education. *Reading and Language in the Elementary School.* Gary, Ind.: Gary Public Schools, 1962.

Brown, D. "Auding as the Primary Language Ability." Unpublished dissertation, Stanford University, 1954.

Brown, R. *Words and Things.* New York: Free Press, 1959.

Durrell, D., and A. Crossby. *Thirty Plays for Classroom Reading.* Boston: Plays, Inc., 1957.

Frye, A. "Syllabus for Speech," mimeographed. Sacramento, Calif.: California State Department of Instruction, 1969.

Giannangelo, D. M., and B. M. Frazer. "Listening: A Critical Skill That Must Be Taught." *Kappa Delta Research,* **12:** No. 2 (December 1975), 42–43.

Lapp, D., and J. Flood, *Teaching Reading to Every Child.* New York: Macmillan, 1978.

Lenneberg, E. H. "On Explaining Language." In *Language and Reading—An Interdisciplinary Approach,* ed. by D. V. Gunderson. Washington, D.C.: Center for Applied Linguistics, 1970.

McKee, P. *Reading for Meaning: Come Along,* Teacher's Manual. Boston: Houghton Mifflin, 1957.

Nichols, R. G., and L. A. Stevens. *Are You Listening?* New York: McGraw-Hill, 1957.

Patin, H. "Class and Caste in Urban Education." *Chicago School Journal,* **45** (1964), 305–310.

Piaget, J. *Plays, Dreams, and Imitation in Childhood.* New York: Norton, 1962.

Poole, I. "The Genetic Development of the Articulation of Consonant Sounds." Doctoral dissertation, University of Michigan, 1934.

Pooley, R. C. *Teaching of English Usage.* Urbana, Illinois: National Council of Teachers of English, 1974.

Rasmussen, C. *Speech Methods in the Elementary School.* New York: Ronald Press, 1949.

Russell, D., and E. F. Russell. *Listening Aids Through the Grades.* New York: Bureau of Publications, Teachers College, Columbia University, 1959.

Schiller, A., and others. *Language and How to Use It,* Book 4. Glenview, Ill.: Scott, Foresman, 1969.

Shaftel, G., and F. Schaftel. *Role Playing, The Problem Story.* New York: National Conference of Christians and Jews, 1952.

Skinner, B. F. *Beyond Freedom and Dignity.* New York: Knopf, 1972.

Smith, M. *Listening Habits and Speech Sound Discrimination.* Haywood, Calif.: Alameda County School Department, 1963.

Van Riper, C. *Nature of Stuttering.* Englewood Cliffs, N.J.: Prentice-Hall, 1971.

Van Riper, C. *Speech Correction: Principles and Methods.* Englewood Cliffs, N.J.: Prentice-Hall, 1972.

Van Riper, C. *Treatment of Stuttering.* Englewood Cliffs, N.J.: Prentice-Hall, 1973.

Van Riper, C., and K. Butler. *Speech in the Elementary Classroom.* New York: Harper & Row, 1955.

Wanat, S. F. "Language Acquisition: Basic Issues." *The Reading Teacher,* **25** (November 1971), 142–147.

Wilt, M. *Creativity in the Elementary School.* New York: Appleton-Century-Crofts, 1959.

Zintz, M. V. *The Reading Process,* 2nd ed. Dubuque: Ia.: Wm. C. Brown, 1975.

Chapter 7
Handwriting

What Are the Objectives of Handwriting Instruction?

Writing is an important means of communication. Therefore, the goal of handwriting instruction should be the introduction of effective and efficient skills. "Good" handwriting is immediately accessible to the reader, which is to say that the single most important criterion in judging handwriting is whether it can be read effortlessly. Other considerations, such as "penmanship," uniformity of size, shape, and spacing, conformity to a standard, printing versus cursive, are of distinctly secondary relevance.

Nonetheless, such considerations and concern for the quality of output may be the means of achieving the primary goal of effective handwriting skills. For this reason, handwriting is taught in the classroom in a manner generally directed toward conformity to a recognized standard. In addition, it is the responsibility of the classroom teacher to encourage students to develop a positive attitude toward handwriting and to nurture enthusiasm about skill attainment. Teachers influence the writing of children by example, by planned lessons, and by establishment and maintenance of standards. Teachers need to be able to use acceptable print script and cursive writing, diagnose the individual needs of children, and plan experiences to meet those needs. Teachers do this by understanding the nature of the task to be done, the materials and tools used, and current procedure and philosophy; by acquiring the personal skills needed; and by understanding the range of individual differences among learners.

Teachers then must become masters of the craft. This chapter will focus on the handwriting of the college student preparing to teach as well as describe the history and research that explain contemporary classroom practices.

When it is said that handwriting should be viewed

as a means of expression and not as an end in itself the purpose is to focus the attention of teachers and learners on the message rather than on the penmanship. This is a proper emphasis. There is no reason to master penmanship unless one wishes to communicate by writing. Unfortunately, some have interpreted this statement as a justification for neglecting instruction in the mechanics of writing. The inconsistency of this thinking is revealed when we look at typewriting. Here, too, the skill is a means of expression. But for a period when the skill is being mastered it becomes a legitimate end to study the habit-forming routines that constitute the skill.

The Role of Practice in the Development of Writing Skills

The psychology of habit formation in teaching handwriting is similar to that used in a sport like golf or tennis or in a skill like piano playing. The learner must first decide to seek mastery of the skill area. After that, each specific movement receives critical attention and drill. In tennis the coach will first illustrate a stroke, then repeat it in slow motion, and finally have the class perform each movement that he has demonstrated. He may even take the learner's arm and guide it through the movements if a correction is needed. The stroke will be practiced separately and in connection with other movements previously taught. In the same way the piano teacher will have the child play simple melodies and then do specific scale exercises to gain finger control. This approach is different from that usually practiced by teachers concerned about meaning and understanding.

Watching an athletics coach at work would be of great help to a handwriting teacher. One would observe that the coach is enthusiastic about the game and concerned about the actions of each player. A good coach or teacher praises good plays but also points out errors. Both are analyzed to make the players aware of their actions, using demonstrations by the coach and selected players. Rewards or trophies are given to the winners. Above all, it should be noted that athletic skills are per-fected through a great deal of individual practice as well as by actual playing of the game.

Although handwriting in the air is justly questioned as it is sometimes done, it may be of assistance in providing a mental image of the letter or word. However, such practice cannot replicate the actual movements involved in handwriting; exercise of the musculature necessary to create letters must simulate the precise activity required in handwriting. As a teacher writes a letter on the chalkboard, she has the class follow her movements, usually on paper but sometimes in the air, as if writing on an imaginary chalkboard. Class observers check variations that indicate confusion or faulty movements. Children learn a great deal from such careful observation of each other. At times, tracing over letters can correct faulty perception or habits.

Maturational Factors and Implications for Handwriting Instruction

Because we are concerned with muscular development and physical maturity in handwriting, there are some factors in the growth patterns of children that should be considered in our teaching.

Primary

The primary child frequently lacks the muscular coordination needed for writing. The powers that are developed are in the big muscles and nerve centers rather than in the small muscles of the fingers. We accept the dominant handedness of little children, which is usually observable at the age of three but may not be fully developed until the age of eight. Because farsightedness is normal in young children, we avoid long periods requiring close work with small details, remembering that patterns of progress will differ widely during the primary grades.

Instructional implications based on these factors would include the following practices. The little child is encouraged to work with clay, finger paint, or other materials that require finger coordination. Large mus-

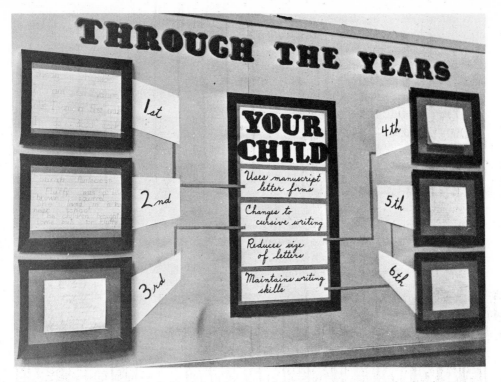

Both students and parents profit from an explanation of the achievement expected in handwriting. (Courtesy of the San Diego City Schools.)

cles are used by forming chalkboard letters about three inches high. When the child is practicing writing at his desk, either lined or unlined paper may be used. There is evidence (Halpin, 1976) to suggest that the kind of paper used at the primary level has no effect on the later quality of handwriting. Standard writing equipment is recommended, but the child should be allowed to use the instrument that he is most comfortable with. Speed is never emphasized. Copy work, which forces constant refocusing of the eye, is avoided. This especially applies to work on the board that the child copies on paper. No effort is made to keep the entire class together for instruction. Each child sets his own progress pattern. The aptitudes or skills of boys and girls should not be compared. Early writing efforts are usually characterized by great deliberateness.

Intermediate

In the intermediate grades the children gain greater control over both large-muscle activities and eye-hand coordination involving the small muscles. These are the years that influence lifetime habits with regard to musical instruments, skill with tools, and handwriting. The longer attention span results in a willingness to accept drill and repetition if the children understand the final goal. As students approach adolescence, the rapid growth of their hands may affect their handwriting. At this stage handwriting can be improved by exercises involving ovals and push-pulls. Older children sometimes express their egos through highly individualized writing, such as ringing the *i*'s instead of dotting them, making triangles of loops below the lines, or crossing the *t*'s in unconventional ways. Insistence on standard practices is left to your discretion and the rules of the school where you are teaching.

As students mature, their handwriting becomes smaller. Depending on school policy, a standardized writing scale may be introduced in the fourth grade. Adherence to the scale should not be mandatory. The scale should be viewed as a guideline by which students may judge their own handwriting and correct discernible defects.

At this time, speed is gradually encouraged and writer's clubs may be established that provide rewards for good penmanship.

The transition from print-script to cursive writing should be deferred until a later time with those children who experience difficulties. However, such children should receive instruction in *reading* cursive writing.

Developmental Sequence of Handwriting Acquisition

The teacher must always be cognizant of the personal variation that exists in skill acquisition and provide individualized attention to each child when necessary. Thus the following sequence of skills acquisition should be interpreted as a guideline only, to be fashioned and modified according to the needs of each child.

Kindergarten

By the end of kindergarten, most children may be expected to possess the following knowledge about handwriting:

1. The child should know that writing is a form of communication. It is a language shared through signs. Signs, names, and other written symbols have meaning.
2. In some cases, a child will be able to write (print script) his first name.
3. There will be some familiarity with the forms of print script writing as the teacher uses it in recording children's stories, labeling pictures, or writing names.

Grade 1

By the end of first grade many students will be able to

1. Write in print script form all letters, both capitals and lower case.
2. Write their name and address in print script.
3. Write simple original stories in print script.
4. Understand and practice proper spacing between letters of a word and between words of a sentence.

Grade 2

By the end of second grade a student should be able to

1. Use print script writing in daily lessons.
2. Understand and use margins, headings on papers, and spacing.
3. Write a friendly letter in print script.
4. Know the correct use of the terms *capital letter, period, question mark,* and *comma* as used between city and state and in dates.
5. Write print script with apparent ease.

Grade 3

By the end of third grade a student should be able to

1. Use both print script and cursive writing to meet his daily needs.
2. Write his own name, his school, city, and state in cursive style.
3. Analyze and improve his own written work.
4. Write with reasonable speed.

Grade 4

During fourth grade a student should be able to

1. Write a friendly letter (one or two paragraphs) in cursive.
2. Write notes to friends and classmates in cursive.
3. Use cursive to write original stories, poems, and reports.

4. Show evidence of retaining print-script writing as a supplementary tool.
5. Meet the grade standards as indicated on a handwriting scale.
6. Recognize and correct errors in letter formation.

Grade 5

By the end of fifth grade the student should be able to

1. Write a business letter.
2. Take notes in class.
3. Plan and present written reports.
4. Use pen and ink neatly.
5. Attempt cursive writing on stationery without lines.
6. Meet grade standards with regard to legibility and speed (fifty to sixty letters per minute).

Grade 6

By the end of sixth grade the student should be able to

1. Proofread and rewrite many first writing efforts.
2. Take pride in submitting neat, orderly papers in all class work.
3. Meet grade standards of legibility and speed.

Grades 7 and 8

By the time a student is in seventh or eighth grade he will have developed a personal style of writing. The language teacher should devote some time to writing instruction each week, especially for the students who have not developed a legible personal style.

History of Handwriting

Much that we teach about handwriting is the result of tradition. In the past "copperplate" writing (examples engraved on copper plate for printing by the early masters) was extensively used. Business schools taught Spencerian script, which was a beautiful, ornate writing, closely related to that devised by the Dutch teachers. Systems based on "arm movement" became popular in the schools. These consisted of a carefully organized series of exercises designed to train the individual to write rhythmically. The writing arm rested on the forearm muscle, and finger movement was avoided. One of the reasons for the wide acceptance of this method is that much of the fatigue associated with long periods of writing was avoided. The exercises consisted of a series of continuous ovals and "push-pulls" or were designed to give practice in writing individual letters and their parts. Students were encouraged to complete sets of exercises of high enough quality to receive certificates of merit and pins awarded by the publishers.

Some have criticized exercises of this type as being so unrelated to actual writing as to be isolated skills; one may learn how to make ovals but not necessarily how to write. A discouraged teacher is apt to accept such criticism and justify neglect of writing practice. On the other hand, there is a great deal of evidence that writing drills did produce excellent and even beautiful handwriting or calligraphy. Many students were actually self-taught by the manuals because their teachers were not masters of the system. Although all students did not become calligraphers, neither did all become excellent readers, mathematicians, musicians, or artists. Nearly all systems used today involve a modification of those in the past.

The reform movement in penmanship instruction that was started in England by William Morris (1834–1896) is still growing. This is an effort to return to the forms used at the time of the Renaissance. In the schools of England one finds systems based on this influence. That of Marion Richardson is an extension of the use of "print-script" writing in the primary grades. It is called Italic writing. This is a form of print first used by Aldo Manuzio in Italy during the Renaissance; Virgil was the first author printed in this type (1501). The current revival is based on the desire to find a script that is both beautiful and legible but that still expresses individuality. No claim is made concerning speed. Italic writing uses a flat pen held at a 45-degree angle, which gives a thick descending line and thin ascending line. The oval, rather than the circle, is its basic movement.

Sing a song of sixpence,
Pocket full of rye;
Four & twenty blackbirds
Baked in a pie.
When the pie was opened
The birds began to sing
Wasn't it a dainty dish
To set before a King.?

An exercise in modern italic script, as used in many European schools.

Many of the letters appear connected and may be so if the writer wishes.

Experiments with the typewriter in the elementary school date back to at least 1927. All such studies have indicated that children enjoy the experience and achieve some skill in the use of the machines. Kindergarten teachers report that as a prewriting experience it is an effective way to teach letter names and aspects of visual discrimination. Children in the upper grades profit from summer schools that have courses in typing. The typewriter appears to provide a bridge between their advanced ideas and the lack of physical maturity for a large amount of handwriting.

It would be impractical to assume that typewriting skill would replace the need for learning to write either print script or cursive writing. The ability to write a neat, legible hand with reasonable speed and without strain is essential in the modern curriculum.

Modern trends in handwriting instruction reflect current understanding of factors in child growth and recent study; however, none can be said to be universally acceptable or based on such absolute information

that future change is impossible. In comparison with the past, these changes may be observed:

1. Cursive writing is losing its place as a recognized part of the early primary program. The simpler print-script writing is preferred (Groff, 1975). Print script is being accepted as desirable writing in all grades.
2. Children no longer trace letter forms except under special circumstances.
3. Children who show a strong preference for writing with the left hand are no longer required to learn to write with the right hand.
4. The use of the rhythmic aids is discouraged. The size and shape of the various letters are so different that an absolute conformity to set rhythm is unnatural.
5. Accessory drills that presumably contribute rhythm and freedom in muscular movement are minimized. Ovals and related exercises are used much less than in the past.
6. There is less emphasis on speed in writing.
7. Fountain, ballpoint, and felt pens are used in classroom practice.
8. Such incentives as penmanship certificates and pins are not widely used, although still available.

For Discussion

1. How can children be led to appreciate the importance of learning to write skillfully?

2. What information do you find in children's encyclopedias that might be used for classroom research on the alphabet?

3. Find an example of Spencerian writing, or, if possible, a person who can write this script. Defend the modern point of view that such art is not needed in writing.

4. Introduce the term *calligraphy* and display illustrations of various styles.

5. Would it be desirable to require all teachers to pass a blackboard writing test before granting them authority to teach?

6. Make a collection of handwriting samples written by children in other countries. Contrast the style and quality of handwriting demonstrated.

7. In the Orient writing instruments such as the ink brush are regarded as objects of art. Should we try to develop an attitude that writing is an art form?

8. How can a typewriter be used as a teaching machine?

How Is Print-Script (or Manuscript) Writing Taught?

Print-script writing (also called manuscript writing) started in England. In 1919 Miss S. A. Golds of St. George the Martyr-School, London, published a copybook called *A Guide to the Teaching of Manuscript Writing*.

In 1922 a course taught by Marjorie Wise of England at Columbia University introduced print script to the American schools. Since that time the use of this simple form of lettering has been accepted in nearly all the schools of the United States.

The term *cursive* means "running" or "connected"; the terms *print script* and *manuscript* refer to writing in which each letter is separately formed, as in printer's type. The major differences are contrasted in Table 7-1.

The use of print script in the primary grades has been accepted for the following reasons:

1. Primary children learn only one alphabet for reading and writing.
2. With its three basic strokes—i.e., circles, arcs, and straight lines—print script is easier for the young child to learn.
3. Print script is more legible than cursive and with practice may be written rapidly.
4. Children who master print script do a great deal more writing of a creative nature than children who must master the cursive form.

Experiences in Writing Readiness

Three kinds of experiences lead to writing readiness:

1. Manipulative Experiences

The first group of experiences can be described as manipulative. These are designed to strengthen muscles needed for writing and to gain control over tools used in writing. Children develop the small muscles of the hands through playing with toys, dialing the telephone, setting the table, changing a doll's clothes, putting puzzles together, cutting with scissors, finger painting, and

TABLE 7-1. Differences Between Print-Script and Cursive Writing

Print Script	Cursive
Letters are made separately.	Letters are joined.
Pencil is lifted at the end of each letter or stroke.	Pencil is lifted at the end of each word.
Letters are made with circles, parts of circles, and straight lines.	Letters are made with overstrokes, understrokes, connected strokes, and ovals.
Letters are spaced to form words. Space between letters is controlled by the shape of the letter. The *i* and the *j* are dotted and the *t* is crossed immediately after the vertical stroke is made.	Spacing between letters is controlled by the slant and manner of making connective strokes. The letters *i* and *j* are dotted and the *t* is crossed after the completion of the word.
Letters closely resemble print and are therefore legible and easy to read.	Letters are unlike those on the printed page.
Small letters and capitals are different except for *c, o, s, p, v, w, x,* and *z.*	Small letters and capitals are different.

clay modeling. They draw or scribble with chalk at the chalkboard or with crayons on large sheets of paper. It is well to remember that scribbling is writing and that it is the child's first means of identifying himself with the writing process until he is ready to be taught the letter forms. In the eighteenth and early nineteenth centuries Johann Pestalozzi (1746–1827) had children draw geometric forms on slates as he told stories. These were actually exercises in writing readiness.

2. Oral Expression

The second group of experiences is designed to increase the child's ability in the use of language. It is futile for children to learn to write before they can express their ideas orally. Beginners must have many experiences that stimulate the desire for self-expression. As they listen to stories and poems, look at pictures, dictate stories and letters, or make up songs, they should be encouraged to comment freely. As children see their ideas written by the teacher in a letter or an invitation, writing becomes a magic tool for extending speech. With this recognition comes not only an understanding of the usefulness of writing but also a strong personal desire to perform the writing task.

3. Practice in Writing Movements

The third group consists of experiences designed to give practice to the basic movements of writing itself. These are usually started at the chalkboard, where only large muscles are involved. The purpose is to understand certain letter forms and how they are created. Circles are first drawn by the children. They are given directions as to the starting place. Following this, the children are asked to look at the number 2 on the clock. When a circle is made it is best to start where the 2 would be if you were making a clock. Children draw clocks, doughnuts, balls, soap bubbles, and Halloween faces, or they "set" a table with a circle for the plate and lines for the knife, fork, and spoon. Some like to attempt such advanced circles as a string of beads, a bunch of grapes, a Christmas tree with ornaments, an umbrella, or a cat.

Children develop the small muscles of the hands through playing with toys, putting puzzles together, and finger painting. (Photo by Linda Lungren.)

Combinations of circles and straight lines can be made by drawing a square wagon with wheels, making a turkey with tail feathers, or making stick figures with round heads.

As children transfer this activity to paper, some supervision is necessary to establish certain habits. All lines are made from top to bottom and left to right. All circles are started at the two o'clock position or where one would start to make the letter *c* and move toward the left.

As soon as possible—even at the readiness period—writing should say something. Children should be encouraged to label their picture of a cat with the word; the letters *c a t* might be copied from a teacher-made example. The child should know the names of these letters before writing them and should realize that he has made a word when he finishes. Thus knowing the letter names and the ability to read what is written are a part of writing readiness.

Introducing Handwriting in the Classroom

The following example illustrates an effective approach that may be used to introduce handwriting: A teacher placed her chair close to the chalkboard while a small group of children stood about her. She remained in a seated position so that she was writing at their eye level. The teacher said, "Today we are going to write. We must first learn to hold the chalk so that it will make a soft, white line. If it squeaks, it is trying to tell you that you are not holding it right."

The teacher then demonstrated how to hold the chalk, first in the right hand and then in the left. "Good writers do it this way. I put my pointer [index] fingertip at the end of the chalk, the middle fingertip next to it, and my thumb underneath. Now let's see if you can do this." After each child had held the chalk, the teacher continued: "I am going to write the name of one of the children in our reader. Watch and see where I start each letter." The teacher wrote each letter slowly, calling attention to the letters that start at the top line and the letters that start in between the lines. "Now I will do it again," the teacher told them. "You will tell me everything I must do." The children, with the teacher prompting, directed the action through a second writing of the word. The original word remained on the board as a guide and reminder. "Let's see how well we have written," the teacher remarked. "Bobby, draw your fingers along the bottom of the letters to see if they sit tightly on the line. Are they all right? Mary, trace your finger along the tops of the low letters to see if they are even. And now, Eric, check the tall letters to see if they start at the top line."

After these checks to sharpen visual discrimination had been made, the teacher continued. "I want each of you to find a place at the chalkboard. I have written the lines on the board. Find the line that is even with your eyes. That is the one you will write on. Find your place and then write the same word that I did." The teacher gave individual help as needed. With some groups it would be better to have one child demonstrate what is to be done before the others try. After each child had appraised his work, the teacher had them write the word a second time.

Other similar lessons teaching spacing between words, as well as other words and letters, should be done at the board before writing on paper is started at the desk.

If a section of the board can be reserved, writing practice during free time will be a popular activity. The teacher can put an assignment at the top of the space such as "Write the names of three boys" or "Write three words that start with *B*."

When making the transition from chalkboard to paper—and until the child is able to write correctly from memory—he must have a copy from which to write. The copy should be made on the same kind of paper that the child normally uses. The letters should be well formed. The amount of work will be controlled by the amount of time free for supervision, as well as by the fatigue factor. Most children tire after writing for about ten minutes.

Mechanics of Script Writing

As illustrated, various systems of print script form the letters in different ways. Usually a school system selects one program and attempts to have a common form throughout all grades. Spacing is a problem in all systems. The instruction to leave the space of the letter *o* between words and of one hump of the *n* between letters means little to beginners. Teachers frequently say, "One finger between letters and two fingers between words." The problem is that letters made of straight lines should be closer together than those with curves in order to give the illusion of uniform spacing throughout.

All writing that is made available to the child for

observation or for copy should be properly spaced and aligned. Occasional comments by the teacher may be used to strengthen the child's impression of well-spaced letters and perfectly straight lines. But in the early stage of writing instruction the child needs to concentrate chiefly on getting a clear visual image of the letters he writes and on learning the correct order of making the strokes. After the child has learned to form the letters properly, there will be plenty of time for him to master the art of letter arrangement.

The paper should be positioned in front of the child in such a way as to facilitate maximum ease in forming letters. The position may vary slightly from child to child but in general will be parallel with the lines of the desk. The paper is moved as the child writes. Standard writing equipment is made available, along with chalk, crayons, and other writing utensils. The child should experiment with the various writing tools to ascertain which affords the most comfortable grip that can be sustained with a minimum of fatigue. Ordinarily, a child can write easily while seated in a properly fitted chair and desk. Some small children write better if they can stand while writing. This is especially true if they are writing on large or oversize easel paper.

Early handwriting instruction should use whole words that have real meaning for the children—words they are interested in and that are easy to write. It will probably be necessary to contrive ways to bring in

When properly positioned, writing can be fun as well as an effective means of communication.

words like *queen, quiet, quail, fox, fix, box, excuse, zebra, zoo, buzz,* and *dozen,* in order to teach the letters *q, x, z,* which are not frequently used. The entire alphabet must be taught.

A study by Coleman (1970) indicated that the lowercase letters presented the following order of difficulty for beginners: *l, o, i, f, x, s, t, v, r, g, a, b, h, j, p, n, m, z, q, k, y, d, c, e, w, u.* The letters *p, q, b,* and *d* give trouble because of their obvious structural similarities. Many programs present the letters in similar groups. One text teaches *o, a, d, q, g, b, p, c,* and *e* as Group One. The letters that use straight lines are Group Two: *l, t, i, f, j, n, m, r, h, u, w, y, r, z,* and *k.* The letter *s* is taught as a continuous series of curves. The capital letters are usually taught in association with children's names. Those identical in shape with their small letter counterparts pose few problems. These are *O, C, S, V, X,* and *Z* in most programs. Making an ABC book gives practice with capital letters.

The following are frequent errors: rounding straight lines and angles, making letters upside down and backward, forming lines so that they do not meet at the proper places, and making incomplete letters. These errors can be prevented by careful initial teaching, although all children make some errors when involved in the thought of what they are writing. With respect to closure errors it is easier for children to join the circle and straight line strokes if the *c* rather than the complete oval is used for parts of the letters *a, d, b, g,* and *q.*

A factor that governs the formation of some printscript letters is that of ease of transfer to cursive writing. The reason for starting the letter *e* with the straight line, then the circle, is simply that this is the way the cursive letter is formed. It may well be that it is wiser to consider the letters in one alphabet unrelated to the other.

As the teacher writes she should call attention to details, naming the letters and commenting on the size, shape, and direction of strokes. She should watch the child write the word, comment favorably on letters that are well formed, and give additional instruction when it is needed. If a particular letter proves difficult, the child should give it additional practice. When introducing letters in a word or isolating a difficult letter for study, the teacher may give more time to demonstration and discussion: "The *t* is a tall letter. We start at the top, go down, and try to make it very straight. We cross it near the top from left to right. The *t* is not quite so tall as an *l,* but it is taller than *i,* or *m,* or *n''* (depending on which letter the children already know).

At this point it is well for you as a teacher to bear in mind that when a child begins to write he cannot remember everything he has been told. Only two things are essential: (1) he must form the letters in fair approximation to the copy, and (2) he must make every stroke in the correct direction as he forms his letters. If he cannot do both, he probably is not ready to write and would profit more from nonwriting activities at this time.

The effectiveness of the practice of tracing, except in special problem cases, has been questioned (Ackov and Greff, 1975). If the child cannot make the strokes without the tedious, time-consuming muscular drill involved in tracing, he is hardly ready for handwriting instruction. And if the child, in tracing, puts all his attention on the segment of line that he is attempting to follow at the moment, he loses sight of the letter or word as a whole, and so at the end of the lesson may be able to write no better than at the beginning.

In learning to write, as in other kinds of growth, all children pass through the same general stages of development. The rate of progress and the time at which each level of achievement is reached will vary according to the individual differences of the children themselves. It is not uncommon for a child to start slowly and then pick up speed as he matures, or for another to start rapidly and then "slow down" later. Nevertheless, at any given time there will be enough children with similar needs to make some group instruction possible. In writing, as in reading, groups must be small enough to permit close personal teacher supervision of each child's work. This is true whether the writing is done on the board or on paper.

A good lesson in handwriting contains five elements: (1) visualization, (2) analysis, (3) practice, (4) comparison or evaluation, and (5) correction.

Note the following in teaching the child to write his name:

1. *Visualization*. The teacher has prepared a card (3 × 5) with the name of each child. "I wonder how many can read each other's names. As I go through the cards, the person whose name it is will call on another child to read it. After all have been read, I will give you your name cards."
2. *Analysis*. "How many have an *e* in their name? Trent, show us how to make an *e*. This is one letter that does not start at the top. Does anyone have an *s* in his or her name? Stacy, show us how to make an *s*. Look at each letter in your name. Are there any you think we should practice?"
3. *Practice*. "Now go to the board and put an *x* at the eye-level line where you will start. Write your name once. When you have finished, go over your name card and see if each letter is correct."
4. *Evaluation*. "How many have all the letters on the line? How many have all the letters right? How many have the space between letters right?"
5. *Correction*. "Now let us write our names once more and make them better. You are to keep the name card at your desk and use it whenever you wish to write your name."

Handwriting Worksheets

In the first grade many lessons in handwriting will require the teacher to prepare a worksheet. Normally these worksheets should meet the following standards:

1. The learner's attention is focused on a few handwriting difficulties.
2. The worksheet contains enough guidance so that possible errors will be avoided.
3. Although the drill is on a single element, the practice results in the feeling that something has been written.
4. There is enough practice to give a sense of purpose to the lesson, but not so much that there is physical strain.

The first thing on the worksheet should be the letters or word demonstrated by the teacher. There may be arrows or other markers to show where the writer starts each letter and to show the direction of the strokes. The first stroke might be in red, the second in yellow, and the third in blue.

The second part of the worksheet may consist of practice on one or two letters. An example should be given and spaces should be made indicating how many "copies" of each letter are required.

Finally, these letters should be put together to form a word or sentence. Sometimes only part of a word is given, with blanks left for the missing letters. Other worksheets may indicate by a picture what word is to be written. As soon as the child is ready, the writing should become personal. The worksheet may start a letter by having printed on it: "Dear Santa, Please bring me . . . . ."

Worksheets and materials can be kept in convenient storage areas so that students may help themselves. (Photo by Linda Lungren.)

Handwriting Practice

After the children have had practice forming letters and combining them into words and sentences, they should be engaged in a great deal of personal writing, using model alphabet charts as a guide. "Home-made" greeting cards provide writing practice. These cards may then be sent to a child who is ill, or they may be used for birthdays, Christmas or Chanukah greetings, Mother's Day remembrance, or Valentine's Day. Labeling also provides excellent writing practice. Children can make their own flash cards for drill in reading. But best of all are the stories written to illustrate a picture or

to entertain the group. Such stories will be discussed later under creative writing.

There are standardized scales to evaluate print-script writing. However, few children can use them. A chart that asks the child to check the following elements will serve for most evaluation needed at this grade:

Did you make each letter the way it is on the chart?
Are your letters on the line?
Are your down strokes straight?
Are your round letters like a circle?
Did you leave enough space between words?

Suggestions for Generating Interest in Handwriting Instruction

There are a number of devices that teachers can use to add interest to the writing practice. Here are some of them:

Ask the children to listen carefully to a word description to see if they can identify a letter that is on the alphabet chart. The teacher says, "I am thinking of a small letter that is made with a circle and then a tall stick." The child who identifies *d* goes to the board and writes it. The teacher then describes another letter.

The teacher asks, "Who can find the letter that comes before *m*? What is its name?" The child who identifies the letter may write it on the board. A variation is to ask, "What letter comes after *m*?"

Each child in turn goes to the front of the room and gives his name and initials. "My name is Mildred Cunningham. My initials are M. C." Then she writes them on the board. Or a child may write a classmate's initials on the board and have the class identify the person.

A magic slate with transparent acetate sheets can be bought at a novelty store. Insert a sheet of paper with the letters, words, or numbers you wish the child to practice. The children trace over these with a crayon—or, better, write under the examples. These can be used many times because the crayon marks can be wiped off.

One teacher starts her group by saying, "We are going to make pumpkins today. Watch how I make one." The teacher uses the guide words "One around.'' After the children have made a row of pump-kins, the teacher says, "Let's put our pumpkins beside a fence post. Now look again," the teacher says, "be-cause you have made the letter *a*.''

Another teacher talks about the letters that are done only on one floor such as *a, c, e, m*. Other letters are upstairs letters like *d, b, h, l*. Basement letters are *g, j, p, y*.

Sometimes children do a better job of alignment if they are told, "Let's see if we can keep our letters sit-ting straight on a shelf.''

After the children have spent several lessons on lines, circles, their names, and single words, one teacher starts with a sentence such as "I am a toy.'' After the unlined paper is distributed the children are asked to fold the paper in half lengthwise, then fold the bottom half to the center fold. This provides folded lines to follow. The children write the sentence on the bottom fold and then draw a picture in the top half to il-lustrate their sentence.

For Discussion

1. Why is it important that early writing practice re-sult in a word?

2. What additional activities can you suggest to make "handwriting" interesting to students?

3. Plan a worksheet that will provide for the steps in a writing lesson suggested in this chapter or evaluate a worksheet in a commercial workbook designed to teach handwriting skills.

How Do Teachers Guide the Child's Learning When Transferring from Print Script to Cursive Writing?

Although there are some school systems that make no effort to teach any form of writing but print script, the majority do introduce cursive writing in either the late second grade or the third grade. This change is more the result of response to cultural tradition than to educa-tional merit. There is evidence (Hildreth, 1960) to in-dicate that, with practice, print-script writing can be written as rapidly as cursive writing. It remains a legi-ble and easy form of writing. It also assumes enough personality so that signatures in print script are now legal. The reason for changing from print script to cur-sive may simply be the child's, parents', and/or teacher's desire. Many children attempt to imitate "adult," or cursive, writing and need direction to do it correctly. Parents may think that cursive writing is "better" than print script. Finally, there is a strong traditional force within the teaching group. Upper-grade teachers using cursive writing often seem unwilling to change. Thus the child must change to conform to the teacher's writing pattern. Another factor in this situa-tion is that cursive seems to be a teaching specific that indicates educational growth. Teachers often like to in-troduce something new; the home reaction is generally that "children in Ms. Hess's class are certainly making progress.''

Surely it makes sense for the child to use print script as often as possible after having mastered this skill. Children may more readily express their ideas in the written form throughout the second and third grades if they use print script. Some children may be ready to make the transition from print to cursive when very young, late in the second grade, whereas others may not be ready for this transition until later in their school career. Even those beginning an early transition should not be rushed. Children should continue to write spell-ing words and answers to test questions in the form of writing that is best for them. Even after cursive has been mastered, there will be occasions throughout all grade levels to use print-script skills in such exercises as filling out forms, writing invitations, and designing greeting cards or posters.

The major aspect of readiness for training in cur-sive writing is the ability to read words written in it. Members of the family will frequently teach a child to "write" rather than "print" his name. Teachers will start using cursive to present assignments and words in the spelling lessons. Children play games with their sight vocabulary in both printed and cursive forms. Other factors—such as desire to write, adequate physi-cal development, and the ability to use print script—

should be considered. Children who are just beginning to understand how to read should not face the additional problem of learning a new way to write.

A few children will make the transfer in imitation of the writing of parents or older children. The change is made with very little guidance, and penmanship instruction is only a matter of perfecting the new forms. These children do not need to follow any of the instructional patterns suggested here.

The transfer to cursive should conform to the principle of moving from the simple to the complex. Experience indicates that the small or lowercase letters should be introduced first, in the following order: *l, e, i, t, u, n, m, h, k, w, o, b, v, x, y, j, f, s, p, r, c, a, d, g, q, z.*

Capital letters, with the exception of *I*, should be taught in association with the children's names. Rather than drill on all of them in the third grade, it is best to practice them in usage with an example and teacher guidance.

The best equipment to use is an ordinary lead pencil at least six inches long, with soft lead (No. 2). In general, the paper should be ruled. Because some children have a tendency to write too small, wide-ruled paper is generally recommended. The following represents a typical sequence of introducing note paper of given specification for each grade:

Grade 1	At first, unruled paper (without lines), 12- by 18-inch, folded. Later, 1-inch ruled paper.
Grade 2	9- by 12-inch, ruled ½-inch alternating light and heavy lines. Ruled 1-inch light, long way.
Grade 3	At first, ½-inch alternating light and heavy lines. Later, ⅝-inch, one space for tall letters.
Grade 4	Reduce to ½-inch as children are ready.
Grades 5, 6	Rules ½-inch, reducing to ⅜-inch. ⅜-inch spacing.

It is good classroom management to have a jar of sharpened pencils ready (having been prepared by a monitor) so that a pencil with a broken point can be exchanged for a new one without class interruption.

Slanted cursive writing is best introduced as a completely new form of writing. Before distributing paper to the class, the teacher might make remarks like this:

Many of you have noticed that your mothers and fathers do not use print-script writing. They may be using a form of writing called "cursive." (The teacher writes *cursive* on the chalkboard.) Some of you have written your names or other words in cursive. Let's see how cursive writing differs from the print script that we have been using. I will write the name of our town on the board in this new writing. You will see that the letters are slanted and joined. We have been writing with our papers directly in front of us. It will be easier to write this new way if you slant your paper. For those who are right-handed, the paper should slant to the left, with the bottom corner pointing toward your heart. If you are left-handed, the paper should slant to the right.

The exact position for each person will differ according to arm length. These variations may be suggested to the individual as the teacher observes his writing.

Introducing Cursive Writing

Minkoff (1975) suggests that the transition from print-script to cursive writing may best be accomplished by discussing the rationale of the "new" writing form. The characters of cursive writing "can be explained as the almost inevitable result of the pressure of speed on print. . . . writing quickly changes the shapes of letters in predictable ways,[resulting] in connected letters, and [requiring] that the pencil be lifted only occasionally" (p. 203). Minkoff concludes that such analysis of cursive letter formation is superior to rote memorization in promoting the acquisition of cursive writing skills.

Once the rationale for the transition has been established, a series of lessons on proper letter formation may be undertaken:

1. Begin by introducing guidelines. The teacher might say: "Watch while I make some lines on the board. Notice how each line slants the same as the other lines. I want them to slant only a little. I am going to leave a space between each pair of lines. Now you may make three pairs of slanted lines. The first letter we make will be the letter *l*. I will start at the

bottom of the first slanted line, make a curved line to the top of the second slanted line, and then make a curved line along the same slant in the middle of the two slanted lines. At the bottom, finish with a small upward curve. Now you try it. Make an *l* with each guideline. Now, make three guidelines and this time we will make two letter *l*'s that join. We might say, 'Up, around, straight down; up, around, straight down.' '' [Observe to see that the letters are neither too wide nor too thin.]

2. Demonstrate the letter *l* using only half of a slanted line as a guide. Use the same three steps. Follow this with the letter *i*.

3. Introduce the letter *t*. Start by making guidelines on two thirds of the writing space. The cross on the *t* is one half the distance between the top and bottom writing lines. The children should now start to use these letters in words. The teacher might say: ''I am thinking of some words that use the letters we have practiced. If I put the guidelines for the words on the board, I wonder how many of you will be able to write the word. Copy the guidelines on your paper before you write the word. Yes, the words are *ill* and *tell*. Can you think of another word that we can write with these letters? Yes, we could write *tile*. What guidelines will we need? See how

Direct assistance should be given in guiding handwriting practice. (Photo by Linda Lungren.)

many other words you can think of using *i*, *e*, *l*, and *t*. We'll compare lists after I have helped some children with their writing.'' Some children will think of only two or three. Possible words include *little, let, lie, lit, tie, title, tell, it, ill, tilt, eel,* and *tee*.

4. Introduce the letter *u*. Start by making two short guidelines in groups of three. Use guide phrases such as ''Up, down, around; up, down, around.'' The letter *n* is made with groups of two small guidelines. This letter begins with a hump that starts a space before the first guideline. Guide words such as ''Up, over, down, up, over, down, up'' may be used. The letter *m* is made with groups of three guidelines. The first stroke is the hump, a space before the first guideline. Now a number of words may be written. ''Instead of starting with guidelines, write the word, then put in the slanted guidelines to see if you have the proper slant. I wonder how many words you can make using *i*, *l*, *t*, *e*, *m*, *n*, and *u*.'' Practice on these letters should continue for several days.

5. Introduce the letter *h*. This is a combination of *t* and *n*. As a guide one needs a long line and a short line. Write words: *hit, hen, hill, him, the, then, them*. The letter *s* presents a special problem. Some prefer a square as a guide rather than a slanted line. The upstroke goes to the corner of the square and the downstroke follows straight down before making the curve.

6. Introduce the term ''bridge.'' The new letters are *w*, *o*, *b*, and *r*. In illustrating the *w*, start by making groups of three lines as for *m*. The teacher might say: ''We will make the letter *w* by starting as if we were making the letter *u*. At the end, we go up once more, then make a bridge. This bridge sags a little. The letter *o* does not need a guideline but the bridge should be stressed. For the letter *b*, we need only a long line as a guide. We first make the letter *l* then close the ending by coming around as one would make an *o* and end with a bridge.''

7. Introduce these words to write: *will, bill, we, be, wet, bet, tub, new, bum*. Practice several days on

words with the bridge. Note that when *e*, *i*, *r* follow a letter with a bridge, they start in a different way. Combinations to be practiced at this point are *os, or, ox, ve, br*. The next letter to study is *k*. This letter is like *h*. It starts as if one were writing *l*, then instead of a letter like *n*, one goes around and makes a little circle, then comes down to finish the letter. If one covers a part of the letters *k* and *h*, one should see *l*.

8. Introduce the letters *a*, *g*, *d*, and *q*, which contain the oval, the most difficult aspect of transfer from print script to cursive. One reason for insisting that when learning print script the child start his circles at the two o'clock position (as in the letter *c*) is to aid in this transfer. Start by having the child make a series of ''eggs that tip or of leaves on a stem.'' If short slanted lines are used, start at the top of these guidelines, make the oval by returning to the starting point, then follow the guideline down to make the connecting stroke.

The Connected Print-Script Approach

Another method that might be described as ''connected print script'' would be handled in the following manner: Have the child print a word like *good*. Then have the child trace the word he has printed, without raising his pencil. This, of course, means that he will connect the letters. As the child retraces, provide directions such as: ''Around, down, make the tail on the *g*; now, without raising your pencil, go up and over to the top of the letter *o*, around the *o*, and, without raising your pencil, slide over to the other *o* and around it, *goo*; without raising your pencil, slide over to the round part of the letter *d*, go around and up on the stick stroke, down again, and add a tail stroke *good*.'' Next let the child try to write the word *good* without retracing the print script.

Only letters that connect almost automatically should be taught by this connective method. The following primary words have letters that are easy for children to connect:

1. act	21. goat	41. hut	61. pail
2. add	22. gold	42. it	62. pat
3. all	23. good	43. lad	63. path
4. at	24. got	44. laid	64. pig
5. auto	25. ha	45. lap	65. pool
6. call	26. had	46. late	66. pop
7. cloth	27. hail	47. laugh	67. pot
8. cloud	28. hall	48. lip	68. pull
9. cold	29. hat	49. little	69. put
10. cup	30. hill	50. load	70. tag
11. cut	31. hid	51. log	71. tail
12. dad	32. hit	52. lot	72. tall
13. did	33. hog	53. oat	73. tap
14. dig	34. hold	54. o'clock	74. till
15. do	35. hole	55. oh	75. to
16. dog	36. hood	56. old	76. too
17. dot	37. hop	57. out	77. tool
18. dug	38. hot	58. pa	78. tooth
19. glad	39. hug	59. pad	79. up
20. go	40. hunt	60. paid	

The teacher starts with words containing letters that are alike in cursive and print script. These would contain the small letters *i, t, o, n, m, e, h, l, u, d, c* and the capital letters *B, C, K, L, O, P, R, U.* A word is written in print script on the board as an example for the children to observe. The word *it* would be printed at a slant. The teacher then adds a "reach stroke," going to the first letter and from the first to the second. An ending stroke for the word is added. Then the teacher says: "Now I am going to do it without patching [guiding dots]. Reach for the *i*. Now make the *i* lean right back against the reach line. Reach high for the *t*. Lean the *t* in the middle and dot the *i*. Let's do it again but this time you tell me what to do. First we will put in patch lines; then we will do it without patching." After this each child practices at the board.

This type of lesson is repeated with *in, me, he, let, nut, do, cut, ice, mud, hut, den, cent, nice, home, mile, come, then, did.* Each lesson contains these steps: the word is written first in slanted print script, reach strokes are patched in, the word is written without patching, and children steer the teacher's chalk through the word before writing it under supervision. Practice cards are provided that illustrate these steps for all the other letters. In the independent writing of the children during this period both cursive and print script appear. Both are expected—and permitted.

When parents ask about teaching their children to

The letters *b, e, f, r, k, s, z* must be taught as specific difficulties because of the lack of form correspondence between the print-script and cursive representations. The cursive that results from the connective method is vertical. Slant is obtained by turning the paper. Some teachers prefer to introduce the connective method by using dotted lines to show the cursive form on top of the print script. Children trace over these dotted lines as they master the new form.

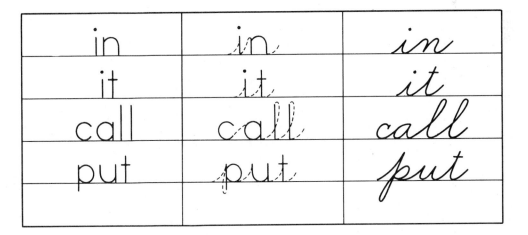

a c d g h i j l m

a c d g h i j l m

a c d g h i j l m

n o p q t u v w x y

n o p q t u v w x y

n o p q t u v w x y

b e f r k s z

b e f r k s z

a clown doll

a clown doll

a clown doll

Connective approach for transition from print script to cursive.

write at home, the teacher may explain thus: "If a child is urged to write before he is ready, he frequently develops a feeling of tension, grips the pencil too tightly, and builds up a dislike for writing. Then, too, many young children's muscles are not developed enough for successful writing. Writing at school is supervised to avoid poor habits, such as gripping the pencil too tightly, incorrect letter formations, and poor position."

If, however, the child is eager to write and seems ready, parents might provide the child with a variety of writing equipment (e.g., pencil, crayon), allowing him or her to select the one best suited, along with unlined paper. Print-script letters may then be taught according to the school's alphabet specifications obtained from the child's teacher. Instruction should deal mainly with lowercase letters; capital letters should be treated only when beginning proper names.

How May Good Cursive Writing Be Achieved and Maintained?

There are a number of well-planned modern handwriting programs available for use in schools. The first step toward achieving good cursive writing is to select or devise a system of handwriting and then follow it with determination and consistency.

Determination is needed because so often the short time allowed for handwriting practice gets crowded out of the school day. In most intermediate grades only about sixty minutes a week, divided into three twenty-minute sessions on Monday, Wednesday, and Friday, are available for handwriting drill. This is enough time if the practices stressed are consistently followed in all the writing of the child. These short sessions are usually planned to provide practice on a single element in writing. It may concern the formation of a letter, spacing, alignment, slant, connecting strokes, or ending stroke. Following the specific instruction, it is important that the new elements be incorporated in meaningful writing activities. A brief period may be set aside when each child may examine his or her writing productions according to a standard.

Handwriting Scales

Handwriting scales are available with nearly all commercial programs. Children find these difficult to use in analyzing their own writing. There is no reason why any class or school cannot collect enough writing samples to develop its own standards or expectancies for each grade. The standardized scales can be used by teachers as they make judgments concerning the samples selected. Probably the most scientifically constructed scale is that devised by Leonard P. Ayres and published by the Educational Testing Service of Princeton, New Jersey. A major consideration is general quality of writing rather than specific style. This is difficult to determine if the writing being judged is vertical or backhand. Most individuals making such appraisals are also influenced by the formation of certain letters, such as capital *R* or small *r*. Noble and Noble and the Palmer Company have scales that diagnose specific writing problems of children practicing the methods published by these firms. The Zaner-Bloser Company makes available a small dictionary of letter forms that each child uses. This dictionary presents the letters of their system with a space for the child to make his own examples. These can be used as a record of a child's progress. As the child compares his present writing with his past work, he can note progress or weakness. This comparison serves much the same purpose as a standardized scale.

Many schools purchase an alphabet strip to place over the chalkboard as a constant point of reference for children as they write. This technique can be effective if it is made significant to the children. Some teachers have pictures drawn to go with each letter. In the lower grades the drawing of an apple for *a* will suffice, but the upper grades may require more challenging words such as *avocado* or *astronaut* to illustrate the letter *a*. Unfortunately, the space over the chalkboard may be an awkward point of reference. For some children the details of the letters are lost because of vision problems. A number of programs provide individual desk cards that are used by the children when they need to recall how a letter is made. In practice, these are more effective than the alphabet strip.

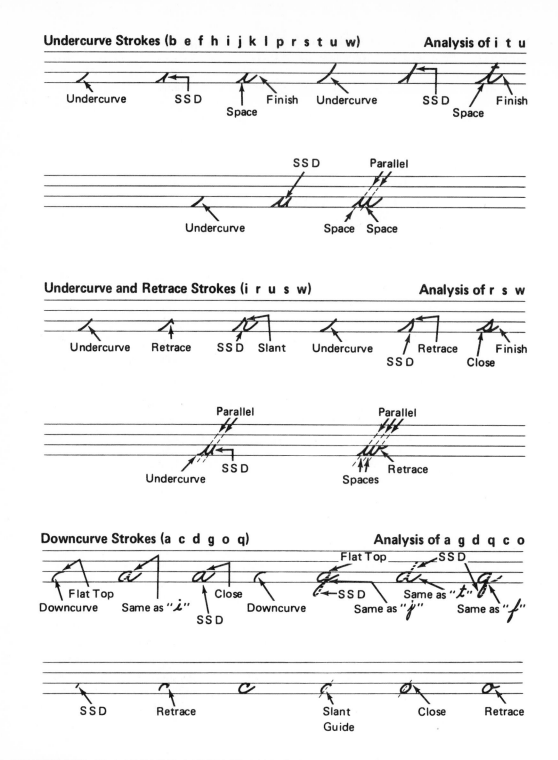

Undercurve Strokes (b e f h i j k l p r s t u w)   Analysis of i t u

Undercurve SS D Space Finish Undercurve SS D Space Finish

SS D Parallel

Undercurve Space Space

Undercurve and Retrace Strokes (i r u s w)   Analysis of r s w

Undercurve Retrace SS D Slant Undercurve SS D Retrace Close Finish

Parallel Parallel

Undercurve SS D Spaces Retrace

Downcurve Strokes (a c d g o q)   Analysis of a g d q c o

Flat Top SS D

Flat Top SS D Same as "*t*"

Downcurve Same as "*i*" Close Downcurve Same as "*j*" Same as "*f*"

SS D Retrace

SS D Retrace Slant Guide Close Retrace

Overcurve Strokes (h k m n v x y z)　　　Analysis of m n v x y z

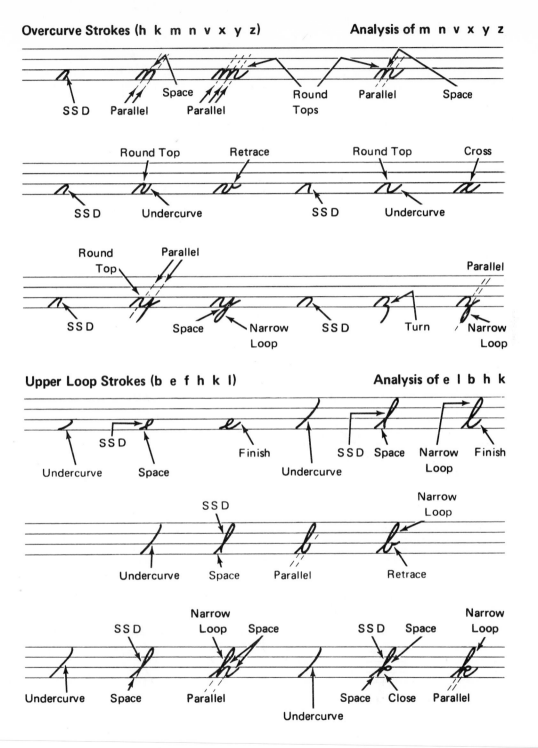

Upper Loop Strokes (b e f h k l)　　　Analysis of e l b h k

Lower Loop Strokes (f g j q y z)　　　　　　　　　　**Analysis of f j p**

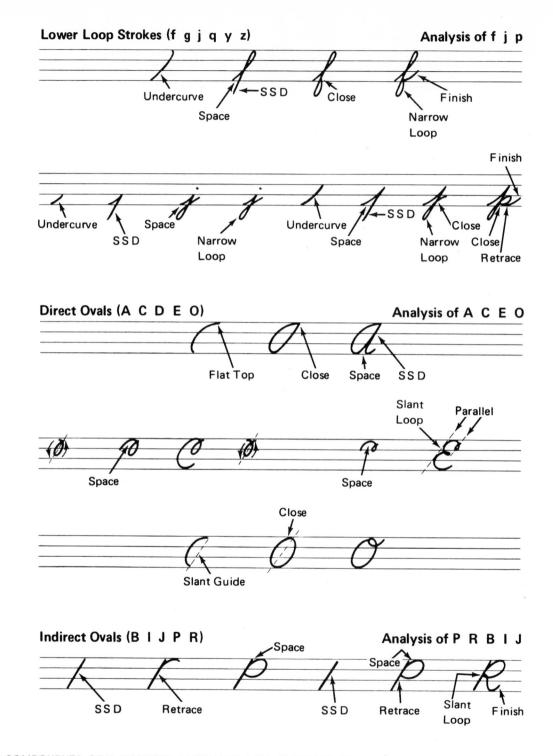

Undercurve　　　←SSD　　　Close　　　　Finish

Space　　　　　　　　　　　　　Narrow
Loop

Finish

Undercurve　　　　Space　　　　　Undercurve　　　←SSD　　Close

SSD　　　Narrow　　　　Space　　　Narrow　Close
Loop　　　　　　　　　　Loop　　Retrace

Direct Ovals (A C D E O)　　　　　　　　　　**Analysis of A C E O**

Flat Top　　　Close　Space　SSD

Slant　　Parallel
Loop

Space　　　　　　　　Space

Close

Slant Guide

Indirect Ovals (B I J P R)　　Space　　　　**Analysis of P R B I J**

Space

SSD　　　Retrace　　　　SSD　　Retrace　　Slant　Finish
Loop

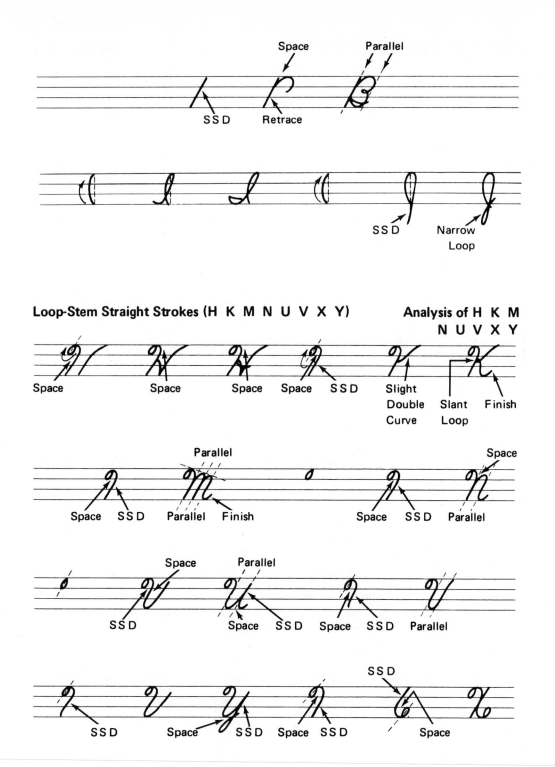

Loop-Stem Straight Strokes (H K M N U V X Y)

Analysis of H K M N U V X Y

Loop-Stem Curved Strokes (Q W Z)

Analysis of Q W Z

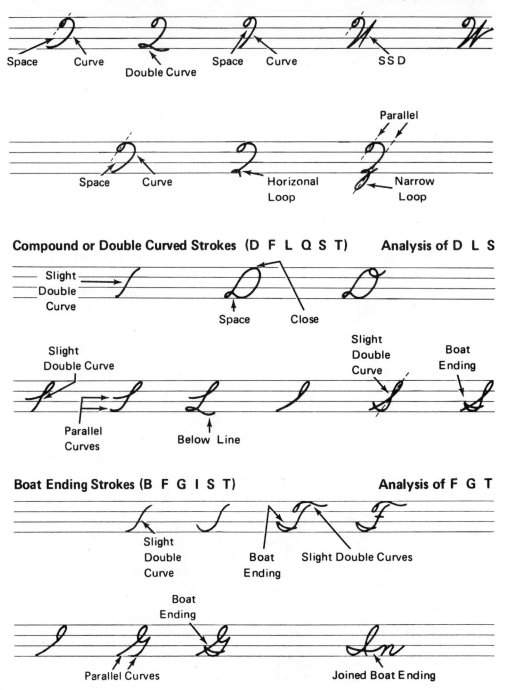

Space   Curve

Double Curve

Space   Curve

SSD

Parallel

Space   Curve

Horizonal Loop

Narrow Loop

Compound or Double Curved Strokes (D F L Q S T)

Analysis of D L S

Slight Double Curve

Space   Close

Slight Double Curve

Slight Double Curve

Boat Ending

Parallel Curves

Below Line

Boat Ending Strokes (B F G I S T)

Analysis of F G T

Slight Double Curve

Boat Ending

Slight Double Curves

Boat Ending

Parallel Curves

Joined Boat Ending

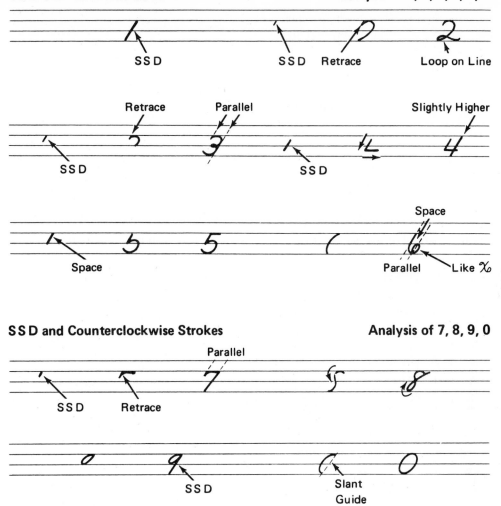

SSD and Clockwise Strokes

Analysis of 1, 2, 3, 4, 5, 6

SSD — SSD — Retrace — Loop on Line

Retrace — Parallel — Slightly Higher — SSD — SSD

Space — Space — Parallel — Like x

SSD and Counterclockwise Strokes

Analysis of 7, 8, 9, 0

Parallel — SSD — Retrace

SSD — Slant Guide

Analysis of Student Handwriting

Writing samples should be collected from each child at least four times during the year and kept in a collection of other examples of his or her work. Some teachers ask the child to write, "This is a sample of my writing on October 1." This inscription is folded back so that it is not visible when the child later writes, "This is a sample of my writing on January 1." Direct comparison can be made to see if skills are being maintained or improvement is being made. Both examples of writing are folded back when the child writes a third or fourth time on the same paper. Such a sample is especially helpful when talking with a parent about a child's work.

The following form, prepared by the Sheaffer Pen Company, is an example of an individual diagnostic device. It is designed to help children establish goals

PUPIL SELF-ANALYSIS SHEET[1]

A. Here is how I write when I am in a hurry:
   (Write: "This is a sample of my writing")

_____

_____

B. Here is how I write when I do my best writing:
   (Write: "This is a sample of my best writing")

_____

_____

C. I would mark my fast writing: (circle one grade) I would mark my best writing:	Excellent Excellent	Good Good	Fair Fair	Poor Poor
D. Here is my analysis of my handwriting:	EXCELLENT	GOOD	FAIR	POOR
1. SLANT .... Do all my letters lean the same way?	_____	_____	_____	_____
2. SPACING .... Are the spaces between letters and words even?	_____	_____	_____	_____
3. SIZE .... Are all small letters evenly small and tall letters evenly tall?	_____	_____	_____	_____
4. ALIGNMENT .... Do all my letters touch the line?	_____	_____	_____	_____
5. LOOPS .... Are *l, f, h, g, y, k, b* well formed?	_____	_____	_____	_____
6. STEMS .... Are all my downstrokes really straight?	_____	_____	_____	_____
7. CLOSINGS .... Are *a, d, g, o, p, s* closed?	_____	_____	_____	_____
8. ROUNDNESS .... Are *m, n, h, u, v, w, y* rounded?	_____	_____	_____	_____
9. RETRACES .... Are *t, i, d, p, m, n* retraced?	_____	_____	_____	_____
10. ENDINGS .... Do my words have good ending strokes without fancy swinging strokes?	_____	_____	_____	_____

[1] From *My Handwriting Quotient* (Madison, Wis.: W. A. Sheaffer Pen Company, 1960).

for their work in handwriting as well as establish meaningful standards.

An additional exercise that might improve a child's handwriting involves him in evaluating the handwriting of a "partner." Either a standardized scale or one developed by the school or classroom may serve as the model for comparison. The purpose of such an exercise is to alert the child to what constitutes "correct" letter formation. This is a cooperative effort; no grades are assigned. The teacher is able to circulate among the students, giving assistance as required.

In the handwriting period there will be times when the entire group will be working on the same problem—perhaps that of word endings or alignment. Because all have a like purpose, group diagnosis is effective. Samples of the writing can be shown on a screen by means of an opaque projector. Because the purpose is to seek a means of improvement rather than providing graded evaluation, most children will welcome the attention and suggestions concerning the next step they should take for improvement. First, attention should be directed toward one or two specific points. After this type of diagnosis has been used for some time, any aspect of the child's writing may be the basis for suggestion. A plastic transparent overlay will help some children examine specific letters. These are available with most handwriting systems. Another device is to cut a small hole in a piece of paper and examine the child's writing one letter at a time.

Frequently only those who have special handwriting problems participate in the classwork, whereas those who have no special needs use the time for independent writing.

Tips for Good Writing

Regardless of the system used, the following five elements enter into the handwriting program; a chart of these made for the classroom can act as a constant reminder:

Formation. Each letter should be made and joined correctly according to whatever penmanship system is followed. Examples of letters that cause trouble can be shown on this chart.

Size. This is to remind students of the need for uniformity in size regardless of the type of letter.

Slant. The problem here is usually one of consistency.

Alignment. Letters that go above or below the line get mixed with other writing and thus are very difficult to read.

Spacing. Even spacing is necessary for rhythmic reading. This chart, based on the program of the New York City schools, emphasizes these ideas.

The final judgment concerning handwriting should be based on the child's daily written work. Occasionally, before and after children complete a written assignment, make a class inventory of writing needs. Have the students look at their papers while you record by number (not name) the results on the chalkboard. Use the following inventory of writing habits:

Alignment
    How many had
        correct top alignment?
        uneven top alignment?
        correct bottom alignment?
        uneven bottom alignment?
        writing under the line?
        writing over the line?

Letter Spacing
    How many had
        correct letter spacing?
        uneven letter spacing?
        letter spacing too close together?
        letter spacing too far apart?

Word Spacing
    How many had
        correct word spacing?
        uneven word spacing?
        word spacing too close together?
        word spacing too far apart?

The secret of continuous improvement is to establish a feeling of achievement. This can be done by setting specific attainable goals. When a goal is achieved, celebrate it fittingly. (Although one can hardly recommend leading a snake dance through the halls whenever the whole class learns to make a good capital *A*, it is no less of an achievement than winning a basketball game.) Examples of such objectives that the entire group can eventually achieve are

Write the small letters of the alphabet correctly four times, joining the letters to each other. The teacher

(or a committee) can be the judge until an acceptable exercise is received from each member of the class.

Write sentences using words with difficult letter joinings, such as *bring, arrows, written, following, uncommon, bewitched, disturbance, suited,* and *delighted.*

Guiding rules for cursive writing of the small alphabet[2]

1. In the lowercase alphabet, every letter, except *c* and *o*, must have a *straight* downstroke, slanting from right to left.

   The downstrokes are straight.

   The downstrokes are not straight.

2. The *space* between two letters should be wide enough to hold an *n* without the upstroke:

   "n spaces" between letters

   Spaces are too narrow.

   Spaces are too wide.

3. All downstrokes must be parallel. Downstrokes are parallel.

   Downstrokes are not parallel.

4. All letters must rest ON the line. Letters rest ON the line.

   Letters do not rest on the line.

5. Letters must be of uniform and proportionate size.

6. The *total* slant of the writing should be parallel to the diagonal of the paper, whether by right-handed or left-handed writers.

[2] From Max Rosenhaus, "You Can Teach Handwriting with Only Six Rules," *The Instructor* (March 1957), 60.

Write sentences using these words: *there, their, they're; here's, hears; were, we're, wear; your, you're.*

Copy a short poem.

Write a good thank-you letter.

Write the alphabet in capital letters.

Write the addresses of three friends as they would appear on an envelope.

Write five quotations.

Make a directory of the class showing names, addresses, and telephone numbers.

Keep the minutes as a secretary of a meeting.

The following sentences contain *all* the lowercase letters of the alphabet. When they are written a few weeks apart, the student may evaluate his progress.

1. The violinist and the zither player were equally fine, so the judge marked both excellent.
2. At the zoo, the children saw an ibex, a jaguar, a kangaroo, a flamingo, and a very queer bird called a pelican.
3. The writer moves the hand quickly but smoothly across the page, watching the sizes of the letters and joining them expertly.

Example: Cursive Writing Lesson Plan

The following example of the cursive writing lesson plan for the fifth and sixth grades is taken from the New York Public Schools.

GENERAL OBJECTIVE

To maintain proper spacing between letters.

SPECIFIC BEHAVIORAL OBJECTIVE

Given instruction in the formation of the small letters with rounded tops, the children will be able to correctly develop all such letters allowing for correct spacing between letters.

MOTIVATION

The teacher shows the class a piece of written work in which many words are illegible (postcard or envelope re-

turned because of illegible address; spelling, composition or social studies papers). On the lined chalkboard, she copies some of the incorrectly written words and writes the correct form next to each. She discusses with the children the causes of the difficulty encountered in reading the words and guides them to the conclusion that the main cause is essentially the pointed tops in certain letters. They also note that other elements, including poor spacing, make words difficult to read.

The teacher writes the letters *m, h, v,* on the chalkboard and adds, at the children's suggestion, other small letters which should have rounded tops, as *n, y, x.* The teacher and children decide which of these letters to reanalyze and practice in order to help them improve the writing of all small letters with rounded tops.

PROCEDURES

Teacher: Writes the letter *y* on the lined chalkboard and discusses it as she writes. . . .
Reviews with the children posture and position of paper and pencil.

Children: Copy the letter, compare it with the teacher's model, note any deviation, rewrite it correctly if necessary, and then write it three or four times more.
Dictate to the teacher, for writing on the chalkboard, words in which the letter occurs at different places, e.g., *you, by, eye.*
Copy these words and check specifically for the correct formation of the letter *y* and the spacing between letters.

Teacher: Moves about the room to assist a few children individually.

Children: Dictate to the teacher, for writing on the chalkboard, a sentence which includes the practice letter and possibly other letters in the related group, e.g., The boys help each other in many ways.
Copy the sentence from the chalkboard once or twice depending upon their individual speed.

EVALUATION

The teacher helps the children to compare their letter *y* in the sentence with their practice writing of the letter. They also note the rounded tops of the related letters in the group. In addition, they compare a piece of writing from their folders with their practice paper to note the improvement in the writing of these letters.

ASSIGNMENT

The children plan to pay particular attention to the writing of the letters with rounded tops in copying their reports for the class newspaper.

Lesson Review

Occasionally a student may need a review of cursive letter construction. The following lesson was designed as part of a rapid review program with intermediate-grade children:[3]

FINISHING STROKES

Ending the last letter of each word with a good finishing stroke makes our handwriting look much better. Most of these strokes swing up with a slight upward curve to the height of the letter *a*. The curve of the final stroke is downward on the letters *g, j, y,* and *z*.

Part 1

Look at yesterday's sample of your best handwriting. Look for the final stroke or "tails" on every word that you wrote on this sample. Put the number of tails that you left off here._____ Count every tail that is poorly shaped or that reaches above or below the height of the letter *a*.

Part 2

Now put your name on the right of the top line of your paper. Put the date just below your name. On the third line just to the left of the center, put the title, "Handwriting." Skip the next line. Using good finishing strokes, write the following sentence three times:

Paul said, "The big brown fox quickly and slyly jumped over the lazy dog."

Skip a line and then write the following words, ending them with good tails:

month	because	windy	high	kite	string
west	held	fell	oak	broke	away
will	where	an	hold	east	air

[3] From Nathan Naiman, *A Blitz Handwriting Program* (San Diego, Calif.: Oak Park School, 1960).

Part 3

Again, look at yesterday's sample of your handwriting. Copy those words needing tails and put good tails or finishing strokes on them. Look closely at the ending of each word to see that you are improving your final strokes.

USING GOOD SLANT IN HANDWRITING—LOWER LOOP LETTERS

Proper slant in handwriting is very important in the making of lower loop letters. Be sure the slanted part of these letters is straight. The lower loop letters are: *g, j, p, y,* and *z*.

Part 1

Take the written work. Put the guide sheet under it. See if the lower loop letters have the correct angle of slant. How would you grade your slant? Is it excellent, good, fair or poor? _____

Now look at the finishing strokes. Put a check by those that do not reach as high as the letter *a*.

Part 2

Today we will practice good slant on the lower loop letters. Put your name on the upper right on the top line of your paper. Put the date just below your name. On the third line just to the left of the center, put the title "Handwriting." Skip the next line.

_____

_____

Carefully write a line of each of these lower loop letters:

g, j, p, q, z

Here are some words that have lower loop letters. Write each two times:

gag pipe gang jig pig

Write this sentence two times: "The big pig danced a jig."

Part 3

Now look at all of the writing you have done today. See if all of your lower loop letters reach half way below the line. See if they have straight backs. Circle those which are poorly formed. Practice writing those words that you circled. How would you grade today's work? Is it excellent, good, fair, poor? _____

Spacing in Handwriting

After one word has been finished, a space is left before the next word is written. This space is just about as wide as the small letter *a*. This space should never be larger or smaller than this.

Part 1

Look back at the sentences you wrote in earlier lessons. See if the spacing between words is about as wide as the letter *a*. Are you leaving too much space or not enough? How would you grade your spacing on these sentences? Is it excellent, good, fair, or poor? _____

Part 2

Put the heading on your paper.

Now here are some sentences for you to write. Be careful to leave a uniform space between your words. Write each sentence twice:

The quick brown fox jumps over the lazy dog.
Whatever is worth doing at all is worth doing well.
Well begun is half done.
Here is a sample of good spacing:

_____

_____

Part 3

Skip a line and write the following:

"Here is another sample of my best handwriting. I am careful with finishing strokes, slant, letter size, and the spacing between letters."

Compare this writing with the writing in the first lesson. Is it better, just as good as, or poorer than this first lesson?_____

The following are other suggestions with respect to handwriting instruction in the intermediate grades that come from experienced teachers:

1. Make the paper on which the final writing will appear have special significance. Make mimeograph copies of a flag, holiday picture, or school letterhead on good-quality "mimeo" bond paper. Explain that the number of copies is limited and that the paper should not be used for the exercise until each person feels that he is prepared. Sometimes attractive stationery will serve the same purpose.

2. Hold a writing clinic with one or two of the best writers acting as "doctors" for specific letters.

3. Exchange handwriting samples with other schools, both in the United States and in other countries.

4. Suggest to parents the value of a good writing instrument as a birthday or Christmas gift.

5. Make art designs formed of alphabet letters.

6. Have an "Each One Teach One" week, during which each child teaches one letter and its formation to another child or small group. Let the children devise worksheets or lessons for this. One fifth grade produced a textbook titled "How to Write Well."

Techniques to Improve Legibility

Because of the diversity of what is considered acceptable handwriting, it is important to assess each child's performance on an individual basis. The major emphasis of handwriting instruction should be legibility coupled with ease of production.

The most significant handwriting problem is illegibility. Illegible handwriting is due to seven errors: (1) faulty endings, (2) incorrectly made undercurves, (3) mixed slant, (4) failure to give letters in the *a* group proper slant, (5) incorrect formation of the initial stroke of such letters as the capitals *W, H, K,* (6) incorrect endings in final *h, m, n,* and (7) failure to make the downstroke of *t* and *d*.

End strokes as spacers between words improve the legibility of writing more than any other single device. Some claim that attention to this factor can improve legibility by 25 per cent.

Ability to make the undercurve of the letter *l* alone improves the shape of many related letters and brings about the orderly appearance of written paragraphs.

The letters that extend below the line should show the same slant as those above the line. The principle of parallel slants brings about harmony in handwriting.

Many letters exhibit an initial stroke shaped like a cane. The stroke consists of two parts, a loop and a downstroke. These should be made so as to conform to the slant of the other letters. There are eleven letters to which this principle applies: *b, d, h, k, l, m, n, p, r, t,* and *w.*

When *h, m,* or *n* appears at the end of a word, there is a tendency to slur the last two strokes. Emphasis on precision in making the last downstroke in writing these letters and in the final upstroke removes a common fault. The letters *t* and *d* constitute a special application of the *l* principle. Once the relationship of these letters to the *l* principle is recognized, errors in letter formation are eliminated.

The letters *e, a, r,* and *t* cause the most confusion. Such combinations as *be, bi, br, by, bo, oe, oi, os, oc, oa, ve, va, vo, vu, we, wi, wa, ws,* and *wr* also cause trouble. The demons of handwriting are *a* that looks like *o, u,* or *ci; l* that becomes *li; d* that appears as *cl; e* like *i* or the reverse; *m* and *n* like *w* and *u; t* like *l* or *i;* and *r* like *e* or *n.*

To make children aware of certain legibility difficulties, have them do the following:

1. Write the words *add, gold,* and *dare* and analyze the letters *a, d,* and *g.* What happens if the letters are not closed at the top?
2. Write the words *no, nail, make,* and *name* and analyze the letters *m* and *n.* What happens if the top is not rounded?
3. Write the words *it, tin, nine,* and *trip* and analyze the letters *t* and *i.* What happens if the letters have open loops?
4. Write the words *late, let,* and *lend* and analyze the letters *l* and *e.* What happens when the loops are not open?
5. Write the words *up, under,* and *run* and analyze the letter *u.* What happens when the tops of *u* are not pointed?

Some writing habits must be changed to increase legibility. Children who write *gt, ot,* or *ju* with short connecting strokes should be told to "swing between each letter" or "spread your letters out like an accordion." At first the distance should be exaggerated, then modified to proper spacing. If a child continues to write all letters close together, let him practice his spelling words on a regular sheet of ruled tablet paper but with the lines vertical rather than horizontal. There should be one letter between each pair of lines.

A tight grip on the writing instrument may produce tense, slow writing. The writer can be helped by having him wad a sheet of paper into a ball. This is held by the lower fingers against the palm of the hand. Such a practice seems to direct the pressure from the pen.

When the writing problem is due to a bad habit in holding the pen, the interesting and inexpensive plastic writing form available from Zaner-Blower may prove helpful. This device positions the writing instrument and aids the necessary retraining.

Speed is the great enemy of legibility. We can think as fast as 250 words a minute and write about twenty-five. Yet eventually some rhythmic speed must be attained.

Drills to increase speed may be one of these types:

1. Write one letter.
2. Write difficult letter combinations that tend to decrease speed of writing, *b, w, v,* followed by *e, i, r.*
3. Write an easy word or words.
4. Write words with thought associations: *clap hands, green grass, blue sky.*
5. Write one- or two-minute time tests.

Suggested sentences containing twenty letters are

1. Working for speed is fun.
2. She will meet you at home.
3. Write all papers neatly.

Suggested rate per minute:

1. Fourth grade, with pencil: 45 letters or better.
2. Fifth grade, with pen: 55 letters or better.
3. Sixth grade, with pen: 65 letters or better.

If a child persists in poor writing, it may reflect an emotional problem. In such cases it is wise to forget about handwriting instruction until the basic problems of the child are cared for. Remember that the basic cause of illegible handwriting is often carelessness. The solution is to make handwriting so important that the learner will care enough to do it well.

What Provisions Should Be Made for the Left-Handed Child?

It is seldom very satisfying to be a member of a small minority or to be considered "different" from other people. The left-handed person faces both these problems. From 4 to 11 per cent of the population is left-handed. The range of these figures may be explained by the extent of tolerance of left-handedness in the segment of the population surveyed. Where no effort has been made to convert the left-handed individual to right-handed writing there are higher percentages of left-handers. (In a society where table manners, writing tools, and student desks conform to the assumption that

What provisions should be made for the left-handed child? From 4 to 11 per cent of the population is left-handed. (Photo by Linda Lungren.)

everyone is right-handed, the left-handed individual certainly is at a disadvantage.)

To expect or require a left-handed person to become right-handed makes no more sense than to expect a right-handed person to develop left-handedness. Many outstanding people have been left-handed: Leonardo da Vinci, former President Harry S Truman, Judy Garland, James V. Cunningham. Historically there has been prejudice against left-handed people. The terms *sinister*—from the Latin *sinistral,* meaning "left-handed"—and *gauche*—French for "left"—reflect the negative characteristics that have been attributed to the left-handed. Sinistrals in school should have the same individual respect that we advocate for all children.

Once we acknowledge the right of a child to write with his left hand, we then have the task of finding ways to help him to do it well. The usual way that left-handedness is revealed is through the individual's activities. Observation of a child while he is using a pair of scissors, bouncing and catching a ball, putting marbles into a jar one at a time, eating with a spoon, or using a hammer and saw will reveal the dominant hand. If a child uses both hands with equal ease, we say that he is ambidextrous. Because of the general convenience that it will provide, these children are taught to write with the right hand.

It is not easy to determine true dominance for some children. They may have a left-eye dominance and still be right-handed. Some children should be referred to trained clinicians to determine true dominance. Handwriting instruction should not be initiated until handedness has been established (Forester, 1975).

A number of simple tests have been suggested to help determine mixed dominance, left-eye preference with right-hand preference, or right-eye preference with left-hand preference. Cases of mixed dominance are evidenced in the problem some children have in keeping their paper in the "arm track." They seem to be maneuvering their paper constantly to try to keep it in place.

The preferred eye can be determined by having the pupil sight a coin on the floor through a cardboard cylinder held at arm's length. The coin is sighted with both eyes open. First one eye and then the other is covered as he looks at the coin. When the dominant eye is covered, the coin can no longer be seen through the cylinder.

A more elaborate device to determine motor-visual preference and to stimulate the development of controlled vision in the eye on the same side of the body as that of the dominant hand is the Leavill Hand-Eye Coordinator produced by the Keystone View Company, Meadville, Pennsylvania.

At one time it was felt that forcing children to change from left- to right-handedness would cause stuttering and other psychological tensions. Some experiments seem to indicate that it is not so much the change as the way the change is directed. Although there is no clear-cut evidence that cerebral damage does take place when a child's natural handedness is tampered with, there is equally little evidence that it does not. As teachers we must ask ourselves this question: Is right-handed writing so important that we are willing to risk creating speech trouble, neuroses, or other evidence of emotional disturbance?

Writing Difficulties Encountered by the Left-Handed

Some of the difficulties faced by the left-handed person learning to write a system devised by right-handed individuals can be experienced by a right-handed person who attempts a few left-handed exercises. Draw a series of squares, first with the right hand and then with the left. Note that the "pull strokes" with the right hand are "pushing strokes" with the left. These strokes involve different muscles according to the hand used. Then observe a right-handed individual writing. He starts at a mid-body position and writes in a natural left-to-right movement, away from the body. An attempt to imitate this will reveal why a left-handed child copying a right-handed teacher will write moving away from his mid-body position toward his natural direction, or right to left. The result is mirror writing, which is completely legible to the writer but cannot readily be deciphered by the rest of us unless it is held up to a mirror. Correction is made by explaining to the child that he must conform

to the left-to-right pattern so that others can read what he writes. Have him copy individual words and letters, always starting at the left side of the paper. This will take considerable time because he is being asked to learn to write words that seem backward to him. Eventually, as these children master reading, the problem disappears. Sometimes it is wise to postpone writing instruction temporarily until reading is well established.

Another result of imitating right-handed writing is that the child develops an awkward writing position. In order to hold a pencil or pen in exactly the way a right-handed person does, a left-handed child may twist his hand around to a backward or upside-down position. Some actually write upside down.

It is very difficult to help these children once such awkward writing positions are well established. The first requirement is that both the child and his parents want to correct it. Without this desire the results of any teaching effort will be limited. For the child it is almost a punishment. Some will write quite well in the "backward" position, but for many it will mean uncomfortable writing for a lifetime.

Writing Instruction for the Left-Handed

Start writing instruction for a left-handed child by adjusting the position of the paper and arm. Place two tape markers on the desk or writing table. Have the child rest his left arm between these two tapes. This will prevent the arm from swinging out. Another tape can be used to indicate the proper position for the paper. Provide a long pencil or ballpoint pen as the writing instrument. Have the child hold this about an inch and a half from the point. The first exercises should be tracing over letters and words written by a left-handed individual. A considerable amount of writing should be done at the chalkboard; it is practically impossible to use the upside-down position there. The teacher might even guide the hand movements to assure the correct response. These children should have a card of letters written by a left-handed person for personal reference at their desks. If the child who has reached the fifth grade is using an awkward position, it is sometimes best to let him continue. Urge instead that he learn to use the typewriter as soon as possible. Some school systems have special summer classes in typing for such left-handed children. Here the left-handed have an advantage over right-handed people; the standard typewriter keyboard was designed by a left-handed person.

There is little experimental evidence to guide a teacher in developing a writing program for the left-handed child. Teachers with experience suggest the following procedures:

1. Group the left-handed together. This makes it easier to supervise instruction and prevents a tendency to imitate right-handed individuals.
2. Begin instruction at the chalkboard where close supervision can be given. Early detection of an error can prevent the formation of a bad habit. Stress left-to-right movement and the starting place when writing each letter. Circles should be made from left to right in print script, even though this may seem awkward at first.
3. When the left-handed child starts writing on paper, it may be wise to have him place an arrow as a "traffic signal" at the beginning of his writing to assure the teacher that he is starting at the correct place and proceeding in the correct left-to-right direction. A left-handed child may be a good helper to another left-hander.
4. The child learning to write print script with his left hand places the paper directly in front of him, just as the right-handed individual does. It will be necessary for him to move the paper frequently as he writes; this is the task of the right hand. Accordingly the writer should be seated at the left-hand side of a table—or alone at an individual desk rather than sharing a table with a right-handed child. Once these first steps have been mastered, the left-handed child might continue writing print script throughout the grades. In the second grade his print script may develop a natural slant if he slants his paper, as he will later for cursive writing, so that his left hand follows a natural arc while moving from left to right. However, some feel that the left-handed child should be started on cursive immediately. Why should he be required to learn two different systems developed for right-handed people?
5. The natural arc of the left hand as it rests on the desk should determine the position of the paper for cursive writing. The upper right corner of the paper will be in line with the centerline of the body. Children can be told that the bottom corner should point "toward your heart." In shifting the paper the right hand presses down on it, holding it firmly until one line is finished, and then moves it up for the next line. The left hand slides lightly along the line of writing while the paper is kept stationary.
6. The pen or pencil is held with the thumb, index, and middle fingers. It should slant toward the writer's left shoulder. The pen should be held a little higher than would be the case for a right-handed writer, so that the child can see what he writes and avoid running the left hand over the written material. Some teachers place a small rubber band around the pen to indicate where to grip the instrument.
7. A good ballpoint or felt pen is a better writing instrument for the left-handed person than a fountain pen. The ballpoint does not dig into the paper with the upstrokes, and the ink dries immediately. Avoid cheap ballpoints that are too short or those that must be held in a tight grip because the sides are too smooth. A strip of adhesive tape on the barrel helps to keep a pen from slipping.
8. Copy for the left-handed writing exercises should be directly in front of the writer, not on the chalkboard. At first some children need to have their hands guided through the proper movements. If a single letter is reversed in any writing, take time to work on that letter alone.
9. Let the child determine his own letter slant after you have established the proper position of the paper for him. Most left-handed children seem to prefer a vertical form of writing. A few find a backhand more natural. Because our objective is legibility and ease of writing, slant should not be predetermined for the left-handed.

10. Special attention may need to be given to the letters *O, T, F,* and *H* to prevent the use of sinistral strokes. Because upward strokes are difficult for some left-handed writers, they may be eliminated on the letters *a, c, d, g, o,* and *q* when they begin a word.

11. A complete set of writing exercises is available for left-handed children learning cursive writing. These exercises were written by Dr. Warren Gardner and are available from the Interstate Press, 19 North Jackson Street, Danville, Illinois.

12. A special meeting with parents of left-handed children is of value. Stress at this meeting the acceptability of being left-handed, stress the problems relating to changing handedness, and give a demonstration of proper left-handed writing.

Research by E. A. Enstron justifies the conclusion that

pupil success in writing with the left hand is basically a problem of teacher understanding. When we know how to help *beginning* left-handed writers, they will, in all normal situations, learn to write successfully with speed and ease, and their writing will have the usual forward slant. There is no need for a left-handed pupil to be stigmatized as an "odd-ball" by writing in a different, absolutely unnecessary, difficult-to-read style [Enstron, 1969].

Individualizing the instruction of left-handed children, providing instruction enabling them to communicate in writing efficiently and effectively, will alleviate greatly the problems encountered by the left-handed (Forester, 1975).

For Discussion

1. What advantages and disadvantages does a left-handed teacher have?

2. Would it be wise to have all left-handed children in the intermediate grades meet together for handwriting instruction?

Suggestions for Projects

1. Assemble enough samples from one classroom or school to construct a handwriting scale. This might be a scale for judging the manuscript writing of children in the third grade, the writing of left-handed individuals of the same age, or of boys in the sixth grade.

2. Plan a display that will explain the handwriting program of your school to the public.

3. Make a comparison of the various handwriting programs now on the market. What are the essential differences with regard to philosophy, equipment, letter-formation drills, and special features?

4. Make a case study of an individual with a handwriting problem.

Bibliography

Ackov, E. N., and K. N. Greff. "Handwriting: Copying vs. Tracing as the Most Effective Type of Practice." *Journal of Education Research,* **69:** No. 3 (1975) 6–8.

Anderson, D. W. "What Makes Writing Legible." *Elementary School Journal* (April 1969), 365–369.

Coleman, E. B. "Collecting a Data Base for a Reading Technology." *Journal of Educational Psychology Monograph,* **61:** No. 4, Part 2 (August 1970).

Enstron, E. A. "Those Questions on Handwriting." *Elementary School Journal* (March 1969), 327–333.

Erickson, L. W., and R. B. Woolschlager. "Typewriting in Elementary School?" *N.E.A. Journal* (October 1962), 54–56.

Forester, L. M. "Sinistral Power! Help for Left-Handed Children." *Elementary English* (February 1975), 213–215.

Furner, B. A. "The Perceptual-Motor Nature of Learning in Handwriting." *Elementary English* (November 1969), 886–894.

Groff, P. "Can Pupils Read What Teachers Write?" *Elementary School Journal,* **76:** No. 1 (1975), 32–39.

Halpin, G. "Special Paper for Beginning Handwriting: An Unjustified Practice?" *Journal of Educational Research* (September 1976), 668–669.

Handwriting Made Easy—Teacher's Manual and Refresher Course. New York: Noble and Noble, 1957.

Hart, L. "Typing Belongs in the Elementary Curriculum." *Business Education World,* **40** (January 1960), 9–11.

Hildreth, G. "Manuscript Writing After Sixty Years." *Elementary English* (January 1960), 3–13.

Horton, L. W. "Illegibilities in the Cursive Handwriting of Sixth Graders." *Elementary School Journal* (May 1970), 446–449.

Leavitt, J. E., and Frances Sigborn Hein. "My Mother Writes Terrible." *Elementary School Journal* (November 1969), 74–78.

Lewis, E. R., and H. P. Lewis. "An Analysis of Errors in the Formation of Manuscript Letters by First Grade Children." *American Educational Research Journal* (January 1965), 25–35.

Minkoff, H. "Teaching the Transition from Print to Script Analytically." *Elementary English* (February 1975), 203–204.

Naiman, N. *A Blitz Handwriting Program*. San Diego, Calif.: Oak Park School (1960).

Chapter 8
Written Composition

How May Imaginative or Creative Writing Be Promoted in the Primary Grades?

The young child can express his ideas in a variety of ways. He can express himself orally, through a dramatic skit, or by creating a picture. As he relates personal experiences and ideas or tells about a picture or an object, the teacher can ask questions and make suggestions to him about his words, ideas, or manner of speaking. At other times the child makes the picture first, then tells what is happening in the picture. This provides a focus for him in determining which of his ideas are important and which are subordinate.

"What would be a good name for Harold's story?" the teacher asks. After several suggestions have been made, the teacher turns to Harold. "Which one do you like best?" After he has decided, the teacher writes the name for all to see. With this beginning, children will soon be dictating stories that the teacher writes and the child reads. As the teacher writes, she points out where she begins and how each sentence ends. "I'll put the first word here, then go to the right. This is the end of the sentence so I will put a period here." A "book" of these stories is placed on the reading table so that children can read and reread the stories they have written. Creative writing can be a class-wide experience, or the efforts of a small group, or an individual working alone with the teacher. Such experience usually follows a discussion period where children "think together" and express themselves freely. In the small-group method, the members work faster and the interest factors and feelings of success are high. The teacher is immediately able to supply needed words or correct spelling, to stimulate thinking, and to build curiosity. In turn, other groups will work with the teacher. Writing experiences of the entire class now involve a common topic, such as "Thanksgiving." During the discussion period, words

Writing is fun and easy. (PHOTO BY LINDA LUNGREN.)

that might be used are placed on the chalkboard. Specific aspects suitable for writing might be listed, such as "My Favorite Thanksgiving," "A Turkey's Ideas About Thanksgiving," "Why I Am Thankful." Thus the individual compositions will vary, although using a similar vocabulary.

Children learn many things when they write. They become familiar with selecting, eliminating, and arranging words, with proofreading, and with correcting errors. The first efforts usually contain misspelled words, incomplete sentences, and meager punctuation and capitalization attempts. The first stories are not corrected, but as the child reads his story to the teacher his

voice indicates beginnings and endings. He then adds, with the teacher's help, his own periods, question marks, and capitals. After children have written many stories and write with ease, the teacher and child correct the first rough draft. The child takes the initiative in finding his errors or in completing the spelling of a word where only the initial letter is given. The child may copy his story and share it with his classmates. Sometimes the story is placed with others in a bound volume. Children frequently offer stories without a title, probably because a title or name inhibits their ease of writing. The teacher or other children may suggest a title when the child shares his unnamed story with them.

Examples of Children's Writing

Here is an early effort of a San Diego boy in the first grade that was published in *Our Writing:*

THE DOME BIRD

(as written by Richard, Grade 1)

One day dome bird thote two + two was twente. One day men buill schools up. and it was time for dome bird to come to school. One day the teacher put up some arethmatik. then dome bird sat down to rite. The dom bird saw two + two on the board. He put twente on the paper. the teacher saw dome Bird arethmatick so she put an X on the paper so the dome bird saw the X so dom bird Learnd how much two + two was.

THE DUMB BIRD

(as read by Richard)

One day dumb bird thought two plus two was twenty. One day some men built schools and

Ideas and freedom to express them have priority over mechanical correctness in this classroom. In time the child will seek correct form and willingly work to achieve the skills needed because he wants to write and knows that such discipline is needed to reach his goal. (COURTESY OF THE SAN DIEGO COUNTY SCHOOLS.)

it was time for dumb bird to come to school. One day the teacher put up some arithmetic. Then dumb bird sat down to write. The dumb bird saw two plus two on the board. He put twenty on the paper. The teacher saw dumb bird's arithmetic, so she put an X on the paper. The dumb bird saw the X, so dumb bird learned how much two plus two was.

As soon as print script has been mastered, the children follow the pattern established by the teacher and write their own story. These will show a great range of interest and expression. But each is important to the writer.

One will laboriously write ''The House'' with many smudges and add his name. Another will cover pages as he writes a story like this:

Robert   Jan. 22, 1958
wonts there was a 1 and a half year old girl. her name was tiny because she was so little. One day she saw a dog. she

wanted to bathe him because he was so dirty. she asked her mother but she said no get that dirty thing out of here. but tiny brahgt a tub in the yard, then she brahgt some waters and put in it. she bathed him. she got wet and dirty. but the dog was not dirty any more. he went away and he did not come back again because he did not like the water.

the end.

The only capital letters Robert knew were those in his name—but that did not stop him. He probably asked for help on *brahgt* and having spelled it wrong once was loyal to his first spelling when the word was repeated. Most revealing of all is a little note in one corner of the page: "I love to make storys."

As children learn to read the pattern of the controlled vocabulary, it is reflected in the material they write. Jon wrote this one:

Jane and Billy play
Run Billy
Billy jumps.

The picture was much more original. Two children were shown with a jumping rope tied to a tree, Billy was jumping while Jane held the rope.

The pattern of teacher-made charts soon appears in the writing of children.

Peggy produced this story:

This is Ann and Linda.
They are looking at the kittens.
The kittens are in the basket.
The basket is yellow and red.
The kittens are cute.

But in the same school another first-grade class was writing these stories:

This is in the Dineohsire's Days. A sea manstre is going to land and eat. a trtaile is under his tail. in those days the were no people.

Jeffrey

This is the sivl war wen the Americans fot the inglish. The Americans wun the wor becas the American's they did not giv up.

by Bobby

It is obvious that two different philosophies are at work here. In one there has been an emphasis on form, in the second on ideas. The natural question to ask is when should these children be expected to spell and write correctly? Teachers who permit the second type of writing say that late in the second grade or sometimes the third grade the children seek correct form. These new standards are the result of wide reading and the gradual mastery of writing mechanics. It is true that unless the principal and parents understand the purposes of the teacher there will be criticism. But it should be recognized that children are not going to attempt words like *monster* or *turtle* if they face criticism with respect to spelling and writing.

News reports of the day are popular subjects for written communications. MacDonald (1975) recommends providing written remarks to supplement letter grades in the assessment of student compositions at the college level. Such a practice would apply similarly to the elementary level.

In encouraging children to write, Parker (1976) urges an expanded writing program that allows for ungraded written exchanges among pupils. Topics that traditionally have been used to elicit composition from students include the following:

Donald brought in a
record for Mrs. Cummins.

A car hit a teacher's
parked automobile
It even hit a house
It almost poured rain too.
by Linda

Today was a happy
day. Today Miss Bovee [student teacher] came.
She will stay until school closes.
Belinda

Holidays receive special notice:

April 7, 1979
Easter Day
On Easter Day we had an egg hunt. I found more eggs than my brother. One egg was under the abalone shell. I

found an egg in both vases. I had fun on Easter. Most of the eggs were in the living room. But some were in the dining room. The eggs were all different colors. They are very pretty. I helped dye the eggs. I had fun on Easter.

Sylvia C.

Before this story was written, certain words were written on the board as the results of a discussion of words needed. Among these were *dye, Easter, colors*. The words *different* and *dining* were corrected before the story was posted. In this class all children wrote on the same topic.

A favorite writing experience at the beginning of second grade is to write "What I Want to Be" stories. These can be reproduced in a little book for parents' night. If the children use a ditto pencil or write on ditto masters, this also provides an example of the child's writing. These are typical examples:

A JET PILOT

I want to be a Jet pilot. You have to learn many things before you can be a Jet pilot. You must know how to fly your plane are you might crash. If the plane runs out of gas I will parachute out

by Billy

A FIRE MAN

I want to be a fire man and put out fires and help people out of fires. I want to be a good fire man I want to slide down the poles. I want to help people to be good and not cause fires

by Richy

A SCHOOL TEACHER

I want to be a school teacher and teach children how to spell and do numbers. I want to teach them how to tell time and many other things I want children who do good work and not spend their time talking

by Diane

Second-grade children advance rapidly. By the end of the year some will write this well. The literary pattern now follows that of favorite books.

FLICKA THE FILLY

Dick's father was at the Johnson's farm getting a colt. Dick was going to train it. When his father came home Dick ran to the truck. The colt was beautiful. It was pure white with a black mane and tail and right on its forehead was a gold star. "What will you name her, son?" asked his father.

"I'll call her Flicka," said Dick.

The next day Dick got up early. He ate his breakfast and went to the stable.

"Come on, Flicka," said Dick. "I'm going to train you." Flicka went with Dick to the pasture.

"First you must learn to obey your master," said Dick. Dick walked away and said "Stay."

Flicka did as he said. Flicka obeyed him with the other tricks, too. And they had lots of fun for the rest of their lives.

by Jayne

After hearing several of the "Just So" stories by Rudyard Kipling, one of the boys wrote this original story:

THE STORY OF THE ELEPHANT THAT HAD NO TRUNK

Once upon a time there lived an elephant. This elephant was very sad because he had no trunk. The way this elephant lost his trunk was.

He was walking along just minding his own business, when out of the blue came a rhinoceros. This rhinoceros was the biggest, fattest rhinoceros you have ever seen. And the elephant crouched down of fright. The rhinoceros stepped on the trunk and off it came. That's the way the elephant lost his trunk.

by Donald

A teacher may plan a lesson in written composition in a six-step sequence. First, the child is either motivated to write or helped to recognize that he has something to express in writing. Second, the vocabulary needed to express the writer's ideas is made available. Third, forms already taught are recalled, because we want the child to practice correct habits. Fourth, time is provided for the writing experience. Fifth, the written material is shared. Sixth, improvements are made in the composition appropriate to the writer's purposes.

This six-step procedure cannot always be completed in one language period. A letter might be started in the language class and completed during the spelling or social studies time. A story or poem might be started on one day, completed on a second day, and, if needed, revised on a third. The amount of writing will depend on the interest and purpose of those involved. Writing should never become "busy work" or a time-filling activity. A limited amount of writing that has a purpose and is carefully guided to prevent the repetition of error will produce the most satisfying results.

The following classroom procedures have been suggested by teachers for each of these six steps:

1. Motivation

PREPRIMER STORIES. Children are encouraged to make their own preprimers. These may be a compilation of the stories of several students or the work of one. Topics may concern Cowboys, Our Town, My Family, Our Pets, Our School.

DIARY OR DAILY NEWS. At first the children will dictate a report to the teacher on "what we did today." Later they will write their own. This may be a rotating activity. One group may be sharing orally for the day or week, another working on a project, and a third keeping the diary. "Our Friday News" is an excellent way to summarize the work of the week for parents and the principal.

WISHES, FEARS, TROUBLES. Feelings stimulate a great deal of creative thought. Expression of such feelings helps the teacher understand the child as well as helping the child to get problems out in the open. Making pictures, then talking or writing about these topics, illustrates this suggestion.

"If I could have my wish"
"I do not like _____"
"Things that scare me"
"If I could be something else I would be a _____
_____"

REPORTS. Most adult writing is done to tell what happened, what a person learned, or what a person did. Simple encyclopedias make it possible for children to share interesting information through written reports. Some even call these "term papers," with sources appropriately indicated.

SEASONS, HOLIDAYS, AND NATURE. The environment is a natural stimulation for writing. Windy days, storms, rain are things to tell about. A "Halloween," "Thanksgiving," or "February Hero" book, made of a compilation of writing, is a rewarding project. In the second grade and beyond children can print directly on ditto masters so that a book for each child can be assembled.

TITLES. All that some children need to start the flow of ideas and the desire to write is a title:

Witches' Brew	Vacation Fun
My Pet	My Toys
Adventures of a Penny	Dear Santa
Chimpanzee Tells All	When I Was Sick
My Old School	Danger
The Old House	Fire! Fire!

FIRST LINES. Getting started is difficult for many. These first lines reproduced on writing paper will often help:

1. Dear Santa, Please _____.
2. My name is _____. I live at _____.
3. Once there was a monkey _____.
4. I am _____. I have _____. I can _____.

"IF" STORIES: SUGGESTED PLOTS

1. If you were a circus pony, what adventures might you have?
2. If you were a lost dog, what might happen to you?
3. If you were a calf that liked to run away, what might happen to you?
4. If you were a dog that saw a turtle in the road, what might happen?
5. If you could go anywhere in the world, where would you go?
6. If you had ten dollars to spend for Christmas, what would you buy?

TELL A STORY ABOUT THESE FACTS

1. I am a crow named Chicago. Tell the story of how I hid some silver and what happened to it.
   Suggested words: thief, chased, claws, dogs, barked, fireman, ladder, afraid, tired.

2. I am a fireman named Jim. One day there was a big fire. Tell what happened.
3. I am a monkey named Bimbo. I love to tease my master. Tell how this got me into trouble.
4. I am a baby brother. I got lost one day. Tell what happened to me.

POST OFFICE. Establish a mail box for each child. At any time any child may write a letter to any other child in the class. The teacher may write a letter as well. Letters may be mailed only at noon and picked up only in the morning before school. To maintain standards it must be understood that no letter will be put in the receiver's box unless it is correctly written.

OUTER SPACE STORIES. Discuss the following: Today we are going to write a space story. Should we take a trip to Venus or stop at the moon? Will it be a dream, or an original story, or a news account in the "Venus Morning News"? Maybe it will be a colony of Pilgrims on the Moon or the diary of one who stayed at home. Perhaps the trip was not planned at all but the result of an accident.

PICTURE STIMULATORS. Picture stimulators are among the best means of motivating a child to write. A picture of a clown cut from a magazine is glued to an idea card. Below it are some stimulating questions: Have you been to the circus? Why is the clown so happy? On the back are words the child might wish to use as he writes a story. Appropriate words might be *clown, circus, tent, laughing, trick, joke, music.* These pictures are equally good as stimulators for oral stories prior to writing.

A WRITER'S CORNER. A technique used by many teachers to stimulate writing is a writer's corner in the classroom. The corner consists of a table and chairs placed below a bulletin board. Questions, pictures, and ideas for word usage can be attractively displayed on the bulletin board for motivation. These are changed frequently. Writing paper, pencils, a dictionary, and needed lists of words are kept on the table. Folders of pictures with words are kept on the table. Folders of pictures with words describing the picture are placed on the table. Large sheets of paper with a mimeographed picture in the corner have been successfully used by some teachers to obtain a variety of stories about one picture.

The materials on the writer's table must be introduced to the children so that they know how to use them correctly. The pictures should be used by the class as a regular writing activity before the materials are placed on the writer's table. This does not mean that every new game or picture placed on the writer's table must be introduced to the group first. It does mean that any different type of material that the teacher places on this table should be explained so that the child knows exactly how to use it.

Periodically some recognition should be given to children who are using the writer's desk. Putting up "The Story of the Week," which can be selected by the teacher or the class, and making a booklet of the best stories are two ways to help stimulate more creative work. Material written may be put in a box and later read aloud by the teacher. The children guess who is the author in the manner of a television quiz program.

One device for the writer's table is a threefold stand made of cardboard. Each fold is about 9 x 11. The center fold has a stimulating picture that is slipped behind a sheet of acetate. On the right is a group of words appropriate to the picture also in an acetate envelope. On the left are reminders to the writer. The teacher can change the pictures and vocabulary as she wishes. The reminders might be "Every story has a title." "All sentences begin with capitals." "All names start with capitals."

There might be envelopes for letters, a calendar, a usable dictionary, a telephone book (for addresses), extra pencils, special paper (stationery), erasers, and other items to make writing attractive.

The writer's desk can be used by children when they have finished other assigned work. It is desirable to have only one child using the desk at a time. However, if the teacher wishes, children may take certain materials to their desks.

In developing language material for this individual activity, teachers should remember that "above average" or "gifted" children are more likely to use them at first, and teachers should plan activities that will be challenging to them.

2. Vocabulary Development

When children write they sometimes wish to use words from their listening vocabulary. One child may ask, "What do you call the signs in the newspaper that tell what people have to sell?" He is seeking the word *advertisement*. The same is true of such words as *alfalfa* (what do cows eat?) or *infinity* (space). At such times the teacher provides the word desired.

In other situations the teacher anticipates that the writing and spelling of certain words will be needed and provides convenient references. Interesting words in stories read should be noticed so that they will be available to future authors. Simple picture dictionaries of the names of things may be consulted or created.

WORD CARDS. Because seasonal words will be needed every year, a packet of cards for Halloween, Thanksgiving, and Christmas can be constructed by older children or the teacher. At the appropriate time these words are spread along the chalkboard to help writers. Pictures on each card, such as a picture of a pumpkin beside the word, will help those still having reading problems.

WORD LISTS. A folder for each child that contains the words most often used will prevent errors as well as make writing easier for the child. This is a combination of a spelling and reading list:

The Words We Use Most Often

These are the words we use most often.
We use them when we write.
We use them when we read.
We can use this as a dictionary.
We can check the spelling of words here.
Check yourself to see how many you know.
Learn the ones you do not know.
Learn to say them very quickly.

a	been	days	from	men	or	snow	think	way
about	before	dear	fun	money	other	so	this	we
after	best	did	gave	more	our	some	thought	week
again	better	didn't	get	morning	out	something	three	well
all	big	do	getting	most	over	soon	through	went
along	book	dog	girl	mother	people	started	time	were
also	boy	don't	girls	much	place	stay	to	what
always	boys	door	give	my	play	still	today	when
am	brother	down	go	name	pretty	summer	told	where
an	but	each	going	never	put	sure	too	which
and	by	eat	good	new	ran	take	took	while
another	called	enough	great	next	read	teacher	town	white
any	came	ever	had	nice	ready	tell	tree	who
are	can	every	happy	night	right	than	two	winter
around	car	father	hard	no	room	that	until	with
as	children	few	has	not	said	the	up	work
asked	Christmas	find	have	now	saw	their	us	would
at	city	fire	he	of	say	them	use	write
away	cold	first	heard	off	school	then	used	year
back	come	five	help	old	see	there	very	years
be	comes	for	her	on	she	these	want	you
beautiful	coming	found	here	once	should	they	wanted	your
because	could	four	may	one	side	thing	was	
bed	country	friend	me	only	small	things	water	

Other Words that Will Help Us

ask	fall
ate	far
black	fast
blue	fly
both	full
bring	funny
brown	goes
buy	green
call	grow
carry	hat
clean	hold
cut	hurt
does	its
done	jump
draw	myself
drink	open

Other Words that Will Help Us

own	stop
please	ten
pull	thank
red	those
ride	together
right	try
round	under
run	upon
seven	walk
shall	warm
show	wash
sing	why
sit	wish
six	yellow
sleep	yes
start	

Based on seminar papers of Catherine Came, Eugene M. Fowler, and Horace McGee of San Diego State College, San Diego, California, the following word book or a card file of frequently used words is suggested as a handy reference for words that are used in certain situations. These are usually created by the teacher after discussion with the children. Contents might include some of the following:

Days of the Week

Sunday	Thursday
Monday	Friday
Tuesday	Saturday
Wednesday	

Months of the Year

January	May	September
February	June	October
March	July	November
April	August	December

Sounds that Animals Make

quack	bow wow
mew	oink oink
cluck	whinny
moo	neigh
coo	

Kinds of Weather

foggy	rainy
cloudy	windy
sunny	hot
clear	cold

Places We Go on Trips

beach	zoo
mountains	harbor
museum	country
desert	farm

Special Words for

tastes	feelings
color	action
smells	sights

Social Studies Unit Words

Words will vary according to unit.

Children may also generate word lists on particular topics suggested by the teacher. For example, the teacher could ask small groups to "brainstorm" all of the words they can think of which describe food, clothes, feelings, etc. The teacher can then paste these word lists on the classroom walls for the children to use in their writings.

Working on a letter as a group helps to establish security among members of the class. Writing a group letter to a sick classmate is a useful writing exercise. (PHOTO BY LINDA LUNGREN.)

TRAINING THE FIVE SENSES. Play games that emphasize sensory response. Have a child do an act while the others listen. Then tell how it sounded. Such actions as tap on the desk, tap on the window, drop a book, drum with two pencils, open a window, and so on are appropriate.

Next imagine that you are a bird that could fly anywhere. Tell what you hear and have the class guess where the bird is.

Close your eyes and picture something you saw at home this morning or on the way to school. See if your words will help others see the same thing. The teacher or a student may ask questions until the complete image is visualized.

Match the beginning and ending of sentences such as these:

The door bell	tiptoed softly
The clock	screamed
Mother	hummed
The whistle	clanged
The fire alarm	whimpered
The baby	blew

3. Standards

Standards are designed to assist expression of ideas, not interfere with them. Yet we do not value a language anarchy. Security built on a knowledge of proper form will aid any writer.

REMINDER CHARTS. Prior to writing, attention is called to certain skills previously used. These can be reviewed rapidly, then posted as a reminder while writing.

CAPITAL LETTERS. Names start with capital letters.

Nancy, Ken, Jay, Erin

Sentences start with capital letters.

See the cat.
Where are you going?

Because all writing involves handwriting skills, the quality practiced is important. Prior to a writing lesson, a five-minute review of the formation of certain letters is valuable. This may involve chalkboard demonstrations by the pupils, an examination of small handwriting reference cards at each student's writing place, or a review of the letter forms usually posted over the blackboard. Second-grade children should know all the letter forms. Primary children should be helped with letters as needed, especially the capital letter forms.

A major use of standards is to direct proofreading of material. Children should not be expected to proofread for all errors, but they should check for certain specifics. The following would be appropriate:

Did I capitalize the words in my title?
Did I keep a margin?
Did I use my best writing?
Did I put only one line through words I wanted to change? (Prevents erasing or scribbling over a word.)

4. Laboratory Writing Exercises

Such activities as the writer's table are individual devices that free the child from classroom pressures. At other times the guidance of the teacher is desirable as certain skills and understandings are practiced.

GROUP COMPOSITION. Working on composition as a group helps to establish security among members of the class, gives the teacher an opportunity to prevent errors in spelling and usage, and builds good human relationships. Some children need this experience before they are able to organize their thoughts and express themselves independently. Subjects for group composition can develop from a common experience or the social studies. The children contribute ideas that the teacher writes on the chalkboard. Later those who wish may copy the product. Letters to a sick classmate, notes sent home about a program, or letters to another class are examples of group composition topics.

STAGGERED WRITING ASSIGNMENT. Although writing will frequently be done by the entire class, a variation is to have only one group write. This makes it possible for the teacher to give more personal help, evaluate with greater care—because there are fewer papers—and provide for the individual differences in a group. There is a competitive element in writing as well as reading. Those operating at approximately the same levels profit most by group instruction.

CLASSROOM HELPERS. At times it will give recognition to a few and help others to appoint one student in each group who may give help with spelling, punctuation, or other problems. Upper-grade children may be given recognition by permitting them to be "human dictionaries" in a lower grade during a writing period.

PREVENTION OF ERROR PRACTICE. Practicing an error tends to fix it as a habit. With experience teachers learn to anticipate problems that the class or individuals will have. To prevent spelling errors and to encourage the use of vocabulary, word cards with illustrations of meaning might be made for the seasons. Halloween words that children want to use would include *gate, witch, ghost, haunted, screamed*. These words might be reviewed, then placed on the chalkboard. A child who wants to use a word has a clue to identify with the picture. After selecting the word he wants, he takes it to his desk, copies it, then returns it to the chalkboard. Review of handwriting and punctuation standards may be carried out before the writing period. The children should be given time to proofread, with questions to guide them. The teacher should never ask a child to do something he knows is beyond the ability of the child. Because some write a dramatic sketch does not mean that all should. It might be well to have some writing as a partner or group activity either at the planning level or at presentation time.

5. Sharing the Written Compositions

Use the sharing time at the beginning of the day to read some of the compositions.

Post compositions on the bulletin board.

Make a booklet, such as "Our Halloween Stories."

Some authorities strongly recommend that the teacher or a parent type stories written by children and correct the major errors. This enhances the child's confidence that he can write and has something to say. There is much testimony that with confidence thus established the children improve in error reduction and clarity of expression.

Collect the written efforts in a folder, which is sent home after the parent conference.

Publish in a school newspaper compositions that have special merit.

Exchange compositions with another class at the same level or a different one (appropriate at the end of a year).

Making Our Sentences Sound More Interesting

Make one sentence from these two short sentences:

1. Spooky was a ghost. He was a friendly ghost.

_____

2. I have a ball. It is a red ball.

_____

3. Lynne has a pencil. It is green.

_____

4. Mary is my friend. She is my best friend.

_____

5. Kelly threw the ball. She threw it to me.

_____

6. This is my wagon. It is big.

_____

7. I have a doll. He is handsome.

_____

8. They have the blocks. There are six.

_____

9. I like your story. It is a good story.

_____

10. It is on the table. The table is large.

_____

6. Improving Composition Skills

The teacher finds something to praise in each composition. "I like the way you used (*a word*)." "The ending is good."

But errors are noted as revealing instructional needs of children. The teacher then composes a story that reflects these errors or, with the permission of a child, uses one of the papers submitted. The problem is presented to the class as "How can we make this interesting paper better?"

The story is written on the board:

SPOOKY

Spooky was a ghost. He was a friendly ghost. He could be everything. But he could not float. He could not moan. He was a funny ghost. He was a happy ghost too.

After the story is read aloud, the class discusses the sentences and the possibility of joining some of them to make the story sound more interesting and flow more easily.

The class may practice on a written drill of the type shown at the bottom of p. 191 (the term *transform* might be used if the students are familiar with the new grammar).

The children then look over their previous stories and change sentences. Other drills of the following nature may be used:

Make a sentence by drawing a line from a group of words in List *A* to a group of words in List *B*. Be sure they belong together.

A	*B*
1. The dog	me his book.
2. The little boy	see the game.
3. Brian gave	ate some ice cream.
4. We went to	ran after the cat.
5. I like	to read.

Write the words you need to finish each sentence. Choose them from the group of words below.

the red ball	ice cream and cake
We have	splashing down
I wish	three blocks to school
She went	four new dresses

1. I like _____ .
2. _____ three new girls now.
3. Every day I walk _____ .
4. _____ I had three dollars.
5. The rain came _____ .
6. Denise has _____ .
7. _____ to the skating party.
8. We are going to have _____ .

Paragraph Drill

Copy these sentences so they tell a story. When you decide which sentence to use first, be sure to indent the sentence. These sentences should make a one-paragraph story.

She ate their porridge and sat in their chairs.

They lived in the woods.

Once there were three bears.

A little girl came to their house.

Reading, Writing, and Rating Stories

Sager (1976) suggests a four-part program, "Reading, Writing, and Rating Stories," which encompasses many techniques to encourage children to improve the clarity and style of their writing. Children are provided with stories that they rate according to vocabulary, elaboration, organization, and structure. They are given the criteria for rating each factor, and in the process of assigning values to the stories in their lessons they develop an understanding of the need for *rewriting* in the achievement of a good written product. Thus children return to their own compositions and apply the same judgments they used in the lessons; they rework and rewrite their own stories.

For Discussion

1. Why is it better to recognize a situation a child will want to write about than to use a device to motivate him to write? Indicate such a situation.

2. Some say that there is a creative element in all writing. For some children, writing their name is creative. Do you agree with this? How would you encourage other writing?

How May Creative Writing Be Fostered in the Intermediate Grades?

It takes more than a permissive classroom climate and a teacher interested in children to produce worthy written work in the intermediate classroom. First of all, writing takes time. If a teacher attempts to suggest a topic and have the child write something in a single language

An attractive display can motivate additional writing of stories. (COURTESY OF THE BURBANK PUBLIC SCHOOLS.)

period, it means incomplete and hurriedly done papers. Creative writing is a questionable homework assignment. There is a suggestion of coercion in homework that will limit the creative expression of some children. Although a child may willingly rework a piece of writing at home, the first draft should be completed under the teacher's supervision. There are a few self-motivated children who like to write, just as others like to study music or play ball. No restrictions should be placed on such children.

A three-day sequence provides adequate time for most writing endeavors. The first period should be used for the stimulation of ideas, discussion of various words and skills needed to develop a topic, and the experimental first drafts of the material. The second period should be a true writing laboratory with each child writing and receiving help as needed. The third day should be used to correct errors, reorganize material, and write the final copy if the child wishes to revise the material. Some projects will take longer. This means that during the year less written composition may be done, but what is done will have purpose and merit.

The teaching sequence is that of motivation, skill development, refinement, and use. Motivation involves any experience that starts a flow of ideas. The discussion helps the student determine the thought he wishes to develop in his writing. Skill development involves planned vocabulary materials, reviews of punctuation, writing, and spelling skills, and help with organization of ideas.

Refinement involves making corrections, proofreading, and writing to improve content, form, usage, spelling, and handwriting. Use is the recognition given the final product as it is read to the class, reproduced in a newspaper, placed on a bulletin board, or shared in a way appropriate to the content.

Just as storytelling pictures are used in the primary grades, so they may be used in the intermediate. Those with great human interest, such as the illustrations of Norman Rockwell, are especially good. But pictures expressing beauty, mood, and action are equally motivating. Class members may select a picture from the group presented by the teacher or all write about the same one. Because children sometimes are impressed by the ideas of other children and thus limit their creativity, it is a challenge to be original and see a story in a picture that no one else imagines. The class discusses two or three before making a choice to use as the basis for a story. The characters are discussed. The children are asked to imagine what is happening now, what happened previously, and what is likely to happen next. Words are selected that describe the action, beauty, or feeling. Possible titles are suggested and first lines written. During a second period the stories are written. Later, children may select pictures from magazines for the writing table or for additional stories.

After the imagination of children has been aroused, it sometimes takes only a title to start them thinking of a story. Such titles as these may be put in a box on the writer's table to help some get started:

The Midnight Visitor
The Falling Star
The Hidden Valley
Lost in a Storm
An Animal Friend
A Secret
My Ambition
Flying at Night
Faster than Sound

In a similar way, opening-paragraph starters help a writer get on his way:

"She's gone! Now I am going to find her diary," muttered Daryl to himself as he crept up the stairs noiselessly.

Daryl stood stock still. His legs refused to go. The sweat broke out on his forehead.

Denny walked to the window to let in a little air. As he began to raise it, something outside caught his eye. He stood with his mouth open. There on the lawn below the window was the strangest thing he had ever seen.

At first the noise was very faint and seemed far away. It was an odd noise, one that the boys didn't recognize. As it moved closer they went out to see what it might be.

Mildred knew that if her mother found out, she wouldn't be able to sit for days, but she was determined to carry out her plan in spite of this.

The children were playing on the beach when they found the strange footprints in the sand. Their curiosity got the best of them and they decided to follow them along the shore.

"Quick, come here," called Trevor, "I want to show you what I've found!" As the others ran to join him, they stopped short, staring in surprise.

When father came home that evening he was whistling happily. The children knew what that meant. He had another of his wonderful surprises.

There was a strange silence about the forest that night. It had an air of waiting for something to happen.

These may be put on cards and placed in an "idea box" to help those who seek ideas.

Some children need only a word or phrase to start a series of thoughts that lead to writing:

ghost
fog
gravy
my worst scare
nightmare
rolling waves
little old lady
a bright idea
late again
mud

some luck
pride
rolling along
long journey
longest day of my life
face like a lion
time to think

The object of writing does not need to be a story. Frequently the purpose is to help children write with vividness and insight. The actual plotting of a story, with beginning, characterization, episodes, climax, and ending, may be too complex for many in the elementary school. It does not matter whether the material is a story, report, autobiography, dramatic play, or sketch. It does matter that the child is learning to express ideas effectively in writing.

Painting word pictures will interest students, yet not demand the time that story writing involves. Ask the children what pictures the word makes them see. Then have them write a word picture. These are examples:

snow   Snow, soft and cold and white, drifted lazily through the air, rested fluffily upon the boughs of the evergreen trees, and in time covered the earth with quiet beauty.

waves   Waves rolled endlessly toward the shore, crashing thunderously against the gray rocks and sending countless sprays of foam skyward.

airplanes Airplanes roared down the runways, then effortlessly left the ground and soared majestically into the sky, soon becoming mere specks in the distance.

Objects will start a child's imagination working. One teacher brought in a bag of old shoes—a football shoe, a tennis slipper, a satin pump, and so on—and presented such questions as "Who wore this shoe?" "Where has it been?" "Why was it thrown away?" The class was motivated, and writing of a highly imaginative nature resulted.

Variations on old themes will help some get started. What happened to Goldilocks on the next day? What did the three bears do at Christmas? What type of queen was Cinderella? Social studies may motivate historical writing in the form of a news account of such events as Columbus's discovery of the New World or the discovery of gold in California. "Hansel & Gretel Go Back to School" by George Creegan, published in *Plays* (October 1966), will remind students of such possibilities.

A "story formula" will challenge some. A good story has five parts: a beginning, a problem, a high point or climax, a following action or solution, and a satisfactory ending. This chart may be used to check the formula:

1. Does your story have a good beginning? Tell the four "W's": Who, When, Where, and What's the problem?
2. Did you make the reader aware of the problem?
3. Does your story reach a high point or climax?
4. Is there an adequate explanation of how the problem was solved?
5. Do all the parts fit together at the end in a way that satisfies the reader?

Five-sentence stories may outline the plot of a story:

1. Mother and I were sitting in the kitchen after dinner one quiet evening.
2. Suddenly we heard a scratching noise at the back door.
3. Mother screamed and jumped up on a chair as a gray mouse darted across the floor.
4. I stood there and laughed at the funny sight, while Mother recovered from terror.
5. I imagine the mouse was more frightened than Mother was.

Charts of this nature may be used as guides:

How Stories Begin

1. With conversation to set the stage for action.
2. With the end of the story, then going back to the beginning.
3. With the middle of the story, then to the actual beginning.
4. With a characterization of the chief character or characters.

Create a Character

When an author writes a story, he creates the characters out of his imagination. You can do that, too. Look at the figure to the left. Can you imagine what sort of person it might be?

Is it a picture of a man or a woman or a boy or a girl? Is it a big person or a little person? What are the things this person likes most? What kind of person is he? What is his name?

Suppose you decided it was a little boy who liked to play baseball, and always wore his uniform and his red baseball cap. His favorite food was hamburgers. He was an absent-minded boy who forgot the things he was supposed to do. His name was Sam.

Try to write a story about Sam. Here is the story that John wrote.

One day, Sam got up early to play baseball. His mother told him she was going to have hamburgers for his lunch. Sam was happy. He played baseball all morning. He was so busy playing baseball, he forgot to go home at lunchtime for his hamburgers!

To the left there is another figure. Ask yourself what kind of person it might be. Make up your own character for this figure, draw his picture, and write a story that shows what kind of person he is.

EMPHASIS
Like the preceding lesson, this one has to do with character description. But now pupils provide the details that help make fictional personalities seem real.

EXPLANATION
Begin this lesson with a discussion of various personalities—real and fictional —whom all the children probably know. For example, have pupils think about what characteristics make these individuals distinct personalities: Crow Boy, Mickey Mantle, Bob Hope, Pippi Long-stocking, Charlie Brown.

Point out that an author gives distinctive qualities to characters so readers will feel they know them as well as they know friends and neighbors.

Then have youngsters read and discuss page 153. During discussion, have children consider what they might tell about a person to bring him alive for readers. A description might include details about the character's interests, likes and dislikes, habits, speech, clothing, physical appearance, and anything that makes him a little different from most other people.

After pupils have followed the lesson's final suggestion, invite them to show their drawings and to read their descriptions aloud. Encourage the class to comment on details in the descriptions that made the characters lifelike. Select several drawings and descriptions for a bulletin-board display.

EXTENSION
At a later date, divide the class into three groups to write a composite story. Let the first group introduce a character with distinctive personality traits. The second group may then develop the plot by presenting a problem. The third group will solve the problem and provide a story ending. Point out that the problem should be one which this type of character would be likely to encounter and that the solution, if it is one that he works out, should also be in keeping with his character.

Working with a friend while imagining an experience often helps the young writer's creativity. (PHOTO BY LINDA LUNGREN.)

5. With a summary paragraph to tell the point of the story.
6. With description.
7. With the time, place, or circumstance.
8. With a question.

Describing Our Characters

1. By a simple statement of fact: Bob is lazy.
2. By describing how Bob does things.
3. By telling an episode to prove that Bob is lazy.
4. By telling how little of his work is done.
5. By comparing him with others who are not lazy.
6. By using synonyms of the word.
7. By reporting what others say.
8. By telling what he is not.
9. By repeating his own characterization of himself.

Self-characterization is easier than describing another. A "Who Am I?" paper that may be read by the teacher while the class identifies the writer may be the beginning of character study. The following example provides this help in guiding children as they describe a character: [1]

Some children, by virtue of personality, home, or early school training, are alert to the details of the world in which they live; others need help in the development of all five senses. These children must be encouraged to find pleasure in observation and in the discussion of what they see.

It is easy to start an enthusiastic discussion concerning the flavor of certain foods. It's fun, too, to put into words the taste of cod-liver oil, an uncured olive, or a mouthful of the Pacific Ocean. Children soon discover that following one's nose may be an interesting

[1] From Andrew Schiller and others, *Language and How We Use It* (Glenview, Ill.: Scott, Foresman, 1969), p. 153.

experience leading to the earthy smell of recently turned sod, the tang of the sea, the fragrance of clean linen just off the line, the musty odor of old newspapers stored in the garage.

Vocabulary is increased and power of expression heightened when pupils are helped to see the importance of contrasting words and ideas. They will enjoy trying it too.

> quietness of the forest
> vs. *clang of the city streets*

> smooth as the snow-covered lawn
> vs. *rough and jagged as the ice on the pond*

Children are easily helped to understand that whole sentences can be built to reflect contrasting ideas that will best express their own feelings:

The forest was dim. Billy thought of the meadow near his home where a sparkling brook with little minnows rushed down mossy rocks in warm sunshine.

Children enjoy the euphony of a sentence or line in which the same first letter or sound in a group of words is repeated a number of times. Alliteration can become stilted when it is used as a mechanical exercise. With older children it should be encouraged not as a game but rather to enhance the meaning of words.

> soft slumbering summer
> lonely leaf
> nodding noon
> whispering wind
> weird white world

Young children use similes naturally and easily. Although they may not label them as such, older children use metaphors in the same manner. Comparison is a natural method of description for young and old alike. Children enjoy completing these phrases:

> as soft as
> as loud as
> as happy as
> as sad as
> as stern as

> as drowsy as
> as bright as
> as cold as
> as easy as
> as hot as
> as muffled as
> as slippery as
> as long as
> as short as
> as pointed as

They become conscious of the use of similes in writing about things that "looked like" or were "as gentle as." One class found that the wind today "was as gentle as"

> a lamb
> my mother's voice
> a soft, furry cloud
> a rose opening
> when night falls

Tactile perception can be used to enrich children's writing. Various objects can be passed among the children and their reactions written on the board. One teacher passed a bowl of ice cubes. In seeking to express their reaction, the children sought and found many words to describe what they had touched. Ice is

> cold
> slippery
> smooth
> hard
> sharp
> shivery

The teacher can use a small figurine, holding it up and asking the class to look at it closely, then putting the figurine behind something. The teacher now asks the class to describe what was seen. The teacher can pretend she has never seen the object, so that she can be very curious about the responses, encouraging accurate, descriptive analysis. After the first attempt, the class tries again, looks at the object once more, develops vocabulary to explain, and goes through the entire object—all responses being verbal. On the third try, using a new object, the class can try writing a description.

After preliminary work on developing "word pictures," the teacher can put three sentences on the board, such as

An airplane went up.
It flew.
It came down.

The class can be encouraged to develop a more interesting and exciting picture of the situation. Action words and descriptive words can be included orally. As a real picture begins to form, children can appreciate the power of such words as *soared, skimmed,* and *floated.*

As a written work experience, children can take another set of three sentences and see how well they can paint another word picture:

The wind blew.
The windows shook.
The storm came.

Ask the children what pictures a word makes them see. Then let them write a word picture.

RAIN

Rain splashed upon the earth, forming puddles on the ground, pelting against the windows, and dripping endlessly from the eaves of the buildings.

WAVES

Waves rolled shoreward in long unbroken lines, each crest forming for an instant a magic crown of transparent green before toppling over into a churning mass of yellow-white foam.

Children are amused by their first encounter with metaphors. Their practical minds create laugh-provoking pictures when they read such statements as "His eyes dropped," "She turned green with envy," "He put his foot in his mouth," "The doctor was tied up," "Someone spilled the beans." Cartoons can be made to accompany metaphors.

Teach shades of meaning by mounting pictures of increasing size on deepening shades of colored paper. Blow "word bubbles" to get synonyms. Start each row with a word, such as *went, pretty, small,* or *old.* Let children blow their bubbles larger by giving synonyms for each word.

While use of a thesaurus is beyond the ability of most children, it does help to make a "classroom thesaurus" of words to use instead of *said, funny, beautiful,* and other overused words. The study of words separated from the situation where children would use them is an isolated and usually ineffective learning situation. Meaningful exercises of this nature, however, are helpful after the need for adequate vocabulary is felt by a writer. Consider the following exercises.[2]

[2] From *Oral and Written Language* (San Diego, Calif.: San Diego City Schools, 1956), with special acknowledgment to Elizabeth Stocker.

To the Pupil:

Life would be pretty dull if we ate the same foods at every meal, or played the same game every day. Life would be equally dull if we said and heard the same words all the time. We need to know enough words so that we don't wear out the same old, tired ones. We can give words a rest by using synonyms. Synonyms are words which have almost the same meaning, like "little," "small," and "tiny."

1. Do you know a word to use in place of "big"?_____
2. Do you know another word which is a synonym for "big"? _____
3. Use your dictionary to help you find three more synonyms for "big."

_____   _____   _____

4. In the exercise below, *circle* the three words that have meanings somewhat alike. Choose the best word to *fill the space* in the sentences. Use your dictionary to help you.

space	distance	New York is a long _____ from here.
expanse	praise	
place	install	

deposit	plan	I will _____ my money in the bank.
crack	split	
break	build	There was a _____ in the plaster.

5. You can find synonyms for these words in the box below. *Write* the correct synonym on the line beside each word. *Check by using your dictionary.*

pair _____   doze _____

jammed _____   funny _____

coast _____   pretty _____

coarse _____   strange _____

nap	lovely	amusing	odd
crowded	shore	couple	rough

To the Pupil:

One day during sharing period Andy told the class this story about his trip to the circus:

"The girl did stunts. Everything she did, the clown tried to do, too. The girl was graceful, but the clown—well, the clown wasn't graceful."

Andy needed a word to tell the opposite meaning of "graceful." He could have used "awkward" or "clumsy," but he just couldn't think of these words. Words which are opposite in meaning to other words are called *antonyms*. To speak and write better we need to know many antonyms.

Circle the word that means the opposite, or almost the opposite, of the first word in each line:

leave	play	sleep	stay
attach	detach	try	wish
powerful	different	homeless	weak
great	small	large	buff
scarce	plentiful	first	thin
most	least	soft	sweet
expensive	late	next	cheap
damp	clean	strong	dry
good	right	bad	ready
give	grow	take	go

To the Pupil:

Think of the word "apple." Does this word do something to you? Now think of "the juicy, red apple." These added words which tell about the apple make us think about the delicious taste of this fruit. When we describe or tell about something we can make it much more interesting by using words which make our listeners or readers see, hear, touch, taste or smell.

Write a word in the blank in front of each word below which will help to describe that word.

1. the _____ car (see)
2. the _____ motor (sound)
3. the _____ flowers (smell)
4. the _____ pie (taste)
5. the _____ satin cloth (touch)

Use these describing words to write in the sentences below:

howling   rough   sour   pungent   glittering

1. The _____ floor scratched his feet.
2. The sky was sprinkled with _____ stars.
3. Pine needles have a _____ odor.
4. The _____ dog kept some people awake.
5. She had a _____ pickle in her lunch box.

To the Pupil:

When we write or speak we paint word pictures in the minds of readers and listeners. These word pictures can be simple black-and-white drawings or they can be wide-screen, 3-D, technicolor, action movies. Compare these two sentences:

1. The fire engine stopped in front of the burning house.
2. Siren screaming and tires screeching, the bright red fire engine braked to a halt in front of the blazing building.

Which sentence painted a better word picture for you? Now see if you can rewrite the following sentences. Make them paint better pictures.

1. Sharon was doing tricks on her bicycle.

_____

_____

2. Susan and Ricky were playing with paper dolls.

_____

_____

3. Mike hit a home run.

_____

_____

4. Irene was wearing a red hat.

_____

_____

5. The horse jumped over the fence.

_____

_____

Proofreading and rewriting are aspects of idea refinement. The fact that the first effort to write is a rough drafting of ideas or an experiment with ideas needs to be established as early as the fourth grade. Because rewriting a long selection can be a burden at this level, the short episode, the humorous incident, the descriptive paragraph, or the news item should be the writing objective.

Standards for proofreading should be established one at a time. Many children need freedom to write without the threat of proofreading or editing all their efforts. The goals of the learner and the teacher will determine the extent to which material should be examined. These will reflect the language skills being taught at the grade level. The following items would be appropriate for the fifth grade:

Proofreading My Story

1. Is my paper headed correctly?
2. Did I skip a line after my heading?
3. Did I capitalize the important words in the title?
4. Did I skip a line before I began to write my story?
5. Did I indent for each paragraph?
6. Do I have a margin?
7. Is each word spelled correctly?
8. Is each sentence complete? Did I omit words?
9. Have I a period or question mark after each sentence?
10. Did I include the important points in my story? Did I tell my story in sequence?

A class may be organized so that each writer has an editing partner. This partner then edits the paper. This report is submitted with the original and rewritten paper.

Proofreading

1. Did this person indent?
2. Did this person watch his margin?
3. Has he checked his spelling?

4. Did he use capitals when they were needed?
5. Is his paper neat?
6. Does this person know when to end a sentence and begin a new one?
7. Has this person used too many "ands"?
8. Do you feel this person checked his paper when it was finished?
   I checked _____ paper.
   My name is _____

Lessons in proofreading should be included in the language period. Exercises of this nature emphasize the skills of proofreading.

Proofread the following story:
1. Does each sentence start with a capital letter? (There should be twelve sentences.)
2. Are all the words correctly spelled? (There are five misspelled words.)
3. Do all the sentences tell about the topic? (There is one that does not belong.)
4. Are the paragraphs indented?

Once upon a time there lived a boy named Billy he lived with his mother and father. Once when his father was outside getting water the Indians came along and burned the house. Only Billy was alive and then he ran to the mountains and stayed there for five days. Billy and his family came from Warren, Ohio.
On the fifth day he saw a nest on a rockey cliffth. In the nest he saw a baby eagle. The mother eagle had been shot with an arrow. He took the baby eagle for a pet. Billy and the eagle grew up in the forest. They ate together and slept together. They had no family but they were not alone.

Displays of work "Before Proofreading" and "After Proofreading" will emphasize the improvement possible. A committee of proofreaders can serve the class. Three students are assigned the task of proofreading stories placed in a box at the reading table. When their work is completed, the work is placed in a "rewrite" box. After a visit to a newspaper, the role of editor can be dramatized in this way.

Classroom recognition can be given to children's writing in several ways. One school makes a scrapbook of "Our Very Best Writing." When the class feels that something is worthy for this collection, the material is added. At the end of the year this is presented to the principal. Scrapbooks made in former years are available on certain occasions.

Children enjoy reading something written by an older brother or sister. Upper-grade children are impressed with material they wrote while in a lower grade. Eventually it may be possible for a child to read material written by one of his parents when the parent was in the fifth grade. The teacher must plan so that the best product of each individual is included and so that no one is left out. During the year a child might substitute a new selection for one previously selected.

Bulletin boards of children's writing provide recognition and encouragement. Some schools have strict rules about the display of imperfect papers. In light of the objectives of creative writing, it seems that a paper with a few errors checked is still worthy of display. Few children are going to find pleasure in rewriting an entire paper just to have it placed on the bulletin board.

Publication in a school paper or magazine is the ultimate recognition for many. Creative writing is not news writing and as such must have a special place in any publication. Many school systems now publish an annual magazine of creative writing. When a selection is considered worthy, it is sent to an editing committee. This committee acknowledges the selection with a letter of recognition explaining that the work will be considered but that not all material submitted will be used. The letter is adequate recognition for many children. If a child's material is selected for the magazine, he receives three copies of the publication and another letter. The existence of such a publication influences many teachers to attempt projects involving creative writing who ordinarily would be more secure stressing drill on the mechanics of language.

Perhaps the most important idea that those who work with children in the area of creative or imaginative writing have found to be true is one of the utmost simplicity. You cannot teach children to write creatively—you can only help them express the original ideas within them. Behind the story, poem, or letter—behind the clear, concise sentence or the stumbling search for words—is the child and all that he can become. Creative writing is one more way to understand him.

As young writers develop confidence a greater awareness of good composition qualities will improve their written expression:[3]

In the intermediate grades many children make definite advancement in the following areas of good composition:

Unity: staying with the subject
Continuity: developing topic statements by addition and illustration
Form: sense of order; organization
Sentence structure: the levels of subordination
Diction: choosing fresh, colorful, precise words
Tone: developing individuality of style

STORY SYNTAX

The following sentences exemplify progress in unity, sentence structure, and diction.

Unity

The following beginning and closing sentences of compositions indicate "staying with the subject":

Grade Four
When the sun comes up, all is still on the lake.
It's very still on the lake when no one's up but me.
I was sitting on the porch watching TV when all of a sudden the TV went out.
From then on the TV was OK.

Grade Six
To have a vacation without any accidents this summer, we should be careful in everything we do. Remember, most accidents can be prevented.
By being careful and using common sense, you will have a very safe summer.

Sentence Structure

The following sentences exemplify logical subordination:

Grade Four
When I look at Brownstone Falls in Mellen, Wisconsin, I think of purple rocks and water falling down them.

[3] From *English Language Arts in Wisconsin*, Robert Pooley, Project Director (Madison, Wis.: Department of Public Instruction, 1968).

When Ranger VI went to the moon he did not bring
back pictures because he met space men and they
took his camera.

Grade Six

Summer would be a lot more fun if people would obey
summer safety rules.

He replied, "I feel that the American people have a
wrong impression of my country of Peru, for my
country is a contrast of old and new, of gaiety and
sorrow."

Diction

The following sentences contain fresh, colorful words:

Grade Four

It was very quiet on the marsh, no fish leaping, no birds
singing.

[The wind] makes the flowers nod their heads and twist
around and rise off the ground.

Grade Six

Cars are speedy now, whizzing by at one hundred miles
an hour.

Whispers come from a motor purring softly.

As a boy I could look down the terraced hillside, to the
green valley snuggled between the mountains; or I
could look upward to the lofty peaks, their diamond
snow shimmering in the blinding sun.

Children use figurative speech as early as fourth grade.
For instance:

[Mars] looked like a big beach ball in the air.

A rhinocerous is big and bold. He has horns like sharp
fat long tacks.

Practical writing is done in any situation where
there is need for it. In comparison with creative writing,
practical writing is frequently more utilitarian and realistic and needs the discipline of correct mechanics to be
acceptable. Correct form seems intrinsically a function
of realistic writing because other people are practically
concerned. This is the type of writing in which the author works more as a reproducer of known facts, conditions, or ideas presented in his own words. Here the
emphasis may be on the mechanics of writing, spelling,
penmanship, neatness, punctuation, and similar external
items without injury to the child's creative expression.

When a child writes creatively, he expresses in one
way or another his feelings or his intellectual reactions
to an experience—something he has seen, heard, or
otherwise come in contact with through his senses. This
expression of personal reactions constitutes the quality
of originality because no one other than the writer can
produce it. It is his own contribution. This type of writing is that of artistic self-expression. It is personal, individual, imaginative, and highly perishable. To keep it
alive there must be complete freedom to experiment and
complete assurance of a respectful reception of the
product regardless of its nature.

Although in a sense the two aspects of writing develop separately and serve different purposes, the child
gradually carries over what he has learned of techniques
in practical writing and applies it where it suits his purpose in personal writing. The emphasis is first and last
on saying something that is worth saying, and saying it
effectively. *A balance between the two types must be
maintained, and to give all writing the same treatment
is to suppress or inhibit the creative spirit of children.*
Lenski stresses the importance of the treatment of creative writing:

It is such a simple thing to help children enter the creative life, to help them to think clearly and to communicate
their ideas to others through the spoken or written word.
Provide the opportunity—let the child talk and let him write,
enjoying both. Share his enthusiasms. All children can and
should learn the free and easy use of words. Creative expression should never be confused with the teaching of the
techniques of writing. These are two distinct procedures.

It should always be remembered that creation is a flowing of ideas. Given a stimulus, ideas come pouring from the
mind like water from a fountain. It is all too easy to stop this
creative flow. Rules for punctuation, spelling, grammar, and
handwriting will stop it. Emphasis on rules is sure to stifle
creative thinking. [Lenski, 1949]

There are some who would not be so negative with
respect to rules as Lenski. Confidence in the craftsmanship of writing and expression also releases creativity. Great writers and artists have also been expert
craftsmen. Certainly no great painter has emerged by
ignoring the disciplines of his craft. By mastering these
disciplines he is able to project his own personal qualities more effectively. Our objective is to use the child's

desire to create to make disciplined craftsmanship acceptable.

Burrows (1965) emphasizes that evaluation of practical writing serves a different purpose than evaluation of personal writing.

One of the acknowledged tasks of the elementary school years is to further the pupil's self-concept. Few experiences in school can so effectively destroy a positive self-image as the teaching of composition. Excessive correction has thwarted the pencil of many a beginner. In other cases, no correction at all has been offered for fear of cramping self-expression. When to correct and when not to correct children's writing has been a dilemma for many teachers.

Solutions arrived at in both England and America reveal surprising agreement. Correction is applied to children's practical writings—letters, reports, records, and other forms of factual prose in which the written paper itself is seen by an audience (Burrows et al., 1964). A British study reaching essentially the same conclusion calls these businesslike forms "recording writing" (Clegg, 1964).

Pride in achieving correct form is developed in these more objective examples. On the other hand, imaginative expression is for enjoyment. Story and verse are to be read aloud to one's class, either by the author or by the teacher, and need not be corrected or rewritten. After being enjoyed by an audience, they are filed privately; their physical form is relatively unimportant. They have already served their purpose in oral communication. Here again the oral basis for learning to write operates with real efficiency. Only when stories or verse are to be made public in a class newspaper or school publication must they be edited and rewritten.

Correction of any writing is best done orally by teacher and pupil in an editing conference, taking turns reading aloud. (PHOTO BY LINDA LUNGREN.)

When they are made public they must be put into good form, as an obligation to others as well as a mark of self-respect.

Correction of any writing is best done orally by teacher and pupil in an editing conference, taking turns reading aloud. Thus they apply the oral-auditory facility established long before the newer learnings of writing and reading.

When writing is an opportunity to reveal one's own feelings and imagination without fear of criticism and with the assurance of respectful listeners, the pupil's picture of himself is enhanced. Not being on the defensive, he can appreciate the good writing of others, both peers and professionals. He can enjoy what is worthy in his teacher's eyes because he too is worthy as a writer. Both his listening audience and those who see his corrected public writing fortify his pleasure and his pride in writing and in himself.

For Discussion

1. Do you consider that children can be as creative in such tasks as letter writing as in imaginative writing?

2. To what extent is it true that the skills of language are the skills of conformity?

3. Alvina Burrows reports, in the *N.E.A. Bulletin*, No. 18, "Certain procedures have not stood up to the testing of research. Among these are encouraging children to plan stories before they write, checking the mechanics as they write, experimenting with words for the sake of using 'colorful' or 'different' ones, studying vocabulary lists, writing for school newspapers, and requiring self-evaluation of writing." Why do you think some of these have proved unsuccessful?

4. Some years ago it was popular to have "picture study" in the language arts. Small reproductions of great paintings were made available to each child. Why do you think the same idea might work as a stimulation of creative expression?

5. Few children will ever become authors or even reporters. Should a greater effort be made in the area of practical writing than in the area of creative writing?

How May the Writing of Poetry Be Fostered?

A teacher is an artist at releasing the creativity in others. Truly creative writing cannot be taught; it can only be released and guided. If we see our task as releasing and guiding poetic expression, certain conditions must be established. First, there must be a climate in which creative effort is fostered. The teacher should point out that certain expressions used by children are imaginative and contain poetic ideas. One day a child mentioned that the sun seemed to be playing peek-a-boo as it hid behind a cloud, then shone again. A comment that this would make a good poem may be enough to get him to write. A quiet place to write, away from the group, is another aspect of climate. Then when such expressions emerge the teacher might ask, "Would you like to go to the writing table and write a poem now while the idea is fresh?" A part of the climate in a room is represented by things valued. The fact that the teacher uses a poem as a central theme for a bulletin board, reads poems to the class with personal enjoyment, or sends a notice home in verse form makes poetry have significance. Second, the teacher provides stimulations that motivate the writer to get started. Sometimes these dramatize a feeling. One student teacher played a recording of a choir singing "The Battle Hymn of the Republic," then asked, "How would you express your thoughts if asked what the United States means to you?" One verse written under these conditions won a national award. Holidays act as punctuation marks in the humdrum repetition of living. Someone has said that one trouble with life was that it is "so doggone daily." When we make some days have special feeing in them it provides all of us with a bit of variety. Halloween, Thanksgiving, Valentine's Day, Mother's Day, and birthdays have emotional associations that stimulate writing.

In addition to a classroom climate that enhances poetry appreciation and personal motivation, the teacher releases creative talents by providing specific writing aids. These include help with the mechanics of writing and spelling, the development of a vocabulary that expresses the right shade of meaning, and the understanding of poetic form. Before the children write Halloween poetry the class might discuss possible words to use. These would include *ghost, witch, haunting, creeping, scare, afraid*. With older children a rhyming dictionary is a great help. Occasionally after a poem has been enjoyed by the group, take time to look at it as one craftsman admires the work of another. The poem "Trees" can be studied in this way without diminishing its beauty. Notice the rhyme pattern. Then discuss the use of words. Why is "lovely" better than "pretty" in the second line? What image did the writer create by using the words "a nest of robins in her hair" and "lifts her leafy arms to pray"? Ask the group to think of similar images, such as "finger chimneys pointing toward the sky" or "little cars pouting in the parking lot."

A combination of words and ideas must be brought together in order to create a poem. Some children are more talented with words and ideas than others, but all children should be able to achieve this combination to a degree. The greater command a child has over words and the more original or varied his ideas, the better will be the quality of the poetry he can create.

The temptation, then, would be to set up a series of lessons designed to build vocabulary and extend ideas. Before doing so it is well to consider the influence of patterns on creativity. Suppose we set up a series of exercises like this:

1. See the cat
   It wears a _____.
2. I have a bill
   It is from the _____.
3. This boy is tall
   He must be _____.
4. This girl is late
   She must be _____.

It would appear that the child *completed* a rhyme, but did he *create* one? At best he learned a small element of the poet's craft concerning words that rhyme.

Another type of exercise provides an idea in the form of a picture, usually of a nursery rhyme. One might be of "Jack and Jill," another of "Jack Be Nimble" or "Mistress Mary." Here again the emphasis is not on creativity, but on the pleasure of repeating familiar rhyme forms. Still another exercise provides lists of words that rhyme:

day	nice
hay	spice
old	mice
told	ice
ball	sail
tall	mail
wall	pail
all	whale
kitten	tree
mitten	see
bitten	free
written	bee

A suggested verse is given:

I threw a ball
High over the wall
And a boy named Jack
Threw it right back.

Although this is patterned, there is the possibility for a bit of original thinking and the satisfaction of completing a verse. Certainly the rhyme words influenced the idea. Instead of starting with a feeling or something to say, the child was assigned the task of manipulating the words of others. The results have little more emotional appeal than the original list of rhyming words.

Creativity from a child's point of view might be thought of as a personal interpretation of experience. The child might ask, "What do certain sounds or sights mean to me? How do I feel when I see or do something? What words can I use that will help others recreate my feelings?"

One group of first-grade children was asked to think of favorite sounds. The following responses were typical:

The sound of nice music.
The sound of the recess bell.

But there were others more personal and possibly more creative, such as those that follow.

The sounds my mother makes in the kitchen getting
  supper ready.
The sound of the slamming of the car door when
  my daddy comes home from work.

One of the charming books for and by children is a
book of definitions of young children. The title is one
of the definitions: *A Hole Is to Dig* by Krause (1952).
The definition of a principal is an appealing one: ''A
principal is to pull out splinters.''

A third-grade class was fascinated by this book and
decided to make some definitions of their own. ''A
desk is to clean up.'' ''A penny is to lose.'' They were
delighted when the comic strip *Peanuts* came up with
''Happiness is an A in spelling.''

These definitions have the novelty of being functional rather than descriptive. They have an unexpected
quality that lends charm to the language. They are probably not poetry, but poetic expression often has this element in it.

From the beginning it would be well to share with
children poetry both with and without rhyme patterns.
Help them discover the beauty or fun of an idea or word
picture in a verse as well as the song of rhyme. ''Fog''
by Carl Sandburg is a good illustration of a poem without rhyme.

The following patterns, free from emphasis in
rhyme, may induce students to express themselves in
free verse as well as rhymed.

Spring Music

Spring is a singing time,
Birds sing in the trees,

  . . . .

  . . . .
And I sing too.

The Feel of Things

I like the feel of things,
The softness of pussy willows,
The smoothness of velvet.

  . . . . .

  . . . . .
I like the feel of things.

Children sense the meter of poetry and eventually
will want to write with this in mind. The teacher might
put a line on the board and have the class count the
beats one would hear if each syllable had equal emphasis.

The man in the moon looked down
— — — — — — —

Then the class experiments with lines like the following and decides which sounds best:

Upon the sleeping little town.
Upon the laughing happy clown.
To see the children gay and brown.
To see that snow had fallen over hill and town.

Then they take some words they know and note
how these words have similar points of emphasis:

altogether   player
manufacture   remember
tangerine   suggestion
doorkeeper   happiness
pleasant

This can be changed with the usual markings for accented and unaccented syllables in poetry:

altogether becomes — — —′ —
remember becomes — —′ —

Then note that in certain poems some words appear
as unaccented syllables. If you say the words *ta* for unaccented and *tum* for the accented syllable you can note
the meter of a poem.

Then the little Hiawatha (or *tum ta tum ta tum ta tum ta*)
Said unto the old Nakomis
All the hills are edged with valleys

Writing words for songs emphasizes meter. One
student teacher interested a group of below-average
sixth-grade children in writing by using Calypso music.
After learning that the singer made up his song as he
went along, the class tried to write ''songs.'' The results begin the next page.

I got a donkey he's a big and fat,
He sits on a pillow and the pillow goes flat.
My donkey, he's a good for nothing beast
Cause he takes all my food for his Sunday feast.
Maxine

One class listened to a recorded reading of translations of famous Japanese haiku.

The ideas of suggestion, emphasized in the last line, and imagery were captured by the children who wrote these lines at the Hunter School in Fairbanks, Alaska.

The boy turned to me
And he smiled with a cute grin.
I did the same thing.

Big Indian Chief
You are brave but very dumb.
Let people rule too!

I hate dogs a lot.
They bark when someone walks by,
Especially me.

I left Alaska, but on the way
I saw purple mountains
And turned back.

A cry is heard. All is still
A pack of wolves
Has made its kill . . . Silence.

The morning sun
Chasing night shadows
Across the awakening world.

The pattern of a haiku poem consists of three lines, the first line having five syllables, the second line seven, and the third line five. Because the English syllable differs from the Japanese it is not always possible to follow this pattern.

Cinquains have much of the same effect in English. The first line has five words and each succeeding line one less:

The white waves bite at
the sandy ocean shore
like a hungry

child eating
cookies.

Or starting with only four words, one gets this result:

The empty house stands
among dead grass
lonely and
still

A second type of cinquain may be developed by initiating a purpose for each line.

First line—one word giving the title.
Second line—two words describing the title.
Third line—three words expressing an action.
Fourth line—four words expressing a feeling.
Fifth line—another word for the title.

Poetic thought does not depend on rhyme. These two selections appeared in the *Albuquerque Public Schools Journal* (March 1970):

I have a tree
With a bee
I love the tree
My friend does too.
Demmy Virgil, GRADE 1, Chapparal

I went to the waterfalls cold and sly,
I waded myself past knee high.
I went to the waterfalls cold and sly,
And I waded through streams of pretty foam.

By then I was tired
Climbing up paths,
Climbing log bridges,
Sliding down sand,
Venturing through groves.

Watching stick boats
Go through one hole
And come out another.

But by and by we went away,
Away from the falls
And all of the play.
Kristina Holm, GRADE 4, Osuna

A ROOM FULL OF SCARY THOUGHTS

It's a stormy night,
All the lights in the house are out
My room is very dark, and suddenly,
I'm alone!

Tall plants and furniture form figures
against the shadow of the blinds.

The rain falling sounds like a million
fingers tapping on my window—as if they want me to let
        them in.

Lights from cars flash through my blinds onto
the wall, and, as the cars move, flashing of the lights
moves from wall to wall as small ghosts.

And I quickly sit my head up and then
sit it back down.

Then suddenly, the storm dies down and the
sound of cars splashing water in the streets seems so close,
        but it's really quite far.

And I sit up in my bed, turn on the light and
realize that I'm in a room full of scary thoughts.

Anna Bain, GRADE 5, Inez

THE CLOWN

Enter the chief clown:
Shouting the age-old line,
"Is everybody happy?"
It used to be that
The audience would answer,
  "Yes!"
But now many reply
with a violent,
  "No!"
Soon there won't
be any clowns left.

Ken Stahl, GRADE 9, Jefferson

Rather than have children start with such a complex task as writing verses about how they feel or things they have seen, some teachers prefer to start with group composition.

The following poem is based on an experience of Eileen Birch, a second-grade teacher who once asked her children to think of quiet things. As each child made a suggestion she wrote it on the chalkboard.

As quiet as snow falling
As quiet as butter melting
As quiet as a cloud in the sky
As quiet as a kitten
As soap bubbles
A tree growing
Santa Claus coming
As quiet as you and I

The children knew that they had created a mood because of the hush in the room. Such experiences can be a step toward individual effort.

A method of writing that will give everyone a sense of participation is the word-stimulus method. The teacher asks the pupils to get ready for a surprise, assuring them that this is not a test and that the papers will be ungraded.

"I am going to tell you a word," the teacher continues, "and you are to write the picture that comes to your mind. You may tell what you see, hear, feel, or imagine. Just tell me the picture that you see in your imagination. Spell as well as you can; we will get the exact spelling later." Then she gives a word like *rain, sunshine, baby, wind, spring,* or *night.*

After the children have finished writing, the papers are collected. Now these individual efforts are assembled into a group poem. This is called a mosaic poem, or cumulative composition, because, like a mosaic painting, it is made from many parts. First the closely related ideas are grouped. One stanza might contain those about gentle rain, another about violent storms, another about the blessings of rain. These are put together with some rearrangement of word order but with no effort to rhyme. Then the class usually has to add several lines at the bottom that create a conclusion.

The following is an interesting account of group poetry with older children.[4]

[4] From S. G. Gilburt, "Cooperative Poetry—A Creative Project," *Language Arts News* (Fall 1957).

When I use the *cooperative technique* in the classroom, I devote the first lesson to the playing of records. I select songs with strong rhythmic undertones such as *"Surrey with the Fringe on Top"* from *Oklahoma!;* Burl Ives' *"Rock Candy Mountain";* an American folk dance, "Golden Slippers." I encourage the pupils to tap out the rhythm with fingers or to clap. It is rough on the teacher's nervous system sometimes, but I have an aim. It does relax the class. They "let go" inwardly and become much more receptive.

I follow up with Vachel Lindsay's "Congo," Masefield's "Sea Fever," and Kipling's "Boots." These are records supplied by the National Council of Teachers of English with readings superbly done by Norman Corwin. As "Boots" is played, I ask for volunteers to march up and down the aisles in rhythm to the poem. The dullest pupil in the class eventually is aroused to a sensitivity to rhythm and thus grasps the simplest aspect of poetry. Now he is ready to feel and enjoy rhythm, and I suggest he try marching.

I follow up with recordings of Tennyson's "Break, Break, Break," Browning's "Boot and Saddle," and Lanier's "Song of the Chattahoochee."

In ensuing lessons, I read in my best orotund manner: "Casey at the Bat," "The Charge of the Light Brigade," or Poe's "The Bells." "The Barrel-Organ" by Noyes and Psalms XXIV and XLVI are rendered by the class chorally. Poetry was meant to be read aloud and heard.

We talk about rhythm in nature—the seasons, night and day. The pupils tell me about rhythm in "boogie-woogie" and "bebop." They bring in their own records and favorite poems. Edgar Guest gets a square deal in my room.

I explain that poetry is far from "sissy stuff." John Masefield was a tough sailor. Joyce Kilmer and Rupert Brooke were topnotch soldiers. Sandburg was a truck-driver. We chat about crowbars and steel spikes and we study "Prayers of Steel." I play Corwin's reading of "Fog" and "Lost," and the class reads with him, softly and lingeringly, absorbing the mood and sound pictures.

We play and sing "Trees," "Road to Mandalay," "Drink to Me Only with Thine Eyes." The class understands by now that songs are poems put to music. We even discuss popular songs and decide whether the lyrics are good or bad. The pupils gradually develop yardsticks of judgment. They select any one poem they enjoyed most for memory purposes.

Throughout, I emphasize the fun, the enjoyment, the movement and the zest of poetry. The feeling for poetry is caught—not taught. The rhythmic exercises, the choral reading, the musical aspects all make for an emotional climate of relaxed interest. These emotional tones, frequently repeated, are associated with poetry and should be retained by the pupil.

By now, the class is eating out of my hand and I come to cooperative writing.

I have had functioning all along in connection with an integrated unit on descriptive writing, a smell committee, a sound committee, a taste committee, etc., who had been compiling actual advertisements from magazines that best reflected these senses in writing. I read Morley's "Smells" or "Swift Things Are Beautiful" by Elizabeth Coatsworth and then invite each pupil to write but *one similar line* on the subject of "Noises." In a few minutes I call on the pupils to read their lines. The class either accepts the line as good, or suggests improvements such as a more picturesque word or phrase. As each pupil's line is accepted, the pupil goes up to the board and proudly writes his line.

A volunteer is alerted to write a brief introduction, another to write a concluding stanza while the class is still working on the body of the class poem. The group composition that follows was turned out in one forty-five-minute period, with a supervisor observing the lesson. We were caught a little short by the bell, hence the weak ending which was not polished up, marring an otherwise interesting piece of work by an average eighth-grade class.

Noises We Like

Most people hate noises,
But a few like them indeed,
Howling, screaming, clicking,
Crying, laughing, walking
These noises some people need.
These be noises one class likes!
The crack of the bat on the first day of spring,
The click of the camera shutter,
The scratch of a pen when writing to a friend,
My dog's bark when he comes to meet me,
The breaking of Rockaway waves at the beach,
The ticking of a clock old and dear,
The beating of drums at a parade,
The tap-tapping of a long wanted typewriter,
The backfiring of a car and the shot of a gun,
The clatter of hoof-beats in the city's street,
The hoot of a train whistle coming round the bend,
The crunching of a dollar and the jingling of a coin,

The light pitter-pat of the rain against the pane,
The chitter-chatter of people in the street,
The gurgle of a baby in the cradle,
The chirp of the sparrows around a crust of bread,
The thump of my heart at report card time,
Roller skates whizzing along pavement streets,
The sound of electricity when I comb my hair,
The crashing and slashing of lightning to earth,
The hiss of a radiator on a cold winter day,
The crackling of an autumn bonfire,
The moo of cows grazing in the field,
The words of a baby who has just begun to talk,
The dancing ivory under the fingers of a "boogie" player.
Hundreds of other noises
Can be acclaimed
But hundreds of others
Cannot possibly be named.

Meanings experienced through poetry call for personal and individual responses. The deep feeling that one person senses in a sentence may be missed by another. We do not seek to have children write a verse in order to please the teacher, to get a good grade, or to participate in a program. Our purpose is to help children discover in poetry some inner satisfaction that is an intimate personal experience. Deserved praise is an important aspect of encouraging children to write. Expect them to present a tremendous range of quality, but encourage each child as he creates at his appropriate level.

An equally important aspect is time to write. Providing a quiet time during the course of the week when children may choose to write or read will reward the teacher with worthy contributions. Occasionally this time has to be scheduled, but often it will have to be taken from some other activity. Sometimes the weather is a deciding factor. During a winter snow when the flakes are sinking slowly to earth or just after a spring rain when every object appears clean-washed would be an excellent occasion for such work. The teacher might say, "Let's have a quiet period now. You may read or write. We will tune in on thirty minutes of silence."

Children like to write poetry in areas that have emotional appeal. Here are some examples:

1. Gripes and Protests

TO THE BOY THAT SITS IN FRONT OF ME

You think that you are funny
You think that you're the best
You think that you're a honey
While you're really just a pest.

In arithmetic you're terrible
In reading you're a dunce
And when you talk the teacher must
Remind you more than once!
            MERRY LEE TASH, GRADE 5

HOBBIES

They tell me that a hobby
Is to help us make the day
To seem a little shorter
And to pass the time away.

But our teachers seem to think
That we have nothing else to do
But to get one of these hobbies
And then write about it too.

They load us up with homework
And then they go and say,
"Children, you need a hobby
To pass the time away."

"Get yourself a hobby"
That's what the teacher said,
Dear teacher, we need hobbies
Like we need holes in the head.

So when we turn in papers
That don't quite meet perfection—
Don't be angry when we say,
"We are building our collection."
            MERRY LEE TASH, GRADE 7

2. Personal Experiences

AFTER SCHOOL

I'm staying after school again.
This is an awful mess;
I might as well get down to work

'Til I can leave I guess.
Let's see, arithmetic's all done,
And so is reading work,
(Just think ME staying after school!
I sure feel like a jerk.)
I could improve my writing,
Oh no, I'd just hate that,
If I could just get out of here
I'd gladly eat my hat,
I guess it's just what I deserve
For acting like a fool,
But you won't catch me here again
Staying after school!

SILAS, GRADE 6

COOKIES

Measure
  Sift
    Beat
Cut
  Cook
    Eat.

VERNON, GRADE 1 (DICTATED)

3. Wonders

GRASS

Green and soft and sweet,
Grass is glistening

Lying on warm grass
I feel relaxed and lazy

With an ant's small size
Grass is probably a kind of jungle.

JANE, AGE 10

4. "If I Were" Poems or Flights of Imagination

If I were a star on the top of the tree,
On Christmas night, here's what I'd see:

Angels and candles, tinsel and balls,
Bright lights and bells and Santa Claus;
Popcorn and long red cranberry string,
Chains of paper—both red and green.

And if I look closely—I'll take my chances—
I see tiny packages tied to the branches.

Around the tree, all over the floor
Are lots of packages—and there's more—
A train, a bike, a doll, a bat,
A DOG? A puppy—imagine that!!

5. Special Days

DEAR MOM

Long years ago, someone decided
That the second Sunday in the month of May,
Should be a day for the women
Who have taught and guided
Their children. Yes, a Mother's Day!
In return for years of dedication
And love and devotion that has never abated;
One day set apart for the mom's of the nation
To show them that they are appreciated.
The gift we give you is modest indeed,
But with this gift is planted the seed
Of a prayer of hope for this family
To spend the next year in harmony.

For all of us know that there is no other
To take the place of you, our mother.

MERRY LEE TASH, GRADE 8

There are others: wishes, surprises, questions, poems "to my doll or dog." But there is one more that should receive special consideration. Sometimes we forget that each child must discover anew the wonders of our world. It is a stimulating experience to watch a group of city boys and girls discovering the beauties of the outdoors in a summer camp. One camp director led a group that rediscovered the place where the Indians long ago had obtained the clay they used in pottery making. As the group rested, he asked them to be still and notice what was happening around them. Imaginations were filled with Indians, of course, but these boys and girls looked at the trees, the brook, the clay bank, the birds and squirrels in a new way. Then the leader asked them how they might share this experience with others. Some sketched the scene, others wrote descriptive letters, but many wrote poems.

The following situation reveals a similar experience of a boy rediscovering the familiar:

HAVE YOU EVER SAT ON THE SHORE OF A HARBOR?

Have you ever sat on the shore of a harbor
And watched the seagulls play?
It's really very interesting
More fun than studying, I'd say.

Have you ever sat on the shore of a harbor
And watched the freighters sway,
Then listened to their whistles
And watched them sail away?
Have you ever sat on the shore of a harbor
And listened to a fog-horn blow,
And wondered where the fog came from
And when and where it will go?

Have you ever watched the sun go down
And have you seen the waves roll in,
Then have you ever wondered,
"When did this all begin?"

BROOKE, GRADE 7

If we accept as our responsibility the releasing of the talents and abilities of the students, there are some teaching practices that should be considered. One does not put a grade on a poem created by a child. Even an evaluative remark such as "Very good" is not appropriate. It would be much more helpful to the writer to receive guidance and encouragement in other ways. A comment such as "What a novel idea. I never would have thought of that!" or "I can feel the snow" indicates the response that a creative talent needs. But young talent will welcome help as well: "Instead of *flat* what do you think of the word *level*?" or "Try *inviting* in place of *nice*." Such comments must be given as suggestions. If the writer accepts them because he feels he must, it can destroy the joy of being creative.

Praise is powerful if it causes continuous growth. Point out the strength of a creative effort. At first teachers are so pleased to get any completed work that a low level of expectancy can be established by excessive praise. The expressions "Your first line is especially good" and "The words *lonely lullaby* create a good

sound and feeling" give praise to the points of best quality.

Two major faults of children's poetry call for special attention. A child may start with a good idea, then come to a dull thump of an ending just to get something that rhymes.

As I looked up at the sky
I saw some planes go flying by
And as I walked home to rest
There came a plane from the west.

After children have achieved some security in the writing of verse it is well to discuss this problem. Encourage them to write nonrhyming poetry until they have discovered how to use many of the aids available such as rhyming dictionaries and a thesaurus.

The second fault is that of writing parodies on familiar verse. It is fun to write parodies when this is the purpose of writing, but the following is questionable as creative poetry. Call it a parody. Then help the child use his idea in a more original form.

I think that I shall never see
An airplane tiny as a bee
A plane that may in summer fly
Into a piece of apple pie.

Closely related to this problem is that of the child who hands in something not his own. Little children sometimes get the idea that the task is to write any poem, rather than one of their own creation. Some misguided older person helps them and they show up with "Roses are red, violets are blue," etc. When this happens, remember that there is no moral issue involved. The child wanted to please. You might say, "That is a cute verse but it has been written before. I think you can write one that no one has ever heard." Or the teacher might suggest, "Maybe instead of writing a poem you could draw a picture or cartoon of your idea." And the teacher might ask herself if she has made poetry writing a bit too important for the present time if children feel pressured to do this type of thing to gain approbation.

Nearly all children and many adults write rhymes and doggerel that have few poetic qualities. As they listen to great poetry with growing appreciation, their writing will reflect the appreciation they have developed. Consumers of poetry are needed as well as writers. Crude efforts produced by experimentation with rhyme may increase a person's awareness of the skills of other poets.

Releasing poetic expression for some who have little inherent talent should not become a challenging burden to the teacher. The object is to release the talent in those so endowed so that all may be enriched by sharing their contributions. Our task is done if we help all to develop this talent to some degree and those gifted in this area to achieve expression in quality that is worthy of them.

For Discussion

1. Assume that you have been selected to judge some children's poetry for a contest sponsored by a local radio station. What basic criteria would you establish to guide your judgment?
2. Collect five poems to enhance a child's concept of seeing or hearing things.
3. Collect five poems that primary children might respond to with rhythm or movement.
4. Poetry might enhance a theme such as a season, rain, the joy of living, protest. Find two or more themes that might be used for poetic expression.

How May Literature Be Used to Influence Written Composition?

In recent years there has been a return to an old practice of using examples from literature to encourage writing by students. At one time students imitated the sentences of Sir Walter Scott or Charles Dickens. Such exercises do influence students who identify with authors and who wish to acquire the disciplines of authorship. Like a knowledge of grammar, the knowledge of plot structure or technique of description and characterization can be useful to some young writers.

We do not know if children grow in ability more from writing a fable than from "writing a story." We do not know if an awareness of story line helps the young writer any more than his intuitive imitation of favorite story patterns. Teachers who are trained in the discipline of English and who believe that simple elements of the discipline should be taught to children frequently gain good results with a planned formal series of lessons on specific writing techniques. Other teachers equally well trained gain impressive results through programs that encourage the child to write creatively without starting with analysis of specific forms. In order to contrast the practice it is necessary to consider the extremes.

Frazier suggests this procedure with respect to a fable: [5]

May Hill Arbuthnot equates writing an original fable to a mathematical prcoedure. She suggets selecting some animal character and a moral such as, "Pride goeth before a fall." If a rabbit is chosen, he cannot be a well-rounded individual with only one weakness; rather, he must be all weakness—and in this case the weakness is *pride*. So the mathematical equation becomes: Proud Rabbit + X (single episode) = Pride goeth before a fall. The writer must solve for X by finding an episode to explain the moral.

Teachers who wish to experiment with fables in their classrooms will find these seven steps for presentation and writing of fables helpful:

1. Read many fables scattered throughout several months.
2. Review the easier fables and those liked by the children. Write the lesson or moral on the chalk board.
3. List other lessons on the chalk board which could appear in a fable.
4. Select one lesson from either group of morals and write a fable together in class.
5. Let pupils select a lesson or moral from these on the board or suggest a new moral and tell how a story or fable could present the idea.
6. Let pupils work in groups or committees and write fables with one of the group acting as secretary or scribe. Go over the fables together in class.
7. Let pupils write their own fables after selecting a moral.

[5] From Alexander Frazier, *New Directors in Elementary English* (Champaign, Ill.: National Council of Teachers of English, 1967), pp. 216–217.

These steps should not be compressed into a tight time pattern but should be extended over a period of time since learning to write fables requires both experience with that type of literature and the development of the intellectual discipline to stay within the form.

The fable which follows illustrates the first type of fable plot pattern. The characters are flat and impersonal, and no one regrets the fate of the lazy chicken. Like most simple fables, this composition by a fourth grade pupil is brief, involving a single incident, and the ending is expected and justifiable. The originality found in other types of writing is not often found in a fable because the form is restricting and the content is prescribed by the moral.

> Once there was a chicken who, even though chickens get up early, this chicken did not. She liked to sleep late in the morning. But her friends who got up early, got the best food. And one day the farmer who owned this chicken was discouraged with this chicken. "She never gets up early, or lays good eggs, or eats good food," said the farmer very discouraged. So the next Sunday that little chicken was on the farmer's plate.
>
> Moral: Laziness does not pay off.

The second fable was also written by a fourth grade boy after a number of fables had been studied in class. Note that the young writer has developed a clear, concise plot and has concluded with a moral.

The Woodsman and the Hawk

> There was once a woodsman who lived alone in a little hut.
>
> One day he was out in front of his hut when all of a sudden he heard two things at once, a hawk screaming and gunfire. He looked around. All of a sudden he happened to hear some flapping of wings. He looked down. There beside him was a panting hawk. The hawk said breathlessly, "Please kind sir, could you help me; a couple of dogs and a hunter are chasing me. Do you have a place to hide me?" "Why of course I do. Go into the hut and eat as much meat from my dog's bowl as you want. But come out when I tell you." In a few minutes the hunter and his two dogs came by the hut. The hunter asked, "Have you seen a hawk in the sky or on the ground around here?" "No, I haven't," he said, but as the woodsman said these words he winked his eye and pointed towards the hut. Anyhow the hunter did not see these signs, and so went on. When the hunter was out of sight the woodsman told the hawk to come out. The hawk

went on its way without saying a word. The woodsman asked, "Why do you go without thanking me for what I have done?" The hawk turned around and said, "I saw what you did as you said those words." Adding to that, he said, "The tongue can be as sly as the hand."

One text, *Composition Through Literature,* approaches the teaching of all written work as well as the study of grammar through literature. Following a selection from *Tales of the Arabian Nights* by Charlotte Dixon the text provides this discussion:[6]

EXAGGERATION IN STORIES

How exaggerated was the account of the trip? You have heard stories exaggerated to the point of ridicule. Too much enlargement becomes ridiculous. But certain types are enjoyable.

Exercise A

The quoted statements or word groups came from the story. Would you accept them as facts or as exaggerations? Explain your answer.

1. The egg "had a circumference of about fifty feet."
2. "I found myself in a hollow surrounded by huge mountains."
3. Its foot "was as thick as a tree-trunk."
4. The snakes "could easily have swallowed an elephant."

Exercise B

Tell in your own words the difference between creating an imaginative story and exaggerating a story in its retelling.

Exercise C

From what you can recall, tell with what each of the following was compared:

1. the bird's shadow
2. the large egg
3. the shining stones
4. the length of trees

STEPS IN YOUR STORY

Even in very imaginative stories, the events must be kept in order. If you have to retrace your steps, the reader becomes confused and his interest lags.

[6] From H. T. Fillmer and others, *Composition Through Literature,* Book C (New York: American Book, 1967), pp. 74–76.

Organization

The following events of the story you have just read are not in sequence. Put them in a step-by-step order.

The ship landed on a deserted island.

His escape from the island was effected by tying himself to the foot of a huge bird.

Sinbad grew restless in Baghdad and decided to set out on a second journey.

He hid in a cave where he remained all night, too frightened to sleep.

Sinbad decided to picnic on the island and do some investigating of the land.

The bird dropped him in a valley of snakes.

Then he discovered a means of escape from the valley.

He fell asleep and on wakening, found the ship had pulled out without him.

Finally, he arrived back in Baghdad.

He found and collected many diamonds in the valley.

COMPOSING METAPHORS

The translator of the story made a number of comparisons, such as "feet as thick as tree-trunks," "snakes as long as trees," and the globe "felt like soft silk." The following comparisons are worn out. Use your imagination and write a fresh comparison for each one.

1. dead as a doornail
2. sick as a dog
3. pretty as a picture
4. clear as a bell
5. smart as a whip
6. cool as a cucumber

INTERPRETATION OF COLLOQUIAL EXPRESSIONS

In the story you found the expression "out of the frying pan into the fire." You know its meaning: jump from one troublesome situation into an even worse one. Write a sentence in which you express each of the following in a straight-forward way:

1. get down to brass tacks
2. chip off the old block
3. snake in the grass
4. calm before the storm
5. hit the nail on the head

WRITING YOUR STORY

It's time to put your imagination to work in a story.

First, select a title and when you write it, be sure to capitalize the first, last, and all important words.

Second, decide how you will reach the place you wish to visit—by train, plane, ship, or any way you like.

Third, decide how many events your story will cover. Plan one paragraph for each event.

Fourth, conclude your story with an account of your return trip.

THE WRITING ASSIGNMENT

Write your story with as much imagination as possible. Remember to keep the events in order, each one leading into the next. Bring the story to a climax with your return trip. Use some exaggeration if you like, but keep it within limits. If you cannot think at the moment of a place you would like to visit, consider one of the following suggestions:

A Journey to Shangrila
A Journey to the Bottom of the Sea
A Journey to the Land of Elephants
A Journey to Hobbitland
A Journey to the Moon
A Journey to the North Pole

A fourth-grade textbook uses the following approach from literature to write a descriptive paragraph: [7]

VARIATIONS IN PROSE

Now that you have read how three poets expressed their feelings about fall, see how four different authors write about the same theme in prose. Each author sets a mood for the changing of the seasons from summer to fall.

The first description of autumn comes from *Farmer Boy* by Laura Ingalls Wilder.

Now the harvest moon shone round and yellow over the fields at night, and there was a frosty chill in the air. All the corn was cut and stood in tall shocks. The moon cast their black shadows on the ground where the pumpkins lay naked above their withered leaves.

In the beech grove all the yellow leaves had fallen.

[7] From Muriel Crosby and others, *The World of Language*, Book 4 (Chicago: Follett, 1970), pp. 275–277.

They lay thick on the ground beneath the slim trunks and delicate bare limbs of the beeches. The beechnuts had fallen after the leaves and lay on top of them. Father and Royal lifted the matted leaves carefully on their pitchforks and put them, nuts and all, into the wagon. And Alice and Almanzo ran up and down in the wagon, trampling down the rustling leaves to make room for more.

When the wagon was full, Royal drove away with Father to the barns, but Almanzo and Alice stayed to play till the wagon came back.

A chill wind was blowing and the sunlight was hazy. Squirrels frisked about, storing away nuts for the winter. High in the sky the wild ducks were honking, hurrying south. It was a wonderful day for playing wild Indian, all among the trees.

Laura Ingalls Wilder

In *My Side of the Mountain,* Jean George expresses her view of the changing seasons.

September blazed a trail into the mountains. First she burned the grasses. The grasses seeded and were harvested by the mice and the winds.

Then she sent the squirrels and chipmunks running boldly through the forest, collecting and hiding nuts.

Then she gathered the birds together in flocks, and the mountaintop was full of songs and twitterings and flashing wings. The birds were ready to move to the south.

Jean George

How have Jean George and Laura Ingalls Wilder differed in their descriptions of squirrels gathering nuts and birds flying south? Which is more appealing to you? Why?

Notice how Marjorie Kinnan Rawlings pays particular attention to the changing weather in her description of fall from *The Yearling.*

The first heavy frost came at the end of November. The leaves of the big hickory at the north end of the clearing turned as yellow as butter. The sweet gums were yellow and red and the blackjack thicket across the road from the house flamed with a red as bright as a campfire. The grapevines were golden and the sumac was like oak embers. The October blooming of dog-fennel and sea-myrtle had turned to a feathery fluff. The days came in, cool and crisp, warmed to a pleasant

slowness, and chilled again. The Baxters sat in the evening in the front room before the first hearth-fire.

Marjorie Kinnan Rawlings

Pay close attention to the way that Virginia Sorensen describes the colors of the trees in this selection from *Miracles on Maple Hill.*

You would think Maple Mountain was on fire.

In every direction the trees were red and yellow. When the sun struck them suddenly, flying through windy clouds, the brightness was almost more than Marley could bear. The redness seemed to come from inside each tree in a wonderful way; it was the red she saw through her hand when she held it against the sun. The yellowness glistened like golden hair, and the wind shook it, and bits of gold spun down upon the grass.

What a lovely world! Every morning on Maple Hill, Marley woke in the very middle of a scarlet and golden miracle.

Virginia Sorensen

Read the descriptions again to look for techniques the authors have used to present their observations about fall.

1. Which senses do the four writers appeal to?
2. What are some of the sensory words and phrases you especially like?
3. Take your senses to an imaginary spring picnic or a summer barbecue. Use pantomime to show what you see, hear, smell, taste, and touch.
4. How does fall come to the city? Think of images that will re-create the sights, sounds, taste, smells, and feel of a city autumn. Build these images into a descriptive paragraph.

Literature is evidence of the success that some individuals have achieved through written composition. As a child identifies with the authors of fine books, the knowledge of technique used will influence his reading and writing. It is possible that overemphasis on literary form and analysis could block effective writing and reading; the student might become so involved with analyzing how the task is done that the content would become secondary. With this caution in mind many teachers will find that children's interest in great writing can motivate their desire to grow in written communication.

For Discussion

1. Is there some value in having a child paraphrase great writing as one might memorize a favorite poem?

2. Why do some teachers feel that enrichment requires children in the elementary school to do something that was formerly taught in high school?

3. The national poetry day is October 15. Plan a school assembly program for this occasion.

How Are Children Taught to Make Reports and Keep Records?

Informal reporting of information and observations and dicussion of this information in small or large groups play major roles in the activities of children. Later these oral expressions may be put into written form. Young children have a need for some written records as they plan together. As the capability for written expression grows in complexity, more detailed plans are possible.

Until such time as children attain sufficient skill in handwriting, the teacher records the information for the group. Later she transfers this information to charts or booklets. Children may then read the written record when they need to review the steps in specific processes, or simply for the pleasure of reliving the experience:[8]

Making Butter

We put cream in a jar. We shook it a long time. Little yellow lumps of butter came to the top.

We poured the buttermilk out and drank it. We washed the butter and tasted it. It needed salt. We added salt. We put it in a mold.

We ate butter on crackers. It was delicious!

[8] *Arts and Skills of Communication for Democracy's Children* (San Bernardino, Calif.: San Bernardino County Schools, 1954) is the source of many of the following examples.

Selection of Topic

There are numerous experiences that may be the subject for simple recording. For example:

The growth of a plant
The date
The daily weather
The daily temperature
The changing appearance of the polliwogs
The days the fish are fed
Monthly height and weight
The number of children present each day

Children enjoy watching the teacher record interesting daily events.

News

Today is Monday.
It is a sunny day.
We are going on a walk.
We will look for wild flowers.
Ted brought a horned toad for us to see.

One group of children carefully recorded the number of days it took for the eggs of the praying mantis to hatch. They recorded:

Roger found a green bug.
It looks like a grasshopper, but it is not a grasshopper.
It is a praying mantis.

Later, they recorded:

Our praying mantis laid some eggs.
It laid them on August 1, 1979.
Then it died.
We are counting the days until the eggs hatch.

After listening to a story, seeing a film or filmstrip, taking a trip, or talking with a resource person, children may wish to record information. As they list the information in the order of occurrence, they gain an understanding of sequence.

After they had seen a filmstrip about a truck farmer, one group made the following record.

After viewing a filmstrip, children may wish to record information. As they observe and then list the information in the order of occurrence, they gain an understanding of sequence. (PHOTO BY LINDA LUNGREN.)

Jobs of a Truck Farmer

The truck farmer plows the soil.
He plants the seeds.
He irrigates the plants.
He sprays the plants.
He harvests the crops.
He sells the produce to a wholesale market.

Children often record individual and group plans for ready reference. The teacher guides the discussion and helps children decide which suggestions will be most helpful. Later, she places these plans on charts for future reference:

How We Clean Up
How We Use Our Tools
How We Go on a Trip
How We Share Together
How We Work Together

Organization of Report

Children are assisted in organizing their thinking by listing questions, recording tentative solutions, testing solutions, and arriving at conclusions. Many of these problems arise in the social studies and related science activities. Problems such as the following may develop after dramatic play:

We Need to Find Out

How the gasoline station gets its gasoline
How the groceries get to the store
How people get money from the bank
What trucks bring to the community

After a group of children had taken a trip to the wholesale bakery, they set up the problem:

What makes bread dough rise?
As children suggested answers to the problem, the teacher recorded their ideas.

DARYL: Because of the warm sun shining on the dough.
BEVERLY: Because of the way the baker beats the dough.
ERIC: Because of the things that are mixed in the dough.
SHANNON: Because of the kind of pan the baker uses for the dough.

This list of suggested answers was held tentative by the group until it could arrive at valid conclusions. The group performed a simple experiment which helped to dismiss the incorrect assumptions and to identify the valid conclusion. The children dictated the following story, telling how their final conclusions were reached:

What Makes Bread Dough Rise?

We wanted to find out what makes bread dough rise.

We took two bowls. We mixed flour and water in one bowl.

We mixed flour, water, and yeast in another bowl.

We took turns beating and stirring the dough in each bowl.

Some of us beat fast and hard. Some of us beat slowly.

We poured the dough from each bowl into two bowls.

The bowls were the same shape and size.

We put the bowls in the sunshine on a table by the window.

Then we went out to recess.

When we came back to the room, we looked at the dough.

We saw that the dough in one bowl was spilling over the edge.

The dough in the other bowl was just as we had left it.

Now we know why bread dough rises. Why? Because there is yeast in the dough!

Girls and boys often wish to record the experiences they have shared or special information they have gained from study trips, special classroom activities, films, filmstrips, or visits of resource people. As children discuss the events that they will include in their story, the teacher guides the group in determining proper sequence, in selecting contributions that best describe the situation, and in choosing words and phrases that are colorful and descriptive.

A group of six-year-olds had carefully watched two caterpillars as each became a chrysalis and later emerged as a purplish-brown "mourning cloak" butterfly. The teacher put captions near the jar, changing them at appropriate intervals. She recorded the children's observations as they watched this sequence of events. Later the children discussed all that had taken place from the first day the caterpillars were brought to their room until the beautiful butterflies emerged. The teacher recorded the following story as the group recalled the experience. She helped the children recall the events in sequential order by referring to the changing captions and to the comments the children had made during the past weeks. Later, the group delighted in hearing their story read back to them.

OUR CATERPILLARS

There were two caterpillars eating geraniums when we found them. They were soft and black, and had real pretty spots on them.

We put the caterpillars and some geraniums into a big jar. We gave them fresh leaves to eat.

One day one made a house. He sort of knitted with his head. He shook it up and down, and up and down. Then he went sideways and up and down. We thought he would get dizzy and fall, but he didn't. Pretty soon he had a brownish, grayish colored house without any door and windows.

The other one made a house too, but he made it when we were not looking. Both houses hung down from the geranium.

After a long time, one moth came out. He sat real still and looked at the jar and everything. After recess he was wiggling his wings. The next day he flew in the jar. By the next afternoon the other moth came out.

They were just alike. Maybe they will be a mother and daddy. They visited together. They were pretty black velvet with pretty yellow trimming on the wings. The spots made the trimming maybe. Anyway it's the same color.

We brought them flowers and leaves. They might lay some eggs and then we'd have lots of moths. We are going to keep them a long time to see. They seem to be happy.

The moths didn't live so very long, but we will still keep them.

Shorter stories may be recorded on the chalkboard and later placed on charts.

As children gain in the ability to write down factual experiences, they begin recording their own stories. To the extent that they project their own personalities into their writing, their stories become more than simply stated facts and a recording of information. These stories become creative as they take on the unique character that is distinct to the child who is the writer. As in all other forms of independently written expression, girls and boys are given all the help they need to set down their thoughts with ease.

Jo Ann wrote:

OUR TRIP

We went to the trucking terminal today. We saw the big trailers and tractors. I got to see the fifth wheel and the dolly wheels. That's what I wanted to see most of all.

Willis wrote:

THE POST OFFICE

The post office is a busy place. There are many workers there. I watched how the mail is sorted and how the letters are canceled.

One man showed us how the mail is put into the boxes. He showed us how the rest of the mail is put into bundles for the mail man.

Taking care of all the mail is a big job.

Nikkie wrote:

WILLIE'S HAMSTER

Willie brought his little hamster to school. His name is Brownie. His eyes are bright and shiny. When he sleeps, he looks like a little ball of fur. He is brown and white and he wiggles all the time. Willie feeds the hamster two times a day. He feeds it oatmeal and lettuce. The little hamster is asleep now. Shhhh.

The development of reporting and recording clearly, accurately, and interestingly expands as children have many and varied experiences in many and varied activities. Girls and boys are helped to gain in the skills of reporting and recording as they are given opportunity to

1. Express themselves orally in many different situations.
2. Dictate and record information that is of real use and value.
3. Set down their own needs and stories independently when they have gained adequate skill and ability in writing.

Children are fascinated with facts. The popularity of information books and children's encyclopedias equals that of story books. This is a report Debra wrote toward the last months of second grade:

COMETS

Comets are the closest thing to nothing that could be something. Comets are made up of: gas, dust, little molecules of dirt and maybe some sparkes. The closer the comet is to the sun the longer its tail is. The farther away the comet is from the sun the shorter its tail is. Comets tails are formed like this: the comet has a very short tail. Then it get longer, longer, and longer untill it's very long. One Comet comes back every 75 year's. It's called Halley's Comet because he was the man who discovered it. He discovered Comets in 1810 many year's ago.

In the fourth grade, Sammy placed a picture of the Rosetta Stone on the bulletin board next to his report, which started:

For many, many years scholars tried to find out what the old Egyptian hieroglyphics meant. Until 1799 there was absolutely no way of telling what the Egyptians had recorded. In that year the Rosetta Stone was found that contained the same message in three languages. Hieroglyphics were used in one of these. The known languages were used to interpret the meaning of the ancient Egyptian writing.

Reporting is a natural outgrowth of a child's interest in his environment. When the material is pertinent, well organized, and interestingly presented, the report serves to enrich the ongoing experiences of children.

Through this medium children project themselves, their understandings of their world, and their feelings about people, animals, things, or situations. They achieve status with their peers while increasing their own knowledge as well as that of the group.

Maturation and experience are factors that have a

cause-and-effect relationship to all communication. Writing a report requires more mature thinking than many of the other written language activities. Because of the difficulties involved, most teachers feel that the written report should not receive much stress until the later elementary years. The background for the organizational thinking required for making written reports, however, is laid during the earlier years in the giving of many oral reports and the occasional writing of group reports.

The writing of a report often serves as a challenge to the exceptional child or to the girl or boy who has some special interest or hobby. Children painstakingly engage in independent research on topics that arouse their curiosity. The research and reporting meet individual needs and at the same time add to the fund of knowledge of the entire group.

The following report was made by a sixth-grade boy whose hobby was collecting rocks:

Mr. Fields has over four hundred specimens in his mineral collection. Almost two hundred of these are geodes. What fun and adventure he has making his collection. He said that finding a geode is like receiving a surprise package. You cannot tell from the wrappings what wonderful treasures are inside. When Mr. Fields discovered his first geode, he would have passed it by had a fellow collector not pointed it out to him. It was somewhat round but irregular and no different in color from the rocks and earth around it.

Have you ever seen a geode after it is cut in two? It is filled with six-sided crystals which are called quartz. How these rose and lavender crystals sparkle! I hope I can find a geode to put in my rock collection.

Facts and imagination can combine to create reports like this:

I WAS THERE WITH LEWIS AND CLARK

I am a flea. I live in Lewis' hat. It all started out in 1803 when Lewis stopped to pet a dog and I jumped on Lewis' leg.

I did not like it there, so I went to higher flesh; that is, his head or hat. Before I knew it, I was boarding a keelboat. From then on I had many adventures. One day we met a grizzly bear. I was going to jump on him, but the men started shooting at him. I then changed my mind. Another

time we were going to see the Sioux Indians. Lewis was all dressed up and his boots were shining. All of a sudden the boat hit something and the boat rolled over. I was almost drowned and Lewis was all wet. I never wished I would go to the dogs so badly in my life. But I was saved.

Later on we came to the Mandan Indians. They were much friendlier than the Sioux. More important, we met a French trapper. Lewis found out he could interpret for them, so they took him along. He had an Indian wife name Sacagawea. He was whipping her one night; when I found out, I leaped over to that trapper and bit him so hard I almost set him in orbit. Another time when our boat turned over, Sacagawea saved some very important papers. One time we saw the Rocky Mountains. Then we came to Sacagawea's people who gave us food and ponies. Soon we came to the Pacific Ocean. I was the first American flea to see the Pacific Ocean. Soon we left for home.

Written by Me, the Little Flea.

Donald, GRADE 5

Children in the middle grades are "joiners." Organized activity clubs give girls and boys a feeling of belongingness and help them to find their places in the social environment. There are many clubs of this type. Some of the most common are 4-H, Brownies, Cub Scouts, Boy Scouts, Blue Birds, and Campfire Girls. Some clubs are formed around interest and service areas, such as science, reading, dramatics, photography, recreation and safety, and the Junior Red Cross.

Most of these clubs have secretaries. Although children enjoy being chosen secretary, they have difficulty learning to keep detailed minutes. Girls and boys are generally so interested in the club activities that they feel little need for more than simple records of the happenings.

Mary showed considerable skill as she recorded the following minutes of the sixth-grade Science Club:

The Science Club met in Room 5 Tuesday afternoon at 2:30. Bill called the meeting to order. I read the minutes. Tom showed us the planetarium he made. He helped us find the Big Dipper and Venus. Mary's mother sent cup cakes.

The acquisition of recording skills should not be limited to the club secretary. After the first meeting the entire group should participate in the writing of the minutes under the teacher's leadership. "How do we start a report of a meeting?" the teacher asks. "Yes, we name the club, the place, and the time." After writing these on the board, the teacher continues, "Who called the meeting to order? What happened first? And what happened next?" Finally the teacher tells them of the form used by club secretaries. "Respectfully submitted" is not needed at the close of minutes. The secretary's signature is adequate. After the minutes are approved, they become an official record.

Simple mimeographed or dittoed newspapers provide an incentive for written reports. Here is a typical page from a monthly paper published by Emory School, South Bay School District, San Diego, California:

MY LETTER BROUGHT RESULTS

After I wrote a letter to the Chula Vista Telephone Co., Mrs. O'Neill got my letter and called my teacher about it, then Wednesday, Mrs. Wallace told the class that my letter had brought results and that we would see a film on telephone service and would have a field trip to see the inside of a telephone building. Telephones mean a lot to us, don't you think so too?

Billy Rinehart

MR. HALSEMA'S GIRLS WON

The girls in Mrs. Wallace's room had a baseball game with Mr. Halsema's girls, Friday, May 2nd. Linda Baker and Carolyn Ferguson were the captains of the two teams. It was a great game. The baseball was flying all over the field. Mr. Halsema's girls won 7 to 6.

Linda Baker

FEELING ABOUT MOVING TO A NEW SCHOOL

It is quite interesting, going to different schools, because some schools have more unusual things than others. Some have bigger and better playgrounds for children to play on. Some have bigger and more colorful rooms and other interesting things. When you first go to a new school, you will probably be afraid, but when you check into school the children will start playing with you, and the second day at school, you will know a lot of kids, and you won't be afraid anymore.

Judith Hawkins

BOOK REVIEW

BIG RED, the dog Danny had always wanted is the name of this book. But first, he must teach the Irish Setter the ways of the woods. Together, they roamed the wilderness meeting nature on her own hard terms. When the outlaw bear injures his father, the boy and his dog must hunt him down. How do they do it? Read the book!

Georgeanna Mulligan

PLAY DAY

On Friday, April 22, we went on a trip to Imperial Beach School. All the sixth grades in the district met there for Play Day.

Research and reporting meet individual needs and at the same time add to the fund of knowledge of the entire group. (PHOTO BY LINDA LUNGREN.)

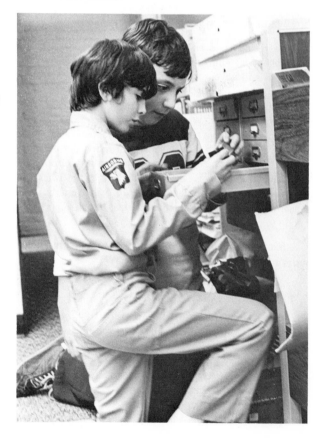

We all met in the auditorium where we sang songs of North and South America. Then we went out on the black top for square dancing. The square dances we danced were: Pop Goes the Weasel, Patty Cake Polka, and Parlez Vouz. After lunch, we divided up into groups for games, dashes and relays. We came back to school in the afternoon tired but happy. Everyone had a good time.

Butch Rurches

OUR PLAYGROUND SETUP

Our playground setup is the only one of its kind in the South Bay Union School District, and is the best one that Emory has had yet. Each class is assigned certain games to play each week. This saves the time of assigning games each day, and also certain areas won't be overcrowded.

With this new plan, everyone will get a chance to play all the games. By the end of the year, you may learn to like a game you never cared for before. It will save a lot of arguments and confusion.

Sherry Hudman

WE'D LIKE YOU TO MEET

Mr. Hanavan, our principal, likes his job. He taught at Pineville Junior High School in Missouri for eight years. He taught in Imperial Beach sixth grade for two years, and taught one year at Fort Growder.

He has a daughter, Connie, ten years old. She is in the fifth grade. He was born in Pineville, Mo. April 5, 1922.

Mr. Hanavan has been at Emory for two years. His favorite foods are baked ham, mashed potatoes, angel food cake, and chocolate milk.

He served in the army during World War 2 and in the Korean War. He is one of our favorite people.

Linda Baker and Diane Wilbur

The teacher should develop, with the class, standards for checking the form and neatness of a written report. This checking method is often called proofreading, editing, or correcting. The standards might be as follows:

Standards for Editing a Report

1. Write the title of the report in the center of the line. Leave a space between the top of the paper and the title. Skip a line after the title.
2. Begin the first word of the title with a capi-

tal letter. Capitalize each important word of the title. Do not capitalize *a, an, at, as, the, of, to, in, from, with,* etc., because they are not considered important words.
3. Have good margins at the top, bottom, left, and right.
4. Use clear writing.
5. Use correct spelling and punctuation.
6. Have "sentence-sense." Do not use incomplete, run-on, or choppy sentences.
7. Indent all paragraphs.
8. Sign your name at the bottom of the last page.

The teacher and the class might develop an editing code using those signs familiar to the newspaper office, as well as other signs which might prove helpful. The signs should be charted as follows:

Editing Signs

sp = spelling
c = capital letter
inc = incomplete sentence
$\mathcal{Y}$ = take out
$\sim$ = transpose, or turn about
lc = small letter (lower case letter)
$\subset$ = join sentences
mb = margins too big
ms = margins too small
// = margins not straight
tkp = punctuation wrong or omitted
wr = making writing clear
ind = indent paragraph
om = something should be omitted
? = material not clear
= space should be left

One of the most valuable activities in association with a school newspaper is the development of a "style sheet," which summarizes the major rules of punctuation, capitalization, and spelling. The local newspaper will usually give a school a copy of the style sheet that guides their writers.

Longer reports employ two areas of skills that involve gathering information and organizing the material. Textbooks provide adequate guidance with respect to note taking and simple outlining. Neither of these skills should be taught in isolation. It is the report that provides the purpose for taking notes. Planning the report provides the outline. These skills should first be studied in association with oral reports. This permits greater concentrated attention on the problems of gathering and organizing information.

The following standards are suggested with respect to note taking:

1. Read the material through before taking notes.
2. Complete one reference before you read another.
3. Use key words, phrases, or sentences to recall ideas.
4. Record the the source of ideas.

With regard to organization, list the big ideas that are to be presented, then add the details under each idea. Children often find the creation of an outline prior to writing the report very difficult to make, but they can outline the report after it has been written. This outlining can be a part of the editing before a report is rewritten. Social studies materials lend themselves to the study of outlining. Normally this is not a skill to be stressed before junior high school.

Following is the standard pattern for an outline:

Simple Outline

     Title
  I.
    A.
    B.
    C.
  II.
    A.
    B.
    C.

Through discussion the children should be made aware that

1. The main topics have Roman numerals. A period is placed after each numeral.
2. The supporting topics (subtopics) are designated by

capital letters. A period is placed after each capital letter.

3. The written report contains as many paragraphs as there are main topics.
4. Each subtopic represents at least one sentence within the paragraph.
5. Each main topic and supporting topic begins with a capital letter.
6. There are no periods at the ends of the main topic or supporting topics unless it is a sentence outline.
7. In the simple outline, Roman numerals are kept in a straight column.
8. In the simple outline, capital letters are kept in a straight column.
9. If a topic is two lines long, the second line begins directly under the first word of the topic.
10. All the topics of an outline are written in the same form. That is, they are written *all in the short form or all in complete sentences.*

Children should be given many experiences of the following kind:

1. Making a group outline for a report.
2. Making a group outline for a current event.
3. Outlining, as a class, a short article in their readers.
4. Making individual outlines.

Reports are motivated by activities such as the following:

1. Write a riddle about an insect, a bird, or an animal.
2. Write one-paragraph reports on famous people.
3. Write an imaginary news report of a historic event, or write the news that must have appeared when the historic event took place.
4. Make believe that you are an animal or a famous person. Write a description of yourself.
5. Visit a museum and report on an object observed.
6. Make comparisons of things we have with those in other parts of the world.
7. Summarize a topic in the encylcopedia in a few sentences.
8. A favorite newspaper feature is "Ask Andy." Put a question on the board and let the children write

the answers as if they were Andy. Make certain first that adequate reference books are available. Questions like:

How far is it to the sun?
What is the brightest star?
How fast does sound travel?
What causes a sonic boom?

9. Provide background comments for a current news story. How large is the Congo? How do people make a living there?

10. Make a travel folder for a city, state, park, or country.

11. Write an autobiography. Parts might be My Birthplace, My Parents, My First School, My Pets and Hobbies, My Ambitions. A baby picture on the cover makes these an appealing Parents' Night attraction. Primary children can make a notebook "About My Family and Me."

12. Write a biography. This would involve interviewing a parent, grandparent, or classmate. In addition to place of birth and school experience, items of the following nature might be included: special likes and dislikes, travel, honors, most important event in his life.

13. Make a class record or folder. This is especially appropriate if the sixth grade is the highest grade in a building. Parts might be History of Our School, Where Our Teachers Were Educated, Our Ambitions, Our Class Will, Twenty Years from Now, Who's Who in the Sixth Grade.

14. The very slow child in the upper grades will find satisfaction in preparing material for young children. Make an alphabet book for the first grade, a farm book for the second, or an animal book for the third grade. These will contain pictures and written explanations. Simple cookbooks and travel records based on a road map are within their level of achievement.

15. Surveys of favorite books, opinions about grammar, simplified spelling, or a school problem, such as social dancing in the sixth grade, are stimulating and involve a great deal of language learning as the material is gathered, organized, and written into a report.

For Discussion

1. How can a teacher discourage research reports that are little more than copied from an encyclopedia?

2. What values would an "in-depth" report have in which each student wrote a book on a country, a holiday, a state, a city? What problems do you foresee in such a project?

3. To what extent should all bulletin boards be student projects?

4. Is the school an adequate community to train reporters to write news accounts?

How Should Punctuation Be Taught?

Human beings learned to talk almost a million years ago and have been using alphabetic writing for several thousand years, but punctuation in the modern sense came into use in our language less than three hundred years ago, and the system is far from perfect. In the system as it stands, the marks are used as follows:

1. For *linking,* use:
   ; semicolon
   : colon
   — linking dash
   - linking hyphen

2. For *separating,* use:
   . period
   ? question mark
   ! exclamation point
   , separating comma

3. For *enclosing,* use:
   , . . . , paired commas
   — . . . — paired dashes
   (. . .) paired parentheses
   [. . .] paired brackets
   " . . ." paired quotation marks

4. For *indicating omissions,* use:
   ' apostrophe
   . omission period in abbreviations (or dot)
   — omission dash

. . . triple periods (or dots)
. . . . quadruple periods (or dots)

Have you ever wondered how the punctuation marks came to be? In pages of Chinese writing there is no punctuation, and as recently as 1945 no punctuation was used in the Korean language. However, when the Koreans decided to write horizontally rather than vertically the need for such marks was recognized.

The ancient Greeks and Romans frequently wrote without separating the words, let alone separating sentences. It was the orators who made the first separations in order to emphasize the thoughts they were expressing. Originally punctuation was built on a single series of pauses. The comma was for a one-unit pause, the semicolon for a two-unit pause, a colon for a three-unit pause, and a period for a four-unit pause. The question mark was a sign to raise the voice at the end of the word. The exclamation point was a little dagger drawn to resemble the real dagger used to fasten important notices to buildings.

One of the first printers, a Venetian named Aldus Manutius, explained the system in this way:

Let us proceed, as it were by steps, from the lowest of the points to the highest.

The least degree of separation is indicated by the comma.

The same mark, if it is used along with a single point, as this is (;) is found in passages in which the words are not opposed in meaning, but the sense depends upon the words in such a way, that, if you use the comma, it is too little; if the double point too much. I was thinking to give an example; but, I felt the point had come out plainly enough, in the immediate preceding sentence.

The doubling of the point is next to be considered: the effect of this doubling is, that the mark thus formed takes rank between the point used in conjunction with the comma, and the point standing alone.

There remains the single point, with which the sentence is closed and completed. It is not difficult to understand, for one cannot fail to notice with what word a sentence ends, although when it is short and another short one follows, I myself use the double point more freely than the single, as for instance: Make ready a lodging for me: for I shall arrive tomorrow: and so again: I give you no orders

concerning my affairs: you yourself will decide what is to be done. [quoted in Flesch, 1954, pp. 114–115]

This is the type of punctuation that was used in the King James Edition of the Bible, which was designed for oral reading and was so punctuated. The original Shakespeare folios were punctuated in this manner, although the modern editions follow conventional punctuation.

An experiment by E. L. Thorndike (1948) illustrates the personal nature of punctuation. Hamlet's soliloquy was punctuated twenty-three different ways by fifty-seven graduate students; the first twenty-four words of The Lord's Prayer were punctuated thirty-two different ways. The study also indicated that after a week the same individuals would punctuate these selections differently.

In the primary grades the child first learns about the period. Three uses of the period are taught:

1. At the end of a sentence: *The books are here.*
2. After an abbreviation in titles of persons and things: *Dr. James.*
3. After initials in proper names: *H. B. Lee.*

The teacher stresses the period in the first reading the child does and in the first sentence written on the board. "This little dot is called a period," she explains. "It tells us to stop because this is the end of a statement." The other uses are taught as an aspect of spelling.

Two uses of the question mark are taught:

1. At the end of a direct question: *Is this your ball?*
2. After a direct question but within the sentence: *"Will you be ready?" the man asked.*

The first can be understood and used by beginners in the first grade. The second should not be presented until late in the third grade. This form is less difficult: *He asked, "Will you be ready?"*

Lord Dunsany once complained that there were so many comma rules that printers could write one of his sentences like this: "Moreover, Jones, who, as, indeed, you, probably, know, is, of course, Welsh, is, perhaps, coming, too, but, unfortunately, alone." In some handbooks one can still find hundreds of rules for the comma. Fortunately for the teacher, eleven seem to be enough to meet the needs of elementary school children.

Four of these eleven rules are those that concern the writing of a letter:

1. To separate the parts of the date and the day of the year: *June 5, 1980.*
2. To set off the name of a city from a state: *Winfield, Kansas.*
3. After a salutation in a letter: *Dear Linda,*
4. After close of a letter: *Your friend,*

Additional comma rules taught in the elementary grades include:

5. To set off short direct quotations: *"We are ready,"* called the boys.*
6. After clauses of introduction: *While they were eating, the bell rang.*
7. Between parts of a compound sentence joined by a short conjunction: *Mr. Hill took Paul, and Jim went in Ms. Thrope's car.*
8. Before and after appositives: *The principal, Mr. Bellus, talked to the parents.*
9. Before and after parenthetical expression: *You told your mother, I suppose, about your report card.*
10. Before and after a nonrestrictive clause: *That boy, who has the dog, is in the fifth grade.*
11. To separate the words in a series: *Sue, Rick, and Billy are cousins.* (Immediately we run into the problem of the comma before *and*. Using one in that position helps to clarify the meaning.)

The colon is quite simple to teach, because there are only four ways it is used:

1. After the greeting in a business letter: *Dear Sir:*
2. Before a long series: *Mother bought the following: oranges, lemons, bread, jam, and cake.*
3. To separate the hour from the minutes: *2:30* A.M.
4. To denote examples: *A proper name should be capitalized: Mary.*

The apostrophe receives a great deal of attention in spelling. It is used in the following ways.

1. With the letter *s* to show possession: *Mary's coat, boys' coats.*
2. To show where letters have been omitted: *don't* (do not), *o'er* (over).
3. To show the omission of number from a date: *Class of '64.*
4. To show the plural of letters and figures: *A's, 2's.*

Quotation marks are a special problem for schoolchildren. Few adults ever write quotation marks unless they are professional writers. The reader is the best textbook for these marks. After a story has been read, go back and have children take the parts of the story characters. Then while the narrator reads all material not in quotations, the characters read their proper lines. Then examine how the material was punctuated so that each person knew what to read. If the class is engaged in story writing, examples of all the varieties of use should be illustrated on the blackboard as a reference. These are two basic usages that all children need to learn:

1. The unbroken quotation with the descriptive element preceding the quotation: *He cried, "Get a new man on first base!"*
2. The reverse of the preceding: *"Get a new man on first!" he cried.*

In order to use a semicolon properly, it is necessary to understand conjunctions. Conjunctions may join either words or groups of words. When a conjunction is preceded by a comma (as when joining two clauses), a semicolon may be used instead of the comma and conjunction. It confuses children to present the semicolon as a compromise between a comma and a period.

Mary was happy, but Joe was sad may be written: *Mary was happy; Joe was sad.* Clauses joined by a semicolon must be related and independent; however, the situation must be related in that it affects both Mary and Joe. One may write: *The sea is beautiful at sunset; the water reflects the brilliant glow of the sky.* But not: *The sea is beautiful at sunset; the cry of the seagulls makes me homesick.* Textbooks contain other rules for the semicolon.

The hyphen is usually considered an orthographic

feature rather than a punctuation mark. It is a growing practice to avoid the hyphen except where a word is divided at the end of a line. Many words formerly hyphenated are now either "solid" (i.e., one word, like *flannelboard*), or two words, like *decision making*. Webster's *Third New International* is a safe guide to follow in hyphenating. Children in the elementary school are not encouraged to use the dash, because they will tend to overuse it. Parentheses seldom appear in children's writing.

Interesting exercises in punctuation can be made by taking material from readers and reproducing it without any punctuation. The child is told how many sentences there are. The exercises can be made self-correcting by putting the title of the book and page number at the bottom of the exercise.

6 Sentences, 10 Capital Letters, 5 Commas, 4 Quotation Marks

she reached into a big box and pulled out a santa claus suit and held it up it was bright red with real fur trimmings billy could see that there was a cap and a set of whiskers and even boots to go with it
isn't that lovely she said to billy the minute i saw it i thought of you im sure it will fit just perfectly she held it up to him

Because some of the punctuation rules are applied primarily in letters, writing a group letter and then copying it from the board is a good way to introduce the comma rules involved. Practice with letter headings is equally good.

Provide the missing capitals and punctuation:

1.   astor hotel
            new york ny
            july 21, 2013
    dear teacher

2.   966 riverview
            madison wis
            june 6 1988
    dear mother

3.   gunnison colo
            dec 5 1994
    dear santa claus

Charts and bulletin boards that act as constant reminders are valuable in the classroom. The children should be involved in the making of these charts.

The following illustrations are suitable for display on bulletin boards:

Watch Your Commas

            713 Olde St.
            Austin, Texas
            Sept. 19, 1979

    Dear Mary,

            Your friend,
            Marty

Capitalize These Words:

1. The beginning of a sentence.
2. Names of months and holidays.
3. Names of particular streets and schools.
4. First word and important words of a title.
5. Names of people, pets, and initials of people.
6. Names of countries, cities, rivers, and mountains.
7. Only names in the greeting; only the first word in the closing of a letter.
8. References to God.

We saw a show
January, Halloween
Biona Ave., Hamilton School
My Visit to the Farm
Beth, Spot, A. J. Boyd
Mexico, Mt. Hood, Columbia River
Dear Sir, Dear Madam, Dear Mr. Hill,
Yours very truly
Lord, Savior, Buddha, God

One teacher makes punctuation marks come alive through dramatization. A question mark with a face and legs, a comma with a smiling face and wearing a hat, and a chubby little period are placed on a bulletin board, each with a caption telling one thing they do. These characters—Chubby Little Period, Jolly Question Mark, Mr. and Mrs. Comma, and Tall Exclamation Point—are introduced via the bulletin board. Each figure with its rule and title is shown. Other rules of punctuation are added as introduced.

The teacher describes how these "punctuation characters" are used:

I have the little people made up into plywood puppets. They are kept on hand in the schoolroom at all times. We use them to point up discussion of punctuation in many ways—in language class, social studies, written work, spelling. For example: in oral reading, we talk about "Chubby Little Period being at the end of a sentence to tell us that we stop here for a short time before going on." "Mr. Comma helps us by telling us this is the place to pause when we are reading a sentence."

I use this lesson in teaching how to begin and end sentences. In this lesson I also introduce the good English habit. "Use a question mark (Jolly Question Mark) after each sentence that asks a question."

Using the wooden "Chubby Little Period," I say,

Chubby Little Period
Runs and sits,
The end of the sentence
Is always his place.

A sentence is written on the board. Using the puppet, I then demonstrate the period's place.

Upper-grade children enjoy a television quiz program in which each punctuation mark appears and is questioned concerning its activities or in which there is a "What's My Line?" or "To Tell the Truth" format, with the punctuation marks appearing as guests. The master of ceremonies starts by saying, "Our guest does four things [or eleven if it's the comma]. We must name all of them to identify him completely."

Older students enjoy trick sentences like the one beginning the next column on this page.

Harry, when Harold had had *had,* had had *had had; had had* had had the teacher's approval. [Omit italics and punctuation when writing this sentence on the chalkboard.]

Have students provide punctuation and capitalization for the following:

The fight over the boys came home.
This is the story of walter who has not heard the story through it walter gained lasting fame a beautiful girl and a glorious name he also gained one autumn day on the grassy field in gridiron play the team was losing the clock moved fast any play might be the last of the game injured walter then called his own signal explaining men ill take the blame if we dont score he ran a full ninety yards or more

Another procedure that illustrates the importance of punctuation in written communication calls for deliberate misplacement of punctuation in a passage with consequent loss of meaning. The same passage can be reproduced several times with varying degrees of distortion. The pupil sees how difficult it is to get meaning from a passage so treated. In the following exercise the first copy completely obscures the meaning, the second copy is frustrating but not impossible, and the third is reproduced correctly:

Billy listened, carefully as the teacher. Explained how punctuation helps. The reader commas periods exclamation marks and question marks? All help a reader get meaning. From the printed page. Billy wondered what would happen. If the printer got the punctuation marks mixed. UP it was hard for him to imagine. What this would do to a story.

Billy listened carefully as the teacher explained. How punctuation helps the reader. Commas periods, exclamation marks and question marks all help. A reader get meaning from the printed page. Billy wondered. What would happen if the printer got the punctuation marks mixed up. It was hard for him to imagine what this would do. To a story.

Billy listened carefully as the teacher explained how punctuation helps the reader. Commas, periods, exclamation marks, and question marks all help a reader get meaning from the printed page. Billy wondered what would happen if the printer got the punctuation marks mixed up. It was hard for him to imagine what this would do to a story.

To emphasize that punctuation marks reflect the pauses and emphasis of speech, reproduce a page from a book such as *Island of the Blue Dolphins* or *Charlotte's Web* or from a story in the reading textbook without punctuation marks. As the teacher reads the story with appropriate stress, pause, and juncture, the students put in the appropriate punctuation. When they check their marks with the original text, the point can be made that punctuation at times is a personal interpretation and that the student and author may disagree and both be correct. In a discussion as to why the author punctuated as he did, rules may be reviewed or clarified.

Students enjoy making up punctuation marks to represent voice signals for which we have no written signals. Tell them that one writer has invented a new punctuation mark to use after such utterances as *How could that be so,* which is actually a question yet requires no answer. This combination exclamation mark and question mark is called an *interbang*.

Ask students to invent punctuation marks to indicate the tone of voice in which a statement is spoken: a low tone of voice, a sad tone of voice, a sarcastic tone of voice, and so on. Then have them use their new punctuation marks in sentences.

For Discussion

1. To what extent is punctuation a personal matter?

2. The newspapers frequently carry stories about errors caused by punctuation. At one time a tariff law was passed to admit fruit trees free of duty. A comma between fruit and trees cost the government a great deal of revenue before it was corrected. Do you know of other examples?

3. Why is it possible for two people to punctuate a paper in different ways and both be correct?

4. Do the following three rules cover most situations?

a. A comma may be used to prevent a possible misreading.

b. A nonessential part of a sentence should be set off with one comma if it comes first or last in the sentence and with two commas if it comes anywhere else.

c. When two or more words or groups of words are similar in form or function, they should be separated by commas.

A textbook for fifth grade suggests this form of evaluation of the children's understanding of punctuation: [9]

1. To see if the students understand the purpose of punctuation ask them (a) why we call punctuation marks *signals;* (b) which punctuation marks stand for voice signals; (c) which punctuation marks do not stand for spoken signals; and (d) why those marks that do not stand for spoken signals are also necessary.

2. To see if the students know how to use the commas, have them insert commas in the sentences below. Have them explain the use of each comma they insert.

a. The knight mounted his black steed(,) passed through the gate(,) rode across the drawbridge(,) and sped to Lady Ann's castle.

b. The dragon arrived on August 21(,) 1100 A.D.(,) at 10 Moat Drive(,) Rhine Valley(,) Germany.

c. Although the knight's horse was fleet of foot(,) Lady Ann could not be saved.

d. Yes(,) the knight was sad.

e. Dragon(,) that was a very rude thing for you to do.

3. To see if the students know when to use exclamation points rather than periods or question marks, have them add end punctuation to the sentences below. Have them explain their punctuation.

a. The king demanded to know if the smith could make a new golden goblet in three short hours(.)

[9] From *New Directions in English* (New York: Harper, 1968), pp. 68–70.

b. Is this rush necessary(?)

c. It is indeed(!) You wouldn't look nice at all without a head(. or !)

d. Stop scribbling on the walls(!)

4. To see if the students can differentiate between direct and indirect quotations, have them add quotation marks wherever necessary in the sentences below. Have them explain their punctuation.

   a. Lady Ann requested that the dragon put her down.

   b. (")Never!(") roared the fire-breathing snorter. (") You shall not go free!(")

   c. Martha said, (")I think this story should end now.(")

   d. The knight said that he, too, was tired of the chase.

5. To see if the students know when to use colons, have them add colons, where necessary, to the sentences below.

   a. Trees have many enemies(:) fire, disease, parasites, and drought.

   b. I saw three people at the party(:) Jane, Dale, and Nancy.

   c. The space station was launched at 4(:)32 A.M.

6. To see if the students know when to use hyphens in numbers, have them write the numerals below in words, hyphenating where necessary.

   a. 98   (ninety-eight) _____

   b. 665   (six hundred sixty-five) _____

   c. 3,479   (three thousand four hundred seventy-nine) _____

   d. 8:55   (eight fifty-five) _____

7. To see if the students know when and how to use the apostrophe, have them insert apostrophes where needed in the sentences below, and then contract words when possible, placing an apostrophe in the correct place.

   a. I can(')t come to the play.

   b. He(')s not home.

   c. She does not (doesn't) understand how the accident dashed that boy(')s hopes.

   d. All the schools(') teams entered the contest.

   e. He has not (hasn't) put the dragon to bed.

   f. We are (we're) seeing your mother tonight.

1. Add commas wherever they are needed in the sentences below.

   a. Alfred, George, Bob, and Don climbed into the capsule.

   b. The launching was to take place on March 31, 1999, from pad sixty-three, Podunk, West Petunia.

c. Marty, I can't stand the noise of the rockets.

d. Besides, it's too hot near the site.

e. Although I would like to see the lift-off, I don't think I'll go out there.

2. Put the correct punctuation mark at the end of each of these sentences:

   a. Dry ice is cold, solidified carbon dioxide.

   b. Watch out! It will give you a frostbite.
      or !

   c. Can't I make it melt?

   d. Hey! Where did it go?

3. Some of the sentences below need additional punctuation. Add the punctuation that is missing.

   a. Sonya asked Bob if he wanted to go on a bike hike.

   b. "I think," said Karen, "that this show could be improved."

   c. "It's horrible!" Ken shouted. "How can you stand to look at it?"

4. Decide what type of punctuation is missing in these sentences. Add the needed marks.

   a. He got up at 5:15 and collected his gear: rod, bait, rope, tent, and knapsack.

   b. Some dinosaurs were small and graceful: the ornitholestes was a dainty dinosaur.

5. Write the following numerals in words.

   a. 32   thirty-two _____

   b. 787   seven hundred eighty-seven _____

   c. 4,999   four thousand nine hundred ninety-nine _____

   d. 8:45   eight forty-five _____

6. In the sentences below, run together any words you can, and insert apostrophes for any letters you leave out.

   a. He is in the bank. he's

   b. We had made an appointment. we'd

   c. You are late. you're

   d. Do not take those flowers yet. don't

7. Explain the difference in meaning between the words with apostrophes in each pair below.

   a. the flutist's notes notes belonging to one flutist or played by him

   b. the flutists' notes notes played by more than one flutist

   c. the clipper ship's sails sails belonging to one clipper ship

   d. the clipper ships' sails sails belonging to more than one clipper ship

8. Punctuate the paragraph below.

How Should Letter Writing Be Taught in the Elementary Grades?

In each classroom beyond the first grade there should be a chart or other ready reference illustrating the form of letters appropriate for the grade. Some teachers put a permanent form on the blackboard with crayons. This shows the lines for date, salutation, body of the letter, and closing. Every language textbook provides adequate examples of various letter forms.

In the primary grades the children start by dictating the letter to the teacher, who writes on the blackboard. Afterward, each child copies the completed note to the person indicated. As soon as the basic pattern is mastered, children are encouraged to write individual messages. These may be to classmates who are ill, to relatives, to the principal, to the janitor, to a speaker who visited the class, or to any individual or group of concern to the child.

The satisfaction of expressing ideas in an accepted social manner seems to be sufficient motivation for most children. But this satisfaction soon ends if the letters are not read and there is no response. Because the post office is usually studied in the second grade, letter writing within the class will interest the children. The letters are carefully written, envelopes prepared, and the letters mailed and delivered as a part of the classroom project. With a little cooperation this can be extended to the second grade in another room or a neighboring school.

As the children advance, letter writing is best motivated by real purposes. Pen pals in other states and countries can be located through the *Christian Science Monitor* in Boston, Mass.; the Junior Red Cross in Washington, D.C.; The International Friendship League, 40 Mt. Vernon Street, Boston, Mass.; and the Parker Pen Company in Janesville, Wis. Sources of free and inexpensive materials are listed in *The Wonderful World for Children* by Peter Cardoza, published by Bantam Books. This inexpensive book will be found wherever paperback books are sold. Some of the major corporations, such as General Foods, Westinghouse Electric, Union Pacific Railroad, and Goodrich Rubber Company, have materials designed for classroom use that will be sent to children who write for them. The highway departments of many state governments will send illustrated highway maps. The National Audubon Society, 950 Third Avenue, New York, N.Y. 10022 and the National Wild Life Federation, 232 Carrol Street, N.W., Washington, D.C. 20012, have interesting material for children concerned with conservation.

However, there are some letters that should not be written. Children's magazines contain many offers to send stamps on approval. Some companies offer free stamps as an incentive. The child who receives such stamps may not understand that he will be expected to pay for them. Another type is the advertisement that offers a bicycle for solving a puzzle. This will involve the child in selling seeds, candy, or other items with a compromise award, such as a camera.

A second type of letter requiring careful consider-

A post office in a rural school provided an incentive for letter writing. There are so many real purposes for letter writing that such a laboratory exercise should be extended as soon as mail services are understood. (COURTESY OF THE SAN DIEGO COUNTY SCHOOLS.)

ation is that written to prominent people. Writing a letter of appreciation to the author of a book is one thing. Writing such a letter to gain information for a book report is another. The author John Steinbeck appealed to high school English teachers to stop assigning such letters. He was getting from seventy-five to a hundred on some days. Congressmen have the help and mailing privileges that do not make this a great burden. Few community leaders are in such a comfortable position.

When the need to write a letter has been established, use the lessons in the textbook that deal with the proper form. Some classes make a ''Letter Form Handbook.'' This is a folder that illustrates the blank form of a letter and contains examples of letters that the children have made or brought from home. If the children come from homes where examples of good letters are available, an excellent bulletin board can be made exhibiting these letters. A collection of letters with spe-

cial offers, which seems to be a modern merchandising practice, might be studied with respect to form and context.

Letters written to express appreciation for a favor or to express interest in a child who is absent provide opportunities for class discussion of the context of such letters. The teacher might start the discussion with the question, ''What are some of the things you would talk about if you could go to the hospital to visit David?'' Let me list the ideas on the board.''

1. Tell about things that have happened at school.
   a. The bicycle test.
   b. The map we finished.
   c. The new bulletin board.
2. Tell something about ourselves.
   a. John has a baby brother.

b. Paula went to visit Disneyland.

c. Colleen lost her glasses.

3. Say something about Joe.

a. Tell him we miss him.

b. Tell him we hope he gets well soon.

c. Tell him to have fun at the hospital.

Then discuss the questions "Should all of us write these ideas in the same order?" "Should all of us write about the bicycle test?"

After the letters are written let the children judge the quality of their own letters. None need to be rewritten, but some children may wish to do so. All should be mailed. Those who wish may read their letters to the group. The following ideas might be used in the evaluation:

1. Does the letter sound like talking?

2. Would you like to receive the letter yourself?

3. Does it tell what the reader would want to know?

The pen pal letter to a stranger is an incentive for descriptive writing. The fact that a child in Alaska has never seen the writer, his home, community, or school provides a good reason for writing about the familiar. Unfortunately, doing this as a classroom assignment detracts from the natural rewards of the activity. After the first letter it is wise to permit the activity to continue as a personal choice. Praise those who do continue writing, let them read the letters received to the class, have displays of letters and items received. Although intermediate-grade children are interested in foreign lands, the children in non-English-speaking countries who wish to write are usually in the upper grades. It thus seems wise to postpone this type of pen pal until children are in junior high school.

Usually a letter to an adult is much more difficult to write than a letter to another child. This seems especially true of "duty letters." "Thank you" notes or expressions of appreciation require specific patterns of language that apparently seem unnatural to some children. Examples of such letters or notes might be used as the beginning of a discussion.

Which of these letters would you like to receive?

11 Agassiz Avenue
Albany, N.Y.
Jan. 6, 1989

Dear Grandmother,

Christmas is so full of surprises. I never expected to have a pair of mittens made by my own grandmother. The colors are just right for my coat. It must have taken you a long time to make them. I'll think of you whenever I wear them.

We gave a Christmas play at school. I was an angel. Daddy says they must have made a mistake to give me a part like that. He is always teasing.

With love,
Jim

Newburgh, Ind.
Jan. 6, 1980

Dear Grandmother,

Thanks for the mittens. I got a sled, a coat, a book, a scarf, a knife, and lots of other things.

I was in a play at school.

Respectfully yours,
Diane

An incentive for letter writing is provided when a child has his own stationery. The paper should be lined. Parents might be encouraged to buy such material as birthday presents for children. The Cub Scouts and Brownies have such stationery for their members. If the teacher gives a gift as a birthday present, it is wise to have a local printer create the type of writing paper the children need. Children might make their own "crests" in art.

Tests of the following type provide a check of the understanding of letter form.

Correct at least eight errors in this business letter form:

4854
chicago illinois
july 4 1988

Sears Co
1616 Grove St
Denver, Colo.
dear sir,

A chart illustrating the terms used in letter writing should be mimeographed and given to each intermediate child. An example of a friendly letter is shown with these parts identified: heading, salutation, body, complimentary close, and signature. A business letter should have these parts identified: inside address, salutation, body, complimentary close, and signature.

A challenging task for all students would be to make a list of salutations and complimentary closings. How would one greet the Queen of England, the Archbishop of a church, a senator, a delegate to the United Nations, or a firm of lawyers?

The following standards may be placed on a chart and used to evaluate letters:

1. Did I tell something interesting? Was I thinking of the receiver and not of myself?
2. Do I have five parts to my letter?
   A heading.
   A greeting.
   A message.
   A closing.
   A name.
3. Did I write neatly so that the person who receives my letter can read it easily?
4. Did I indent the first word of each paragraph?
5. Did I align the margins on each part of my letter?

For Discussion

1. In addition to reports and letter writing there are other functional language situations when a child needs to write. When would a child need to write a description, an advertisement, a notice, an invitation, a biography, a joke?

2. Do you think writing postal cards should be a part of the letter writing program in school?

Closing and Name

Name _____

Begin the first word in the closing with a capital letter. Copy over the following closings correctly.

your friend, _____

sincerely yours, _____

with love, _____

Write the closing you would use if you wrote a letter to your mother.

_____

Write the closing you would use if you wrote a letter to a friend.

_____

Write the closing you would use if you didn't know the person very well.

_____

Put a comma after the closing. Write the following closings correctly.

Your friend _____

Sincerely yours _____

With love _____

Begin each part of your name with a capital letter. Write the following names correctly.

ginny vanek _____

alan wan _____

liz cimino _____

jack hall _____

3. Because schools have publications for creative writing, do you feel that outstanding reports, letters, and other such material should receive similar recognition? How might this be done?

Suggestions for Projects

1. Mauree Applegate suggests an I-W-S formula to start some children in creative writing. This means: *I*deas, *W*ords, and *S*timulators. Use this formula to devise materials that might be used in the classroom.

2. Problems stimulate the able child. Create some folders that present a series of problems and the suggested means whereby the answers may be found to use with such students.

3. Make an anthology of poetry written by children.

4. Evaluate ten films or filmstrips that might be used to stimulate imaginative writing. "The Hunter in the Forest" is suggested in many school courses of study.

5. Evaluate a specific suggestion with respect to creative writing. Such suggestions as the following may be used: Have children write the story of a comic-book episode or write a summary of a television show; encourage children to experiment with flannelboard characters or puppets as they develop a story or play before writing.

6. Investigate the procedures used with respect to publication of a collection of creative writing. How are the materials selected, who pays for the publication, how is the material distributed?

7. Make a study of worthy free materials that may be secured through letters written by children. Use the following sources as a guide:

Where to Get Free and Inexpensive Materials, by David L. Byrn and others, Fearon Publishers, 2263 Union St., San Francisco, Calif.

Elementary Teachers Guide to Free Curriculum Materials, by Educators' Progress Service, Randolph, Wisconsin. Annual.

Free and Inexpensive Learning Materials, 9th edition, Peabody College for Teachers, Nashville, Tenn.

So You Want to Start a Picture File.

Sources of Free and Inexpensive Pictures for the Classroom.

Sources of Free Travel Posters and Geographic Aids.

All the above by Bruce Miller and available from him, c/o Box 369, Riverside, Calif.

Sources of Free and Inexpensive Educational Materials, Field Enterprises, Merchandise Mart Plaza, Chicago, Ill.

Bibliography

Applegate, M. *When Teacher Says to Write a Poem* and *When Teacher Says to Write a Story.* New York: Harper & Row, 1968.

Arnstein, F. *Poetry in the Elementary Classroom.* New York: Appleton-Century-Crofts, 1962.

Burrows, A. T. "Children's Language." *National Elementary School Principal* (1965), 16.

Burrows, A. T. *Teaching Composition—What Research Says to the Teacher.* No. 18. National Education Association, 1969.

Burrows, A. T., C. Jackson, and D. O. Saunders. *They All Want to Write.* New York: Holt, 1964.

Carlson, R. K. "The Sunset Is a Pretty Pink Dove—Children's Voices in Poetry." *Elementary English* (October 1969), 748–757.

Clegg, A. B. *The Excitement of Writing.* London: Chatto and Windus, 1964.

Crosby, M., and others. *The World of Language,* Book 4. Chicago: Follett, 1970, pp. 275–277.

English Curriculum Study Center. *Project English: Written Composition—A Guide for Teachers in Elementary Schools,* Bulletin No. 101965. Athens, Ga.: University of Georgia, 1964.

Fillmer, H. T., and others. *Composition Through Literature,* Book C (about grades 5 and 6). New York: American Book, 1967.

Flesh, R. *How to Make Sense.* New York: Harper, 1954.

Frazier, A. *New Directors in Elementary English.* Champaign, Ill.: National Council of Teachers of English, 1967.

Gilburt, S. G. "Cooperative Poetry—A Creative Project." *Language Arts News* (Fall 1957).

Hofsteiler, A. N., L. A. Anderson, and R. Frame. *Cooperative Evaluation of Proficiency in English and Creative*

Writing. Charleston, W.V.: Kanawha County Schools, 1962.

Holbrook, D. *The Secret Places*. London: University Paperbacks, Methuen, 1964.

Joseph, S. M. *The Me Nobody Knows*. New York: Avon Books, 1969.

Joy, J. *Nonsensical Nuances of the ABC's*. Haywood, Calif.: Alameda County Schools Dept. (224 West Winton Avenue, Haywood, Calif. 94544), 1968.

Kahl, H. *36 Children*. New York: Signet Books, 1968.

Kids (a magazine written for and by children). (Write to Box 30, Cambridge, Mass. 02139, for sample copy.)

Koch, K. *Wishes, Lies and Dreams*. New York: Chelsea House, 1971. (Paperback: Random House, 1971.)

Krause, R. *A Hole Is to Dig*. New York: Harper, 1952.

Lenski, L. "Helping Children to Create." *Childhood Education,* **26** (November 1949), 101–105.

Lewis, R. *Miracles*. New York: Simon & Schuster, 1969.

MacDonald, R. "Grading Student Writing: A Plea for Change." *College Compositional Communication* (May 1975), 154–158.

McCord, D. "Excerpts from 'Write Me Another Verse.'" *Horn Book* (August 1970), 364–369.

Meams, H. *Creative Power—The Education of Youth in the Creative Arts*. New York: Dover, 1958.

New Directions in English. New York: Harper, 1968.

Northwestern University Curriculum Center in English. *Project English: A Teacher's Experience with Composition*. Evanston, Ill.: Northwestern University, 1965.

Parker, R. "Who Says Johnny Can't Write?" *English Journal* (November 1976), 42–46.

Petty, W. T., and M. E. Bowen. *Slithery Snakes and Other Aids to Children's Writing*. New York: Meredith, 1967.

Pooley, R., Project Director. *English Language Arts in Wisconsin*. Madison, Wis.: Department of Public Instruction, 1968.

Redkey, N. "Free Writing for Fluency," *Elementary School Journal* (May 1964), 430–433.

Right On (a magazine by youth in East Harlem, New York City). (East Harlem Youth Service, 2037 Third Avenue, New York, N.Y. Send 50¢.)

Sager, C. *Reading, Writing and Rating Stories*. Wellesley, Mass.: Curriculum Associates, 1976.

San Diego City Schools. *Oral and Written Language,* 1956.

Schiller, A., and others. *Language and How We Use It*. Glenview, Ill.: Scott, Foresman, 1969.

Teachers and Writers Collaborative Newsletters. Pratt Center for Community Improvement. (244 Vanderbilt Avenue, Brooklyn, N.Y. 11205. $3 for four issues.)

Thorndike, E. L. "Punctuation." *Teacher's College Record* (May 1948), 533.

Torrance, P. E. "Creative Thinking of Children." *Journal of Teacher Education* (December 1962), 448–460.

Torrance, P. E. *Guiding Creative Talent*. Englewood Cliffs, N.J.: Prentice-Hall, 1962.

Wilt, M. *Creativity in the Elementary School*. New York: Appleton-Century-Crofts, 1959.

Chapter 9
Spelling

A BOY AT SAULT STE. MARIE

A boy at Sault Ste. Marie
Said, "Spelling is all Greek to me,
   Till they learn to spell 'Soo'
   Without any 'u,'
Or an 'a' or an 'l' or a 't.' "
             Anonymous

SOLILOQUY ON PHONICS AND SPELLING

This year—I firmly made a vow—
I'm going to learn to spell.
I've studied phonics very hard.
Results will surely tell. . . .

"I thought I heard a distant cough
But when I listened, it shut ough."
Oh, dear, I think my spelling's awf.
I guess I meant I heard a coff.

"To bake a pizza—take some dough
And let it rise, but very slough."

That doesn't look just right, I noe.
I guess on that I stubbed my tow.

"My father says down in the slough
The very largest soybeans grough."
Perhaps he means "The obvious cloo
To better crops, is soil that's nue."

"Cheap meat is often very tough.
We seldom like to eat the stough."
I'm all confused—this spelling's ruff.
I guess I've studied long enuph.
             Isabel Smythe

A SMALL BOY WHEN ASKED TO SPELL "YACHT"

A small boy when asked to spell "yacht,"
Most saucily said, "I will nacht."
   So his teacher in wrath,
   Took a section of lath,
And warmed him up well on the spacht.
             Anonymous

What Is the Place of Spelling in the Language Arts Program?

Correct spelling may be considered the counterpart of legible handwriting in effective written communication. Poor spelling and poor handwriting interfere with comprehension, which is the major criterion of communication. Furthermore, poor spelling may result in lost employment opportunities (Medway, 1976). Although overemphasis on spelling may be detrimental if it constricts a child's written output, the inculcation of a positive attitude is an important step in motivating the child to spell correctly.

Your task as a teacher is to guide the student's growth in the ability to spell the language. It has been assumed by many that if the teacher supervised the student's use of a spelling book or workbook, this objective would be realized. Sometimes this has resulted in efforts to master the content of the book, much as if it were a geography text, rather than to develop individual spelling skills. Many young teachers are so influenced by their own memories of spelling classes that their efforts are directed toward motivating students to mastery of twenty words each week regardless of the usefulness of these words to the student.

Spelling Skills

Some of the major skills needed to spell are

1. The ability to relate phonemes (sounds of the language) with the graphemes (letters) used to represent them in writing. This means being able to understand the relationship between the beginning sound of *put* and the letter *p* and knowing that the sound of the group of letters at the end of *seeing* is represented by *ing*.
2. The ability to recall and represent consonant-vowel patterns as used in English spelling.
3. The ability to recognize sound variations represented by vowels and such consonants as *g* in *garage*.
4. The ability to use the dictionary to ascertain correct spelling and pronunciation of words.

In addition, a knowledge of the origins of words can be of assistance in learning to spell. For example, the word *know* shows its Scandinavian source and contains a letter no longer pronounced. According to some linguists, *kn* is a phoneme.

Word Knowledge Skills

Because spelling is seldom done for the purpose of creating nonsense words, there are skills related to understanding the meaning of words. These include understanding word roots and the changes produced by bound morphemes (prefixes and suffixes), knowing how to use a dictionary, and seeking to conform to the widely accepted standards of correctness that facilitate communication.

A person who wants to spell a word starts with an idea of what he wishes to express in writing. The idea must be associated with its speech symbol, or word, such as *pain* or *cake*. After selecting the word, the speller thinks of the separate sounds in it. These sounds are identified with the letters of the alphabet that represent them. Then the speller reproduces the letters in the sequence that will spell the word in its approved form, so that the letters *c-a-k-e*, rather than *kak, cak,* or *kake,* are used.

After one has mastered the spelling of a word, parts of this sequence are performed without conscious effort. If you learned to use the typewriter, you will recall how you progressed from a conscious effort involved in striking each letter to an automatic "cluster" of whole words and phrases. Similarly, the fluent writer expresses abstract ideas or involved concepts without having to grope for words letter by letter. A dictionary and thesaurus may be kept at hand to enrich one's output and to ascertain the spelling of difficult words.

It may help to clarify the steps in the spelling process to note that they are the opposite of the steps in the oral reading process. In reading, one starts by seeing the printed word. If the reader is not completely familiar with the word, the letters are examined. These are associated with the sounds they represent in the oral *vocabulary* of the reader. This oral word is next connected with its meaning in the *experience* of the reader.

Chomsky (1972) suggests that beginning readers might profit from using plastic letters on alphabet blocks to create their own spelling patterns for words with which they are already familiar. Montessori (1967) and Sylvia Ashton-Warner (1963) employed similar methods when teaching Italian and Maori children. The suggestions of Chomsky and the programs of Montessori and Ashton-Warner parallel the Piagetian view that children have a more thorough understanding of what they themselves solve.

The process used to read and spell differs with individuals. The present analysis may not be descriptive of what *you* do. Some will use sound associations much less than others, substituting visual associations. "Seeing" the word for spelling involves a problem that is not present in "seeing" the word for reading. In spelling, the word form must be supplemented by a clear impression of different letter elements in correct sequence. This impression requires not only a longer period of time to see the word for spelling than reading but also better visual memory and discrimination.

Phonetic Inconsistencies

A serious spelling problem is posed by the phonetic inconsistencies in the way our language is written. Horn analyzed the word *circumference* by syllables and by letter in order to determine the possibilities for spelling the word by sound. He discovered 288 possible combinations when each letter is analyzed. In summarizing this study, he states:

It is no wonder that a few months after a word has been temporarily learned in a spelling lesson, and subsequently used only occasionally in writing, the child is sometimes confused by the conflicting elements which his pronunciation of the word may call out of his past experience. With so little of the rational character to guide him the wonder is that the child fixes as easily as he does upon the one arbitrary combination which constitutes the correct spelling. [Horn, 1954]

This point can be illustrated in its most extreme form by spelling *potato* as "gh-ough-pt-eigh-bt-eau" by using these sounds: *gh* in *hiccough*, *ough* in *though*, *pt* in *ptomaine*, *eigh* in *weigh*, *bt* in *debt*, *eau* in *beau*.

Everyone knows the uncertainty of the English graphic form *ough* in such words as *though, through, plough, cough, hiccough, rough*. Only slightly less troublesome to the learner are such ambiguities as *doll–roll, home–come, sword–word, few–dew, break–squeak, paid–plaid*.

When the child meets the letter *a* in a word, it may have one of these sounds: *all, allow, nation, want; e* is different in *legend, legal; i* in *fin* and *final; o* in *pot, post, come; u* in *cub, cubic; y* in *cyst* and *tyrant*. The combinations of vowels are still more perplexing; *ea* has such variations as *clean, bread, hearth; ei* in *receive*, in addition to being different from *ie* in *siege*, has a different sound in *neigh* and *weight* and still another in *height*. The *o* combinations give forms like *blood–bloom, cow–crow, shout–should, shoulder–tough, though–rough, couple–court, cough–enough, plough–rough*. Final *e* is generally mute and is supposed to affect the preceding vowel as in *van, vane; rob, robe;* but in *change* and *sleeve* it has no effect and there is a series—*come, dove, love, some, have*—in which the vowel is shortened rather than lengthened.

In our writing of the language, the letter *a* has forty-seven different sound associates. There are three hundred different combinations that express the seventeen vowel sounds.

The short *i* sound is especially difficult. It is spelled at least fifteen ways in common words and only in a little more than half the time with the letter *i* alone. Examples are *i* (*bit*), *e, y* (*pretty*), *ie* (*mischief*), *ui* (*build*), *ey* (*money*), *a* (*character*), *ay* (*Monday*), *us* (*busy*), *ee* (*been*), *ei* (*foreign*), *ia* (*marriage*), *o* (*women*), and *ea* (*forehead*). There are other spellings in less common words. In these words one would expect the long vowel sound: *furnace, mountain, favorite, minute,* and *coffee*.

Another sound, the schwa (ə), is found in half of the multisyllabic words of the ten thousand commonest words. It is spelled thirty ways with almost any vowel or vowel diagraph: *about, taken, pencil, lemon, circus, teacher, picture, dollar, nation*. Although the use of the schwa may simplify the pronunciation of the unstressed syllables, the implication for spelling is quite different.

Good auditory perception and careful listening habits are a part of the spelling study procedure. If children use common pronunciation as a guide for spelling, they face many difficulties. If the pronunciation of a word is somewhat blurred in reading, the sound is still near enough to carry the meaning. In spelling, the word must be exact. Any word with a schwa calls for careful visual discrimination in order to learn the pattern used to spell the sound.

Silent letters are especially perplexing in spelling. If one includes letters not pronounced in digraphs, as in *please* or *boat,* and double letters where only one is pronounced, nearly all letters of the alphabet are silent in some words. In reading we can call them ghosts or use them to identify words that may be confused with others, but in spelling all these silent letters must be remembered. There is no phonetic clue to their presence in a word.

To alleviate the problems encountered in both reading and spelling, various authorities since the time of Noah Webster have called for changing the spelling of words to coincide with phonetic pronunciation. There does, indeed, appear to have been some very minor movement in that direction, as may be seen by the acceptance of such spellings as *donut* and *drafty.*

Phonetic Consistencies

Phonetic aids do exist in the spelling of the English language. An analysis of the 3,381 monosyllables in our language and the separate syllables of 2,396 polysyllables in words from the Jones spelling list shows that the English language is 86.9 per cent phonetic. Hanna and Moore report that our system of writing is basically alphabetic and that for almost every sound there is a highly regular spelling:

Eighty per cent of all the speech sounds contained in words used by elementary school children were spelled regularly. Single consonants are represented by regular spellings about 90 per cent of the time.

The vowel sounds cause the most spelling difficulty but even here the short *a* is spelled with an *a* about 90 per cent of the time as is the short *i* at the beginning of a word. Short *e* is spelled with an *e* about 89 per cent of the time, short *o* with an *o* 92 per cent, and short *u* with the letter *u* 72 per cent of the time.

The long vowel sounds cause much more trouble in spelling than short vowel sounds. All the long vowels may be written in a variety of ways. [Hanna and Moore, 1952]

Others have indicated that some of the frequently used words of our language do have phonetic consistency. Of the first thousand words on the Rinsland spelling list, we find the sound *a* is spelled as follows, the figures in parentheses representing percentages:

a	=	able (57)
ay	=	lay (23)
ai	=	laid (13)
ei	=	reindeer (3)
ea	=	break (3)
ey	=	they (1)

The sounds of the consonants are more consistent:

Phoneme		Grapheme correspondence	
b	=	bad	(100.0)
d	=	dog	(99.5)
f	=	fun	(85.3)
f	=	phone	(10.5)
j	=	age	(58.4)
j	=	jump	(31.5)
k	=	came	(60.0)
k	=	keys	(15.9)
l	=	lit	(89.7)
l	=	ball	(10.3)
m	=	me	(100.0)
n	=	no	(99.8)
p	=	pin	(100.0)
r	=	run	(100.0)
s	=	sit	(67.3)
s	=	city	(25.1)
t	=	time	(99.8)
v	=	vine	(99.4)
z	=	his	(75.5)
z	=	zero	(17.4)

However, even with apparently consistent consonants such as *b, d,* and *p,* there are spelling irregularities. For example, the letter *b* presents spelling problems in words where it is silent, as in *bomb, debt, doubt,* or *subtle.* The letter *d* is silent in *handkerchief, handsome,* and *Wednesday,* and in *soldier* it has a *j* sound. The *p* is silent in *raspberry, receipt, cupboard, corps,* and in words like *psalm, pneumonia,* and *psychology.*

Spelling Errors

An analysis made by Wolfe (1952) of spelling errors in a fifth grade indicated that 36.3 per cent were phonetic mistakes. Vowel substitution formed 8.1 per cent—*sence* for *since, togather* for *together, eny* for *any, lissen* for *lesson.* Vowel omissions formed 6 per cent—*busness* for *business.* Doubling or nondoubling caused 5 per cent—*refuell* for *refuel.* Consonant substitution, ending, and diphthongs caused the remaining errors—*pance* for *pants, feels* for *fields.* Vowel and consonant insertions were not grouped with phonetic errors, but are related—*pagun* for *pagan, leater* for *later, stolden* for *stolen, finely* for *finally.*

Phonetic errors seem to indicate a need for emphasis on visual and auditory imagery, but it is apparent that there are elements of unreasonableness in the way our language is spelled. Smith, Goodman, and Meredith (1970) suggest that phonic misspellers naturally misspell words according to the speed, style, and dialect of their spoken language.

It would only confuse the child more if this problem were presented to him as he started to learn to spell, but as teachers we need to understand the phonetic complexity of the task we seek to impart.

Spelling is an area in which there is little systematic relationship between growth and the amount of time spent in teaching. It appears probable that growth in ability to spell is related to extensive reading, maturational factors, and the specific needs for oral or written communication. A successively larger number of children spell a given word correctly in each grade. However, the progress does not appear to be closely related to the presence or absence of the word in the formal curriculum. In one study a spurt caused by using a sixth-grade book in the fifth grade was followed by a decline to normal rate. Apparently substantial gains made in special drives, as in spelling contests, prove ephemeral. Perhaps the results are to be expected because of the significance of total maturation in individual spelling abilities when all children have adequate opportunity for learning.

Building Spelling Skills

A teacher can build a good spelling program that is consistent with modern psychology and can gain additional time in the curriculum with the following program:

1. Be aware of the words used frequently in everyday speech as revealed by a word list and make occasional checks to see if these are being mastered. The New Iowa Spelling Scale (Greene, 1955) can serve as a guide in judging the appropriateness of specific words for the children in a class.
2. Have the children keep a notebook of words they have misspelled and once a week have a lesson pertaining to these words. A class list may serve as well. Students should print "difficult" words as encountered on flipchart paper, visible to the entire class.
3. Have planned worksheets available for use by those who are not able to make letter-sound association; divide words into syllables, identify base words, use abbreviations, apply generalizations, etc. These should be ungraded and are appropriate to some children's needs in each of the intermediate grades.

Modern textbooks reflect the careful thinking and planning of many individuals. Used as a means for teaching spelling rather than the end of spelling instruction, these textbooks will serve the teacher well. The teacher should feel free to change the words in the assignment to meet the needs of her students. The fact that grade placement of words follows no absolute rules should encourage her to select the lessons in any sequence that seems wise. Above all, she must remember that the average textbook deals with the minimum needs of children. Only the teacher can meet the spelling needs represented by each child's desire to express his ideas in words that are uniquely his own.

New words from social studies texts or the news are added to the bulletin board as a challenge to good spellers. The notebooks contain an alphabetical list of new vocabulary added by the children.
(COURTESY OF THE SAN DIEGO CITY SCHOOLS.)

In light of this, Smith et al. make an interesting proposal:

Perhaps schools and teachers need to take a new view of spelling. If the demand for absolute perfection in spelling at all stages in all written expression were abandoned in favor of a developmental approach—that is, movement *toward* correct spelling—then children would eventually become more effective spellers. Spelling should facilitate communication with words they can spell correctly, children should be encouraged to use their language in as rich a form as possible. They will tend to learn to spell the words they use. [Smith et al., 1970, p. 241]

Paul utilizes this developmental approach to introduce spelling to children in kindergarten:

1. Single letters are used to represent the sounds of phonemes (*PPL = people, FRN = friend*).
2. Nasal sounds appearing before consonants are omitted (*m* in *bumpy, n* in *pen*).
3. Single letters, particularly *L, R, M,* or *N* may represent a whole syllable (*TABL = table, NHR = nature*).
4. A sophisticated set of criteria is used in deciding which vowel letter to use when the child has not yet learned the spelling of short vowel sounds (both *fill* and *feel* are spelled *FEL*).

Children who learned initially to spell according to this system were given the opportunity to express their ideas independently. As they began reading and learning standard spelling, they began substituting standard forms in their own writing.

Geedy (1975) reports that learning may best be effected by making word meanings important to the child. "The best learning occurs when spelling is related to purposes real to the child. Teachers must create situations where children *need* to know how to spell" (p. 235).

What Words Should a Child Study in the Spelling Period?

Study of words from word lists has been shown to be more effective than the study of words in context in promoting spelling skills (Horn, 1962). Results indicate that words studied from lists are learned more quickly with greater retention and transfer more readily to new contexts.

There are over 600,000 words in a modern dictionary. Textbook writers must determine how many of these should be included in a spelling program. Their decisions have been guided by the Research of Horn and Rinsland. Horn (1927), of the University of Iowa, examined correspondence of business firms to learn

what words were most frequently used by adults. Rinsland (1945), of the University of Oklahoma, conducted a nationwide study of children's written material.

In addition to these research efforts, other scholars have examined the words most frequently misspelled at each grade level, words that are of frequent usage in both adult and children's word lists, words common to reading lists, and words that contain special difficulties.

When a group of authors starts to write a spelling textbook, the authors consult all these studies and make a list of their own that reflects their personal philosophy about what should be done with respect to spelling instruction. Those who feel that success motivates students will usually have a rather short list. Those who stress phonics may include words that are not used very often, yet provide phonetics practice. Those who feel that children learn to spell many common words outside of school will emphasize the words in the language that cause misspelling. Usually they include about 4,000 words. A survey of twenty-four of the most popular spelling textbook series revealed that there were approximately 10,000 different words to be found in all these texts (Betts, 1949).

More recently, Geedy (1975) summarized the diverse notions concerning criteria for inclusion of words to be studied. "There appears to be greatest agreement in making selections based on children's present needs in writing and frequency of need at a given grade level" (p. 233).

Studies by Johnson and Majer (1976) as well as others reveal the interesting fact that a few words of our language are used over and over again. Over one half of our writing consists of a repetition of the following 100 words:

a	big	doll	had
all	boy	down	has
am	but	eat	have
and	can	for	he
are	Christmas	girl	her
at	come	go	here
baby	did	going	him
ball	do	good	his
be	dog	got	home

house	mother	said	to
how	my	saw	too
I	name	school	tree
I'm	not	see	two
in	now	she	up
is	of	so	want
it	on	some	was
just	one	take	we
know	our	that	went
like	out	the	what
little	over	then	when
look	play	them	will
made	pretty	there	with
make	put	they	would
man	red	this	you
me	run	time	your

Horn (1927) noted that after the first thousand words the addition of the next thousand added a very small percentage of the words used by writers.

A person who learns 2,800 words knows 97 per cent of the words in common use. If he learns the 1,200 words next in frequency he increases his writing vocabulary only 1.1 per cent or up to 98.3 per cent of all the words he will write, which are found among the frequently used words of our language.

TABLE 9-1. Frequency of word usage in the ages of the word count derived from the horn basic writing vocabulary

Different words	Percentage of total word count
100	58.83
500	82.05
1,000	89.61
1,500	93.24
2,000	95.38
2,500	96.76
3,000	97.66
3,500	98.30
4,000	98.73

Reprinted by permission of E. Horn from the Twenty-third Yearbook of the National Society for the Study of Education.

Rinsland (1945) discovered similar facts, as illustrated in Table 9-2.

TABLE 9–2. Frequency of word usage in the Rinsland vocabulary*

Different words	Percentage of total word count
25	36
50	40
100	60
200	71
300	76
500	82
1,000	89
1,500	93
2,000	95

* For example, 10 words comprise about 25 per cent of all children's word usage.

Reprinted by permission of Henry D. Rinsland and Macmillan Publishing Co., Inc., from *A Basic Vocabulary of Elementary School Children*, copyright 1945 by Macmillan Publishing Co., Inc.

Hildreth explains:

The richness of the English language results in infrequency of use for the majority of words. Beyond the short list of words learned in the elementary school years is a tremendous store of thousands of words from which people may wish to select. There are relatively few words used as frequently as *girl* or *get*, but a word such as *gigantic* can be matched by 5,000 other words that are used with about equal frequency in English writing. Ten thousand words is a conservative estimate of a person's life writing needs. It is practically certain what 2,500 of these words will be, but not the remaining 7,200. Some persons will use two or three times ten thousand words in a lifetime of writing. [Hildreth, 1955, p. 141]

Research by Hanna et al. (1966) disagrees fundamentally with the principles of functional frequency in the grade placement of words. A Stanford University team studied the sound-letter correspondence or relationships of over 17,000 of the most frequently used words. They sought to find the percentage of these words one could spell correctly on the basis of knowledge of certain phonetic generalizations. They discovered in their research that knowing the phonological structure of written language would allow one to spell correctly 85 per cent of the words one needed. These researchers have given "Some Suggestions for the Study."

The selection of vocabulary for a modern spelling curriculum should begin with a linguistic analysis of American English. The study words should illustrate the principles, generalizations, and correspondences considered appropriate for a child at a given time.

Spelling is not only a process of mastering the orthography of the spoken vocabulary a child possesses at a certain age; it is at the same time an exercise of continuously expanding both his speaking and writing vocabularies. . . . By building into the child the analytic power that comes from a knowledge of the structure of the American-English orthography, there will be almost no limit to the eventual size of his spelling vocabulary—except the size of his aural-oral vocabulary itself. [Hanna et al., 1966]

The authors note that the purpose of learning to spell a word is related to the application of the word. If the word has immediate application for the individual, then learning to spell it will be immediately useful. However, if the purpose of studying a word or group of words is to strengthen the individual's understanding of the structure of the language, then it is the understanding or generalization that becomes functional.

Horn summarizes the rationale for specific instruction about individual words:

1. More than one-third of the words in a standard reference work on the pronunciation of American English showed more than one accepted pronunciation.
2. Most sounds can be spelled in many ways, one spelling not being sufficient to call it the most "regular" spelling.
3. Over one-half of the words in a conventional dictionary of American English contain silent letters, and about one-sixth contain double letters when only one letter is actually sounded.
4. Most letters spell many sounds, especially the vowels.
5. Unstressed syllables are especially difficult to spell. [Horn, 1960]

Thus research suggests the following as an effective spelling program:

1. Weekly selection from an approved word list of the words to be studied.
2. Administration of selected words on a pretest, followed by immediate self-correction.
3. Review of appropriate study methods and subsequent application of study methods on words missed on the pretest.
4. Retest followed by self-correction; further instruction as indicated.
5. Final test.

The preceding approach was piloted by Hillerich (1968). Comparisons were made on a pretest-posttest basis between an experimental group employing the method and a control group using a commercial program. Results indicated no significant differences between the two groups in terms of posttest scores on words studied. However, children in the experimental program scored significantly better on words not studied, despite the fact that the commercial program purports to build spelling power. The experimental group studied twice as many words per week as the control group but devoted only three days a week to spelling, as compared with the five days a week required by the commercial spelling program.

The two periods normally spent in spelling instruction were devoted to additional experiences in written language: writing, revising, and the teaching of proofreading skills. As a result, teachers reported a great increase in interest in spelling correctly.

As an added bonus, children using the experimental approach were able to do at least twice as much in the way of written language as they had done in the past, because of the two added periods. Spelling is thus put into proper perspective.

There is *no point* in learning to spell orally, and there is *no point* in learning to spell words that one is not going to *use* in his writing. Spelling is a communication skill whose sole import derives from written expression.

When Should Words Be Introduced into the Spelling Curriculum?

Equal in importance to the problem of *what* words should be taught is the question of *when* a word should be taught. This problem might be emphasized by asking yourself, "At what grade level should the word *school* or *elephant* be taught?" Textbook authors have been guided by the answers to these two questions: "When do children want to use this word? How difficult is it to spell?"

It is a complex task to decide about the difficulty of a word. If we were to take a single word, such as *elephant,* and give it to ten children in each grade in school, we would learn that some children in each grade would spell it correctly and that others would misspell it. If the following figures indicated those who spelled it correctly in each grade, we would have the beginning of a scale to measure how difficult the word is.

Grade	Number spelling word correctly
2	2
3	4
4	7
5	9
6	9
7	10
8	10

On the basis of both need and possible error, it would seem that these students needed help on the word during the third and fourth grades. It may be that the word is too difficult for the second and would challenge no one in a seventh-grade class.

The first spelling scale was designed in 1913. In 1955 Harry A. Greene designed the New Iowa Spelling Scale, which is still widely used.

The extent of the New Iowa Spelling Scale indicates the amazing scope of modern research. Approximately 230,000 pupils in almost 8,800 classrooms in 645 different school systems were involved. Because each pupil undertook to spell 100 words, a total of over 23 million spellings comprise the data for this scale. With respect to the words *elephant* and *school* the scale provides the following information:

Grade	Per cent of class spelling word correctly	
	Elephant	*School*
2	0	32
3	5	68
4	24	86
5	55	92
6	57	97
7	74	99
8	82	99

It is evident from the preceding table that the correct spelling of the word *school* occurs much earlier and more completely than does the correct spelling of the word *elephant*. However, we still do not know how interested the child in your room is in using the word *elephant*. As a teacher you need a copy of this scale on your desk at all times to give you information about other words that grow out of classroom writing.

Although the New Iowa Spelling Scale may serve as an indicator, there still remain uncertainties about the grade placement of individual words. When we recognize that the linguistic maturity of children differs, it is apparent that a formal graded list will be unrelated to the needs of certain children in a classroom.

The first lesson in a spelling textbook may be as difficult as the last. Thus if there are units designed for Halloween, Chanukah, or Christmas, it is good judgment to skip to those units at the appropriate time. Similarly, the words in a fourth-grade speller may actually be more difficult for a specific child than those in a fifth-grade lesson. Spelling lists must be examined so that word selections reflect the individual needs of the child or group of children being taught.

Results from the Stanford Study indicate the following ordering of linguistic information: [1]

Grade 1—a. Presentation of CVC patterns of monosyllabic words which appear in the child's spoken vocabulary (e.g., *cat, run*).
   b. Instruction in upper and lower case lettering which represent the phonemes being learned as words.
   As skills are developed more challenging correspondences may be introduced such as single sounds (e.g., *s*) spelled with two different letters (e.g., *s*it, *c*ity), and consonant beginning and ending clusters (e.g., *brick*).

Grade 2—a. Provision of experiences to lead pupils to the discovery of rules and generalizations to help explain both consistencies and peculiarities of phoneme-grapheme behavior.
   For example—
   1. various spellings of "long" vowel sounds (e.g., *gate, fete, wait, they*)
   2. formation of plurals and third person singular
   3. irregular spellings of "short" vowel sounds (e.g., *have, build*)
   4. introduction to syllabication
   b. Instruction to the importance of alphabetical order and its value in relation to dictionary usage.

The spelling program in subsequent grades should continue to expand the pupil's knowledge of the orthography of his language and be concerned with increasing emphasis upon examination of factors that influence the correct choice of graphemic representation in increasingly complicated words. Both phonological and morphological bases for mastery of phoneme-grapheme correspondences will become part of his program of study as he becomes more sophisticated in his analysis of the relationships between spoken and written American English. [Hanna et al., 1966, p. 129]

[1] From Paul Hanna and others, *Phoneme-Grapheme Correspondence as Cues to Spelling Improvement* (Washington, D.C.: U.S. Department of Health, Education, and Welfare, 1966).

For Discussion

1. Why do classroom teachers frequently favor a workbook in spelling? What advantages and what disadvantages exist in such a program?

2. Why is a word easy for one child and difficult for another in the same grade?

3. What words do you think will be in the adult needs of children now in school that are not included in the studies listed, such as *computer* and *transistor?*

4. How can you explain the frequent misspellings of such words as *going, Chanukah, Christmas, knew,* and *hear?*

5. Because the basic list of 100 words appears over and over again in the writing of children, why do they need to be isolated for spelling instruction?

6. Think of the number of words you spell correctly that were never in a spelling lesson. How did you learn to spell them?

7. What are some words that would be used in the vocabulary of children in your locality that are not frequently used nationally?

8. Would it be necessary to put all the words in a spelling lesson that children want to use in a special report?

A Laboratory in Spelling for Teachers

Psychology confirms two ideas that teachers use to guide their activities. One is to start with the needs and goals of the learner and the other is to make learning an active process. It will help you as you plan for classroom work to experience some of the activities suggested in this chapter for children.

The following words are considered "spelling demons." Decide whether the spelling is correct or not. If a word is correct, mark a check by it; if it is incorrect, rewrite it correctly.

1. achieve   4. anoint
2. alright   5. battalion
3. analize   6. coolly

7. definately
8. dependant
9. descendant
10. disappate
11. dissapoint
12. drunkeness
13. ecstacy
14. embarrassed
15. indispensable
16. inimitible
17. inoculate
18. irresistable
19. irridescent
20. liquefy
21. neice
22. occassional

23. occurence
24. perseverance
25. proceed
26. putrify
27. reccomend
28. recieve
29. sacreligious
30. seize
31. seperate
32. supercede
33. superintendant
34. tyranny
35. ukelele
36. vilify
37. wierd

KEY: 1. √ 2. all right 3. analyze 4. √ 5. √ 6. √ 7 definitely 8. dependent 9. √ 10. dissipate 11. disappoint 12. drunkenness 13. ecstasy 14. √ 15. √ 16. inimitable 17. √ 18. irresist-ible 19. iridescent 20. √ 21. niece 22. occasional 23. occurrence 24. √ 25. √ 26. putrefy 27. recommend 28. receive 29. sacrilegious 30. √ 31. separate 32. supersede 33. superintendent 34. √ 35. ukulele 36. √ 37. weird

Now compare your responses with the answer key. Among the word list were there common misspellings? What are the patterns of letters that persistently cause confusion? What explanation might be given for the erroneous spelling? How did those who spelled each word correctly remember the standard sequence of letters? Did anyone follow a rule to spell correctly? How may individual errors be analyzed in a manner that will avoid repetition of the error?

One of the simplest spelling games is Endless Chain. A third grade might start with three-letter words. The first child spells *cat*. The next child must then start with a three-letter word starting with the last letter of the previous word, which in this case is *t*, so he might spell *ten*. The next child's word must then start with *n*, such as *not*. When a child cannot think of a word or misspells the one he selects, the chain is broken. Some-

times each child writes the words being spelled orally in order to get a visual image. A college class might start with five-letter words. For variety the words may be adjectives (any number of letters) or names of places (thus involving capital letters). Very soon the students want to use their dictionaries. It adds to the game to let each child have one so that he can find a five-letter word starting with *o*, or whatever letter happens to be the last one in the word previously spelled. See how many words you can make into a chain in two minutes. You might start, for example, with *stand–draft–teach*. . . .

A review of alphabetical order might be given in the fourth grade by having the following message put on the chalkboard:

Can you break the code?
Bmm tuvefout bsf jowjufe up b usftvsf ivou gsjebz jo uif hznobtjvn

Clue: Write the alphabet in sequence and note position of the letters in the message.

How Should Spelling Be Taught?

We have noted the efforts that have been made to find *what* words should be taught and *when* they should be taught. The problem of *how* words should be taught has been of equal concern. In the late nineteenth century, Rice (1897) suspected that the methods of spelling instruction were not very efficient. He conducted experiments that convinced many schools that they were spending too much time on the direct teaching of spelling. (To this day we have not been able to decide whether it is best to teach spelling in association with other school work or to have a specific period each day.) The amount of time spent in the spelling period has been reduced to about seventy-five minutes a week, and the child who has demonstrated spelling mastery is permitted to engage in other instructional activities.

As mentioned, Horn (1960) demonstrated the efficiency of the test-study plan of organizing a week's work. In this plan the students take a pretest of the weekly assignment the first day. This separates the words they know how to spell from those that need drill. Exercises and other activities to encourage writing of the words that were misspelled are used during the week; a final test of all the words is given at the end of the week. A chart of progress is kept by each student, words missed are added to the next week's lesson, and review lessons are given at intervals to assure a respelling of words studied.

A variation of this plan is the *study-test* plan, in which fewer words are given each day but they are words known to be difficult for most of the class. There are daily tests as well as one at the end of the week on all words. The following plans for spelling instruction are typical of many school programs:

PLAN A

First Day

1. Introduce the words in the new lesson in a meaningful way.
2. Discuss meanings of words.
3. Use words in sentences.
4. Note which words are phonetic.
5. Note likenesses to words previously learned.
6. Note any unusual spellings.
7. Form visual images and sequence of letters in each word.
8. Write the words.
9. Develop word lists, which are on continuous display.
10. Integrate use of these words throughout the curriculum.

Second Day

1. Use the words in a worksheet.
2. Do the exercises in the spelling book.
3. Write sentences using the words.
4. Write a story suggested by the words.
5. Play bingo or other games which call for use of the words.

Third Day

1. Test and check words with the children.
2. Design plans for further study (games, worksheets, word practice).

Fourth Day

1. Study the words missed on the test and words from individual card files.
2. Give additional words to children who have mastered the list by the third day. (This may be done earlier in the week.)
3. Teach additional words by making derivatives.
4. Work with individuals and small groups with special needs.

Fifth Day

1. Give the final test. It is advisable for each child to have a booklet in which to write the words.
2. Check the tests with each child.
3. Test children on additional words learned.

PLAN B

1. Present the lesson on Monday.
2. Test on Tuesday, giving additional words to children who need no further study on the regular lesson.
3. Study the words and use them on Wednesday and Thursday.
4. Give the final test on Friday.

PLAN C

Give a pretest on Monday and then plan the following days according to the results of the test.

Make tests more interesting and valuable by variety in method. For example, test certain other abilities:

1. Circle or underline vowels in certain words.
2. Mark long or short vowels in certain words.
3. Select the words of more than one syllable.
4. Divide words into syllables and mark accents.
5. Write abbreviations of words.
6. Alphabetize the words.
7. Change all singular words to plurals.

8. Show contraction or possession.
9. Introduce words similar to those in the word list to apply generalizations.

Although students sometimes may profit from grading each other's tests, this task is best done by teachers. Students should understand the standard for scoring a test. A word is marked wrong if the letters are not in correct order, or if a capital letter is omitted in a word always capitalized, or if either the apostrophe, period, or hyphen is omitted.

After the papers have been returned to the pupils, a short discussion of the common errors is valuable. Review the steps used in individual study by asking:

1. Did you pronounce and *hear* the word correctly?
2. Did you try to spell by sound when the sound does not agree with the letters?
3. Did you forget the letters in one part of the word?

Each misspelled word should be written correctly in the pupil's individual review list or workbook. Teachers should praise pupils who initiate their own review work. This is one of the habits of the good speller. He is concerned over his misspelling and makes an effort to correct it.

Spelling Errors: Cause and Effect

The learner and the teacher should recognize the fact that testing in spelling is done to guide learning. Errors should help the student to direct his study efforts. After the children have rewritten each misspelled word in the review list correctly, the class and teacher should analyze words to diagnose the nature of error. The *types* of errors commonly made are as follows:

1. Omission: *the* for *they*.
2. Carelessness: *surily* for *surely*.
3. Phonetic spelling: *Wensday* for *Wednesday*.
4. Repeating or adding a letter: *theeth* for *teeth*.
5. Transposition: *esaily* for *easily*.
6. Ignorance of the word: *parell* for *parallel*.
7. Failure to hear or perceive words correctly: *bureau* for *mural*.

The frequent *causes* of spelling errors are summarized in Table 9-3.

TABLE 9-3.

Error	Cause
acurate for *accurate*	faulty observation
docter for *doctor*	group pronunciation or faulty teacher pronunciation (Break into syllables and point out difficult spots.)
laffun for *laughing*	inaccurate auditory and visual perception
horse for *hoarse*	inaccurate visual perception.
athalete for *athlete*	pronunciation error
ate for *eight*	incorrect meaning association
bying for *buying*	incorrect root word association
non for *none* *opn* for *open* *Wensday* for *Wednesday*	too dependent on phonics (Children must be helped early in spelling to note orthographic irregularities of our language.)
beyoutey for *beauty* *exampull* for *example*	overemphasized pronunciation (Words should be spoken naturally.)
cents for *sense* *except* for *accept*	incorrect meaning association (Such words should be taught in pairs.)
askt for *asked* *berrys* for *berries* *largist* for *largest*	unfamiliarity with common word endings (These should be taught as they apply to many common words.)
dissturb for *disturb* *preevent* for *prevent* *bysect* for *bisect*	unfamiliarity with common prefixes
acke for *ache* *bucher* for *butcher* *juge* for *judge*	failure to note silent letters that appear in some words (Help children to form correct mental images.)
bill for *bell* *brin* for *brain* *alog* for *along*	lack of phonics or faulty writing habits
allright for *all right* *goodnight* for *good night*	unfamiliarity with expressions that must be written as two words (Specific teaching is required.)

TABLE 9-4.

Word	No. of misspellings III	IV	V	VI	Total	No. of ways	Common type	No. of occurrences III	IV	V	VI	Total	Specific errors	No. of occurrences III	IV	V	VI	Total
almost	21	23	28	15	87	26	almost	6	14	19	8	47	ll for l	13	17	20	10	60
													n for m	4	4	6	4	18
already		46	45	25	116	44	allready		13	11	8	32	ll for l		28	19	12	59
													y omitted		11	12	7	30
													e for ea		10	8	4	22
													a for ea		8	3	1	12
family		45	53	31	129	66	famly		10	7	7	24	i omitted		15	21	15	51
													ey for y		6	13	3	22
													n for m		8	10	4	22
													l misplaced		7	9	3	19
first	45	36	27	16	124	35	frist	12	4	18	9	43	ri for ir	14	8	19	9	50
lock	69	38	10	6	123	33	loke	17	14	2	1	34	e added	24	15	3	1	43
													c omitted	21	14	3	1	39
													a for o	10	3	2	1	16
makes	55	33	25	16	129	32	maks	24	15	8	3	50	e omitted	45	21	11	3	80
passed	52	48	58	47	205	22	past	28	44	38	34	144	t for sed	34	44	39	35	152
													st for ss	5	3	18	4	30
vacation		58	51	37	146	86	vaction		9	20	23	52	2nd a omitted		30	26	30	86
													c omitted		10	6	1	17
													ca omitted		6	6	4	16
													k for c		10	2	0	12
while	33	25	22	23	103	54	wile	9	9	5	9	32	h omitted	24	17	12	19	72
													ll for le	6	2	2	6	16

Source: G. C. Kyte, "Errors in Commonly Misspelled Words in the Intermediate Grades," *Phi Delta Kappan* (May 1958), pp. 367–371.

An analysis of the errors made by a class will reveal a wide variety of spellings of a single word. Table 9-4 illustrates the number and variety of spelling errors that may occur in a given word. For example, the word *almost* was spelled twenty-six different ways! The most frequent error was a doubling of the *l*. Study exercises are planned to place emphasis on such parts of words without identifying them as "hard spots." It is apparent that other irregularities also cause spelling trouble.

To, Too, Two

Some persistent spelling errors demand specific attention. *To, too,* and *two* are often confused. The error is usually of the following type:

I am to tired to play.

Children seldom make such errors as the following:

The game is two easy.
To more days until Christmas.

In order to reinforce proper identification and usage of *to, too,* and *two,* have the children make charts of this type:

Too = more than enough:
The window is too high.
Too = also: *Jack went too.*

Use *to* like this: *I rode to town.*
I went to see the game.

two = 2 (1 + 1): *We found two pennies.*

Note that each is a different part of speech. *Too* is an adverb, *to* a preposition, and *two* an adjective.

The drill found in Table 9-5 will provide meaningful contrast. The class is divided into teams and captains are chosen. The captain gives each pupil on his team one of the words listed in the table. The pupil writes a sentence on a slip of paper, using the word he has been given with *to, two,* or *too.* For example, a pupil on Team 1 may be requested to compose a sentence using *loudly.* The pupil may write, "We sang too loudly." He then writes "Team 1" and his name on his slip and gives it to his captain. The captain tells him whether or not the usage is correct. The entire sentence

TABLE 9-5. The teaching of spelling

Team 1	Team 2	Team 3	Team 4	Team 5
loudly	cold	hot	exciting	sneeze
quietly	run	help	wrestle	whistle
stoves	town	movies	camp	swim
marbles	dogs	puppies	the circus	sing
young	heavy	automobiles	carrots	thin
jump	bad	fast	school	books
dark	the beach	slippery	icy	warm

is examined for capitals, periods, and correct spellings.

Each team may now choose a pupil to write his sentence on the board. Is each sentence correct? If so, the team scores a point. Then a second pupil is chosen from each team. When any pupil makes an error, his team fails to score. The team that scores the highest wins the game.

When a team has a perfect score, the teacher may dictate sentences of greater complexity to that team while the other teams continue the game. The following sentences may be dictated for further practice:

1. You have far too many apples to go in that basket.
2. I have two pencils too many.
3. I came to school too late to see the exhibit.
4. Were you too late to go with Tom to town?

It's, Its

Another frequent error is confusion between *its* and *it's.* Make the charts of this type to help students see the difference:

It's is a contraction meaning "it is."
Examples: *It's a new desk. It's too sweet.*

Its is a possessive, like *his* or *your:*
The motor hummed its tune.

Have the children make up sentences to illustrate each definition.

What Is It?

The following stories may be written on the chalkboard for further practice. Have the children write the numbers 1 to 23 on a sheet of paper. Either *its* or *it's* is supplied for each blank in the stories according to its appropriate usage.

A Red Breast

    __1__ breast is red. __2__ song is "Cheer up!'' __3__ home is a nest of grass and twigs. What is it? __4__ a robin.

Man's Best Friend

    __5__ called man's best friend. __6__ eyes are kind. __7__ tail wags when __8__ friendly and happy. __9__ teeth are sharp, but __10__ heart is all gold. What is it? __11__ a dog.

Fenders Easily Bent

It has four wheels. __12__ motor hums. __13__ tires screech. __14__ steering wheel is round and smooth. __15__ fenders are easily bent or battered. What is it? __16__ an automobile.

Good for Bones and Teeth

    __17__ something to drink. __18__ color is creamy white. __19__ good for bones and teeth. Butter is made from __20__ fat. __21__ best when __22__ cold. What is it? __23__ milk.

A useful extension of this idea is for each pupil to write a "What Is It?'' story. The teacher may give a category such as *toys* or *animals* with a requirement that the possessive (*its*) be used, for example, at least two times in the story. The personal application of a principle is one of the most effective means of ensuring learning and retention.

Capital Letters

Capital letters are a cause of spelling confusion. Have the children note the words that are capitalized in their social studies books, then make a chart of this nature:

A CAPITAL LETTERS CHART FOR ME

Do Capitalize

1. The first word of each sentence:
   This afternoon we went to the game.

2. The names of months of the year, days of the week, and holidays:
February	*Wednesday*
Halloween	*New Year's Day*

3. The names of particular streets, schools, and buildings:
Adams Avenue	*Central School*
Riverview Street	*State Office Building*

4. The first word and all important words in the titles of books, movies, stories, magazines, and poems:
Skid	*My Visit to the City*
Charlotte's Web	*The Star Spangled Banner*

5. The names of people and pets, the titles and initials of people, the word *I*:
   Miss Mary A. Cunningham   My dog, Dingle
   Denise, Daryl, and I

6. The names of countries, states, cities, mountains, and rivers:
New York City, New York	*Rocky Mountains*
Warren, Ohio	*Colorado River*

7. The first word in the greeting or closing of a letter:
Dear Nancy,	*Sincerely yours,*
Gentlemen:	*Yours very truly,*

8. Words referring to the deity:
God	*Holy Ghost*	*Jehovah*
Lord	*Savior*	*He*

Do Not Capitalize

1. The names of seasons:

 spring *winter*
 summer *autumn*

2. The names of games, birds, trees, flowers, vegetables, fruits, and animals:

baseball	*carrots*	*robin*	*chickens*
oak	*apples*	*rose*	*maple*

The following exercises may be useful in reinforcing the concept of capitalization:

1. Write the answer to such questions as the following:

 Where do you live?
 What is your father's name?
 What school do you attend?
 What countries would you like to visit this summer?
 When is your birthday?
 What is your favorite subject in school?
 How would you address a letter to your principal?
 What is the title of your favorite book?

2. a. Change the small letters to capitals:

 my cousin lives in denver. her name is linda lou. she attends jefferson school. each wednesday they have a class in spanish. last year she went east for her vacation. she heard the president in rhode island. her favorite book is the little house in the woods.

Children who find the preceding too difficult might be helped by omitting the initial letter of each capitalized word. (This also avoids showing an error.)

 ____y cousin lives in ____enver.

 b. Copy this letter and supply appropriate capital letters:

 115 south hill street
 san diego, california
 september 6, 1981

 dear jim,
 our girl scout troop just made an overnight trip to palomar mountain. it was fun since i slept in my own sleeping bag. please write and tell me how the evanston little league made out.

 your friend,
 sharon

Mnemonics

A mnemonic device is one that aids the memory. Such devices are highly personal; although they may help some children, they may be merely an additional burden to others, because in order to remember one thing the child must remember the association among several things.

Following are a few association ideas that may help some children who are having specific spelling difficulties:

all right	*All right* is like *all wrong.*
cemetery	Watch the *e*'s in *cemetery.*
principal	The *principal* is a prince of a *pal.*
principle	A *principle* is a *rule.*
separate	There is a *rat* in *separate.*
balloon	A *balloon* is like a *ball.*
familiar	There is a *liar* in *familiar.*
parallel	*All* railroad tracks are *parallel.*
almost	*Almost* always spelled with one *l.*
capitol	There is a *dome* on the capit*o*l.
bachelor	The *bachelor* does not like *tea.* (Common error is *batchelor.*)
yardstick	A *yardstick* is in one piece.

A mnemonic association that works for one person does not always work for another. The associations you think up for yourself are better than the proclaimed masterpieces of others. The more startling an association is, the better it will be remembered:

```
l
e
t
t          station*ary*
station*ery*    t
```

hear   You have to use your *ear* for this one.

indepen*dent*   We made quite a *dent* in England in 1776.

gram mar   Anyone can spell the first half. Copy the second part from the first, in reverse order.

The hardest spelling rule concerns when to double a final consonant and when not to. Note how a single consonant favors a long sound and how a double consonant favors a short sound. Examples will make it clear:

hated	(hatted)	bated	(batted)
mated	(matted)	dined	(dinned)
fated	(fatted)	planed	(planned)
rated	(ratted)	writing	(written)

An association between related words will clarify some spellings. One can remember the *a* in *grammar* by relating it to *grammatical*. One can remember the *a* in *ecstasy* by relating it to *ecstatic*. These blanks can be filled properly by noticing the vowel in the associated words.

dem__cratic	democracy
pres__dent	preside
prec__dent	precede
comp__rable	comparison
comp__sition	composer
hist__ry	historical
janit__r	janitorial
manag__r	managerial
maj__r	majority
ill__strate	illustrative
ind__stry	industrial
imm__grate	migrate
ab__lition	abolish
comp__tent	compete
si__n	signal

bom__	bombard
cond__mn	condemnation
mali__n	malignant
sof__en	soft
mus__le	muscular

For Discussion

1. Classroom management of testing procedures needs to be planned. How would you distribute workbooks and collect them? Should children check their own papers or exchange them? How do you handle individual words in a test? (Each child will have different errors.)

2. Should one have a "100 per cent club" for those who always achieve 100? Should some who are perfect in an early test be excused from the final? Should a student who is assigned only five words and gets them correct receive the same grade as one who is assigned ten and spells them correctly?

3. Should some students become spelling tutors to help the less able? What would such a student learn from the experience?

4. Are there some students who respond favorably to competition and grades and others who don't? Is it possible to provide differential treatment without seeming to discriminate?

5. Why is the term *remedial* inappropriate with respect to teaching a developmental skill?

6. The following examples of phonetic irregularities in the way we spell might be used to help parents understand the spelling problem. What others might be made of such information?

   a. What common word could you get by pronouncing the letters *ssworps?*
      Sure. Ss as in *mission, wo* as in *two,* and *rps* as in *corps.*

   b. What common word could you get by pronouncing the letters *psolocchouse?*
      Circus. Ps as in *psychology, olo* as in *colonel, cch* as in *Bacchus, ou* as in *famous,* and *sc* as in *science.*

c. *Sugar* is the only English word beginning with *su* sounded as *shoo*.
"Are you sure?"

d. What common word could you get by pronouncing the letters *ghoti*?
Fish. Gh as in *rough, o* as in *women,* and *ti* as in *fiction.*

e. What word has five consecutive vowels?
Queueing.

f. What word has five *e*'s and no other vowels?
Effervescence.

g. Pronounce *Pothzwabyuckeling.*
There's nothing to pronounce! Every letter is silent: the *p* as in *pneumonia, o* as in *leopard, t* as in *ballet, h* as in *catarrh, z* as in *rendezvous, w* as in *wrong, a* as in *dead, b* as in *dumb, y* as in *today, u* as in *four, c* as in *czar, k* as in *knock, e* as in *blue, l* as in *would, i* as in *cruise, n* as in *condemned,* and *g* as in *gnu.*

Effective Approaches to Teaching Spelling

In the primary grades the child's individual development in relation to the school objectives strongly influences his spelling needs. It must be remembered that the child is attempting to master the physical skill of writing and that the major teaching objective during these years is to establish sound reading habits.

The peculiar phonetic nature of our language has created a teaching dilemma. We want the child to establish some competence in the use of sounding so that he can learn how to pronounce new words. Reading programs have been designed to help the child do this by means of a carefully selected group of words to practice on. As long as spelling and reading involve the same vocabulary there is a limited amount of conflict. But the reading vocabulary in primary readers is more like the vocabulary of the normal three-year-old. The six-year-old child of today has a relatively large vocabulary. When he writes, it is normal for him to use the words in his oral language, some of which contain the spelling irregularities peculiar to English. Any demand for conformity to accepted spelling places a serious limitation on the child's willingness to write his ideas. For this reason we accept phonetic spelling in a primary child's writing. The primary child writes to express his ideas. He uses the letters that will make the proper word sound. The teacher who has been trained to expect it will not be confused when she sees *elephant* spelled *lefant* or *once* spelled *wants.* The acceptance by the teacher of such unconventional spelling seems to give the child confidence in writing.

If the teacher wishes to introduce a spelling period late in the first grade, the words should be related to reading words and should be phonetically simple. Thus spelling can be a successful experience and the child begins to think of himself as a *good* speller.

The close association of the skills of handwriting, reading, listening, and spelling at the primary level creates a number of factors that must be considered carefully. Nearly all that is done to achieve what is called reading readiness leads also to spelling readiness. When the child notes sounds, makes his first phonetic associations, practices at the easel to coordinate hand and eye, or works with clay to develop small hand muscles, his growth in these areas will influence his subsequent developments in spelling.

Spelling starts when the child first seeks to produce a written word in order to tell something. First-grade children do this as they label, do reading exercises, write at the chalkboard, or compose group charts.

Many schools do not have specific spelling books or a formal spelling period in the first three grades: instead, the work is directed by means of reading workbooks and writing instruction. When a textbook is used, the following procedure is effective:

1. Introduce the word (recognition and meaning):
Teacher writes the word on the board.
Children point to it in their books.
Children find it in the story.
Children use the word orally in meaningful sentences.

Flashcards can be used in teaching spelling. The child first identifies the word and then spells it.
(PHOTO BY TOM WOLFE.)

2. Identify letters (visual and auditory imagery):

"What letters are needed to write the word?"

"Have we a new letter in this word?" If so, the teacher shows on the board how to write the new letter.

Children practice the letter. (Teacher observes and helps where help is needed.)

Say again: "What letters are needed to write the word?"

"Shannon [Roger, all the girls, all the boys, row two, row five, etc.], say the letters needed, fingers point to the word and eyes taking a picture of it."

"Who can tell the letters [spell the word] without looking at the book?"

3. Write the word (visual and motor imagery):

Teacher writes the word on the board, calling attention to the details of letter formation. (Uses ruled lines to set example for height of letters.)

Teacher writes the word again, and a third time if necessary, to strengthen visual imagery and the know-how of writing the word. Children write the word once. (Compare.)

Repeat until the word has been written four or five times, not more.

Teacher in the meantime observes and helps where necessary.

4. Same procedure for the next word.

5. Recall:

Children spell orally new words learned during a particular study lesson.

Children recall and spell orally words learned the day before.

If time permits, children may take a written trial test on words learned thus far (in a given week).

Drill

At the primary level the following drill procedures are suggested:

Flashcards: Teacher flashes a spelling card. Child identifies the word and spells it, or all children write the word. In the latter case, children check written words and write those misspelled in a notebook for further study.

"I am thinking of a word." "I am thinking of a word that rhymes with *cat* but begins with *h.*" Child identifies the word *hat* and spells it orally or all the children write the word.
"I am thinking of a word that tells [means] the kind of weather it is when you need to bundle up to keep warm." (*cold*)
"I am thinking of the base [root] word in *farmed.*"
"I am thinking of a word that means the opposite of high." (*low*)

Word recall: List a number of words on the board. Children put heads on desks while the teacher erases one word from the list. Then a child recalls the word and spells it. Repeat until the entire list is erased. Everyone can participate in the game if all children *write* the words as they are erased.

Spelling Lesson Plans

The following are examples of specific spelling lessons:

STRUCTURAL ANALYSIS: GRADE 2

Objective

To develop ability to recognize variants formed by adding *es* to root words.

Procedure

1. Write the following: "I found a mother fox. She had two baby foxes." Have the sentences read; then point to the first and ask, "How many does the next one tell about? What letters are added to *fox* to make it mean more than one?"
2. Write the following: "Harold rolled the potato across the floor. Harold rolled the potatoes across the floor." Have the sentences read silently and ask, "Which sentence means that Harold rolled more than one potato across the floor?"
3. Write the following: "I wish I had some cake. Patty wishes she had some cake."

Point to *wishes* and ask, "What ending is added to *wish* to make *wishes?* Does -*es* make *wishes* mean more than one?" Explain that we say "I wish" but we say "Patty wishes" or "he wishes." Read the sentences using the word in the incorrect ways: "I wishes" and "Patty wish."

INFLECTED FORMS: GRADE 2

Objective

To develop the ability to attach inflected and derived forms of known words in which the final *e* is dropped before an ending.

Procedure

1. Write the word *ride* on the board and have it pronounced. Erase the final *e* and add -*ing*. Call attention to the dropping of the *e*. Have *riding* pronounced.
2. "What is the root word of *riding*?" Write *ride* opposite *riding*. "How many vowel letters do you see in *ride*? What vowel sound do you hear? Does dropping the silent *e* and adding -*ing* change the sound of

the root word? Can you hear *ride* in riding?''
3. Write *talking* on the board. Ask pupils to
tell what ending they see and to what root
word *ing* was added. Write the root word.
4. Repeat with *coming*.
5. Use the same procedure with *nice–nicer;
bake–baker; fine–finer*.
6. Lead the children to formulate the generalization that when a word ends in final *e*, the
e is usually dropped before adding an ending.

Seatwork

Write the root words after each word:
finest _____
making _____
talking _____
slower _____
liked _____
finer _____
colder _____
moving _____
faster _____
baker _____
longer _____
riding _____
fired _____

INFLECTED ER-EST FORMS: GRADE 2

Objectives

To promote ability to recognize inflected forms
by adding *-er* and *-est*.
To express ideas in comparative terms.

Procedure

1. Write these sentences on the board and have
it pronounced.
2. Add *-er* to make it *shorter*. What word is
this?
3. Erase *-er* and add *-est*. Now what word is
this?
4. Repeat with *long.* (*longer, longest*)

5. Draw three lines and write these sentences
and fill in the blanks:

first   The _____ line is the longest of
         all.
second   The _____ line is shorter than the
         second.
third   The _____ line is the shortest of
         all.

6. Write the following words on the board,
have each pronounced, and have pupils use
them in sentences: *cool, cooler, coolest;
hot, hotter, hottest; big, bigger, biggest;
deep, deeper, deepest.*

Seatwork

1. Write these sentences on the board and have
the children copy the sentences and all the
comparative endings.
I am big _____ than you are.
It is hot _____ today.
He is the nice _____ boy I know.
She is much nice _____.
The wind is getting cold _____.
He is the fast _____ boy on our team.
2. Write *-er* endings and *-est* endings for
*fast   big   cold   hot
nice   deep   slow*

OBSERVING, LISTENING, WRITING: GRADE 2

Objective

To teach the children how to spell words
through observing, listening, and writing.

Materials

Spelling story. (On board.)
Pencils. (In desks.)
Paper. (Distribute before children come into
the room.)
The story: *Our News*
    There are thirty-six at *school* today.
    We will *read* a new book.
    We have a *new* turtle.

Method

Have the children:

1. Put name on paper and fold into four columns.
2. Look at the story and be able to read it.
3. Read the story, one sentence at a time.
4. Frame the words (e.g., *school, read*).
5. Put a box on the board with letters in it (e.g.,

s	o	o
h	l	c

).

Ask the children:

6. "What spelling word do we have that has all of these letters?" (e.g., school)
7. "What letter goes first?" (e.g., *s*)
8. "Can you use it in a sentence?" (Call on a student.)
9. "What can you tell me about the word?" (e.g., silent *h;* double vowel)
10. "Let's close our eyes and think of the word. Think of the silent *h,* double vowel, size. Spell it to yourself."
11. "Look at the board to see if you spelled it right."
12. "Close your eyes and spell the word for me." (Call on a student.)
13. "Write the word in your first column. Write it in the second."
14. "Let's spell the word once."
15. "Who can read this word for the class?" (Point to *read.*)
16. "Can you use it in a sentence?"
17. "Let's look at the word carefully. What can you tell me about it?"
18. "Let's close our eyes and think of the word. Think of the two vowels, silent *a,* three short letters, and one tall letter. Spell it to yourself. _____. Can you spell it?"
19. "Let's look at the word and spell it once again."
20. "Write it on your paper."
21. "Write it in the second column."
22. "Write it in the third column by memory."

How Are Generalizations Formed in Spelling?

In psychology the word *generalization* describes the process of discovery in a learner as he notices identities in different situations. If one teaches generalizations made by others, these become the traditional spelling rules. Good spelling teachers plan situations in which the elements of identity needed for a generalization may be discovered by the learner. For example:

TEACHER: *Quick* is an interesting word. The *qu* sounds like *k.* What other words do you know that start like *quick*? *(These words are listed on the board.)* Do you notice anything about these words? Yes, they start with *q.* Let's look in our dictionary and notice the words that start with *q.* What do you notice about spelling words that start with *q*? Yes, initial *q* is followed by *u,* except in a very few foreign words that are sometimes used in English.

Follow these suggestions:

1. Before considering a generalization be certain that enough words of the given category are known to the child to form it.
2. Help the child to notice why there are exceptions, such as attempting to pronounce the plural of *dress* only by adding an -*s* rather than -*es.*
3. Consider only one generalization at a time. The following generalizations are usually taught:
   a. Forming plurals of nouns by adding -*s* to the singular.
   b. Forming plurals by adding -*es* to words ending in *s, x, sh, ch.*
   c. Forming plurals by changing *y* to *i* and adding -*es.*
   d. Forming plurals by changing the singular forms (*women, halves*).
   e. Using an apostrophe in a contraction.
   f. Using a period after abbreviations.
   g. Forming singular possessives by adding -'*s.*
   h. Dropping final *e* when adding a suffix beginning with a vowel.

Many new words are developed from root words by simply adding -s, -ed, *or* -ing *to a root word without any other change.* (PHOTO BY LINDA LUNGREN.)

    i. Keeping the final *e* when adding a suffix beginning with a consonant.

Lesson Plans

The following two lessons will illustrate the development of generalizations with children:[2]

TYPE OF LESSON: SIMPLE GENERALIZATION

Generalization: "Many new words are developed from root words by simply adding -*s*,

[2] From *Thinking About Spelling* (Grosse Point, Mich.: Grosse Point Public Schools, 1948).

-*ed*, or -*ing* to a root word, without any other change."

Aims

1. To show that by adding -*s*, -*ed*, and -*ing* to many words one can spell three or four more words after learning to spell the root word only.
2. To extend gradually the concept of generalization so that pupils can use it as an aid in discovering correct spellings.

Materials

The words were chosen from word lists for second and third grades.

play	rain	help	spell
want	garden	burn	clean
need	open	paint	pull

This list was chosen for the simple meanings at the grade 3 level and because they are basic words to which the suffixes -*s*, -*ed*, and -*ing* can be added to make new words without any other change. Thus, if the child learns to spell *play*, he should be able to generalize and spell *plays*, *played*, and *playing*.

Procedure for the Week

Monday

1. Present root words somewhat as follows: "Here are the new words to be learned this week. Some of them you already know because you had them in the second grade. Who can point out one that we know?"
2. Have a child point out one and spell it. Continue somewhat as follows: "This week we have chosen some words that we already know how to spell because we are going to learn to use a spelling trick that will save us time and work. We will take the word *play*. Let us call this a root word. *Root word* means the simplest form of a word. In talking, writing, and spelling, we use many forms of a root word by adding

one or more letters to it to make new words that we need. Let us see what happens to *play* when we add an *s*. What word does this make?''

3. Use both in sentences and demonstrate on the board. ''Barbara and Bill play with the dog.'' ''Barbara plays with the dog,'' etc.
4. Have pupils demonstrate with other words in a list, until you are sure they understand. Have the pupil tell what he does as he changes the word at the board. Have a pupil spell the new word without looking at the board.
5. Use remainder of the period for supervised study period. *Pronounce, use,* and *study* each word.

Tuesday—Review

1. Have the root words written on the board. Give ample opportunity for recall of the new spelling trick. Select several pupils to go to the board and change a word by adding *s*, spelling it as they do so.
2. Point out again that we only had to add one letter to make a whole new word, which we could spell without studying.
3. Suggest that there is another trick by which one can add another ending and get another word. (Perhaps some child will be able to show this step.)
4. One of these endings is *-ing*. Using *play*, add *-ing* to show that the new word now becomes *playing*. Example: ''Bobby is *playing* with James.''
5. Call for a volunteer at the board to change *help* to *helping*.
6. Go through the whole list, showing by pupil demonstration how each word may be changed and used.
7. In the same manner add *-ed* and get *played, rained,* etc.
8. Have all pupils make a chart as follows. Pronounce several of the words. Have pupils spell the other forms.

Base Word	New Words Formed		
	+ *s*	+ *ing*	+ *ed*
1. play	plays	play*ing*	play*ed*
2. rain	rain*s*	rain*ing*	rain*ed*

9. Announce that there will be a test on Wednesday. Suggest that maybe only the root word will be given and the students will be asked to build three new words from it.
10. How many new words should we be able to spell by Friday (count) (thirty-six new words) (forty-eight words counting root words)?

Wednesday

The trial test may be a game. Explain that different forms of the words will be given, such as play*ed*, jump*ing*, help*s*. Each pupil must spell the word correctly and then write the root word following the form pronounced. Give children time to correct the mistakes and rewrite the words. (NOTE: Do not give words that end in *k* for examples of the *-ed* ending. The pronunciation is not clear enough. It sounds like *t*. Example: *bark, barked.* Explain this later to the pupils.)

Thursday

1. Reproduce chart on board.
2. Give only the root word. Have individual children fill in the spaces under careful guidance. (Choose those who had errors on Wednesday.)
3. Have pupils spell orally all four forms.
4. To show a working knowledge, give about three new base words, such as *learn, fill, hunt,* and have the children discover the derived forms from them.
5. Select only words to which the generalization will apply.
6. Caution the children that there are some words that have other changes before *-s*, *-ed*, or *-ing* is added. To explain an in-

stance in which other changes in words are necessary, select the word *grow*. Try the generalization. Show pupils that they do not say *grow—ed*, but use *gr—w*. See if some child can supply the *e*. Such exercises develop *thought spelling*.

Friday—Final Test

1. At this time, as many of the derived words as desired may be used.
2. After the derived word is pronounced, the group could be asked to give orally, then write the root words beside the other as an aid to spelling.
3. Check papers. Make note of pupils who do not understand the process. Repeat this type of lesson soon for these pupils.

Individual needs may be met in these ways.

1. Pupils who are able to learn more words could be allowed to take their readers, find words with these endings, and write the root word, followed by other derived words. These should be checked individually.
2. A few extra words from the second- or third-grade list could be given, such as *add, hunt, wheel, seat*.
3. Those pupils who did not learn the trick should be given copies of the chart and several of the easy words to work on the following week for extra practice.

After a generalization is discovered it is important that a maintenance program be planned to use this knowledge.

1. Every subsequent list of words should be studied for new words, derivatives of which are formed by adding *-s, -ed,* and *-ing.*
2. A number of words in the third-grade list are formed with other generalizations, which will be learned later. The teacher should explain this to the pupils as they discover them.
3. One group of words that may confuse them—such as *know, hear, grow, bring,*

buy, fall, find—may be used to show how new words are formed by adding *-s* and *-ing,* but a different word is used to form the past, such as *knew* or *heard,* instead of simply adding *-ed.*

4. Extending the pupils' experiences to include the spelling of derived forms as they learn the base words will prepare them to write more fluently and with fewer errors in written English situations. Individual discovery of spellings creates an interest in the various forms of words they use and causes pupils to scrutinize more carefully the arrangement of letters in all words. The feeling of success in achievement (learning the spellings of forty-eight new words in a week) has a tonic effect on attitude toward learning to spell.
5. This generalization is a valuable one at this level for there are many words to which it applies.

Other words that can be used for this generalization are the following:

Second-Grade List

ask	look
call	last
end	show
milk	snow

Third-Grade List

add	land	park
count	learn	part
fill	light	pick
jump	nest	pull

The following lesson might be taught in the fourth grade and above to establish the silent *e* generalization.

TYPE OF LESSON: GENERALIZATION

Generalization: "Many words ending in silent *e* drop the *e* before adding suffixes beginning with a vowel (e.g., lov*ing*, lov*ed*, lov*able*) but retain the silent *e* when the suffix begins with a consonant (e.g., love*ly*, care*ful*, same*ness*, home*less*).

General Aims

1. To provide children with adequate methods of word study, so that they may gradually solve their spelling difficulties individually.
2. To increase child's written vocabulary.
3. To stimulate pride in correct spelling in all written situations.

Specific Aims

1. To introduce the use of the generalization: "Many words ending in silent *e* drop the *e* before adding *-ing* or *-ed*."
2. To extend gradually the use of the silent *e* generalization to include the use of other common suffixes, such as *-er*, *-est*, *-able*, beginning with a vowel.
3. To emphasize the fact that in adding suffixes, such as *-ly*, *-ful*, *-ness*, *-less*, beginning with a consonant, do not drop the final *e*.
4. To develop the concept of learning to spell by the use of insight or transfer of training as well as automatic memory.
5. To emphasize the economy of time and effort in becoming a good speller when insight is used.

Materials

The following word list was selected from the word list for third and fourth grades:

skate	hope
dance	bake
close	chase
share	divide
vote	smoke
move	love
place	trade
line	

Approach

A very easy group of words ending in silent *e* was chosen from the third- and fourth-

Attractive bulletin boards emphasizing silent e *words are a constant reminder of correct spelling.* (PHOTO BY LINDA LUNGREN.)

grade list so as to present as few spelling difficulties as possible in mastering the root words. Attention here should be focused on what happens to the root word ending in silent *e* when the endings *-ing* and *-ed* are added to make new words. When this is clearly understood, the fun of discovering new words and their spellings by adding these endings to other silent *e* words should follow.

Procedure for the Week

Monday

1. Teach or review meaning of *root word, syllable, vowel, consonant, silent letter, de-*

rived. Illustrate and ask for examples to make sure pupils understand.

2. Begin the lesson in the following way: "Most of you already know how to spell some of these words, for several of them you learned in the third grade. The others are easy. Let us look carefully at these words. What final letters do you see in all of them? Yes, it is *e*. (Bring out the fact that it is silent by having words pronounced.) This week we are going to learn how to spell twenty-four or more new words without studying them. To do this, we will use a spelling trick on these root words. Before we are ready to learn the trick we must be sure we can spell the root words. Remember, they all end in a silent *e*."

3. Study base words. Make sure pupils can spell them.

Tuesday

1. "Yesterday we noticed some things that were alike in all these root words. What are they?" (Each ends in *e*. Final *e* is silent.)

2. "You often learn to use new words by adding new endings to root words. (Illustrate with *skate-s*.) Each ending changes the meaning and the spelling of the word. Let us see what happens when we add the ending *-ing* to *skate*. This is the trick." Write *skate* on the chalkboard. Erase *e*, adding *-ing*. "What new word does this make? What happened to the final *e* when we added *-ing?*"

3. Write *skate* on the board and say, "Let us see what happens when we add the ending *-ed*." (Erase *e* and add *-ed*, calling attention to return of the *e* when we added *-ed*.) Illustrate on board the need for dropping final *e*, to avoid skat*eed*.

4. Repeat same procedures with *dance, close, share*.

5. Let pupils make new words with *vote, move, place*, by adding *-ing* and *-ed*. Carry on with pupils at chalkboard and in seats. Bring out the fact that the trick works for all words in the list.

6. Let pupils try phrasing the generalization for all of these words. A simple wording is this: "Most words ending in silent *e* drop the *e* before adding *-ing* or *-ed*." Write this on the chalkboard and leave for further reference.

7. Let several pupils come to the board to illustrate by stating the rule and spelling the word formed.

8. Address class somewhat as follows: "This week's spelling words should not be difficult. When you learn the base words you can easily spell the derived words by following the rule. How many words will we have in our final test?" (Three times the number of root words.)

Wednesday

1. Turn to the list of base words on the chalkboard. Have one child pronounce all the words. Review the application and statement of the generalization.

2. Pass out duplicated sheets (see sample) and say: "Complete this chart by adding *-ing* and *-ed* to the words you learned Monday. The new words are called derived words. The first one is done for you. Perhaps you will need to read the generalization before you start to work."

3. Call attention to the increase in pleasure and the decrease in work that comes from spelling by transfer.

4. Check the work of poor spellers as they proceed.

Thursday

1. Pass out duplicated sheets again. Explain to children that you will pronounce the root

words or their derivatives and they are to put them in the correct spaces. See that the children are following directions.

2. Be sure that the children think of the generalization as a way to increase their ability to spell without study.

Friday

1. Test on generalization: "dropping the final *e*." Have pupils prepare three columns on their papers.

2. Mastery test: spell root word and both derivatives for each as pronounced.

3. To give practice in recognizing word variants by identifying the base word, the following lesson might be used: Write the following words on the chalkboard. Have pupils copy in a single line on paper. Then opposite these words write the word from which the derived word was formed. (Example: *glancing–glance.*)

faced	saving	smoking
sneezing	poked	graded
taking	prancing	stating
chased	loving	becoming
noticing	taken	blamed

4. Children may show that other derived words can be made by adding other suffixes such as *-er* or *-est,* or *-able,* to *love, notice, move,* etc. Continue to show how many new words they can spell by using this generalization.

5. In order to avoid the development of incorrect ideas concerning the addition of *-ed* to all base words when we wish to make them tell what happened yesterday rather than today, it is advisable to call attention to other ways of changing a root word. We say *lost* not *losed, took* not *taked, drove* not *drived,* etc. These changes should be noted, not as exceptions to our present generalization ("Most words ending in silent *e*

drop the *e* before adding *-ing* or *-ed''*) but rather as unusual changes in root words in order to change the meaning of the word.

6. There are a few exceptions that may well be noted. We do not drop the silent *e* in such words as *see, free, agree,* when we add *-ing,* although we do so when we add *-ed* in order to avoid *freeed.*

Lessons of the following type should follow in order to reinforce the learning.

1. Extension of the use of generalization—for words ending in silent *e* to include *all* common suffixes.

a. Use small groups of words ending in silent *e* to which common endings or suffixes, such as *-er, -able,* or *-est,* can be added. (Note that *-ed, -ing, -er, -est, -en,* and *-able* all begin with vowels.)

love loved loving lover lovable
use used using user usable

Pupils should be encouraged to note other words ending in final *e* that they use often in their writing to add to spelling lists.

b. Use groups of words to show that final *e* is *not dropped* when adding common endings such as *-s, -ly, -ness, -ful, -less,* and *-ment.* (Note that these suffixes begin with consonants.) Use only the forms of words that pupils understand readily and can use in meaningful sentences. The following words are appropriate.

voice	voices	voice*less*	
care	cares	care*less*	care*ful*
love	loves	love*ly*	
bare	bare*ness*	bare*ly*	
brave	braves	brave*ly*	
case	cases	case*ment*	
sore	sores	sore*ness*	

Have pupils suggest others that they use.

c. Formulate a statement of the generalization for suffixes beginning with a consonant.

2. Maintaining and developing skill in the use of the generalization as a spelling aid.

 a. Pupils should be exposed to many new situations with root words in which they are asked to discover spellings of derived words. They should say orally the derived form for a given use of a base word, try to spell it by substituting other letters or adding syllables, then write it. "Checking guesses" is an important step in this procedure. This play with words combines ear, eye, and thought spelling so that pupils have several types of associations to aid in recall. Games based on such procedures can be devised. Saving of effort and time and having fun with words should be stressed.

 b. When selecting words for spelling lists in third, fourth, fifth, and sixth grades, make sure that representative root words or their derivatives are used each week so that the new word list can be analyzed for the purpose of detecting words with which pupils have learned to deal through generalization, i.e., include a -y word; one ending in silent e; others to which -s, -ed, or -ing can be added without change; and so on.

 c. Group root words included in grade list ending in silent e to which pupils are to add common endings beginning with vowel or consonant through using generalization, such as nicer, nicest, nicely; careful, caring, careless, cared; closer, closest, closely, closeness.

 Make hectograph chart as follows:

d. Other words in the list for fourth grade that can be used for the application of this rule should be noted.

e. Note important exceptions, such as tie, die, lie, tying, dying, lying. (Final e preceded by i is dropped and the i changed to y.) Teach these individually, because they are common words often used. See if children can think of others.

f. Emphasize the value of using generalizations by having pupils select certain derivatives or root words formed from words in list that they agree to add to list without study. Provide opportunity each week for pupils to practice use of generalization with these unlearned words. A limited number of such words should be pronounced and spelled in the final test each week.

g. A correlate lesson with reading will extend the use and understanding of this generalization dealing with the spelling of one-syllable words. Change the emphasis of the reading aid, "Words of one syllable containing two vowels, one of which is a final e, the first vowel is usually given long sound."
 Apply it as an aid in spelling one-syllable words when they are pronounced. Take such a word as safe—ear spelling would stop at saf, but applying the reading rule for final e spelling would help the children to remember to add the silent e—safe, also side, shake, cave, and so on.

In the middle and upper grades a number of generalizations may be drawn inductively from experience with words. Examples of such generalizations were

Base Word					Derived Words				
-ing	-ed	-er	-est	-s	-able	-iess	-ful	-ness	-ly

suggested in 1953–1954 by the City of New York. Remember, these generalizations are *not* to be memorized by your students: [3]

1. Plurals of most nouns are formed by adding -s to the singular: *cat, cats,* etc.
2. When the noun ends in *s, x, sh,* and *ch,* the plural generally is formed by adding -es: *buses, foxes, bushes, churches.*
3. A noun ending in *y* preceded by a consonant forms its plural by changing the *y* to *i* and adding -es: *body, bodies.* Words ending in *y* preceded by a vowel do not change *y* to *i: boy, boys.*
4. Plurals of a few nouns are made by changing their form: *woman, women; mouse, mice; scarf, scarves.*
5. An apostrophe is used to show the omission of a letter or letters in a contraction: *aren't, we'll.*
6. An abbreviation is always followed by a period: *Mon., Feb.,* etc.
7. The possessive of a singular noun is formed by adding an apostrophe and *s: father, father's.*
8. The possessive of a plural noun ending in *s* is formed by adding an apostrophe: *girls, girls'.*
9. A word that ends in silent *e* usually keeps the *e* when a suffix beginning with a consonant is added: *nine, ninety; care, careful.*
10. A word that ends in silent *e* usually drops the *e* when a suffix beginning with a vowel is added: *breeze, breezing; live, living; move, movable.*
11. A one-syllable word that ends in one consonant following a short vowel usually doubles the consonant before a suffix that begins with a vowel: *fat, fattest; big, bigger, biggest.*
12. A word of more than one syllable that ends in one consonant following one short vowel usually doubles the final consonant before a suffix beginning with a vowel provided the accent is on the last syllable: *commit, committed, committing; forget, forgetting.*
13. A word ending in *y* and following a consonant usually changes the *y* to *i* before a suffix is added unless the suffix begins with *i: cry, crying.* A word that ends in a *y* and follows a vowel usually keeps the *y* when a suffix is added: *buy, buys, buying.*
14. The letter *q* is usually followed by *u* in a word.
15. The letter *i* is usually used before *e* except after *c,* or

[3] From *Teaching Spelling,* Curriculum Bulletin, Series No. 6 (New York: Board of Education of the City of New York, 1953–1954).

when sounded like an *a* as in *neighbor* and *weight.* Exceptions: *neither, either.*

16. Proper nouns and adjectives formed from proper nouns should always begin with capital letters: *America, American.*

Other phonic generalizations that apply two thirds of the time or more are

1. If the only vowel letter is at the end of a word, the letter usually stands for the long sound (*he, she, me*).
2. The *r* gives the preceding vowel a sound that is neither long nor short (*horn, more, worn*).
3. When a vowel is in the middle of a one-syllable word, the vowel is short (*rest, grass, glad*).
4. The first vowel is usually long and the second is usually silent in the digraphs *ai, ea,* and *oa* (*nail, bead, boat*).
5. Words having double *e* usually have the long *e* sound (*seem, tree, week*).
6. In *ay* the *y* is silent and gives *a* its long sound (*play, say, day*).
7. When the letter *i* is followed by the letters *gh,* the *i* usually stands for its long sound and the *gh* is silent (*high, fight, might*).
8. When *y* is the final letter in a word, it usually has a vowel sound (*dry, my, fly, happy*).
9. When there are two vowels, one of which is final *e,* the first vowel is usually long and the *e* is silent (*bone, home, write*).
10. When *c* and *h* are next to each other, they make only one sound, usually pronounced as in *church* (*catch, child, watch*).
11. When *c* is followed by *e* or *i,* the sound of *s* is likely to be heard (*cent, city, circle*).
12. When the letter *c* is followed by *o* or *a,* the sound of *k* is likely to be heard (*camp, came, code, come*).
13. When *ght* is seen in a word, *gh* is silent (*fight, thought, might*).
14. When a word begins with *kn,* the *k* is silent (*knew, knot, knife*).
15. When a word begins with *wr,* the *w* is silent (*write, wrist, wrong*).

16. When two of the same consonants are side by side, only one is heard (*happy, called, guess*).
17. When *ck* appears together in a word only the *k* is pronounced (*black, brick, sick*).

Many old rules must be evaluated carefully not only as to their accuracy but also as to the child's ability to use the rule in practice. It was once taught that when two vowels are found together in a word, as in *each*, the second is silent but helps the first to "say its own name" or have the long vowel sound. If you check the words in spellers, you will find numerous exceptions to this rule (*break, height, through*).

It is not true that one can spell correctly by "spelling the word the way it sounds." In fact, thiss staytment iz enuff to mayk won shreek. However, some phonetic generalizations should be mastered in the intermediate grades. The polysyllabic words in the Rinsland list contain 23,000 syllables. Of these, fifty are key syllables spelled consistently the same way. The fifty are listed in Table 9-6.

The syllable that occurs most frequently is *ing*, which is found in 881 words. Thus a child who has learned to spell the *ing* syllable in one word will know it in 880 more. A test might be given asking that only the first syllable heard be spelled, as the words in the first column are pronounced, the second syllable as the next column is heard, and so on.

A test of the following type might be given to intermediate-grade children to discover those who already are able to apply some phonetic knowledge to spelling.

To the students: I am going to pronounce some words that do not have a meaning. You are to spell these words as they sound to you.

băb	lib	ving	clace	theet
dod	mif	med	cray	spug
fim	nam	yim	flest	quam
gog	paber	zet	gloil	shork
huf	rading	blash	plold	
jil	sim	chad	brays	

When the regular spelling test is given, check the ability to transfer phonetic knowledge in this manner:

Word in Spelling Lesson	Pronounce This Word and Use in a Sentence
stop	stopping
blow	black
shrill	drill
nation	vacation

There are some learners who do not form generalizations with ease and thus need special help in spelling. If you have a poor speller who is an able student capable of doing better work and who *wants* to spell correctly, suggest the following steps used in learning to spell a word: [4]

Step 1. Look at the word very carefully and say it over to yourself. If you are not sure of the pronunciation, ask the teacher to say it for you, or look it up in the dictionary yourself.

Step 2. See if the word can be written just the way you say it. Mark any part of the word that cannot be written the way you say it.

Step 3. Shut your eyes and see if you can get a picture

TABLE 9-6. Key syllables of spelling consistencies

Initial syllable	Medial syllable	Final syllable
re ceive	an i mals	go ing
in to	Jan u ary	start ed
a round	sev er al	mat ter
de cided	dec o rated	on ly
con tains	af ter noon	hous es
ex cept	el e phant	va ca tion
un til	pe ri od	ver y
com mon	reg u lar	pret ty
dis covered	In di an	re al
en joy	won der ful	ta ble
an other	car ni val	af ter
o pen	gym na si um	base ment
e ven	ar ti cle	sto ry
pro gram	ear li est	long est
ac ci dent	o ver alls	sev en

[4] From Grace M. Fernald, *Remedial Techniques in Basic School Subjects* (New York: McGraw-Hill, 1943).

of the word in your mind. If you cannot get a clear picture of the word, you can remember the parts that are written the way you say them by pronouncing the word over to yourself or feeling your hand make the movements of writing the word. If you are learning the word *separate,* all you need to do is to say the word to yourself very carefully and then write what you say. If there are any parts of the word that you cannot write the way you say them, you will probably have to remember them by saying something you can write. Say the letters, if necessary, for these syllables of the word, but not for the rest of the word.

Step 4. When you are sure of every part of the word, shut your book or cover the word and write it, saying each syllable to yourself as you write it.

Step 5. If you cannot write the word correctly after you have looked at it and said it, ask the teacher to write it for you in crayon on a strip of paper. Trace the word with your fingers. Say each part of the word as you trace it. Trace the word carefully as many times as you need to until you can write it correctly. Say each part of the word to yourself as you write it. After you have learned words in this way for a while you will find you can learn them as easily as the other children do without tracing them. (Some teachers have the child trace the word in sand or on fine sandpaper in order to achieve a greater touch impression.)

Step 6. If the word is difficult, turn the paper over and write it again. Never copy the word directly from the book or from the one you have just written, but always write it from your memory of it.

Step 7. Later in the day, try writing the word from memory. If you are not sure of it, look it up again before you try to write it.

Step 8. Make your own dictionary. Make a little book with the letters of the alphabet fastened to the margin so that it is easy to see them. Write any new words you learn, or any words that seem especially difficult for you, in this book. Get this book out often and look these words over, writing again, from time to time, those that seem difficult. When you write these words by yourself, do just as you did when you learned them the first time. Say them, looking at them while you say them, and then write them without looking at the word in your book.

For Discussion

1. What pressures cause children to cheat on a test?

2. Why are students unmotivated by continuous failure?

3. Are there some words you habitually misspell? What would you suggest?

4. Make a tabulation of errors from one final test of a class. Detect common needs suggested by the errors.

5. Recall an association you have used to help remember the spelling of a word. These are called mnemonic devices. Sometimes the more absurd they are, the easier they are remembered. For example, one could say *dessert* has *ss,* where *desert* has only one *s,* because one would rather have more of it. Or remember the stationery you write on has *er,* just like *letter.* Make a collection of these devices used in your class.

6. For some children, understanding a generalization such as "Adding *s* makes more than one," or "Each syllable has a vowel" is quite difficult. How would you teach one of these generalizations?

7. What spelling rules help you spell a word? How do you use them?

8. Do you think it might be possible to omit a spelling period in some classes? Give reasons for your answer.

9. Are there words in your listening or reading vocabulary that are not in your speaking and writing vocabulary? Why? Which vocabulary is largest? Why?

What Dictionary Skills Do Children Need?

Children need to appreciate the tremendous effort that has gone into the production of the dictionary they use. Let them discuss what it must be like to live in a country that does not have a dictionary for reference. There are many such countries.

The idea of a dictionary is not new. The Assyrians prepared a dictionary of their language nearly 2,600 years ago. Other people, notably the Greeks and Romans, prepared dictionaries, but these included only the rare and difficult words to be found in their language. With the coming of the Renaissance, during the fourteenth and fifteenth centuries, a great deal of attention was turned to the early literature of the Greeks and Romans. This brought about the preparation of lexicons and glossaries containing the translated meanings of foreign words.

It was not until about the middle of the eighteenth century that any attempt was made to catalogue the common words in the English language. The most complete work was done by Samuel Johnson, who brought out his famous dictionary in 1755. Johnson spent nearly eight years in getting his book ready and did make an effort to include the most accepted spelling and definition for each word that he used.

The first American dictionary of 70,000 words came from the pen of Noah Webster in 1806. The Merriam brothers brought out their dictionary in 1864 with 114,000 words. The second edition (1934) contained over 600,000 entries. The last revision of the second edition contained a little more than 750,000 words, of which over 100,000 were new entries. In 1962 the radically new third edition appeared, causing considerable controversy among scholars because of its inclusion of many words and expressions previously considered to be substandard or slang. The third edition contains 100,000 "new" words, but the total number of entries is less than that of the second edition. The fact that many words were dropped explains the lack of increase in the number of entries.

The last twenty-five years have brought a newcomer to the dictionary field, the dictionary designed for elementary classroom use. Up until now each classroom, regardless of the age of the pupils, usually had a large Webster's Unabridged Dictionary on a stand or shelf for use by the entire class. A few of the more enterprising pupils might have had small dictionaries of their own, but these were rather drab, uninviting books with diminutive type, few illustrations, perplexing definitions, and a selection of words ill suited to the pupils' needs. The newer dictionaries have hundreds of illustrations of plants, animals, and objects, with their scale indicated by a numerical fraction. The point-size of the type has been increased, the format has been made more attractive, the definitions have been clarified, and illustrative sentences added. All words are carefully appraised before inclusion in an effort to eliminate rare, obsolete, or obsolescent words. A good modern dictionary is one of the most valuable books the pupil can have. It is as essential as any textbook.

Picture dictionaries have been developed for use in the primary grades. The picture-word association does help some children as they look up words for spelling.

In all classroom work with the dictionary, the words to be alphabetized, located, or discussed should be carefully chosen to contribute some real purpose in the pupils' writing or reading. The children, as well as the teacher, should recognize the need or use.

Some fourth-graders will be more ready to begin with more advanced work than will some sixth-graders. The teacher should determine each child's ability and then work with small groups having common needs. She should vary and repeat practice at intervals until the children achieve mastery of a given skill. Besides a list of words, the dictionaries for schools frequently contain other information: the story of language, flags of nations, foreign words, biographies, geographical names, pronunciation, syllabication, and even instructions on how to use the dictionary.

Promotion of Dictionary Skills

Steps in teaching the use of the dictionary are discussed here in an approximate sequence of difficulty, but teachers may vary the order of presentation and omit or add material to meet the needs of their classes.

Alphabetical Sequence

The first dictionary skill to be taught is the location of a word. Some children may not know the alphabet sequence because it has not been used frequently prior to this time. Check to be sure that the children know the sequence of letters in the alphabet, and then practice until they can find words in the dictionary by their first letters. To avoid the necessity of having some children recite the alphabet before they can locate a word, discuss the relative placement of letters. Have the children discover that when the dictionary is opened in the center we find the words that start with *l* and *m*. If it is opened at the first quarter we find the words with *d* and *e,* and at the third quarter we find the *r* and *s* words.

Discuss how this will help them to locate a word more rapidly than if they just start at *a* and go through the alphabet.

Next, have the children suggest a word. Have them open their dictionaries near the place the initial letter would be found without thumbing through the pages. Then have one pupil stand in front of a group and open the dictionary at random while the other members of the group guess the initial letter of words on that page.

Another dictionary game would have a student locate in the dictionary a word from that week's spelling list. Each student would then take turns at saying a test word from the spelling list. The "leader" would say whether the test word appears before or after the chosen word in the dictionary. The objective is to guess the word in the least number of tries.

To teach pupils how to arrange words in alphabetical order, have them alphabetize brief lists in which no two words begin with the same letter. When this has been mastered, alphabetize by second letters (*sat* before *seven*); by third letters (*share* before *sheep*); and so on. For additional practice, ask children who finish work early to arrange the books in the classroom library alphabetically according to authors, write an index page for a class book, make a card catalogue for a collection of pictures, or find in a telephone directory the telephone numbers of absentees.

Guide Words

The second skill to be learned is the use of guide words. After discussing the advantages of being able to find a word quickly, show the group that at the top of each page in the dictionary there are two words. The one at the left is the same as the first word on the page. The one at the right is the same as the last word on the page. These are called guide words. For practice give a page number. Have the children turn to that page and read the guide words.

Arranging books or records in alphabetical order is excellent practice for more advanced students. (PHOTO BY LINDA LUNGREN.)

The dictionary is helpful to students in learning alphabetical sequence, using guide words, learning definitions, locating correct spelling, and learning correct pronunciation. (PHOTO BY LINDA LUNGREN.)

Then write on the board a word that the group wishes to find. Above this, write the guide words on the page where you happen to open the dictionary. Have the group decide whether you must look nearer the front or nearer the back of the book. Continue the process in this manner until you find the right page and word. To check understanding, write a word on the board. Have the pupils find the word, keeping count of the number of times pages are turned to find the word. Thus, opening the dictionary to the correct initial letter would count as one "turn." The next "turn" would seek to find the approximate vicinity of the word. Each successive approximation would count as a turn until the word

was found. The children with the least number of turns might be recognized by hand-raising or by having their names written on the board as "Word-Finders" or some such heading. This type of work should be repeated many times under supervision and then independently.

Chalkboard drills may be used to develop skill in the use of guide words. Start by writing on the board a pair of guide words taken from the dictionary. Below them write a group of four or more words, some of them selected from the dictionary page. Have the children select and check the words that belong on the page of the dictionary. For example:

> *kent* khaki *kindred*
> kennel
> kine
> kidnap

This kind of work should be repeated on successive days. At first it should be done under teacher guidance at the board. Later the children may do it independently at their own desks. Individual children may create exercises of this nature for the class to do.

The following game is helpful as a review: Divide the group into two teams. Write a word on the board. Ask children to find the word and hold up their hands when they have found it. The first child to find the word scores one point for his team. The first team to finish scores one point. (Check by page number.) The game should be limited by using a certain number of words (e.g., ten) or by playing for a certain number of minutes.

Another exercise is built on word meanings. The teacher prepares a list of words that the children will need to know, locates each word in the dictionary, and notes the guide words for each word. When the game begins, the teacher writes a pair of guide words on the board and gives a brief definition of the word that the group is to find. The pupils find the page and scan it for the right word. For example:

> Guide words: *springboard* and *spurt*
> Definition: a short run at full speed
> Answer: *sprint*

Definitions

The third major area of dictionary skills has to do with definitions. Explain to students that whenever a word is found in their reading that cannot be defined from context, they should use the dictionary. Many words have only vague meanings. Use the dictionary for more exact meanings. Explain the difference in meaning between the following pairs of words: *climate* and *weather; less* and *fewer; hotel* and *restaurant.*

Some words get so overworked that we call them tired words. The dictionary can suggest other words to use for *said* or *big.*

Considerable thought is required in selecting the right meaning from several meanings given in the dictionary. For a few children it will be a discovery that words have more than one meaning. Introduce this work with the word *run.* Have the group think of several meanings, writing each new meaning on the board before looking it up in the dictionary. Underneath the definitions suggested by the children, write those definitions from the dictionary that were not mentioned. Then have the children, either as a class or independently, write a sentence incorporating *run* to illustrate each definition. Have the pupils select another common word, such as *safe, strike, husband,* or *signal,* and discover how many different meanings for it they can find and illustrate.

Interesting lessons can be planned to show how the illustrations in the dictionary clarify meaning. The arithmetic in the ratio should be studied so that the phrase *one-sixth actual size* has meaning. An interesting discussion can be planned around the topic "Which words can be illustrated and which cannot?"

An understanding of prefixes and suffixes is another aid to word meaning. When the children understand that *trans-* means "across" or "over" in *transportation, transfer, translate,* and *transcontinental,* they have a meaning clue to other words with this prefix. They can discover that the dictionary gives the meanings of many prefixes.

A discovery or inductive lesson is easy using the dictionary. Have the students read a series of definitions of words starting with another prefix, *sub-,* then decide what meaning the prefix gives to the words.

One of the basic clues to meaning is the ability to identify the root word. Start by supplying a root word and have pupils list other members of the same family: *kind (kindly, kindness, unkind, kindliness).* Discuss the fact that these words are similar in meaning as well as in appearance. Children need help in learning how the dictionary deals with word families. The root word is listed at the margin in heavy type and other members of the family are not listed marginally but are explained under the root word. In spelling and reading, root words should be identified and sometimes checked with the dictionary. This is important when the word is to be divided into syllables. Even though we divide the word as we pronounce it, the basic root is seldom divided in writing. Some children will enjoy knowing about a few common Greek and Latin roots which will help them guess word meanings. These were used by a fifth grade:

Latin

annus (year)	annual
	perennial
	anniversary
aqua (water)	aqueduct
	aquaplane
	aquarium
audio (listen or hear)	auditorium
	audible
	audition
avis (bird)	aviary
	aviation
	aviator
ducere (to lead)	conduct
	educate
	aqueduct
via (way)	viaduct
	trivial
	deviate

Greek

aster (star)	aster
	astronomy
	asterisk

cycle (ring or circus)	bicycle
	motorcycle
	cyclone
graphein (to write)	autograph
	telegraph
	graph
logos (word)	catalogue
	dialogue
	astrology
metron (measure)	meter
	thermometer
	speedometer
phone (sound)	phonics
	telephone
	phonograph

The interest in looking up words and learning definitions should also be developed by selecting sentences from the children's reading material. For example: "The initial expense was about thirty dollars." Have the children find *initial* in the dictionary. Discuss the meanings given, and choose the one most applicable.

A list of "difficult" words from the children's readings should be compiled by the teacher and/or pupils and tested at the end of each week in one of the following ways:

1. Give the words and have the children supply the definitions.
2. Give the words and have the children use them appropriately in sentences.
3. Supply both words and definitions in scrambled order and have the children match them appropriately.
4. Supply the words in scrambled order along with the sentences from the readings which incorporated the words, leaving blanks where the words are to be filled in.

Have the children keep a record of their own "problem words," words missed on the preceding exercises. These should be presented to the teacher at designated intervals (e.g., each month). The teacher can then compile individualized word lists to strengthen vocabulary skills. Such words may also be used in "vocabulary bees" or as team exercises.

The most frequent use of a dictionary is to locate the correct spelling of a word. This is not easy when it is a word that the child cannot spell. Take as an example a word that a child has asked you to spell for him, such as *usable*. The group will be sure of the first two letters. Have the children look up the word as far as they are sure and then glance down the page until they find the word. Even after looking up a word it is possible to make a mistake. Before the spelling is copied from the dictionary, the definition must be read in order to prevent such errors as the use of *complement* for *compliment*, *calendar* for *calender*, *complaisant* for *complacent*, or *obsequies* for *obsequious*.

Sometimes a word is located through the trial-and-error method. Words with difficult beginnings, such as *cistern*, after they have not been located under *s*, must be sought under other letters having the same sound. It takes real detective work to track down some words, such as *light*.

Other spelling help in the dictionary concerns abbreviations, capital letters, and plural forms, but children must be shown how to locate each of these items.

Pronunciation

Another area of dictionary skills concerns pronunciation.

SYLLABICATION. The first step in pronunciation involves dividing words into syllables. These rules are usually taught in third-grade reading. This is a good time for children to discover that the dictionary can act as a check on their syllabication. A few listening lessons in which children tell how many syllables they hear when words are pronounced will reveal that the number of vowels we hear in a word tells us how many syllables there are in it.

ACCENT MARKS. While dividing words into syllables, point out to the students that we pronounce some syllables with more force or accent than others. Then show how the dictionary indicates this stress with the accent mark. Children will be interested in words where a change in accent may indicate a change in meaning, as in "Use the movie machine to *pro ject'* the picture" or "He found that building the dam was a difficult *proj'ect.*"

Some dictionaries indicate a secondary as well as a primary accent, as in *mul' ti pli ca' tion.* To check understanding of accent, give the children sentences containing blanks and a choice of the same word syllabized and accented in two different ways. The pupils decide which form to use in the blank and then write a sentence of their own using the other form. For example: "The chairman will (*pre'sent* or *pre-sent'*) the speaker."

DIACRITICAL MARKS. Another skill involves the use of diacritical marks as an aid to pronunciation. The pronunciation key at the bottom of each page (or on the endpapers of the book) is a basic reference. Although this key may differ from dictionary to dictionary, its use remains the same. If the children can read the key words, there is no great need to be able to identify all the markings. The sound association can be made between the key pronunciation word and the one in the dictionary.

Instruction needs to be given that involves marking long and short vowels and then discovering that vowels have other sounds as well as the long and short. Illustrate how these are indicated in the key words on each page in the dictionary.

Have available such assignments as the following as spare-time work for students:

> Underline the word or words which have the *same* vowel sound as the word on the left.

ă as in *at*	*rattle, sale, athlete, clasp, gas*
ā as in *age*	*pale, name, display, radio, pat*
â as in *care*	*square, maple, fair, compare, dare*
ä as in *art*	*harvest, tame, star, depart, arm*
à as in *ask*	*grass, vast, grant, brave*

Teach the children to use the phonetic respelling given in the dictionary as an aid to pronunciation. Have the group make a list of words in which

ph or *gh* sounds like *f* (*elephant, tough*)
ch or *ck* sounds like hard *c* (*chorus, tack*)
d, dg, or soft *g* sounds like *j* (*soldier, ridge, ages*)

c sounds like *s* (*cent*)
c sounds like *k* (*act*)
c, x, or *s* sounds like *sh* (*ocean, anxious, sugar*)
l, w, k, or *b* is silent (*calf, wrong, know, comb*)

Teach the children that for some words there is more than one pronunciation and that the preferred one is given first.

Introducing Dictionary Skills

Although the dictionary is usually not introduced for the student's use until fourth grade, there are several good practices that will familiarize the students with dictionary procedure prior to the fourth year of school.

In the second and third grades children should be encouraged to keep their own file of words they have learned in reading. A brightly painted shoe box makes an excellent file of this sort. Each divider cut from cardboard should be labeled with a letter of the alphabet in both small letters and capitals. Children write the words they want to keep on file on cards or construction paper, or they can find words in magazines to cut out and paste on the cards. Then the words are filed behind the proper letter of the alphabet.

Another device is to make picture dictionaries for either individual or class use. Children choose a big scrapbook, label the pages with each letter of the alphabet, and write the words on the scrapbook pages, complete with accompanying pictures.

After the dictionary is introduced in either the third or the fourth grade, the following exercises may be used to facilitate its use:

1. A dictionary is placed on the first desk of each row. The teacher writes any ten words on the board. At a given signal, the first pupil in each row looks up the first word. When he finds it, he jots down the page number and passes the dictionary to the person behind him, who does the same for the second word, and so on. The first row finished is the winner. If a mistake is made in a page number, the second row finished is the winner.
2. The same game is played with definitions or pronunciations.

3. The same game may be played with names of mythological characters.
4. Each student brings to class a sentence containing a difficult word. A dictionary is placed on each student's desk and the class is divided into two teams. A pupil reads his sentences and states the word he wants defined. The opposing team is given approximately half a minute to look up the word in the dictionary. At a signal from the teacher, dictionaries are closed and the one who presented the sentence calls a pupil from the opposing team to define the word. If the pupil misses, he is eliminated and another is called. The game is continued until all of one team has been eliminated.

Worksheets like the following are sometimes used to practice dictionary skills:

DICTIONARY ACTIVITIES

These are individual activities. Each individual has a dictionary, paper, pencil. Questions for the contest have been put on the board and covered with a map or newspaper.

What letter or letters if any have been omitted?

pro__dure	picni__ing
dorm__tory	place__able
vac__um	cartil__age
super__ede	indel__ble
reform__tory	privil__ge

Plurals

Give the plurals of

alumnus	stratum
bandit	court-martial
basis	bacillus
index	teaspoon
mother-in-law	spoonful

Alphabetical Order

Write in alphabetical order:

Denver	St. Louis
Milwaukee	Chicago

Nashville	San Francisco
New York	St. Paul
New Orleans	Los Angeles
Miami	Seattle
Warren	Bloomington

Give the comparative and superlative degrees of *silly, polite, tidy, wet, sad, old, good, little, many.*

Prefix

The children find the meaning of the following prefixes or bound morphemes; then write words that use them. Example: Prefix *re-* means "again," "back," or "down" (*retreat, return, relate*).

Use these prefixes: *re-, in-, sub-, ex-, inter-, intra-, de-, con-, pre-, dis-, ante-, bi-, contra-, extra-, post-, trans-, dia-, hemi-, semi-, demi-, poly-, peri-, syn-, mis-, pro-, over-, be-, un-, mal-, ultra-, super-, medi-, tri-.*

Words of All Nations

The following English words have been adapted or borrowed from other languages. Look up the word and list the country from which it comes:

ski	canoe
coffee	circus
kimono	sky
sonata	radio
garage	dachshund
kindergarten	piano
tobacco	menu
sauerkraut	ranch
waltz	cafeteria
rodeo	assembly
fiesta	

Where Are They Found?

After each word in the following, write on the blank line the place where each is found; that is, in the air, on the land, or in water.

Use of the dictionary is an essential aspect of spelling instruction. (COURTESY OF THE BURBANK PUBLIC SCHOOLS.)

1. sturgeon ————————————————
2. tripod ————————————————
3. amoeba ————————————————
4. dromedary ————————————————
5. octopus ————————————————
6. linnet ————————————————
7. prawn ————————————————
8. eglantine ————————————————
9. oracle ————————————————
10. obelisk ————————————————

Who Uses What?

In this group a word is given, such as *plane.* Opposite the word is listed the worker or profession, such as *lawyer, carpenter, taxi driver.*

You are to underline the one who uses the tool or item named. In the example it is the *carpenter* who uses the *plane* in his work.

1. splice   aviator, tea taster, sailor
2. snaffle   jockey, marine, auctioneer
3. palette   miner, artist, keypunch operator
4. girder   knight, builder, gardener
5. font   minister, librarian, horticulturist
6. harpsichord   undertaker, druggist, musician
7. foil   teacher, fencer, cyclist

8. awl   cobbler, grocer, sculptor
9. pestle   judge, jeweler, druggist
10. creel   student, angler, mail carrier

Alphabetizing

Give the students a list of words such as the following and have them arrange the words in alphabetical order:

bewitch	boiler
offend	tan
suspect	scrape
peanut	penny
hog	hold
under	understand
custom	cart
please	plea
summer	sum
reach	suit
custom	wag
you	wall
real	task
piano	plot
home	hook
understood	underneath
cult	cartridge
pedal	pleasure
sit	simmer
tank	wander

Synonyms

A synonym is a word that has the same meaning as another word. Write a synonym for each of the following:

craven	aspect
lucid	wrath
irksome	adept
fickle	soothe
robust	rebuke

Abbreviations

Write down the meanings of the following abbreviations:

bbls., A.D., bldg., no., cong., gal., Rev., St., P.M., doz., ans., Capt., inc., Gen., Hon., Gov., P.O., M.D., R.F.D., B.C., supt., Y.M.C.A., mfg., wk., R.R., P.S., etc., i.e., A.M., vs., O.K., Pvt., D.D., Fem., adv., Apr., dept., vol., S.W., Ry., pp., U.S.N., S.S., viz., riv., nat., I.O.U.

Syllabication

Words divided at the ends of lines in printing, typing, and handwriting should be divided between syllables. Copy from your dictionary the following words, showing their proper division into syllables. Spell them correctly and omit the diacritical marks.

nicety	miraculous
geranium	phraseology
locomotive	European
suburban	statistics
democracy	burglar
originate	armistice
comparable	dirigible
finale	lamentable
heroine	despicable
seizure	syllable

Identification Exercises

Tell whether the following are bird, fish, or tree: tanager, barnacle, almond, vulture, cardinal, flicker, anchovy, gannet, yew, warbler, vireo, sumac, auk, toucan, acacia, tarpon, avocado, sucker, bittern, rock, cinnamon, sycamore, sole, chestnut, ebony, starling.

Tell whether the following are flower, animal, or vegetable: anemone, gherkin, hyena, syringa, kohlrabi, yak, gibbon, jasmine, mammoth, gentian, okra, lemur, rhubarb, poinsettia, puma, sloth, arbutus.

Tell who uses the following: trowel, platinum, rifle, scissors, snaffle, accordion, kilt, adze, splice, anvil, kayak, davits, lute, calumet, palette, mosque, girder, auger, font, percolator, brig, puck, discus, strop, calk, doily, epaulet, hoop, canister, creel, scepter, awl, lasso, mangle, metronome, easel.

Tell where the following are found: sturgeon, autogiro, bison, tripod, cobra, weevil, amoeba, dromedary, chalet, brougham, veranda, dolphin, constellation, corral, caisson, cheetah, squid, sloop, mollusk, phoebe, ketch, manatee, osprey, obelisk, ferret, coot, ermine, merganser, scrole, elevator, eglantine, phaeton, grebe.

Matching

Match the ending in the right-hand column with the correct beginning in the left-hand column, and write it in the blank space:

acci	ize	_____
sever	fy	_____
special	ance	_____
tick	pose	_____
uni	dox	_____
veri	dent	_____
trans	et	_____
wheth	fy	_____
para	er	_____

Homonyms

In our language we have a number of words that are pronounced alike but that have different meanings. The words *to, too, two* are homonyms. Try to find a homonym for each of the following and write it on the line after the word given:

bear____	days____
pair____	there____
him____	whole____
way____	tacked____
ewe____	right____
feet____	meet____
here____	blue____
peace____	our____
ate____	rain____
ball____	sun____
be____	rode____
air____	sea____

sew____	cent____
deer____	would____
won____	steak____

Word Analysis

Use a dictionary to do these exercises. Write the words in the blanks provided. Find a word beginning with the indicated prefix and having the indicated meaning.

Prefix	Definition	Word
ab-	to take a person away by force	____
ab-	to go away hurriedly and secretly	____
ab-	to free a person from debt or a duty	____
ad-	to stick fast	____
ad-	to be next to	____
ad-	to warn	____
ad-	to move forward	____
ad-	to give notice of something	____
anti-	to be against society	____
anti-	a remedy that prevents poison from taking effect	____

The following exercise is done in the same manner as the one preceding.

Prefix	Definition	Word
com-	to fight with someone	____
com-	to speak of something with approval	____
com-	to find fault with something	____
com-	to mix with	____
de-	to keep from entering	____
de-	to grow less in size	____
de-	to protect from danger	____
dis-	to not be honest	____
post-	afternoon	____

For Discussion

1. Compare the definition of a word in an elementary dictionary with that in a collegiate edition. Why is at least one collegiate dictionary needed in an intermediate classroom?

2. Compare the glossary in an intermediate science or social studies text with a dictionary.

How May Spelling Games Be Used to Motivate One to Learn to Spell? [5]

Games provide extra motivation for some of the drill that children need to master spelling. Although it is unlikely that spelling will ever have the fascination of baseball for some children or golf for some adults, interest in words and their spelling can be heightened by using a spelling game.

Games call for considerable planning to be successful. In introducing the game, first give the name, then have some children "walk through" each step as you describe it. After that, have a trial run to be certain that everyone understands. Establish a few rules during the practice period. Choosing partners or teams can create considerable social tension. This can be avoided by using row against row or counting and having "odds" versus "evens."

The timing of a game is important. Just before recess is usually a good time, because it avoids the necessity of a difficult transition from an exciting game to an uninspiring page in a history book. Do not make a game last too long unless it is a special privilege. Ten to fifteen minutes should be the maximum. To be of value the game should provide drill on needed words or skills.

College students using these games will find this list of words that were missed by the finalists in the National Spelling Bee a challenge.

Famous Last Words

The following list consists of thirty of the words on which national championships have been won or lost

[5] Unless otherwise noted, this material is adapted from Paul S. Anderson, *Resource Materials for Teachers of Spelling* (Minneapolis: Burgess, 1958).

since the National Spelling Bee began in 1925. Can you spell them?

abbacy	interning
abrogate	knack
acquiesced	luxuriance
albumen	oligarchy
asceticism	onerous
brethren	plebeian
canonical	promiscuous
chrysanthemum	pronunciation
deteriorating	propitiatory
dulcimer	psychiatry
flaccid	sacrilegious
foulard	sanitarium
fracas	semaphore
gladiolus	stupefied
intelligible	therapy

A Fateful Fifty

The fate of fifty contestants in National Spelling Bee championship finals in recent years was determined by the following fifty words. On each of them a boy or girl finalist missed, and a championship chance was lost. See if you know them.

aeriferous	febrile
agglomeration	fission
aggression	foment
aplomb	glacial
archetype	guttural
assonance	herbaceous
bier	homiletic
catalyst	imitator
consensus	imposter
coruscation	indissoluble
cuisine	insouciant
disputatious	jocose
effeminate	manumit
efflorescence	mattock
elision	medallion
emendation	meretricious
ennoble	minatory
exacerbate	obloquy

pallor   saponaceous
peripatetic   scintillate
peroration   shellacked
pomegranate   urbane
qunadary   vilify
requiem   wainscot
rue   yawl

Games for Primary Grades

1. PUZZLE ELEMENTS

a. I am in *see, sing,* and *say*. What sound am I?
b. I am in *took,* but I am not in *look*. I am _____.
c. *Baby, book, ball.* The *b* is at the _____.

2. MAKING NEW WORDS BY CHANGING A VOWEL

bat	fur
bet	far
bit	ham
but	hum
cat	him
cot	pen
cut	pan
bug	pin
big	pot
beg	pat
for	pit

3. WRITING ALLITERATIVE SENTENCES

Bob bought big blue balloons.

This might be a team affair with two or three working together to produce the sentence. Older children like to make advertising slogans:

Buy Billie's Best Boston Beans

Can Charlie's Canaries Comfort Charlie's Comrades?

✓4. TREASURE BOX. Words are written on separate slips of paper that are then folded and put into a box called the treasure box. Each child in turn draws out a slip, which he hands to the teacher without opening. The teacher pronounces the word and the child attempts to spell it. Any misspelled words are handed back to the children who had difficulty with them. The object is for the pupil to end the game with no slips of paper. Those who do have slips learn to spell the words that are on them. This exercise can be performed by two children in a quiet corner.

5. TURN UP LETTERS. The players are seated at a table. Before them on the table face down are a number of alphabet cards. The players decide on some category for the game—animals, birds, cities, flowers, and so on. Then each player in turn picks up a card and exhibits the letter. The first child to write a word beginning with that letter, belonging to the category decided on and spelled correctly, gets the card. The spelling of the word may be challenged. If it is incorrect, the challenger gets the card. When all the cards have been turned up, the player having the most cards wins.

6. ALPHABET JUMBLE. Two sets of the alphabet are placed in a long chalk tray. Two children compete to see which one can be first to arrange one set in correct alphabetical order.

7. FIND IT. Words are listed on the chalkboard. The teacher or a student gives the definition of the word and the children in turn spell the word defined.

8. HEAR IT. The words are listed on the board. The leader says, "I am thinking of a word that starts with the same sound as one hears at the beginning of _____," or "one that rhymes with _____." The children write the words indicated and gain a point for their own score for each correct selection.

9. GUESS AND SPELL. "It" selects an object that is in plain sight in the room. The other children start guessing the first letter of that object. When the first letter is guessed, they start working on the second, then the third, until the word is spelled. The correct letters may be put on the chalkboard as they are spelled by the one who is "it." When any student thinks that he may be able to spell the total word after the first few letters have been guessed, he may challenge the leader and complete the word. He then becomes "it."

10. NOVELTY SPELLING. Instead of calling words from a spelling list, the teacher asks questions such as "Can you spell a word that rhymes with *joint*?" "Can you spell a word containing *ph* which sounds like *f*?" "Can you spell a word that means _____?" Have

members of the class in turn read their lists. The variety adds interest and influences vocabulary.

11. CHALKBOARD SPELLING. Primary children feel that it is a privilege to write on the chalkboard. Reserve a place at the board where a child may go during his free time just as he might go to the library corner. Put a different exercise on the board for each child, such as

What children in our room have names that start with *B?*

What do you want for Christmas?

What do you like to eat?

Where would you like to visit?

How many words do you know that start with *wh?*

12. USE THE WORD. The words of the spelling lesson are placed on the board and left during the day. Each time one of the words is used in a child's writing during the day counts one point for his side. This can be row-against-row competition. The word does not count unless the one who writes the word reports it for the count.

13. PEAR TREE. How many pear (pair) trees can you develop with your class? Synonyms and antonyms? But how about such pears (pairs) as *horse, colt; cow, calf?* Or *hands, gloves; feet, shoes?* Or *swimming, swimmer; archer, archery?* Divide your class into committees to develop these trees. Each committee draws a large tree and puts pairs of words on yellow or light green pears. Add leaves for effect.

Spelling Games for Upper Grades

1. DICTIONARY GAMES. One child opens the dictionary at random, saying, "I have opened the dictionary to an *sp-* page." Each child then writes as many words starting with *sp-* as he can. Two teams may compete, each child in turn adding a word. To prevent careless or poor writing, each team may have a "recorder" who writes the words suggested by the team. Have three to five on a team. The winning team may be challenged by another team.

2. MEMORY GAME. Several picture cards, each portraying a single object, are shown to pupils (or it might be the objects themselves). The pictures or objects are then concealed and the children are asked to write the names of all the objects they remember. To vary this game, expose a list of words and then have pupils write as many as they can recall. It is more difficult if the words must be written in alphabetical order. For some children a test of listening is valuable. Start by having them listen to three words, then write them. Keep increasing the number of words.

3. BASEBALL. One form uses word cards and is especially good for practice on words frequently misspelled. Each card contains a word, a value such as one base hit, home run, and so on, and the position of the player who is to catch the ball if it is misspelled. The cards would look like this:

all right 2-base hit 3rd baseman	separate home run pitcher	February 3-base hit right field

Sometimes children take positions in the classroom as if it were a baseball diamond. It is equally interesting to use a chalkboard diagram with players remaining at their seats while the team captain indicates their movement on the diagram.

In another form, four diamonds are drawn on the chalkboard. The first member of the team at bat goes to the first diamond. The first word is given by the pitcher. The pitcher may be the teacher or a member of the opposing team. The child at the board writes the word. Those at their seats write the word for practice. If the word is spelled successfully by the batter, he moves to the second diamond (first base) and a new player goes to the first diamond. Again the teacher pronounces a word to be spelled. Both players at the board write the word. If both spell the word correctly, each player moves to another diamond and a third player goes to the first diamond. If either player misspells the word, he is out. Thus it is possible for two or more players to be put out by one word. When a player advances through all four diamonds, a score is made for the team he represents.

4. THE MAIDEN AND THE DRAGON. At one chalk-board area a "maiden" is drawn, tied to a rock by five ropes. On the other side a dragon is drawn facing five waves. (Flannel-board figures make this easier.) One group represents the maiden, the other the dragon. The game proceeds in the manner of a traditional spelldown. Each time a member of the team of the maiden misspells a word, one of the waves is erased. The waves are protecting the maiden from the dragon. Each time a member of the dragon team misspells a word, one of the ropes is erased. When the five waves are gone, the dragon will be released to devour the maiden. But if the five ropes are cut, the maiden is freed and the dragon dies. Suspense develops although no player leaves the game.

5. ROOTS AND BRANCHES. This game is intended to develop awareness of parts of words. Make four cards for each of several root words: for example, *march, marched, marching, marcher; fear, feared, fearing, fearful;* and so on.

Make enough copies of each set of words for four "books." Shuffle the cards and deal six cards at a time to each player. Players sort their cards as in playing "Authors." If a player holds four cards of words from the same root, he can make a "book." Each player in turn may call for a card by naming the card he holds and may continue to call as long as other players hold wanted cards. When there are no more available cards of the kind he calls, he discards, and the next player takes his turn. The objective is to get as many books as possible. Care should be taken in preparing the cards for this game not to introduce different elements too fast for slow readers: for example, doubling the final consonant of a root, or changing the sound, as *lose* and *lost.*

6. WORD ADDITION. To facilitate the use of word endings and prefixes, words are listed on the board. Each child uses that list of words to see how many new words can be made by adding beginnings and endings. Plural forms and *-ing, -er, -est, -ed, -r, pre-,* and *im-* may be used. Words that may be used are *run, occupy, view, prove, write, large, build, hear, stand, call, part, play.*

7. GHOST. One child starts with a letter that is also a word, as *I* or *a*. The next child adds another letter to make still another word, as *in*. The next child might spell *tin*, the next *into*. The letters may be rearranged, but each previous letter must be included and just one letter added. The child who cannot make a new word in this way is a "ghost," the object of the game being to avoid becoming one. This is a good game for a large number of players.

8. SPELLING JINGLES. When the children come across a new word, they can help establish its spelling in their minds by writing jingles using the word in rhyme. The children enjoy composing the jingles and, at the same time, learn to spell the new word and other similar words. When the word *night* was learned, for example, the following was written:

When it is night
We need a light.

9. WHAT'S MY WORD? Each child has a different word. One stands in front of the group. Each student in turn may ask one question, then spell the word he thinks is the word of the one in front. The questions may concern the meaning, the beginning sound, a rhyming word, or the word root. The student who identifies the word takes the leader's position.

10. TRAVEL. Ticket salespeople are appointed for various points, such as "Airplane ride to New York," "Bus ride to Los Angeles," and so on. Each has a group of words. Students in turn apply for tickets and are given them after spelling all the words on the salesman's list. A variation might be a county fair or a circus, with the ticket admitting the speller to special events.

11. SMOKED BACON. Make two or more sets of cardboard letters with the letters of *smoked bacon.* Teams face each other with each child holding one letter. The teacher calls out a word that can be spelled by these letters. The first team to get in correct positions gets a point. These letters form at least a hundred words.

This can be a chalkboard game. Write *smoked*

bacon on the board. Let each team write a word in turn. The winner is the one who writes the longest list of words in a certain time limit. As a flannelboard game, this may be a group or individual activity.

12. NEW SPELLDOWN. The fifteen to sixteen words of the week's lessons are put on the board. Each child is assigned one word, which becomes his "name." (Two or more may have the same word.) The leader goes to the front of the room and calls on one of the students. This child faces the rear of the room (because the words are still on the chalkboard) and is asked to spell the leader's word. If he is incorrect, he sits down; if correct, he asks the leader to spell his word. The class, looking at the words on the chalkboard, acts as judges. When the leader misses, the challenger takes his place.

13. FOURTH-GRADE SCRAMBLE. Take any week's lesson and scramble the letters in each word. The teacher scrambles the letters of a word on the board and the children write the word correctly on their papers. If each letter of the word is on a separate card, they may be placed on the chalk rail. One child unscrambles the word, writes it on the chalkboard, and uses it in a sentence. The class watching this may write the words as each one is unscrambled. A true scramble avoids placing the letters in a horizontal sequence but writes all over the board. Letter cards may be so scrambled on a flannelboard.

14. YOU CAN'T CATCH ME. As the teacher gives the first word, each child writes it on his paper. Then the papers are passed in a predetermined order (to the left, for example). The child receiving the paper checks the last word and writes the word correctly if necessary. Then the teacher gives the second word and the papers are passed. Every paper should be perfect if all errors are caught. While this may not always happen, those words needing review will have received attention in a different way.

Fun for All Ages

1. SPELLDOWNS. Traditional spelldowns involve one team that competes with another. If a child mis-spells a word and the person whose turn it is to spell on the opposite team spells it correctly, that child is "spelled down" and takes his seat. He can be saved if the opponents misspell the word and the next person on his team spells it successfully. A good P.T.A. feature is to have a group of girls spell against their fathers. Ordinarily, "boys-versus-girls" is not a fair contest, but sometimes Boy Scouts will challenge Girl Scouts, or a fifth-grade team will challenge a sixth-grade team. (The National Education Association has a clever play available that uses a spelldown dramatically. Write for "Command Performance," by Tom Erhard.) Rather than using oral spelling alone it adds to the educational value to have the words written neatly on the chalkboard by the contestants.

2. CHECKERS. Checkers is a spelldown in which the student who spells a word correctly "jumps" two persons in the direction of the end of the line. When he reaches the end, he goes to his seat. The advantage of such procedure is that those who need practice remain, whereas those who know the words have time for independent work. This may be called a spellup and the students may move from the end of the line to the top when they drop from the line.

3. SPELLUPS. Spellups are the same as the traditional spelling bee with one exception—instead of the teams lining up, each team member remains seated until he misses a word; then he stands. When a player misses a word, the person standing is given a chance to spell the word correctly. If he succeeds, he sits down. Remember this is a game. If errors are embarrassing to any individual, it would be wise to avoid such direct comparison.

For Discussion

1. Why is it better to use one or two instructional games at a single grade level?

2. How can a teacher give recognition to the successful students without discouraging those less competent?

3. Should games be used at a time when a parent or a supervisor is visiting a classroom?

How May the Spelling Program Be Enriched to Challenge All Students?

In every intermediate classroom there are children who do not respond to formal spelling instruction or who are far beyond the spelling level of the class. The suggestions that follow may be used in light of the teacher's knowledge of the children's needs.

These may be assigned by the teacher or self-assigned by the student as is appropriate to the situation. The child who gets 100 per cent in the week's assignment in spelling instruction or who is far beyond the class might profit by doing one of these activities. The child who never succeeds with the words in a spelling assignment may find motivation for proper spelling through an interesting writing experience. Correct spelling is a refinement of writing, and a writing approach to spelling makes sense to many students.

Write a news report of an event in the school or classroom.

Find other meanings for words in the spelling list and write a sentence illustrating the meaning.

Write a paragraph about a secret wish, or a wish you make but do not really want, such as being a baby again or a dog.

Write a story of the first Thanksgiving (or any holiday) you remember.

How did people first learn to use fire, the wheel, or glass? Make up a story answer or find the material in a reference book.

Take an old story or fable and make it modern, such as "Christmas [or Chanukah] with the Three Bears."

What was the bravest thing your father or mother ever did?

Make up a story of a dog hero (or any pet).

Write a description of a bird or flower.

Make a list of first-aid suggestions that should be in every automobile.

Look up in an encyclopedia and report how long these animals usually live: dog, horse, bear, elephant.

Write a description of someone in the room; let the class guess who it is.

Try to write twenty compound words.

How many words can you list that end with -le (or -age, or any other common ending)?

Report on a radio or TV program that you think your class would enjoy.

Make up a Paul Bunyan story.

Make a list of words that have tele- in them (or any other base Latin or Greek form).

Cut out a newspaper story and do one of the following: Underline each adjective (or noun, adverb, etc.). Underline each compound word. Underline the topic sentence. Make an outline of the story.

Correct the English used in a comic strip or book.

Discover different ways in which the same meaning is expressed in different parts of the English-speaking world; for example, in England: *lift* for *elevator; cinema* for *movie; petrol* for *gasoline; sweets* for *dessert* or *candy;* in Canada: *spool of cotton* for *spool of thread; tap* for *faucet; window blind* for *window shade;* in Australia: *sundowner* for *hobo.*

Report on the origin of some of the words we use.

Collect and discuss words that have come to us from other peoples. For example:

African	zebra, chimpanzee
American Indian	hominy, persimmon, squaw
Arabian	admiral, alfalfa, magazine
Australian	kangaroo, boomerang
Chinese	silk, pongee, tea, ketchup
Dutch	skipper, sleigh, waffle, boss
French	cafe, bouquet, aileron, dinner
German	hamburger, waltz, kindergarten
Greek	theater, botany
Hebrew	amen, hemp, shekel

Hindu	calico, jungle, chintz, dungaree
Hungarian	goulash, tokay
Irish	brogue, colleen, bog
Malay-Polynesian	gingham, bantam, tattoo
Persian	scarlet, caravan, lilac, seersucker
Portugese	veranda, marmalade, yam
Scandinavian	ski, squall, smelt, keg
Scots	clan, reel (dance)
Slavonic	sable, polka, robot
Spanish	barbecue, bronco
Turkish	tulip, coffee, fez
Welsh	flannel, crag

Collect and discuss words that have been derived from place names. For example:

italics	Italy
cashmere	Cashmere (Kashmir, India)
morocco (leather)	Morocco
calico	Calcutta
milliner	Milan

Discuss new words invented to meet new needs: for example, *airplane* (1870); *vitamin* (1930); and *jeep* and *radar,* in the last few years. Explore the ''new words'' section of the dictionary.

Find out how the days of the week and the months of the year got their names.

Discuss and list the origin and meaning of the names of members of the class. (Example: John = Hebrew *Yohanan,* ''God Is Gracious.'') The following references will be helpful:

Adelson, Leone. *Dandelions Don't Bite.* New York: Pantheon Books, 1972.

Epstein, Sam, and Beryl Epstein. *The First Book of Words.* New York: Franklin Watts, 1954.

Ernst, Margaret. *Words.* New York: Knopf, 1954.

Funk, Charles E. *Heavens to Betsy.* New York: Harper & Row, 1955.

Funk, Charles E. *Thereby Hangs a Tale.* New York: Harper & Row, 1950.

Garrison, W. B. *Why You Say It.* Nashville: Abingdon, 1955.

Laird, Helen, and Carlton Laird. *Tree of Language.* Cleveland: World, 1957.

Bibliography

Anderson, P. S. *Resource Materials for Teachers of Spelling.* Minneapolis: Burgess, 1958.

Ashton-Warner, S. *Teacher.* New York: Simon & Schuster, 1963.

Betts, E. A. *Spelling Vocabulary Study: Grade Placement of Words in Seventeen Spellers.* New York: American, 1940. *Grade Placement of Words in Eight Recent Spellers.* New York: American, 1949.

Blake, H. E., and R. Emans. ''Some Spelling Facts.'' *Elementary English* (February 1970), 241–249.

Board of Education of the City of New York. *Teaching Spelling.* Curriculum Bulletin, Series No. 6 (1953–1954).

Chomsky, C. ''Invented Spelling in First Grade.'' Unpublished paper, Harvard Graduate School of Education, May 1974.

Chomsky, C. ''Write Now, Read Later.'' *Language in Early Childhood Education,* ed. by C. Cazden. Washington, D.C.: National Association for the Education of Young Children, 1972.

Dunkeld, C., and L. Hatch. ''Building Spelling Confidence.'' *Elementary English,* **52:** No. 2 (February 1975).

Fernald, G. M. *Remedial Techniques in Basic School Subjects.* New York: McGraw-Hill, 1943.

Geedy, P. S. ''What Research Tells Us About Spelling.'' *Elementary English* (February 1975), 233–236.

Graham, R. T., and E. H. Rudorf. ''Dialect and Spelling.'' *Elementary English* (March 1970), 363–375.

Greene, H. A. *The New Iowa Spelling Scale.* Iowa City: Bureau of Educational Research and Service, University of Iowa, 1955.

Groff, P. *The Syllable: Its Nature and Pedagogical Usefulness.* Portland, Ore.: Northwest Regional Educational Laboratory (500 Lindsay Building, 710 S.W. Second Avenue, Portland, Oregon 87204).

Grosse Point Public Schools. *Thinking About Spelling.* Grosse Point, Mich., 1948.

Hall, R. A. *Sound and Spelling in English*. Philadelphia: Chilton Co., 1964.

Hanna, P. R., and J. T. Moore, Jr. "Spelling—From Spoken Word to Written Symbol." *Elementary School Journal* (February 1953). (Republished as a pamphlet by Houghton Mifflin, Boston.)

Hanna, P. R., J. S. Hanna, R. E. Hodges, and E. H. Rudorf, Jr. *Phoneme-Grapheme Correspondences as Cues to Spelling Improvement*. Washington, D.C.: U.S. Department of Health, Education and Welfare, Office of Education, 1966.

Hildreth, G. *Teaching Spelling*. New York: Holt, 1955.

Hillerich, R. L. "A Spelling/Writing Project Becomes an English Program." *Illinois ASCD Newsletter of Curriculum and Supervision,* **14:** No. 2 (March 1968), 1–3. Springfield, Ill.: Illinois Association for Supervision and Curriculum Department.

Horn, E. *The Basic Writing Vocabulary*. Iowa City: University of Iowa, 1927.

Horn, E. "Phonics and Spelling." *Journal of Education* (May 1954). See also E. Betts. "Phonics: Practical Considerations Based on Research." *Elementary English* (October 1956).

Horn, E. "Spelling." *Encyclopedia of Educational Research,* Vol. 26, ed. by Hanna Chester Harris. New York: Macmillan Publishing Co., Inc., 1960.

Horn, E. *Teaching Spelling: What Research Says to the Teacher,* No. 3. AERA of the NEA, 1962.

Johnson, D. D., and E. Majer. "Johnson's Basic Vocabulary: Words for Grades 1 and 2." *Elementary School Journal* (September 1976), 74–82.

Key, M. R. "The English Spelling System and the Initial Teaching Alphabet." *Elementary School Journal* (March 1969), 313–326.

Lillard, P. P. *Montessori: A Modern Approach*. New York: Schocken Books, 1972.

Mazurkiewicz, A. J. "Toward a Spelling Reform." *Reading World* (December 1976), 81–87.

Medway, P. "Let Down by Spelling." *Times Educational Supplement* (London, May 28, 1976), 19.

Montessori, M. *The Montessori Method*. Cambridge, Mass.: Robert Bently, 1967.

Paul, R. "Invented Spelling in Kindergarten." *Young Children* (March 1976), 195–200.

Rice, J. M. "The Futility of the Spelling Grind." *Forum* 23 (1978), 169–172.

Rinsland, H. D. *A Basic Writing Vocabulary of Elementary School Children*. New York: Macmillan Publishing Co., Inc., 1945.

Smith, E., K. Goodman, and R. Meredith. *Language and Thinking in the Elementary School*. New York: Holt, Rinehart and Winston, 1970.

Tiedt, S. W., and I. M. Tiedt. *Exploring Words*. San Jose, Calif.: Contemporary Press, 1964.

Wolfe, R., Sr. "A Study of Spelling Errors." *Elementary School Journal* (April 1952).

Chapter 10
Exploring Literature
for Children

What Is the Purpose of Teaching Literature in the Elementary School?

All children have an imagination, though its power may vary. As some children grow older, their imagination seems to diminish rather than expand. The literal-minded child, through literature, can strengthen his skills of imagination and his ability to empathize with others. The literature teacher can thus help the growing child cultivate and extend his powers of imagination.

Teachers hope that their efforts in literature instruction will lead children to find in books an appreciation of the richness of life, with all its experiences and its feelings, that will enlarge their lives. Reading about others who solve problems similar to his own can help the reader to feel confident about his ability to face life. Each person needs to feel that he belongs, has a contribution to make, and will be respected by others. Stories contribute to these feelings in many ways. It is

comforting to know, for example, that others feel the same way about a situation as you do or that others are sometimes motivated by envy, as you occasionally may be. When the story depicts an honorable way of behaving, the reader feels confident because he too would have acted that way. Contrasting one way of living with another helps a reader to appreciate qualities in both.

All children have a right to their literary culture, and experience with this literature is an important aspect of reading skill. To be knowledgeable, the child must know the meaning of such sayings as "Don't be a dog in the manger" and "He is a regular Tom Sawyer." One textbook cannot give all that is needed, but the heritage of folk literature should be a discovery of young readers. Many selections in contemporary reading programs are designed to lead to wider personal reading. The classic plots and themes found in such tales as "Cinderella," "Puss-in-Boots," and "Snow White" are a part of the literary background needed to understand the many stories based on overcoming evil with wit or innocence, gaining success in spite of great odds, and changing the ugly into the beautiful.

Certainly the child learning to read needs to know that reading can be a pleasure, whether in the form of listening to material well read or participating in silent or oral group reading. Children should also know the pleasure of personal writing, which can be stimulated by literature.

Salient Issues and Children's Literature

Today it is realized that children's literature can be an important influence in shaping a child's self-concept as well as his concept of the world. The issues of sex and racial stereotyping, empathy, and death are among those of concern to both authors and teachers.

Sex Stereotyping

The issue of sex stereotyping in children's literature has received considerable attention in recent years. Taylor (1973) reports of the California elementary reading textbooks that they "fail to prepare girls for future realities, [and] they contribute subtly and significantly to the formation of negative self-images" (p. 1045). Males are far more frequently portrayed as the main characters in the first six grades, and when females do appear they often are stereotypes, being emotionally flighty, ridiculous, or uninteresting.

Greater value and prestige are attached to the male role. Boys are portrayed as more competent than girls in physical tasks and in creativity. Girls lack the freedom to inquire, explore, and achieve.

The ubiquitous and pervasive nature of sex stereotyping was illustrated by Jennings (1975) at the preschool level. Her study revealed that, in general, girls found the male role much more acceptable than the boys found the female role. The portrayal of women in occupational roles has been examined at the preschool level (Murphy, 1975) and in comparison with the literature of the 1930s (Hillman, 1976). Hillman found little

Motivation is a byproduct of interest. (PHOTO BY LINDA LUNGREN.)

change in the range of occupational roles of women in children's literature despite the recent political, social, and economic changes.

Awareness of the existence of sex stereotyping is a beginning. The teacher and school librarian should make available books portraying women in roles traditionally considered to be men's roles. Books that might be provided are *What Can She Be? A Veterinarian?*, *What Can She Be? A Lawyer?*, *What Can She Be? A Farmer?*, *What Can She Be? A Police Officer?*, and *What Can She Be? A Musician?* by Gloria and Esther Goldreich; *Challenge to Become a Doctor: The Story of Elizabeth Blackwell* by Leah Lurie Heyn; *Johnny*

Attractive bulletin boards emphasizing reading of everyday articles will encourage the idea of reading as a necessity. (PHOTO BY TOM WOLFE.)

Racial Stereotyping

Children's literature may be a source in shaping a child's concept of race as well as sexual identity. Mathis (1974) has cited passages from recent children's literature that portray Blacks in negative and stereotypic roles. To counteract such possible bias, Thompson and Woodard (1972) list the following books as depicting Blacks in positive settings with positive identities: *Gabrielle and Selena* by Peter Desbarats; *Hooray for Jasper* by Betty Horvath; *The Snowy Day, Whistle for Willie, Peter's Chair,* and *A Letter to Amy* by Ezra Jack Keats; *Sam and Big Cowboy Western* by Ann Herbert Scot; and *What Mary Jo Wanted* and *What Mary Jo Shared* by Janice May Udry.

In selecting interracial books for inclusion in the class library, the teacher should determine that they portray all races as composed of individuals with positive traits and personalities in a variety of social positions. Such books should have appeal for all children.

Empathy

The development of the characteristics that contribute to our humanity is a gradual process with roots in early childhood. Children's literature may be instrumental in the development of such qualities as empathy. Wolf (1975) proposes four stages in the development of empathy during the preschool years: (1) trust in the constancy of the object world; (2) trust in the constancy of the human world; (3) experience of emotional pain when faced by problems lacking ready solutions; and (4) desire and quest for resolution of complex emotional dilemmas. Wolf recommends the following books, which correspond to these developmental stages: (1) *Goodnight Moon* by Margaret Wise Brown, (2) *Little Bear* by Elsie Holmehind Minarik, (3) *Sam* by Ann Herbert Scott, and (4) *Crow Boy* by Taro Yashima.

When we read meaningful books to children in groups, over and over, throughout the early years, we provide chances to share important feelings, to connect in powerful ways to others, peers as well as elders, and to develop the

Learns to Type by Mabel Crain; *William's Doll* by Charlotte Zolotow; and *Henry Reed's Baby-Sitting Service* by Keith Robertson.

Not only is there a need for reorientation in depicting women's role behaviors, but men should more frequently be portrayed in tender, caring, and empathetic roles. The goal is to provide children with positive role models regardless of sex to allow for self-expression and enhancement.

potential for the full dimensions of empathy, which is, after all, the capacity for being human. [Wolf, 1975, p. 49]

Death

The concept of death has largely been avoided in children's literature until recent years. There is recognition (Swenson, 1972; Sadker, 1976; Grollman, 1969; Feifal, 1959) that children do have perceptions about death, although such notions may not coincide with reality.

Sadker (1976) provides selections that may contribute to a child's awareness and acceptance of death and the attendant realization of the value and wonder of life. Books designated for preschool and primary grades include *The Tenth Good Thing About Barney* by Judith Viorst, *Growing Time* by Sandol S. Warburg, *The Dead Bird* by Margaret Wise Brown, and *Annie and the Old One* by Miska Miles.

Death is treated in the following books for older children: *A Taste of Blackberries* by Doris Buchanan Smith, *By the Highway Home* by Mary Stolz, *The High Pasture* by Ruth Harnden, *The Magic Moth* by Virginia Lee, and *Death Be Not Proud* by John Gunther. Two other outstanding books that deal with the process of death are the children's favorites *Charlotte's Web* by E. B. White and *Little Women* by Louisa May Alcott.

Concept Development and Children's Literature

The following list of books illustrates the extent to which children's literature may satisfy a child's curiosity about himself and his world: [1]

CURIOSITIES OF CHILDREN THAT LITERATURE CAN SATISFY

1. Curiosity about themselves.
   a. *Where Do Babies Come From*—Sheffield
   b. *The Human Body*—Lewis and Rubenstein
   c. *What Makes Me Feel This Way?*—LeShan

[1] From R. E. Toothaker, "Curiosities of Children That Literature Can Satisfy," *Childhood Education* (March 1976), 262–267.

2. Curiosity about the natural world.
   a. *Let Me Take You on a Trail*—Hawkinson
   b. *Come Along!*—Caudill
   c. *The House That Nature Built*—Kalina
   d. *What's Under a Rock?*—Gannon
3. Curiosity about people and places.
   a. *Natural Wonders of the World*—Stocks
   b. *The Seven Seas*—Clemons
   c. *Me and Willie and Pa*—Manjo
   d. *Bloomers and Ballots: Elizabeth Cady Stanton and Women's Rights*—Mary Stetson Clarte
   e. *Rosa Parks*—Eloise Greenfield
4. Curiosity about machines and how they work.
   a. *Making Tools*—Zim and Kelly
   b. *Hoists, Cranes and Derricks*—Zim and Kelly
   c. *What Makes a Computer Work?*—Halacy
   d. *Hold Everything*—Sam and Beryl Epstein
   e. *How Automobiles Are Made*—Cooke
5. Curiosity about facts and proofs of facts.
   a. *Guinness Book of World Records*
   b. *Statistics*—Srivastava
   c. *Science Experiences: Observation*—Bendicks
   d. *The Chemistry of a Lemon*—Stone
6. Curiosity about the ideals by which men live.
   a. *The First Book of Ethics*—Black
   b. *Religions*—Haskins
   c. *The Quakers: The Religious Society of Friends*—Elgin
7. Curiosity about the social world.
   a. *Families Live Together*—Meek and Bagwell
   b. *Behind the Magic Line*—Erwin
   c. *Somebody Go and Bang a Drum*—Cavdill

Literary Analysis for the Young Child

In the early years of a reader's life the literary emphasis should be on verse, fable, and folklore. For some children the only literary abilities that need to be developed will be those required in order to identify these types of reading material. Eventually children will note the different ways stories start and end, that some characters seem real and others remain as flat as the paper in the book, and that writers, by the use of words, can make the reader feel happy or sad. All of this in time becomes an awareness of writing style. When a child discovers that a single writer writes a kind of story that he is able to identify, the reader has made a basic literary discovery.

Teachers who wish to extend emphasis on literature should limit their efforts to the following types of analyses:

1. *Character*. What are the clues to characters suggested in the writing? From what is said or the action taken, what inference can be made about the individual? Why does the character act the way he does? What are his values? Did anyone change in the story? Why?
2. *Setting*. Can you see where the story is happening? How do those in the story act because of the setting? Is there a basic struggle between the people in the story and the nature of the place where they live?
3. *Mood–feeling–tone*. What words are used to tell you how the writer feels? What is the tone of voice of the storyteller? Is it serious? Humorous? Is this a true experience?
4. *Story pattern*. What story would you tell if you had only the first paragraph to guide you? Can you tell what happened by reading only the last paragraph? Is there a theme or lesson that the writer is illustrating? Who is telling the story? What difference does it make?

The teacher's goal is to enhance what is read, such as discovering the subtle bits of humor and character that might be lost as the reader becomes involved in the plot.

The child's appetite for more reading can be stimulated by individualizing the selections along the following guidelines:

1. Guiding the child to reading that will broaden and deepen his experiences.
2. Fitting the library book to the child, not the child to the book.
3. Bringing masterpieces of children's literature from the past and those of the present into proper perspective.
4. Challenging, but not pushing, the child.

5. Waiting with wisdom and patience for the child's own pattern of reading growth to unfold.

Teachers have encouraged wide reading by using the following procedures:

1. *Storytelling and oral reading* carefully selected from various types of literature that children might otherwise miss. Certain books or passages from books for increased appreciation of skillful use of language, vivid characterization, or dramatic incident are savored best when they are shared.
2. *Book talks,* including introductions to authors, illustrators, background material, stories behind stories, and sampling of passages to broaden reading interests and add zest to reading.
3. *Roundtable, thought-provoking discussions* to help children discover for themselves the deeper meanings and values that transcend the plot in good books. This does not mean overanalysis, which would destroy the pleasure of a good story for children, but it does mean a voluntary sharing of the fresh, individualized interpretation of the universal truths of a good story as a child sees them in relationship to his own experience.
4. *Literature* presented in such a way as to vitalize and enrich all areas of study and school experience so that children will come to recognize reading for pleasure and self-enlightenment as a natural part of living. Teachers should not feel that every literary experience must be followed by a related activity. However, frequently the interest of the children and the nature of the literature enjoyed guide individuals or groups quite naturally into creative writing, art experiences, creative drama, quizzes about authors or stories, or other interpretive activity.

There is a place for personal reading in the curriculum. This is an opportunity for the child to follow his interests and read for his own enjoyment. Many teachers feel that motivating such reading through records, visits to the library, book talks, and other such activities constitutes an adequate program. Others feel that children need guidance to find the books that have lasting merit. Few children will read more than four hundred books of children's fiction in their lifetime. It is important that some of these be true literary experiences.

Promotion of Group Discussion and Appreciation of Literary Works

Children may acquire an appreciation of literature by *in depth* discussions of prudently selected works. The following plans illustrate the means of incorporating literature into the child's experiences, thereby bringing a personal relevance and interest into the study of stories and books:[2]

Children, on returning from a trip to the zoo, expressed interest as to how the bears were caught. The teacher discerned that this interest would serve to introduce the story of *The Biggest Bear* by Lyn Ward.

The teacher read the story and shared the illustrations with the interested group around him. The children gasped as they learned that Mr. Pennell had killed three bears and therefore had three bearskins nailed to his barn, but Johnny's family had none. Like Johnny, the children became more and more attached to the bear cub in the story. The antics of Johnny's bear as he grew bigger and bigger brought intermittent squeals of delight and gasps of horror, especially details of the chaos in mother's kitchen and the damage in father's shed. They sympathized with Johnny as his father explained that the bear must go back to the woods.

"The bear really liked Johnny, didn't he?" a child exclaimed.

"Yes he did! But now Johnny had to do something that was very difficult for him to do," explained the teacher.

The sad-eyed audience gave visual testimony that they experienced vicariously what Johnny was feeling as he and his father took the bear into the forest, and all three fell into a bear trap. How delighted the students were to eventually find that some kind men would take care of Johnny's bear if Johnny would let them have him for the zoo.

At this point the teacher asked Jamie if he knew one way of capturing bears for the zoo. The teacher was pleased when Jamie replied, "They set traps; but I hope all people are as kind as these zoo people were."

[2] These plans are largely derived from *English Language Arts in Wisconsin*, Robert Pooley, Project Director (Madison, Wis.: Department of Public Instruction, 1968).

The teacher could tell that the children were anxious to talk about the book and he therefore asked the question, "Was there any part of the story you liked best?" He called on extrovert Tommy, who was wildly waving his hand.

"I liked the part where Johnny took the bear in all directions. May I make a map of Johnny's trip with the bear?" he asked, "and can I call on someone else to answer next?"

When the teacher nodded his head, Tommy called on Larry, who only now was emerging from his shell. Larry timidly smiled and said that he liked the part when Grandpa Orchard said, "It's better to have a bear in the orchard than an Orchard in the bear." The group laughed with Larry because they liked him and were happy that he was no longer afraid to share his ideas with them.

The teacher then presented these questions and watched the children's reactions in order not to destroy the pleasure they had derived from the story: "When Johnny first found the bear cub, why didn't he kill him? After all, he did want a bearskin for their barn." "Was it all right for Johnny to have the bear for a pet?" "Why did Johnny try to do what his daddy wanted him to do even though it was hard for him?" "How did Johnny feel?"

At the close of the lesson a young girl asked if she could take the book home to share with her little brother, and when others echoed this request, the teacher knew that *The Biggest Bear* would be one of their favorite stories.

The next day another child brought his record of *The Biggest Bear* to share with the group, and once more the class relived the story.

In addition to generating enthusiasm about a given story through personal experiences, a teacher's careful guidance may bring about observation and inference concerning plot, characterization, mood, and setting.

The following examples of lessons on children's literature illustrate how children may derive interpretations and definitions of literary attributes through thoughtful questioning.

The Good Master by Kate Seredy was used in an intermediate class. Setting was ascertained by having a child locate Budapest and the Hungarian Plains on a map. Discussion ensued concerning the time (prior to World War I) during which the story takes place.

The following questions were raised in order to bring about the realization of the plot: "At the beginning of the story, what particular feelings did the family have about Kate's actions? What caused her to become more gentle in

her ways? What was the feeling at the end of the story?"
Such questions exemplify the interrelation of story attributes. Through answering such questions a child derives
not only the theme but also the delineations of the characters and their moods and feelings, which in turn convey the
tone of the story.

Direct questioning was instrumental in evoking plot
definitions of the following works. The plot of *Wheel on the
School* was brought out by this question: How do Lina and
the people of the Dutch fishing village get the storks back?
In discussing *My Side of the Mountain* by Jean George, the
children saw that Sam had dozens of problems to solve in
living off the land for a year. In reading *Hans Brinker* by
Mary Mapes Dodge, the teacher helped the children identify
the main plot by asking, "Why does everyone try so very
persistently to restore Raff Brinker's memory?"

As mentioned, investigation of characterization and
mood contributes to the manifestation of the plot. In reading *And Now Miguel* by Joseph Krumgold, the children followed Miguel's experiences as he grows up to be a man in
his father's family. The plot of *Mary Poppins* by L. Travers is
revealed through the following discourse: Mary Poppins
was a magical character, vain and stern. Would you like Mary
to sit beside you? Why? To direct their thinking about the
plot of *Johnny Tremain* by Esther Forbes, the teacher asked
the children how the story would be different if Johnny lived

A library corner in the classroom supplements the school library. (COURTESY OF THE SAN DIEGO
COUNTY SCHOOLS.)

today. In discussing *Henry Huggins* by Beverly Cleary, the teacher asked, "Have you experienced some of the frustrations Henry had? How did Henry meet his problems?" In an activity to develop plot for *The Secret Garden* by Frances Burnett, the teacher suggested that the children portray Mary's bad temper by role playing. Similarly, children may gain understanding of the feelings of the Cratchit family in Dickens's *A Christmas Carol* by reading expressively the episode of Christmas dinner at the Cratchits'.

The following are further examples of developing insights as to the nature of setting, mood, and theme:

The setting of *Blue Willow* by Doris Gates was represented in a mural composed by the class. Attention to illustrations and the author's name suggested the Japanese setting for *Crow Boy* by Taro Yashima. Pictures and slides were used to show the environment for the story *Wheel on the School* by Meindert DeJong. A recording and filmstrip provided setting and mood for the story *The Sorcerer's Apprentice* by H. H. Ewers, translated by Ludwig Lewisohn. In the study of *The Silver Llama* by Alida S. Malkus, pictures of Peru were helpful. A sense of time and place setting was developed for *The Tree of Freedom* by Rebecca Caudill by making a table map of clay showing the mountain and the passes in Kentucky at the beginning of the westward movement.

Children may particularly enjoy stories in familiar settings. For example, children from Wisconsin would recognize scenes from *Caddie Woodlawn* by Carol Brink as similar to their own environs. In *King of the Wind* by Marguerite Henry, the teacher explained that Henry lives in Virginia and asked the children why they thought the author could write so vividly about horses. In *Paddle to the Sea* by Holling C. Holling, the children quickly discerned how the illustrations show the beauty of the Great Lakes, the St. Lawrence, and the Atlantic.

The teacher developed sensitivity to mood in the following stories by asking appropriate questions: How is a mood of suspense created in *Matchlock Gun* by Walter Edmonds? In *Call It Courage* by Armstrong Sperry, the children felt the excitement of being marooned on a desert island and sighed with relief at the outcome of the story. They admired the courage of Mafatu. They were asked these questions: what makes this story exciting? What other feelings do you have as you read the story? In *The Story of Doctor Dolittle* by Hugh Lofting, although the animals are continually in trouble and are fearful, the story is very humorous. The children were asked: Why is this story so funny? Do you like this kind of humor?

An awareness of theme was developed by discussion of the main idea in a story. In *Beatinest Boy* by Jesse Stuart, the teacher asked, "What is the relationship of the boy and his grandmother?" After reading *Apple and the Arrow* by Mary Buff and Conrad Buff, the children were asked how the Swiss people won their struggle for freedom against the Austrian tyrant, Gessler. Before reading *Door in the Wall* by Marguerite De Angeli, the children saw a filmstrip showing the fortification of a castle so that they would be better able to visualize the difficulties of the small invalid boy who was able to save a castle.

It is hoped that the foregoing discussion will provide a useful resource for the teacher in involving her students in the quest for meaning in literature and in the appreciation of the value of studying literature.

Sources of Children's Literature

In recent years one of the great changes in publishing emphasis has taken place in the area of children's literature. Today nearly every major publishing house has a children's editor who selects or develops manuscripts for books suited to the interests and abilities of modern children. There are some publishers who specialize in books for young readers. There are over four thousand new titles published each year for children and youths in the United States.

The bulk of this material is of only temporary importance, as is true for most fiction and nonfiction published for adults. But many books of real worth may go undiscovered because busy teachers and parents do not have the time to keep informed in this rapidly expanding field.

An early task for one preparing to teach is to explore this segment of the child's world. At first, read at all grade levels in order to find out what type of material is available. Later, concentrate on the grade levels that most concern you.

One source of information concerning children's literature is the *Children's Catalog* published by The H. W. Wilson Company, New York. This is primarily a reference work for use in libraries. In it are listed recently published books considered of highest merit as well as works of the past of enduring value. If you are establishing a library for the first time, you will find in it a special list recommended for initial purchase as a nucleus for future growth. The *Children's Catalog* is expensive and therefore should be made available by the school district with library funds.

A promising guide to children's literature is *Children's Literature Review,* Volume 1 (Block and Riley, 1976) and Volume 2 (Riley, 1976). A resource that is published semiannually, the *Children's Literature Review* provides critical reviews of selected works, submitted by well-known children's authors and book reviewers. A biographical sketch is given of each author along with the plots of the works represented.

Other sources of children's literature that may be consulted are *The Bowker Annual* (published yearly), *Children's Books in Print, Subject Guide to Children's Books in Print, Index to Children's Poetry, Negro Heritage Reader for Young People,* and *Index to Black Poetry.*

In order to recognize merit and to direct the attention of the public to children's literature, a number of awards are made each year. The John Newbery Medal is awarded to the book considered the most distinguished contribution to American literature for children. Following is a list of the most recent Newbery Medal winners.

The Caldecott Medal honors the best-illustrated book for children. The most recent winners of the Caldecott Medal are listed below.

Newbery Medal awards

Title	Author	Date and publisher
Sounder	William Armstrong	1970; Harper
The Summer of the Swans	Betsy Byars	1971; Viking
Mrs. Frisby and the Rats of NIMH	Robert O'Brien	1972; Atheneum
Julie of the Wolves	Jean George	1973; Harper
The Slave Dancer	Paula Fox	1974; Bradbury
M. C. Higgins the Great	Virginia Hamilton	1975; Macmillan
The Grey King	S. Cooper	1976; M. K. McElderry/Atheneum
Roll of Thunder, Hear My Cry	M. D. Taylor	1977; Dial
Bridge to Terabithia	Catherine Patterson	1978; Crowell

Caldecott Medal awards

Title	Author	Date and publisher
Sylvester and the Magic Pebble	William Steig	1970; Windmill/Simon and Schuster
A Story—A Story: An African Tale	Gail Haley	1971; Atheneum
One Fine Day	Nonny Hogrogian	1972; Macmillan
The Funny Little Woman	Arlene Mosel	1973; Dutton
Duffy and the Devil	Harvey and Margot Zemach	1974; Farrar
Arrow to the Sun	Gerald McDermott	1975; Viking
Why Mosquitoes Buzz in People's Ears: A West African Tale	Retold by V. Aardema	1976; Dial
Ashanti to Zulu: African Traditions	Margaret Musgrove	1977; Dial
Noah's Ark	Peter Spier	1978; Doubleday

There are other awards that call attention to books of merit. These include The Laura Ingalls Wilder Award and The Regina Medal. In Canada there are two Book-of-the-Year-for-Children medals. The Hans Christian Andersen Award is an international children's book award. In England the Carnegie Medal and Kate Greenway Medal correspond to the Newbery and Caldecott awards in the United States. There are awards given in France, Germany, Norway, Sweden, and Switzerland for outstanding children's books published each year in these countries.

The book reviews that appear in *The Horn Book, Childhood Education, Elementary English, The New York Times, The Christian Science Monitor,* and *Kirkus Reviews* provide other sources of aid in selecting books for children.

The Children's Book Council, 175 Fifth Avenue, New York, New York, 10011, promotes the nationwide Book Week. Posters, book jackets, wall charts, and other materials are available for school use at very low cost.

With all this emphasis on newness it must not be forgotten that we share a great cultural heritage from the past. There are constant references in our language that assume that we know the meaning of such expressions as "my man Friday," "the golden touch," "the patience of Job," and "whitewashing the fence."

Anthologies of children's literature contain collections of old and new verse, fairy tales and folktales, short selections from modern writers, notes on authors and illustrators of children's books, and excellent suggestions for their classroom use. In time most elementary teachers will want to purchase one of these anthologies to keep on their desks as a constant source of classroom material. A book of this nature is as basic to good instruction as chalkboard and chalk, but some districts hesitate to spend funds for individual teacher references. In that case the teacher has no choice but to purchase the book as a basic tool of the profession and use the expense as a tax deduction.

The *Anthology of Children's Literature* by Edna Johnson, Evelyn R. Sickels, and Frances Clark Sayers, published by Houghton Mifflin Company, and *Story and Verse for Children* by Miriam Blanton Huber, pub-lished by Macmillan Publishing Co., Inc., are outstanding single-volume collections. May Hill Arbuthnot has written several books: *Time for True Tales, Time for Fairy Tales, Time for Poetry,* and *Children and Books,* all published by Scott, Foresman and Company.

A number of special bibliographies have been issued to help teachers locate material appropriate to the needs of a child. Some of them are periodically brought up to date. The following are helpful: *Reading Ladders for Human Relations,* edited by V. M. Reid (Washington, D.C.: American Council on Education, 1972); *Behavior Patterns in Children's Books* by Clara J. Kircher (Washington, D.C.: Catholic University Press); *About 100 Books, a Gateway to Better Group Understanding* by Ann G. Wolfe (New York: The American Jewish Committee Institute of Human Relations); and Ethel Newell, "At the North End of Pooh: A Study of Bibliotherapy," *Elementary English* (January 1957). Leland Jacobs of Columbia University has provided a series of four programs for adults about children's books that is available in *How to Choose Children's Books* (Board of Missions of the Methodist Church Service Center, 7820 Reading Road, Cincinnati, Ohio 45237).

In the area of children's literature we are endowed with great riches. Our problem is to share them with wisdom.

For Discussion

1. What sources of information concerning new books for children are available in your teaching community? What responsibility must a teacher assume for this information to be used?

2. Would you consider such old favorites as *Mrs. Wiggs of the Cabbage Patch* or *Black Beauty* appropriate for contemporary children?

3. How do you explain the popularity of series books with young readers?

4. Comic books are a favorite form of leisure reading for some children. Are they of literary merit? How should such material be handled in school?

5. Have you had an experience that would justify the following statement?

> As children, most of us were turned off and away from literature by teachers' instructions to read selections of prose or poetry to find their "true" meaning—dissecting, analyzing, and finally giving succinct summaries of what the authors were attempting to communicate to us. We came to view literature not as an encounter with life as it is or might be, but as a formal, dull learning experience in which the teacher engaged in literary criticism with an uninvolved audience.

6. Can you recall reading any book that influenced your beliefs or attitudes?

7. How concerned should parents and teachers be when they discover children reading books that they consider inappropriate? What countermeasures would you suggest?

8. How should such topics as death, divorce, and propaganda be treated in children's literature?

9. Comment on the following statement:

> Children read books, not reviews. They don't give a hoot about the critics. They don't read to find their identity. They don't read to free themselves of guilt, to quench the thirst for rebellion, or to get rid of alienation. They have no use for psychology. They detest sociology. They don't try to understand Kafka or *Finnegan's Wake*. They still believe in God, the family, angels, devils, witches, goblins, logic, clarity, punctuation, and other such obsolete stuff. They love interesting stories, not commentary, guides, or footnotes. When a book is boring they yawn openly, without any shame or fear of authority. They don't expect their beloved writer to redeem humanity. Young as they are, they know that it is not in his power. Only the adults have such childish illusions. [Singer, quote from *Saturday Review,* March 21, 1970, p. 18]

How Can Teachers Involve Parents in the Literature Program?

Our objectives in the teaching of literature will never be realized if our efforts are limited to what can be accomplished in the school day. Appreciation of literature as a personal enrichment takes time. The rhythm of the school day, with its schedules and demands, is not right for some literature. It is when the reader is alone, unscheduled and undisturbed, that a story can truly come alive. But children will complain that they do not have time to read at home. There is so much time needed for music lessons, homework, chores—and television. Once the "rhythm of the night" was the inspiration of storytelling. Parents shared the stories of their youth and children discovered the world of imaginative writers. Today the rhythm of the night has come to mean the sound of ricocheting bullets on television, the wearisome exhortations of announcers, and the tasteless prolixity of commercials. Somehow we must work with parents to find time for children to read. Our first task is to show parents the values of literature in contrast to the thirty-minute exercises in violence or inanity of TV drama. Annis Duff's book *Bequest of Wings* tells of the joys shared by a family as modern books were used in the home. If a teacher cannot get parents to read this book, it might be wise to discuss it with them at a parent-teacher meeting or conference.

Most parents will respond to the teacher's appeal for their help in providing good books for their children. Explain to them why we need so many children's books and how difficult it is to secure the right ones. Suggest that at Christmas or on a birthday they buy a book for their child that might be shared with the class. A group of parents and teachers might suggest a list of books to be purchased or the criteria to be followed when buying books for children.

Ownership of a book means a great deal to a child. A recent study asked the members of a sixth-grade class to list their three favorite books. The final list failed to correspond to any bibliography of children's books, but one element was noted: If a child owned a book it was listed as a favorite.

Another way of making parents aware of the material available for children is a planned summer reading program. As summer approaches, a fifth-grade class might ask the sixth grade to suggest books that it would enjoy. The fifth-graders should also note the books their class has enjoyed but which some members have not

Letting children browse in a bookstore is one way the parent may encourage children to discover the fun of reading.
(PHOTO BY LINDA LUNGREN.)

had time to read. From these two sources each child might select six or eight books that he plans to read during the summer. A simple folder or notebook can be made and used for an early report at the beginning of the next school year.

When parents sponsor a book fair they discover the modern world of children's literature. Material for such an enterprise can be secured from the magazine *Scholastic Teacher* (50 West 44th Street, New York).

Parents are sometimes concerned about the expense of children's books. It does seem like an extravagance to pay $3 for a picture book that only takes twenty minutes to read. Nancy Larrick, in *A Parent's Guide to Children's Reading,* makes an important point by comparing the costs of good books with toys, and then pointing out that long after the toys are broken or dis-

carded the books are still available for rereading. This is one criterion to use in buying a book: Will it be worth rereading? If not, don't buy it. There are other sources for books of only temporary interest.

There are good, inexpensive books available. *Scholastic Magazines* publishes a series of paperback books for children. These are reprints of the finest modern books available. The E. M. Hale Company of Eau Claire, Wisconsin, also publishes reprints of outstanding children's books. Some of the ''grocery-store'' or ''supermarket'' books are also good. A committee of the P.T.A. might evaluate some of these and suggest a few for purchase.

'' 'Tis a strange sort of poverty to be finding in a rich country.'' These are the words spoken by an immigrant lad in Ruth Sawyer's *The Enchanted School-*

house. Though his words refer to the inadequate and dilapidated school facilities to be found in a wealthy and thriving city in America, they can well apply to all of America today—a land wealthy with a multitude of fine books that children and parents have not discovered.

For Discussion

1. What influence would this poem have on the parents of the children you teach?

MY MOTHER READ TO ME

Long ago on winter evenings,
I recall, my mother read;
There beside our old base-burner
Just before my prayers were said.

Here she gave me friends aplenty,
Friends to fill my life for years;
Meg and Jo and Sister Amy
For little Beth I shed my tears.

Scrooge and Tim and Mrs. Wiggs
Robin Hood and Heidi too,
Young Jim Hawkins and his treasure
Saved from Silver's pirate crew.

Can it be that one small lady
Could, just by her magic voice,
Change a room so, in a twinkling
To the scenes from books so choice?

Poor we were, as some might count us,
No fine house, our clothes threadbare,
But my mother read me riches
From the books she chose with care.

Now in times of fear and struggle
When woe and want about me crowd,
I can use reserves of courage
From the books she read aloud.

E. H. Frierwood

2. Is involvement through concern for the reading of all children a better approach than one of concern for a specific child?

How Is Poetry Presented in the Modern Curriculum?

Our culture is rich in poetic tradition. In many communities there is a Longfellow School or one named for Lowell, Whitman, Field, or Stevenson. The respect for poetry was reflected in the curriculum of the recent past, which frequently specified selections that were to be studied and memorized in each grade. Some schools had as many as a hundred ''pieces'' to be mastered in the seventh and eighth grades.

This requirement was intended to ensure that each child would know this aspect of our cultural heritage. Although it was recognized that some of this material was beyond the understanding of the students, and that memorization added a burdensome routine, teachers sincerely felt that eventually this material would enrich lives. Many adults today get great satisfaction in reciting ''Abou Ben Adhem'' or ''Snowbound.'' Some will say, ''This poem did not mean much to me when I was in school but each year I seem to enjoy it more.'' On the other hand, some who were taught this way learned to detest poetry and still think of it as a disciplinary activity.

In the curriculum of the past, poetry was frequently associated with programs. One learned a piece to recite on Friday afternoon or at a parents' meeting. Grandparents especially were delighted with this accomplishment and usually rewarded the speaker with a gift. Contests were held in which all the participants recited ''The Highwayman.'' Audiences would spend an afternoon listening to ten or more elocutionists repeat the same selection.

Good poetry is sometimes found in popular magazines and daily papers. Although many of these poems are of transient value, some very good material undoubtedly goes unrecognized in the great mass of published verse. Some of the more talented poets of our day may turn to songwriting or prose because of the greater financial returns involved. Just as such poems as ''Trees'' and ''America, the Beautiful'' have been made into fine songs, the lyrics of many popular songs have merit as verse.

In a modern classroom poetry serves many purposes and needs. It is used to enrich all curriculum areas. Modern anthologies contain a great deal of verse appropriate to the age and reading level of the child for whom the book is intended, although this places a severe limitation on the choice of material. May Hill Arbuthnot has a useful collection in *Time for Poetry* that the teacher reads to children rather than having them read it aloud themselves.

Most teachers today start with the children with whom they work rather than with a collection of poetry which they feel must be mastered. They recognize the truth of Carl Sandburg's statement:

Poetry for any given individual depends on the individual and what his personality requires as poetry. Beauty depends on personal taste. What is beauty for one person is not for another. What is poetry for one person may be balderdash or hogwash for another. [Sandburg, 1930, p. 20]

The teacher seeks to present material that will meet the immediate appreciation level of students as well as build sensitivity for growth in appreciation. Many teachers keep a file of poetry and draw from it when appropriate throughout the school day. As the seasons change, verses are used to express the children's feelings or to call attention to the flight of birds or the budding of our pussywillow. Holidays are made special days through poems that may be used as the theme of a bulletin board display. In social studies, the life of the Indian becomes more accessible as the group recites a Navaho prayer or chant. On the playground the ideals of fair play and good sportsmanship are remembered because a verse suggests meaningful behavior. Throughout each day and year the child grows in perception and understanding through the planned use of poetry. He learns to listen to words for both meaning and sound. He finds that some words create an atmosphere that is sad or frightening, whereas others have a warm or relaxing effect.

To accomplish this, the teacher starts with herself. Teachers who experience the most difficulty at the beginning are those who have a love for great poetry yet are unwilling to discover the appreciation level of the children with whom they work. Walt Whitman's "When Lilacs Last in the Dooryard Bloom'd" will probably not be accepted by a student who delights in "Little Orphan Annie" by Riley. The most important consideration in selection of material is to avoid any value judgment as to what children *should* like. Stated positively, the most important consideration is to discover what they *do* like.

Start by reciting a poem to the children. Avoid any discussion of word meanings. Children do not need to understand every word in order to enjoy a poem. After you have recited it, a child may ask what a certain word means. If he does, by all means tell him in a sentence or two. Then repeat the poem a second time. Select for recitation a few of the very best children's poems.

Reading poetry to the children requires preparation. The teacher should read the verse aloud to herself, noting the punctuation, the mood of the poem, and any unusual expression or words. Before reading aloud, a few remarks help the listener orient himself. Introduce "Little Orphan Annie" in this manner: "Here is a poem your parents liked, and I think you will like it, too. There are a few words like *hearth* and *rafter* that you may not know; they mean. . . ." Then, the teacher might ask a few questions after the first reading. Appropriate ones would be "Why do you suppose the author repeats the words *If you don't watch out?* Notice how they are written in the poem to show how they might be read." After the children have been shown the printed poem, another question would be "How do you feel when you hear the words *the lamp wick sputters and the wind goes whooo?* What was the writer trying to do?" If the children wish, the teacher might read the poem a second time, then place it on the reading table for those who wish to read it themselves.

Some children will bring poems they have found and offer to read them to the class. Others will respond to the invitation to bring poems for the teacher to read. Reading poetry aloud is difficult, and many children do not do it well. As a result it may be a deadly listening experience. We want to develop good listening habits, but there are better ways of doing it than by forcing attention to poorly read poetry.

The poems found in children's readers are much more fun to read if they have first been heard with pleasure. These selections are the basis for instruction concerning the oral reading of poetry, but that instruction should follow an appreciative listening. Good oral reading is largely imitative and the example followed should be a worthy one. It is the poet who has to speak through the oral reader. It is not the reader speaking poetry. May Hill Arbuthnot gives the following advice about one of the problems teachers face:

If you discover a group of children or young people who groan, "Oh, not poetry!", it means one of several things. They have been fed poems too old, too difficult or too "precious" for them. Or they have been set to analyzing poetry—finding all the figures of speech, marking the meter, putting the poem into their own words, picking out the most beautiful line or some such nonsense. The cure for these victims is, take it easy. Begin with nonsense verse or the simplest and most objective verses about everyday experiences and activities. After all, you don't start children's musical experiences with symphonies and sonatas. Even John Ciardi, a serious adult poet and poetry critic, starts his own children with nonsense or humorous verse. But please note his verses are never banal doggerel, but skillfully written by a master craftsman.

Another starting point for reluctant poetry-tasters is the narrative or story poem, long or short. The rapid, on-going meter of verse heightens the sense of action and makes the ballad irresistible to children. From "The Night Before Christmas" for the youngest, to the gory old Scotch-English ballads for the oldest, the story poem will hold them enthralled.

In conclusion, never forget that, like music, poetry is an aural art. It should be spoken and heard to be fully understood and enjoyed so read poetry aloud whenever you have a chance. Even at your loan desks, have a book of poems on hand, show it to your youthful customer and say casually, "Listen to this and see if you like it," and read a short one. Even our young teenage sophisticates, when they hear poems vigorously and unaffectedly read, say wonderingly, "Read it again." While the children bounce enthusiastically and cry, "Sing it again!" That is your reward. [May Hill Arbuthnot, 1962, p. 377]

Sometimes a poem is presented by having it read well by the teacher or pupil, then read in unison by the class. At other times a carefully prepared lesson plan helps children identify with the purposes of the poet and the beauty of language used.

Sample Lesson Plan

The following sample lesson plan is intended to be a guide or outline to be expanded on or altered to meet the demands of the individual teaching situation: [3]

GRADE 4: SAMPLE LESSON PLAN FOR TEACHING MARGARET WIDDEMER'S *"THE SECRET CAVERN"*

Objectives

1. To introduce the poetry of introspection.

2. To point out how the speaker's character is revealed through the imaginative experience of the poem.

3. To lead the child to introspect, i.e., to reason about himself, his desires, his imaginative experiences, his actions.

4. To indicate to the child the close affinity that usually exists between his natural desires (his likes and dislikes), his imagined experiences, and his actions.

5. To point out to the child that in many cases when his actions run counter to his desires and plans it is a result of his having thought (reasoned, intellectualized) about those planned courses of action, a result of his visualizing the actions and their consequences. He decided beforehand that the desired action would be wrong or unwise.

Presentation

1. Introduction: Life would be quite dreary if we didn't have any pals or playmates, wouldn't it? I am sure I would be unhappy and lonely if I didn't have any friends. I like to be around people, but there are also times when I like to be alone. Sometimes when I am alone I like to read; sometimes I like to think; and sometimes I like to let my imagination wander.

[3] From *A Curriculum for English Poetry for the Elementary Grades* (Lincoln: University of Nebraska Press, 1966), pp. 21–28.

Perhaps some of you can tell me what you like to do when you are alone?

2. After the children respond, continue: I would like to read a poem to you about an adventurous child whose imagination often wandered.

See if you can tell why I think this is an adventurous child.

THE SECRET CAVERN

Underneath the boardwalk, way, way back,
There's a splendid cavern, big and black—
If you want to get there, you must crawl
Underneath the posts and steps and all.
When I've finished paddling, there I go—
None of all the other children know!

There I keep my treasures in a box—
Shells and colored glass and queer-shaped rocks,
In a secret hiding-place I've made,
Hollowed out with clamshells and a spade,
Marked with yellow pebbles in a row—
None of all the other children know!

It's a place that makes a splendid lair,
Room for chests and weapons and one chair.
In the farthest corner, by the stones,
I shall have a flag with skulls and bones
And a lamp that casts a lurid glow—
None of all the other children know!

Some time, by and by, when I am grown,
I shall go and live there all alone;
I shall dig and paddle till it's dark,
Then go out and man my pirate bark:
I shall fill my cave with captive foe—
None of all the other children know!

Margaret Widdemer

3. Discussion: Now can any of you tell me why I think this is an adventurous child? (Responses will probably be related to the dark cavern. If children are unfamiliar with the word "cavern," explain its similarity to "cave." The children may suggest the "treasures," "chests," "weapons," "flag with skulls and bones" and the "pirate bark.")

4. Why do you suppose there is just one chair? (The child wanted this as a private, secret place.)

5. Do you think the child truly wants to live there all alone when all grown? What tells us in the poem that the child really does like to be around other people? (The child is going to fill the cave with "captive foe.")

6. I am going to read the poem again, and this time I want you to notice what kinds of pictures the poem helps you to see. (Read the poem again. Children often close their eyes while creating images. The atmosphere must be such that the children are relaxed and feel free to close their eyes or put their heads on their desks, if they wish.)

7. Now let's talk about the mental pictures the poem helped us to see. (The children will probably describe the cave, the colorful treasures, and so forth. Try to elicit responses about the feelings they experienced while listening. Some children may think the dark cave seems "spooky." The sensation of "dampness" may also be mentioned by the children. The sound of the paddle of the boat as it swishes in the water is a possible response. At this point the children may be eager to paint or draw the scenes which you and they have pictured.

8. Creative writing: Just think of all the pictures and feelings we have been talking about. By choosing certain words the poet was able to help us see these pictures. Let's see if we can think of a picture we might like to paint using words. We've had so many good ideas about the poem, about secret places and being alone that I think we would all enjoy painting some pictures with words. You might like to describe a place you know—a cave, a treehouse, a quiet place or perhaps your own room. We will need two sheets of paper. We will call one our "Idea Paper." We will jot down on this paper ideas that come to our minds. Then we may want to think about our

ideas for a while and decide how we'd like to put them together. Some of you may want to write a paragraph that will make a picture for us, or help us to "hear" certain sounds. Some of you may want to write a poem using your ideas. Perhaps some of you already have a short story in mind. I see that everyone has his "brush" (holding up pencil) and his "canvas" ready (hold up paper), so let's start "painting." (The teacher who takes this time to write creatively along with the children will see many satisfying results. The experience seems to become more enjoyable and worthwhile to the children when the teacher is writing also. After their poems or paragraphs are finished, the children may want to exchange papers for proofreading or to form into small groups to read them aloud. Compositions could be recopied for a bulletin board or a composition booklet. The central objective is to make certain the experience has been enjoyable for the children and that they feel their compositions are noteworthy.)

Although the feeling for poetry is often caught rather than taught by the informed and enthusiastic teacher, the schools should provide for ever-increasing depths of appreciation. It is not enough to expose children just to the poems they can feel and readily understand. We must expose them also to "a sense of a margin beyond, as in a wood full of unknown glades, and birds and flowers unfamiliar," as Andrew Long said in his introduction to the *Blue Poetry Book*.

Teachers need to expose children to ever-increasing depths of appreciation. Following are some specific ideas and suggestions of poems to use to help children understand the concepts:[4]

1. Enjoyment of rhythm, melody, and story.
   a. *Rhythm*
      "Barbers' Clippers," by Dorothy Baruch—child listens for rhythm in this unrhymed poem.

---

[4] From *Find Time for Poetry*, Primary Curriculum Supplement (Oakland, Calif.: Oakland Public Schools, July 1960).

   b. *Melody*
      "Sea Shells," by Amy Lowell—hear the sea in the alliteration of *s*.
   c. *Story*
      "The Little Elfman," by John Kendrick Bangs—hold a conversation between a child and a puppet elf.
2. Appreciation of seeing one's own experiences mirrored in poetry.
      "Choosing Shoes," by Efrida Wolfe—children tell how they felt when they went shopping for shoes and compare experiences.
3. Projection into a world other than that in which one lives.
      "Radiator Lions," by Dorothy Aldis—a child who lives in a home may be helped to understand George's predicament, living in an apartment, housing unit, etc.
4. Understanding of symbolism and hidden meanings.
      "Boats Sail on the Rivers," by Christina Rossetti—see clouds as ships and rainbow as a bridge.
5. Sensitivity to patterns of writing and literary style.
      "Merry-Go-Round," by Dorothy Baruch. If this poem is put on a chart, young children can note that the shape of the lines as well as the words convey the movement of the merry-go-round.

For Discussion

1. Why do teachers sometimes start with poems they feel children should like rather than with what children do like?

2. What contemporary poetry do you respond to? Share some of the words of popular songs or of the popular poems of Rod McKuen in class. If children are to find satisfaction in poetry, the teacher must find and present poetry that gains a response equal to that she feels toward poetry that speaks to and for her.

3. Why is it unfair to ask children to name a favorite poem?

4. Why do teachers feel more secure presenting a poem by a recognized poet than one containing ideas and rhyme that children enjoy?

5. Should sentimental verse or rhymed doggerel be considered subliterature to be ignored by the school?

How May a Verse Choir Encourage the Classroom Use of Poetry?

The oral reading of poetry has long been a tradition in the British Isles. The verse choir in some areas is as highly organized as an orchestra. High and low voices are balanced to gain special effects and the number in a choir is limited to certain voice qualities. A performance by such a group is as effective as that of a singing choir. We do not seek the same standards with verse choirs in the elementary school. Our primary object is to delight those who are taking part rather than to perfect a performance for the entertainment of others. The result of accomplishing this will be a satisfying self-expression that leads to a high degree of appreciation of the material used.

In achieving this primary objective there are a number of parallel benefits. The shy child feels that he is a contributing member of the group. He is able to participate in a public appearance without any agonizing emotional pressures. The greatest benefits are in the area of speech. The values of precise enunciation and careful pronunciation are obvious to the most slovenly speakers. The slow or fast speaker is made aware of the effect of such speech on the listener. Not only is the quality of voice tone brought to the level of awareness, but also those whose voices are unpleasant receive needed attention.

From the beginning the approach should be one of enjoyment. With any group start with familiar material so that there is no problem of memorization. A favorite with all ages is "Hickory Dickory Dock." After writing it on the chalkboard, the teacher might point out that the poem has the rhythm of a clock ticking. Then add the words *tick-tock* three times at the beginning and end.

Tick-tock, tick-tock, tick-tock
Hickory Dickory Dock
The mouse ran up the clock
The clock struck, One!
The mouse ran down
Hickory Dickory Dock.
Tick-tock, tick-tock, tick-tock

The teacher might say, "Now watch my arm. I will move it as if it were a clock pendulum or metronome. When I go this way, say *tick,* and this way say *tock.* Let's practice it once to see how much we can sound like a clock." After one round of practice, go ahead: "That was fine! Now we will have one row be a clock and tick all the way through the verse while the rest of us say it. Notice that we must pause after the *tick* to allow time for a *tock* sound. We might say the last *tick-tock* very softly as if the clock was stopping."

Later a way might be discussed to emphasize the word *one.* Sometimes emphasis is secured by having only one person say the word, sometimes by clapping hands or ringing a bell, and sometimes simply by having everyone say it louder.

Another verse with a dramatic effect is one with a "wind" idea in it. Have the entire group hum to sound like a wind blowing, then while some continue to hum, the verse is said with the humming quietly fading away at the end. Most children will know "Who Has Seen the Wind?"

Who has seen the wind?
Neither I nor you;
But when the leaves hang trembling
The wind is passing through.

Who has seen the wind?
Neither you nor I;
But when the leaves bow down their heads
The wind is passing by.

Christina Rossetti

Before saying a verse together it is wise to note the punctuation. If a group pauses at the end of each line an unpleasant singsong effect destroys the meaning of the poetry. Sometimes this can be avoided by a slight pause after words that should be emphasized, such as *seen* in the first line or *leaves* in the third.

Usually the signal "Ready, begin" is used for primary children. A hand signal can serve the same purpose. The opening of a closed fist might be the sign to start.

Choral Readings with Refrains

The simplest type of choral reading is that using a refrain. One student may be selected to read the "solo."

THE CHRISTMAS PUDDING

(Read faster and faster with each line.)

Solo:	Into the basin put the plums,
Refrain:	Stirabout, stirabout, stirabout.
Solo:	Next the good white flour comes,
Refrain:	Stirabout, stirabout, stirabout.
Solo:	Sugar and peel and eggs and spice,
Refrain:	Stirabout, stirabout, stirabout.
Solo:	Mix them and fix them and cool them twice,
Refrain:	Stirabout, stirabout, stirabout.

Lillian Taylor

Additional selections may be found at the end of the chapter.

Another simple form is the two-part arrangement. Half of the children say one part and the other half the other part. Question-and-answer poetry is often used for the two-part arrangement.

A third arrangement is the line-a-child pattern. Each child has a chance to speak one or more lines by himself. In some poems certain lines can be spoken by individual children and other lines can be spoken in unison.

THE SONG OF THE POP-CORN

Unison:	Pop-pop-pop!
1st Child:	Says the pop-corn in the pan;
Unison:	Pop-pop-pop!
2nd Child:	You may catch me if you can!
Unison:	Pop-pop-pop!
3rd Child:	Says each kernel hard and yellow;
Unison:	Pop-pop-pop!
4th Child:	I'm a dancing little fellow,
Unison:	Pop-pop-pop!
5th Child:	How I scamper through the heat!
Unison:	Pop-pop-pop!
6th Child:	You will find me good to eat.
Unison:	Pop-pop-pop!
7th Child:	I can whirl and skip and hop.
Unison:	Pop-pop-pop-pop!
	pop!
	Pop!
	POP!!

Louise Abney

Choral Readings Involving a Group

The most difficult of all choral reading is that involving the total group. Much practice is required in speaking together; in drilling on articulation, enunciation, inflection, and pronunciation; and in blending the voices into workable balance while maintaining satisfactory timing. Sometimes it is wise to divide a class into high and low voices.

Solo parts should be used to encourage all children rather than to display a few stars. Frequently solo parts should be spoken by small groups of three or four whose voices are similar.

After children are interested in choir work, they will accept some special speech exercises, such as rolling their heads for relaxation, or such tone exercises as saying *ba, be, bi bo, bu* toward the front of their mouths. If the teacher starts with these, most children think they are ridiculously funny and no worthy results are achieved.

A verse choir should perform because it motivates both effort and interest, but the teacher must avoid the temptation to use material beyond the appreciation level of the children or material unworthy of memorization. At Christmastime little children in their night clothes with candles make an appealing group. A sixth-grade graduation class might prepare a patriotic verse, "I Am an American," from *Book of Americans* by Stephen Vincent Benet. Inviting visitors from another room to hear a choir perform is as motivating as more elaborate presentations.

Poems suitable for choral presentations are provided at the end of this chapter.

For Discussion

1. What were some of the poems you memorized in elementary school? Why did you memorize them?

2. Are the words of any current popular song of poetic quality?

3. What would you do with a poem a child brought to school that you considered not worth spending time on in class?

4. Do you feel that a more analytical approach to poetry should be made in the intermediate grades than is suggested in this chapter?

5. What type of tests should be given to children with respect to poetry taught in the classroom?

What Verse May Be Used with Young Children?

Action verses or finger plays are found in all cultures. The Chinese have them, our American Indians have them, and new ones are invented daily. Friedrich Wilhelm August Froebel, the father of the kindergarten, collected many of his time and called them mother's-play. You may recall the delight you felt as your mother moved your toes and said, "This little piggie went to market, this little piggie stayed home," etc. We suspect that one of the most interesting experiences of childhood is that of self-discovery, and these verses reflect the charm of that experience. The following are among the best known:

PAT-A-CAKE

Pat-a-cake, pat-a-cake, baker's man
Make me a cake as fast as you can.
Roll it, prick it, and mark it with T,
And put it in the oven for Tommy and me.

THUMB MAN

Thumb man says he'll dance,
Thumb man says he'll sing,
Dance and sing my merry little thing,
Thumb man says he'll dance and sing.
Where is thumb man?
Where is thumb man?
Here I am. [*Fist forward with thumb standing.*]

Here I am. [*Other fist forward, thumb standing.*]
How do you do this morning? [*Wriggle one thumb in direction of other.*]
Very well, I thank you. [*Wriggle other thumb.*]
Run away, run away. [*Hands behind back again.*]
[*Can be sung to the tune of "Are You Sleeping?"*]

The poem is repeated with each of the digits of the hand using the following names: *pointer, tall man, ring man,* and *little man.*

In using action plays, it is better to use too few than too many. The fun seems to be in repetition of the familiar favorites. The teacher first demonstrates the entire verse, then asks one or two children to come to the front and do it with her. After that, each line is done by the group and repeated until a few have mastered it. Needless to say, parents delight in watching a verse choir use these materials.

After these become old favorites, children will want to make up their own. To do this, start with a movement such as holding up an arm with the fist closed.

"This is an airplane searchlight,"
[*Arm held up, wrist bent.*]
"It turns to the left," [*Open the fist.*]
"And the airplane came home" [*Movement of both hands of airplane landing.*]
"On a dark, dark night."

Other movements might be holding hands together to indicate something closed, fingers raised as candles on a cake, fingers "walking" to indicate movement either on the table or for an insect on the bend of the arm or opposite palm, fists pounding to indicate marching, building, or loud movements. Soon total body action is needed and eventually one reaches simple pantomime.

When using nursery rhymes, children's names may be substituted for those of the rhyme characters. Let each child select the person he wants to be, to avoid this being used in a way that might hurt the child. Let children join in on a repeated refrain. This may also be done in such a story as "Little pig, little pig, let me in!" "No, no, no, not by the hair of my chinny-chin-

chin.'' Poems involving the use of body and hand motions appear at the end of the chapter.

Supervisors and principals sometimes use finger play as a means of establishing acceptance on the part of little children. A principal who can teach a new one in the kindergarten will always be welcome. Froebel saw in this common interest a mystic relationship. Perhaps he was right. But it is obvious that these simple verses help children to speak better, notice sounds in words, learn about rhyming endings, and gain social recognition in a way that is pleasant to both the child and the teacher.

Action stories may be developed after the pattern of the old nursery rhyme in which one child says, ''I went upstairs,'' and the other child replies, ''Just like me.'' A leader tells a part of a story and the remainder of the group does the action, saying at the same time, ''Just like this.''

LEADER: Goldilocks went for a walk in the forest.
GROUP: Just like this.
LEADER: She stopped to look at a bird.
GROUP: Just like this.
LEADER: The bird said, ''Cheer up! Cheer up!''
GROUP: Just like this, ''Cheer up! Cheer up!''

After reading the story *Copy-Kittens* by Helen and Alf Evans, the children may want to act it as it is reread. Other stories of this nature may be ''played'' as the beginning of creative dramatics.

For Discussion

1. What contemporary activities might be made into body play? Do the following suggest pantomime: airplane beacon, cars parking, flowers blooming, airplane landing?

2. How are finger plays related to the chants of childhood used when jumping rope or playing games? See Ione Opie and Peter Opie, *The Lore and Language of School Children* (London: Oxford University Press, 1959).

What Values Are There in a Teacher's Poetry File?

A poetry file assures the teacher of having interesting material available. Most teachers prefer to put in the file a few old favorites that they know will be used. Without a file it sometimes takes hours to locate such well-known verses as E. L. Thayer's ''Casey at the Bat'' or Joaquin Miller's ''Columbus.''

After teaching the same grade for some time, many teachers prefer to put favorite verse in a notebook classified by the months. The beginning teacher usually finds a card file most convenient. Then as the teacher borrows and clips, she selects those that are most useful. She will then have a collection from which selections are readily available for incorporation into class activities.

There are many ways to organize such a collection. One heading might be *Holiday and Seasonal Poems*. Later these might be divided under the titles *Halloween, Christmas, Chanukah, Valentine's Day, St. Patrick's Day, Winter, Summer, Spring,* and *Fall*. Although there are many poems about holidays, it is sometimes difficult to find one appropriate to your group.

Another broad category for a poetry file might be that of *Curriculum Enrichment*. In time this too could be divided into the various subjects.

In the first grade one teacher used the following poem while her class was studying the post office:

A LETTER IS A GYPSY ELF

A letter is a gypsy elf
It goes where I would go myself;
East or West or North it goes;
Or South, past pretty bungalows,
Over mountain, over hill,
Any place it must and will,
It finds good friends that live so far
You cannot travel where they are.
                    Annette Wynne

In science the following might be used:

CLOUDS

Over the hill the clouds race by
Playing tag in a blue, blue sky;
Some are fat and some are thin.
And one cloud has a double chin.
One is a girl with a turned up nose
And one wears slippers with pointed toes;
There's a puppy dog too, with a bumpity tail,
And a farmer boy with his milking pail.

Sometimes they jumble all in a mass
And get tangled up with others that pass.
And over the hill they go racing by
Playing tag in a blue, blue sky.
    Helen Wing, The Christian Science Monitor

CLOUD NAMES

Cumulus clouds
Drift over the sky,
Fluffy as soapsuds
Billowing by.

Along the horizon
In layers of light
The stratus clouds glow
In the sunset bright.

Cirrus clouds hang
So loosely together
Their cottony film
Means a change of weather.

Nimbus clouds threaten
With blackness of storm
Shut the door, light the fire
Be cozy and warm.
    Los Angeles City Schools

One of the major reasons for having children write poetry is to release strong feelings. Poems that express these feelings for children probably act the same way. There are some children who will find these poems delightful "because they say exactly how I feel." As a category for a poetry file they might be listed under *Expression of Strong Feelings*.

ONE DAY WHEN WE WENT WALKING

One day when we went walking,
    I found a dragon's tooth,
A dreadful dragon's tooth,
    "A locust thorn," said Ruth.

One day when we went walking,
    I found a brownie's shoe,
A brownie's button shoe,
    "A dry pea pod," said Sue.

One day when we went walking,
    I found a mermaid's fan,
A merry mermaid's fan,
    "A scallop shell," said Dan.

One day when we went walking,
    I found a fairy's dress,
A fairy's flannel dress,
    "A mullein leaf," said Bess.

Next time I go walking—
    Unless I meet an elf,
A funny, friendly elf—
    I'm going by myself!
    Valine Hobbs

CHOOSING SHOES

New shoes, new shoes,
    Red and pink and blue shoes.
Tell me, what would you choose,
    If they'd let us buy?

Buckle shoes, bow shoes,
    Pretty, pointy-toe shoes,
Strappy, cappy low shoes,
    Let's have some to try.

Bright shoes, white shoes,
    Dandy-dance-by-night shoes,
Perhaps-a-little-tight shoes,
    Like some? So would I.

    But
Flat shoes, fat shoes,
    Stump-along-like-that shoes,
Wipe-them-on-the-mat shoes,
    That's the sort they'll buy.
    Ffrida Wolfe

Probably the most charming of all poems for children are those that allow adults to regain insight into the child's world, to rediscover the simple ways of life again. Such poetry is childlike rather than childish. In your poetry file you will want a section on *Enrichment of Daily Life*. Those who work with primary children will especially want material by Dorthy Aldis. Another author for this age is Aileen Fisher, who wrote this favorite:

COFFEEPOT FACE

I saw
my face
in the coffeepot.
Imagine
a coffeepot face!
    My eyes
were small
but my nose was NOT
and my mouth
was—every place!
        Aileen Fisher

An example of poetry without rhyme that creates a mood is this poem by Beatrice Schenck De Regniers:

LITTLE SOUNDS

Underneath the big sounds
underneath the big silences
listen for the little secret sounds.
Listen.
ts   ts
That is the little sound of the sugar,
The little loaf of sugar
deep inside the cup of hot black coffee.
ts   ts
That is what the sugar says.

Listen for the little secret sounds.
Sh! be very quiet and listen.
tck tck tck tck tck tck tck tck
That is the little sound of your father's watch.
tck tck tck tck tck tck tck tck
It makes such a tiny hurrying scurrying sound.

Listen for the little sounds always.
When a pussycat licks her fur
can you hear a little sound?
When someone is licking an ice-cream cone
can you hear?
Did you ever hear
a rabbit biting a lettuce leaf?
a cow switching her tail?
a tiny baby breathing?

Listen
to the little sound of
a letter dropping into a letter box,
a pin falling to the floor,
a leaf falling from a tree,
dry leaves crunching under your feet.

Listen to the little secret sound
of a pencil writing on paper,
of a scissors snipping your fingernails,
of a flower stem breaking when you pick a flower.

Listen for the little sounds always—
Listen.
        Beatrice Schenck de Regniers

Primary teachers will want a special section for poems that can be told with the flannel graph. ''Waiting at the Window'' by A. A. Milne requires only three figures: two raindrops and a bright yellow sun. When the teacher first shares the poem, she guides the drops down. On the next telling, a child may do so. Eventually some children will learn the poem because it is so much fun to tell with these flannel figures.

Verses that suggest a way to act will always be popular with teachers. Some of these suggest standards of conduct, others are gentle reminders, and a few use a bit of ridicule to guide behavior.

LITTLE CHARLIE CHIPMUNK

Little Charlie Chipmunk was a talker
Mercy me!
He chattered after breakfast
And he chattered after tea
He chattered to his sister
He chattered to his mother
He chattered to his father

And he chattered to his brother
He chattered till his family
Was almost driven wild
Oh, Little Charlie Chipmunk
Was a very tiresome child.

Helen Cowles le Cron

THREE CHEERS FOR PETER

When Peter eats a lollypop
He doesn't walk or run or hop
He sits upon the bottom stair
Or in the kitchen on a chair
He doesn't try to chew or bite
Or swallow chunks; he just sits tight
And sucks. And he is careful not
To let it make a sticky spot
On furniture. Three cheers for Peter
He's a good safe candy eater.

Alice Hartich

You will find many verses that are worthy of a poetry file simply because they are fun and add humor to life. These include limericks, nonsense verses, and those with clever use of words. The whimsical couplets of Ogden Nash are recorded with musical background. Children especially enjoy his ''The Panther'' (which ends with ''Don't anther'') and his ''The Octopus.''

A bit of wisecracking doggerel like this has its place in your file:

MODERN LIGHT

Twinkle, twinkle little star
I know exactly what you are
You're a satellite in the sky
And why my taxes are so high.

Another group of verses in your file should consist of poems that help the child relate himself to all nature. In the fall children will sense the rhythm of nature when you read to them Rachel Field's ''Something Told the Wild Geese.'' Children who have found animal tracks made in sand or snow may listen with appreciation to ''The Tracks'' by Elizabeth Coatsworth. The following poem employs delicate and sensitive imagery:

SOFT IS THE HUSH OF FALLING SNOW

I like the springtime of the year
When all the baby things appear;
When little shoots of grass come through
And everything is fresh and new.

But, oh, I like the summer, too.
When clouds are soft and skies are blue
Vacation days are full of fun
I like being lazy in the sun.

But when the fall has once begun
I'm glad that summer then is done
I love the frosty biting air
The harvest yield seen everywhere.

But winter is beyond compare
For though the world seems black and bare
It's rest time for the things that grow
And soft is the hush of falling snow.

Emily Carey Alleman

Even arithmetic has been a subject for writers:

COUNTING

Today I'll remember forever and ever
Because I can count to ten.
It isn't an accident any more either,
I've done it over and over again.

I used to leave out five and three
And sometimes eight and four;
And once in a while I'd mix up nine
As seven or two, but not any more.

I count my fingers on one hand first,
And this little pig is one,
And when old thumb goes off to market
That's fine, and one of my hands is done.

So when I open my other hand
And start in counting again
From pick up sticks to big fat hen,
Five, six, seven, eight, nine and ten.

Harry Behn

The effect of reading a poem like ''I Wish'' by Nancy Byrd Turner or ''A Mortifying Mistake'' by

Maria Pratt after a dull arithmetic period will justify all your efforts to create a poetry file.

A MORTIFYING MISTAKE

I studied my tables over and over, and backward and
    forward, too;
But I couldn't remember six times nine, and I didn't know
    what to do,
Till sister told me to play with my doll, and not to bother my
    head.

"If you call her 'Fifty-four' for a while, you'll learn it by
    heart," she said.

So I took my favorite, Mary Ann (though I thought 'twas a
    dreadful shame
To give such a perfectly lovely child such a perfectly horrid
    name),
And I called her my dear little "Fifty-four" a hundred times,
    till I knew
The answer of six times nine as well as the answer of two
    times two.

Next day Elizabeth Wigglesworth, who always acts so
    proud,
Said "Six times nine is fifty-two," and I nearly laughed
    aloud!
But I wished I hadn't when teacher said, "Now Dorothy, tell
    if you can."
For I thought of my doll—and sakes alive!—I answered,
    "Mary Ann!"

Maria Pratt

Poetry that will help us understand other cultures is needed. Poems of this type follow.
From Korea:

SONG OF FIVE FRIENDS

How many friends have I? Count them.
Water and stone, pine and bamboo—
The rising moon on the east mountain,
Welcome, it too is my friend.
What need is there, I say,
To have more friends than five?

They say clouds are fine; I mean the color.
But, alas, they often darken.
They say winds are clear; I mean the sound.

But, alas, they often cease to blow.
It is only the water, then,
That is perpetual and good.

Why do flowers fade so soon
Once they are in their glory?
Why do grasses yellow so soon
Once they have grown tall?
Perhaps it is the stone, then,
That is constant and good.

Flowers bloom when it is warm;
Leaves fall when days are cool.
But O pine, how is it
That you scorn frost, ignore snow?
I know now your towering self,
Straight even among the Nine Springs.

You are not a tree, no,
Nor a plant, not even that.
Who let you shoot so straight;
What makes you empty within?
You are green in all seasons,
Welcome, bamboo, my friend.

Small but floating high,
You shed light on all creation.
And what can match your brightness
In the coal dark of the night?
You look at me but with no words:
That's why, O moon, you are my friend.

author unknown

From Senegal:

FOREFATHERS

Listen more often to things rather than beings.
Hear the fire's voice,
Hear the voice of water,
In the wind hear the sobbing of the trees,
It is our forefathers breathing.

The dead are not gone forever.
They are in the paling shadows
And in the darkening shadows.
The dead are not beneath the ground,
They are in the rustling tree,
In the murmuring woods,
In the still water,

In the flowing water,
In the lonely place, in the crowd;
The dead are not dead.

Listen more often to things rather than beings.
Hear the fire's voice.
Hear the voice of water.
In the wind hear the sobbing of the trees.
It is the breathing of our forefathers
Who are not gone, not beneath the ground,
Not dead.

author unknown

Children need to recognize the poetic appeal in material without rhyme.

GOOD NIGHT

Many ways to spell good night.

Fireworks at a pier on the Fourth of July spell it with red
    wheels and yellow spokes.
They fizz in the air, touch the water and quit.
Rockets make a trajectory and gold-and-blue and then go
    out.

Railroad trains at night spell with a smokestack
    mushrooming a white pillar.

Steamboats turn a curve in the Mississippi crying in a
    baritone that crosses lowland cottonfields to a
    razorback hill.
It is easy to spell good night.
    Many ways to spell good night.

Carl Sandburg

Sharing poems related to the same topic will help children see how different points of view come to be.

You might say to your class, "In these poems each writer is talking about houses. Do they agree in any way?" Then share with them "Sometimes a Little House Will Please" by Elizabeth Coatsworth, "Our House" by Rachel Field, "Our House" by Dorothy Brown Thompson, and "Song for a Little House" by Christopher Morley.

Teachers will find that the building of such a file increases their own appreciation of poetic expression. However, what has been said concerning individual dif-ferences of pupils applies to teachers as well. If you do not truly feel some pleasure and delight in sharing poetry with children, possibly it will be well for you to spend time on those aspects of the curriculum about which you are enthusiastic. In a few cases you may learn with the children or from the children. Start where you are, even if the only poetry that stirs you in any way is "The Star Spangled Banner" or "Home on the Range." That is a beginning.

For Discussion

Evaluate two poems for preschool children, two for third-graders, and two for sixth-graders. This bibliography will locate the sources for you. (Note that asterisked items are for primary grades only.)

Aiken, Joan. *The Skin Spinners: Poems*. New York: Viking, 1976.
Aldis, Dorothy. *Hello Day*. New York: Putnams, 1959.
_____. *All Together*. New York: Putnams, 1952.
*_____. *Is Anybody Hungry?* New York: Putnams, 1964.
Austin, Mary. *The Sound of Poetry*. Boston: Allyn & Bacon, 1963.
Behn, Harry. *The Little Hill*. New York: Harcourt Brace Jovanovich, 1949.
_____. *Windy Morning*. New York: Harcourt Brace Jovanovich, 1956.
_____. *The Wizard in the Well*. New York: Harcourt Brace Jovanovich, 1956.
_____. *Cricket Songs: Japanese Haiku*. New York: Harcourt Brace Jovanovich, 1964.
Cole, William, ed. *Humorous Poetry for Children*. Cleveland: World, 1955.
_____, ed. *Beastly Boys and Ghastly Girls*. Cleveland: World, 1964.
_____, ed. *The Birds and the Beasts Were There: Animal Poems*. Cleveland: World, 1963.
_____. *Oh, What Nonsense!* New York: Viking, 1966.
_____. *Poems for Seasons and Celebrations*. Cleveland: World, 1961.
*De Regniers, Beatrice Schenk. *Something Special*. New York: Harcourt Brace Jovanovich, 1958.
Dwyer, Jane E. *A Book About the Animals and Me; 21 Poems About Animals*. New York: Western, 1971.
Fisher, A. *Cricket in a Thicket*. New York: Scribners, 1963.

————. *Going Barefoot*. New York: Crowell, 1960.

————. *Like Nothing at All*. New York: Crowell, 1962.

*Frank, Josette. *Poems to Read to the Very Young*. New York: Random House, 1961.

Hopkins, Lee Bennett. *Girls Can Too! A Book of Poems*. New York: F. Watts, 1972.

Kuskin, Karla. *Alexander Soames: His Poems*. New York: Harper & Row, 1962.

————. *In the Middle of the Trees*. New York: Harper & Row, 1958.

————. *Square as a House*. New York: Harper & Row, 1960.

————. *The Animals and the Ark*. New York: Harper & Row, 1958.

————. *The Rose on My Cake*. New York: Harper & Row, 1964.

Lewis, Richard. *In a Spring Garden*. New York: Dial, 1965.

————. *The Moment of Wonder: A Collection of Chinese and Japanese Poetry*. New York: Dial, 1964.

Livingston, Myra Cohn. *I'm Hiding*. New York: Harcourt Brace Jovanovich, 1961.

————. *Listen Children, Listen: An Anthology of Poems for the Very Young*. New York: Harcourt Brace Jovanovich, 1972.

————. *See What I Found*. New York: Harcourt Brace Jovanovich, 1962.

*————. *Wide Awake*. New York: Harcourt Brace Jovanovich, 1959.

McCord, David. *Far and Few*. Boston: Little, Brown, 1925.

————. *Take Sky*. Boston: Little, Brown, 1961.

Merriam, Eve. *Catch a Little Rhyme*. New York: Atheneum, 1966.

————. *It Doesn't Always Have to Rhyme*. New York: Atheneum, 1964.

————. *There Is No Rhyme for Silver*. New York: Atheneum, 1962.

Milne, A. A. *Now We Are Six*. New York: Dutton, 1927.

————. *When We Were Very Young*. New York: Dutton, 1924.

Nash, Ogden. *A Boy Is a Boy*. New York: Watts, 1960.

————. *Custard the Dragon*. Boston: Little, Brown, 1959.

————. *Parents Keep Out*. Boston: Little, Brown, 1951.

————, ed. *The Moon Is Shining Bright as Day*. Philadelphia: Lippincott, 1953.

————. *The Pocket Book of Ogden Nash*. New York: Pocket Books, 1955.

O'Neill, Mary. *Hailstones and Halibut Bones*. Garden City, N.Y.: Doubleday, 1964.

————. *People I'd Like to Keep*. Garden City, N.Y.: Doubleday, 1965.

————. *What Is That Sound?* New York: Atheneum, 1966.

————. *Words, Words, Words*. Garden City, N.Y.: Doubleday, 1966.

Orska, Krystyna. *Illustrated Poems for Children; A Special Collection*. Northbrook, Illinois: Hubbard, 1973.

Powell, Meredith. *What to Be?* Chicago: Childrens Press, 1972.

Tripp, Wallace. *A Great Big Ugly Man Came Up and Tied His Horse to Me; A Book of Nonsense Verse*. New York: Little, Brown, 1973.

Worth, Valerie. *Small Poems*. New York: Farrar, Straus and Giroux, 1972.

Should a Teacher Read to Children?

There are many books that children enjoy and need to know before they have achieved the ability to read them independently. Shared experiences act as bridges between those involved. The quiet moments with a parent while Huckleberry Finn drifts down the Mississippi or with an entire class as the teacher leads it through *Alice in Wonderland* or Dorothy's wonderful land of Oz establish kindred spirits and high morale.

In many schools throughout the nation teachers read selected books to children. In the intermediate grades the first fifteen minutes after lunch is usually set aside for this purpose. While the pupils relax after strenuous play, the teachers read from old and new classics. Favorites include Lewis Carroll's *Alice in Wonderland*, Joel Chandler Harris's *Uncle Remus Stories*, Virginia Sorensen's *Miracles on Maple Hill*, L. Frank Baum's *The Wonderful Wizard of Oz*, E. B. White's *Charlotte's Web*, Betty MacDonald's *Mrs. Piggle Wiggle's Magic*, Kenneth Grahame's *The Wind in the Willows*, Walter Edmond's *The Matchlock Gun*, Glen Round's *Blind Colt*, Lucretia Hole's *The Peterkin Papers*, Armstrong Sperry's *Call It Courage*, Hildegarde Swift's *Railroad to Freedom*, Alfred Olivant's *Bob, Son of Battle*, Rudyard Kipling's *The Jungle Book*, Howard Pyle's *Otto of the Silver Hand*, Glen Round's *Ol Paul the Mighty Logger*, A. Sommerfelt's *Road to Agra*, Margot Benary-Isbert's *The Ark*, Mark

"Ear literacy" is far ahead of reading literacy throughout the elementary school. In many schools throughout the nation teachers read selected books to children. (PHOTO BY LINDA LUNGREN.)

Twain's *The Adventures of Tom Sawyer,* and the many books about space travel.

Preparation for Oral Reading

There are only a few hints that the teacher needs to remember to be a good oral reader. First, enjoy the story yourself. If it is a book that you do not mind rereading as each new group of children comes to your room, you can be certain not only that the book is worthy of your efforts but also that your appreciation will be sensed by the children. Second, interpret the mood and differentiate between the principal characters in dialogues; be a bit dramatic when the plot is exciting, but don't explain the action while reading. Let some of the new words be interesting enough for the children to discover their meaning from the context; if there is a moral, let the listener discover that too. Third, because of time limitations, scan a new book and note the good stopping places. Sometimes it spoils a story just as it does a movie to come in late or to have the film break in the middle of a scene. Finally, always keep in mind that your purpose is to guide the children toward an appreciation of good literature and excellent writing. This period is not a time to spend with material of only passing interest or mass production quality.

Reading to Young Children

Reading a picture book to little children requires special preparation. The books for kindergarten and primary children must be selected with care. Although little children will respond to almost any material presented by a teacher whom they love and respect, it should always be kept in mind that the materials read establish the standards the children will form for later reading. A book such as *Petunia* by Roger Duvoisin presents animals with childlike characters with which the child easily identifies. Humanized machines in books such as *Mike Mulligan and His Steam Shovel* and *The Little Engine that Could* tie together the worlds of fantasy and reality. The humanized animals of the old, old favorite *Peter Rabbit* continue to charm children because of their intimacy with all living things. Rhyme adds charm but is not necessary. To be avoided at this level are stories with dialect; fairy tales of giants, dragons, and cruel stepmothers; and stories that are overemotional or overexciting.

The story should be short or in episodes that cover easily divided parts. Establish standards as to behavior during story reading. Routines should be known to all so that stories are expected at certain times or at a certain signal. Children should not be expected to stop an especially interesting activity without a "getting ready" or "finishing up" time. At the beginning, some teachers prefer to start the story hour with only a part of the group.

To regain a wandering child's attention, call him softly by name, or smile directly at him to bring his attention back to your voice. In some groups, the more mature may need to work together. This may be the beginning group for the story hour while others rest or color. The teacher usually does as much telling as reading, using the pictures in the book to guide the questions and interest of the listeners.

Although it may be handled well by some teachers, a child's retelling of the stories read seldom holds the attention of other children. A story book brought from home should be identified as "Billy's book." After the teacher has examined the material, she may feel that the stories are appropriate for the group. Otherwise, a chance to see and talk about the pictures usually satisfies everyone.

To help some develop better habits, two children may be chosen to sit on each side of the teacher. These children in turn help show the pictures in the book. A special honor on a birthday or when there is a new baby at home might be to select an old favorite for the teacher to read that day. It is well to remember that some children have never listened to a story read to them before coming to school.

One of the major purposes of presenting a book to a child of this age is to enable him to select the book to peruse with pleasure by himself. Watch children as they thumb through a new set of library books. They will pick one up, glance through a few pages, then discard it for another. In many classrooms it is wisest to put books on the library table only after they have been read to the children. With this experience, the child can make a meaningful selection. Here are nine suggestions for reading a picture book:

1. Gather the children closely around you either on low chairs or on the floor.
2. Sit in a low chair yourself.
3. Perform unhurriedly.
4. Handle the book so that children can see the pages at close range.
5. Know the story well enough so that you do not need to keep your eyes on the page at all times.
6. Point out all kinds of minute details in pictures so

that pupils will look for them each subsequent time they handle the book.

7. Encourage laughter and spontaneous remarks.
8. Make illustrations as personal as possible by relating them to the pupils' own experiences.
9. Impart your own enjoyment of the book.

Many teachers feel that there should be no interruptions the first time a story is presented. With a picture book the reader and listener are involved in a rhythm of learning the words and seeing the pictures. The reader does not intrude anything, such as explanations of word meanings or personal reactions. For some children and some books this is the only way a story should be read. In many cases the first reading of a story should proceed in this way so that the total book experience will be felt by the child. For other books and other children careful attention to detail and involvement through personal association with story incidents enrich the experience. Experience will determine the most effective procedure for a new teacher.

Here is the way one teacher presented *Wag Tail Bess* by Marjorie Flack: [5]

Boys and girls, the name of our story today is *Wag Tail Bess*. [*Run fingers under the title from left to right.*] Can anyone tell me what kind of a dog this is on the cover? [*Accept all suggestions.*] Maybe the story will tell us. [*Open the book.*] This is an envelope that shows that this book belongs to the library. This little card in the envelope says our class has the book and this slip of paper tells us when the book must go back to the library. This is done to remind us that other children would like to read the book when we have finished it. That is why children should not tear out such things. Sometimes inside the cover of a book there are very interesting pictures that tell us what the book is about. What do you see on these end papers? Yes, there is the dog again. There is an old friend of ours. Do you remember Angus? Do you think those are ducks or geese? Maybe the story will tell us. There is one other little animal on this page. Yes, there is a little kitten. You can just see his tail. [*Turn the page.*] This is the title page. There again is the title, "Wag Tail Bess."

[5] From Marie E. Taylor, "Instant Enrichment," *Elementary English* (February 1968), 229–233.

And this is the name of the person who wrote the story, Marjorie Flack. At the bottom it tells the name of the company that published the book. [*Turn the page and read.*]

Once there was an Airedale puppy. (*Aside:* Yes, you were right, John, the dog is an Airedale.) Once there was an Airedale puppy and she was named Wag Tail Bess because her mother's name was Bess and her father's name was Wags. But Wag Tail Bess never wagged her tail or stuck up her ears or smiled as an Airedale should, so she was called plain Bess.

Bess was so shy she was afraid of almost everything although she was big enough to know better. [*Look at the pictures of Bess.*] See how afraid she looks. [*Continue reading.*] When Bess was outdoors she was afraid to come indoors, and when she was indoors she was afraid to go outdoors. When Bess was taken walking she was afraid to walk forward, so she would try to walk backward, and when she couldn't go backward—she would lie down. [*Show the pictures.*] See how Bess would pull back. Notice the other dogs looking at Bess. What do you suppose they were thinking? [*Continue reading.*] Bess was even afraid to eat her dinner. She would sniff at it on this side and sniff at it on that side, until at last she would get so hungry she would gulp down her dinner without chewing it at all. [*When you reach the words* get so hungry, *read them slowly and show them to the children.*] Then Bess would be afraid because her tummy ached. [*Look at Bess.*] This is the way she would eat. This is the way she felt when her tummy ached. [*Continue reading.*] At nighttime Bess was afraid of a strange, black creature. Sometimes it was small and sometimes it was large, but always it would stay with Bess wherever she went; crawling on the floor and climbing up the stairs and down the stairs, and sometimes on the wall. What do you think it was? [*Show the picture.*] Yes, it was her shadow. How do you feel about Bess? Don't you feel a little sorry for her?

One day when Bess was outdoors because she was afraid to go indoors, she heard these sounds come from the yard next door: "Meowww! Quack, Quack! Wooof-Wooof!" [*Show the picture and repeat the sounds as you point at the words. Turn the page while the children are still watching the page. Read while they look.*] Then up in the tree jumped a cat! [*Again while they are looking at the book turn the page and while they look, read.*] Through the hedge came scuttling a duck, then came [*again read while they watch the action of the story in the pictures*] another duck! And then came [*turn the page*] Angus! (See the ducks and the cat and Angus. What will happen now? Well let's read and see.)

The foregoing excerpt is enough to show how one teacher would conduct a typical story hour session. Such a procedure takes time but it is effort well invested. A teacher who takes such pains to ensure her pupils a pleasant acquaintance with a picture book is providing those pupils with many later periods of recurring pleasure. They will relive in imagination all the activities she described, enjoy again the color and detail of the pictures, and rediscover familiar details in the scenes she has pointed out. The book will become a familiar friend which they will enjoy again and again.

Recommended Books for Oral Reading

The revised list of books that follows was originally prepared by Taylor (1968). It has been classroom tested. However, success in one situation does not guarantee a response in another.

Kindergarten

Angelo the Naughty One, by Helen Garrett. Viking, 1944. Children love this story about a boy who hates to take baths.

Angus and the Ducks, by Marjorie Flack. Viking, 1944. A favorite picture book about a sassy little scottie. Other books in the series are *Angus Lost* and *Angus and the Cat.*

Bedtime for Frances, by Russell Hoban. Harper, 1960. A badger child tries to delay bedtime just as other children do.

The Biggest Bear, by Lynd Ward. Houghton, 1952. A Caldecott Medal Book about a boy's pet bear cub that becomes overwhelming when he grows up. *Nic of the Woods,* by the same author, is equally successful as a dog story.

Blueberries for Sal, by Robert McCloskey. Viking, 1948. Anticipation is strong in this story about Sal and her mother, and little bear and his mother, getting all mixed up while gathering blueberries.

Contrary Woodrow, by Sue Felt. Doubleday, 1958. About kindergarten and Valentine's Day.

The Country Bunny and the Little Gold Shoes, by DuBose Heyward. Houghton, 1939. A favorite Easter story.

Curious George, by H. A. Rey. Houghton, 1941. Only one of many monkey stories: *Curious George Flies a Kite; Curious George Learns the Alphabet; Curious George Goes to the Hospital;* and others.

Daddies, by Lonnie C. Carton. "Tender, amusing rhymes about daddies and their children."

Edith and Mr. Bear, by Darr Wright. Doubleday, 1964. All the Darr Wright books are highly recommended.

George and the Cherry Tree, by Aliki. Dial, 1964. One of the few simple picture books available for seasonal demand.

The Happy Lion, by Louise Fatio. McGraw, 1934. All the people who visited the zoo were the lion's friends until he got out of the cage. More titles in this series.

The Magic Tree, by Gerald McDermott. Landmark Productions, 1973. A story of twins, one ugly, one handsome, and their lives in the African heartland.

Make Way for Ducklings, by Robert McCloskey. Viking, 1941. A family of mallard ducks makes their home in the middle of Boston. Outstanding Caldecott Award book.

May I Bring a Friend? by Beatrice S. De Regniers. Atheneum, 1964. Children are carried away as each successive caller at the queen's tea party is more ridiculous. Rare illustrations and delightful rhymes.

No Roses for Harry, by Gene Zion. Harper, 1958. Indomitable Harry knows that no self-respecting dog would wear a sweater with roses, even one knitted by Grandma.

Old MacDonald Had a Farm, by Pam Adams. Grosset Publishers, 1976. A mildly amusing version of this familiar rhyme. Each new animal appears in a cutout.

Paddy's Christmas, by Helen Monsell. Knopf, 1942. A bear story with the subtle meaning of Christmas.

Read-to-Me Storybook, by the Child Study Association of America. Crowell, 1947. Excellent collection of contemporary stories for young children.

The Red Balloon, by Albert Lamorisse. Doubleday, 1957. An imaginative picture book that leads to discussion.

Rosebud, by Ed Emberly. Little, 1966. Delightful turtle story.

Swimmy, by Leo Lionni. Pantheon, 1963. Like *Rosebud,* a book for sharp eyes. *Inch by Inch,* by the same author-illustrator, uses the concept of size.

Told Under the Blue Umbrella, by the Association for Childhood Education International. Macmillan, 1933. Excellent collection of recommended stories for children.

The Train, by David McPhail. Little, Brown, 1977. A boy and his train play in the middle of the night.

Willy Bear, by Mildred Kantrowitz. Parent's Magazine Press, 1976. A well-done story about the anxieties a small boy faces on his first day at school.

You Can't Catch Me, by Joan Kahn. Harper, 1976.

First Grade

Andy and the Lion, by James Daugherty. Viking, 1938. Andy, who likes to read about lions, meets one on his way to school. The thorn-pulling episode is a modern version of *Androcles and the Lion.*

Babar and Father Christmas, by Jean deBrunhoff. Random, 1949. A fine introduction to the other Babar books. Children squeal when Babar falls through the roof.

The Five Chinese Brothers, by Claire Bishop. Coward, 1938. A modern classic. Exaggeration and repetition delight youngsters.

Giants, Indeed! by Virginia Kahl. Scribners, 1974. A humorous story about a boy who assumes giants are his size and what happens when he meets a family of giants.

The Gift of Hawaii, by Laura Bannon. Whitman, 1961. A little Hawaiian boy has "a great big love for his Mamma."

Hailstones and Halibut Bones, by Mary O'Neill. Doubleday, 1961. Intriguing book of verse that invites creativity with color.

Hattie Be Quiet, Hattie Be Good, by Dick Gackenbach. Harper & Row, 1977. The story of Hattie, a helpful rabbit.

Jeanne-Marie Counts Her Sheep, by Francoise. Scribner's, 1951. A simple story, picture, counting book.

Katy No-Pocket, by Emmy Payne. Houghton, 1944. An amusing story of how a mother kangaroo solves the problem of having no pocket.

Miss Nelson Is Missing, by Harry Allard. Houghton, 1977. A well-illustrated fun book in which the lenient Miss Nelson teaches her misbehaving class a lesson by becoming a strict teacher.

Nine Days to Christmas, by Marie Hall Ets. Viking, 1959. A Caldecott book about a Mexican Christmas, introducing the pinata.

A Pocketful of Cricket, by Rebecca Caudill Holt, 1964. A quiet story about a boy's affection for his pet cricket and the first day of school.

Red Is Never a Mouse, by Eth Clifford. Bobbs, 1960. A book of color.

Ski Pup, by Don Freeman. Viking, 1963. Hugo, a Saint Bernard rescue dog, accidentally becomes a ski dog.

The Snowy Day, by Ezra Jack Keats. Viking, 1962. An experience in visual perception. A little boy tries out the snow.

The Story About Ping, by Marjorie Flack. Viking, 1933. A little duck in China does not wish to get a spanking if he is the last one on board.

Time of Wonder, by Robert McCloskey. Viking, 1957. One can feel the fog and the other sensations of beach life at the ocean.

Where the Wild Things Are, by Maurice Sendak. Harper, 1964. A very imaginative monster book about a little boy who gets even after being sent to his room.

Whistle for Willie, by Ezra Jack Keats. Viking, 1964. Willie's day is full of the small discoveries of all children.

Second Grade

And to Think That I Saw It on Mulberry Street, by Dr. Seuss. Vanguard, 1937. Nonsense rhyme about a street where the ordinary becomes the extraordinary.

"B" Is for Betsy, by Carolyn Haywood. Harcourt, 1939. The day-by-day incidents in the Haywood books make them completely realistic and entertaining. At the end of the year many children will enjoy reading them.

The Bears on Hemlock Mountain, by Alice Dalgleish. Scribners, 1952. Everyone told Jonathan there were no bears on the mountain. Suspense mounts as Jonathan crosses the mountain.

Brighty of the Grand Canyon, by Marguerite Henry. Rand, 1953. Highly recommended, this story of a lone burro found by an old prospector has magnificent drawings of the Grand Canyon.

Charlotte's Web, by E. B. White, Harper, 1952. The gentle friendship of a pig, a spider, and a little girl who could talk to animals.

Clown Dog, by Lavinia Davis. Doubleday, 1961. A boy defends his dog in a new neighborhood until his pet becomes a hero by discovering an orphaned fawn.

Crow Boy, by Taro Yashima. Viking, 1955. A shy Japanese boy is recognized by his classmates through his teacher's understanding.

Down, Down the Mountain, by Ellis Credle. Nelson, 1961. Two Blue Ridge Mountain children want creaky-squeaky shoes more than anything else in the world.

Easter in November, by Lilo Hess. Crowell, 1964. A surprise Easter story about an unusual breed of chickens that hatches colored eggs.

Good-bye Ruby Red, by Geraldine Kaye. Children's Publishers, 1976. A fantasy in which a paper doll comes to life.

King Orville and the Bullfrogs, by Kathleen Abell. Little, Brown, 1974. A fairy tale with humorously detailed drawings.

Lentil, by Robert McCloskey. Viking, 1940. Lentil's harmonica saves the day. Illustrations large enough to be seen by the class.

Little Runner of the Longhouse, by Betty Baker. Harper, 1962. A much needed easy treatment of Iroquois life.

Marshmallow, by Clare T. Newberry. Harper, 1942. A pet cat cannot understand when a little white bunny comes to live at his home. Exceptional illustrations, fine story.

Mike's House, by Julia Sauer. Viking, 1954. Most second graders have been introduced to *Mike Mulligan and His Steam Shovel,* by Virginia Burton, and will chuckle at this story of a boy who will not make a compromise.

Millions of Cats, by Wanda Gág. Coward, 1928. How does a little old woman choose one from millions of cats?

Mouse Soup, by Arnold Lobel. Harper & Row, 1977. A mouse tale where a mouse and a weasel put stories into soup.

Reindeer Trail, by Berta and Elmer Hader. Macmillan, 1959. "How the fleet-footed reindeer brought to Alaska by the friendly Lapps save the Eskimos from starving."

The Story of Helen Keller, by Lorena Hickel. Grosset, 1958. This version of a great lady's life is simple enough to be enjoyed by second and third grades.

Tom Tit Tot, illus. by Evaline Ness. Scribner's, 1965. The comic illustrations fit the "gatless" girl in this refreshing variation of Rumplestiltskin.

Two Is Company, Three's a Crowd, by Berta and Elmer Hader. Macmillan, 1965. Fine to use when the geese are migrating. The story of how Big John and his wife feed a few and soon have more than they can handle.

Third Grade

The Borrowers, by Mary Norton. Harcourt, 1953. If you can't find your stamps or thimbles, the Borrowers are probably using them for pictures or footstools. One third grade constructed a home for the little people.

The Courage of Sarah Noble, by Alice Dalgleish. Scribners, 1954. The true story of a brave little girl who, in 1707, went with her father into Indian territory.

Dancing Cloud, the Navajo Boy, by Mary Buff. Viking, 1957. Excellent story of Navajo life with striking full-spread illustrations.

The Day the Hurricane Happened, by Lonzo Anderson. Scribners, 1974. An adventure story of two young people in a Virgin Island Hurricane.

The Enormous Egg, by Oliver Butterworth. Little, 1956. Young Nate Twitchell finds an oversized egg in his chicken nest that hatches into a baby dinosaur and complications.

Henry Huggins, by Beverly Cleary. Morrow, 1950. All the Henry books are enthusiastically recommended.

Homer Price, by Robert McCloskey. Viking, 1943. Each chapter is its own story. *The Doughnuts* and *Super Duper* are samples of the humor.

The Hundred Penny Box, by Sharon Mathis. Viking, 1975. The story of an old woman and a young boy and the love they share.

The Indian and the Buffalo, by Robert Hofsinde. Morrow, 1961. This author has given us much authentic Indian material.

Just the Thing for Geraldine, by Ellen Conford. Little, Brown, 1974. Story of Geraldine and her attempts at various pasttimes.

The Limerick Trick, by Scott Corbett. Little, 1960. Kerby needs to write a limerick to win a contest. A chemical mixture solves one problem but leads to another when Kerby finds he can't stop rhyming.

The Light at Tern Rock, by Julia Sauer. Viking, 1951. Excellent Christmas reading. A boy learns patience the hard way when he is forced to spend Christmas tending the lighthouse beacon.

Little House in the Big Woods, by Laura Ingalls Wilder. Harper, 1953. The entire Wilder series, depicting the author's childhood in the Midwest, is highly rated and always enjoyed.

Little Navajo Bluebird, by A. N. Clark. Viking, 1943. A fine picture of present-day Navajo life.

Mary Poppins, by P. L. Travers. Harcourt, 1962. Remarkable things happen when Miss Poppins blows in as the new Nanny.

The Matchlock Gun, by Walter Edmonds. Dodd, 1941. Historical fiction set in the Mohawk Valley during the French and Indian War. A boy is left to protect the family when the father answers the call for help from a settlement under attack.

The Missing Piece, by Shel Silverstein. Harper & Row, 1976. An "it" looks for the missing piece to "it."

The Nightingale, by Hans C. Andersen; illus. by Harold Berson. Lippincott, 1963. A fine retelling of a favorite story.

The Nutcracker, trans. by Warren Chappell. Knopf, 1958. An excellent selection for Christmas. May be used with the music.

The Otter's Story, by Emil Liers. Viking, 1953. Like *The Beaver's Story,* recommended as an absorbing, unsentimental animal story.

Paddle-to-the-Sea, by Holling C. Holling. Houghton, 1941. An Indian boy carves a toy canoe and launches it in the waters of northern Canada. The story traces its journey through the Great Lakes, over the Falls, into the Atlantic. Striking illustrations showing landscape and industry native to the area.

Tatsinda, by Elizabeth Enright. Harcourt, 1963. A fantasy with weird creatures, strange names, and a little girl pursued because she is different.

A Weed Is a Flower: The Life of George Washington Carver, by Aliki. Prentice, 1965. Fine introduction to biography.

Fourth Grade

Away Goes Sally, by Elizabeth Coatsworth. Macmillan, 1934. Sally moves from New England to Maine wilderness in the original house trailer—a log cabin on runners.

The Bee Man of Orn, by Frank Stockton. Holt, 1964. A man wishes to live his life over. The surprise ending delights the children.

The Beetle Bush, by Beverly Keller. Coward, 1976. About a born loser who finally achieves success.

The Bluejay Boarders, by Harold Keith. Crowell Co., 1972. Three children take over the care of a nest of newborn bluejays.

The Children of Green Knowe, by L. M. Boston. Harcourt, 1955. A beautifully written fantasy. Children will differ about what is real and what is imagined.

Chitty-Chitty-Bang-Bang, by Ian Fleming. Random, 1964. A magic car becomes a boat or airplane when the family escapes from gangsters. Highly recommended.

Families Are Like That, by the Child Study Association of America. Crowell, 1975. A book of short stories concerning children and the problems they face in family life.

Ice King, by Ernestine Byrd. Scribners, 1965. Sensitive story of a friendship between an Eskimo boy and a bear orphaned by hunters.

The Magic Bed-Knob, by Mary Norton; in *Bed-Knob and Broomstick.* Harcourt, 1957. Sheer fantasy about English children and their magician friend who gets the book off to a fine start when she falls off her broomstick and sprains her ankle.

Mama Hattie's Girl, by Lois Lenski. Lippincott, 1953. This regional book gives meaning to the place of Black people in the North and South and is also excellent for the relationship between child and grandmother.

Matilda Investigates, by Mary Anderson. Atheneum, 1973. The story of an eleven-year-old girl who tries to become New York's first woman detective.

Misty of Chincoteague, by Marguerite Henry. Rand, 1947. A captivating horse story that begins with Pony Penning Day, still held on Chincoteague Island.

The Moffats, by Eleanor Estes. Harcourt, 1941. A family story full of humorous incidents. The Halloween chapter is hilarious.

Navajo Sister, by Evelyn Lampman. Doubleday, 1956. Excellent tale about the adjustment necessary when Navajo children leave the reservation for boarding school.

Pippi Longstocking, by Astrid Lindgren. Viking, 1950. A Swedish story about an uninhibited little girl who lives by herself and does only what she pleases in very unusual ways.

The Shy Stegosaurus of Cricket Creek, by Evelyn Lampman. Doubleday, 1955. George is the dinosaur who escaped extinction.

Strawberry Girl, by Lois Lenski. Lippincott, 1945. A realistic story about a family of Florida Crackers; strong regional background.

Stuart Little, by E. B. White. Harper, 1945. The mouse-man has been a "smash" in one fourth grade. "Good for the first day of school."

Wind in the Willows, by Kenneth Grahame. Scribners, 1961. A classic that few children will enjoy unless it is first shared aloud.

The Witch of Blackbird Pond, by Elizabeth Speare. Houghton, 1958. Excellent background of Puritan America and the witchcraft movement. A Newbery Medal winner.

Young Mark Twain and the Mississippi, by Kane Harnett. Random House, 1966. One of the excellent Landmark Series.

Fifth Grade

And Now Miguel, by Joseph Krumgold. Crowell, 1953. Authentic picture of sheep raising in New Mexico and a boy who longs to become a man.

The Animal Family, by Randall Jarrell. Pantheon, 1965. A mystic story of a woodsman, a mermaid, and the animals. Like *The Children of Green Knowe,* children will puzzle over the story.

Call It Courage, by Armstrong Sperry. Macmillan, 1940. A South Sea Island boy, shamed by the tribe, redeems himself by his bravery. Adventure at its best.

The Complete Peterkin Papers, by Lucretia Hale. Houghton, 1960. The uninhibited Peterkin family finds solutions peculiar only to them. Ridiculous humor.

F*T*C* Superstar! by Mary Anderson. Atheneum, 1976.

Story of an actor-cat who succeeds in his profession with help from a pigeon friend. Clever caricatures.

Farmer Boy, by Laura Ingalls Wilder. Harper, 1933. "Good to show how people lived before modern conveniences." Early New York state.

The Gold-Laced Coat, by Helen Fuller Orton. Lippincott, 1934. Fine to read before a field trip to an early American fort. This setting is Ft. Niagara.

The Island of the Blue Dolphins, by Scott O'Dell. Houghton, 1960. Based on the actual life of the sole inhabitant of the island, this Newbery winner has had great appeal for intermediate grades.

Li Lun, Lad of Courage, by Carolyn Treffinger. Abingdon, 1947. A courageous boy proves himself by achieving the impossible on a mountain.

Miss Pickerell Goes to Mars, by Ellen MacGregor. McGraw, 1951. Miss Pickerell shuddered at the thought of a ferris wheel or stepladder. Her jaunt on a spaceship is a complete surprise. One of many in a series.

Pancakes-Paris, by Claire Bishop. Viking, 1947. A realistic story about a typical friendship between a French boy and American soldiers during World War II. A little French vocabulary.

Road to Agra, by Alic Sommerfelt. Criterion, 1967. Boy and sister make a long journey to gain help from World Health Association.

Shadow of a Bull, by Maia Wojciechowska. Atheneum, 1964. The future is decided for the nine-year-old son of a famous bullfighter when he is born. A fine treatment of a child's reaction to public pressure in a setting rare to children's literature. A Newbery Award winner.

Susy's Scoundrel, by Harold Keith. Crowell, 1974. Story of Susy's pet coyote who outwits hunters who think that he is killing sheep.

The Talking Tree, by Alice Desmond. Macmillan, 1949. A fine book for the study of Alaska; about totem poles and a young Tlingit Indian who must reconcile past with present.

Twenty and Ten, by Claire Bishop. Viking, 1952. Twenty school children in France befriend ten Jewish children fleeing from the Gestapo during World War II.

Sixth Grade

Adam of the Road, by Elizabeth Gray. Viking, 1942. An interesting picture of life in 13th-century England.

Aunt America, by Marie Halun Block. Atheneum, 1963. Life behind the Iron Curtain. Children need to understand the concepts of freedom.

The Bronze Bow, by Elizabeth Speare. Houghton, 1961. An unusual setting portraying the hatred of the Jews for their Roman conquerors during the time of Christ. Used before Easter each year by one fifth-grade teacher. A Newbery Medal book.

The Christmas Carol, by Charles Dickens. Many editions. The descriptive flavor of Dickens's words is not heard in the television versions.

The Door in the Wall, by Marguerite deAngeli. Doubleday, 1949. A crippled boy, despairing in a society of medieval knighthood, triumphs over his handicap. Excellent background for monastic and feudal study. A Newbery winner.

Emma's Dilemma, by Gen Leroy. Harper, 1975. The story of Emma, whose problems grow when she finds her dog must go because grandma, who comes to live with them, is allergic to the dog.

Follow My Leader, by James Garfield. Viking, 1975. A boy adjusts to blindness at the age of eleven.

The Incredible Journey, by Sheila Burnford. Little, Brown, 1961. Fascinating adventure of a motley group of animals traveling together.

Last Night I Saw Andromeda, by Charlotte Anker. Walck Co., 1975. Determined to find a scientific interest to please her father, Jenny starts collecting fossils.

It's Like This, Cat, by Emily Neville. Harper, 1963. Sophisticated sixth-graders will enjoy this story of New York City and a boy who never quite understands his parents, and vice versa. A Newbery book.

The Loner, by Ester Wier. McKay, 1963. Excellent character study of a boy who travels with migrants until he meets "Boss" and desperately wants to please her. Fine picture of sheep raising.

The Magic Meadow, by Alexander Key. Westminister, 1975. A fantasy about a crippled boy in a hospital who takes the nurses and his bedridden companions to a happy place in the future.

Martin Rides the Moor, by Vian Smith. Doubleday, 1965. A wild pony is the salvation of a boy deafened by an accident.

My Name Is Pablo, by Alice Sommerfelt. Criterion, 1966. Youth problems in Mexico City.

Onion John, by Joseph Krumgold. Crowell, 1959. A close friendship develops between the boy and the town junkman. Excellent human relations: humorous but realistic.

Second Hand Family, by Richard Parker. Bobbs, 1965. An up-to-date treatment of teenage interests. Concerns a group that plays rock and roll. Enjoyed by preteens.

The White Panther, by Theodore Waldeck. Viking, 1941. A fast-moving story about a panther stalked by man and beast because he was born white.

A Wrinkle in Time, by Madeleine L'Engle. Farrar, 1962. Science fiction at its best.

For Discussion

1. Can you recall the names of any of the books your teachers read aloud to your class in school?

2. Do parents still read aloud to children at home? How is this a beneficial experience?

3. What other sources are available for read-aloud stories?

4. How would you handle the criticism that reading aloud to a class is just entertaining the children when you should be teaching them?

How May Book Reports Be Effectively Used in the Classroom?

Surveys of the school subject preferences of children usually reveal that language class is rated the favorite by one in ten but is the least liked by about three in ten. Within the specifics of the language course the item most frequently listed as the least preferred is book reporting. It is probably safe to assume that book reporting has not been a very popular activity with many children.

There are a number of reasons why this may be so. At one time children were required to read a prescribed number of books from a specific list each month or each report-card period. The books were frequently not appropriate to the readers and the motivation was coercion. It may not have been so distasteful to read the books, but to be required to review them in prescribed uniform style was an artificial writing assignment. It was not uncommon that children would copy from one another or from book summaries found in libraries.

Boehm has expressed a concern of many teachers:

Why don't more students seek . . . out [good books]? Because we discourage them. We make reading a penalty. We insist that our pupils write book reviews, naming the principal characters and important events in a format unchanging for a hundred years. So our youngsters read the short, the concise, the easily remembered books. And teachers should be the last to criticize them. The challenging, the thought-provoking books are to be shunned because teachers want only dates and names. [Boehm, 1960; p. 37]

A related reason for the unpopularity of this activity is what has been described as the "FBI approach" to literature. The teacher's purpose might be stated: "Has the child really read the book? Has he just leafed through or looked at the pictures? He must answer certain questions so I'll be sure that he read it."

Another approach is that of account keeping. This listing of books often incorporates a competitive spirit. Many readers are going to feel embarrassed if others read ten books while they read only two.

In a third grade one teacher reports stimulating a high interest in books that the children were to select independently. A rule accepted by the group was that once a book selection was made, that book was to be completed. One child selected an excellent but long and difficult book. She was still reading this while other children were on a second or third book. Because a public record was kept, this had an effect. The next book she selected was short and had many pictures. Because the element of competition is difficult to eliminate, this factor can be corrected by allowing a number of points for each book so that the more difficult ones will be allotted more points and thus will not be avoided.

There are many worthwhile purposes for book reports. First, reports are a way of learning from the reading of others. When a child has had a reading adventure or learned some interesting information, others like to share it with him. Second, reading can be motivated by a report. One child's stamp of approval on a book will encourage others to want to read it. "Even the boys will like Laura," exclaimed one child after reading *Little House on the Prairie*. Third, reports meet a social need. Sharing the fun of *Freddie, the Detective* is as important in the conversation of fourth-graders as discussing the current bestseller is among adults. Fourth, specifics need to be noticed in order to appreciate a book thoroughly. Such specifics can include an author's use of words, descriptive passages, or illustrations. Fifth, reports give recognition to children. For many children reading a book is an achievement. Each one is a trophy that attests to greater mastery of a complex skill that has been put to use. Sixth, reports tell the teacher about the child's interests and needs. Misinterpretation or confusion revealed in a report indicates special needs that guide the teacher in planning work with the child. Although literature is largely for enjoyment and appreciation, the reading process can be observed and help can be given in its improvement so that further experiences in literature will prove more satisfying and rewarding.

In all grades, both oral and written reports are used. Oral reports require careful direction and planning to be worth the attention of the class. Time required to prepare peep shows, cartoon strips, dioramas, dressed characters, flannelboard figures, and other such accessories for book reports is often questioned. Some children have both the time and interest needed to make such comment, and such visual devices add to the effectiveness of a presentation. A balanced approach in terms of the overall needs of a child must play a part in any consideration by the teacher.

Primary children may give book reports as a part of the sharing period. Or an opening exercise one morning a week might emphasize books they find interesting. At such times teachers make suggestions like the following: Show only the cover of a book and tell why the reader liked it. Show one picture and incite curiosity as to what is happening in the story. Show a sea shell, leaf, model airplane, space ship, or rock, that some books explain. Show a flannel-board figure or a picture for a part of a story read by a child. Form a book club and follow a simple outline in making reports. Such an outline might include

1. What kind of a story is it? Is it true?
2. What is it about?
3. Is it about this country or some other? When did it happen?
4. What are the pictures like?
5. Is the book easy to read?

6. Who wrote the story? Do we know any other stories by that person?

These items are only suggestions. Certainly every book does not fit into the use of each question. Any item-by-item checking can become monotonous. We merely want to help children become conscious of the many qualities that books have and the substance that develops real appreciation of literature. The forms on page 329 have been used by teachers.

Intermediate children have a wider range of possibilities with respect to book reports, both because of greater maturity in oral language and in writing facility and because of greater breadth of reading interests. The purposes of reporting are to interest others in expanded reading, to share information, to communicate the pleasure of ideas from reading, and to emphasize the achievement of having read a book that was significant for one reason or another to the reader. Often children themselves have useful suggestions for accomplishing these purposes. The person who read the book pretends to be one of the characters. The audience is to guess the name of the book from what he says or does. A series of clues may be given and the listeners and observers may write the name of the book opposite the number of the clue. These guessing games give all children a chance to participate. A group of children may also present a panel. They may discuss a book they have all read, or the subject "Dog or Horse Stories I Have Liked."

A good way to emphasize authorship is to have a "Lois Lenski Day" or a "Newbery Award Day (or Week)." Students may be curious to find the qualities that made certain books worthy of awards. Such qualities as characterization, picturesque words, descriptive passages, ingenious plot, appropriate illustrations, imaginative humor, and range of experiences take on meaning and importance as children learn to recognize them. The group might create an award for a favorite book.

An oral synopsis of a story is good practice in arranging events in sequence and in learning how a story progresses to a climax. It also helps children who are interested in writing stories of their own.

READ FOR FUN

Name _____ Date _____
Book title _____
_____

Main character _____
_____

People who like
_____ animal stories
_____ stories about children
_____ stories about _____
_____
_____ adventure stories
_____ funny stories
_____ exciting stories
_____

will like this book.

Did you enjoy this book? _____
It was
_____ easy to read.
_____ hard to read.
_____ just right.   (*Used in Grade 2*)

BOOK REPORT   (*Grades 3 and 4*)

Name of book_____
Author _____
Illustrator (if any) _____
Name some of the characters: _____
_____

Tell which character you liked best: _____
_____
_____

The part of the book I liked best was _____
_____
_____
_____

Do *one* of these things:
  1. Tell your class part of the story.
  2. Make a picture.
  3. Make something suggested in the book.

My name is _____ Room No. _____

Broadcasting a book review over the public-address system or radio is a challenge for careful preparation and ingenuity in planning sound effects, background music, or dramatic reading. Clear enunciation and good voice modulation will also be important.

Telling a story, telling about a new book, or reading a small excerpt to another class may be good for the child who wants to share the experience, and it may stimulate the audience to learn more about the book or others by the same author.

During an informal "book club" session the students meet in small groups and talk about books they have read. The object is to whet the book appetites of the group.

An oral comparison of two books related in theme is a good exercise in critical evaluation. The problems of the Black girls in *Shuttered Windows* by Florence Means and *Mary Jane* by Dorothy Sterling might be compared; so, too, the humor in the *Paul Bunyan Stories* might be compared with that in *Pippi Longstocking.*

Such projects as constructing a miniature stage, making preparations for a television show, planning and decorating a bulletin board, dressing dolls as book characters, impersonating book characters, and planning quiz programs about books may all on occasion stimulate interest in both oral and written reports. Displaying such related objects as a cowbell for Heidi, wooden shoes for Hans Brinker, a Japanese doll, travel pictures, or pioneer relics is a good device for vitalizing both reading and reporting. In social studies the study of a country can be personalized through a story character, thus providing broader understanding of both the literature and the geography of the country.

Written reports may take many forms. Letters of appreciation may be written to authors or librarians. A letter to a friend or relative recommending a book should actually be mailed. Advertisements may be written for the school paper, a bulletin board, or a book jacket. Short reviews may be written for "We Recommend" bulletin boards or for "Before You Read" or "My Opinion" scrapbooks. Sometimes the local paper will publish well-written book reviews. Some classes keep a file of brief summaries that is consulted when a child wants a certain type of book. These are usually limited to a few sentences. Some children like to keep a "Personal Reading Notebook" in the form of a diary like the following one:

PERSONAL READING NOTEBOOK

Here are some ways in which information about the things in my book have helped people:

_____
_____
_____

Below are some unsolved problems or questions (about things in my book) that scientists are still working on:

_____
_____
_____

I recommend this book because _____
_____

Name _____ Date _____

MY BOOK REPORT

Title _____

Author _____ Number of pages _____

Illustrator _____

The biographer (one who writes about a real person) tells the following childhood incident in the life of his subject:

_____
_____
_____

The subject of the biography is

_____

The following people were important in helping this real person to grow into a famous adult:

_____
_____
_____

A problem that this person had to overcome was

_____
_____

This person overcame his problem in this way:

_____
_____

This person had the following characteristics that I admire:

_____
_____

I think the most exciting adventure that this person had was

_____
_____
_____

Teachers have developed many techniques to encourage children to read widely. A bulletin board on which each child has a small book in which to record the titles and authors of each book read is quite popular. Sometimes this is done on a bookshelf and each child has a cardboard-bound book cover in which to do his recording so that the bulletin boards are not occupied for such a long period of time. One class used the space idea by putting the name of each new book read on a small paper satellite. The caption was "We Are Really Orbiting."

Children sometimes are inclined to limit their reading to a single interest. To encourage a more balanced reading program, teachers sometimes use a reading wheel divided into areas of biography, foreign lands, animals, science, adventure, or folklore. As each child reads a book, his name is placed in the proper area on the wheel. The object is to have one's name in each area. Many publishing companies provide a free wall chart designed to encourage a well-rounded program in reading. The *News-Journal* of North Manchester, Indiana, has several forms of "My Reading Design" that also serve this purpose.

Another plan to widen the reading interest involves

the use of a map. The object is to "Take a World Cruise" or "See America First." Books appropriate to each region are suggested. Sweden might be represented by "The Sauce Pan Journey," France by "The Big Loop." After a book is read about one country or area, the child moves on to the next until the tour is completed.

Bulletin boards or charts frequently motivate the reading of a book. The teacher might make a list under the title, "These Are Ms. Smith's Favorites." A group of children might list others under such titles as "We Recommend for First Purchase," "Interesting Travel Books," "Books to Grow On," "Books About This Area."

In most situations the reading is more important than the reporting. The teacher needs to know the quality of the child's reading to be sure he is getting the most from each reading adventure. This can be done in class situations through observances of a child reading independently, in teacher-pupil conferences, and in some of the discussions and reporting that he does. There is no need for a report on every book. Some children need more of these reporting experiences than other children. In the final analysis the best reports may be a child's heartfelt spontaneous statement, "Ms. Collins, do you know another like that?"

For Discussion

1. If your state has a Reading Circle, try to learn these things about it. How are books selected? What motives are given the children for reading these books?

2. Do you feel the criticism of book reports is justified in terms of your own experience?

3. Do you think book reports might be individualized? One child might limit his report to those new words he learned; another might limit his to finding an interesting sentence.

4. How can we prevent embarrassment for a child who must read books much below the reading level of others in the class?

How Do Teachers Become Effective Storytellers?

There are no basic rules to ensure the proper telling of a story. Some of the greatest story craftsmen cannot agree as to best methods to use. Storytelling is as individual an art as acting or playing a musical instrument. Each person must develop his own techniques, style, and selection of stories to suit his taste and abilities.

There are a few basic considerations, however, on which most storytellers agree.

1. The story must be appropriate to the audience. The very young child likes simple folk tales, but he does not respond to stories that are completely make-believe, with goblins, elves, and fairies. He does not understand the completely abstract. There must be some elements in the story that relate to his personal experiences. In the story of "The Three Bears" we have chairs, beds, bowls of soup, and activities that are familiar. Having them associated with bears adds mystery and adventure, but the events are familiar, everyday experiences. The child accepts the unreal because it is close enough to the real world he knows.

Little children love rhymes and jingles, and many old story favorites have a marked rhythmic quality. In stories this rhythm is the result of repetition of words and phrases in a set pattern. Such phrases as "Not by the hair of your chinny-chin-chin" or "Then I'll huff and I'll puff and I'll blow your house in" always bring delighted responses.

Children like to play with words. That is the way words become more meaningful and a lasting part of their vocabulary. Children cannot keep from repeating "a lovely, light, luscious, delectable cake" as the teacher reads "The Duchess Bakes a Cake." In telling some stories the teller prepares the listeners by saying, "This story contains some wonderful new words. One of them is _____ which means _____; another is_____ which means _____. Listen for them." One or two words presented before a story would be enough. The story will do considerable teaching by providing context for the words.

Make-believe is most important to children in the

years from six to ten, because it helps them understand the world about them and increases their imaginative powers. In the stories that they read and hear the youngsters are the heroes, at least for the time being. They know they are pretending, but as the story unfolds, each child wishes to become Jack the Giant Killer or Cinderella.

2. The storyteller knows that some stories are good to tell and other stories are better to read. The rich dialogue and description of *Winnie the Pooh* and *The Jungle Book* should remain intact. A story for telling must be simple and direct. The plot must be strong and develop rapidly. In storytelling there is no place for long analyses of characters or situations. The mental pictures must be supplied by a few words or a phrase. Each incident must be vivid and clear-cut in the listener's mind. The climax must be emotionally satisfying. This can be a surprise, the solution of a problem, or something achieved.

The charm of simplicity can best be learned through experience. We know that children respond to cumulative repetition, such as one finds in ''The Gingerbread Boy.'' They want the characters to talk. Descriptions are simple because children supply so much with their own imaginations. Good must triumph, but it is all right for the bad people to be very bad as long as in the end they are punished. Some prefer stories of animals to those with people in them. For many, the gentle stories about raindrops, flowers, and insects are a new discovery in contrast to the rapid pace of television and movie cartoons. A story that lasts six or eight minutes is quite long enough, and many favorites take less time than that.

''The Three Little Pigs'' is an example of a good story for telling little children. Each step is an event. No time is spent in explanation or unnecessary description. The story tells what the characters did and said and the events are linked in the closest kind of sequence. There are no breaks and no complexities of plot. Each event presents a clear, distinct picture to the imagination.

Ordinarily it is wisest not to change traditional stories. If you question any element in a story, it is usually best to select another story. There is a trend in the direction of removing much of the horror aspects of the old folk material. The three bears are now friendly bears. They are provoked by Goldilocks because she enters their home without permission. The wolf now chases Red Riding Hood's grandmother into a closet instead of devouring her. In the original version of the ''Three Billy Goats Gruff'' the troll had his eyes gouged out and was crushed to death. In the modern version he is merely butted into the river and swims away unscathed, never to return. The first two of the Three Little Pigs are no longer eaten by the wolf but make an exciting escape to the house of the wise pig.

Any idea that may cause the young child to lie awake at night is best omitted from the program. It is well to discuss make-believe with children. Let them be assured that there are really no dragons and that wolves are unlikely visitors in the suburbs.

Another common theme in many of the old tales is the cruelty of stepparents and other kin related by remarriage. Stereotypes that stigmatize kin, old age, or social groups have no place in the story hour.

A discussion before reading some of these stories can take care of such questionable elements. The story of a good stepmother like Abraham Lincoln's provides a balance to ''Cinderella.'' There are many good and kind old ladies to offset the cruel old hag in Hansel and Gretel. Teachers should remember that the horror that an adult senses in a story such as ''Snow White'' is quite different from a child's point of view. Torture and even death have only incidental significance for many children. Death is frequently an acceptable solution to a problem. Children play Cowboys and Indians, ''good guys'' and ''bad guys,'' with violent shouts, agonizing mock deaths, and melodramatic hardships one moment and listen with rapt attention to a poem of delicate beauty the next.

Sometimes children themselves will suggest changes in these stories. This frequently happens as they dramatize a story. Another interesting variation on the traditional material is to put the characters in a new situation. Make up a story of visiting the Three Bears during summer vacation or let Cinderella go to school.

3. A storyteller knows that preparation is needed to make a story vivid to listeners. After a careful reading, put the story aside and think about it until you can picture the story to yourself, clearly in all details. Check any doubts by reading the story again. It is better for a beginning storyteller to know a few stories well than to attempt so many that none can be told with complete confidence. The ''tell it again'' quality of stories is a great safeguard for beginners. Any storyteller is almost sure to tell a story better each additional time he tells it. A beginner might plan an introduction, plan the sequence of the events, plan an ending, and then practice telling it aloud by himself.

4. A storyteller knows that the audience must be comfortable and free from interruptions during the story, and that the story must end before the audience becomes weary or bored. Wait a few moments before starting a story so that there is a hush of expectancy in the room. If some children are inattentive or noisy, pause until quiet is restored. If many grow restless it is quite obvious that you have the wrong story. Don't blame the children; just say, ''I guess this isn't the right story, so let's stand up and stretch.'' Then go on with some other group activity such as marching, singing, or finger play. Start another story only when there are expectancy and readiness for wholehearted listening.

Certain devices can be used to hold the attention of listeners. When Hans Christian Andersen entertained the children of Denmark with his stories, he used to cut out silhouettes in order to make his characters more vivid. In ancient China the storyteller would cast shadows to illustrate the characters in his tales of magic and ancient ways. Movie cartoon favorites use a combination of silhouette figures and movement to hold attention. In the modern classroom the flannelboard provides the storyteller with the means of achieving similar types of movement, magic, and characterization.

As the child listens to the storyteller, his visual attention is focused on character and movement as figures representing the main characters are moved about on the flannelboard.

Flannelboard stories should be looked on as a means of stimulating the imagination and improving the quality of oral language of children. Many teachers find that permitting children to make their own flannelboard stories and then tell them helps expand their language power, self-confidence, and creative talents. Another prospect is the emotional release that can be observed in some children as they plan, cut out, and manipulate figures to illustrate some story they especially like or that they create.

Although the term *flannelboard* is used here, the device may be made with felt or coat lining. Those made for children's games are sometimes sprayed with ''flocking.'' A store that specializes in window-display materials will have this for sale. If flannel is used, get the heaviest available. Coat lining is usually obtainable from a dry goods store. If you have a large bulletin board that you wish to cover, use felt or coat lining. Each figure needs to have a large piece of flannel or felt glued to the reverse side. Then as it is placed on the board the teller should run his fingers over the figure, causing it to adhere to the board. Some use rough sandpaper or flocking on the figure. For some figures bits of flannel about an inch square in three or four places serve to hold better than one large piece.

Children seem to respond better to cutouts made of bright and heavy construction paper than to drawn figures. Apparently cutouts allow more scope for the imagination. However, illustrations cut from books and made into figures for the flannelboard also appeal to them. In a sense this type simply transfers the book illustrations to the flannelboard. Faces and clothes can be drawn with ink or wax crayon or made of bits of construction paper pasted to the figure.

Some stories need scenic backgrounds—a big woods, a lake, a castle. Rather than make these of paper, it is easier to draw them with crayon on a large piece of flannel. Then the figures will stick to the scenery as the story is told. Regular outing flannel is good for this purpose.

Most flannelboards are made of plywood or heavy composition cardboard about two feet wide and three feet long. The felt or flannel should be about three feet by four feet in order to allow adequate overlap on the back of the plywood. Staples from a regular paper stapler will hold it well. Do not glue the flannel to the board, as the glue reduces the static charge that causes the figures to adhere. The size should be large enough to hold the figures, but not so large that it is uncomfortable to carry or awkward to store away. Some teachers like to have handles on the board, others hinge them so they will fold. It costs about as much to make a board as to buy one. The only advantage to a homemade one is that you have exactly what you want.

The following story is a flannelboard favorite:

QUEER COMPANY[6]

A little old woman lived all alone in a little old house in the woods. One Halloween she sat in the corner, and as she sat, she spun.

Still she sat and
Still she spun and
Still she wished for company.

Then she saw her door open a little way, and in came

A pair of big, big feet
And sat down by the fireside
"That is very strange," thought the little old woman, but—

Still she sat and
Still she spun and
Still she wished for company.

Then in came

A pair of small, small legs,
And sat down on the big, big feet
"Now that is very strange," thought the old woman, but—

Still she sat and
Still she spun and
Still she wished for company.

Then in came

A wee, wee waist,
And sat down on the small, small legs.
"Now that is very strange," thought the old woman, but—

Still she sat and
Still she spun and
Still she wished for company.

[6] From Paul Anderson, *Flannelboard Stories for the Primary Grades* and *A Second Book of Stories to Tell* (Minneapolis: Denison, 1962 and 1969).

Then in came

A pair of broad, broad shoulders,
And sat down on the wee, wee waist.
But—

Still she sat and
Still she spun and
Still she wished for company.

Then in through the door came

A pair of long, long arms,
And sat down on the broad, broad shoulders.
"Now that is very strange," thought the little old woman,
    but—

Still she sat and
Still she spun and
Still she wished for company.

Then in came

A pair of fat, fat hands,
And sat down on the long, long arms.
But—

Still she sat and
Still she spun and
Still she wished for company,

Then in came

A round, round head
And sat down on top of all
That sat by the fireside.

The little old woman stopped her spinning and asked

"Where did you get such big feet?"
"By much tramping, by much tramping," said Somebody.

"Where did you get such small, small legs?"
"By much running, by much running," said Somebody.

"Where did you get such a wee, wee waist?"
"Nobody knows, nobody knows," said Somebody.

"Where did you get such broad, broad shoulders?"
"From carrying brooms," said Somebody.

"Where did you get such long, long arms?"
"Swinging the scythe, swinging the scythe," said
    Somebody.

"Where did you get such fat, fat hands?"
"By working, by working," said Somebody.

"How did you get such a huge, huge head?"
"Of a pumpkin I made it," said Somebody.

Then said the little old woman,
"What did you come for?"

"You!" said Somebody.

The following techniques should be used as a story is told with the flannelboard:

1. Place the flannelboard where it will remain securely in a place that can be seen by all students. The chalkboard is good if the group is in a small circle seated before it. An easel is better if the board must be seen by an entire room. If children are seated on a rug, they must be farther away from the teacher than when she uses a picture book. Those in front will be under a strain looking up if too near the board.

2. Arrange the figures to be used in the sequence needed for telling the story. It is best to keep them in a folder away from the sight of the listeners. Otherwise, some of the surprise and suspense are lost as they are introduced. A manila folder used in file cabinets makes a good container. Staple a pocket on one side of the folder to hold the figures and staple the story to the other side.

3. There is a tendency to look away from the listeners to the figures as they are placed on the flannelboard. Of course, this is necessary. Try to use this movement to direct the listeners' eyes but turn back to the audience as you tell the story. Otherwise, you will find yourself talking to the flannelboard, thus creating a hearing problem for your audience.

4. Plan your follow-up before you tell the story. Are you going to evaluate the story? Are you going to have the children retell parts of the story? Are you going to have them create a favorite story? When a story ends in the classroom it is a bit different from the ending of a play in the theater or a television program. The audience is still with you. Instead of going home or turning on another station you must plan the transition to the next school task.

In the Orient there are still storytellers who earn a living walking along the street. They signal their approach by tapping two pieces of wood together. Each child offers a small coin and is given a piece of hard candy. While he eats the candy, the storyteller entertains with some of the famous folk stories of the land or the latest adventures of Mickey Mouse. As the story unfolds, the storyteller illustrates it by a series of color prints from books, or hand-drawn pictures. These *Kamishe-bai,* or picture stories, might well be used in our own country.

Stick figures and simple puppets used as characters in a story or as the teller of the story will hold the attention of those children who need something to see as well as to hear. An important object in a story such as a lamp, old coffee mill, glass slipper, shaft of wheat, apple, miniature rocker, spinning wheel, or toy sword may be used. If the story involves a fable, the teacher may provide an explanation of the core of an apple, the way a seed or feather is formed, or the shape of a flower or leaf, because the fable was a means of explaining a fact of nature. And one should not neglect the chalkboard or simple stick figures to illustrate a scene or character.

In addition to a pleasant voice, clear speech, adequate vocabulary, and a relaxed appearance, today's storyteller needs the resources of inner grace that come from sincerity and a respect both for the audience and for the art of storytelling. When you have a clear visual picture of each character and scene, know the plot thoroughly, can establish a mood for listening, and are able to end the story so that your audience is satisfied, you are a good storyteller.

For Discussion

1. Do you think that every child should have a contribution to make in the social situations of his life by being able to tell a joke, relate a humorous family experience, do a trick, or tell a story at the campfire? In what ways does such an ability influence personality?

2. How can we find time in the school day to provide opportunities to tell stories and listen to them?

3. Should the oral interpretations of literature be limited to fiction and poetry?

Suggestions for Projects

1. Review ten books that might be read by children in a single grade to improve their understanding of a foreign land or an ethical value (a different book for each country or value).

2. Review ten books that might be read by children in a single grade to improve their historical or geographical concepts of our country.

3. Make a collection of twenty-five poems that will appeal to children in the fifth and sixth grades. Indicate in general how such poetry would be introduced and used.

4. Make a collection of ten poems appropriate to the purposes of a verse choir at a grade level.

5. Select three stories or ballads that might be dramatized by children.

6. Make a bibliography of dramatic material to use in the intermediate grades.

7. Indicate the skills needed and how they may be developed with regard to the dramatic presentation of a play.

8. Collect a group of ballads or stories that might be read aloud while a group presented the action in pantomime.

Choral Readings

FUNNY THE WAY DIFFERENT CARS START

Solo 1: Funny the way different cars start.
Row 1: Some with a plunk and a jerk,
Row 2: Some with a cough and a puff of smoke—
   Out of the back,
Row 3: Some with only a little click—
   With hardly any noise.
Solo 2: Funny the way different cars run.
Row 4: Some rattle and bang,
Row 5: Some whirrr,
Row 6: Some knock and knock,

Girls: Some purr
Boys: And hummmmm
All: Smoothly on with hardly any noise.

                 Dorothy Baruch

THE GIANT SHOES

Solo 1: There once was a Giant who needed new shoes,
Refrain: Left! Right! Tie them up tight!
Solo 2: Said he, "I'll go to the shoestore and choose."
Refrain: Left! Right! Tie them up tight!
Solo 3: "High ones, and low ones, and black one and
   brown."
Refrain: Left! Right! Tie them up tight!
Solo 4: "Give me the biggest you have in the town."
Refrain: Left! Right! Tie them up tight!
Solo 5: The shoeman said, "These are the biggest I've got."
Refrain: Left! Right! Tie them up tight!
Solo 6: "Take them and try them and keep them or not."
Refrain: Left! Right! Tie them up tight!
Solo 7: "They fit," said the Giant, "and squeak, I'll buy
   them."
Refrain: Left! Right! Tie them up tight!
Solo 8: He wore them all year 'cause he couldn't untie them,
Refrain: Untie them! Untie them!
Solo or Group: He wore them all year 'cause he couldn't
   untie them.

                 Edwina Fallis

Choral Readings Involving a Group

BUNDLES

(Good for stressing enunciation)

A bundle is a funny thing
It always sets me wondering;
For whether it is thin or wide,
You never know just what's inside.
Especially on Christmas week,
Temptation is so great to peek;
Now wouldn't it be much more fun
If shoppers carried things undone?

                 John Farrar

THE AMERICAN FLAG

Solo: There's a flag that floats above us,
          Wrought in red and white and blue—

A spangled flag of stars and stripes
Protecting me and you.
Unison: Sacrifices helped to make it
As men fought the long months through—
Boys: Nights of marching
Girls: Days of fighting
Unison: For the red and white and blue.
Girls: There is beauty in that emblem
Boys: There is courage in it, too;
Girls: There is loyalty
Boys: There is valor
Unison: In the red and white and blue.
Solo: In that flag which floats unconquered
Over land and sea
There's equality and freedom
Unison: There is true democracy.
Solo: There is glory in that emblem
Wrought in red and white and blue—
Unison: It's the stars and stripes forever
Guarding me and guarding you.

Louise Abney

LITTLE ECHO

All: Little Echo is an elf
Who plays at hide and seek.
You never, never find him.
But you can hear him speak:
Low: Hello *High:* Hello
Low: Hello *High:* Hello
Low: I'm here *High:* I'm here
Low: Come near *High:* Come near
All: I'm here.

Los Angeles City Schools

LOCOMOTIVE

Unison: Mobs of people
Lots of noise
Rattling baggage.
Porter boys.
Grinding brakes.
Shifting gears
Merry laughter,
Parting tears!
Solo: All ab-o-o-ard! All ab-o-o-ard!
Dark: Slowly
Slowly

Turning,
Massive engine moving on.
Medium: Smoking
Smoking
Higher
Higher
Smokestacks hurl the smoke anon.
Light: Fuel
Fuel
Fire
Fire
Faster
Faster
Speed
Speed!
Unison: Got to reach my destination.
Got no time for hesitation.
Have to please the population.
I am working for the nation.
Hurry, hurry to my station.
Medium: Past the valleys, past the hilltops,
Past the river, past the pond,
Past the farmhouse or the city
Quickly covering the ground.
High: I'm racing the sun
I'm racing the moon
I'm racing the stars
I'm faster than time
Low: The mountains clear away for me.
They build a bridge across the sea.
The iron weight above my wheel
Medium: Trembles even rails of steel
Dark: Through tunnels, black, a sooty black
With dusty smoke and grime,
Light: Faster, faster, night's decending
All: I must reach my place on time!

Rodney Bennett

Poems Involving Finger Play

LITTLE JACK HORNER

Little Jack Horner sat in a corner
[*Sit straight in chair; left hand held in lap in the pie.*]
Eating his Christmas pie.
[*Pretend to eat pie with right hand.*]
He put in his thumb and pulled out a plum
[*Stick thumb of right hand into pie; pull out the plum.*]

And said, "What a good boy am I!"
    [Hold hands high in air.]

FLAG SALUTE

(This salute to the flag may be used the first semester in school; then gradually introduce our national salute.)

The work of my hands
    [Cup both hands in front of you.]
The thoughts of my head
    [Both hands on top of head.]
The love of my heart
    [Hands folded over chest.]
I give to my flag.
    [Extend hands and arms toward flag.]

TWO DICKEY BIRDS

Two little dickey birds sitting on a wall;
    [Fists clenched, thumbs erect.]
One named Peter, the other named Paul.
    [Nod one thumb, then the other.]
Fly away, Peter; fly away, Paul.
    [One hand, then other moved to behind back.]
Come back, Peter; come back, Paul
    [One hand, then the other reappears.]

FIVE LITTLE SQUIRRELS

Five little squirrels
Sitting in a tree,
The first one said,
"What do I see?"
The second one said,
"I smell a gun."
The third one said,
"Quick, let's run!"
The fourth one said,
"Let's hide in the shade."
The fifth one said,
"Oh, I'm not afraid."
But—bang! went the gun
Away they did run!

LITTLE TURTLE

There was a little turtle.
    [Upper right index finger.]

He lived in a box.
    [Place in cupped left hand.]
He swam in a puddle
    [Move finger in circle.]
He climbed on the rocks.
    [Move up on left fingers.]
He snapped at a mosquito.
    [Snap right hand in air.]
He snapped at a flea.
He snapped at a minnow.
He snapped at me.
    [Snap toward self.]
He caught the mosquito.
    [Close right fist in air.]
He caught the flea.
He caught the minnow.
But he didn't catch me.
    [Point toward self, shake head.]

TWO TELEGRAPH POLES

Two tall telegraph poles
    [Pointer fingers erect.]
Across them a wire is strung.
    [Middle fingers outstretched to touch between pointer fingers.]
Two little birds hopped on.
    [Thumbs to position against "wire."]
And swung, and swung, and swung.
    [Sway arms back and forth from body.]

CATERPILLAR

Roly-poly caterpillar
Into a corner crept,
Spun around himself a blanket,
Then for a long time slept.
Roly-poly caterpillar
Wakening by and by—
Found himself with beautiful wings,
Changed to a butterfly

ITSY, BITSY SPIDER

Itsy, bitsy spider went up the water spout.
    [Hands make a climbing motion; or thumbs on index fingers of opposite hands, one after the other.]
Down came the rain and washed the spider out.
    [Drop hands.]

Out came the sun and dried up all the rain.
  [*Arms circled overhead.*]
Itsy, bitsy spider went up the spout again.
  [*Make "spider" motion again.*]

GRANDMOTHER

Here are grandmother's glasses,
  [*Circle thumb and finger, each hand, over eyes.*]
Here is grandmother's hat.
  [*Fingertips together on head.*]
This is the way she folds her hands
And puts them in her lap.

READY FOR BED

This little boy is ready for bed.
  [*Hold up forefinger.*]
Down on the pillow he lays his head.
  [*Place finger in palm of opposite hand.*]
Covers himself all up tight,
  [*Fold fingers over forefinger.*]
Falls fast asleep for the night.
  [*Cock head toward shoulder, close eyes.*]
Morning comes, he opens his eyes,
  [*Quickly lift head, open eyes.*]
Throws back the covers with great surprise,
  [*Open palm to uncover forefinger.*]
Up he jumps and gets all dressed,
  [*Quickly raise forefinger off palm.*]
To hurry to school to play with the rest.
  [*Move finger off to the side.*]

FIVE LITTLE SOLDIERS

Five little soldiers standing in a row
Three stood straight and two stood so,
Along came the captain, and what do you think
They all stood up straight just as quick as a wink.

FIVE LITTLE PUMPKINS

Five little pumpkins sitting on a gate.
The first one said, "My it's getting late!"
The second one said, "There are witches in the air."
The third one said, "But we don't care."
The fourth one said, "Let's run, let's run!"
The fifth one said, "Isn't Halloween fun?"
"Woo-oo-oo" went the wind, out went the light.
Those five little pumpkins ran fast out of sight.

Bibliography

Anderson, P. *Flannelboard Stories for the Primary Grades*. Minneapolis: Denison, 1962.

Anderson, P. *A Second Book of Stories to Tell*. Minneapolis: Denison, 1969.

Arbuthnot, M. H. "Helping Children Enjoy Poetry." *Wilson Library Bulletin*, **36** (January 1962), 377.

Arbuthnot, M. H., and Z. Sutherland. *Children and Books*, 4th ed. Glenview, Ill.: Scott, Foresman, 1972.

Boehm, C. "What You Don't Know About Your Schools." *Saturday Evening Post* (May 14, 1960), 37.

Chambers, D. W. *Storytelling and Creative Drama*, Dubuque, Ia.: Wm. C. Brown Co., 1970.

Cohen, D. W. "Word Meaning and the Literary Experience in Early Childhood," *Elementary English* (November 1969), 914–925.

Duff, A. *Bequest of Wings*. New York: Viking, 1959.

Duff, A. *Longer Flight*. New York: Viking, 1959.

Feifal, H. "The Child's View of Death." *Meaning of Death*. New York: McGraw-Hill, 1959. (Reprinted from the *Journal of Genetic Psychology*, 1948.)

Fenner, P. *The Proof of the Pudding*. New York: John Day, 1957.

Gilpatric, N. "Power of Picture Books to Change Child's Self-Image." *Elementary English* (May 1969), 570–574.

Grollman, E. *Explaining Death to Children*. Boston: Beacon Press, 1969.

Guilfoile, E., and others. *Adventuring with Books: A Booklist for Elementary Schools*. Champaign, Ill.: National Council of Teachers of English, 1966.

Haviland, V. *Children's Literature: A Guide to Reference Sources*. Washington, D.C.: Library of Congress, 1966.

Helson, R. "Fantasy and Self Discovery." *Horn Book* (April 1970), 121–134.

Highland Park Independent School District. *English Language Arts* (1967). (Address: 7015 Westchester Drive, Dallas, Texas.)

Hillman, J. S. "Occupational Roles in Children's Literature." *Elementary School Journal* (September 1976), 1–4.

Huck, C., and D. Y. Kuhn. *Children's Literature in the Elementary School*. New York: Holt, Rinehart and Winston, 1968.

Hundler, J. "Books for Loving." *Elementary English* (May 1970), 687–692.

Jennings, S. "Effects of Sex Typing in Children's Stories on

Preference and Recall." *Child Development* (March 1975), 220–223.

Klugman, L. *Newbery and Caldecott Medal Books*. Boston: Horn Books, 1965.

Larrick, N. *A Teacher's Guide to Children's Books*. Columbus, O.: Charles E. Merrill, 1960.

Mathis, S. "True/False Messages for the Black Child: Racism and Children's Literature." *Black Books Bulletin* (Winter 1974), 12–19.

Murphy, C. "Sex Stereotyping in Literature During Early Childhood." *Counseling and Values* (April 1975), 186–191.

Pooley, R. *English Language Arts in Wisconsin*. Madison, Wis.: Department of Public Instruction, 1968.

Reid, V. M. (ed.) *Reading Ladders for Human Relations,* 5th ed. Washington, D.C.: American Council on Education (in cooperation with NCTE), 1972.

Sadker, D. "Death—A Fact of Life in Children's Literature." *Instructor* (March 1976), 75–84.

Sandburg, C. *Early Moon*. New York: Harcourt Brace Jovanovich, 1930.

Sawyer, R. *The Way of the Story Teller*. New York: Viking, 1962.

Sikes, G. *Children's Literature for Dramatization*. New York: Harper & Row, 1964.

Smith, J. S. *A Critical Approach to Children's Literature*. New York: McGraw-Hill, 1967.

Swenson, E. J. "The Treatment of Death in Children's Literature." *Elementary English* (March 1972), 401–404.

Taylor, M. "Instant Enrichment." *Elementary English* (February 1968), 229–233.

Taylor, M. E. "Sex-Role Stereotypes in Children's Readers." *Elementary English* (October 1973), 1045–1047.

Thompson, J., and G. Woodard. "Black Perspective in Books for Children." *The Black American in Books for Children*. Metuchen, N.J.: Scarecrow Press, 1972.

Toothaker, R. E. "Curiosities of Children That Literature Can Satisfy." *Childhood Education* (March 1976), 262–267.

Whitehead, R. *Children's Literature: Strategies of Teaching*. Englewood Cliffs, N.J.: Prentice-Hall, 1968.

Widdemar, M. *Little Girl and Boy Land*. Harcourt Brace Jovanovich, 1952.

Wolf, L. C. "Children's Literature and the Development of Empathy in Young Children," *Elementary English* (May 1975), 49.

Chapter 11
Reading: Comprehension of Written Discourse

What Reading Skills Are Taught in the Language Arts Program?

Throughout the history of American reading education millions of dollars have been spent on research attempting to determine the best methods and materials for the teaching of reading. Important differences among programs with different emphasis have been found, but none of these differences is as significant as the finding that different teachers using the same materials and methods produce a greater range of results than any range found for the different programs. Some teachers, because of unique abilities to understand the needs of a learner and to make the available materials relevant, are successful in developing reading abilities regardless of method.

This does not mean that reading methods and materials are unimportant. It does mean that a competent teacher, using materials in which she has confidence, is essential to a successful program in reading instruction. If the teacher knows *why* she is using a certain book with a child or *why* she is helping a child master a specific reading skill, she is operating at a professional level that assures positive results.

Reading is a process of comprehending written discourse that involves decoding and recoding. One aspect of decoding is to relate the printed word to oral language meaning, which includes changing what is seen in print into meaningful sound. Consistent sound clues in a synthetic language such as English may be represented by total words, word groups, or bound morphemes such as *-ing*. A child learning to speak a language usually associates sounds with meanings; that is, he hears sounds as words or sentence parts. A child's first association between writing and reading is usually based on meaning. The child of three or four can select his favorite record or book through visual clues; he visually recognizes the names of stores, the names of

Purposeful, enjoyable reading can happen anywhere. (PHOTO BY LINDA LUNGREN.)

streets, and the names of some of the products advertised in commercials on television.

There are ideographs in our language as well. The $ sign contains no clues to its sound, but you know its meaning. All our numbers are ideographic. The symbols 9, 10, 11 contain no sound clues but represent only meanings.

Few books read by adults are printed "talk." Certainly, the authors of this textbook have never talked in the manner in which it is written. When the teacher works with comprehension and understanding as reading skills, he has a controlled situation that permits him to prepare the oral language and the experience background of the reader that are essential to interpret the thought presented by the writer. It does not matter if these are called reading-thinking skills as listed in many courses of study since 1900, or creative or critical reading skills, as in more recent publications.

A part of our problem in the language arts is that the term *reading* has many meanings. Some of these have to do with purpose, such as *oral* reading, when a

writer's ideas are projected through speech; reading that describes an *area* in the curriculum; reading that means *action* and may refer to anything from a child's telling what he sees in a picture to a judge's interpretation of a point of law. A child may read a word by changing it to sounds that he recognizes in his language, or he may change it to sounds and discover that it is still meaningless. Another may understand a word's meaning without being able to pronounce it. In terms of response a word means different things. Sometimes the response is careful and profound thought, at other times it is an imaginative fantasy. There may be great emotional feeling in the response or only casual notice.

Eventually all aspects of reading are mastered by most students. But to the beginner the problem is one of looking at words in their printed or written form and discovering the meaning intended by the one who wrote them. Reading is the method by which we communicate to ourselves—and sometimes to others—the meaning contained in printed symbols.

Reading may be thought of as looking *through*

TABLE 11-1. Classification of word structure elements together with examples and word recognition processes

Words in a compound word	Stem or root word	Inflectional forms	Prefixes	Suffixes	Possessive forms	Contractions	Syllables
Example: *snowman*	Example: *joy*	Examples: Words changed by adding *s—cats* *es—boxes* *ed—walked* *ing—walking* *er—sweeter, trainer* *est—sweetest*	Examples: *re—return* *dis—disappointed*	Examples: *ment—amusement* *less—helpless*	Examples: *John's hat* *the girl's doll*	Examples: *didn't* *aren't* *haven't*	Examples: *dan ger* *wis dom*
Children learn to identify the two separate words in a compound word as *snow, man,* when having difficulty in reading a compound word.	Children learn to look for the stem word in words changed by adding affixes as *joyful, enjoyed, enjoyment* as needed when meeting unrecognized words.	Children learn to recognize and pronounce these endings when encountered in reading words.	Children learn to recognize prefixes and their meanings when encountered in reading words.	Children learn to recognize suffixes and their meanings when encountered in reading words.	Children learn to identify possessive forms by noting apostrophe *s* in reading words.	Children learn that the one word stands for two words, and that the apostrophe shows where a letter was left out.	Children learn the concept of a syllable, and learn several ways of dividing words into syllables, when reading words.

Nila Banton Smith, *Reading Instruction for Today's Children* (Englewood Cliffs, N.J.: Prentice-Hall, 1963).

Structural analysis and phonic analysis are different in content and application. Phonics is concerned with the sound elements in words; structural analysis, with the units that make up the structure of a word or that change the meaning of a word. Structural analysis can be put into effect more rapidly than phonic analysis; it does not take as long to perceive whole structural units in a word as it does to sound out letters or letter combinations. Structural analysis is most useful from third grade on where children frequently need to pronounce new words of two or more syllables. Pupils should be encouraged to use structural analysis first in attacking an unrecognized word, and if that does not work, then to use phonics. The two should be combined frequently.

words to the fields of thought *behind* them. The degree of relationship between the meaning of the writer and the interpretation of the reader determines the accuracy of the reading. The meaning is not on the printed page, but in the mind of the reader. Thus meanings will differ, because each reader possesses different experiences in terms of which he interprets the words.

To the beginner each word represents a puzzle to be solved. A word like *mother* or *baby* presents little or no difficulty because the meaning is definite, the word is familiar, and the feelings associated with the word are usually pleasant. A word like *fruit*, however, which can mean *apples*, *bananas*, *oranges*, *grapes*, *lemons*, or *peaches*, is a different problem. A word like *here*, which may mean *at school*, *by the teacher*, *where I stand*, *on the desk*, or almost anyplace, is a puzzle indeed. Then there are words like *at*, which even the teacher cannot define without talking a long time. Some printed words are interesting visually, such as *look*, which has a pair of eyeglasses in the middle, and *oh*, the first letter of which is the shape of the mouth when you say it. Each new word that is recognized and remembered represents a satisfying experience when one is learning to read.

From the teacher's point of view the process is one of repetition, encouragement, reteaching, searching for material, making special material, being pleased by the success of some, and being concerned about the needs of others. Teachers do not expect beginners to identify words that are strange in meaning or new to their oral language. Effort is directed toward the establishment of word analysis skills that will help a child change the printed words to their proper sounds and meanings, which are already part of his oral vocabulary. The focus of teaching effort is on the individual child. Reading is not taught to a child, but rather a child is taught to read.

Word Analysis Skills

A beginner probably remembers each word through the same kind of association process that an adult uses in recalling the identity of people. Such factors as age, hair color, size, profession, place of meeting, and topic of conversation serve as memory aids. If we are seeking to recall a person's name, we use these factors as clues. In much the same ways a child learns to look for certain clues that will help him to recognize the message of the printed word. Five types of reading clues are taught as a part of a child's word skills:

1. *Phonetic clues.* None of the reading programs widely used today neglects the importance of this knowledge. Phonetic clues should probably be called linguistic clues because both individual sounds and the language flow of words, sentences, and story are involved.

2. *Word-form clues.* These are sometimes called configuration clues. They are the forms of the word that give it some identity. *Christmas* and *grandmother* are relatively easy words because of their meaning and length. *Elephant*, with its silhouette or shadow of tall and long letters, may be recognized because of its form. For some words these configuration clues render little assistance. Words like *such*, *said*, and *word* have similar silhouettes or, as some teachers say, have like shadows. Recent studies suggest that beginners use these clues far less than experienced readers. It may be that, as Williams (1970) suggests, there are few exceptions when word-form clues should be taught above the second grade.

3. *Structural clues.* These are noticed in common endings such as *-ing*, *-ed*, and *-tion*. Compound words contain structural clues when children recognize the two combined words. The ability to use prefix and suffix meanings or to recognize the root word represents an advanced use of these clues, as is evidenced in Table 11-1.

4. *Sight word clues.* These are clues that must be memorized through repetition. Words with indefinite meanings, such as *of*, those with difficult phonetic combinations, such as *one*, and some proper names are examples of sight words. Children with keen visual memories will usually learn almost all primary words by sight. Certain words need many repetitions before they are mastered. Words like *here*, *there*, *who*, *what*, and *where* are especially difficult. Others will be remembered after only a

few repetitions. Dictionary skills are sometimes referred to as a reading clue. Certainly for older students the dictionary is a way of determining the meaning of a word.

5. *Context analysis clues.* These are found in the pictures in a book, in the meaning of known words in the sentence, or in the oral discussion of the class. It is always wise to discuss the pictures in a story first, or the children will move their eyes away from the new word to look at the picture for help. If the oral discussion has set the story in Africa, the child may use that clue to understand a new word when he comes to it.

Carter and McGinnis delineate various context clues: [1]

Definition

The unknown word is defined in the descriptive context. For example: A house on a boat is called a *houseboat.*

Synonym

This type of contextual clue consists of a known synonym for the unfamiliar word. For example: Mother was angry and father was *irate* too.

Familiar Expression

This type of clue requires a background and knowledge of common expressions and acquaintance with familiar language patterns. For example: She was as proud as a *peacock.*

Experience

Children and adults may depend upon their experience and mental content to supply the meaning of the new word. For example: The color of grass is *green.*

Comparison or Contrast

The unknown word may be compared or contrasted with something known. For example: John is extravagant, but his brother isn't. John's brother is so miserly he could almost be called *penurious.*

[1] From Homer J. Carter and Dorothy J. McGinnis, *Teaching Individuals to Read* (Boston: Heath, 1962), pp. 84–85.

Summary

The new or unknown word may summarize the ideas that precede it. For example: Down the street they came. First there were the girls twirling batons, then the marching band, and then the men in uniform. It was a *parade.*

Reflection of Situation or Mood

The general tone of the sentence or paragraph provides a clue to the new or unknown word. For example: The clouds were black and ominous. Occasionally streaks of lightning slashed the sky while low rumblings of thunder could be heard in the distance. Silhouetted against this threatening background was the dark and foreboding house where I hoped to secure refuge against the storm. Without warning, a strong feeling of *apprehension* gripped me.

In practice, clues are combined. Word form and phonics are combined in locating the base word and the ending in a plural like *birds.* Even sight words often contain a structural or phonetic clue that an individual child will use.

In addition to these word-attack skills, skills relating to thinking about what is read are of equal concern. The word-attack skills enable the reader to examine a printed word and determine its language sound and meaning. The *skills of response* help the child organize and interpret what the writer has said. These refer to understanding the main idea expressed, noticing details that add meaning, determining whether the idea is true, and noting the personal responses of appreciation. Another group of skills is usually called the *study skills.* These include the ability to locate information, read maps and charts, and select pertinent information.

The understanding of meaning is closely related to purpose or incentive for reading. A problem or question leads to meaningful reading experiences.

Here are several purposes that focus attention in reading:

Read to find out what discovery the character made, what the character did, what happened to a particular character, or to answer the questions the group had about Indian life or space flight. (Reading for details or facts.)

Read to find out why it was a good title, what the

The understanding of meaning is closely related to purpose or incentive in reading. This student desiring to assemble a model car is involved in a meaningful reading experience. (PHOTO BY LINDA LUNGREN.)

problem is in the story, what the character learned, and to summarize what the character did to achieve his purpose. (Reading for main ideas.)

Read to find out what happened in each of the parts of the story, what happened first, second, and third—each step taken to solve a problem, scenes and events for dramatization. (Reading for sequence or organization.)

Read to find out why the characters feel the way they do, what the author is trying to show us, why the characters changed, what qualities the characters had that helped them succeed or caused them to fail. (Reading for inference.)

Read to find what was unusual about a character, what was funny in the story, or whether the story was true. (Reading to classify.)

Read to find out how the character changed, how his life is different from the life we know, how two stories are alike, how the character is like the reader. (Reading to compare or contrast.)

Read to find out whether the character was successful or lived by certain standards, whether you would like to do what the character did or work the way he did in the story. (Reading to evaluate.)

A modern reading program seeks a content so interesting and so related to what is known about children that it serves as the instrument for the mastery of the reading process. Recent material recognizes the importance of relating content to the familiar family life of the reader. Urban children are interested in folk and traditional literature, but they also need stories with which they can identify in terms of their daily experience.

The reading process involves a number of specific skills, such as the use of word analysis techniques. At times the mastery of process is the focus of instruction, but it is not the end purpose of a reading program— which is to help the child attain a level of reading that will enable him to acquire, organize, and share ideas as an intelligent member of society.

Comprehension

As Stauffer (1969) and many other reading educators have suggested, reading requires engagement of the thinking process by an active participant. *Active* is the key word here; if the reader's cognitive abilities are not engaged, he does not receive or retain anything. For this reason, passivity and successful reading comprehension are mutually exclusive. As for retention of material read, Jenkins (1974) suggests that reading comprehension is closely linked to memory. He maintains that what is best remembered is what has been experienced:

I think we will eventually conclude that the mind remembers what the mind *does,* not what the world does. That is, experience is the mind at work, not the active world impinging on a passive organism—and experience is what will be remembered. [Jenkins, 1974, p. 11]

Comprehension of written material requires many kinds of processing. The activities of a proficient reader include operations performed both on the text that he is reading and on his knowledge of the world. Flood and Lapp (1977) have demonstrated that readers must process by inference before they can extract meaning from the text. Inference unites the text with the world through the reader's knowledge. For example as Lapp and Flood (1978, p. 285) suggest, a successful reader performs the following operations to extract the meaning of a sentence:

The text says: The duck is ready to eat.
Operation 1: The reader must resolve the ambiguity of this sentence.
Operation 2: The reader must apply his world knowledge (experience).
  a. The reader generates the possibilities of the meaning of the sentence.
    i. The duck is ready to eat *corn, his supper, a worm . . .*
      or

ii. *Andy is finished cooking and* the duck is ready to be eaten.
  b. The reader waits for more contextual information from the passage; that is, he reads farther.
The text says: *The duck is ready to eat. He always squawks to announce to the farmer that he is hungry.*
Operation 3: The reader extracts the implicit meaning of the first sentence (i.e., the duck is ready to eat something).

These operations occur almost simultaneously if the reader is an active participant in the process of reading. If the reader is passive, none of the critical operations can occur and no comprehension will result. Long ago, Thorndike stressed the importance of recognizing reading as an active participating task:

Understanding a paragraph is like solving a problem in mathematics. It consists in selecting the right elements of the situation and putting them together in the right relations, and also with the right amount of weight or influence or force for each. The mind is assailed as it were by every word in the paragraph. It must select, repress, soften, emphasize, correlate and organize, all under the influence of the right mental set of purpose or demand. [Thorndike, 1917, p. 329]

Theories of Reading Comprehension

Recognizing that comprehension demands work on the reader's part does not mean that we have a totally adequate understanding of the reading comprehension process. Good teaching requires that we consider research findings and our own experience in order to determine the most effective instructional program. Many recent research studies have contributed toward explaining the reading comprehension process. These attempts are essential for our understanding and for curriculum planning and change. Instead of following an absolutely traditional curriculum, we must decide on appropriate instruction with reference to first-hand and research findings. The result of reading is the comprehension of written material. For over fifty years, reading educators have defined the process of reading as "thought-getting" (Farr, 1971). Kingston (1961) elaborated this concept with the statement that "Reading comprehension can best be understood as a product of communications that results from interaction between the reader and writer" (p. 10). Trabasso (1972) and Chase and Clark (1972) present comprehension as information processing, whereas the theories proposed by Dawes (1966) and Frederiksen (1972) illustrate the analysis of connected logical discourse. Other models that explicate the reading process include those of Gough (1972), LeBerge and Samuels (1974), Smith (1971), and Rumelhart (1976).

For Discussion

1. What sight words might a child learn from watching television? Should such words be used in beginning reading instruction?

2. In what sense would the term *reading* by synonymous with *thinking*? Are there thinking skills that should be taught? In what way is thinking influenced by reading? Is the detection of propaganda a reading or a thinking skill? Is the response to poetry a reading or a thinking activity? Is it a learned response?

What Are the Basic Reading, Language-Oriented, and Individual Approaches to Reading Instruction?

As suggested by Lapp and Flood (1978), all existing reading approaches may be classified into three major subdivisions: *sequential reading approach, spontaneous reading approach,* and *managed language/reading systems approach.*

Sequential Reading Approach

Sequential reading approach refers to all methods of teaching reading that emphasize objective, tightly structured, logically organized content primarily directed toward the intellectual dimension of the student. Such methods include the basal reader or programmed instruction.

Basal Readers

Basal readers are designed to evidence a whole word influence, a phonics influence, or a linguistic influence.

The term *basal reading series* is usually applied to a planned program of instruction presented in a series of books written by an author or a group of authors and put out by a single publisher. Because the publisher has the missionary task of spreading the author's ideas about reading instruction, there is a tendency to stress one or two ideas in order to attract attention to a series. Competing series in basic reading necessarily must contain much that is similar; however, each series will have methods as well as content that differ from others. One will stress a carefully selected vocabulary or phonetic controls. Another will emphasize the teacher aids in the manual or workbooks that will make the task "easier." Still another will emphasize content of stories, which may correlate with social studies or be selections from children's literature.

Basal reading series usually have one or two reading-readiness books, three or four preprimers, a primer, a first reader, and two books for each grade up to sixth grade. Each book has its own workbook. Some series use the workbook to present the new words before they are encountered in the textbook. Others use the workbook for additional practice, testing, and independent reading. A few series introduce some words in the readiness books. Between 45 and 60 words are used in the preprimers. All of these are used in the primer. A primer usually adds 90 to 100 words and the first reader 140 to 160 to complete a total of about 300 words in the first grade. Second readers will add from 350 to 600 words and the third readers from 600 to 900. The total number of words used in the primary readers of different authors varies from about 1,100 to 1,800. A number of additional words are derived from these basic words lists. The actual number of different words the child will see in print in the first three grades will range from 2,500 to 4,000.

There are two reasons for the careful control of vocabulary in many series. First, a small sight vocabulary can become the foundation for development of phonetic and structural analysis skills. Second, it makes it possible for the child to read something that satisfies him without too much difficulty. Piano lessons are planned in much the same way. Simple melodies provide a feeling of accomplishment and the reading of notes can be limited to simple techniques.

Each reading series contains a different vocabulary, but a large percentage of words in all series will be from the first 1,000 of the Thorndike Word List. This is a study of 20,000 frequently used words in children's books and is referred to by all publishers.

Words that are taught in one series and used in another are called overlap words. If *come* has been taught in one preprimer, the child will be able to read it in another.

Overlap of vocabulary in five preprimers

A	B	C	D	E
Tom	go	Tip	Ted	Bill
ride	Dick	no	run	come
Betty	help	here	jump	see
fast	look	come	Sally	and
Susan	Jane	Jack	Boots	Linda
Bunny	Sally	is	Mother	Ricky
see	Puff	not	to	here
Flip	here	with	come	Rags
and	Spot	me	look	run
Mother	run	Janet	at	fast
come	oh	find	and	to
airplane	at	home	Father	midnight
the	me	go	play	me
can	Tim	the	splash	look
Pony	get	ball		work
Father	down	will		at
apple	jump	you		home
get	come	I		can
toys		and		
		play		

The following facts should be noted. No two series use exactly the same vocabulary. Words such as *come, look, and,* and *here* do overlap. Although no single book contains more than 21 words, the combined

number of different words in these first preprimers is 65.

Because of these facts, teachers find it best to go through the preprimers of one series first; then the preprimers of other series may be used for free reading while a child is studying in the primer.

The question of vocabulary control involves all materials available for classroom use. Simple library books with controlled vocabulary are being produced in great numbers. If this vocabulary does not have considerable overlap with the basic readers, the children may find it difficult. However, word count alone does not determine the interest a child has in certain material. A child may find that a book of great interest to him is not so difficult as a vocabulary study would indicate.

Schools sometimes adopt one basic series and then use books from other series as supplementary readers. This usually means that equipment such as flash cards and workbooks for the basic series is available. A common practice is to use three basic series in some grades to provide for differences in ability. The major advantage gained is in the area of content.

From the child's point of view a reader is interesting or "good" according to its content. But the teacher looks upon the stories as the vehicle whereby certain skills are developed. The writers of a basic series first determine the method of teaching, which they build into the teacher's manual. Stories and vocabulary are selected that will best support the method employed. The manual is the key to the teacher's success. A student beginning to teach starts with the manual of the series used, adjusts the suggestions in terms of what is known about the children, and adds material when needed. Although the manual is not a teaching plan, it does make suggestions for use as such. Basic reading instruction is a carefully organized activity designed to develop specific reading skills as well as an intensive consideration of the writer's ideas. Reading instruction is not a race to get to the end of a book or to cover a great mass of material in a short time.

Efforts have been made to organize the reading skills into levels of development. A textbook series often considers the reading-readiness and preprimer books as being level 1. The primer would be level 2. Because many series have divided the second and third grades into two levels, there are seven levels of skill development in the first three grades. Charts showing the plan of skill development may be secured from the textbook publishers. In practice, the reading skills do not develop in such an orderly fashion. The language we use has a less apparent order of difficulty than, for example, arithmetic.

Passages taken from contemporary basals are presented in the following pages. The first two selections are taken from the primary level 5 (first grade) basals of the Ginn 720 series. Note the print size, the illustrations, the repeated vocabulary items, and the controlled syntax.

The next selection is taken from level 12 (sixth grade) of the Ginn 720 series. Note the print size, the sophistication of the illustrations, and the advanced vocabulary. Sentences, at the beginning levels, are usually a line or less in length. The content complexity and the story length are adjusted to meet the students' maturity levels.

Basal series have been the focus of much criticism throughout the last decade. Many disparaging references have been made about Dick and Jane, principal characters in the basal series that at its peak was the most widely used elementary school series ever. Poor Dick and Jane bore the insults aimed at many similar basal series, for they became the symbols of all such beginning materials.

Following are some of the common criticisms of the basal series:

1. The vocabulary and sentence patterns do not match the spoken language of children.
2. The content is not interesting to children.
3. The books are developed for graded levels and the child is forced to read in the book for his grade level.
4. The manual must be followed to the last letter. As a result, the program is not adjusted to individual needs and instruction often becomes sterile and uncreative.
5. Use of a basal leads to a uniform three-achievement-level grouping plan whether or not relevant to the performance of the individuals in the group.
6. Children are asked to do workbook pages indiscriminantly.
7. The basal reader provides the sole source of material used in teaching reading skills to children.
8. Basals do not provide for different learning styles or different modes of instruction.
9. Basals are not based on a sound theory of learning.
10. Basal series do not provide instructional procedures.
11. The content often furthers sexual and class stereotypes.

RESPONSES TO THE CRITICISMS. The previous statments provide a sampling of the many criticisms of basal reading programs. The classroom observer may very well have experienced some situation that supports each of these critical statements. The important point, however, is whether the actual problem lies with the basal series itself or with the use of the series in the classroom.

The beginning levels of a basal series do not reflect the extensive oral vocabulary demonstrated by many beginning readers, and the sentence patterns are not those used by many children. It is well known that there is much need for improvement in these areas, and some changes have been made in the more recent basal series. However, no series can reflect the oral vocabulary of every child in the United States. The effective teacher must supplement the basal series in order to match the experience levels of her students. Furthermore, it is quite possible that in teaching a child *to read* it is not necessary or desirable to achieve lexical diversity.

There are many variations among basal reading programs. The authors and producers of each series attempt to build in content and activities that give this program unique characteristics. Some series (Economy, 1975) provide a strong word recognition program; some (Macmillan R, 1975; Ginn 720, 1976) purport to be

Pigeons and Popcorn

Toni looked up at the big buildings.

Pigeons came down from the buildings, looking for food.

A woman came down the street.
" Are you lost? " she said to Toni.
" You're not lost, are you? "

" No. " Toni said.
" My sister is going to meet me here. I'm not lost. "

60

Theodore Clymer et al., May I Come In? (*Boston: Ginn & Co., 1976*), *Reading 720, p. 60.*

Old Buildings and New

Men are at work here.
Some old buildings have to come down.

The men work with big machines.
Men and machines are everywhere.
Down come the old buildings.

Theodore Clymer et al., May I Come In? (*Boston: Ginn & Co., 1976*), Reading 720, p. 78.

IMAGINE SUCCESS

SOMETIMES REACHING A GOAL you have set for yourself can seem almost impossible. Such was the case with Damyan,[1] a Ukrainian boy, who began to feel he never would be a champion swimmer—at least not until he could find the key to success.

Luckily, in swimming class Damyan was making such good progress that at almost every session he got a nod. And one day the coach even went so far as to say, "Good." Damyan was steadily nudging Kolya[2] for top place. Maybe, before long, the coach would tell him that he was ready for the advanced class. Wouldn't that be something to tell his friend Igor[3] and Igor's father!

But then, all of a sudden, the coach began finding fault with his crawl. There was something wrong with the rhythm, the coach kept declaring, as time and time again he blew his whistle. The harder Damyan tried, the worse he got. But he didn't know how to

[1] Damyan (DAM-yan) [2] Kolya (KOHL-yah) [3] Igor (EE-gor)

404

From Measure Me, Sky, *Reading 720 Series (Lexington, Mass.: Ginn, 1976), pp. 404–405.*

help himself, and with every lesson he felt he got steadily worse.

Then finally one Monday, disaster came. The day began like any other. Damyan went to school and after school to his swimming class. From the beginning that swimming lesson went badly. Damyan had never swum so poorly. His whole body seemed filled with lead, and only with effort could he move his limbs.

Time after time the coach blew his whistle and singled him out for correction.

Damyan tried again.

Again the coach blew his whistle.

Suddenly, Damyan had had enough.

The instant the coach finished still another demonstration of what he wanted Damyan to do, with one swift upward lunge Damyan lifted himself out of the pool and ran blindly for the locker room. Even before he reached it, he was filled with horror at what he was doing.

But it was too late to turn back.

more creative than the average in their content and suggested follow-up activities; and others are developed around classical children's literature. Some series, as recently as five years ago, attained uniqueness by shifting from graded levels to nongraded levels; consecutive letters and numbers, e.g., *J, K, L, M,* marked increased difficulty of material. This shift to nongraded materials has become a trend among all basal series.

Teacher's manuals are the basis for many strong arguments for the use of basal series. They provide step-by-step procedures that offer the inexperienced teacher security and assistance and also provide real continuity to the program.

The Chandler Language Experience Readers by Carillo et al. and the Bank Street Readers by Black have been developed in response to the criticism that basals tend to reflect the values and mores of white middle-class families. These programs deal with multiethnic urban environments and also contain many motivating illustrations. Following are examples taken from the Bank Street Readers.

All basal series will probably continue to be criticized. However, a basal program can be a real asset to any classroom teacher if used properly. In recent years publishers have been successful in making their stories more relevant and in providing technical assistance to teachers. We urge you to avoid being swept away by current propaganda and encourage you to examine the basal series for yourself to decide whether it is useful for your purposes.

WHOLE WORD INFLUENCES. In whole word instruction children are expected to identify a word immediately. The method involves instant identification rather than subdivision of the word into parts, analyzing the parts, and stating the word. Each time the classroom teacher asks a student, "What does that word say?" he is utilizing the whole word method of instruction. Because the children are not engaged in letter-by-letter, sound-by-sound analyses, this process differs from the phonics approach. The whole word approach for teaching unfamiliar vocabulary is often referred to as the *look and say* method.

Most basal readers utilize the whole word method as one process of instruction. One reason is that the En-

glish language is not purely alphabetic; its twenty-six letters represent approximately forty-five sounds. In addition, many words in English have irregular pronunciations with respect to the general sound patterns and principles of the language. The sounds of some of the most frequently used words, such as the basic sight words *saw, was, them, they, it, that, under, over,* are difficult to predict through phonetic analysis. Foreign words and those derived from foreign languages also pose problems: *chamois, hors d'oeuvre, suite, savoire faire, vein, depot.* Other instances include homographs:

Denny *wound* the yarn for us.
The patient's *wound* is severe.

Have you *read* the paper today?
Please *read* the directions carefully.

and homophones:

It was a question of their *right* to demonstrate.
Mary promised that she would *write.*

Julio told us tall *tales* until we wept.
Imagine how people would look with *tails.*

The teaching difficulties presented by these examples are obvious. In such cases, advance knowledge of whole word structures is more valuable to the reader than efforts to analyze letter-sound patterns.

In the teaching of whole words there is heavy reliance on *visual discrimination ability.* Studies by Barrett (1965), Durrell (1958), Samuels (1972), Silvaroli (1965), and others suggest that the *major* visual discrimination skill highly correlated with reading success is the ability to discriminate alphabet letters. The need for this skill is immediately apparent in the teaching of similar whole words:

This word is *pat.*
It looks like *bat,* except
pat begins with *p* and
bat begins with *b.*

After several exposures to these words, students will incorporate them into a sight vocabulary of whole words. The whole word approach is an aid in vocabulary ex-

Room for a Pet

One day in the park Pedro saw
a policeman on a horse. It was a big horse
with a long black tail.

The horse stopped by Pedro. When Pedro
put up his hand, the horse put his wet nose
right in it.

The policeman smiled. "I think my horse
likes you," he said.

"Well, I like your horse," said Pedro.
"I like him a lot."

He watched the policeman ride away
on his big horse.

Then Pedro ran home.

79

Irma Simonton Black et al., eds., My City, *The Bank Street Readers, Bank Street College of Education (New York: Macmillan, 1965), pp. 79–80.*

"Mother," said Pedro. "I am thinking.
I am thinking about a pet for me."

"What kind of pet?" his mother asked.

"A horse," said Pedro. "I am thinking
of a horse with a long black tail."

"A horse in this little apartment?"
said Pedro's mother. "You must think
again, Pedro."

Pedro went out again.

Pedro walked and thought.

Jean's Father Goes to School

"My father goes to school," said Jean.

"He can't," Arthur said. "Fathers don't go to school."

"They do so," said Carmen. "My father goes to school at night. He learns how to read and write English."

"See!" Jean said to Arthur. "Fathers do go to school."

"Jean," asked Carmen, "what does your father do at his school?"

"Well, today he has to jump out of a window," said Jean.

210

Irma Simonton Black et al., eds., My City, *The Bank Street Readers, Bank Street College of Education (New York: Macmillan, 1965), p. 210.*

There Was a New Boy

There was a new boy on the block. He
moved into the house next door to Henry.

Henry looked him over. He looked O.K.,
but you can't really tell by looking.

Henry told Jack about the new boy.
"A new boy moved in next door to me,"
he said.

Irma Simonton Black, ed., et al., My City, *The Bank Street Readers, Bank Street College of Education (New York: Macmillan, 1965), p. 57.*

pansion for older children and in the teaching of contractions: *can't, I'm, it's, she'll, we'd.*

PHONICS INFLUENCE. The phonics influence on reading materials and instruction dates back to the 1880s, when reading educators found that the use of letter-sound relationships was an aid to the identification and pronunciation of unfamiliar words. Although the value of this process is obvious, it is necessary to remember that phonics can serve only as a partial word analysis process. A look at the English alphabet explains the reason for this: twenty-six letters are used to represent approximately forty-five sounds. The adaptation of words with foreign origins (*chamois, depot*) serves as another case in point where an exact one-to-one sound-symbol correspondence is impossible. In spite of these examples, phonics instruction has been an important part of basal materials for decades, with good reason. Let us now consider two teaching aids once popularly believed to alleviate the problem of phonic inconsistencies.

ITA. The *ITA* or *Initial Teaching Alphabet* is an augmented alphabet. Anyone who reads and writes English realizes the problems arising from the use of a twenty-six-letter alphabet for a system of almost twice that many sounds; by necessity, some symbols must be used for more than one sound. In addition, particular sounds can be represented by a number of different spellings, a situation that guarantees spelling confusion.

To correct these problems, an Englishman named James Pitman (1964) devised an augmented alphabet, also called an artificial orthography, having forty-four symbols. In its formulation an effort was made to preserve the upper half of letters as they are in the traditional orthography, the logic being that a child who learned to read with the ITA would have an easier time during the inevitable shift to traditional orthography. Although Pitman's efforts to produce an improved English sound system were not the first, the ITA has been more widely employed than any other similar method.

Use of the ITA is not tied exclusively to a particular method of teaching reading. Basal programs in both England and America employ it. As part of the Early-to-Read program (1966), it has been circulated throughout a number of American school systems. The ITA can also be readily employed in a language experience program. Because of the limited quantity of materials available in the ITA, however, it would be virtually impossible to develop an individualized reading program using only the ITA. Even if sufficient materials reach the market, their cost is likely to be prohibitive. In addition, the program is applicable only in the primary grades, with a transition in second or third grade to traditional orthography. The greatest use of individualized reading programs is on the intermediate skill levels.

Words in Color. A second aid for phonics instructions is *Words in Color,* devised by Caleb Gategno in 1962. Instead of a single letter or combination of letters as the symbol for a speech sound, thirty-nine different colors are used to represent the sounds of English. The materials of the system consist of charts of words with the color representations for traditional letter configurations.

Eight of these charts are phonic code charts, and twenty-one others contain word illustrations. One example of the letter and letter-combination charts is this selection of phonic codes, representing the sound of long *a:*

a—able	eigh—weigh
ey—they	aigh—straight
ay—they	ei—their
ai—mail	ea—great

These long *a* sounds are coded *green* every time they appear. Similarly, short *a* sounds are coded *white* at each occurrence, and long *e* sounds are coded *vermillion.* The thirty-six other English sounds represented in this system have other distinctive color codes.

One of the drawbacks to this and other phonics systems is that there are few materials and a limited selection of reading materials. As with any other phonics program, children using the Words in Color program rely heavily on letter sounds and word parts instead of whole words and letter names. Another difficulty with this system is the need for sophisticated visual discrimination; the variations in color are highly significant.

When the color codes include a range of greens—for example, from dark green, olive green, and emerald green to leaf green, light green, and yellow green—the color discrimination problem may impede phonics analysis.

LINGUISTICS INFLUENCE. Linguistics is the scientific study of language. It includes an investigation of the sounds used in language, the combinations of sounds that make up words, and the meanings attached to these sounds. The patterning of these words into thought-expressing units is also a major concern of structural linguistics.

The influence of linguistics on basal reading instruction is relatively new. A variety of "linguistic" reading programs have appeared, beginning with the Bloomfield-Barnhart *Let's Read* (1961) stories. The Palo Alto Linguistic Program, the Miami Linguistic Reading Program, and the Merrill Linguistic Readers are other examples of series that use strict vocabulary control in beginning materials. Vocabulary control facilitates the teaching of certain phonetic principles. For example, students learn the sound-symbol relationships for specified consonants and the short sound of one or two vowels, then as many different words as possible that can be made from the combination of these letters. Declarative and interrogative sentences are developed using these words. The following group of sentences illustrates the content typical of the beginning levels of linguistic programs:

> Dan is a man.
>
> Dan is tan.
>
> Dan is a tan man.
>
> Is Dan tan?
>
> Fan Dan, the tan man.

Many linguistic materials avoid the use of illustrations to accompany stories, for their authors feel that pictures provide an unnecessary crutch for the reader. Some authors utilize very simple illustrations involving only one or two colors in order to achieve a compromise between starkness and ordinary illustration.

Linguists have sometimes criticized the unnatural language patterns of basal reading programs, e.g., *See*

Spot run. The expression *Dan, the tan man* also seems unnatural. However, sentence patterns do reflect ordinary language usage as the program moves to more advanced levels. In fact, sentences in the linguistic readers often appear more complex that those in other basal materials on an equivalent level.

Reading programs with a linguistic influence have appeared in various formats. Some have taken the form of a basal series, whereas others have been composed of a series of small paperbacks. At least one series has appeared in a programmed format. Regardless of format, the series have all attempted to deal systematically with mastery of sound-symbol relationships and to avoid attention to irregularly spelled words.

The rather monotonous content resulting from strict attention to spelling patterns and letter substitution has provoked much criticism but has also attracted some strong support. Some teachers find it very difficult to generate real enthusiasm for Dan the tan man. Advocates of linguistic programs argue that this is of little significance in beginning reading. They feel that the security children gain from the contact with consistent sound-symbol patterns more than compensates for the lack of content substance.

Following are selections from various linguistic reading programs.

Programmed Instruction

Another example of the sequentially planned approach to teaching reading is programmed materials. Programmed instruction consists of the presentation of a block of information broken down into small units. Through linear or branched patterning these small blocks are organized for logical and sequential teaching.

In a branched configuration one unit or frame of information is presented to the learner for response. If a correct response is given, the learner may bypass several frames to move only through those containing unknown information. This allows for specific instruction and adjustment of the ratio between mastered and unfamiliar areas of knowledge.

In a linear program every learner moves step by step through the same series of frames. The factor for

Fly, Kite, Fly

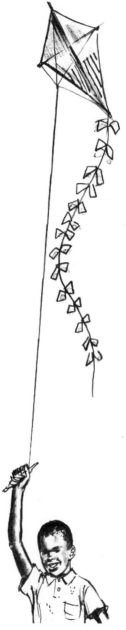

Fly, kite, fly

Far up in the sky.

Feel the wind.

Grab the breeze.

Fly, kite, fly.

Wag, kite, wag.

Be a sky-ride flag.

Jag and skip.

Zag and zip.

Wag, kite, wag.

Glide, kite, glide.

Sit on the wind and ride.

Scrape the sun.

Be my pride.

Glide, kite, glide.

Theodore E. Glim, The Palo Alto Reading Program, Sequential Steps in Reading, *Book 8, 2nd ed. (New York: Harcourt Brace Jovanovich, 1975).*

Look at the Man

Look at Dan.

Is Dan at bat?

Dan is not at bat.

A man is at bat.

Look at the man bat!

The man ran.

Dan sat.

26

Wayne Otto et al., I Can, *Merrill Linguistic Reading Program (Columbus, Ohio: Merrill, 1975), pp. 26–27.*

can

man

ran

Dan

fan

pan

van

to

fat
fan

pat
pan

man
fan
pan

fan
pan
van

27

The Fastest Hound Around

Away down south
In Sourwood County
Lived an old hound dog.
His name was Bounty.

Asleep all day,
Stretched out on the ground,
No lazier dog
Could ever be found.

Now Bounty belonged
To farmer Hal Prouse.
They lived alone
In an old farmhouse.

The Palo Alto Reading Program, *Book 19, 2nd ed.* (*New York: Harcourt Brace Jovanovich, 1973*).

individualization in linear patterning is the rate at which the learner progresses through the complete series.

Two advantages of programmed instruction are instant feedback and instant error correction. The programmed instruction method is usually structured so that the learner completes one small block of the program per frame and checks to determine whether his response is correct before moving to the next frame. Immediate correction of errors prevents continued use of incorrect data.

The formats of such instructional programs vary. They may come as workbooks or as something more mechanical, e.g., audio or television tapes. In conjunction with the differences of format may be differences in mode of response. Whatever these variations are, their design will require individual response and provide immediate feedback with reinforcement of correct answers and correction of incorrect ones.

There has been some variety in partially programmed systems, but to date the Sullivan Programmed Reading system (1963) seems to be the most complete one designed for developmental reading instruction. This linear program reflects a linguistic approach.

Spontaneous Reading Approach

The spontaneous reading approach emphasizes methods such as *language experience* and *individualized instruction*, which encourage personalized reading instruction or curricula.

Language Experience

In recent years *Language Experiences in Communication* by Dr. R. Van Allen (1976) has encouraged interest in the language experience method. The approach was not conceived as one to rely on published materials. Rather, it is meant to grow out of the oral expressions of individual or groups of children.

The following example from *From My Front Door* illustrates materials that have been developed and published in an attempt to encourage language experience programs:[2]

[2] R. Van Allen, *Language Experiences in Communication* (Boston: Houghton Mifflin, 1976).

Preparation for Day 21
What to have on hand

Materials	Quantity	Purpose
Resource Cards 41 through 45, *Neighborhoods Near and Far*		Discussion Center
Resource Card 46, *Making Papier-Mâché*		Art Center
Reading Experience 20, "An American Indian Home"		Reading Center

UNIT 2; DAY 21

Discussion/Planning Period: Discussion Center

Help review the previous week's activities.

Explain that this week the children will be dealing with places beyond the neighborhood. Encourage a discussion of other places, using Resource Cards 41 through 45, *Neighborhoods Near and Far*.

Activity Period: General

Children may be working on the *Class Magazine* or discussing Listening Experience 7, "This Land Is Your Land."

Choice 1. Invite the children to look for mini-cities while on a class walk.

Choice 2. Encourage the children to write picture stories about *A Walk on the Moon*.
   Exploring writing (I,6): Elaboration

Activity Period: Art Center

Ongoing activities include making posters, *Punctuation Pictures*, illustrations of the story "Stone Soup," *Neighborhood Pictures*, *Recycling Projects*, pomanders, *Ideal School Pictures*, and improvements in the *Neighborhood Model*.

Choice 1. Suggest that the children make *Mars Maps*.
   Responding in personal ways (III,7)

Choice 2. Invite the children to draw pictures of things every neighborhood should have.

Choice 3. Urge the children to paint pictures showing what they would do in a place portrayed on Resource Cards 41 through 45, *Neighborhoods Near and Far*.

Choice 4. Children might make figures using Resource Card 46, *Making Papier-Mâché.*

Activity Period: Reading Center

Ongoing activities include comparing versions of the story "Stone Soup," working with Reading Experiences 14, "A Very Special Place" and 17, "The Tree," and looking for examples of good and bad environmental conditions.

Choice 1. Encourage the children to read and prepare to share Reading Experience 20, "An American Indian Home."
    Extending vocabulary (II,3)

Choice 2. Read the poem "Very Lovely," and urge the children to talk about other ideas it gives them.

What to prepare in advance

1. If one is available, prepare a foreign language recording for playing in the Listening/Viewing Center.

Activity Period: Writing Center

Ongoing activities include writing *Stone Soup Stories, Random Poems,* answers to want ads, *If I Were Mayor* stories, an invitation, and *Special Smells Poems,* and working with Ditto-sheet U11, *Sights, Sounds, and Smells from My Front Door.*

Choice 1. Suggest that the children write stories about what the neighborhood was like in the past.

Choice 2. Invite the children to write *Neighborhood Wish Books.*

Choice 3. Urge the children to write reports about people of other cultures in response to Resource Cards 41 through 45.

Activity Period: Listening/Viewing Center

Children may be working with "Who Am I?" from Listening Skill Lesson 20, *Poems about People,* with "Dance Poem" from Listening Skill Lesson 19, *Poems of Movement,* or with Listening Experience 7, "This Land Is Your Land," looking at pictures of environmental conditions, or preparing a *Sound Collage.*

Choice 1. Invite children to listen to a foreign language record and then try to invent a new language.

Activity Period: Discovery Center

Ongoing activities include working with *Sniff-It Jars* and preparing a *Size Chart.*

Other

Discussion/Planning Period: Discussion Center (Whole Class)

After the children talk briefly about last week's activities, explain that for the last four weeks their activities have been associated with places, things, and people in their neighborhood. This week the children will be writing, discussing, drawing, and learning about places beyond the neighborhood.

You might ask the children: "If you could live any place you wanted, where would you like to live?" If you could make any place be the way you wanted it, what would you do?" Display and pass around Resource Cards 41 through 45, *Neighborhoods Near and Far.* Suggestions given on the cards may be helpful in guiding the discussion. Talk about other human places, animal places, strange and mystical places, magical places, and places in outer space—planets, moons, and asteroids.
    Discussing and conversing (I,5)

Activity Period: General

Choice 1. Take a class walk to look for mini-cities, little worlds within the larger environment. Look down for anthills and worm holes. Look up for nests and tree houses. Look way up to see if any cities can be found in the clouds. Encourage the children to pretend they are ants or birds or that the streets are canals. After the walk the children can write about what they saw, felt, or imagined.
    Responding in personal ways (III,7)

Choice 2. When you are back in the classroom, pull out the *Move Book* introduced on Day 7. Are there any words there that would describe what walking on the moon would be like? Maybe you'll have to add one. How about *bounce?* Suggest that the children write picture stories about *A Walk on the Moon.*
    Exploring writing (I,6); Elaboration

Activity Period: Art Center

Choice 1. Suggest that the children make *Mars Maps.* They can show a Martian city with houses, a spaceport, and any other features they think a Martian city should have.
    Responding in personal ways (III,7)

Choice 2. Some children might draw pictures of something they think every neighborhood should have.

Choice 3. Encourage the children to imagine themselves in any one of the places shown on Resource Cards 41 through 45, *Neighborhoods Near and Far.* They can paint pictures showing what they would do in the place they pick.

Choice 4. Resource Card 46, *Making Papier-Mâché,* shows how to make papier-mâché constructions. Children might follow instructions on the card to make something they imagine—a family from outer space, perhaps.

Comprehending what is heard (III,2): Following directions

Activity Period: Reading Center

Choice 1. Encourage some children to read Reading Experience 20, "An American Indian Home," to find out how the Dakota Sioux Indians built their houses long ago. The children can share what they learn from their reading during the Sharing/Assessment Period.

Extending vocabulary (II,3)

Choice 2. Read the poem "Very Lovely" by Rose Fyleman aloud. Encourage the children to talk about it. What other ideas does it give them? Could they substitute snow or ice for water and imagine what it might be like?

Very Lovely by Rose Fyleman

Wouldn't it be lovely if the rain came down
Till the water was quite high over all the town?
If the cabs and buses all were set afloat,
And we had to go to school in a little boat?

Wouldn't it be lovely if it still should pour
And we all went up to live on the second floor?
If we saw the butcher sailing up the hill,
And we took the letters in at the window sill?

It's been raining, raining, all the afternoon;
All these things might happen really very soon.
If we woke to-morrow and found they had begun
Wouldn't it be glorious? *Wouldn't* it be fun?

Activity Period: Writing Center

Choice 1. Suggest that some children write stories about what their neighborhood was like in the past. They might find something in the Reading Center helpful, or they might interview an older person who has been in the neighborhood all his or her life.

Organizing ideas (III,3)

Choice 2. *Neighborhood Wish Books* might be written. Each could contain a story or poem about something the children wish for or something about the neighborhood. The stories or poems could be written on gaily colored papers of different shapes, and the completed books might be displayed in the Reading Center.

Authoring individual books (I,7): Author's purpose; author's point of view

Choice 3. Some children might want to examine Resource Cards 41 through 45, *Neighborhoods Near and Far,* as a beginning step to preparing written reports about people of other cultures.

Activity Period: Listening/Viewing Center

Choice 1. Some children might like to listen to a foreign language record and then make up a language of their own. They could use a few words from an existing language or a language system such as pig latin or even create a new language, "Martian" perhaps. If they wrote a dictionary giving a few of their words and the English equivalents, they could challenge other classmates to use the dictionary to decipher messages.

Exploring sounds (II,2): Recognizing sound-spelling relationships

Sharing/Assessment Period: Discussion Center (Whole Class)

Invite the individual children to share with the rest of the class any of the work they have done. Encourage class involvement with the many projects. Especially encourage the children to compare any of the imagined places they have thought of today or any of the faraway places they have investigated with the place where they live. Help them to think about how the places are different and how they are the same. Do the children think it would be a good idea to adapt some of the features of the other places to their own place?

Assimilating and integrating ideas (III,4): Comparison and contrast

Suggest that the children ask their parents, grandparents, older friends, and relatives about experiences that they've had living in other places—other houses, neighborhoods, cities, or countries. How were these experiences different from the ones the children have now?

The extension of the child's language is reflected in the points outlined by Lee and Ellen (1963) when they delineated their definition of language experience:

1. What a child thinks about he can talk about.
2. What he can talk about can be expressed in printing, writing, or some other form.
3. Anything he writes can be read.
4. He can read what he writes and what other people write.
5. As he represents his speech sounds with symbols, he uses the same symbols (letters) over and over.
6. Each letter in the alphabet stands for one or more sounds that he makes when he talks.
7. Every word begins with a sound he can write.
8. Most words have an ending sound.
9. Many words have something in between.
10. Some words are used over and over in our language and some words are not used very often.
11. What he has to say and write is as important to him as what other people have written for him to read.
12. Most of the words he uses are the same ones which are used by other people who write for him to read. [pp. 5–8]

The implementation of a language experience program encourages the development of an individualized/personalized curriculum.

Individualized Instruction

The reason teachers have turned to a program of individualized reading instruction is the range in abilities found in the normal classroom. It is not uncommon for the thirty-five children in a fifth-grade room to have a range that extends from below that of average third-grade readers to above that of average ninth-grade students. In such situations the teacher divides the class into groups for instruction. The books or assignments for each group will be determined by the reading achievement of the individuals in that segment of the class. In a small rural school that has one teacher for all the grades, similar grouping practices are followed. It is customary for an able second-grade child to read with those in the third or fourth grade. The term *personalized reading* is sometimes used to describe such practices.

A special method of individualizing instruction within a classroom has been identified by the terms *self-selection* and *language experience approach*. The self-selection program allows each child to seek whatever reading material stimulates him and to work at his own rate with what he has chosen. The major elements of a self-selection reading program include the following:

1. Children themselves select their own reading materials.
2. Children read at their own rate.
3. Teachers work almost entirely with individuals.
4. The best elements of recreational reading and one-to-one skill teaching are combined.
5. Groups are organized not by ability but by purpose or goals.

Individualized reading is not a single method but rather a plan of instruction that can be adapted to any method. Individualized reading does not eliminate the use of groups. Instead, it changes the way groups are organized, how long they exist, and what their purposes are.

The child does not decide whether or not he will participate in developing skills, what materials will be supplied, what skills he will work on, or any other matter that pertains to professional competence. This is the teacher's role. An individualized reading program is planned, designed, and organized into an instructional program. Individualized reading is not recreational reading. Recreational reading does not usually involve reading instruction. In individualized reading, definite provision is made for the teacher to teach, for the children to read aloud to the teacher at reasonable intervals, and for reading instruction to take place daily.

Materials are a basic consideration of individualized reading. If children are to have any degree of self-selection, then materials in large quantities must be available, typically a hundred or more titles at any one time in the classroom. Material for individualized reading includes, of course, all varieties: basal texts, supplementary readers, library books, texts in the various subject fields, trade books, pamphlets, brochures, teacher-made and pupil-made materials, magazines, and newspapers.

Management procedures and arrangements in individualized reading are flexible. The teacher does have well-defined purposes; goals are firmly fixed in mind, and an organization and structure are provided that re-lease children to learn. But materials, time allotments, and procedures are used and developed in terms of the individual learner's growth in reading and self-develop-ment.

Usually teachers plan scheduled periods to meet the following objectives:

1. For selection of reading materials.
2. For individual reading conferences between teacher and pupil.
3. For independent activities for children not reading independently.
4. For class or small-group discussion and sharing.
5. For children in pairs or small groups to engage in creative work growing out of common reading.
6. For small groups or the whole class either with the teacher or independently to develop needed skills and to work on common difficulties in reading.
7. For children to read independently.

Time allotments vary. No two teachers work ex-actly the same way, nor are all of these activities pro-vided each day. Some teachers set aside special days for certain activities; other teachers have them for short times throughout the day.

The typical daily program follows a routine of this nature: The teacher gives some direction to the class as a whole before starting other activities. During this time the children have an opportunity to raise questions about their work, to clarify committee work assign-ments, to decide reading plans, and to get a clear under-standing of the day's plans.

Depending on the day's purpose, planned activi-ties, and needs and interests revealed, the teacher would work in one or more of the following ways:

1. Hold individual reading conferences while others work on independent activities.
2. Work with a small group on a particular skill while others read independently.
3. Hold individual reading conferences while some children read independently and others work in pairs or small groups on creative activities.
4. Circulate to provide help as children read indepen-

dently, carry on other independent activities, or work in groups.

Balance in the program is maintained by looking at the daily activities for a period of time. Some teachers keep a diary to record past activities and plan future programs. In this way they soon discover that a fixed daily routine is not necessary to achieve desired results with each pupil contact.

Grouping is flexible in time span and composition. Some groups work only a day together, others longer. Depending on their needs, some children may partici-pate in several groups at a time or perhaps none at all. After reviewing her notes, the teacher recognizes a common need and plans a group activity; or after four or five reading conferences, volunteers are designated to form a group. Test results may indicate good possi-bilities for group work. Groups are formed in different ways but always for a specific task at a particular time. When the purpose is accomplished, the group is dis-banded. Grouping frequently occurs in individualized reading, but it is organized to focus on the individual learner.

Direct attention is paid to skills in individualized reading. The skills are no different from those found valuable in any basic reading program. The emphasis is on determining which skills are to be developed in indi-vidual children and how much practice each should have.

Procedures used for skill development vary from day to day, but teachers generally find these basic steps helpful:

1. Provide individual guidance during the reading conference.
2. Perform group work with children who share a common need.
3. Encourage pupils to assist each other—working in small groups.
4. Divide the class into practice groups alternating teacher guidance and self-responsibility.
5. Make plans for the entire class.

Any program that encourages children to read in many areas for a variety of purposes at different speeds demands some kinds of records. In individualized reading many types of records are useful:

Running diaries of reading activities.

Individual plans for reading, sharing, or activity.

Records of reading difficulties—new words, meanings of words, development and completion of comprehension worksheets, and so on.

Records of kinds and amount of reading.

The teacher keeps individual cards or a page in a notebook for each pupil, recording dates when books were started and finished, difficulties encountered, strengths noted, attitudes, and personal observations.

Although some teachers prefer an individualized reading program, it is a growing practice to combine group and individualized, managed programs. Some of the students may follow a basic reader as it was planned by those who created the series; others may follow an individualized program guided by the teacher.

Managed Language/Reading Program

The content of a *managed language/reading program* may be defined as being logically organized while emphasizing individualized instruction. It capitalizes on the strengths of both the sequential and spontaneous reading approaches. Such programs have been developed in an attempt to provide classroom teachers with a manageable program. Many of the newer programs include basals with interesting and relevant stories. Often included are filmstrips and tapes of the stories, ditto worksheets, teacher manuals, criterion-referenced tests, and elaborate recordkeeping systems. These supplementary components are intended to help teachers to individualize their reading programs.

To the extent possible, these systems are language experience based, for they attempt to include stories that closely reflect the language of real children in true-to-life situations. The management systems help the teacher to *diagnose, prescribe,* and *evaluate* each child's program.

Following is a description of the management system of Ginn's Reading 720 program. Other programs have also attempted to develop management systems. [3]

The management system for an instructional program is neither the content of that program nor the teaching method by which content is presented to pupils. Rather, it represents a kind of framework or pattern by means of which content and teaching methods can be organized to assure that some specific outcomes occur. Usually, the desired effects of managing instruction are as follows: (1) that pupils are systematically taught at least a core set of specified educational objectives, with the exception of those pupils who have previously become proficient in certain of these objectives, (2) that evidence is generated to show whether pupils learn these objectives at a level of proficiency pre-specified as desirable, (3) that provision is made for systematic re-instruction of pupils on any of the objectives for which they have failed to demonstrate proficiency, and (4) that teaching pupils to acceptable proficiency on this set of core objectives is accomplished in the minimum reasonable time.

When the core strands of Reading 720 are taught in the management mode, the foregoing outcomes can be realized. Using a management system, the teacher may select from the rich pool of hundreds of objectives, those specific ones that represent the core skills of Reading 720, drawn from the comprehension, vocabulary, and decoding strands. The teacher may then build lesson plans emphasizing, or even restricted to, these core objectives and teach those children known to need them. Additional Reading 720 components allow the teacher to evaluate with precision the proficiency of pupils on the core objectives. Other Reading 720 resources can then be used to reteach missed objectives to just these pupils who need re-instruction. Because managed instruction focuses so tightly on core essentials and attempts to limit instruction within the core strands to that demonstrably required, whether initial or reteaching, it moves pupils with maximum efficiency toward attainment of the desired outcomes.

Implementing a management system in teaching Reading 720 aids the teacher in the following ways:

[3] For example, T. Harris et al., *The Economy Company Readers* (Boston: The Economy Company, 1975); William Eller et al., *Laidlaw Reading Program* (River Forest, Ill.: Laidlaw Publishing, 1976); C. Smith, *The Macmillan Reader* (New York: Macmillan Publishing Co., Inc., 1975).

—in helping to select what pupils are to learn

—in systematic planning for and provision of supplementary instruction

—in individualizing instruction according to pupil needs

—in establishing an instructional pace that is efficient yet accomplishes desired goals

A successful managed language/reading system integrates its various components into the existing basal program. Such integration is exemplified by the following example and materials taken from Ginn 720: [4]

COMPONENTS OF READING 720 MANAGEMENT SYSTEM

A management system is integrated or built into Reading 720. All the directions needed for managing core skills instruction are found in this Teacher's Edition. Instructions will be found placed sequentially as needed, throughout the various sections of the lesson plans and in the manuals accompanying the various components that are essential to managing instruction in Reading 720. All such manuals are supplied with these components when purchased separately, and are also reproduced in this section of the Teacher's Edition.

The following are necessary for managing the instruction of the core skills. These items are also available as separate components.

Activities in Part 4 of the Lesson Plan

Activities in Part 4 of each plan are designed to introduce and give practice reinforcement of objectives taught in the unit.

Unit Criterion Exercises

The Unit Criterion Exercises may be used to assess pupil proficiency on the specified core skills of a unit. Pupils scoring at or above Suggested Criterion Score (SCS) are assumed to have attained acceptable proficiency on the tested objective. The rationale for establishing the SCS is described in the Criterion Exercise manual and is found beginning on page 251 of this Teacher's Edition.

[4] T. Clymer et al., *Ginn 720 Reading Program* (Lexington, Mass.: Xerox Co., 1976). Copyright 1976 by Ginn and Company.

Criterion Exercise Record Sheets (CERS)

The CERS are forms for recording and organizing groups of pupils' Unit Criterion Exercise scores and referencing them to specific supplemental instruction or enrichment resources. Instructions for using the CERS are found on page 264. The CERS for each unit are found on pages 265–267.

Booster Activities

Paper-and-pencil instructional activities are designed to give practice or reinforcement to pupils scoring below Suggested Criterion Score on any of the objectives tested in a Unit Criterion Exercise. All the Booster Activities for Level 5 are found on pages 271–280 and the manual of directions for their use is on pages 268–270. Instructions for selecting the proper Booster Activity are found in the manual. It is important to note that Booster Activities ''boost'' marginally performing pupils to an acceptable level. When pupils score very low on an objective, especially if they get none of the items right, they need reteaching. After reteaching has been accomplished, the Booster or the other practice activities may be given.

Use of the following component, while not essential, is strongly recommended:

Reading Achievement Card

The Reading Achievement Card is a chart for recording and organizing all of an individual pupil's criterion exercise scores for one level. This component is reproduced in this Teacher's Edition. It is also found on the last two pages of each Unit Criterion Exercise booklet, and, in addition, is available separately printed on tag board.

Several other Reading 720 components are optionally usable with management mode instruction and, except for the Informal Reading Inventory, do not appear in this Teacher's Edition. Each has its own manual or other Directions describing its use. These components include the following:

Initial Placement Test

The Initial Placement Test aids in determining the level in which to start pupils new to Reading 720.

Reading 720 Initial placement test
Class work sheet

Teacher's Name
School   Date
City   Grade

Pupil's name	IPT level	Initial assigned level	Assigned level after 2 weeks	Comments
1.				
2.				
3.				
4.				
5.				
6.				
7.				
8.				
9.				
10.				
11.				
12.				
13.				
14.				
15.				
16.				
17.				
18.				
19.				
20.				

Informal Reading Inventory

The Informal Reading Inventory helps in making initial individual placement decisions or in post-instruction diagnosis as a supplement to the Unit Criterion Exercises.

Unit Decoding Pretests

The Pretests are an aid in determining which decoding skills pupils already know before they start a unit.

Level Mastery Tests

Level Mastery Tests may be used for surveying pupil achievement on an entire level, or for providing a cumulative, final check on pupil proficiency on the level's objectives.

Reading Progress Card

The Reading Progress Card serves as a device for recording cumulative reading achievement tests and other data for all thirteen levels. It is available in file-folder-format.

How Has the Readiness Concept Influenced Instructional Practice in Reading?

In the development of each child there is a time when his language facility, experience, or social development indicates that he is ready for a particular aspect of read-

Reading 720
Reading achievement card
Level 2

Pupil's Name _____

School _____

_____

Key: Total = Number of Items; SCS = Suggested Criterion Score; PS = Pupil's Score

Directions: Record in the appropriate box the pupil's score on each part of the Criterion Exercise. At the end of a level, sign and date the card.

Unit 1
DECODING
initial consonants
/b/b, /l/l, /r/r, /h/h

Total	SCS	PS
12	10	

Notes: _____
_____
_____
_____
_____

VOCABULARY
Word Recognition

Total	SCS	PS
8	6	

_____
_____

Unit 2
DECODING
initial consonant /j/j

Total	SCS	PS
4	3	

Notes: _____
_____
_____
_____

VOCABULARY
Word Recognition

Total	SCS	PS
10	8	

_____
_____

Unit 3
DECODING
initial consonant /k/c

Total	SCS	PS
4	3	

Notes: _____
_____
_____
_____

VOCABULARY
Word Recognition

Total	SCS	PS
12	10	

_____
_____

Unit 4
DECODING
initial consonants
/l/l, /y/y, /n/n

Total	SCS	PS
9	7	

Notes: _____
_____
_____
_____

VOCABULARY
Word Recognition

Total	SCS	PS
10	8	

_____
_____

ing instruction. Table 11-2 indicates the aspects of readiness that a teacher would consider in the first grade. Some of these factors are developmental and cannot be influenced directly by instruction, whereas others, of course, may be influenced by the work of the kindergarten.

TABLE 11-2. Russell checklist for reading readiness

Physical readiness	*Yes*	*No*
1. Eyes:		
a. Do the child's eyes seem comfortable? (Does he squint, rub eyes, hold material too close or too far away from eyes?)	_____	_____
b. Are the results of clinical test or an oculist's examination favorable?	_____	_____
2. Ears:		
a. Does he respond to questions or directions, and is he apparently able to hear what is said in class?	_____	_____
b. Does he respond to low-voice test of twenty feet, a whisper test of fifteen inches?	_____	_____
c. Is his audiometer test normal?	_____	_____
3. Speech:		
a. Does he speak clearly and well?	_____	_____
b. Does he respond to correction readily?	_____	_____
4. Hand-eye coordination:		
a. Does he make his hands work together well in cutting, using tools, or bouncing a ball?	_____	_____
5. General health:		
a. Does he give an impression of good health?	_____	_____
b. Does he seem well nourished?	_____	_____
c. Does the school physical examination reveal good health?	_____	_____
Social readiness		
1. Cooperation:		
a. Does he work well with a group, taking his share of the responsibility?	_____	_____
b. Does he cooperate with the other children in playing games?	_____	_____
2. Sharing:		
a. Does he share materials without monopolizing their use?	_____	_____
b. Does he share his home toys with others?	_____	_____
c. Does he wait his turn in play or games?	_____	_____
d. Does he await his turn when classwork is being checked by the teacher?	_____	_____
3. Self-reliance:		
a. Does he work things through for himself?	_____	_____
b. Does he work without asking teacher about the next step?	_____	_____
c. Does he take care of his clothing and materials?	_____	_____
d. Does he find anything to do when he finishes an assigned task?	_____	_____

Social readiness	Yes	No

4. Good listening:
   a. Is he attentive? _____ _____
   b. Does he listen rather than interrupt? _____ _____
   c. Does he listen to all of a story with evident enjoyment so that he can re-tell all or part of it? _____ _____
   d. Can he follow simple directions? _____ _____
5. General:
   a. Does he take good care of materials assigned to him? _____ _____
   b. Does he follow adult leadership without objection or show of resentment? _____ _____
   c. Does he alter his own methods to profit by an example set by another child? _____ _____

Emotional readiness

1. Adjustment to task:
   a. Does the child see a task (such as drawing, preparing for an activity, or cleaning up) through to completion? _____ _____
   b. Does he accept changes in school routine calmly? _____ _____
   c. Does he appear to be happy and well adjusted in school work, as evidenced by good attendance, relaxed attitude, pride in work, eagerness for a new task? _____ _____
2. Poise:
   a. Does he accept a certain amount of opposition without crying or sulking? _____ _____
   b. Can he meet strangers without unusual shyness? _____ _____

Psychological readiness

1. Mind set for reading:
   a. Does the child appear interested in books and reading? _____ _____
   b. Does he ask the meanings of words or signs? _____ _____
   c. Is he interested in the shapes of unusual words? _____ _____
2. Mental maturity:
   a. Does the child's mental test show him sufficiently mature to begin reading? _____ _____
   b. Can he give reasons for his opinions about work of others or his work? _____ _____
   c. Can he draw something to demonstrate an idea as well as children of his own age? _____ _____
   d. Is his memory span sufficient to allow memorization of a short poem or song? _____ _____
   e. Can he tell a story without confusing the order of events? _____ _____
   f. Can he listen or work an average length of time without restlessness? _____ _____
   g. Can he dramatize a story imaginatively? _____ _____
3. Mental habits:
   a. Has the child established the habit of looking at a succession of items from left to right? _____ _____
   b. Does he interpret pictures? _____ _____
   c. Does he grasp the fact that symbols may be associated with pictures or subjects? _____ _____

TABLE 11-2. (*continued*)

Psychological readiness	*Yes*	*No*
d. Can he anticipate what may happen in a story or poem?	_____	_____
e. Can he remember the central thought as well as important details?	_____	_____
4. Language:		
a. Does he speak clearly?	_____	_____
b. Does he speak correctly after being helped with a difficulty by the teacher?	_____	_____
c. Does he speak in sentences?	_____	_____
d. Does he know the meanings of words that occur in preprimers and primers?	_____	_____
e. Does he know certain related words such as *up* and *down, top* and *bottom, big* and *little?*	_____	_____

From David Russell et al., *Manual for Teaching the Reading Readiness Program,* rev. ed. (Boston: Ginn, 1961), pp. 55–57.

Activities for Cognitive Development

As suggested by Brown, the following activities tend to put an emphasis on mental development:[5]

The child's language ability develops and extends in environments which encourage individual expression. The slow-to-start would benefit from experiences in listening, observing, looking, talking, interpreting; experiences in feeling, seeing, smelling, hearing, identifying; experiences in musical and rhythmic expression; experiences in dramatic play and game activities; talking over, sharing, telling stories, singing songs, chanting rhymes, and many other experiences to develop free and easy oral expression.

Observation

Many opportunities for individual and group participation should be provided to check on the accuracy and understandings children gain through observing, watching, noting, interpreting, perceiving, listening, touching, smelling, tasting. Activities such as:

1. Ask the children to tell what they saw on the way to school.
2. Play a musical record. Have the children tell what they heard.
3. Provide many different kinds of materials—such as lace, burlap, velvet, and brocade—and have the children describe the material and tell how it feels or how the children feel—happy, sad, etc.
4. Have them listen and identify different sounds they hear in the classroom.
5. Ask the children to identify the smells they might notice on a trip to the grocery store.

Observations may be visual, auditory, kinesthetic, or in combination.

Interpretation

Children need to be given opportunities to interpret their environments. Interpretation is a process of putting meaning into and taking meaning from an experience. Children interpret their experiences in the light of their past experiences. We all recall the experiences of the six blind men and an elephant. A picture, a story, a trip, or a book may provide the medium for interpretation.

1. Have the children look at a picture of clouds. Is it summer or winter? A fair sunny day or a rainy day? What makes you think so?
2. Have the children observe a new book. What kind of story do you think this will be? Will it be a happy story? Will it be a funny story?

Classification

Classifying calls for examining, grouping, bringing about order. Classifying involves the process of analysis and synthesis. Children have to think on their own to come to a conclusion or decision on classification. Collections of pic-

[5] From Salome Brown, "The First Grade Child Not Quite Ready for Reading Instruction," *Reading in Action in the Sixties* (Bellingham, Wash.: Western Washington State College, January 1965).

Opportunities should be provided to check on accuracy and understandings children gain through observing, watching, and noting. These students are studying about snakes through reading, observing, and discussing. (PHOTO BY LINDA LUNGREN.)

tures may be used again and again for different kinds of grouping. The classification may be weather. The children then place the pictures into groups according to pictures of summer and pictures of winter.

Comparison

Perceptive observation is sharpened through comparison. Children need to be aware of likenesses and differences. Children may compare many things, such as a bird and an airplane, two pictures, two stories which have been read by the teacher, two songs the children sing, a tree and a bush, two pets, two holidays.

Imagination

The drawing of mental pictures calls for inventiveness and originality. Children need to create, to invent, to pretend. Imagining can free a child to leave a prosaic environment and go into a world of make-believe and creativeness. The imaginative teacher can develop many activities such as the following: What would you do if you could fly? If you were an elephant? If you were a teacher? If you were a president? What would you do if you had a dollar? If you had a lot of money? Where would you spend the winter if you were a bear? If you were a grasshopper?

Other activities would include collecting, organizing, making associations, dramatizing, predicting, investigating, hypothesizing, making assumptions.

Table 11-3 will help teachers follow up the diagnostic results of the inventory questions.

Readiness is determined by interest in the topic, familiarity with the vocabulary, and the intellectual ability to respond to the ideas.

Concepts such as the following from fourth- and fifth-grade books will cause reading difficulty unless the teacher anticipates the language background of the students and helps provide meaning for these terms:

Most of the *infectious* and *contagious* diseases are caused by *bacteria*.

Birds help to keep the *balance of nature*.

The *red corpuscles are racing through the capillaries*.

Business and industry were *paralyzed*.

Science has *unlocked* the greatest force in nature.

Such figures of speech and strange terms often cause trouble, but the child may also not be aware of the meanings of simpler terms. If the child understands the term *stag* to mean a boy without a date, imagine the meaning that might be read into Scott's line, "The stag at eve had drunk his fill."

Often it is the thought, rather than the words, that requires a readiness to understand. Even a beginning reader can recite Hamlet's "To be or not to be," but to understand these words requires a psychological orientation far beyond the child's mental capacity.

For concepts to be clarified after reading there must

TABLE 11-3. Reading readiness handicaps and their correction

Handicap	Evidence of handicap	Helpful procedures
Low in general intelligence	MA is below 6–0 on a test. IQ is below 90 on a test. Seems lacking in curiosity. Ideas seem vague and confused. Comprehension is poor. Range of information is poor. Unable to give explanations. Language development is retarded.	Mental age will increase steadily as child gets older. If child has been handicapped by poor environment, sometimes shows increase in IQ with good schooling. If MA below 5–0 or IQ below 80, may take a year or more to become ready for reading instruction. General readiness work with little emphasis on reading until child has reached MA of at least 6–0 is recommended.
Poor memory	Forgets instructions. Unable to recall events of story. Memory span below four digits or words. Poor memory for visual details. Memory is tested in various ways in the Gates, California, Betts, Monroe, Stevens, Van Wegenen tests.	Give motive for wanting to remember; send on errands with oral messages. Tell a simple story; ask child to retell story after other children have done same. Play memory games: One child says something, second tries to repeat it; if correct, he takes lead. Several objects on table. Child who is "it" turns back, tries to tell which one was removed. Have children inspect picture. Remove picture, ask for list of things in picture.
Inability to follow directions	Needs repetition of directions. Becomes confused if given more than one direction at a time. Look for evidence of low intelligence, language handicap, or poor hearing. Difficulty in following directions on any readiness or intelligence test.	Give directions slowly and clearly. Gain child's attention before starting. Play "following directions" games. At first, give one direction at a time, then two, then three. Allow children to take turns in giving directions for games and other classroom activities. Check for possible hearing difficulty.
Poor attention	Does not listen when directions are given. Tires of activity quickly. Is very distractible. Seems dreamy, absorbed in own thoughts.	Check for possible hearing difficulty. This is normal in young children. Watch for signs of restlessness and change to another activity. For individual activities, give a seat away from other children. Give opportunity to tell his stories and ideas. In general, provide interesting activities.
Poor visual perception	Insensitive to similarities and difference in pictures, words, letters. Draws and copies drawings poorly. All readiness tests contain subtests to measure visual perception.	Practice in clay modeling, drawing, cutting around outlines. Assembling picture puzzles. Finding missing parts in pictures. Describing pictures in detail. Exercises for noting visual similarities and differences, such as those in reading readiness workbooks. If very poor, delay reading. Check for possible visual deficiency.

Handicap	Evidence of handicap	Helpful procedures
Poor auditory perception	Seems to have poor hearing but does well on hearing test. Speech is indistinct or defective. Does not recognize rhymes. Is insensitive to similarities and differences in word beginnings or word endings. Cannot recognize (or blend) a word if it is sounded out. Tests of auditory perception are included in Gates and Monroe tests.	Provide a good model of speech. Encourage accurate pronunciation. See suggestions under "Defective speech." Much use of rhymes, jingles, poems, and songs. Call child's attention to difference between two words that he confuses. Play "word family" games. One child says a word; next child has to say a word that begins (or ends) the same way. Say a list of words. Have child listen for one that does not sound like others. Many teachers do much of their training in auditory or phonic readiness after children have begun to read.
Poor general health	One or more of these: overweight; underweight; pale, looks anemic; listless, tires easily; frequent colds; mouth breather; poor posture; other signs of poor health. Report from physical examination or nurse.	Recommend a thorough medical examination. Take special precautions to avoid strain and fatigue for frail or sickly children. Give rest period. Discuss with mother the child's eating and sleeping habits. Check up to see that defects are corrected.
Poor vision	Does poorly on vision tests. Teacher observes that eyes tear or become bloodshot; child squints or closes one eye to see better; gets close to board or chart to see; complains of headaches.	Refer for eye examination. If glasses are needed, see that they are obtained and used. Place in a favorable seat. If difficulty is severe, sight-saving activities and materials may be necessary.
Poor hearing	Does poorly on whisper or watch test. Teacher notes that child: has a chronic ear infection; seems inattentive; misunderstands directions; asks to have statements repeated; comprehends better in conversation than at usual classroom distances.	Refer to an ear specialist or hospital clinic. Give child a favorable seat. Speak slowly and distinctly to child. Emphasize visual approach in reading. Poor hearing is no reason for delay in starting reading, unless other handicaps are present.
Poor muscular coordination	Clumsy: poor at walking, running, skipping, hopping, dancing, climbing stairs, throwing, catching. Often drops and spills things. Poor hand-eye control in using scissors, crayon, pencil.	Be patient; clumsiness and slowness are not intentional. In severe forms, lack of coordination may be sign of neurological difficulty. Refer for medical examination. Rhythmical games to music: dancing, skipping, etc. Rhythm band. Show careful ways of holding objects. Simple types of handwork: cutting, pasting, coloring, weaving, constructing. Use of manipulative toys: pegboards, form-boards, etc.

TABLE 11-3. (*continued*)

Handicap	Evidence of Handicap	Helpful Procedures
Limited vocabulary	Limited comprehension. Has difficulty finding words to express his ideas; uses circumlocutions. Nearly all readiness and intelligence tests contain vocabulary tests.	Vocabulary develops normally out of rich, varied experiences. Acting games. Teacher says a sentence, children (taking turns) act it out. Different games can be played in which children act out nouns (animals, etc.), verbs (walk, run, hop), adverbs (quickly, quietly), prepositions (under, behind, in). Pictures are used for introducing new concepts. Children list all words they know of one type (tops, pets, flowers, etc.) Those not generally known are described and illustrated.
Poor use of language	Speaks in one or two words, or in fragmentary sentences. Uses immature speech forms ("I runned," etc.). Uses awkward or confused word order. Uses undesirable speech forms which are characteristic of his cultural background.	Put child's idea into a complete sentence, have him repeat it. All statements should be in complete sentences. Gently correct grammatical errors, awkward constructions, slang, etc., by stating child's idea in more appropriate language; praise him when he repeats teacher's statements. Provide opportunities for natural growth in language ability through free conversation, group discussions, telephone conversations, radio broadcasts, composing group stories, telling experiences, dramatization of stories.
Defective speech	Speaks too fast, runs words together. Lisping Baby talk; defective pronunciation of consonant sounds. Marked hesitation, stammer, or stutter.	Speak slowly and distinctly to children. Encourage child to take his time. Promote relaxation. Is normal in children who have lost baby teeth. If marked, requires special training in production of speech sounds. Mild cases usually clear up without special attention. This is a problem for a speech correctionist or psychologist. Classroom teacher should encourage relaxation, rhythmical activity, freedom from strain.
Emotional instability	Extreme sensitivity; crybaby. Specific nervous habits. Poor concentration.	Teacher should show warmth, liking for the child, appreciation. Underlying cause of nervousness needs to be removed. Severe cases of emotional instability should be referred to a psychologist or mental hygiene clinic.
Lack of self-reliance	Child makes excessive requests for help. Child gives up quickly when he meets difficulties.	Encourage child to try to do things. Provide help and support when needed. Build self-confidence through experience of success in a graded series of activities, starting with very easy ones.
Poor group relations	Child is bossy; picks fights and quarrels.	Remove from group temporarily. Look for cause in the home situation.

Handicap	Evidence of Handicap	Helpful Procedures
	Submissive, shy, afraid to speak up.	Ask child easy questions. Praise generously. If too shy to talk in front of group, allow to recite to teacher privately.
Bad family situation	Interview with mother or older children in family. Look for evidence of: poor discipline—too harsh, too lax, or inconsistent. Quarreling and dissension. Child is unloved. Child is overprotected.	When family situation is very bad, parents should be encouraged to seek help of social service agency or mental hygiene clinic. Some mothers are receptive to tactfully given suggestions concerning discipline and child management.
Lack of interest in reading	Child seems restless, uninterested, when teacher reads or tells stories. Child shows no interest in books or in learning to read.	Language may be too difficult or ideas too strange for child's comprehension. Vary type and difficulty of stories. Provide library table with interesting picture and storybooks. Read stories from books in class library. Have a bulletin board. Post simple notices, etc. Build simple reading stories from children's own experiences. Praise generously the first signs of interest or attempts to read.

Chart by Battle Creek Public Schools, Battle Creek, Michigan.

be teacher planning prior to reading. However, such clarification is also a part of long-range readiness training in that the children form a habit of demanding meanings that make sense as they read. Other long-range readiness practice may be illustrated by the way primary grades provide readiness for the work study skills of the intermediate years. Getting the main idea essential for the study of social studies and math, as well as outlining in language, can be started in the primary grades by listening to decide what is the best title for a selection. Drawing conclusions can be presented in terms of listening to decide what will happen; the important skill of understanding association between ideas can be presented in terms of noticing the meaning of such words as *it, there, they,* which are referents to persons or things in preceding sentences.

As the children mature, the responsibility with respect to readiness for meaningful reading is shared with them by the teacher. In all areas of the curriculum the teacher accepts responsibility for these tasks:

Help students construct the concepts that are needed to understand what is read.

Express the assignment in questions that are stated and organized cooperatively by the teacher and the pupils. Such cooperative activity defines the assignment, sets purposes that motivate the reading, and provides opportunities for the pupil to evaluate and organize ideas read.

Provide for individual differences in reading by supplying a variety of books that can be read by children with various reading abilities.

Set purposes for the discussion and additional activities that give the pupil opportunities to evaluate, organize, and plan for the retention of ideas gained through reading.

Give attention to each pupil's deficiencies in the reading-thinking jobs. The point of breakdown in locating information, arranging ideas, and so on, must be diagnosed for each student.

In classroom practice the readiness concept has led to some specific ways to handle individual differences. These include (1) dividing the class into groups of children with similar needs, (2) creating reading material that will interest older children yet will not be too difficult in terms of word-attack skills, (3) planning so that children will learn from each other, (4) providing special rooms for those who need additional instruction, (5) individualizing all reading instruction in a single classroom, (6) organizing the curriculum as a non-graded primary school, (7) planning summer school programs that are both remedial and enriching.

What Is the Place of Phonics in the Language Arts Program?

As suggested earlier in this chapter, *phonics* and *phonetics* are terms that are often confused. Phonetics is the science of speech sounds in actual use. Phonics is the application of phonetics in the teaching of reading and spelling. The phonetic symbol in speech for the *s* sound would be the same in all these words: *bus, kiss, scene, face, psalm, listen, schism, six, answer, city.* Yet in the use of phonics a child must remember that the sound is made by various letter combinations. The sound element is called a phoneme. In the words listed above, the sound /s/ is a phoneme.

One point must be understood from the beginning of any discussion of phonics. Communication involves an exchange of meaning. It is quite possible for a child to learn to sound out the letters of a word like *d-a-w-k-i-n*, but unless the sounder then associates the word with its meaning (stupid), he is not reading. In such a case all that he has done is to write a design with letters of the alphabet. Although phonic skills can be used in such meaningless ways, it does not follow that they are valueless skills. Indeed, the ability to use the sounds of our language as it is written, combined with a demand for meaning, is basic to both reading and spelling. However, because ours is not a strictly phonetic language it is inappropriate to rely solely on phonics as a reading program.

In reading, children use phonics to do these major reading tasks:

1. To identify the initial sound of a word.
2. To divide a word into syllables in pronunciation.
3. To check a guess when a strange word is identified from context.
4. To identify prefixes and common endings.
5. To identify the word root.

The phonics problem in reading is that of changing printed letters to sound and then giving meaning to the combination of sounds that makes a word. Without a meaning clue this process is difficult; if the word is completely unknown to the child, it is almost impossible. Relatively simple words like *adage* and *adobe, table* and *tablet,* or *tamable* and *tamale* require distinctions of pronunciation that are not easily discoverable by phonetic analyses.

On the market today are programs that teach sounds independently and then apply them to words. Some start with vowels, others with consonants, and still others with consonant-vowel combinations, such as *fe, fi, fo, fu.* When this material is well taught, children memorize many of the sounds and alphabet letter associations of our language.

In application of the sounds, this material usually ignores the many nonphonetic words common in our language, such as *was, been, have, come,* and *you,* and does use those that can be built phonetically, such as *gun, sun, fin, mold, ill, dill,* and *kill,* which are not very useful in the reading material of the primary grades.

A more serious problem is that the skills learned do not apply to the analysis of longer words. The ability to sound *pat* simply does not apply to *patriot, pathetic,* and *patience.*

In the classroom one observes wrong teaching practices concerning phonics. Some teachers confuse visual similarity with sound similarity. Words like *grow, snow, low,* and *grown* are included with exercises on the *ow* sounds in *owl, cow,* and *clown.*

Finding little words in big words gives a sound clue less than half the time, yet teachers persist in telling children to look for the little word. There is no sound like *an* in *thanks, fat* in *father, is* in *island, of* in *often,* or *all* in *shall.* Finding the little word may give a false sound value as *bat* in *bathe, am* in *blame, doze* in *dozen,* and *row* in *trowel,* or prevent proper syllable identification as *am* in *among, even* in *eleven,* and *beg* in *began.* Finding the base or root word is quite another matter. Finding *father* in *fatherly* or *forget* in *unforgettable* is quite different from attempting to find *fat* in *father* or *table* in *unforgettable.* Take any page of material and note the little words in the big ones. In the previous sentence a child might find *an* (any), *age* (page), *at, ate, mat* (material), *an* (and), *no, not* (note), *he* (the), *it, lit* (little), *or* (words), *on* (ones). In none of these is the meaning of the small word a clue to the meaning of the large word. If a child considers *no* as a meaning, the meaning of the little words read into the larger word could create confusion or establish a habit of not seeking meaning.

An observation of a first- or second-grade class will reveal that the teachers do a great deal of prompting with phonetic clues. Suppose the child is trying to read the word *mumps.* After the child has got the initial sound, the teacher will say, "It rhymes with *jumps.*" With that help the child says the word. It should be noted that alone he would never have been able to provide the clue "It rhymes with *jumps.*" If he could do that, he could have read the word. We do not know if such figuring out with teacher clues helps the child remember the word. Some evidence indicates that the beginning sound and meaning are all some children need. If they cannot identify the word, it should be told to them and be taught as a sight word along with some nonphonetic words, such as *laugh, each,* and most proper names or place names.

Basic reading series differ considerably in their use of phonic material. Some use any device that will work with specific new words as they are introduced. One new word will be remembered by the shape, another by the fact that it starts with the *m* sound, still another because it rhymes with a known word. Other programs attempt to teach patterns of attack that the child should use with each new word.

At present the following sequences of learning are commonly followed:

1. Listening to and understanding oral language.
2. Recognizing names that begin alike.
3. Recognizing the beginning sound of a word.
4. Recognizing letters and word differences.
5. Matching letter and word forms.
6. Expressing speech sounds and using language.

1. Hearing and recognizing in the context of words the following single consonants in the initial position: *b, c* (hard sound only), *d, f, g* (hard sound only), *h, j, l, m, n, p, r, s, t,* and *w.* Omit *k, v, x, y,* and *z.*
2. Hearing and recognizing in the context of words the speech consonants *ch, sh, th,* and *wh;* the consonant blends such as *sk, sm, sn, sp, st, sw, tw, br, bl, gl, pl, fr,* and *tr* in initial positions.

Any one of the initial sound items may be introduced as soon as the pupil knows two or more words that begin with that item.

1. Introducing, in the context of a word, *v* and *y* in addition to reviewing the initial consonants presented in first grade, and later presenting *g* and *k.*
2. Continued teaching of blends *gr, fr, cr, dr, bl, cl, gl, sw, tw, scr,* and *thr,* in the context of a word.
3. Emphasizing the short vowel sounds.
4. Introducing the long vowels (the terms *vowel, long,* and *short* are used).
5. Teaching the speech consonants in final position.
6. Introducing the vowel blends *ow, ou, oi, oy, ew, au, aw,* and *oo.*
7. Teaching the double vowels *ai, ea, oa, ee, ie, ay,* and *oe.*

1. Maintaining single consonants and consonant blends.
2. Teaching the silent letters in *kn, gh,* and *wr.*
3. Teaching the variant consonant sounds *c, g, s, z, ed,* and *t.*
4. Continuing work on double vowels.
5. Teaching the influence of final *e.*
6. Teaching the vowels followed by *r.*
7. Teaching the prefixes *a-, be-,* and *un-.*
8. Teaching the suffixes *-y, -ly, -er, -est, -less, -ful,* and *-en.*
9. Teaching the division of words into syllables.
10. Teaching alphabetization.

11. Teaching the three-letter blends: *str, thr.*
12. Teaching contractions: *can't, don't.*

1. Maintaining all previously taught skills and addition of appropriate difficulties.
2. Teaching the prefixes *dis-, ex-, in-, out-, re-, trans-,* and *un-.*
3. Teaching the suffixes *-eenth, -ese, -ical, -ion, -ous, -ship, -sun,* and *-ty.*
4. Teaching the placement of accent on words divided into syllables.
5. Teaching the use of key words for pronunciation in dictionary.
6. Teaching the use of diacritical marks.

A survey of studies on generalizations in phonics drew these conclusions:[6]

Certain generalizations appeared to be commonly taught but to have very limited usefulness according to the included studies. The following fell in this category:

The vowel in an open syllable has a long sound.
The letter "a" has the sound (ô) when followed by "e."
When there are two vowels, one of which is a "final e," the vowel is long and the "e" is silent.
In many two and three syllable words, the "final e" lengthens the vowel in the last syllable.
When a word ends in "vowel-consonant-e," the vowel is long and the "e" is silent.
When two vowels are together, the first is long and the second is silent.
If the first vowel sound in a word is followed by a single consonant, that consonant usually begins the second syllable.
When two sounds are separated by one consonant, divide before the consonant, but consider "ph," "ch," "sh," and "th" to be single consonants.

It is recommended that teachers be particularly cautious when instructing children in situations in which these generalizations might apply in two or more specific ways until oral recognition is achieved. For example, the following generalizations might be helpful:

Single vowels are usually short, but a single vowel may have a long sound in an open syllable (approxi-

[6] From Lou E. Burmeister, "Usefulness of Phonic Generalizations," *The Reading Teacher* (January 1968), 350–356.

mately 30 percent of the time), especially in a one syllable word.
If a word ends in "vowel-consonant-e" the vowel may be long or short. Try the long sound first.

The following generalizations are those from the studies which seemed most useful, except for the "final e" generalization and the phonic syllabication number 2 generalization. The latter two generalizations were formulated by the current author as a result of the findings of the utility level studies.

Consonant Sounds

1. "C" followed by "e," "i," or "y" sounds soft; otherwise "c" is hard (omit "ch"). (certain, city, cycle, attic, cat, clip; success)
2. "G" followed by "e," "i," or "y" sounds soft; otherwise "g" is hard (omit "gh"). (gell, agile, gypsy; gone, flag, grope; suggest)
3. "Ch" is usually pronounced as it is in "kitchen," not like "sh" as in "machine."
4. When a word ends in "ck," it has the same last sound as in "look."
5. When "ght" is seen in a word, "gh" is silent. (thought, night, right)
6. When two of the same consonants are side-by-side, only one is heard. (dollar, paddle)

Vowel Sounds—Single Vowels

1. If the only vowel letter is at the end of a word, the letter usually stands for a long sound (one syllable words only). (be, he, she, go)
2. When "consonant + y" are the final letters in a one syllable word, the "y" has a "long i" sound; in a polysyllabic word the "y" has a "short i" (long e) sound. (my, by, cry; baby, dignity)
3. A single vowel in a closed syllable has a short sound, except that it may be modified in words in which the vowel is followed by an "r." (club, dress, it, car, pumpkin, virgin)
4. The "r" gives the preceding vowel a sound that is neither long nor short. (car, care, far, fair, fare) [single or double vowels]

Vowel Sounds—Final "Vowel-Consonant-e"

When a word ends in "vowel-consonant-e" the "e" is silent, and the vowel may be long or short. (cape, mile, contribute, accumulate, exile, line; have, prove, encourage, ultimate, armistice, come, intensive, futile, passage)

Vowel Sounds—Adjacent Vowels

1. Digraphs: When the following double vowel combinations are seen together, the first is usually long and the second is silent: ai, ay, ea, ee, oa, ow (ea may also have a "short e" sound, and ow may have an "ou" sound) [main, pay; eat, bread, seen; oat, sparrow, how]
2. Diphthongs (or blends): The following double vowel combinations usually blend: au, aw, ou, oi, oy, oo ("oo" has two common sounds). [auto, awful, house; coin, boy; book, rooster]
3. "io" and "ia": "io" and "ia" after "c," "t," or "s" help to make a consonant sound: vicious, partial, musician, vision, attention (even ocean).

Syllabication—Determination of a Syllable

Every single vowel or vowel combination means a syllable (except a "final e" in a "vowel-consonant-e" ending).

Syllabication—Structural Syllabication

These generalizations take precedence over phonic syllabication generalizations.

1. Divide between a prefix and a root.
2. Divide between two roots.
3. Usually divide between a root and a suffix.

Syllabication—Phonic Syllabication

1. When two vowel sounds are separated by two consonants, divide between the consonants but consider "ch," "sh," "ph," and "th" to be single consonants. (assist, convey, bunny, Houston, rustic)
2. When two vowel sounds are separated by one consonant, divide either before or after the consonant. Try dividing before the consonant first. (Consider "ch," "sh," "ph," and "th" to be single consonants.) [alone, select, ashamed, Japan, sober; comet, honest, ever, idiot, modest, agile, general]
3. When a word ends in a "consonant-l-e" divide before the consonant. (battle, treble, tangible, kindle)

Accent

1. In most two syllable words, the first syllable is accented.

a. And, when there are two like consonant letters within a word the syllable before the double consonant is usually accented. (beginner, letter)
b. But, two vowel letters together in the last syllable of a word may be a clue to an accented final syllable. (complain, conceal)
2. In inflected or derived forms of words, the primary accent usually falls on or within the root words (boxes, untie) [Therefore, if "a," "in," "re," "ex," "de," or "be" is the first syllable in a word, it is usually unaccented.]

For Discussion

1. Why might the phonetic principles of a language be more apparent to one who can read than to one learning to read? Have you mastered the reading of a foreign language? If so, how did phonics help?

2. Are phonics generalizations useless to a beginner?

3. Can you explain the following inconsistencies?

OUR QUEER LANGUAGE

When the English tongue we speak
    Why is *break* not rhymed with *freak*?
Will you tell me why it's true
    We say *sew* but likewise *few*;
And the maker of a verse
    Cannot cap his *horse* with *worse*?
Beard sounds not the same as *heard*;
    Cord is different from *word*.
Cow is *cow,* but low is *low,*
    Shoe is never rhymed with *foe*;
Think of *comb* and *tomb* and *bomb*;
    And think of *goose* and not of *choose*;
Think of *comb* and *tomb* and *bomb*;
    Doll and *roll*, *home* and *some*;

And since *pay* is rhymed with *say,*
    Why not *paid* with *said,* I pray?
We have *blood* and *food* and *good*;
    Mould is not pronounced like *could*
Wherefore *done* but *gone* and *lone*?
    Is there any reason known?
And in short it seems to me
    Sounds and letters disagree.
                Lord Cromer

How Are the Consonant Sounds Taught?

To use a consonant sound in reading, the child must do two things. First he must identify the sound of the letter, then he must use that sound in combination with the other letters to make a word.

In order to identify the sound of *b*, this type of exercise or combination of them may be used. There are others used in workbooks and suggested in teachers' manuals.

1. The teacher says, "Listen to find in what way these words are alike: *ball, bell, bent, bill, book.* Yes, they all have the same sound at the beginning."
2. "Now look at these words while I say them: *ball, box, beg.* In what two ways are they alike? Yes, they sound alike at the beginning and start with the same letter. The letter is *b.*"
3. "I am thinking of a girl in class whose name begins with *b*. Who is she?"
4. "Here are some pictures of toys. Which ones start with the letter *b? Ball, bed, bat, bus.*"
5. "Listen while I say a sentence. Name the words that start with *b*. 'The big ball is baby's. Bobby will buy a book.'"
6. "Put a marker on each picture that starts with *b*."

button	box	cane
cat	basket	book
banana	duck	bonnet

7. "I am thinking of something that is good to eat that starts with *b*. Can you name it?"
8. "Say 'Little Boy Blue' and 'Baa Baa Black Sheep.' When you hear a *b* hold up a finger."
9. Mark *b* on four letter cards. Do the same for some of the other letters. Put them all together. Show the letter *b*, have the children find others like it. Or place all letters that are like it in a row.
10. The teacher says, "I am thinking of a *b* word that rhymes with *fall, cone, maybe, cat.*"

Once the sound is identified in words and associated with the letter, then the task is to substitute the sound into a word in a way that helps identify the word. This type of substitution exercise is widely used. The teacher reviews the sound. "You know these words on the board: *ball* and *big*. I have put a line under the new word in the sentence: 'The apples are in the box.' With what letter does it start? Yes, it is a *b*. What sound does it have? What is the sentence talking about? What words do you know that will make sense that start with a *b*?"

Sometimes the substitution must be made in other parts of the word. "What letter does the new word start with in this sentence? 'Daddy has a new *job*.' Yes, it is a *j*. What word do you know that would make sense? No, it is not *jet*. Look at the last letter in the new word. What sound does it have? Does *jet* have the sound of *b* at the end? Can you think of a word that would make sense that starts the way *jet* does but has a *b* sound at the end?"

Or the sentence may be *Mary has a red ribbon.* "No, the word is not *raincoat*. What letters are in the middle of the word? What words do you know that start with an *r*? Use that sound and the other words to read the new word."

Special practice in substitution should be done with exercises like this: "You know these words: *ball, big.* You also know these words: *get, look.* What new word do we make when we take away the *g* in *get* and put a *b* in its place? What new word do we make when we take away the *l* in *look* and put a *b* in its place?"

In order to construct this type of exercise follow these steps:

Start with words that contain the letter on which the children are to practice. In the preceding example start with *book* and *bet*. Then change them to words such as *look, took, cook* and *get, jet, let*. Select the one that is best known by the children. These words can be used in substitution exercises for the letters indicated:

c not, ball, now, look

f ball, box, can

l dog, tip, not

n cap, hot

p will, not, get, can, big

w bent, hill, lake

s get, funny, no, Jack

*Games provide additional drill
with word recognition skills.*
(PHOTO BY TOM WOLFE.)

t	Jack, ball, down, can, look
r	can, make, fun
j	will, big, may
k	will, sick, deep
wh	tip, kite
st	sand, make, may, jump, sick, keep
str	may, feet, like
sh	take, not, look, my, mine, make
bl	bed, show, came
pr	hide, mint
cr	sleep, show, back, thank, down, just
cl	down, hear, Dick
i	(short) but, better, fast, had, let, lamb, lock, pull
	(long) none, done, rope
e	(short) but, ball, band, follow, bunch, full, hold, not, sat, shall
ea	bad, but, fast, hit, not, sat
ee	but, choose, did, said, stop
a	(short) ten, pet, trick, dish, fun
a	(long) time, while
o	red, put, cut, let
o	mist, ride, wire
oo	feet, head
u	big, bad, cap, dog, hit, not, pop
oa	get, cut, bet
th	first, jump, tick
tr	may, got, cap, just, made, by
tw	dig, fine, girl

Another form of substitution exercise asks the child to choose between two words in a sentence.

Write the word *live* on the board. "Who can read this word? Tell me what happens to the word *live* when the first letter is changed." Write *give* under *live*. Have the new word pronounced. Then ask the children to select the proper word in these sentences:

John and Paul $\frac{give}{live}$ on High Street.

John will $\frac{give}{live}$ Paul a cake.

"Can you tell these new words that are made from words you know?" Write the words *dog, get, night,* and *cake* on the board. Substitute *l* for the first letter in each of these words. Follow this by having the children select the proper word in a sentence using these words.

Consonant blends present some difficulties. The major error to avoid is that of adding an extra vowel sound at the end of the blend. *Clear* becomes *cul-ear, blue* becomes *bul-oo, scream* becomes *sker-eam,* and *stream* becomes *struh-eam* or *stur-eam.*

Gray (1961) believes that in presenting the consonant blends through many listening experiences there is an advantage in presenting all the possible blends involving an identical consonant letter in a group, as *bl, cl, fl, gl, pl,* and *sl.* In this way children will become aware that the consonant *l* is often used as part of a blend. This is true as well of the letters *r* and *s.*

In some words a trigraph, or three consonants blended together, can be sounded before the vowel sound, as in *scratch, stream, splash, sprint, scream.* At the end of words there are many possible combinations of two or more consonants that form blends in words such as *bulb, self, held, hard, large, earth, spark.*

To develop skill in attacking new words through the visual and auditory recognition of consonant blends, proceed as follows:

1. Write *bring* and *bread* on the chalkboard. Have the words pronounced and the letters *br* underlined in each word. Say: "Listen as I say *bring, bread* again. Do the letters *br* have one sound or two?" Call attention to the sound of *b* in *ball* and *r* in *ride.* "Let me hear both sounds when you say *bread, bring.*" Have several children in turn repeat the words.

   "Listen as I read some sentences to hear other words that begin with the same two sounds as *bring.*" Read the following sentences, pausing after each for a child to repeat the *br* words.

Throw the *broken branch* in the *brook*.

The *bridge* over the *brook* is not *broad*.

Write the following sentences on the chalkboard and have them read silently and orally. Help the group to identify *brook* by comparison with *bring* and *book*.

Bring this *book* to the *brook*.

Go *down* to the store and get some *brown bread*.

2. Use the method given in the preceding activity to develop recognition of the consonant blend *tr*. Use the known words *train, tree, truck* and the following sentences on the chalkboard:

Will you *try* to make my *train* go?

Dick can do a *trick* with his *truck*.

3. Provide each child with a pair of cards 1 × 4 inches on which has been written *br* or *tr*. Ask the children to listen as you pronounce the following word groups and to hold up the card that has the two letters with which all the words begin.

tr: traffic, trick, traveler, trip, tractor

br: break, brothers, breakfast, brook

Drill on consonants and blending can be done with a "word wheel." Two circles are cut from heavy paper or oak tag. One is larger than the other. The upper circle has a consonant or consonant blend aligned with a slot that exposes the remainder of the word on the other disk. As the top disk is revolved, the words are formed for the pupil to call.

Picture dictionaries or student-made charts are helpful. The children may gather pictures, bring them to school, and paste them on the page in the dictionary where the apppropriate beginning consonant sound is printed or on the chart labeled with that consonant. This should be a group activity because children usually tire of making individual sound dictionaries.

An initial consonant game based on "word families" provides a check on a child's understanding. The student has a card on which an entire word is written or printed. Used with this card are a number of single-consonant cards that may be placed one at a time over the initial consonant to make another word. For example, if one uses the word card with the word *man* on it, the consonants *p, r, t, f, b, c,* and *v* may be written

on the smaller cards. By superimposing each small card on the first letter of *man,* the child may form the words *pan, ran, fan, ban, can,* and *van.* When not in use, the small cards may be clipped to the large one.

Exercises in which the child writes an initial consonant to complete a word and then says the word give him the opportunity for *seeing, saying, hearing,* and *doing* activities. These are effective in all phonics work and are particularly good in corrective work. Such an exercise appears here:

Directions: Write the initial consonants indicated in each of these words. Then say the words.

m	c	b
____ad	____at	____all
____other	____ome	____ig
____ud	____old	____oy
____ay	____up	____ack
____eat	____ar	____ox
____op	____all	____ell
____ill	____ap	____ut
____itt	____an	____ook

In studying individual consonant sounds, there are many word-card devices that can be used. A card is made so that the initial consonant shows only when the card is folded. When the card is unfolded, a key picture replaces the initial consonant. For example, with the word *cat,* when the card is not folded, the child sees the key picture of a cat and the element *at;* when it is folded, the *c* appears, making the word *cat.*

One of the card devices resembles the first one mentioned for use with initial single consonants. It differs only in that there is a consonant blend that may be superimposed on the initial letter of a *known* word to make a *new* word. For example, the known word may be *black.* On separate cards, the consonant teams *tr, st,* and *cr* are printed. By manipulating these cards, the child can make *track, stack,* and *crack.*

Children may easily make their own individual consonant key cards by using heavy folded paper. One side of the card contains the consonant. When the card is opened, the picture and key word appear. These cards serve as excellent helps when children are still learning the initial consonant sounds and need frequent help with them. On the back of the folded card a simple sentence is written to help the child to see the word in context.

A knowledge of the consonant sounds is one of the most helpful ways phonics can be used in reading. Teachers frequently ask the children to ignore the vowels but to use only the consonants in sounding a word. A sentence in which all vowel letters have been omitted can be read by most children. For example: Th__ m__ther w__s s__ h__pp__ t__ f__nd h__r ch__ld wh__ h__d b_____n l__st th__t sh__ cr_____d.

How Do Children Learn to Use the Vowel Sounds?

The first step in use of vowels is the ability to recognize a, e, i, o, and u as letters that represent vowel sounds. As recognition is being mastered, the child should also understand that when these letters make the same sound as their names we call them long vowels and put a straight line over them. The letters a and I are little words that children know. The e in be and o in no are long because we hear the letter names in them. The long u as in use and Utah is quite rare in the basic reading vocabulary.

McKee suggested the following pattern of instruction with respect to the short a:

Step 1 (see). Print bad, can, and hat on the board. "Here are three words we have learned to read. Look at the middle letter in each word. Do all these words have the same letter in the middle? What is that letter? Is it a vowel?"

Step 2 (hear). "Now I am going to say six words. Listen for the sound you hear in the middle of each word." Say map, bad, rag, can, last, and hat. (Slightly elongate but do not isolate the sound of the vowel a. Do not print these words or try to teach pupils to read them.) "Did all those words have the same sound in the middle?"

Step 3 (associate). Point to the words on the board. "Let's all look at these three words and say them together. In what two ways are all three words alike?" (They all have the same letter and the same sound in the middle.) "That sound is the same as the sound we hear at the beginning of

and, am, and at. It is one of the sounds that the vowel a very often has in a word. It is called the short a sound."

Step 4 (apply). "We have now learned the short sound that the vowel a often has in words. Let's see if we can use that vowel and its short sound to decide what some new words are." (Print but on the board.) "What is this word? Now watch while I take out the vowel u and put the vowel a in its place." (Erase the u and print a in its place to make bat.) "Who can tell us what this new word is?" (Follow the same procedure to change cut to cat, him to ham, put to pat, and top to tap.) [McKee, 1967]

The short e is one of the most difficult phonetic elements a child is asked to master. Here is one way of presenting it:

(Print men, bed, get, let, red, and neck on the board.) "Let's look at these words and say them together." (Point to men.) "What is the vowel in this word?" (e). "Do you hear the long e sound or the short e sound in men?" (The short e sound. Continue in the same way with the remaining five words.) "What did you notice about the e in each of these six words? (Each e has the short sound.) "When e is the only vowel in a word and it is followed by one or more letters, the e usually has the short sound." . . . "Let's use what we have learned about the short e sound to help us read some words that we may not know." (Print the following short sentences on the board.)

Ben had a pet dog named Shep.

Shep sat up to beg for his bones.

Ben put a bell in Shep's pen.

Shep could make Ben hear the bell when he wanted to be fed.

Then say: "In the sentences on the board, some words are underlined. Read the sentences to yourself. Use what you know about the short sound of e to help you decide what the underlined words are. Be sure the word you decide on makes sense in the sentence. Will you read the first sentence aloud?" (Have two or more pupils read each sentence aloud. Then have one or two pupils read all four sentences aloud.)

Ea presents a special problem because it may be either long or short. Print the words ready, head, and breakfast on the board. "Let's look at these words and say them together. What two vowels are used together in these words?'' (*ea.*) ''Do you hear the long *e* sound or the short *e* sound in these words?'' (The short *e* sound. Print *clean, cream,* and *read* on the board. Point to *clean.*) ''What is this word?'' (*clean.*) ''Do you hear the short *e* sound or the long *e* sound in *clean?*'' (The long *e* sound. Treat *cream* and *read* in the same way as *clean* was treated.) ''The vowels *ea* usually stand for the long *e* sound. When you see the vowels *ea* in a word you don't know, try the long *e* sound first for those vowels. If that doesn't give a word you know, try the short *e* sound. Let's see whether we can use what we know about the sounds of the vowels *ea* to help us read some words that we may not know.'' (Print the following sentences on the board.)

> Ann went to one store for some <u>beans</u>, some <u>bread</u>, and some <u>meat</u>.
>
> She went to another store for some <u>white thread</u>.

Then say: ''Read the sentences on the board to yourself. Use what you have learned about the sounds that the vowels *ea* can stand for to help you decide what the underlined words are.'' Then say to a pupil: ''Will you read the first sentence aloud?'' (Have two or three pupils read each sentence aloud.)

With upper-grade students the first step is to discover the nature and extent of the child's knowledge of vowels. Write four or more familiar words on the board and ask the students to identify a vowel sound that may appear in only one or two of them. For example, write on the board the words *cake, man, ran,* and *made.* Ask the child to say the words to himself. Then ask in which words he hears the short form of the sound *a.* Some of the vowel elements and some suggested words that may be used in the exercise are the following:

Vowel Rules

There are some rules that will help a few children. Rather than ask the children to remember these rules, it is wiser to place them for reference somewhere in the room. Of course, this should be done only after they have been made meaningful.

RULE 1. If you do not know what sound to give to a vowel, try first the short sound. If you do not get a word that makes sense, try the long sound of the vowel.

This rule is most useful with the short words of our language and does have considerable consistency in books that follow a controlled vocabulary. There will be some vowels that will be neither long nor short. When the child discovers one, the teacher might explain this. There is no reason why the child needs to learn all the variations of the vowels before he has the help of a dictionary.

RULE 2. When a word has only two vowels and one of them is *e* at the end of the word, the first vowel is usually long.

This is the old ''silent *e*'' rule. It is least helpful when most needed. Such exceptions as *gone, have, love,* and *come* are introduced early in primary reading. One teacher called this *e* ''company that had come for a visit.'' Then she would say, ''Once there was a little girl named Elizabeth but at school people called her Betty. But whenever her name was on a program or the minister came to visit, her friends called her Elizabeth. That is the way with some vowels. When they are alone they have one name but when they have company they have another.''

RULE 3. When a word has only one vowel and it is the last letter in the word, the vowel is usually long.

Such a rule would help only with the little words

Short Sound of		Long Sound of	
a	cake, man, ran, made	*a*	late, band, mail, catch
e	bed, deep, feet, bread	*e*	fresh, green, neat, left
i	give, light, mind, twin	*i*	city, did, find, hide
o	lot, hop, joke, hope	*o*	both, toast, cloth, chop
u	jump, music, mumps, use	*u*	puppy, puff, use, mule

such as *me, be, go, no, so,* but there are also *to, ha, ma,* and so on.

When a child does not recognize one of the vowel sounds, the same steps that were used in teaching the consonants may be followed. The *first step* is to help the child hear the sound. Print on the board the words *an, and, am, at.* Say, "We know these four words. Let's say them together. Now listen while I say them again. What did you notice about the way these words begin? What other words do you know that begin with the same sound?" (With some vowels it is wise to use the medial position such as *bad, can, bat.* In this case the children are asked to note that the words sound alike in the middle. Other words they might recall are *had, ran, sat, fat, cat.*)

The *second step* is to see the letter and associate it with the sound heard.

The *third step* is to substitute the letter and sound to make new words. Use the words *fed, miss.* Substitute the *a* as heard in *an, am* to make *fad, mass.*

The following words may be used for this step:

long *a*	bone, hole, glide, woke
short *a*	bread, quick, fed, hitch
ai	boat, bread, get
aw	drown, flew, down
short *e*	beat, pack, flash, him
ee	boat, did, stood, had
long *i*	bend, spoke, race, grape
short *i*	bud, butter, fast, wet
long *o*	clever, grape, mile, sale
short *o*	bag, rid, map, left
long *u*	late, done, care, fame
short *u*	back, hill, dance, desk

Many combinations of two vowels are used to represent vowel sounds. Teachers often use a rule, "When two vowels go a-walking, the first one does the talking." This is to help the child use a long *e* sound in words like *meat* and *bead.* Overdependence on this generalization can lead to mispronunciation of many words. A better warning might be, "When two vowels go a-walking, there's danger a-stalking."

The danger is that the two vowels are blended together in a diphthong or that two vowels may form a digraph in which one vowel sound is made. The last vowel rather than the first may be the sound made. Vowel combinations which form diphthongs are *oi* as in *boil, oy* as in *boy, ou* as in *mouse, ow* as in *crowd.* Two vowels together which make a digraph may have the sound of the first or the second vowel. *Ai* as in *mail* and *aisle, ea* as in *beam* and *steak, ie* as in *pie* or *believe, ui* as in *suit* or *guide.* The digraph may not present the long sound of either vowel as in *head, foot, fruit, canoe, would,* and *could.*

Activities

The following activities designed by Herr are practical for drill with vowel sounds:[7]

1. When introducing the long and short sound of vowels, write the word *dim* on the blackboard, and ask the children to tell you the word. Then add an *e* and ask the children to tell you the word. Do this with several words until the children notice that a final *e,* although silent, makes the long *i* sound. Divide the class into two groups. One group looks in books for words with short sounds. The other group finds words where the final *e* makes the other vowel long.

2. For a long-and-short-vowel game, collect pictures of objects with long and short vowel sounds, such as *bell, shoe, cat, cone,* and *glass.* Paste these on 3- × 5-in. cards and place in a box. Paste a picture of a short-sound vowel word in the lid and one of a long-sound vowel word in the bottom. The children sort the cards and put them in the right places. Later use words instead of pictures. Provide a key for self-checking.

3. Play a detective game to find the silent letters. Prepare a list of words from reading or spelling lessons. The children circle the letters that are silent: *before, coat, high, blue, leaves.*

4. List several words on the blackboard. The children rewrite them, substituting another vowel for the one given: *went, want; wish, wash; dish, dash;* and so forth.

5. Give the group a duplicated list of words. They add

[7] From Selma E. Herr, "Phonics Clinic," *The Instructor* (May 1957), 35–39.

another vowel to make a new word: *mad, made, maid; led, lead; din, dine.*

6. Everyone numbers his paper. The teacher says, "I am going to say some words that have either a long or a short sound of *a* in them. When I say the word, write *S* on your paper beside the number of the word if the *a* has a short sound. Write an *L* if the word has a long *a* sound in it." Be sure that the words are short and, of course, familiar.

7. Eight words (*bow, brow, cow, how, now, plow, sow,* and *allow*) are the only words primary children need with the *ow* sound. They meet these words in which *ow* has the sound of long *o*—*blow, crow, flow, glow, grow, know, low, mow, row, show, slow, snow, throw, tow, sow,* and *below*. Once their meaning is clearly understood, have several activities to provide further study. Put them on flash cards and show. Have the children stand up if they have an *ow* sound, sit down if they have an *o* sound. (Notice that *bow* and *sow* are in both groups.)

8. Make separate flash cards for practice on phonic irregularities. Have a bulletin board with pictures and words that have unexpected sounds. Let children pair off and show the cards to each other. For variation show them in the opaque projector. Avoid words with many irregularities.

Duplicate a list of common words involving the hard and soft *c*. Read over the list with the group, then have the children write these words in two separate columns. Do the same thing with *g*.

9. Present *ar, er, ir,* and *ur* separately, rather than treating the vowels alone. Use groups of words such as *sir, were,* and *blur* to show that *ir, ur,* and *er* have the same sound. Point out that with *ar,* the *r* usually says its own name.

For Discussion

1. Identify a common vowel sound in these words: *fur, fir, mother, cellar, myrrh, word, journal, search, cupboard, colonel, acre, avoirdupois, were.* What is it called?

2. Should phonics instruction start with the vowels? Examine a series that does, such as that published by Economy Press of Oklahoma City.

How Are Reading Skills Taught at the Primary Level?

The first step in word recognition is to help the child realize that the printed letters represent language. In preprimers the story is told through the pictures. The children discuss what is happening, and at first the teacher reads what the book characters are saying. As the story progresses and one of the characters is calling to his mother (or dog or baby) the teacher asks, "What would you say if you were the boy in the story?" Eventually a child will say, "Come here, Mother." "That is exactly what the story says," explains the teacher. "Now you read the words that tell us what the boy says."

The clue used here is the context or meaning clue. Through repetition of the words the child eventually remembers what the word says whenever he sees it. Some words cannot be developed from the meaning alone. Such words as *said, at, was, am, is,* and *blue* must be learned through planned repetition.

The beginner seldom depends on sound clues alone to recognize a word but uses the sound represented by a letter in combination with meaning or word form. As soon as the child knows by sight two or more words that start the same way, he has a clue to the sound of all words beginning with that letter. Some letter-sound associations seem to be used by most children. The consonants *m, s, b, t, n,* and *j* appear to be quite easy as sound clues.

Primary sight vocabulary is based on words that the children use frequently and with meaning in their oral language. Familiar objects in the room are labeled. Words to be presented emerge from the discussion and are written on the board or on the chart. "This is what Joe said," the teacher comments as she writes, " 'Come, Ann, Come here.' Who will read these words for us?" Then the word will be used in other situations until it is repeated many times and the children recognize it without prompting. Small cards with words printed on them are used. The children place the words on the proper article in a picture. Or the words are distributed and in turn each child puts his label on the proper article in the room. A box of variety-store items may provide the models. Names of the articles are pasted on a large cardboard designed to lie flat on the table. The children in turn place their article on the correct word. Color names are learned by matching two cards—one with only the name, the other with the name and color. The children in turn place their article on the correct word.

Word-form clues are indicated in a number of ways. Have the children notice the form of a word, its general length, shape, size, and configuration, without reference to individual letters. This is always done with a left-to-right motion of the hand under the word. After a short sentence, phrase, or word is read to the children, the word or words are displayed. The children are then asked to choose one of several pictures that illustrates what the word says. After a word is shown to the children, it is taken away. Children then close their eyes and try to "see" the word. Check by showing two words and have the children select the one they saw first. During this period words of unlike appearance are used, such as *name, bed, funny*. Attempting to distinguish between words that look alike, *this* and *that* or *funny* and *bunny,* will only cause confusion at this time.

Structural analysis starts with the *-s, -ing,* and *-ed* endings on words. Emphasis is placed on the part of the word that helps a child to remember which is the base or root word. Too great an emphasis on these endings will cause children to start looking at the wrong end of the word. The left-to-right habit of observing words can be stressed by presenting some words for drill in this fashion:

$$help + s = helps$$
$$or \quad help + ed = helped$$

or by direct contrast:

help   help
helps   helped

Phonetic analysis at this time is directed toward auditory discrimination. Speech jingles that repeat sounds should be used. If two or more words start with the same sound, the fact should be noted. Names that start the way words do provide a personal association with a sound. The emphasis is still on hearing parts of words, hearing the beginning of a word, or hearing the ending of a word. Names of letters are still being learned by some children during this period.

In preprimers the story is told with the pictures, and the reading is usually what the characters in the book say. Some stories are more easily reviewed if the pages are mounted in sequence like a cartoon strip. Have the children tell the story, then have them read what the story people are saying. Many series have the first preprimer in the form of a big book. This can be used for group instruction without the physical handling of the reading material during the initial introduction periods. When the child does get his own book it is a tremendous psychological experience for him to be able to read the first story independently.

The preprimer level will be completed by many children during the first half of the year. Some children will remain at this level throughout the first grade; a few need to start at the preprimer level in the second grade.

Most children arrive at primer level after reading the preprimers of the basic series. Children are ready to read a primer story when their interest has been aroused, their previous experiences have been keyed in with the story, and their speaking vocabularies have become adequate to deal with the concepts. Guided discussion and sharing of experiences pertinent to the story to be read give the children experience in talking and listening and develop readiness. A motivating question before silent reading helps children to read for meaning. Good reading and study habits are developed during the silent reading of the story. The children learn to identify their own problems of word recognition and comprehension and ask for help when needed. In the beginning, a lesson may consist of only one page of a story. As reading skills are developed, the children can manage larger units.

Discussion following silent reading helps the children to clear up comprehension problems. They can enjoy the humor of the story together and discuss relationships of characters. The teacher is able to check comprehension further by asking questions.

Rereading may be done after the silent reading of each page or after the reading of the entire story. The motivation of rereading should be to find the answer to a question, to find out how the characters felt, to enjoy the story, or to find the most interesting parts.

With respect to phonics, the children and teacher start to build a chart of "key" words to use in working out new words. This chart is built slowly, adding words as they are met in reading.[8]

The following single consonant chart is a typical example. Words used on the chart should be words in the reading series being used. One series would use *work* instead of *wagon;* another, *look* instead of *little*.

From the very beginning, children should be taught how to skip over a word and then think it out from context, because they must necessarily do a great deal of this in later independent reading. After the student becomes familiar with the sounds of initial consonants, he should be taught to check his guessed word with the beginning sound of its printed form. The following procedure is suggested as one means of helping him acquire his skill.

In the sentence "Tom saw a bird fly to the

Bb	baby	*Pp*	pet
Cc	candy	*Qq*	quack
Dd	day	*Rr*	run
Ff	father	*Ss*	something
Gg	go	*Tt*	toy
Hh	house	*Vv*	valentine
Jj	jump	*Ww*	wagon
Kk	kite	*Xx*	
Ll	little	*Yy*	yes
Mm	mom	*Zz*	zoom
Nn	none		

(The word after *x* is omitted because the children will encounter *x* mostly at the end of words, as in *box*.)

ground," we assume that *fly* is the only word which the child does not know.

TEACHER: Look at the word. What is another word that starts with the same sound?
CHILD: *Fun.*
TEACHER: What does a bird do that starts like *fun?*
CHILD: *Fly.*
TEACHER: Now read the sentence again to see if the word fits.

The following purposes and exercises are appropriate at the primer level.

---

[8] Devices presented here are from many sources, the major one being the 1960 Language Arts Course of Study of Grand Rapids, Mich. Other suggestions came from teachers.

PRIMER EXERCISES

Purpose

To develop greater comprehension and emphasize reading for meaning.

Exercise

From a pack of cards with words on them, choose the ones that fit in each of the following sentences:

See the _____ red car.
  (little)
Find _____ big cars for me.
  (two)
Find a big _____ ball.
  (red)

Draw a picture illustrating a riddle. Copy the riddle and paste it below the picture.

Purpose

To develop auditory and visual discrimination and encourage meaningful associations of sight words through the use of picture clues.

To develop the use of structural analysis as a means to better word recognition by providing opportunities to recognize the variant *s*.

Exercise

Make cards with a picture on one side and the word on the other side. Say the word and then turn the card over to see if it is correct.

Provide pictures of two boats with the words *boat* and *boats*. Have the children look at the pictures and put a circle around the correct word. Repeat with many different pictures.

The same words beginning with a capital and small letter are like two completely different words to first graders. You can put two lists on the board:

come	not
do	Do
Not	will
Will	come
Go	go

Touch two children and say a word. The children go to board, frame the word, and say it. Have a child touch and say the word in the first column and another child find it again and say it in the second. Direct a child to draw lines between the two words that say the same thing. Ask a child to erase the words he can say. Later these same words may be used in sentences on the board. This should give further meaning to words and provide an added reading situation.

First-Reader Exercises

At the first-reader level the children show more independence in reading. They are able to read and grasp the meaning of longer and more involved stories, to use context clues, to predict outcomes and draw conclusions in stories, to feel success and joy because they have a substantial reading vocabulary. Many children are at this level at the beginning of their second year in school, others will have mastered this material by the end of the first year.

In auditory and visual discrimination the children begin to recognize initial consonant blends such as *bl*— black, *fr*—friend, *sp*—spell, and *dr*, *gr*, *pl*, *st*, *tr*.

Words are added to a chart of consonant blends as they are met in reading. Some will not be met until second-reader level. The consonant blend and digraph chart would appear like this:

bl	black	*gl*	glad	*sp*	spell
br	brown	*gr*	green	*st*	stop
ch	children	*pr*	pretty	*sw*	swing
cl	clown	*sc*	scat	*th*	this
cr	cry	*sh*	she	*tr*	train
dr	dress	*sk*	skate	*tw*	twin
fl	flag	*sm*	small	*wh*	white
fr	friend	*sn*	snow		

Children at the first-reader level begin to learn the following final consonant sounds:

d	red	*g*	pig	*k*	book
l	wheel	*m*	him	*n*	hen
p	up	*s*	us	*t*	bat

Picture dictionaries made by the children will reinforce most of the consonant sounds as well as establish a dictionary concept. Such an activity might be an early homework assignment. Use a notebook or single sheets that may later be assembled. At the top of each quarter space the child may paste a picture of some familiar object. Each object picture must start with a different sound. He then cuts words starting with those sounds from old magazines and pastes them in the correct column.

With respect to word structure, children begin to recognize the *-ed, -d, -ing,* and *-s* endings. After the children have studied a story with the teacher, sentences such as the following may be written on the board:

The man stopped at the house.

The big black bear walked in.

The baby climbed on his back.

Purpose

To check the children's understanding.

The children marched around the room.

The door opened.

The teacher then gives the following directions:

Draw a line under the word that tells what the man did when he came to the house.

Draw a line under the word that tells how the bear came in.

Draw a line under the word that tells how the baby got on the bear's back.

Draw a line under the word that tells what the children did.

Draw a line under the word that tells what the door did.

The teacher will then call attention to the endings of all the words underlined on the board. The teacher says, "Very often we come to a word that looks like a new word to us when it is really an old word with *-ed* on the end of it. I'll write a word on the blackboard and then I'll ask one of you to write *-ed* on the end of the word and tell what it is after you have changed it." (Writes such words as *help, look, call, walk,* and so on.) Individuals write *-ed* on the end and pronounce the word.

The following exercises may be used at the first-reader level:

Exercise

Write the best word on each line:

1. A rabbit _____ in a hole under a tree.
   live lived
2. The rabbit said, "I _____ I had red
   wish wished
   wings."
3. He _____ in the Wishing Pond.
   look looked
4. The rabbit _____ around three times.
   turn turned
5. He _____ home to show his wings to his
   start started
   mother.

To develop the ability to comprehend more involved stories, provide opportunities for answering questions about a story. Children may be urged to make inferences with exercises like this.

Comprehension of words may be checked in a game of this nature.

Classification exercises will also check comprehension.

Exercise

Draw a circle around the correct word.

Dick liked Spot.	Yes	No
Sally was happy.	Yes	No

Play "Going Places":
A pack of cards is placed upside down at the front of the room. Two or three players are chosen. A starting line and finish line are designated. Each in turn takes a card from the top of the pack. One may read, "Take two steps." "Take one big step." Another, "Go back one step." "Jump." "Stay where you are." A "Run" card allows the child to go to the good line at once and win.

Put these words under the correct heading:

Things to wear	*Things to ride*	
coat	train	cap
boat	horse	mitten
airplane	dress	hat

The Reading Lesson

During reading instruction the teacher must be concerned with the attention span of individuals in the group, the need for physical movement, the handling of material, and the activities of the remaining members of the class, in addition to the immediate aspects of the lesson. Handling of these details is indicated in the following lesson. In 1958 a group of students in a class of Dr. Constance McCullough created this material. The story being read is "Little Red Riding Hood."[9]

The teacher and pupil activities are indicated first; then an explanation of the points remembered by the teacher is given as the class proceeds throughout the lesson.

The first aspect of the lesson is to build a common background for the group and to build the forms and meaning of the vocabulary used in the story.

1. The children are in a circle in the front of the room.

[9] From Constance McCullough, *Handbook for Teaching the Language Arts* (San Francisco: Paragon Publications, 1958).

The teacher starts by asking, "How many of you have ever been to the woods?" "What is it like in the woods?" "Are there woods near here?" "How is it different from the town or city?"

Set the mood for reading. Develop unfamiliar concepts. Find out what is known; have children inform each other; determine what, if anything, you must explain to them. Contrast is an effective teacher.

2. "Our story today is about a girl who lives near the woods. Read this silently as I write it and be ready to read it aloud." Write: The little girl lives near the woods. As you start to write the *w* for *woods,* say "woods," for this is the one word the children do not know. (If the word were polysyllabic, like *hunter,* you would say "hunt" as you wrote the *h* and say "er" as you wrote the *er.*)

Silent reading before oral encourages efficient reading unimpeded by lip movements. Stand to one side as you write, so that *all* can see. Seat children so that this is possible. Say new words as you write them, so that children may have *simultaneous* impressions of the word from ear and eye. Write the word in a phrase or sentence so that it appears in a normal setting, making normal demands upon the reading eye and providing clues for later identification.

3. "Let's all read it together." Run hand under the sentence as the children read, to stress left-to-right observation.

All children thus experience seeing, hearing, saying—of the new word in a setting that emphasizes its meaning as well as its form. Unison activity tends to keep all children involved, watching and thinking.

4. "The little girl's name was Little Red Riding Hood." Write, and say as you write, "Little Red Riding Hood." "Let's all say it." "Who can find the new word in this name and frame it and say it for us?" Child comes up, puts hand on either side of "Hood" and says "Hood." "Is he right?" "Let's read that word together." Pass hand under word as they read.

Children watch you write the words and are forced to observe them from left-to-right. Their first impression, at least, cannot be reversed or confused about which word says what. Have children take special notice of the new word. Framing of the words focuses the attention of the group and shows clearly which word the child thinks he is "reading." "Is he right?" makes whole group think and react rather than being silent and passive spectators. "Who can find" rather than "John, show us" puts all children on their toes.

5. "Red Riding Hood met someone in this story. You can solve the word for yourselves. Watch carefully as I write and be ready to read the phrase." Write: met a hunter. The children know *hunt* and *-er* from word analysis training. Pause to give children time to read. "Who will read it for us; Bill?" Bill comes up, frames phrase and reads. "Is he right?" "How do you know? Jane?" Jane explains that the word contains *hunt* and *-er*. She comes up, frames separate parts and says them as she does this. "Let's read the phrase together." Have children discuss what a hunter does, what he might be hunting, etc. Show picture if necessary to clarify idea.

Have children solve for themselves the words that follow principles of word analysis they have learned. All children should engage in word analysis which they have been taught. Those who don't understand can learn from another child's explanation. All experience multisensory approach to the word in a meaningful setting. Develop the concept of *hunter*.

6. Suppose that all words that are new in the story have been introduced as above. On the chalkboard now are the sentences and phrases: The little girl lives near the woods, Little Red Riding Hood, met a hunter, carried a basket, a big wolf. The teacher says, "Let's read together now the phrases and sentences on the chalkboard." Some children will need much repetition of the words, others very little. For extremely slow readers (learners), the teacher may not even introduce the story itself that day, but invent a story of her own on the chalkboard and pocket chart, which gives additional practice with new words and phrases.

7. *Comprehension check:* "Who can find, frame, and read the line that tells where someone lives? Jerry?" "Who can find the phrase that tells whom she saw in the woods? Janet?" "Who can find the name of our little girl? Buster?" "Who can find the phrase that tells about a man? Dick?" "Who can find what Little Red Riding Hood took with her? Jo?"

Recognition of the word should stress its meaning as well as its form. Here, you are not just testing one child; you are giving others a chance to see and hear the words again. Make sure that all are watching, not tying shoestrings.

8. *Word recognition check:* "Stand when you think you can find, frame, and read to us one of our new words. Pat?" Do this for all the words. "We read our words from left to right. Underline the new word from left to right as you say it." (Pat doesn't know what to do.) "Janet, will you help him?"

Change of position relieves physical fatigue and keeps children with you. Young children need these changes more frequently than older. Chair-scraping, wiggling, and inattention are your signals. Stress left-to-right direction. Give children experiences in helping each other. Encourage them to feel that being shown the way is help rather than negative criticism or a cause for embarrassment.

9. *Flash-card exercise:* Have flash cards containing words they know and the new words, so that you can build phrases and sentences with them. Sit to the right of the pocket chart so that you will not cover the cards as you set them in from left to right. "I am going to make a story; but, instead of telling it to you, I am going to have you read it to me. Watch carefully and be ready to read my first sentence."

Maintain the left-to-right observation of print by the order in which you insert the cards. Give children a purpose for watching before you start. Children who know what is expected of them are more apt to do it.

10. Put into the pocket chart the cards: I went into the woods one day. Have a child read the sentence. Have all stand who agree that this is right. Add other sentences similarly. Finally, have whole story read, then new words identified.

Do not summarize here the story they will read in the book; make a different story. Physical relief through movement is provided again if needed.

11. "Now, I am going to show you some words. If you recognize the word I show, stand." Show *hunter.* Children stand. "Jim, will you read it for us?" "Let's all say it together: *hunter.* Be seated. Are you ready for the next word?" Etc.

Test of word recognition without context fosters careful study of the word. Speed is not nearly so important as care, here. Call on one child; otherwise, children who don't know the word will stand for the honor of looking smart and get away with it.

12. *Chalkboard exercise:* This can be similar to the pocket chart exercise or a variation such as: Trees grow in the woods; A hunter shoots animals. "I shall write a sentence on the chalkboard. If you can read it, stand." Have a child read it. "Is this a true statement? Do trees grow in the woods? Can you prove it?" Have the child show the picture you used for the concept of woods earlier, showing the trees in the woods.

These sentences make children think of the meanings of the new words. Have an established signal such as standing, raising hand, to reduce chaos. When true-false statements are given, always require proof. Otherwise, you are teaching guessing, not reading or thinking.

13. *Chart or newsprint exercise:* Prepare a story on a chart, using the new words. Have the children read it to you and reread parts in response to your comprehension clues. Or have children make up their own cooperative story using the new words. Draw stick figures on the chalkboard and have child read the sentence your picture refers to. Have child pantomime a meaning and have another child read the word or sentence so illustrated.

Words are best learned in meaningful settings of known words. Repeated exposures to the new words in varied settings finally cause learning. Creative expression is an effective way of cementing impressions. The drawings provide interest of guessing and variety for the same old purpose; getting the child to read the sentence. Pantomime also lends variety and gets the wiggliest temporarily off the squeaky chair.

The second aspect of the lesson concerns the directed reading of the story.

14. "Who would be a good person to pass books today? Petunia?" "Let's open our books to the table of contents. How many have found the page with the table of contents on it? George, you could find it faster with the book right-side up. There; that's right." "Look down the page, now, for the name of our new story, *Little Red Riding Hood.* Let's read the name of our story and the page it is on aloud, together: *Little Red Riding Hood,* page forty-five.

Keep the books safely tethered until you need them. Make passing the books an honor—incidentally, another reason for good behavior and attention. Some children get D in reading because they get A in horseplay. Much better than drawing attention to George would be a quiet signal to him or turning his book. Give him credit when he does it right.

15. "Who will write our page number on the chalkboard? Angus?" "In which half of our book will we find page forty-five? Esther?" "When you have found the page, study the picture at the top of it and be ready to tell me what you see."

Do this if writing numbers is still difficult for the children. Help children judge how far back into the book to look for a page. Reading the table of contents is learned by using every opportunity to read it. Even primers have a table of contents.

16. "What is happening in the picture?" (Little Red Riding Hood is talking to a lady—must be her mother. Little Red Riding Hood must be ready to go to the woods—she has her basket her mother is just filling with cookies and she has her little red riding hood on.) "Who is talking in the picture?" (her mother) "Read the first page and be ready to tell what her mother said." "Look up when you are ready." Aside to Everett: "Are you sure you read it carefully and know the answer?" "What did Mother say? Alec?" (Take this here baskit to gramma's and doan say nuttin to strangers and come straight ta home.)

The general question brings out main idea and some details, whereas "Who is in the picture" gives you just one detail. In guiding the reading of young readers, give them something to look for in a paragraph, a page, or in two pages. Older readers (such as high third or fourth grade average readers) may have a purpose set for reading an entire story alone. In all cases, however, a purpose is set. Children need to learn to read for a variety of purposes. Therefore, try to vary the objective of the reading throughout the lesson.

17. "Why do you think she wanted Grandmother to have the cookies?" "Why did she warn Little Red Riding Hood about strangers and coming straight home?" "Who will read what she said and make it sound the way she must have said it?" "Let's look at Joe and listen while he reads, to hear how she sounded." "What do you think Little Red Riding Hood will say? Let's read the next page to find out." Proceed through the story, asking questions and discussing points, until the end.

Make children aware of the human relationships and feelings, reasons behind behavior. Oral reading should have a listening audience. Oral reading is optional here, depending upon how much is needed for practice. Oral reading here serves the purpose of increasing children's awareness of mother's feeling and concern. Have children predict events. Here, again, a purpose is set for silent reading. The third aspect of the instruction is to provide purposeful rereading of the material.

18. "We talked yesterday about how Little Red Riding Hood's mother felt about her going into the woods alone. How do you think Little Red Riding Hood herself felt? Find the place that makes you think that, and read it aloud to us."

A single reading of a basal reader story does justice neither to the story nor to the learning of the new words. Basal reading experience should give the child more insight into the story meaning than he would have derived alone or in one reading. "Intensive reading" is the term.

19. "Let's listen carefully while Harry reads and decide whether that part does show that Little Red Riding Hood was happy and excited as Harry said. . . ." (Harry reads.) "Do you think Harry is right? Does any other place in the story make you think that she was glad? Billy?" Etc. "Why do you think she was happy and excited? Any other reasons?" "Did Little Red Riding Hood remember everything her mother said? How many of you think she did? No one? Find the place that makes you think she didn't. . . . What should Little Red Riding Hood have done instead of stopping to talk?" (Children can act this out if you wish, to get the feeling for situation.) "What kind of person do you think Little Red Riding Hood was?" Various answers here will lead to reading various parts for proof. Put the adjectives used by the children on the chalkboard. "What words describe your idea of the wolf?" Put these in parallel column.

Oral reading should have an audience that listens for meanings. Children should not always watch the page as a child reads aloud, for this practice puts the children's attention on the accuracy of the reading rather than on the ideas expressed. Have the audience either look at the speaker, "breast" their books, or hold their fingers in the partly closed book. In any case, impress the children with the fact that this is a *listening* time.

Purposeful rereading time is a time for asking questions which require a variety of types of comprehension, skimming to find answers, and oral reading activities.

20. As children discuss wolf's characteristics, have them notice these points of plot in relation to him: "Why did the wolf use a special voice, as Esther said, when he talked to Little Red Riding Hood? Why did he tell her to pick a bouquet? Why didn't he eat her then instead of going for her grandmother? Pretend you are the wolf talking to himself about what he did and what he is going to do. Who would like to do that? Did the wolf succeed in fooling Little Red Riding Hood when he sat in bed dressed like Grandmother? No? Find the place that makes you think she began to doubt."

Make children aware of cause and effect, motives and results, effect of certain choices upon plot. Have children grasp the point of view of each important character. Give children the experience of skimming for evidence.

21. "Do you think this story could really have happened? Why or why not? What in the story seems real? What seems untrue to life? What do we call a story like this?" "If your grandmother were in trouble in her home, would a hunter come to rescue her? Who would? Who protects us? Who could give her the best help?" Have the children observe that the kind of helper would depend on grandmother's trouble: illness, burglary, fire, etc.

Have the children judge the real as opposed to the fanciful. Have them learn the terms applied to fanciful tales of this kind. Feature the relationship of the story to the child's own living.

22. "We can take better care of our grandmothers than Little Red Riding Hood could in the woods." "Do you think this story is a story of today or of long ago? Do you get any clues in the pictures or the story that make you think this? What are they?" "Why do you think this story was called Little Red Riding Hood? Can you think of a better name for it? What if this story appeared in a newspaper. . . . What would the headline be?" (Hunter De-Grandmothers Wolf.)

Protect the children from nightmares! Study the illustrations for a purpose. Have children express the main ideas in a variety of ways.

The fourth aspect of the lesson provides practice and application of skills taught.

23. "The author of this story had a good way of telling how things looked and acted and felt and tasted. How did he say Little Red Riding Hood skipped down the path? (like a bouncing ball) How did he say the wolf's eyes looked when he saw the cookies?" (like two ripe plums) Write these expressions on the chalkboard, under one another. "What do you notice about these two lines?" (They both begin with "like." They both liken something to something else to make it clear.)

Skill-building of various types (word recognition, word analysis, comprehension, interpretation, study skills) is done in five- or ten-minute exercise periods. Preferably they are done at the end of a period (group meeting), so that you may assign individual follow-up work at the children's desks to prove individual grasp of the work done. Usually reader manuals suggest from two to five such exercises. You should use all of them at some time during the days involved in the story, unless you are sure that the children can do them well enough without practice. Each exercise is a link in a chain of learnings. To leave one out is to risk worse performance later on, or forgetfulness of the technique. Reading skills rust out from disuse.

24. "As I pass out these sheets of paper to you, read the directions at the top to see what authors can do with words. Will you read the directions to us, Henry?" "What does that mean we should do? Yes, we are to read each sentence, find it in our story, and complete it. Read the first one to us, Bill." (Little Red Riding Hood skipped down the path like a _____ _____.) "What should we write in the blanks? . . . Yes. Now you are to do the others in the same way. At the bottom of the page you are to write your own endings to sentences. You are to tell how you think Little Red Riding Hood looked as she skipped down the path. What could you say she looked like when she skipped?" "These expressions are called similes." Write *similes* on the chalkboard. Have the children repeat the word with you. Face them so that they can see your lips.

Help children read directions. Have one child read aloud, or all in unison. Don't assume they know what is meant. Ask them to tell what is meant. Go through the sample with them. This is creative work. Each lesson desirably has some imitative activity and some creative; something that takes a short time, something that takes time, thought. Use the technical term the children will have to become accustomed to in later work. Strange words are better grasped when the lips of the speaker can be seen.

25. "Now, who will tell us what he is going to do on this page? Douglas?"

Have a child tell what the job is, in summary, so that no question remains.

26. "Does everyone understand? If you finish early, what can you do?" Have a list of activities somewhere on a chart or on the chalkboard which are legitimate uses of reading time if a child finishes early.

Waiting for the class causes restlessness if a child finishes early. Use reading time for reading activities, not bead stringing, sawing, unrelated to reading.

27. Later, either that day or at the next meeting with the group, go over the papers with the children, either individually or as a group. "Who will read the first sentence? Do you all agree with his answer? No? What do you have, Jerry? How can we find out who is right? Let's look in our books and find the place. Now, read it aloud, please, to us, Jerry."

Rereading of the papers provides another reading experience. Proofreading to find one's own rights and wrongs is more effective for learning than teacher-marked papers. Teach the children to refer to authority rather than languish on a "tis-taint" basis.

28. The following exercise was designed to make children aware of author's style, to give them a new language tool of their own, and to reexperience the words of the story. As you read this story of life in the woods many years ago, was there anything you wondered about that the story did not tell? List the questions the children ask. Decide where they might find the answers. This may lead to a visit to the library, the reading of books you have collected on woodland animals, etc., the seeing of a film, the listening to a story you read—then having the children tell what they found out. Perhaps, then, having collected this information, they will wish to express it in pictures or in a scrapbook as well as in discussion. Other creative activities might be such as these: to have the children pretend they had been Little Red Riding Hood and write or tell the story as it would have happened to them; to write the story cooperatively as a news story; to write a story about another wolf, etc.; to make illustrations for the story the child makes up.

Enrichment activities are of two kinds: informational and creative. Informational activities are those which add to the child's knowledge. Creative are those in which he expresses his own ideas regarding the story. Both are important and desirably we should have both in a lesson plan for a story. Children should have the incentive of being read to as well as the work of reading for themselves. Creative work can be a natural outcome of research activities. Telling a story involves the use of concepts being learned; sometimes it reveals misconceptions which must be straightened out. Writing a similar story means writing the new words the children are still trying to master—an effective left-to-right experience with the new symbols. Drawings or other artistic expression related to reading not only give children a pleasant association with reading but crystallize impressions for the child and reveal any misconceptions to the teacher.

For Discussion

1. Observe a first-grade teacher at work. Note the similarities between what she does and what was described in the preceding.

2. Would it confuse a beginning teacher to attempt to explain all aspects of a lesson that she has taught?

3. To what extent could these activities be imitative of those of an experienced teacher without one's knowing the reason why they are done and still be a part of a good teaching performance?

4. Do you agree that vocabulary is best developed in situations that require its use, or would you plan lessons involving lists of new words for lessons similar to spelling lessons for vocabulary development?

5. Would you defend the use of special-skill textbooks in addition to the readers being used?

6. Do you think that primary children should make greater progress in reading than we now expect? How might this be done? What factors other than reading skill should be considered in instruction?

7. Defend or criticize this statement: "The teacher should spend as much time finding the right reading material for a child as instructing him in reading."

8. Would it be possible for two different children to use different clues to recognize a word? If possible, illustrate different ways of recognizing a word.

9. Children may recognize a word that is familiar in their language, but they must identify a word that is strange in meaning as well as form. What skills are more associated with identification than recognition? At what grade levels are identification skills used?

10. Although some children will have mastered much of the reading process by the end of six months, we know that it is quite normal for others of equal mental ability to reach the fourth grade before this happens. How can we explain this to parents? How can we give these children praise and recognition in a nonreading activity? What are the children learning that is as important as learning to read?

11. What special problems does a child face in learning to read when he comes from a home where English is not spoken? What are his major educational needs? Should such children be grouped with slow-learning children from English-speaking homes?

How Are Charts Used in Reading Instruction?[10]

Many children enter first grade with great enthusiasm for learning to read. Some fully expect to read the first day. We know that the best quality of learning takes place when there is thirst for it. If a class "has its mind set" on wanting to read, there is a simple way to begin that not only satisfies the eager child but also paves the way for the more formal type of reading. The first group experience to be recorded and read may be as simple as a brief record of play. It might look like this:

We played dodge ball.
It was fun.

The teacher may need to create the brief statements of the very first recorded experiences. Very soon, however, children catch on to the idea and there is ready response to: "What might we say about what we did?"

Interest span of first graders at the beginning of the year is very brief, so care must be taken to get a few brief statements on the blackboard rather rapidly. Then with the teacher using the pointer to help scan the line from left to right, the group repeats what has been written. Then the pointer moves to the beginning of the next line and moves smoothly to the end of the sentence as it is read with the teacher. There is no stopping at words. It is saying what has been said, with attention to two lines of symbols that are as unfamiliar to the children as the scratchings on the Dead Sea Scrolls would be to most adults. After it has been read once or twice the teacher might say, "That is reading and you can do it." Her enthusiasm and pleasure reassure the children that reading is fun and they anticipate their next experience. That would be enough for one time and the group would proceed to other types of activities. During the day the teacher might copy the sentences on a sheet of newsprint and bring it out just before the children go home. Again they would read it together with the teacher and go home with the feeling that they had learned to read, just what they had expected to do, and

---

[10] Much of this material is from curriculum publications of the Madison, Wisconsin, and Long Beach, California, public schools.

parents are convinced from the first day's report that the children are off to a good start.

Each day new experiences are recorded. The teacher gives guidance in getting variety into the sentences, in keeping them simple, and in supplying appropriate words or phrases as needed. Sometimes charts are reread from day to day as long as interest is maintained. They are discarded as they lose significance.

This classroom example will illustrate a part of the teacher planning that takes place as an experience chart is developed.

The children have completed the construction of a barn. The teacher considered possibilities for stories that would include words from the reading list, such as

Look, look.	See, see.
Look at our barn.	See our barn.
It is big.	It is green.
Hay, horses, and feed are in it.	It is white.
	Animals live in the barn.

These two stories, thought out by the teacher, should be compared with the story finally composed by the group. The teacher guided the children to make up their story and accepted their contributions, even though she had several ideas as to how it might develop. The preplanning helped her to control vocabulary and length, even though the resulting story dictated by the children was different.

With this preparation the teacher guides the children's discussion:

TEACHER: What are some of the things we could write about our barn?
CHILD 1: Bobby, John, and Mary helped to make it.
CHILD 2: It is big.
CHILD 3: It is painted.
CHILD 4: I helped.
CHILD 5: I saw one. It was red.
TEACHER: What color is ours?
CHILD 3: White and green.
TEACHER: What is in a barn?
CHILD 1: Horses.
CHILD 2: Food for the animals.
CHILD 3: Cows to be milked.
TEACHER: You've told many interesting things about our

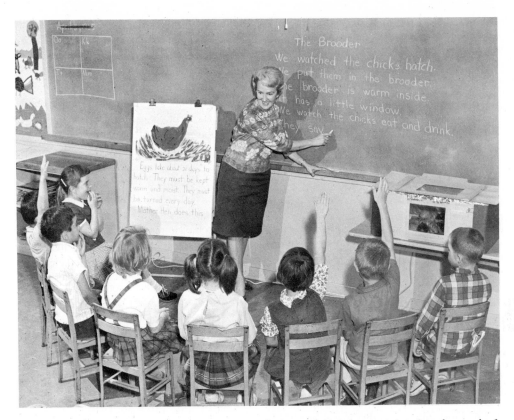

Dictated stories grow out of a common experience. Seeing one's own language in print takes much of the mystery out of early reading attitudes. (COURTESY OF THE BURBANK PUBLIC SCHOOLS.)

barn. Do you think we could tell in a story the things which are most important?

CHILD 4: You mean a story like we did about the trucks?

TEACHER: Yes.

CHILD 3: Yes, a story like the truck story.

As the teacher asks questions in logical order and the children respond, their sentences are written on the chalkboard by the teacher.

TEACHER: You've made a fine barn. What could you say to make others look at the barn?

CHILD 2: See our barn. (*Teacher records.*)

TEACHER: That would make us look, wouldn't it?

TEACHER: What color is it?

CHILD 1: White and green.

TEACHER: What can you tell about the colors in a sentence?

CHILD 3: It is white and green. (*Teacher records.*)

TEACHER: What is kept in the barn?

CHILD 4: The farmer goes in there.

TEACHER: That's right. Is that where he lives?

CHILD 4: No, but the horse does.

TEACHER: Yes, and what else would we find in the barn?

CHILD 2: Hay.

CHILD 3: Feed.

TEACHER: Who can give us a sentence with the things you mentioned in it?

CHILD 1: The farmer stays in the barn sometimes; the horse, the feed, and hay are in the barn.

TEACHER: You've included everything that was said. Would it be all right if I left the farmer out since he doesn't live there, and say, "Hay, feed, and horses are in the barn"? (*Teacher records.*)

CHILD 1: Yes.

TEACHER: We've said many good things about the barn. Let's read the story together, and as we are reading, maybe you can think of a title for the story. (*Class reads together.*)

CHILDREN: (*In unison.*) See our barn. It is white and green. Hay, feed, and horses are in the barn.

TEACHER: Does someone have any idea for our title?

Titles are not necessary for all stories. When they are used the teacher will guide children to select a title quickly.

CHILD 1: See Our Barn.

CHILD 2: The Green and White Barn.

CHILD 3: Our Barn.

TEACHER: Shall we use that one?

CHILDREN: (*In unison.*) Yes. (*Teacher records "Our Barn" above the story.*)

Follow-up activities may include such things as drawing a picture to illustrate the story; work on basic words as *look, at, our, it, big, see;* writing one sentence or word, and, of course, rereading the story the next day.

In making charts, keep the printed matter well centered so there is a balance of space around the story. The print must be large enough so that it can be easily read by all the children. It is a good idea to draw very light lines if newsprint is used, or to scratch lines with a pin if oak tag is used. Tall letters should be about 3 inches high and small letters about an inch and a half. An inch should be allowed between lines. Use a medium-sized felt pen to do the lettering and be sure to make correct letter forms with proper spacing between letters and between words.

In addition to group-experience charts other types of charts are needed.

PICTURE CHARTS. For variety a large, colorful picture may be introduced and short sentences written about the picture. Sometimes the class will dictate short sentences telling about the picture; later, when a sizable sight vocabulary has been established, the teacher may bring in a surprise illustrated story using words the children know.

WEATHER CHARTS. The first type of recording might be: This is a sunny day; or, Today is cloudy. Children might advance to: Today is December 4. It is cloudy and cold. We saw snowflakes this morning. It may snow tonight.

Sometimes symbols for clouds, wind, sun, rain, and so on, are inserted in slots on a chart. If turnover pages are kept, at the end of the month children may count the number of cloudy days, and so on. The days of the week may be added to such a chart as time goes on. The months of the year as well as temperature readings may be added as children are ready for such experiences. Third-grade children might have a rather complete weather record including the direction of the wind and barometric readings.

NEWS ITEM CHARTS. As children share news with the class a teacher might record such items as:

Linda has a baby brother.
Paul's father went to Chicago.
Barbara has new shoes.
Jim has a birthday today.

As the year advances the news might extend to what is happening in the community and in faraway places.

PLANNING CHARTS. These may start with something as simple as:

We will listen to a story.
Next we will play a game.
Then we will sing.
Our work period comes next.

As time goes on such charts could include specific directions the group will follow such as:

Tomorrow we will make butter.
We will need:

— — —

etc.

A listing of names of those responsible for bringing certain things or doing each of the tasks involved may be included.

Directions for a new game, social studies procedures, choice of work experiences, household duties, and rules for fair and safe play may go into various charts which the children play a part in planning.

RECORD CHARTS. Record charts would indicate progress or growth. There might be a height and weight chart. One might indicate the changes that take place as children observe bulbs or plants grow and bloom. Another might keep the scores of games that are played from time to time. Still another might record the names of stories the teacher reads so it can be referred to for later choices of favorites. Later in the year records can be kept of books the children read, of achievements in other learning activities, and of items they might wish to include in a "First-Grade Yearbook."

REFERENCE CHARTS. A color chart to which children may refer when they are learning colors, a number chart, a picture dictionary type chart for word recognition, a phonics chart, and a bird or flower chart are all examples of the reference chart.

In summary, the use of charts with young children serves the following purposes:

1. Classroom-created charts give the reading process real meaning and significance, because the children's own experiences are the basis for them.
2. The mechanics of reading are practiced. These include

   a. Left-to-right eye movement.
   b. The sweep from the end of one line to the beginning of the next.
   c. The significance of words and sentences.
   d. Observation of the use of simple punctuation.

3. Children are helped to see that reading serves many purposes.
4. Much language development takes place (producing clear, simple sentences; expansion of vocabulary; thought organization; putting events in proper sequence).
5. Charts can serve as a beginning in the development of perceptual clues:

   a. As certain words are used repeatedly, they can be identified and used on flash cards to become fixed as sight vocabulary.

   b. Whole sentences can be printed on oaktag strips so children can match them on the chart to note likenesses and differences.
   c. Children note that many words start alike. As these words are said they hear the likenesses in beginning sounds and you have an introduction to phonics.
   d. As the beginning of a sentence is read, children anticipate what follows and this becomes groundwork for use of the context clue in later reading.
   e. Children understand that the picture at the top of the chart is a clue to what the printed matter relates.

There are limitations in the use of charts. Charts seldom accomplish within themselves all that we hope to do in the area of reading. The range of words used on charts is very broad. No attempt is made to teach all the words used. Only those that are used commonly are pulled out and used on cards to become sight words and a part of each child's reading vocabulary. Of course, some children will learn many words simply by seeing them used on the various charts—which is to be encouraged. Charts do not provide for all the development of perceptual clues. Charts merely serve to introduce, to reinforce, or to make use of such clues that are developed in the reading program.

For Discussion

1. Some authorities feel that one weakness in a chart story is that no new meaning is revealed to the child as he reads such material. "It is as if the child has written a letter to himself." Do you agree or disagree with this point of view?

2. Some teachers construct the chart story with the children, then cut up the story to create flash cards. What would be their purpose in such a procedure?

3. Some teachers have created chart stories which they use year after year. This saves the time taken to create a story and provides simple reading material for practice. What weakness would you see in such a program? What strength?

4. Could adequate charts be made by putting words in a pocket chart so that sentences were formed? What would the children miss in a chart so constructed?

What Plans Must Be Made for Independent Work in the Primary Grades?

With any type of individualized instruction the teacher has the responsibility of planning work that will keep the rest of the class busy while the teacher works with a small group. The basic reading series provides in the workbook purposeful individual activities. When the basic workbook is not available, it is a growing practice to employ outstanding teachers during the summer months to produce this type of material for a district. If the material created meets a local need with special content, the time is well spent. If, however, the material is merely a copy or adaptation of existing published work, the effort may be questionable professional conduct. There are companies that provide master copies of worksheets printed with a special ink so that they can be reproduced. Although these may not be directly related to the material being taught, a busy teacher will often find them better than those she might hurriedly produce. Some manuals for basic readers now recognize this problem and suggest work that is designed for reproduction.

When worksheets are used, demonstrate to the children how to mark each activity when the work is first presented. The vocabulary of the directions sometimes must be taught. Later only brief directional sentences need to be addressed to the pupils until they are able to read and carry out the directions independently. There are often general directions or questions at the beginning of a page. They are there for the purpose of motivating pupil reading of the text. They require thought, and oral responses are expected; the pupils write on the lines provided or on lined paper. Enrichment suggestions may require children to use books and materials other than their reading textbooks. A teacher's daily reading plans should include the reminder to provide all needed materials.

In order to establish standards with children on how to obtain the materials necessary to complete enrichment activities, discuss the location of books, desirable traffic patterns as children move about the room, the way items are returned to the proper places. Some work-type activities may be too varied for the slow groups. If so, use only the portions that are suitable. Use the remainder at another time when the teacher is able to be with the groups.

Independent activities should be checked by the teacher to give children a feeling of security in accomplishment and to know the day-by-day effectiveness of pupil work. The teacher will then know what to review and when to provide additional independent work. A quick check may be sufficient on some days, but a detailed evaluation should be made at least twice a week. Papers sent home should be carefully checked; errors should be marked.

A sample and an analysis of a good reading worksheet follow.

To provide additional oral reading the independent reading circle has been established by some teachers. In late first grade the children who are in the top group are permitted to form an independent group that reads to each other without the teacher being present. The material provided is easy reading for the children involved. For children working in a basic first reader the group may read from a preprimer of a series not used in their previous work. The leader has a set of cards with the names of those in the group. These are rotated to determine who will read next. Should a child need help with a word, the leader calls on members of the group to help.

Because being a member of such a group is a special privilege, these children must assume responsibility for their own behavior. At the designated time the children form a circle in a secluded corner of the room. Monitors distribute the books which are stored in that area. Each child has a marker that is left at the page where the reading will start. In turn, the students read aloud. At times the teacher may visit the group or ask them to tell the class about the story they are reading. The period lasts for fifteen to twenty minutes. In second grade, all groups may participate, limited only by avail-

ANALYSIS OF A GOOD READING WORKSHEET

BOOK: *Finding New Neighbors*   "Baby Bears," 110–117

Adequate space should be provided when writing is required.

Name_____

_____

Read pages 110–117 carefully so that you can discuss these questions:

1. How did the bears feel about Iva?
2. Why were the bears happy at the end of the story?
3. Do you think this story could really have happened? Why or why not?

Guide questions should establish purpose for reading. Answers should be *oral*, not written.

Number the following sentences in the order they came in the story:

_____The bears were given a home in the cottage.

_____A man found two baby bears in the forest.

_____The bears enjoyed doing their tricks for the children.

_____The bears played tricks on people in the entire neighborhood.

_____The man carried the bears in a hat.

_____A hunter took the bears to the city.

_____The hunter sold the bears to the circus.

Activities should require thought. Writing should be kept to a minimum.

R usually gives a vowel a special sound if it comes after the vowel in the word, as *ir* in *stir*.

Say each word softly and circle each vowel-with-*r* sound that you hear.

her	for	herd	burn	river
girl	acorn	circle	turtle	squirt
barn	story	far	purple	cart

Word study skills should be practiced after they are taught at the circle.

Usually you can tell how many syllables are in a word by softly clapping the rhythm as you say the word. Write on the line before each of the following words the number of syllables it has.

(Avoid excessive picture drawing.)

_____ only	_____ important	_____ shell	_____ promise
_____ village	_____ apron	_____ slowly	_____ which
_____ market	_____ molasses	_____ bananas	_____ curtains
_____ mind	_____ sneeze	_____ doctor	_____ swish

Fast workers should be encouraged to make additional contributions to the class by finding and sharing interesting and pertinent information. For the "Early Birds": Can you find some interesting facts about bears? Look in your science books or in the dictionary.

able material, and in the third the low group. The other third-grade groups profit more by individual reading of library books.

Individual games that provide drill are needed to supplement worksheets. Each game must be taught at the circle, then placed on a shelf to be chosen by the child when he is given that opportunity. Any worksheet that involves drawing lines to match a picture and a word, a singular and plural form, a contraction and the two words that form it, words that start alike, or words that rhyme may be put on a shoestring board. This is a heavy piece of cardboard with two parallel lines of words written on it. A shoestring is attached to the words in the first column and a brad or a hole is put near the words in the second column. Instead of drawing a line, the child connects the shoestring between the appropriate words. After the board is checked, the strings are disconnected and the drill may be used by another child. Sometimes rubber bands can be used as well as shoestrings.

Another way of matching words is to use clothespins. The snap-type clothespin is used. On a card one list of words is presented. The words to be matched are written on the clothespins. The child snaps the pins opposite the appropriate words. Each cardboard should have a cloth bag attached, which contains the pins to be used in that drill. Clothespins can be used in many exercises that would require the child to fill in a blank. Prefixes or suffixes might be on the clothespins and the base word be on the card. Beginning consonants may be on the clothespins and the remaining part of the word on the card. Sentences may be on the card, with a word omitted. The proper word would be selected by the child as he reads it on the clothespins and snaps it next to the sentence that it completes.

Boxed drills have a game appeal. The most convenient boxes for these games are hosiery boxes. Stores will usually save them for a teacher if she requests them. The directions for the game are pasted in the top of the box. Sometimes the correction key can be included so that these will be self-correcting. The box may contain a picture with words on small cards to be placed on the object named. There may be a series of questions that the child answers yes or no by putting all the yesses on one side and the noes on the other. The sentences on the strips of cards may be reassembled to tell a story. Vowels may be put in their proper places in words. Old workbooks and readers may be cut up and put in these boxes in the form of dozens of interesting game drills.

A manila folder with a pocket or envelope to contain the cards with the words, vowels, or sentences used in the exercise is another convenient form. The following type of exercise is used:

Short *a*	Long *a*
⎯⎯ ⎯⎯	⎯⎯ ⎯⎯
⎯⎯ ⎯⎯	⎯⎯ ⎯⎯
⎯⎯ ⎯⎯	⎯⎯ ⎯⎯
⎯⎯ ⎯⎯	⎯⎯ ⎯⎯
Pocket	Pocket

Make a cardboard folder with space for short vowels on one side, for long vowels on the other. On small pieces of cardboard, words with both long and short vowels are written.

To Play: The pupil places the words on the right page. When not in use, the word cards may be placed in the pockets at the bottom. Folders for each vowel may be made by choosing words from pupil's needed vocabulary.

Sentences using words often substituted for one another are used:

⎯⎯ time is it? ⎯⎯ is my book. ⎯⎯ boy is eating my cake.	⎯⎯ do you like to play? ⎯⎯ is the way
Pocket	Pocket

That	What	That	What

To Play: The pupil places the word cards in proper places on the blank lines. One pupil checks another.

Or prefixes and suffixes can be used:

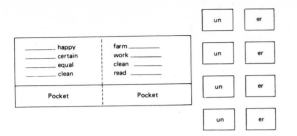

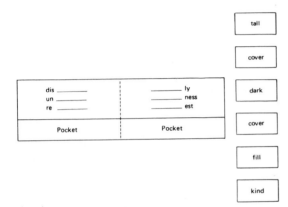

To Play: The pupil puts the prefix and suffix cards in the proper blanks and pronounces the words.

To Play: The pupil puts the word cards in blanks beside proper prefix or suffix.

Some teachers make their own magic slates out of a sheet of heavy cardboard (9 × 12 inches) and a sheet of clear acetate the same size. The acetate is taped to the board at both sides but left open at top and bottom. A skill-building exercise slipped between the board and the acetate sheet can be marked with a china-marking pencil. The pencil marks rub off easily with a cloth, leaving the slate ready for another child to use. Both the acetate and china-marking pencils can be purchased at art supply stores.

Acetate envelopes made of two transparent sheets fused together are obtainable at most stationery stores. These envelopes will accommodate two exercise pages placed in the envelope back to back, with perhaps a thin sheet of cardboard between them for stiffening.

Worksheets that present a word over and over again in context provide better drill practice than flash cards. It is possible for a child to recognize a word in isolation and not be able to read it in a sentence. The meaning in flash card drill is sometimes ignored. Thus it becomes important that teachers find ways of presenting work material that serves this purpose yet is easily evaluated and administered.

For Discussion

1. How may parents be involved in the creation of some of the materials described?

2. There is much discussion of teaching machines at this time. In what sense is an independent work device a teaching machine?

3. Evaluate some of the following devices as independent reading equipment:

Garrard Press; 119 West Parke Avenue; Champaign, Ill.
    Basic Sight Vocabulary Cards. Grades 1–3
    Consonant Lotto. Grades 1–4
    Group Sounding Game. Grades 1–8
    Picture Word Cards. Grades K–1
    Group Word Teaching Game.
    Syllable Game. Grades 2–4
    Vowel Lotto. Grades 1–4
    Sight Phrase Cards. Grades 1–4
Kenworthy Educational Service, Buffalo, N.Y.
    Doghouse Game. Grades 2–4
Steck Company; Box 16; Austin 61, Texas Reading
    Essentials Reading Aids. Grades 1–3

How Is Reading Taught as Children Advance in Primary Reading Skills?

The Second-Grade Level

Children at second-grade level are beginning to develop independence in word recognition, realization of the many happy experiences that they get from books, and an understanding that reading can help them to solve problems and to satisfy their curiosity. Creative reading and creative problem solving may be encouraged through selection of stimulating materials, sensitive questioning, and a nurturing environment. Growth in reading skill continues through exercises of the following nature to achieve the purpose stated. The exercises are illustrative. Similar ones constructed for drill purposes would be longer and at a difficult level to challenge the student.

Purpose	*Exercise*
Develop comprehension and provide opportunities for children to make judgments.	Read and choose the correct reason: Jane liked to read books about birds. One morning she saw a book about birds in Mr. Brown's store. Jane wanted the book. She went home for money because _____. She had to pay for the book. She wanted to buy candy.
Provide opportunities for children to find the main idea of a story.	Choose a sentence that tells what a story is about. What would be a good name for this story? What did we learn by reading the story?
Provide opportunities for children to remember logical sequence.	Review the action in a story using such words as *first, then, next, after that,* and *finally* in brief sentences. Then skim the story to note words or phrases that cue the reader to the time when certain events occurred and how long a period of time the events covered. Number events in correct sequence: _____ Bill went to school. _____ Bill got out of bed. _____ Bill ate his breakfast.
Provide opportunities for children to make inferences.	Underline the best answer to the question: Mr. Hill put a dish of food outside his back door. He called his dog, but the dog did not come. So Mr. Hill left the food near the door and went into the house. Soon a big brown dog came by. When the Hills' dog came home, he did not find any dinner. Why didn't the Hills' dog find his dinner? Mr. Hill did not feed him. A cat ate the dinner. A big brown dog ate it.

Purpose	Exercise
Provide opportunities for children to perceive relationships of time and place, manner, sequence, cause and effect.	After reading a story, underline the correct phrase. When did Tom hide? during the night before breakfast at noon Where was father working? in the yard near the tree near the river
Provide opportunities for children to experience sensory images.	Choose the words to use when talking about the weather: branch voice penny cloudy cold stormy mother sunny rainy
Develop vocabulary through the understanding of fundamental concepts; provide opportunities for children to understand related values.	Fill in the blanks in the following sentences: Apple pies are _____ than apples. Mother's pies are _____ than apples. Lynne liked apple pies the _____ of all. good better best
Provide opportunities for children to use chronological sequence.	Fill in the blanks: Wednesday is the _____ day of the week. (fourth) Lynne is the _____ child in the row. (third)
Provide opportunities for children to understand complementary concepts.	Supply the proper word: Pies are made by a baker; clothes are made by a _____. A cat runs on its legs, but a car runs on _____.
Provide opportunities for children to strengthen the ability to perceive analogous relationships.	Cross out the word which does not belong: house door road roof eight dress ten four lunch dinner nail breakfast
Provide opportunities for children to develop the ability to anticipate meaning.	Write on the line a word that makes the sentence true: The color of the grass is _____. The name of the dog is _____. Write on the line a word that makes the sentence true:

Purpose	Exercise
	Bob wanted a _____.
	Tom _____ home.
	Mother gave _____ a new doll.
	Mary went boat
Provide opportunities for children to develop an understanding that a word may represent more than one meaning.	Notice that some words have more than one meaning:

a bank of snow
money in the bank
post a letter
a fence post
an Indian trading post

Provide opportunities for children to identify sounds and the meanings of homonyms.

Insert the correct homonym cards in the blank spaces on a large chart:

A _____ has horns.
Denise is a _____ little girl.
Do you like a _____ sandwich?
I will _____ you at the corner.
I _____ my dinner at twelve o'clock.
Juan has _____ pennies.
This book is _____ my brother.
Two and two are _____.

deer	dear	meat	meet
ate	eight	for	four

Draw a line from the word in the first column that sounds the same as the word in the second column.

bear	mail
male	blew
sail	bare
blue	sale

The first two weeks of the second school year should be spent in reviewing the subject matter of the first grade. At the end of this period the teacher will have discovered children which are not yet able to make use of these skills in attacking unknown words. Such children may be grouped together and given instruction suited to their needs.

The remainder of the class can begin their work with the short and long sounds of the vowels. The ability to make intelligent use of the long and short sounds of vowels in attacking unknown words has been acquired with difficulty by the average and below-average child. Therefore, these sounds should be developed with particular care.

The order of development of the word elements and phonograms depends on the difficulties the children encounter in their reading and on words used for study in drill or practice periods. For example, one group working in a practice period with such words as *harder*, *start*, *sharp*, and *arms* would profit from a study of the phonogram *ar*, whereas another group who finds words such as *mouth*, *shout*, and *loud* difficult should study the phonogram *ou*.

1. To develop the short sound of *a*:

a. The short sound of *a* must be introduced.

TEACHER: What sounds do you hear first in these words? (*Points to such familiar words as* at, am, apple, *and while the children pronounce them.*) See if you can hear that sound in these words. (*Points to such words as* cat, ran, sat, fat, back *as different children pronounce them.*) What sound do you hear first in these words? (*Points to* at, am, *and so on.*) Which letter in these words has the same sound? (*Points to* cat, ran, sat, *and so on.*) Think of another word in which you hear that same sound. (*Write words on the blackboard as they are given.*)

b. At another period such a list as the following may be written on the board:

bag   tap   bad
pan   sad   lap

TEACHER: Yesterday we found out the sound of this letter. (*Write* a *on the blackboard.*) What was it? Find that letter in these words. (*Individual children point out the letter* a *in the different words.*) That letter has the same sound in these words that it had in *apple* and *at*. See if you can think of all the sounds in the first word and tell us the word.

Have various children respond as the different words are indicated. If a child calls the word *bag*, *bad*, have him give the sound of the final letter *g* and then say the word as a whole. The child should never be allowed to pronounce the word as *ba-aa-gu* or *baa-gu*, but should *think* the separate sounds and pronounce the word as *bag*.

c. The following exercise will help children differentiate between the long and the short sounds of *a* in words with which they are familiar. In arranging words of this type, the teacher must include *only known words*.

Write on the blackboard a list of words such as the following:

can   play
had   sang
baby   fat
last   place
stand   bank
name   stay
ran   apples
ate   that

Individual children should take turns pronouncing these words and drawing a ring around those words where the *a* sounds like the *a* in *at*. Such an exercise may later be hectographed and used for independent seat work. The short sounds of the remaining vowels may be developed similarly.

2. To develop the long sound of *a* review the words in which *a* has a short sound.

TEACHER: Sometimes the letter *a* has another sound. Listen for the sound of *a* in these words. (*The teacher will point to and pronounce such familiar words as* ate, make, came.) What was the sound which you heard in every word? What is this word? (*Write* at *on the board.*) Now what is it? (*Change* at *to* ate.) What did I do to change the sound of *a*? (*Do the same with* mad *and* made.) What is the difference between these words? (*Write* cap *and* cape *on the board.*) What is this word? (*Point to* cap.) What is this one? (*Point to* cape.) What have we found out?

A child should be able to state the generalization in words such as these: When there is an *e* on the end of a word with *a* in it, the *a* says its own name.

3. To develop the long sound of *e*, review the short sound of *e* in such known words as *pet*, *left*, *held*, *went*, *nest*, *get*, *hen*, *tell*, and so on.

TEACHER: Here are some other words with *e* in them. (*Points to the following list of familiar words on the chalkboard:*

wee, three, weeks, sleep, feet.) Find a word that means very small. (*Child points to* wee *and pronounces it.*) Find a word that is the name of a number, and so forth. The other day when we studied words like *pet* and *hen* we found one sound that *e* has. Sometimes it has a different sound. Listen for the sound of *e* in these words. (*The teacher pronounces* wee, three, *and so forth, very distinctly.*) What sound do you hear? When *e* changed the sound of *a* where did we find the *a*? Instead of coming at the end of the word, where does the second *e* sometimes come in these words? That is another thing we must remember when we are working out new words for ourselves. (*Follow this by changing* met *to* meet, step *to* steep, fed *to* feed, *and so on.*)

4. To develop the phonogram *ay*, write such words as the following, which the children have already encountered in reading, on the board.

play   stay   gray   away

TEACHER: Find the word that tells the color of the squirrel. Find the word that tells what the squirrel liked to do. Find the word that tells what Sally wanted the squirrel to do. Find the letters that are the same in all four words. (*Individually children may frame* ay *in each of the four words.*) See if you can find out for yourselves what these words are. (*The following words are written on the blackboard and the children are helped to work them out independently as already described above.*)

gate   sale   fade
lame   tame   fake

An exercise such as the following will be of value in helping the children discriminate independently between long and short vowels and at the same time grow in the skill of using contextual help effectively. The following exercise would not be used until the long and short sounds of the letters *a*, *e*, and *i* have been developed.

Read each sentence. Look for the word which belongs on each line. Write the word on the line.

One morning Tom _____ up.
　　　　wake woke

He _____ out of bed.
　got goat
"I _____ I am not late," he said.
　hop hope

TEACHER: Listen while Billy pronounces the words and see if you can hear the sound of those letters. What is it? Here is another word with that same sound in it. (*Write* say *on the board.*) What is it? I'm going to change *say* into a new word. Watch and see if you can read the new word. (*Erase* s *and write* m.)

Continue to change the initial consonants, using *d*, *h*, *l*, *p*, *r*, *w*.

To provide opportunities for discriminating between words containing the phonogram *ay*, after the phonogram has been developed, a seat work exercise of the following type may be given:

Write the word that makes the sentence true.

1. One _____ Tom went to the farm.
　　pay way day hay
2. He rode all the _____ in a car.
　　　　day say may way
3. He saw the cows eat _____.
　　　　　lay hay pay ray
4. One cow _____ down in the barn.
　　　lay hay pay ray
5. Tom said, "_____ I try to milk
　　　way say may ray
a   cow?"

The Third-Reader Level

When children come to the third-reader level, they have already met many words of more than one syllable, some of which they have learned as sight words. They have had experiences in listening to spoken words to identify the number of parts in each. At the third-reader level the term *syllable* is introduced. The children are beginning to develop skill in noting the number of syllables and whether the vowel is long or short.

At the third-reader level they have a directed-reading class daily—a time when they work with the teacher in reading groups or individually for basic reading instruction. During the silent reading, they receive help when needed in attacking new words.

By the end of the third-reader level, the children have gained much skill in attacking words independently. They should use and apply these skills in all school work. Periodic checks must be made to be sure previous learnings are not forgotten.

Application of word-attack skills is achieved through the following activities:

Purpose	*Exercise*
Develop the ability to perceive visual and auditory differences; provide opportunities for children to hear the sounds of letters.	Listen to the teacher pronounce a series of words, most of which rhyme. Clap hands when a non-rhyming word is heard.

Complete orally very short rhymes begun by the teacher.

> The funny clown
> Jumped (*down*)
> How much does a farmer pay
> For a wagon load of (*hay*)

Listen to and imitate the sounds of animals, birds, or machines.

> tick-tock of the clock
> ch-ch-choo of the train
> peep-peep of a chicken

Provide opportunities for children to recognize the letters and combinations of letters.

Use rhyming words to fit content.

> lunch-punch

> Soon it will be time for _____.
> He made a hole with a _____.

> matter-fatter

> Do you think it will _____.
> If you are a little _____.

Provide opportunities for children to blend sounds in order to pronounce unknown words.

Complete the rhyming word at the left. Then write the correct word in each sentence.

> (*clown*) Billy had a little br_____ puppy.
> The king wore a gold cr_____.
> The bright sun made Sally fr_____.

Provide opportunities for children to recognize vowel sounds and identify them.

Underline the vowels in each word:

thing	ball	find	day
red	he	let	she
solo	hop	long	wing
sang	mind	sun	hat

Purpose

Develop the ability to analyze the structure of words and give the children opportunities to become aware of endings such as *-er*, *-est*, *-s*, *-ed*, *ing*, and *-es*.

Give the children opportunities to learn the structure of compound words.

Give the children opportunities to learn to identify contractions.

Give the children opportunities to learn possessive forms.

Develop the ability to alphabetize; provide opportunities for children to alphabetize words by the first letter.

Exercise

Add *-s*, *-ed*, and *-ing* to the end of the word *shout* to make new words to fit in the blanks.

Fisherperson Karen heard some _____.
It was Jack. He _____ again and again.
''Who can be _____?'' asked Fisherperson Karen.

Combine the words in the first column with those in the second column to make compound words.

after	way
door	ball
air	noon
gold	fish
class	room
base	plane

Make a list of the compound words in a paragraph in a reader.

Match contractions with the words from which each was contracted.

she'll	it is
it's	she will
won't	cannot
can't	will not

Write the name of the person who owns these things:

Jane
Jane's dog _____
The girl's doll _____
My mother's dress _____
Tom's cat _____
Father's car _____

Write the correct word in each blank.

A pilot flies in it.	a_____
We read it.	b_____
It is a baby bear.	c_____
It can bark.	d_____

Children may be challenged to go on as far as they can with other clues.

Purpose	Exercise

Develop the ability to interpret the written page; give children the opportunity to follow written directions.	Follow simple directions written on slips of paper or on the chalkboard.
	
	    Walk to the window.
	
	Perform several written directions in the order given:
	
	    Write *go* on the chalkboard.
	    Tap Teddy on the head.
	    Walk around a table.
	    Open the door.
	    Sit down.

Give children the opportunity to arrange words into sentences.	Unscramble a jumbled sentence written on the board. Choose teams. Unscramble several jumbled words. The team unscrambling them first wins. Play "Grab Bag": Choose an envelope containing words that will make a sentence. Arrange the words in order.

Give children the opportunity to interpret ideas by planning riddles.	Compose riddles:
	
	    I start with *w*.
	    I live in a frame.
	    I am in schools, homes, and stores.
	    What am I?
	
	                    (A window.)

Give children the opportunity to skim to find something quickly.	After reading orally in class, take turns pantomiming a part of the story for others to find in the book. The first one finding it may read it aloud.
	
	Find the one element that is not right in each paragraph:
	
	    Sam's mother was getting dinner. She cooked beans, potatoes, meat, and rubber, and she made a cake.
	
	    Tom and Ernestine were playing in the snow. They both wore warm clothes. Ernestine had on her winter coat, mittens, woolen scarf, pajamas, and a cap.
	
	    Tom had on a warm sweater, his sister's dress, his mittens, cap, and boots.

Give children the opportunity to interpret a story and follow the sequence of events.	Interpret through dramatization a story studied and read during a directed reading class.

Purpose	*Exercise*
	Choose a chairman to lead the discussion and to direct the play. Discuss what should be done to make the story into a play.
	List important events in proper sequence. Discuss what the characters would do and say. Draw pictures of each main event in a story. Arrange them in sequence. Write a sentence about each.
Give children the opportunity to form sensory images.	Answer questions such as the following:

What would *smell* this way?

spicy _____   sweet _____
strong _____   unpleasant _____

What would *feel* this way?

furry_____   soft _____
smooth_____   prickly_____

What would *taste* this way?

sweet _____   bitter _____
sour _____   salty _____

List all the words possible which describe a familiar object.

Develop the ability to clarify and learn new meanings and provide opportunities to enrich vocabulary.

Draw a circle around the word that means the same as the underlined word:

My brother <u>hurt</u> his hand.

repaired   injured

I listened to his (tale.)

story   music

Develop functional understanding of word relationships and provide opportunities for children to organize and classify types of things.

Draw a line under the family name of a group of words:

lamb   beef   <u>meat</u>   pork

Draw a line through the word that does not belong in each group:

book   ~~girl~~   page   word

Arrange a list of words in categories:

Animals	*Food*	*Clothing*
bear	coat	antelope
milk	shoes	trousers

Purpose	Exercise
Provide opportunities for children to perceive relationships of time, place, manner, and sequence.	Arrange the following words and phrases in the proper column:

Where?	*When?*	*How?*
in the car	this noon	
later	under the tree	
one day	into the school	
with a bang	in his room	
everywhere	every night	
that morning	at the window	
fast	as fast as he could	

Purpose	Exercise
Provide opportunities for children to strengthen meaning associations.	Respond with the opposite of a given word:

forget (remember)	laugh (cry)
tired (rested)	cross (happy)
top (bottom)	hot (cold)

Provide opportunities for children to discriminate in multiple meanings.

Choose the correct word for each sentence:

wraps   patch   change

See the pretty strawberries in the _____.
Did your mother _____ your dress?
Put your _____ in the cloakroom.
My sister _____ her Christmas presents.
_____ your shoes.
The clerk gave me the right _____.

Develop an awareness of phonetic elements and provide opportunities for children to discriminate between hard and soft sounds of *g.*

In each sentence fill in the blank with the word which has the soft sound of *g:*

The _____ was eating the seeds.
    goose pigeon
The _____ came from Sue's aunt.
    message gift

Fill in the blank with the word which has the hard sound of *g:*

We could see the beautiful _____.
                      bridge gate
The _____ animals crowded close
    strange greedy
together.

Purpose

Provide opportunities for children to discriminate between hard and soft sounds of *c*.

Provide opportunities for children to organize and develop phonics rules.

Develop an awareness of the meaning and sound of prefixes and suffixes, and skill in identifying root words and structural changes; give the children the opportunity to learn how new words are formed by adding suffixes to known root words.

Exercise

List these words in the proper column:

	Soft c		*Hard c*
take	cellar		dancing
circus	cups		package
count	cabbage		ice
lettuce	city		cap

The Phonics Express: Write a phonics rule on each car. Add new cars as new rules are learned.

Form known root words with alphabet blocks or scrabble tiles. Add a prefix or suffix to the root word and discuss the change in the meaning of the word:

	kind			fair
un	kind		un	fair
	kind ly			fair ly
	kind ness			fair ness

The children in a word study period have worked with a group of words such as the following which have been written on the board by the teacher:

raccoon	enough
waddles	hardly
several	perhaps
hollow	special

TEACHER: I am going to write some things for you to do on the board. (*After the teacher writes each of the following directions she calls upon a child to respond. The other children check the response.*)

> Put a cross before *waddles*.
> Draw a line between *several* and *perhaps*.
> Draw a line below *enough*.
> Draw a ring beside *special*.

In each sentence there is a group of words which told you exactly *where* to put your mark. Look at the first sentence. Draw a line under the words which told you where to put the cross. (*Continue in this way with the remaining sentences.*)

Read the first word that is underlined in each of those sentences. What do you notice particularly about those words?

Purpose

Provide opportunities for following written directions that necessitate careful attention to detail. These procedures offer suggestions for work of this kind and at the same time call attention to the prefix *be-*.

Exercise

Very often we find *be* at the beginning of words just as it is here. Think of some words you know which begin that way. (*Write on the board such words as* because, begin, become, behind, *and so on, given by the children.*)

This may be followed at a later period by an exercise in which the children must discriminate between words with the prefix *be-* and so give careful attention to meaning. Such an exercise as this must, of course, be based on the actual experience of the group.

Write the right word on each line:

1. Tom sits _____ Joe.
   because behind belong
2. Mary sits _____ Sally and
   between began become
   Jane.
3. The table is _____ the clock.
   between begin below
4. The Indian dolls _____ to
   become belong beside
   Dick.
5. Tom is at home _____ he
   between beneath because
   has a cold.

Develop an understanding of how the ending *-ful* changes the form of known words.

Choose phrases from the child's reading, such as *very kind and faithful, a very useful work animal, a wonderful sight*.

TEACHER: In the first phrase find a word which tells you that the elephant was trustworthy. What is it, Suzanne?

In the second phrase find a word which tells you what kind of a work animal the elephant was. What is it, Jim?

In the third phrase find a word which tells you that it is a marvelous sight to see elephants at work. What is it, Lewis?

What interesting thing do you notice about those three words? Underline the part that is the same in all three.

Purpose	*Exercise*

Read the word that you have left if you leave that ending off each word, Carol.

Very often in our reading we will find words that end in *-ful*. Let's make a list here on the blackboard of words which you know that end in *-ful*. (*Such words as* thankful, thoughtful, careful, *as they are given by the children.*) What meaning is added by the ending *-ful* to the root words?

Identify root words and structural changes that may be necessary for adding suffixes.

An exercise like this one may be used:

Place many cards on a table and root words that have been changed when suffixes were added.

circling	smoky
happily	racing
noisy	writing

Ask the children to identify the root word in each and tell what happened when the suffix was added. If the right response is given, the child takes the card. The child who has identified the most words wins.

Develop skill in recognizing syllables and learning to apply rules; provide practice in applying known rules of syllabication as an aid in the pronunciation of words.

Make fish-shaped cards (2½ x 4½ inches). On each write a one-, two-, or three-syllable word. Attach a paper clip to the tail. Place mixed-up cards, word down, on a table. With a magnet pick up a fish. Look at the word, say it, applying known rules, and tap out the syllables, with a louder tap for the accented ones.

Develop skill in alphabetizing; provide experiences for children to associate first-letter word position in the alphabet.

Place words on large cards. Use colored string as dividers between the syllables of the words.

fur/ni/ture	au/to/mo/bile
ta/ble	ap/ple

Place the words listed below in the proper column:

abcdefg	*hijklmnop*	*qrstuvwxyz*
happy	girl	cried
little	sorry	Tim
ladder	when	inch
apple	Judy	tall

Provide experiences for children to alphabetize by the first and second letters.

Write a set of cards by having each child write his first name on one. Spread the cards on a table and

Purpose	Exercise

Purpose

Exercise

pick them up in alphabetical order. At first alphabetize by only the first letter, later the second.

Choose a card on which three words beginning with the same letter have been written. While holding it so that others can see it, read the words in alphabetical order. If it is done correctly, keep the card until the end of the period.

slipped	chasing
strong	company
splash	carpenter

Number in ABC order the three words on each line below:

_____ people	_____ outdoors
_____ window	_____ almost
_____ look	_____ close

Exercises such as those that have been described are used as a step in a reading lesson. The teacher's plan will be based on the materials read by the children.

This plan outline is suggested for *groups reading at or above third-grade level*. How might the plan be modified for an individualized program?

THIRD-GRADE LESSON PLAN

Date _____   Group _____

Book _____   Pages _____

MOTIVATE FOR CIRCLE ACTIVITIES.

_____

CHECK COMPREHENSION. (Use guide questions as a basis for discussion.)

_____
_____
_____

PURPOSEFUL ORAL READING. (To support a point, to share an exciting portion, and so forth.)

_____
_____
_____

DEVELOP OR REVIEW SOME WORD-ATTACK OR COMPREHENSION SKILLS.

_____
_____
_____

MOTIVATION OF NEW MATERIAL. (*Arouse interest.* Tie the story to children's own experiences and extend by using children's experiences to relate or contrast. Develop the meaning of any concepts that may be outside the reader's experience.)

_____

Select words from the new vocabulary that should be presented to the group. (Words are prewritten on board or chart. Introduce the words in sentence or phrase form.)

_____

Ask questions to guide silent reading. (Have these listed on the chalkboard, a chart, or a worksheet. These questions usually determine the purpose for which children read. See "Guiding Group Activities" for examples.)

_____

_____

Explain independent reading activity. (See "Guiding Group Activities.")

_____

Indicate activities for early finishers.

_____

How Is Reading Instruction Directed in the Intermediate Grades?

Teachers seek to achieve the following purposes in the reading program of the intermediate grades:

1. *Continue* development of word-recognition skills started in the primary grade. There will be many at this level who are operating at second- and third-grade levels of reading. Some of normal ability follow a delayed pattern of achievement in reading. For a number of reasons, about one boy in ten does not read comfortably until late in his tenth or eleventh year of age. A part of this is lack of purpose. Apparently the reading materials of previous years did not appear worth the effort to read them. But now that he needs to read directions to make model airplanes or is exploring vocational interests, reading assumes a new importance.

2. *Develop* discrimination with respect to reading material. This involves elements of critical judgment, appreciation of literary quality in writing, and the ability to select material needed to solve a problem from material less important.

3. *Teach* the reading skills needed in association with the school program. Intermediate children need to practice increasing reading speed, skimming, using the index or other aids to locate material, and interpreting new concepts, terms, and representation of ideas such as graphs. The dictionary is studied in detail.

4. *Help* the child *integrate* all the language art skills so that they reinforce each other. The close association of these skills may be noted in the parallel columns of skills on the next page.

In the classroom the teacher uses sets of basic readers, library books, weekly and monthly magazines, and daily newspapers to teach reading. At the beginning of the year it is wise to use a reader at least one grade below the level of the children as a review reader. This gives the teacher a chance to get to know the students without discouraging those below grade level. It is normal that from one fourth to one third of an average fifth-grade classroom will be able to read only third- or fourth-grade material. Social studies books and some science books will be difficult for many to read until concepts are established through experience that provides meaning and language experience.

Intermediate teachers soon learn that many of the

Reading for a specific purpose is an aspect of group instruction. A second or third reading, thus motivated, adds to individual reading efficiency. (PHOTO BY LINDA LUNGREN.)

Listening-Reading Skills	Speaking-Writing Skills
Getting the main idea	Finding the topic sentence
	Paragraphing
	Note taking
Reading for details	Outlining
	Giving directions
	Organizing ideas in sequence
	Summarizing
Determining author's meaning of a word	Developing vocabulary
	Using the dictionary
	Interpreting drama
Using context skills	Understanding sentence structure and paragraphing
Using word analysis skills	Spelling
Reading orally	Pronouncing
	Enunciating
	Interpreting drama
Interpreting poetry	Reading in unison, writing creatively
Visualizing	Describing
Understanding modifiers and referents	Using pronouns, adverbs, adjectives, clauses, and phrases
Drawing conclusions	Organizing material logically
Learning social sensitivity to ideas presented	Expressing emotional feelings

study skills, such as drawing conclusions, reading for detail, getting the main idea, and locating information, are developed in materials other than the reading textbook. Intermediate readers are a source for some of these skills, but the major contribution is made in the area of literature.

Because a great range of ability exists in any intermediate class, lesson planning is usually done in terms of groups with similar needs. These steps in a reading lesson are suggested in most basic programs.

1. Silent reading of the new story is motivated. Pictures, questions, and the experience of the child or teacher are used to arouse interest. At this time teachers anticipate and present some of the language and vocabulary needed to read the story.
2. A few of the key concepts and words are introduced. Seldom is it necessary to present all new words, because the children need to practice the word-attack skills they know. Some of these skills may be used in the presentation of the new words as review or reteaching.
3. Any related work in the form of workbooks, chalkboard work, or follow-up assignment is presented and explained.
4. The activities at the circle or with the group are developed. These may start by the teacher's checking previously assigned work. This work may remain with the student for further practice or be collected for checking. The story that has been read silently is then discussed. This discussion will involve questions concerning the main idea, evaluating characters and conduct, drawing conclusions, enjoying humor or literary style. Oral reading is often a part of this period as children clarify points, read dialogue for expression, choose parts, or check understanding. Interest and purpose in the next lesson are established. Some of the new words may be analyzed or checked for meaning. Nearly every lesson provides some opportunity to strengthen phonetic and research skills.

Before leaving the group, the teacher asks some child to repeat the assignment as a means of reinforcing

the memories of others. Circle procedures need variations to avoid monotony. One device that seems to appeal to intermediate children is to create problem-solving situations rather than having the teacher always provide answers and directions.

Certain activities of the class must follow established routines. These involve handling papers, distribution of books, and movement within the room. After a group has left the circle, the teacher will require a few minutes of time to check the work of those who remained at their desks.

In order to encourage and guide recreational reading, at least one period a week should be devoted to this type of activity. This may involve the entire class or only a single interest group, depending on the type of books being read or the level of reading. Those reading at an easier level often hesitate to talk freely about books that other children have already read.

Other special needs may be provided for in weekly one-hour periods. Those who are working in a skill text that is below grade level or in special editions of the *Reader's Digest* may meet several times during a week for special instruction.

To determine the needs of students, a teacher may secure information about students from available guidance records. To obtain standardized test scores quickly in vocabulary, comprehension, and speed, investigate the Nelson Silent (grades 3–9) and Nelson-Denny Reading (grades 10–college) tests, published by Houghton Mifflin Co. in Boston, Massachusetts. These require only thirty minutes of time (ten for vocabulary and twenty for comprehension), provide both percentile ranks and grade levels, and demand a minimum of teacher work in scoring because of a carbon answer sheet.

For additional analysis of other aspects of reading, the following are suggested.[11]

1. For a complete phonics summary:
   McKee Phonics Inventory, Houghton Mifflin Co.,

[11] These suggestions are through the courtesy of Dr. J. E. Sparks, Chairman, Reading and Study Skills Department, Beverly Hills Unified School District, Beverly Hills, California.

Boston, Massachusetts. *Botel Informal Inventory,* in Morton Botel's *How to Teach Reading,* Follett, Chicago.

2. For an estimated comprehension level:
   Gray Oral Reading Test, Bobbs-Merrill Co., Indianapolis, Indiana.

3. For a test of phonogram understanding:
   Remedial Reading Drills, George Wahr Publishing Co., Ann Arbor, Michigan.

4. To establish an individual reading level:
   Wide Range Achievement Test, Chas. L. Story Co., Wilmington, Delaware.

5. For an easy determination of intelligence:
   The Quick Test, Psychological Test Specialists, Missoula, Montana.

6. For suggestions to follow diagnosis:
   Standard Diagnostic Reading Test, Harcourt Brace Jovanovich, New York.

7. For suggestions to prepare for standardized tests:
   Reading Skills Workbooks, Evansville Public Schools, Evansville, Indiana.

Test results should be explained to each student to help plan the next step needed. A child eventually will recognize his needs in this area as he does in other activities and accept his work as something he seeks rather than that imposed by the authority of the teacher.

It will help many students to discuss a story or unit in advance to set goals in terms of what they know about the subject, to anticipate what might happen, and to establish oral vocabulary appropriate to the topic.

Lessons on vocabulary are often needed. A successful technique would be to have each student survey the material to be read to locate new words and then to build his own individualized vocabulary. To do this Word Profiles (3 × 5 cards) may be set up in the manner shown at the top of the next column.

word	definition derivation original sentence
front of card	back of card

Cards enable the student to manipulate words better than if they are listed on a notebook sheet. Cards can be filed after mastery of a word has been achieved; new ones can be added easily. Students can hand their packs to classmates for partner testing.

This approach to vocabulary will result in a better list than one taken from the book by the teacher.

Intermediate grade children like the idea of "cracking paragraphs," which implies reading paragraphs for complete understanding.

The student needs to find the topic noun, the word or phrase around which the paragraph revolves. Then the reader finds the sentence that makes the most general statement possible about the topic noun. This is the topic sentence or main idea.

In about 90 per cent of nonfiction or textbook paragraphs, students may expect to find this main idea in the first sentence. In the remaining paragraphs, this main idea may be in any sentence (often last) or it may be implied.

After much experience with finding main ideas in paragraphs, students could search for the details or the specifics, primarily found by asking *who, what, when, where, why,* or *how* about the general statement.

Until students can "crack paragraphs" with competence in independent, silent reading, they may do it in small groups using charts or using this teacher-made material.

A teacher provides a large number of highly structured paragraphs from books at levels from grade 4 through high school to be used for practice by those needing it on 5 × 8 cards. The students complete the information in the chart below.

Topic Noun	General Statement	Specific Statements
The word around which the entire paragraph revolves.	The main idea; the topic sentence.	The details; the facts that support the general statement.

Those students who are experiencing a secure knowledge of content of reading matter should learn to probe that content in depth, through critical reading-thinking skills.

Text-Explicit, Text-Implicit Information and World Knowledge

Questions may involve text-explicit information. For example:

That February up in the woods was one to be remembered. The wind moaned and shrieked around the corners of the cabin, but the boys were warm and cozy inside. In some of the blizzards it wasn't easy to do the chores, but the boys were toughened to it. The cattle crowded together for warmth under their shelter and came through in good shape.[12]

1. *Text Explicit*. How did the wind sound? How did the boys feel? Why did the cattle crowd together?
2. *Text Implicit*. Were the boys able to complete their chores during the winter?
3. *World Knowledge*. Why was it important that the cattle come through in good shape? Why do people choose this type of work?

Diagnostic teaching depends on continuous evaluation by both the teacher and learner. The usual methods used are informal tests, oral questioning, and student reports. In addition the student should be learning to evaluate his own achievement. When an error of understanding is made, he must analyze why he misunderstood. Did he skip an important word? Did he use the wrong meaning for a word? All errors are simply learning opportunities when handled in this way. At no time should the learner be concerned about being better than another reader. He may know this as he would in any other activity, but such comparison is not the basis for diagnostic teaching.

Conclusions from evaluation by a learner may be similar to the following: "This book is too difficult—I need to know more about finding root words—I need to know how to locate words in the dictionary—I need to learn how to locate places on a map—The illustrations will provide meaning clues—This writer does not organize carefully-—I want to find out more about a topic."

Self-determined "next steps" by teacher and learner provide the motivation for continuous growth in reading skills.

A positive approach would be a record such as, "Today I learned _____." Another way to do this is to keep records at times of only the things that were done right until the recognition of needs loses any negative feeling in much the same manner an athlete uses when he says, "I need to practice _____," or a businessman says, "I need to improve _____."

In order to free the teacher's time to meet individual and group needs, purposeful work must be found for those at their desks. Some able children like to prepare challenging materials for others to read. These may be a series of questions concerning an article from a magazine or newspaper. If mounted in a manila folder, the article on one side and questions on the other, they may be used many times or sent to another room. The circulars children receive when they write to firms or communities are also interesting reading experiences when prepared in this fashion. There are well-planned workbooks for all the intermediate grades. Although few classes would use one of these for all students, small sets of this material will save hours of teacher time as she helps children who have been absent, who need special help, or who are above average and need challenging material.

The following activities have been found to be of value as seatwork practices:

Reread the first paragraph of the story. Answer the following questions:
1. Who are the characters introduced?
2. Where does the beginning of the story take place?
3. When does the beginning of the story take place?
4. What problem is being introduced?
Make a list of the leading characters in the story and skim story to find descriptive phrases of each.

Appearance	Characteristics
Action	Expressions
Feelings	Attitudes

[12] From Verne T. Davis, *Times of the Wolves* (New York: Morrow, 1962).

Write a description in your own words, one for each character.

Choose your favorite character. Pretend you meet this person. Write a conversation you might like to have with this person.

Choose two characters in the story. Write a conversation between them.

Choose a character from this story and one from another story your class has recently read and write a conversation between them.

Choose one location mentioned in the story. Make a list of all descriptive words and phrases used in the text about this location.

Write in your own words a description of this place.

Read the ending of your story. Make a picture as you see the scene.

Choose a title for the picture. Write a short paragraph to go with the picture.

Read the first three paragraphs of the story and make an outline of them:

1. What is the first paragraph about?
   a. People
   b. Places
   c. Action
2. What is the second paragraph about?
   a.
   b.
   c.
3. What is the third paragraph about?
   a.
   b.
   c.

Skim the story and make lists of words ending with -ing, -ed, -s, -es. Decide if any words are examples of the following rules, and if so, list the examples under the rule number.

Rule 1. If a word of one syllable ends with a single consonant by a single vowel, the final consonant is usually doubled before a suffix beginning with a vowel is added.

Examples: run, running; fun, funny; hop, hopping

Rule 2. When a word of more than one syllable ends with a single consonant preceded by a single vowel, the consonant is usually doubled before adding a suffix beginning with a vowel when the accent is on the last syllable.

Examples: omit, omitted

Rule 3. If a word ends with a single consonant immediately preceded by more than one vowel, the final consonant is not usually doubled when a suffix is added.

Examples: weed, weeded; dream, dreaming

Rule 4. If a word ends with two or more consonants or a double consonant, the consonants are usually retained when adding the suffix.

Examples: jump, jumped; dress, dresses

Rule 5. If a word ends with silent *e,* the *e* is usually dropped before a suffix beginning with a vowel is added.

Examples: hope, hoped

Rule 6. In words ending with *y* immediately preceded by a consonant, the *y* is usually changed to an *i* before a suffix is added.

Examples: cry, cries

Rule 7. Words ending with *y* retain the *y* when a suffix beginning with *i* is added.

Examples: hurry, hurrying

Rule 8. If a word ends in *y* immediately preceded by a vowel, the *y* is usually retained when a suffix is added.

Examples: play, played

Choose words from the story that will go with the following:

1. Words telling how high.
2. Words telling how low.
3. Words telling how fast.
4. Words telling how slow.
5. Words telling when.
6. Words telling where.

Look through the story and study all illustrations.

Skim the story and choose one or two sentences as titles which you feel are appropriate.

Read the story again. Choose a scene as a subject for a peep box. Make a peep box for this scene.

Reread the story. List the scenes presented. Make characters for each scene to use on flannelboard.

Practice the story using the pictures to illustrate.

Work with a committee to chose one scene from the story that can be told in pantomime. Plan for one pupil to read from text while others pantomime what happens.

Choose one character from today's story and one from another story you have read. Plan a meeting of these two characters. Decide what you would have them doing at this meeting. Paint a picture of this scene. Choose an appropriate title. Write conversation.

Choose an experience one of the characters had in the story. Write about an experience you have had similar to this.

Choose a situation as described in the story. Write a myth or a "whopper" about this siutation.

Write a personal, newsy letter to one of the characters in the story telling about your activities and inquiring about something the character has been doing.

Write a personal letter as from one character to another. Write an answer to the letter as from the other character.

Make up a limerick about a person, place, or thing mentioned in the story.

Make a sequence chart of things that happened.

You may want to make illustrations to go with the chart.

Choose a scene in the story. Make stick puppets to go with this scene and plan to put on a show for the class.

Choose a character. Pretend something he owns that has been mentioned in the story has been lost.

Write an advertisement fore the "lost and found" column of the daily paper.

Write riddles using characters, places, or objects from your story.

Pretend you are the news editor of the daily paper published in the city where the characters of the story live. Write articles which may appear in this paper mentioning the doings of these characters.

Plan some headlines, and so on.

Choose one of the characters who is in trouble.

Write a short play for the class to act out, using the other characters as needed.

Look for words in the story and list them under the following headings:

dr	tr	fr	fl	bl	cl	sl	st	sw
st	sw	sn	sm	cr	gr	pr	br	qu
pl	sp	spr	str	thr	ch	sh	wh	th

Look for words ending with -ck, -ng.

Look for words ending with -al, -aw, -ai, -ay, -oa, -oi, -oy; -ow as in slow; ow as in cow; -ar, -er, ir, -ur.

Find words starting with soft g, hard g, soft c, hard c.

Find words illustrating the following:

1. Silent e at the end of the one-syllable word.
2. Silent vowel in a word in which two vowels come together.
3. Silent letter in double consonants.
4. When c or g is followed by e, i, or y, it usually has the soft sound.
5. When there is only one vowel in a one-syllable word it is usually short unless it is at the end.

Find words that have root words within them.

Find compound words.

Find hyphenated words.

Find words to which you can add -y, -ly, -er, -est, -ful, -en, -able. Make the new words by adding these endings.

Find words that start with re-, un-, be-. Find other words to which these prefixes may be added. How are they related in meaning?

Find contractions in the story such as I'm, what's, we're, that's, haven't, there's, aren't.

Find words that end in -e to which -ing, -ed, -est, or -y may be added to form new words. Make new words by adding these endings. Note that the *e* must be dropped in adding these.

Look for figures of speech in the story. Explain the meaning.

Choose single words that describe each character.

In a column to the side of these lists, write words that are opposite in meaning. For example: *happy, sad; laugh, cry*.

List all the words on a certain page that express action; things a character did.

Tell briefly why you think each character did the things he did in the story.

Use the table of contents in the reader to find another story similar to this one and tell why you chose that particular one.

Read in some source book in the room more information about something mentioned in the story.

List all the words of whose meanings you are not sure. Find them in the dictionary or glossary if the book has one. Choose the meaning that you think best applies to the use made of the word in the story.

Write statements from the story for others in the class to decide whether true or false. Be sure you know the correct answer.

Write sentences for others in the class to complete.

Find passages in the story that make you feel sad, happy, drowsy, excited.

Find parts of the story you feel are humorous.

Write a fable, legend, or fairy tale about some incident or character in the story.

Look back through the book. List the stories you have read under the following headings: fanciful tale, biography, true story, realistic.

Find words that begin with *dis-, en-, in-, un-, re-*.

Words that end with *-ion, -ist, -ment, -ant, -er, -ance, -ish, -able, -ful, -less*. Note the influence of these elements on meaning.

Select an advertisement or news story and note the words that have emotional appeal in them.

Take a circular of a city or park and make a series of questions that a visitor might find answered in this circular. Clip a week's TV schedule from the Sunday paper. Make a series of questions that might be answered by reading this schedule. Read an advertisement of something you would like to buy—a bicycle, toy, car. What questions are *not* answered in the material?

For Discussion

1. When should children be permitted to read library books in the classroom?

2. Should a child in the sixth grade who reads as well as an adult be expected to participate in the reading class?

3. Why do you feel a teacher is justified, at the beginning of the year, in having the better readers do a great deal of oral reading in the social studies and science classes?

4. Why are some more likely to enjoy reading circulars they have received in the mail, or a Scout Manual, or an item in *Popular Science Magazine* than a story in the reader?

5. Examine some of the study skills such as reading for details, drawing conclusions, and getting the main idea in association with the content subjects. Find examples of reading details in a mathematics problem, in a science experiment, and in a geography book. Would it be possible for a child to use the skill in one area and not in another? What factors are operating to make these situations similar or different?

6. In *The Reading Teacher* (October 1965), a Detroit teacher tells of using the words of songs by the Beatles for reading instruction with retarded readers. The ten songs had a total of 173 words, used 1,072 times. Of the 173 words, 139 appear in Dolch's Word List. There is much repetition, *I* appears 54 times, *you* 64 times, *love* 53 times. Would such a program help such a child establish word-attack skills? What popular songs of today might be used in such an approach?

Supplementary Reading

Because supplementary reading books reinforce rather than introduce the basic reading skills, pacing in the supplementary books should be accelerated. Approximately four to six weeks will be required to complete a reader, depending on the length of the book and the ability of the pupils.

It is a good plan to progress systematically through the book. In planning supplementary reading, the teacher gives less attention to detailed presentation of the new vocabulary and skills. Reading assignments should be considerably longer than in the basic program. It may be necessary to use several supplementary books before the group is ready to move up to the basic reader at the next level of difficulty. Caution should be exercised in moving a child into the basic reader before he is ready.

The period of supplementary reading affords an excellent time for a child with changing needs to move to a group where his needs can be better met. For example, if the child consistently misses three or four words on a page, his needs for challenge and success will probably be met by moving him to a level where he can succeed. If the material presents little or no challenge to a child, he should probably be moved to a more difficult level. It is usually advisable to make a gradual move by letting him work for a time in both the old and the new groups.

The elements of a lesson taught from a supplementary reader involve added emphasis on comprehension and interpretation of what has been studied. A maximum of silent reading and a minimum of writing exercises should be included in periods of independent study. If study-type exercises are provided in the reader, they should be carefully selected to serve the purpose of the lesson. How would you modify this third-grade lesson?

I. *Text:* Charles E. Merrill, *Treat Shop*

  A. *Purposes:* To build comprehension skills, to build oral reading skills, to review skills of structural analysis, to increase vocabulary, and to appreciate the author's ability to create feeling.

  B. *Assignment* (*at previous circle period*).

    1. Pages 56–71 were to be read silently. Pupils were instructed to be

prepared to answer these questions orally:

    a. What problem did the Tollivers have? How did they solve the problem?

    b. Why did Joey appreciate his job more at the end of the story than at the beginning?

  2. Children were given the following written assignment: Reread the selections to find the page numbers and the paragraph numbers that tell:

    a. Why the Tollivers decided to get rid of the cats.

    b. How the Tollivers' house seemed with no cats around.

    c. Why the cats caused no more trouble at mealtime in the Tolliver house.

    d. Why Joey was discontented in the city.

    e. How Joey felt when he first reached the farm.

    f. Why Joey changed his mind about life on the farm.

  C. *Procedure* (*at the reading circle*).

    1. Check on work prepared independently.

    a. Build interest: "In what ways were the two stories you read yesterday alike? Have you ever felt like Joey?"

    b. Discuss guide questions.

    2. Do purposeful oral reading.

    a. Set a standard: "Today, let's try to make our reading sound just like we're talking."

    b. Check assignment that was prepared independently by having pupils read to prove a point.

    c. Evaluate in terms of standards.

3. Build word-study skills.

   a. Review the meaning of *un* as a prefix.

   b. Write the following words on the chalkboard:

   unnecessary   unsuccessful
   uncomfortable   unpack

   c. Identify the root word and the prefix in each of the four words.

4. Motivate the new story.

   a. Read the introductory poem on page 73 aloud. Ask, "Did you ever see a fairy? Why is it fun to read about elves and giants today?" Discuss pictures briefly in the first two stories.

   b. Show a book of *Grimms' Fairy Tales*.

   c. Suggest that pupils who enjoy the stories in the reader will probably enjoy other fairy tales.

   d. Introduce key words of vocabulary (prewritten on the board).

   better weather   powerful *crow*
   beautiful *bray*   goblins
                         screamed
   fine *mouser*   The *Bremen
                         Town
                         Musicians*

   e. Present guide questions (list on chalkboard, chart, or worksheet).

      (1) Why do you think the shoemaker and his wife were good people?
      (2) Tell why the title "Bremen Town Musicians" does not fit the story.

5. Make assignment,

   a. Read pages 74–85. Be able to discuss the guide questions.

   b. Reread the stories. As you do, list the page number and the paragraph number for each story that has:

   A sad part.
   An exciting part.
   A funny part.

For Discussion

1. Under what circumstances would you retain a child at grade level because of a reading deficiency?

2. What values do you see in a pre-first-grade year between kindergarten and first grade?

3. If a class were grouped on the basis of equal reading skill development at the primary level, how long would it stay that way?

What Activities May the Teacher Use in the Circle to Promote Interest and Practice?

There are usually five steps in a primary basic reading lesson. The first is a preparatory or readiness phase in which the concepts needed to read the material are developed and new words are introduced. A part of this period is to arouse the interest of the student.

The second phase involves a guided reading of the material. This is usually silent and then oral, followed by a discussion. The manuals provide well-planned questions that establish purposes for the reading and check on comprehension.

After the total story is completed there is a discussion which involves additional comprehensive check and interpretation of the story.

The fourth step is drill on word-recognition skills.

The fifth is an application of what has been learned, an enrichment or a creative application of the information or skills mastered.

Although the manuals are rich in suggestions, teachers need resource materials to review the vocabulary of the previous day, to provide interesting drill on new words, and to meet special needs of children.

The following suggestions were made by a group of experienced teachers in a summer school class. Select only a few that seem to appeal to the group you teach. Although children like a little variety, too much may be overstimulation.

1. List on the chalkboard words that may be causing difficulties. Give meaning clues and challenge the children to find the correct word, as, "Can you find a word that means something we do with our eyes?" (*look* or *see*). "Can you find a word that joins other words?" (*and*) "Can you find a word that means a color?" (*brown* etc.) When children get the idea of clues relating to the meaning of words, each child who guesses the correct word may give the clue for a next word for the others to guess. This may be done with phrases, too. In this way the children are not merely calling out words but are associating them with meanings, which is fundamental in reading.

2. One child is asked to leave the room momentarily. The others agree on a word from a list on the chalkboard. The first child returns and is given a pointer. He points to one of the words and says, "Is it *wagon?*" The children respond with, "No, it is not *wagon*" or "Yes, it is *wagon*," as the case may be. In this way all children's attention is focused on the words and all maintain interest in the repetition that takes place.

3. Divide the class into two, three, or four groups with a balance of fast and slow learners in each group. Present a pack of troublesome words to each group and challenge them to help one another until all members of the group can be checked individually on the entire pack. Those who know all the words are eager to help the slow learners during free time or whenever there is time before school starts or during bad-weather recesses. Group records may be kept and the competition continued as more words and phrases are presented in other packs.

4. Troublesome words during a reading-class period are recorded on the chalkboard. Allowing five to eight minutes at the end of the class time, check each child before he proceeds to his seat. Those who are most likely to know the words are checked first and the slow learners remain for more help. Words of which some children are not sure may be put on flash cards and given to the children to work on at home or during free moments with other children.

5. The children sit on the floor in front of their chairs. Each child in turn is asked to recognize a flash-card word or phrase. If he identifies it correctly, he sits up on his chair and the teacher proceeds around the circle of children on the floor. This gives slow learners more chances for help. If a child does not know the word or phrase, a child who is seated on a chair is challenged. This keeps all children attentive, as those seated in chairs do not know when they may be called on; if they cannot give immediate response, they are again seated on the floor.

6. Place four or five difficult words along the chalk tray. Have the children repeat the words with you several times. Then have all children close their eyes while you remove one word. Mix up the remaining words. Then the children are to open their eyes and determine which word is missing.

7. Give each child a flash card with a word that he has found especially difficult. Have him take a good look at it. Then call out three words and the children having those words are to place them on the chalk tray. All the children then say the words, after which the teacher mixes them up and the original children go up and get their own words and identify them.

8. Each child is given several flash cards. The teacher calls out an initial sound and children having words starting with that sound place them on the chalk tray. Errors are detected and children who do not respond correctly are helped.

9. Each child stands behind his chair. A flash card is placed on each chair. A child who needs help with the words is chosen to identify them. He picks up each card he can identify correctly. These are handed to the teacher. The children standing behind the chairs on which words appear that the child does not know may go with the child to a corner of the room and help him learn them. The game is repeated with the remaining words and another slow learner is helped.

10. A word is printed on the chalkboard beside the

name of the child who has been having difficulty with that word. It is his "word for the day." Frequently during the day at odd moments the teacher challenges him to identify it.

11. The semicircle of chairs on which the children are seated is referred to as the streetcar. One child is chosen as the conductor. He stands behind the first chair. A word is flashed and if the conductor can identify it before the child on the chair he moves on behind the next chair and another word is flashed. If he is first to identify each word all around the class, he goes to his seat for other activity. If a child on the chair is first to identify a word, he becomes the conductor and exchanges places.

12. Children are given one or two flash cards. The teacher calls for words that rhyme with a given word, or words that are action words, or words that are foods, or number words, or people's names, and so on.

13. At the end of the reading class period the difficult words from the lesson are printed on the chalkboard. A child is given an eraser and asked to identify one of the words. If he says it correctly he may erase it and go to his seat. Another child is asked to identify another word, and so on until all words have been erased.

14. A list of ten difficult words is printed on the chalkboard. Each child starts at the bottom of the list and sees how far up he can go identifying the words. When he misses a word, his initials are placed beside that word and the next child starts at the bottom. If a child can identify them all, his initials are placed at the top of the list. The second time the children who missed a word are asked to identify the word they missed and then proceed up the list until they reach the top.

For Discussion

1. Would any of the foregoing devices be useful in a tutorial situation in which the children worked in teams of two to drill each other?

2. Would any of the foregoing devices be useful in the home where a parent wanted to help a child in reading?

What Reading Problems May a Beginning Teacher Anticipate?

A number of problems may surprise and dismay the beginning teacher. Space does not permit a discussion of all the special and remedial techniques used. These situations, which are accepted as normal by the experienced teacher, include the following:

Children frequently lose the place while they are reading.

Children continue to move their lips during silent reading.

Children reverse words such as *on* and *no* or *stop* and *spot*.

Children finish the worksheets too soon or not at all.

The books seem too difficult for a child.

Children will not read loudly enough to be heard.

Children say the words but do not understand what is being read.

Children doing seatwork keep interrupting the teacher when she is working with a group.

A child fails to recognize a word in a story even though he always knows it when it is used on a flash card.

Parents wish to teach the child out of the basic reader.

Children continue to lose their place for three reasons. (1) The width of the line of type (or *measure*) may be too great in proportion to the print size so that the eye cannot follow the line without "wandering" to the beginning of the next line. Newspaper columns are designed to permit rapid reverse eye movements for adults. Adults frequently lose the place when the reading lines of small type extend longer than five or six inches. In all cases, however, the size of the type is a factor, as well as the measure. Reading textbooks are usually designed with these factors in mind, but the library books that children read aloud are sometimes difficult typographically. The otherwise excellent books of Holling C. Holling, such as *Paddle to the Sea* and

Pagoo, illustrate this problem. A related physical factor is the placement of illustrations on the page so that they tend to draw the eyes away from the beginning and ending of the line. (2) Interruptions in reading may cause children to lose the place. The interruption may be a difficult word. The reader may look at the picture on the page or in the previous paragraph in order to find help and then be unable to scan rapidly to the place where he is reading. A question from the teacher or a correction that causes the reader to look away from his material to the chalkboard or a chart is a common occurrence. (3) Boredom may cause a child to lose the place. Sometimes this results from waiting his turn to read in a large group of slow readers or from lack of interest in the story. Books seem to grow heavier when held for a long period of time, and merely following the page while others read aloud is not a highly motivating situation.

Teachers sometimes have students use strips of heavy paper as place markers. These are held under the line the child is reading to guide his eyes. This can be done comfortably only when the child is at a table or desk. In a circle children must rest their books on their laps, steady them with one hand, guide the marker with the other, and bend their bodies into unnatural shapes in order to read. Place markers are a great help when kept clean and used in situations where the children are physically comfortable. Sometimes it is better for the teacher to go to the child's desk or table rather than have him come to the circle.

Oral reading of information material is usually difficult. Beyond the primary level a child should not be asked to read orally unless the material has first been read silently. The skilled oral reader actually scans ahead of the material he is voicing. This is a specific skill developed in the middle grades.

Lip movement or vocalization is natural for a beginner in the reading of any language. Adults studying a foreign language can be observed moving their lips as they silently pronounce the words they read. Many adults do not move their lips, but according to some physiologists vocal cords are unconsciously activated by the speech center in the brain and take on all the necessary configurations as in actual audible speech.

College students complain of "tired throats" after a night of study without realizing that this silent reading may actually be the cause. Silent voicing of all words results in slow, plodding reading.

At first, all silent reading means "saying the words to yourself." In the third grade and beyond, children are encouraged to scan material for the ideas presented rather than the sounds written on the page. Although many are taught to do this before third grade, it is at this level that the child usually has mastered the basic reading skills and faces the need for such a skill in extensive reading situations.

To remind children that their lips are moving, teachers sometimes have them hold a pencil on the upper lip as they read. This will make them conscious of any lip movement. An extended reading of simple material for the enjoyment of the ideas usually develops adequate speed of reading that causes the vocalization to be reduced or to disappear.

The problem of deciding which books are easy or difficult is a puzzle indeed. The use of various readability formulas is discussed in connection with children's literature. The concept of frustration levels of reading refers to the number of new words a child must be told as he reads. If there are more than three in any sequence of nineteen words, the books are considered difficult. Intermediate children face one new word in every ten because of the rapidly expanding vocabulary of the textbooks used. Such factors as print size and leading (from the lead metal used to make spaces between lines) cause printed material to look either easy or difficult. The attitude of the reader is important. When children say that a book is "too easy" their judgment may be influenced wholly by this factor of typographic appearance. The subject matter is also a factor in a child's judgment of a book. A book about "Cowboy Sam" may be accepted by a fourth-grade reader while an animal fable in a more difficult vocabulary will be rejected.

Each child has a level at which he can succeed and grow. To find this instructional level the teacher should:

1. Estimate the child's reading level from his previous records and tests.

2. Choose a book one level lower than the estimated level.
3. Choose a page approximately one third from the front of the book.
4. Have the child read orally without preparation 100 running words. (Use a shorter passage if testing at a low reading level.)
5. Record as errors the following:
   a. Substitutions.
   b. Mispronunciations.
   c. Words pronounced by the teacher.
   d. Repetition of more than one word.
   e. Insertions.
   f. Omissions.
6. Test at the next lower level if the child misses more than one out of twenty running words.
7. Test at a higher level if he reads fluently.

The child's instructional level has been found when he averages no more than five errors out of 100 running words. This method does not check comprehension, but it is an easy device for grouping. When groups are formed, the teacher can check comprehension. If a child consistently fails to comprehend 75 per cent of the material read, he should be moved to a less difficult book.

Modern reading programs provide plateau reading experiences or absorption periods during which no new vocabulary difficulties are added. These periods are designed to fix skills previously taught or to provide opportunity to increase reading speed. Frequently neither the teacher nor the child, strange to say, recognizes these periods as easier than others.

In some cities kits of materials relating to a unit topic are prepared for a class. In theory, these books are selected to care for the wide reading range of the normal classroom. Although the extremes of very simple and difficult are relatively obvious, the intermediate range is difficult for both teachers and children to distinguish. Intermediate readers are especially confusing. Some fourth-grade books seem more difficult to certain children than others designed for the sixth grade.

The child who reads *was* for *saw* is obviously starting at the wrong end of a word. A clear understanding at the start of reading instruction of where to start to look at a word will prevent this. Noticing which words are alike at the beginning is a readiness exercise that is widely used. Too much emphasis on rhyming will cause children to look at the wrong end of a word for a reading clue. The tendency to reverse a word, which is revealed when a word like *no* is read as *on,* may apply to other words, even though the child pronounces the misread word correctly. A great emphasis on phonetic formulas like *will, dill, sill* may cause the child to look at the *-ill* first, then the beginning. When he does this to all words, it is natural that confusion as to the word meaning and pronounciation results.

Worksheets provide extra drill, simple tests, and independent activity. Certain types are unpopular with teachers. The most undesirable are those that require the child to cut and paste. This type of activity can seldom be done without supervision. Probably the most difficult are those that have a story cut into parts that the child is asked to rearrange in logical order. (This is a good activity but should be done as a boxed individual game.) Nearly all worksheets provide an opportunity for children to add a colored sketch when they complete the work. This may be a device to keep children busy while the teacher works with others.

Routines that provide the child with a place to put his work when finished and something to do while other complete the work are established by wise teachers. One teacher has three folders, one for each group. As soon as a child completes his work it is placed in this folder. The work is corrected that evening and returned to the children in the reading circle the next day. Those who finish their papers are permitted to read a library book, go to an interest center in the room (usually with established rules on how many may be in one place), or select an individual game. When workbooks are used, the drill sheets for the day are removed. The child cannot be expected to care for all the material that he does not use or need in these books. Normally they are an awkward size for desks and difficult for little hands to handle. Individual cardboard folders in which worksheets are inserted are especially helpful when some of the work is done in the circle where there is no adequate support to mark worksheets.

It is also wise to anticipate the reasons children come to the teacher for help. Perhaps there is a child who makes a practice of not listening to directions, or one who does not easily comprehend them when they are given. This child might be asked to repeat the directions after you have given them so everyone will be sure they know what to do (and you will know that he understands). Then a check must be made to see that everyone has a pencil or other needed materials. Seating the children far enough apart will eliminate complaints of copying or annoyances. Then it can be explained to the children that, because they know how annoying it is when someone interrupts their group procedures, it will be a good policy to rule out interruptions except for extreme emergencies. When interruptions do take place, the teacher needs to be firm in her judgment as to whether the interruption is a real emergency. Especially at the beginning of first grade the interruptions are often merely to get attention, and such interruptions should be discouraged at the outset. Be sure that after a group has finished reading you recognize good independent workmanship. Children need attention and praise but help them to understand that there are occasions when the needs of the group are more important than the needs of individuals.

The soft-voiced child has many desirable qualities, but he may be a source of distraction to other children if he cannot be heard beyond the first row. Low-voiced tones may be based on shyness or fear of making an error. Some beginners have been so frightened by wild rumors of school disciplinary methods that they practically refuse to talk.

Teachers put these shy children in small groups, sometimes bolstering their confidence by giving them a reading partner or letting them sit next to the teacher. Dramatic play, use of flannelboard characters, verse choir, and singing help this type of child.

More of a problem for a beginning teacher is the loud child with a short attention span. Each one of this type is different. Some are the center of attention at home and expect to be accorded the same status at school; some get no attention at home and therefore demand it at school. The "grasshopper" interests and activities of such children can disturb an entire classroom and create extreme tension for the teacher.

Establish a few patterns of behavior and insist that they be followed consistently. Some of these patterns will be negative. The more effective will be those that suggest alternate activities for the undesirable ones. It is not a teaching weakness to permit these children to act as leaders in the few classroom practices that they like. If activity is an essential, such errands that must be made to the principal's office may be assigned to this type of child. Chores like wrapping or unwrapping books from the central office or serving as playground monitors use up some of the boundless energy of these children. Peer judgment has some influence, but do not place the responsibility for disciplinary decisions on the other children.

Some children in the second or third grade develop the ability to verbalize the words of the reader without any clear understanding of what is being said. Sometimes these are children with a foreign-language background. They apparently have mastered all the word-attack skills except that of understanding word meaning. These children are sometimes good spellers as well. Each word is an interesting design in type rather than a thought symbol. Rather than more reading and writing these students need a great deal of speaking and listening with meaning. Word calling happens at all levels of education. As the attitude of demanding meaning is developed—not just meaning in the abstract, but the specific meaning of the speaker or writer—this type of verbalizing disappears. Too great an emphasis on scope or speed of reading may develop an attitude of "covering ground" rather than assimilating thoughts or comprehending ideas. Exercises that require rephrasing or finding words of similar or opposite meaning focus attention on what the words mean rather than how they are pronounced.

A child was once asked how he knew the word was *the* on the flash card, and he said, "I always remember that the card with *the* on it has a bent corner." Such a remark may indicate that flash-card drills often become too detached from word meanings. As each word is presented it is well to give the children a chance to use it in their own sentences. Attention is then drawn to the first letter of the word and to any peculiarities in the word form, such as preponderance of tall letters, length of the word, and so on. If several copies of the flash card are available, it is best to mix them with other words and call on children to find all the cards that have the word *the*. Then give each child a book and ask him to find the word, put his finger under it, and raise his other hand. After you have checked to see whether they are correct, the children of one group can be looking for another *the* while you are busy with a second group. Another form of drill is achieved by placing cards along the chalk tray and giving such clues as "find the card that has a girl's name on it," "find the word that joins other words together," "find a color word," or "find an action word," so that children think about word meanings as they recognize them.

More and more schools are adopting the policy of not sending home the book used for basic reading instruction until the child has completed this book at school. A child attempting to follow the suggestions of two authorities, his teacher and his mother, can become confused. Some mothers are excellent teachers, but there are many who in their zeal "push" children too much and take the joy from the reading experience. Coercion or prolonged sessions of reading when the child wishes to do something else tend to destroy the best teaching efforts at school. Belittling remarks or sarcasm from older children exaggerate a beginner's errors and lower the self-esteem of a sensitive child. The child who needs the most help with reading at school seldom benefits from home instruction. The careful diagnosis of individual problems is a professional task not to be attempted by a well-meaning parent. Supplementary readers and library books that provide practice on reading skills taught at school are designed to be read at home. Because these will contain some words that do not follow phonetic principles, parents might be informed that they can be of most help to their child by listening to the stories he reads, praising his efforts as he struggles with new words, and prompting him occasionally so as to avoid long pauses. Shared reading experiences, in which parent and child alternately read parts of bedtime stories from newspapers or books, are among the most precious memories of childhood.

For Discussion

1. The content of much primary reading consists of stories about children with a pony, Daddy's new car, or grandmother's big farmhouse. Children of lower socioeconomic groups seldom read about situations similar to their own. In what way may this influence reading instruction?

2. Do you think that television has influenced children's interest in reading? How might the teacher influence home television habits?

3. At times it may be necessary to use a textbook that the child has already used in a previous grade or in another school. How can you justify this to the learner?

Bibliography

ARTICLES

Barrett, T. C. "Predicting Reading Achievement Through Readiness Tests." *Reading and Inquiry*. Newark, Delaware International Reading Association, 1965, pp. 26–28.

Brown, S. "The First Grade Child Not Quite Ready for Reading Instruction." *Reading in Action in the Sixties*. Bellingham, Wash.: Western Washington State College, January 1965.

Burmeister, L. E. "Content of a Phonics Program." *Reading Methods and Teacher Improvement* (ed. by Nila Banton Smith). Newark, Del.: International Reading Association, 1971, pp. 27–33.

Burmeister, L. E. "Usefulness of Phonic Generalizations." *The Reading Teacher* (January 1968), 350–356.

Calvin, A. D. "How to Teach with Programmed Textbooks." *Grade Teacher* (February 1967).

Chase, W. G., and H. H. Clark. "Mental Operations in the Comparison of Sentences and Pictures." *Cognition in Learning and Memory* (ed. by L. W. Gregg). New York: Wiley, 1972, pp. 205–232.

Clymer, T. "The Utility of Phonic Generalizations in the Primary Grades." *The Reading Teacher*, **16** (1963), 252–258.

Dale, E., and J. S. Chall. "A Formula for Predicting Readability." *Educational Research Bulletin,* **27** (January 1948), 11–20.

Dawes, R. M. "Memory and Distortion of Meaningful Written Material." *British Journal of Psychology,* **57** (1966), 77–86.

Durrell, D. "Success in First Grade Reading." *Boston University Journal of Education,* **140** (February 1958), 2–47.

Durrell, D., and H. A. Murphy. "Boston University Research in Elementary School Reading, 1933–63." *Journal of Education,* **145** (December 1963).

Emans, R. "Phonics: A Look Ahead." *Elementary English* (May 1969), 575–582.

Farr, R. "Measuring Reading Comprehension: An Historical Perspective." *Reading: The Right to Participate* (ed. by Frank Green). National Reading Conference, 20th Yearbook, 1971, pp. 187–197.

Feeley, Joan T. "Teaching Non-English-Speaking First-Graders to Read." *Elementary English* (February 1970), 198–208.

Fisher, J. A. "Dialect, Bilingualism and Reading." *Reading for All* (ed. by Robert Karlin). Buenos Aires, Argentina: International Reading Association, 1974.

Flood, J. "A System for Scoring Readers' Recall of Propositions from Texts and Cumulative Effects of Information on Inference Making." In *Reading: Disciplined Inquiry in Process and Practice,* P. D. Pearson and J. Hansen, eds. 27th Yearbook of the National Reading Conference, 1978.

Flood, J., and D. Lapp. "Prose Analysis and the Effects of Staging on Prose Comprehension." Paper presented at the Second Annual Reading Association of Ireland Conference, Dublin, Ireland, 1977.

Flood, J., and D. Lapp. "The Role of Selected Text-Internal Stimulants on Inference," paper presented at 28th National Reading Conference. St. Petersburg, Fla., December 1978.

Frederiksen, C. H. "Discourse Comprehension and Early Reading." *Washington Basic Skills Group.* Washington, D.C.: National Institute of Education, 1976.

Frederiksen, C. H. "Effects of Task-Induced Cognitive Operations on Comprehension and Memory Processes." *Language Comprehension and the Acquisition of Knowledge* (ed. by J. B. Carroll and R. O. Freedle). Washington, D.C.: V. H. Winston, 1972, pp. 211–245.

Frederiksen, C. H. "Inference and the Structure of Children's Discourse." Paper for the Symposium on the Development of Processing Skills, Society for Research in Child Development Meeting, New Orleans, 1977.

Fry, E. "Programmed Instruction and Automation in Beginning Reading." *Elementary Reading Instruction* (ed. by Althea Beery et al.). Boston: Allyn and Bacon, 1969, pp. 400–413.

Gough, P. "One Second of Reading." *Language by Ear and Eye* (ed. by J. F. Kavanagh and I. G. Mottingly). Cambridge, Mass.: MIT Press, 1972, pp. 331–358.

Harris, A. J. "Key Factors in a Successful Reading Program." *Reading Teacher* (January 1969), 69–76.

Herr, S. E. "Phonics Clinic." *The Instructor* (May 1957), 35–39.

Jenkins, J. J. "Can We Have a Theory of Meaningful Memory." *Theories in Cognitive Psychology: The Loyola Symposium* (ed. by R. L. Solso). Hillsdale, N.J.: Erlbaum, 1974, pp. 1–20.

Jenkinson, M. D. "Reading—An Eternal Dynamic." *Elementary School Journal* (October 1970), 1–10.

Kingston, A. "A Conceptual Model of Reading Comprehension." *Phases of College and Other Adult Reading Programs* (ed. by Emery P. Bliesmer and Albert J. Kingston, Jr.). Tenth Yearbook of the National Reading Conference, 1961.

LaBerge, D., and S. J. Samuels. "Toward a Theory of Automatic Information Processing in Reading." *Cognitive Psychology,* **6** (1974), 293–323.

Lapp, D., and J. Flood. "Differences Between Teacher and Student Decomposition and Recall of the Propositional Structure of Student Texts." Paper presented at the 28th National Reading Conference, St. Petersburg, Fla., December 1978.

Lorge, I. "Predicting Readability." *Teachers College Record,* **45** (March 1944), 404–419.

Oliver, M. E. "Key Concepts for Beginning Reading." *Elementary English* (March 1970), 401–402.

Rutherford, W. "Learning to Read: A Critique." *Elementary School Journal* (November 1968), 72–83.

Samuels, S. J. "The Effect of Letter-Name Knowledge on Learning to Read." *American Educational Research Journal,* **9** (Winter 1972), 65–74.

Sartain, H. W. "The Place of Individualized Reading in a Well-Planned Program." *Readings on Reading Instruction,* 2nd ed. (ed. by Albert J. Harris and Edward R. Sipay). New York: David McKay Co., 1972, 193–199.

Sartain, H. W. "Do Reading Workbooks Increase Achievement?" *Elementary School Journal* (December 1961), 157–162.

Serwer, B. L. "Linguistic Support for a Method of Teaching Beginning Reading to Black Children." *Reading Research Quarterly* (Summer 1969), 449–467.

Shuy, R. W. "Some Considerations for Developing Beginning Reading Materials for Ghetto Children." *Journal of Reading Behavior,* **1** (Spring 1969), 33–44.

Silvaroli, N. J. "Factors in Predicting Children's Success in First Grade Reading." *Reading and Inquiry.* Newark, Del.: International Reading Association, 1965, 296–298.

Smith, N. B. "The Many Faces of Reading Comprehension." *Reading Teacher* (December 1969), 249–260.

Spache, G. D. "Psychological and Cultural Factors in Learning to Read." *Reading for All* (ed. by Robert Karlin). Newark, Del.: International Reading Association, 1973, 43–50.

Stauffer, R. G. "The Language Experience Approach." *Perspectives in Reading,* No. 5 (ed. by J. F. Kerfort). Newark, Del.: International Reading Association, 1965.

Strickland, R. G. "The Language of Elementary School Children: Its Relationship to the Language of Reading Textbooks and the Quality of Reading of Selected Children." *Bulletin of the School of Education, Indiana University,* **38** (1962), 4.

Thorndike, E. L. "Reading as Reasoning: A Study of Mistakes in Paragraph Reading." *Journal of Educational Psychology,* **8** (1917), 323–332.

Trabasso, T. "Mental Operations in Language Comprehension." *Language Comprehension and the Acquisition of Knowledge* (ed. by J. B. Carroll and R. O. Freedle). Washington, D.C.: V. H. Winston, 1972, pp. 113–137.

Wardhaugh, R. "Is the Linguistic Approach an Improvement in Reading Instruction?" *Current Issues in Reading* (ed. by Nila Banton Smith). Newark, Del.: International Reading Association, 1969, pp. 254–267.

Williams, J. P., E. L. Blumberg, and D. Williams. "Clues Used in Visual Word Recognition." *Journal of Educational Psychology* (August 1970), 310–315.

Willis, B. C. "Communication Skills, Games, Techniques and Devices—Grades K-1-2-3." Chicago: Board of Education, 1964.

BOOKS

Allen, R. Van. *Language Experiences in Communication.* Boston: Houghton Mifflin, 1976.

Allen, R. Van. *Report of the Reading Study Project.* Monograph No. 1. San Diego: Department of Education, San Diego County, 1961.

Aukerman, R. C. *Approaches to Beginning Reading.* New York: Wiley, 1971.

Bloomfield, L., and C. L. Barnhart. *Let's Read: A Linguistic Approach.* Detroit: Wayne State University Press, 1961.

Carter, H. J., and D. J. McGinnis. *Teaching Individuals to Read.* Boston: Heath, 1962.

Dallman, M., L. Rouch, L. Y. Chang, and J. J. DeBoer. *The Teaching of Reading,* 4th ed. New York: Holt, Rinehart and Winston, 1974.

Durkin, D. *Teaching Them to Read,* 2nd ed. Boston: Allyn and Bacon, 1974.

Durkin, D. *Teaching Young Children to Read.* Boston: Allyn and Bacon, 1972.

Flesch, R. F. *Marks of Readable Style: A Study of Adult Education.* New York: Bureau of Publications, Teachers College, Columbia University, 1943.

Fries, C. *Linguistics and Reading.* New York: Holt, Rinehart and Winston, 1962.

Fries, C. *Reading in the Elementary School.* Boston: Allyn and Bacon, 1964.

Gray, W. S., and B. E. Leary. *What Makes a Book Readable.* Chicago: University of Chicago Press, 1935.

Hafner, L. E., and H. B. Jolly. *Patterns of Teaching Reading in the Elementary School.* New York: Macmillan, 1972.

Harris, A. J. *How to Increase Reading Ability,* 5th ed. New York: David McKay Co., 1970.

Harris, L. A., and C. B. Smith (eds.). *Individualized Reading Instruction: A Reader.* New York: Holt, Rinehart and Winston, 1972.

Johnson, D. D., and P. D. Pearson. *Teaching Reading Vocabulary.* New York: Holt, 1978.

Karlin, R. *Teaching Elementary Reading: Principles and Strategies.* New York: Harcourt Brace Jovanovich, 1971.

Lapp, D., and J. Flood. *Teaching Reading to Every Child.* New York: Macmillan, 1978.

McCullough, C. *Handbook for Teaching the Language Arts.* San Francisco: Paragon Publications, 1958.

McKim, M., and H. Caskey. *Guiding Growth in Reading,* 2nd ed. New York: Macmillan, 1963.

Pearson, P. D., and D. D. Johnson. *Teaching Reading Comprehension.* New York: Holt, 1978.

Robinson, H. A. (ed.). *Reading: Seventy-five Years of Progress.* Supplementary Educational Monograph No. 96. Chicago: University of Chicago Press, 1966.

Rumelhart, D. E. *Toward an Interactive Model of Reading.*

Technical Report No. 56. University of California, San Diego: Center for Human Information Processing, 1976.

Savage, J. F. *Linguistics for Teachers.* Chicago: Science Research Associates, 1973.

Schulwitz, B. S. (ed.). *Teachers, Tangibles, Techniques: Comprehension of Content in Reading.* Newark, Del.: International Reading Association, 1975.

Smith, F. *Understanding Reading.* New York: Holt, Rinehart and Winston, 1971.

Smith, H. P., and E. V. Dechant. *Psychology in Teaching Reading.* Englewood Cliffs, N. J.: Prentice-Hall, 1961.

Smith, J. A. *Creative Teaching of Reading in the Elementary School,* 2nd ed. Boston: Allyn and Bacon, 1973.

Spache, G. D., and E. B. Spache. *Reading in the Elementary School,* 3rd ed. Boston: Allyn and Bacon, 1973.

Stauffer, R. G. *Directing Reading Maturity as a Cognitive Process.* New York: Harper & Row, 1969.

Stauffer, R. G. *Directing the Reading-Thinking Process.* New York: Harper & Row, 1975.

Stauffer, R. G. *The Language-Experience Approach to the Teaching of Reading.* New York: Harper & Row, 1970.

Strang, R. *Diagnostic Teaching of Reading.* New York: McGraw-Hill, 1964.

Tinker, M., and C. McCullough. *Teaching Elementary School,* 3rd ed. New York: Appleton-Century-Crofts, 1968.

ELEMENTARY CLASSROOM MATERIALS

Barbe, W. *Barbe's Reading Skills Check List.* New York: Parker Publishing Co., 1975.

Bloomfield, L., and C. L. Barnhart. *Let's Read: A Linguistic Approach.* Detroit: Wayne State University Press, 1961.

Buchanan, C. D. *Sullivan Programmed Readers.* New York: McGraw-Hill, 1963, p. 68.

Clymer, T., et al. *Ginn 720 Reading Program.* Lexington, Mass.: Xerox Company, 1976.

Dolch, E. W. *Dolch Basic Sight Word Test.* Champaign, Ill.: Garrard Publishing Co., 1942.

Downing, J. "Bandy's First Jump." *The Downing Readers.* Southampton Place, London: ITA Publishing Co., Ltd.

Gategno, C. *Words in Color.* Chicago: Learning Materials, Inc., 1962.

Glim, T. E. *Miami Palo Alto Readers.* New York: Harcourt Brace Jovanovich, 1968, p. 73.

Gray, W. *On Your Own in Reading.* Chicago: Scott, Foresman, 1961.

Harris, L. A., and M. D. Jacobson. *Basic Elementary Reading Vocabularies: The First R Series.* New York: Macmillan, 1972.

Lee, D. M. and R. V. Allen. *Learning to Read Through Experience.* New York: Appleton-Century-Crofts, 1963.

Mazurkiewicz, A. J., and H. J. Tanyzer. *Early to Read Program,* Revised Phases 1, 2, 3. Belmont, Calif.: i/t/a/ Publications, 1965–1966.

McKee, P. *Come Along,* Teacher's Manual. Boston: Houghton Mifflin, 1967.

Pitman, Sir J., with A. J. Mazurkiewicz and H. J. Tanyzer. *The Handbook on Writing and Spelling in i/t/a/.* Belmont, Calif.: i/t/a/ Publications, 1964.

Russell, D., et al. *Manual for Teaching the Reading Readiness Program,* rev. ed. Boston: Ginn, 1961.

Index

Dictionary(ies) (*cont.*)
  in study of spelling, 246
  teaching use of, 274–84
    activities in, 280–83
    alphabetical sequence, 274–75
    definitions, 277–78
    games, 276, 279–80, 286
    guide words, 275–76
    introducing, 279–83
    pronunciation, 278–79
Digraph chart, 398
Digraphs, 387, 394
Diphthongs, 387, 394
Directions, inability to follow and reading
      readiness, 380*t*.
  written, exercise for following, 425
Disability, language, 80
Discussions, to encourage reading of lit-
      erature, 296
  group, for appreciation of literary
      works, 297–99
Dixon, Charlotte, 216
Dramatics. *See also* Plays
  in classroom, 129–35
    creative, 129–33
    formal, 133
    memorization in, 133
    pantomime as preparation for, 130
    plays for, and sources of, 133
    puppets used in, 132–33
  for radio and television, 133–35
    script writing for, 131–32
  sociodrama related to, 131
Drill, effectiveness of, 13
Durkin, D., 17, 18, 19
Durrell, D., 125, 129, 356

Ear training, for speech habits, 114
Early-to-Read program, 361
Economy reading series, 351
Editing, of report, standards for, 225
Editing signs, 225
Eimas, P. D., 69
Electric Company, The, 20
Emotional instability, reading readiness
      affected by, 382*t*.
Emotional needs, of young child, 23
Empathy, development of, through
      children's literature, 294–95
Encoding, 39
Endings. *See also* Root word; Suffixes
  generalizations about, in spelling,
      263–71

English language. *See also* Bilingual edu-
      cation
  cultural influences on, 47–49
  as Foreign Language (EFL), 61
    drills for, 108–109
  history of, 50–56
  Middle, 53
  modern, 53–56
  modern influences in, 58
  Old, 51–53
  as Second Language (ESL), 22, 61,
      120–21
    games for working with children
      learning, 121–24
  speaking, before reading, 85–86
  Standard, 85
  trends throughout development of,
      56–57
Enrichment, for spelling program,
      289–90
Enstron, E. A., 178
Environment, classroom, 4
  to encourage listening, 93–94
  home, 16–17, 19. *See also* Parents
Environmental aspects, in language de-
      velopment, 69–70
Epstein, Beryl, 290
Epstein, Sam, 290
Ernst, Margaret, 290
Evaluation. *See also* Standards; Tests
  of child, by parent, 19
  of handwriting, 161
  of letter writing, 236
  of punctuation, student's understanding
      of, 232–34
  of reading skills, 373, 374
  of written composition, 205
Exclamation point, 228, 232
Experiential-conceptual-informational
      background, of bilingual child,
      86
External learning stimulants, 16–19

Fable, writing, 215–16
Family. *See also* Home environment; Par-
      ents
  bad situation in, and reading readiness,
      383*t*.
  verbal discourse within, 16–17
Farb, P., 66
Farr, R., 348
Feelings. *See also* Emotional entries
  expressed through poetry, 313

Feifal, H., 295
Ferguson, C. A., 77
Fernald, Grace M., 272*n*.
Fillmer, H. T., 216*n*.
Finger plays, 311–12
  poems involving, 338–40
Finocchiaro, Mary, 116*n*.
First Thanksgiving, The, 133–34
Fisher, Aileen, 314
Flag courtesy, 136
Flannel graph, poems told with, 314
Flannelboard, construction of, 334–35
  for storytelling, 334–36
Flash cards, 442–43. *See also* Cards
Flood, J., 62, 90, 348, 349
Folk tales, suitability of, 333
Foreign-speaking children. *See* Bilingual
      child
Forester, L. M., 175, 178
Forgetting. *See* Memory
Formal operations, 15
Fowler, Eugene M., 188
Fraser, C., 75
Frazer, B. M., 100
Frazier, A., 215
Frederiksen, C. H., 349
Fromkin, V., 70
Frustration levels, in reading, 440
Frye, Agnes, 112*n*.
Funk, Charles E., 290

Games. *See also* Activities
  consonant, 391
  dictionary, 276, 279–80, 286
  for foreign-speaking children, 121–24
  for independent working, 412
  for pronunciation of consonants,
      115–17
  for public usage habits, establishing,
      108–110
  for speech improvement in primary
      grades, 116–17
  spelling, 251, 284–88
Gardner, Warren, 178
Garrison, W. B., 290
Gategno, Caleb, 361
Geedy, P. S., 246
Gelman, R., 77
Generalizations. *See* Phonics, generaliza-
      tions; Spelling, generalizations
George, Jean, 218
"Get Set," parent training program, 18
Giannangelo, D. M., 100